MICROSOFT EX
EXAM 70-215: INSTALLING, CO
MICROSOFT WINDC

MW00721049

Installing Windows 2000 Server	er(s):
Perform an attended installation of Windows 2000 Server	3
Perform an unattended installation of Windows 2000 Server	3
Upgrade a server from Microsoft Windows NT 4.0	3
Deploy service packs	3
Troubleshoot failed installations	3

Installing, Configuring, and Troubleshooting Access to Resources	Chapter(s):
Install and configure network services for interoperability	4
Monitor, configure, troubleshoot, and control access to printers	4
Monitor, configure, troubleshoot, and control access to files, folders, and shared folders	4
Monitor, configure, troubleshoot, and control access to Web sites	4

Configuring and Troubleshooting Hardware Devices and Drivers	Chapter(s):
Configure hardware devices	5
Configure driver signing options	5
Update device drivers	5
Troubleshoot problems with hardware	5

Managing, Monitoring, and Optimizing System Performance, Reliability, and Availability	Chapter(s):
Monitor and optimize usage of system resources	6
Manage processes	6
Set priorities and start and stop processes	6
Optimize disk performance	6
Manage and optimize availability of System State data and user data	6
Recover System State data and user data	6

Managing, Configuring, and Troubleshooting Storage Use	Chapter(s):
Monitor, configure, and troubleshoot disks and volumes	7
Configure data compression	7
Monitor and configure disk quotas	7
Recover from disk failures	7

Configuring and Troubleshooting Windows 2000 Network Connections	Chapter(s):
Install, configure, and troubleshoot shared access	8, 9
Install, configure, and troubleshoot a virtual private network (VPN)	8
Install, configure, and troubleshoot network protocols	8, 9
Install and configure network services	8, 9, 10
Configure, monitor, and troubleshoot remote access	10
Install, configure, monitor, and troubleshoot Terminal Services	10
Install, configure, and troubleshoot network adapters and drivers	8, 9

Implementing, Monitoring, and Troubleshooting Security	Chapter(s):
Encrypt data on a hard disk by using Encrypting File System (EFS)	11
Implement, configure, manage, and troubleshoot policies in a Windows 2000 environment	11
Implement, configure, manage, and troubleshoot auditing	11
Implement, configure, manage, and troubleshoot local accounts	12
Implement, configure, manage, and troubleshoot Account Policy	12
Implement, configure, manage, and troubleshoot security by using the Security Configuration Tool Set	11

MCSE™ Windows® 2000 Server

David Johnson
Dawn Rader

The Coriolis Group, LLC
14455 N. Hayden Road, Suite 220
Scottsdale, Arizona 85260

480/483-0192
FAX 480/483-0193
http://www.coriolis.com

Library of Congress Cataloging-in-Publication Data
Johnson, David, 1970-
  MCSE Windows 2000 server exam prep / by David Johnson and Dawn Rader.
    p. cm.
  Includes index.
  ISBN 1-57610-696-9
  1. Electronic data processing personnel--Certification. 2. Microsoft software--Examinations--Study guides. 3. Microsoft Windows 2000 server. I. Rader, Dawn. II. III. Title.

QA76.3.J63985 2000
005.7'13769--dc21

                                          00-031755
                                          CIP

President and CEO
Keith Weiskamp

Publisher
Steve Sayre

Acquisitions Editor
Shari Jo Hehr

Development Editor
Deborah Doorley

Marketing Specialist
Cynthia Caldwell

Project Editor
Sharon Sanchez McCarson

Technical Reviewer
Jeff Dowdy

Production Coordinator
Meg E. Turecek

Cover Designer
Jesse Dunn

Layout Designer
April Nielsen

CD-ROM Developer
Michelle McConnell

Printed in the United States of America
10 9 8 7 6 5 4 3 2 1

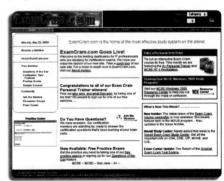

The Coriolis Group, LLC • 14455 North Hayden Road, Suite 220 • Scottsdale, Arizona 85260

ExamCram.com Connects You to the Ultimate Study Center!

Our goal has always been to provide you with the best study tools on the planet to help you achieve your certification in record time. Time is so valuable these days that none of us can afford to waste a second of it, especially when it comes to exam preparation.

Over the past few years, we've created an extensive line of *Exam Cram* and *Exam Prep* study guides, practice exams, and interactive training. To help you study even better, we have now created an e-learning and certification destination called **ExamCram.com**. (You can access the site at **www.examcram.com**.) Now, with every study product you purchase from us, you'll be connected to a large community of people like yourself who are actively studying for their certifications, developing their careers, seeking advice, and sharing their insights and stories.

I believe that the future is all about collaborative learning. Our **ExamCram.com** destination is our approach to creating a highly interactive, easily accessible collaborative environment, where you can take practice exams and discuss your experiences with others, sign up for features like "Questions of the Day," plan your certifications using our interactive planners, create your own personal study pages, and keep up with all of the latest study tips and techniques.

I hope that whatever study products you purchase from us—*Exam Cram* or *Exam Prep* study guides, *Personal Trainers*, *Personal Test Centers*, or one of our interactive Web courses—will make your studying fun and productive. Our commitment is to build the kind of learning tools that will allow you to study the way you want to, whenever you want to.

Help us continue to provide the very best certification study materials possible. Write us or email us at **learn@examcram.com** and let us know how our study products have helped you study. Tell us about new features that you'd like us to add. Send us a story about how we've helped you. We're listening!

Visit ExamCram.com now to enhance your study program.

Good luck with your certification exam and your career. Thank you for allowing us to help you achieve your goals.

Keith Weiskamp
President and CEO

Look for these other products from The Coriolis Group:

MCSE Windows 2000 Accelerated Exam Prep
By Lance Cockcroft, Erik Eckel, and Ron Kauffman

MCSE Windows 2000 Professional Exam Prep
By Michael D. Stewart, James Bloomingdale,
and Neall Alcott

MCSE Windows 2000 Network Exam Prep
By Tammy Smith and Sandra Smeeton

MCSE Windows 2000 Directory Services Exam Prep
By David V. Watts, Will Willis, and Tillman Strahan

MCSE Windows 2000 Security Design Exam Prep
By Richard Alan McMahon and Glen Bicking

MCSE Windows 2000 Network Design Exam Prep
By Geoffrey Alexander, Anoop Jalan,
and Joseph Alexander

**MCSE Migrating from NT 4 to Windows 2000
Exam Prep**
By Glen Bergen, Graham Leach, and David Baldwin

**MCSE Windows 2000 Directory Services Design
Exam Prep**
By J. Peter Bruzzese and Wayne Dipchan

**MCSE Windows 2000 Core Four
Exam Prep Pack**

**MCSE Windows 2000 Server
Exam Cram**
By Natasha Knight

**MCSE Windows 2000 Professional
Exam Cram**
By Dan Balter, Dan Holme, Todd Logan,
and Laurie Salmon

**MCSE Windows 2000 Network
Exam Cram**
By Hank Carbeck, Derek Melber, and Richard Taylor

**MCSE Windows 2000 Directory Services
Exam Cram**
By David V. Watts, Will Willis, and J. Peter Bruzzese

**MCSE Windows 2000 Security Design
Exam Cram**
By Phillip G. Schein

**MCSE Windows 2000 Network Design
Exam Cram**
By Kim Simmons, Jarret W. Buse, and Todd Halping

**MCSE Windows 2000 Directory Services Design
Exam Cram**
By Dennis Scheil and Diana Bartley

**MCSE Windows 2000 Core Four
Exam Cram Pack**

and...

MCSE Windows 2000 Foundations
By James Michael Stewart and Lee Scales

ABOUT THE AUTHORS

David Johnson, a.k.a. "DJ," is a manager at a large systems integration and maintenance company in Austin, TX. He served many years in the networking trenches, working his way up the food chain. When not working or writing, DJ enjoys billiards, food, cigars, and wine. DJ can be reached at **count0@texas.net**.

Dawn Rader has been a networking writer, editor, and researcher since 1993. Since joining LANWrights, Inc. full-time in 1996, she has performed duties as Managing Editor on over 95 books. In her spare time, Dawn enjoys doing Hatha yoga, dancing, reading, and shooting pool. When not doing one of those, she's usually being walked by her 120-pound black Labrador Retriever, Benjamin, or being bossed around by her fat black cat, Boo.

ACKNOWLEDGMENTS

We would like to thank the following individuals for their contributions to this manuscript: Libby Chovanec, Jacqui King, Grant Miller, Barry Shilmover, James Michael Stewart, and Lee Scales. In addition, we would like to extend our thanks to Martin Grasdal for his attention to detail in performing a technical review of this manuscript.

Finally, to the wonderful people at The Coriolis Group: a big thank-you to Shari Jo Hehr, for her continued support of efforts on behalf of LANWrights; to Paula Kmetz and Sharon McCarson, for their guidance and support throughout this project; and finally to Anne Marie Walker and Jeff Dowdy, for their editorial and technical reviews of this book.

—Collectively

My thanks, as always, to the teams at LANWrights and Coriolis for giving me the opportunity to challenge myself and do something I enjoy.

Thanks to Stephanie for understanding and coping with the difficulties that come with working and writing.

And, as always, thanks to Mama Kitty for reminding me that nothing, absolutely nothing, is more important than eating and sleeping.

—David Johnson

I have so many wonderful people to thank for the myriad blessings in my life. First off, my continued thanks to Ed Tittel, my good friend and great boss. Ed: Thanks for giving me a chance and sticking by me over the past six and a half years…who woulda thunk it?!

Next up is my dearest friend, Mary Burmeister. Mary: You have shown me the true meaning of friendship over and over; I'm so fortunate to have you in my life! Thanks to Laura Nelson for always being there for me. Thanks to Tri, James, and Manny: Life just isn't worth living without dancing! To my beautiful mother and my extraordinary grandmother: Thank you for always loving me and believing in me. To Susan Arnold Lange: Thank you so much for helping me find the person I was meant to be.

—Dawn Rader

CONTENTS AT A GLANCE

TABLE OF CONTENTS

EXAM INSIGHTS

Welcome to *MCSE Windows 2000 Server Exam Prep*! This comprehensive study guide aims to help you get ready to take—and pass—Microsoft certification Exam 70-215, titled "Installing, Configuring, and Administering Microsoft Windows 2000 Server." This Exam Insights section discusses exam preparation resources, the testing situation, Microsoft's certification programs in general, and how this book can help you prepare for Microsoft's Windows 2000 certification exams.

Exam Prep study guides help you understand and appreciate the subjects and materials you need to pass Microsoft certification exams. We've worked from Microsoft's curriculum objectives to ensure that all key topics are clearly explained. Our aim is to bring together as much information as possible about Microsoft certification exams.

Nevertheless, to completely prepare yourself for any Microsoft test, we recommend that you begin by taking the Self-Assessment included in this book immediately following this Exam Insights section. This tool will help you evaluate your knowledge base against the requirements for an MCSE under both ideal and real circumstances.

Based on what you learn from that exercise, you might decide to begin your studies with some classroom training or some background reading. You might decide to read The Coriolis Group's *Exam Prep* book that you have in hand first, or you might decide to start with another study approach. You may also want to refer to one of a number of study guides available from Microsoft or third-party vendors. We also recommend that you supplement your study program with visits to **ExamCram.com** to receive additional practice questions, get advice, and track the Windows 2000 MCSE program.

We also strongly recommend that you install, configure, and fool around with the software that you'll be tested on, because nothing beats hands-on experience and familiarity when it comes to understanding the questions you're likely to encounter on a certification test. Book learning is essential, but hands-on experience is the best teacher of all!

HOW TO PREPARE FOR AN EXAM

Preparing for any Windows 2000 Server-related test (including "Installing, Configuring, and Administering Microsoft Windows 2000 Server") requires that you obtain and study materials designed to provide comprehensive information about the product and its capabilities that will appear on the specific exam for which you are preparing. The following list of materials will help you study and prepare:

➤ The Windows 2000 Server product CD includes comprehensive online documentation and related materials; it should be a primary resource when you are preparing for the test.

➤ The exam preparation materials, practice tests, and self-assessment exams on the Microsoft Training And Certification page (**www.microsoft.com/trainingandservices/**). The Testing Innovations page offers samples of the new question types found on the Windows 2000 MCSE exams. Find the materials, download them, and use them!

➤ The exam preparation advice, practice tests, questions of the day, and discussion groups on the **ExamCram.com** e-learning and certification destination Web site (**www.examcram.com**).

In addition, you'll probably find any or all of the following materials useful in your quest for Windows 2000 Server expertise:

➤ *Microsoft training kits*—Microsoft Press offers a training kit that specifically targets Exam 70-215. For more information, visit: **http://mspress.microsoft.com/prod/books/1959.htm**. This training kit contains information that you will find useful in preparing for the test.

➤ *Microsoft TechNet CD*—This monthly CD-based publication delivers numerous electronic titles that include coverage of Directory Services Design and related topics on the Technical Information (TechNet) CD. Its offerings include product facts, technical notes, tools and utilities, and information on how to access the Seminars Online training materials for Directory Services Design. A subscription to TechNet costs $299 per year, but it is well worth the price. Visit **www.microsoft.com/technet/** and check out the information under the "TechNet Subscription" menu entry for more details.

➤ *Study guides*—Several publishers—including The Coriolis Group—offer Windows 2000 titles. The Coriolis Group series includes the following:

  ➤ *The Exam Cram series*—These books give you information about the material you need to know to pass the tests.

➤ *The Exam Prep series*—These books provide a greater level of detail than the *Exam Cram* books and are designed to teach you everything you need to know from an exam perspective. Each book comes with a CD that contains interactive practice exams in a variety of testing formats.

Together, the two series make a perfect pair.

➤ *Multimedia*—These Coriolis Group materials are designed to support learners of all types—whether you learn best by reading or doing:

➤ *The Exam Cram Personal Trainer*—Offers a unique, personalized self-paced training course based on the exam.

➤ *The Exam Cram Personal Test Center*—Features multiple test options that simulate the actual exam, including Fixed-Length, Random, Review, and Test All. Explanations of correct and incorrect answers reinforce concepts learned.

➤ *Classroom training*—CTECs, online partners, and third-party training companies (like Wave Technologies, Learning Tree, Data-Tech, and others) all offer classroom training on Windows 2000 Server. These companies aim to help you prepare to pass the Server test. Although such training runs upwards of $350 per day in class, most of the individuals who partake find them to be quite worthwhile.

➤ *Other publications*—There's no shortage of materials available about Windows 2000 Server. The complete resource section in Appendix C should give you an idea of where we think you should look for further discussion.

By far, this set of required and recommended materials represents a nonpareil collection of sources and resources for Windows 2000 Server and related topics. We anticipate that you'll find that this book belongs in this company.

TAKING A CERTIFICATION EXAM

Once you've prepared for your exam, you need to register with a testing center. Each computer-based MCP exam costs $100, and if you don't pass, you may retest for an additional $100 for each additional try. In the United States and Canada, tests are administered by Prometric (formerly Sylvan Prometric), and by Virtual University Enterprises (VUE). Here's how you can contact them:

➤ *Prometric*—You can sign up for a test through the company's Web site at **www.prometric.com**. Or, you can register by phone at 800-755-3926 (within the United States or Canada) or at 410-843-8000 (outside the United States and Canada).

➤ *Virtual University Enterprises*—You can sign up for a test or get the phone numbers for local testing centers through the Web page at **www.vue.com/ms/**.

To sign up for a test, you must possess a valid credit card, or contact either company for mailing instructions to send them a check (in the U.S.). Only when payment is verified, or a check has cleared, can you actually register for a test.

To schedule an exam, call the number or visit either of the Web pages at least one day in advance. To cancel or reschedule an exam, you must call before 7 P.M. pacific standard time the day before the scheduled test time (or you may be charged, even if you don't appear to take the test). When you want to schedule a test, have the following information ready:

➤ Your name, organization, and mailing address.

➤ Your Microsoft Test ID. (Inside the United States, this means your Social Security number; citizens of other nations should call ahead to find out what type of identification number is required to register for a test.)

➤ The name and number of the exam you wish to take.

➤ A method of payment. (As we've already mentioned, a credit card is the most convenient method, but alternate means can be arranged in advance, if necessary.)

Once you sign up for a test, you'll be informed as to when and where the test is scheduled. Try to arrive at least 15 minutes early.

THE EXAM SITUATION

When you arrive at the testing center where you scheduled your exam, you'll need to sign in with an exam coordinator. He or she will ask you to show two forms of identification, one of which must be a photo ID. After you've signed in and your time slot arrives, you'll be asked to deposit any books, bags, or other items you brought with you. Then, you'll be escorted into a closed room.

All exams are completely closed book. In fact, you will not be permitted to take anything with you into the testing area, but you will be furnished with a blank sheet of paper and a pen or, in some cases, an erasable plastic sheet and an erasable pen. Before the exam, you should memorize as much of the important material as you can, so you can write that information on the blank sheet as soon as you are seated in front of the computer. You can refer to this piece of paper anytime you like during the test, but you'll have to surrender the sheet when you leave the room.

You will have some time to compose yourself, to record this information, and to take a sample orientation exam before you begin the real thing. We suggest you take the orientation test before taking your first exam, but because they're all more or less identical in layout, behavior, and controls, you probably won't need to do this more than once.

Typically, the room will be furnished with anywhere from one to half a dozen computers, and each workstation will be separated from the others by dividers designed to keep you from seeing what's happening on someone else's computer. Most test rooms feature a wall with a large picture window. This permits the exam coordinator to monitor the room, to prevent exam-takers from talking to one another, and to observe anything out of the ordinary that might go on. The exam coordinator will have preloaded the appropriate Microsoft certification exam—for this book, that's Exam 70-215—and you'll be permitted to start as soon as you're seated in front of the computer.

All Microsoft certification exams allow a certain maximum amount of time in which to complete your work (this time is indicated on the exam by an on-screen counter/clock, so you can check the time remaining whenever you like). All Microsoft certification exams are computer generated. In addition to multiple choice, you'll encounter select and place (drag and drop), create a tree (categorization and prioritization), drag and connect, and build list and reorder (list prioritization) on most exams. Although this may sound quite simple, the questions are constructed not only to check your mastery of basic facts and figures about Windows 2000 Server, but they also require you to evaluate one or more sets of circumstances or requirements. Often, you'll be asked to give more than one answer to a question. Likewise, you might be asked to select the best or most effective solution to a problem from a range of choices, all of which technically are correct. Taking the exam is quite an adventure, and it involves real thinking. This book shows you what to expect and how to deal with the potential problems, puzzles, and predicaments.

When you complete a Microsoft certification exam, the software will tell you whether you've passed or failed. Results are broken into several topic areas. Even if you fail, we suggest you ask for—and keep—the detailed report that the test administrator should print for you. You can use this report to help you prepare for another go-round, if needed.

If you need to retake an exam, you'll have to schedule a new test with Prometric or VUE and pay another $100.

Note: *The first time you fail a test, you can retake the test the next day. However, if you fail a second time, you must wait 14 days before retaking that test. The 14-day waiting period remains in effect for all retakes after the second failure.*

In the next section, you'll learn more about how Microsoft test questions look and how they must be answered.

EXAM LAYOUT AND DESIGN

The format of Microsoft's Windows 2000 exams is different from that of its previous exams. For the design exams (70-219, 70-220, 70-221), each exam consists entirely of a series of case studies, and the questions can be of six types. For the Core Four exams (70-210, 70-215, 70-216, 70-217), the same six types of questions can appear, but you are not likely to encounter complex multiquestion case studies.

For design exams, each case study or "testlet" presents a detailed problem that you must read and analyze. Figure 1 shows an example of what a case study looks like. You must select the different tabs in the case study to view the entire case.

Following each case study is a set of questions related to the case study; these questions can be one of six types (which are discussed next). Careful attention to details provided in the case study is the key to success. Be prepared to toggle frequently between the case study and the questions as you work. Some of the case studies also include diagrams, which are called *exhibits*, that you'll need to examine closely to understand how to answer the questions.

Once you complete a case study, you can review all the questions and your answers. However, once you move on to the next case study, you may not be able to return to the previous case study and make any changes.

The six types of question formats are:

➤ Multiple choice, single answer

➤ Multiple choice, multiple answers

➤ Build list and reorder (list prioritization)

➤ Create a tree

➤ Drag and connect

➤ Select and place (drag and drop)

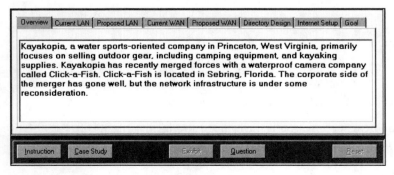

Figure 1   This is how case studies appear.

*Note: Exam formats may vary by test center location. You may want to call the test center or visit **ExamCram.com** to see if you can find out which type of test you'll encounter.*

Multiple-Choice Question Format

Some exam questions require you to select a single answer, whereas others ask you to select multiple correct answers. The following multiple-choice question requires you to select a single correct answer. Following the question is a brief summary of each potential answer and why it is either right or wrong.

Question 1

What is the best method to use for encrypting a compressed file?

○ a. Ensure you are a member of a group with administrative privileges, and use the Advanced Attributes button to set encryption settings.

○ b. Decompress the file, and use the Advanced Attributes button to set encryption settings.

○ c. Set up a recovery agent to encrypt the file.

○ d. Move the file to a folder that is encrypted.

The correct answer is b. Compressed files cannot be encrypted. You must first decompress the file, then encrypt its contents through the file's Properties | Advanced Attributes area. Answers a, c, and d are incorrect; because compressed files cannot be encrypted; these settings are mutually exclusive.

This sample question format corresponds closely to the Microsoft certification exam format—the only difference on the exam is that questions are not followed by answer keys. To select an answer, you would position the cursor over the radio button next to the answer. Then, click the mouse button to select the answer.

Let's examine a question where one or more answers are possible. This type of question provides checkboxes rather than radio buttons for marking all appropriate selections.

Question 2

Which of the following operating systems can be upgraded to Windows 2000 Server? [Check all correct answers]

❑ a. Windows NT Server 3.51

❑ b. Windows 98

❑ c. Windows NT 4 Workstation

❑ d. Windows NT 4 Server

Answers a and d are correct. Windows NT 4 Server and Windows NT Server 3.51 can be upgraded to Windows 2000 Server. Answers b and c are incorrect, because Windows 98 and Windows NT 4 Workstation cannot be upgraded to Windows 2000 Server.

For this particular question, two answers are required. As far as the authors can tell (and Microsoft won't comment), such questions are scored as wrong unless all the required selections are chosen. In other words, a partially correct answer does not result in partial credit when the test is scored. For Question 2, you have to check the boxes next to items a and d to obtain credit for a correct answer. Notice that picking the right answers also means knowing why the other answers are wrong!

Build-List-and-Reorder Question Format

Questions in the build-list-and-reorder format present two lists of items—one on the left and one on the right. To answer the question, you must move items from the list on the right to the list on the left. The final list must then be reordered into a specific order.

These questions can best be characterized as "From the following list of choices, pick the choices that answer the question. Arrange the list in a certain order." To give you practice with this type of question, some questions of this type are included in this study guide. Here's an example of how they appear in this book; for a sample of how they appear on the test, see Figure 2.

Question 3

From the following list of famous people, pick those that have been elected President of the United States. Arrange the list in the order that they served.

Thomas Jefferson

Ben Franklin

Abe Lincoln

George Washington

Andrew Jackson

Paul Revere

The correct answer is:
George Washington
Thomas Jefferson
Andrew Jackson
Abe Lincoln

On an actual exam, the entire list of famous people would initially appear in the list on the right. You would move the four correct answers to the list on the left, and then reorder the list on the left. Notice that the answer to the question did not include all items from the initial list. However, this may not always be the case.

To move an item from the right list to the left list, first select the item by clicking on it, and then click on the Add button (left arrow). Once you move an item from one list to the other, you can move the item back by first selecting the item and then clicking on the appropriate button (either the Add button or the Remove button). Once items have been moved to the left list, you can reorder an item by selecting the item and clicking on the up or down button.

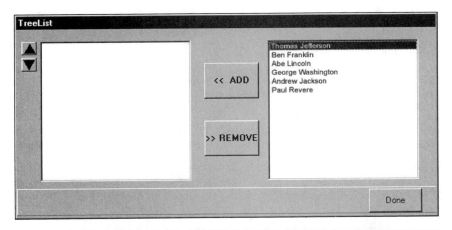

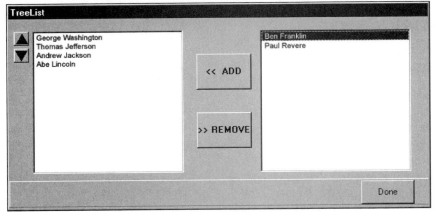

Figure 2   This is how build-list-and-reorder questions appear.

Create-a-Tree Question Format

Questions in the create-a-tree format also present two lists—one on the left side of the screen and one on the right side of the screen. The list on the right consists of individual items, and the list on the left consists of nodes in a tree. To answer the question, you must move items from the list on the right to the appropriate node in the tree.

These questions can best be characterized as simply a matching exercise. Items from the list on the right are placed under the appropriate category in the list on the left. Here's an example of how they appear in this book; for a sample of how they appear on the test, see Figure 3.

Question 4

The calendar year is divided into four seasons:

    Winter

    Spring

    Summer

    Fall

Identify the season when each of the following holidays occurs:

    Christmas

    Fourth of July

    Labor Day

    Flag Day

    Memorial Day

    Washington's Birthday

    Thanksgiving

    Easter

The correct answer is:

    Winter

        Christmas

        Washington's Birthday

    Summer

        Fourth of July

        Labor Day

Spring
    Flag Day
    Memorial Day
    Easter
Fall
    Thanksgiving

In this case, all the items in the list were used. However, this may not always be the case.

To move an item from the right list to its appropriate location in the tree, you must first select the appropriate tree node by clicking on it. Then, you select the item to be moved and click on the Add button. If one or more items have been added to a tree node, the node will be displayed with a "+" icon to the left of the node name. You can click on this icon to expand the node and view the item(s) that have been added. If any item has been added to the wrong tree node, you can remove it by selecting it and clicking on the Remove button.

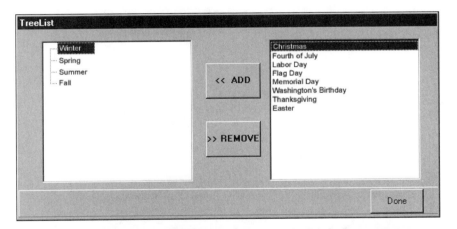

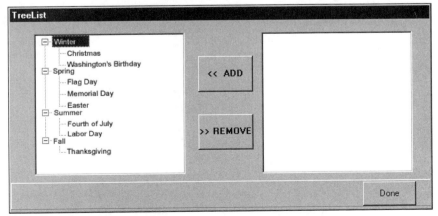

Figure 3   This is how create-a-tree questions appear.

Drag-and-Connect Question Format

Questions in the drag-and-connect format present a group of objects and a list of "connections." To answer the question, you must move the appropriate connections between the objects.

This type of question is best described using graphics. Here's an example.

Question 5

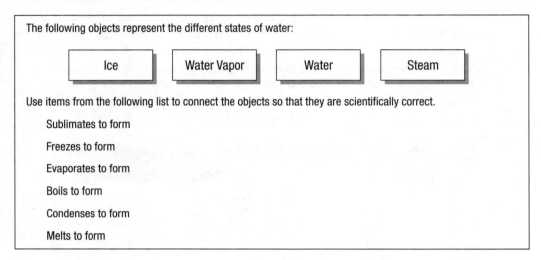

The following objects represent the different states of water:

| Ice | Water Vapor | Water | Steam |

Use items from the following list to connect the objects so that they are scientifically correct.

Sublimates to form

Freezes to form

Evaporates to form

Boils to form

Condenses to form

Melts to form

The correct answer is:

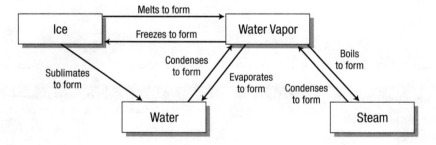

For this type of question, it's not necessary to use every object, and each connection can be used multiple times.

Select-and-Place Question Format

Questions in the select-and-place (drag-and-drop) format present a diagram with blank boxes, and a list of labels that need to be dragged to correctly fill in the blank boxes. To answer the question, you must move the labels to their appropriate positions on the diagram.

This type of question is best described using graphics. Here's an example.

Question 6

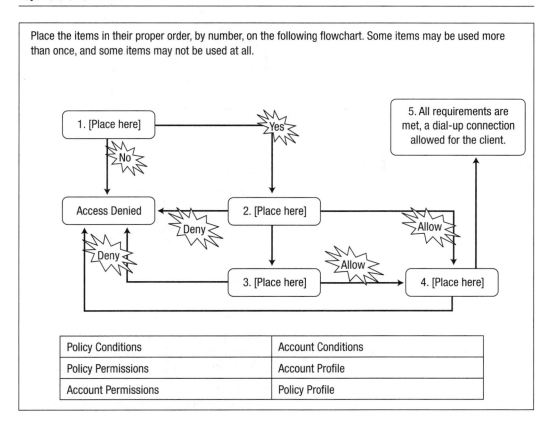

Place the items in their proper order, by number, on the following flowchart. Some items may be used more than once, and some items may not be used at all.

Policy Conditions	Account Conditions
Policy Permissions	Account Profile
Account Permissions	Policy Profile

The correct answer is:

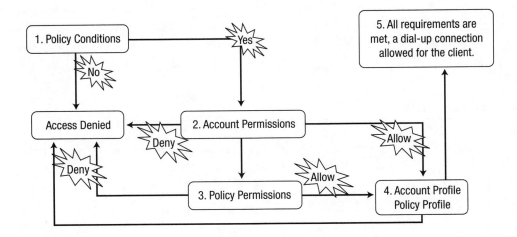

MICROSOFT'S TESTING FORMATS

Currently, Microsoft uses four different testing formats:

➤ Case study

➤ Fixed length

➤ Adaptive

➤ Short form

As we mentioned earlier, the case study approach is used with Microsoft's Windows 2000 design exams. These exams contain of a set of case studies that you must analyze to enable you to answer questions related to the case studies. Such exams include one or more case studies (tabbed topic areas), each of which is followed by 4 to 10 questions. The question types for design exams and for Core Four Windows 2000 exams are multiple choice, build list and reorder, create a tree, drag and connect, and select and place. Depending on the test topic, some exams are totally case-based, whereas others are not.

Other Microsoft exams employ advanced testing capabilities that might not be immediately apparent. Although the questions that appear are primarily multiple choice, the logic that drives them is more complex than older Microsoft tests, which use a fixed sequence of questions, called a *fixed-length test*. Some questions employ a sophisticated user interface, which Microsoft calls a *simulation*, to test your knowledge of the software and systems under consideration in a more or less "live" environment that behaves just like the original. The Testing Innovations page at **www.microsoft.com/ trainingandservices/default.asp?PageID=mcp** includes a downloadable practice simulation.

For some exams, Microsoft has turned to a well-known technique, called *adaptive testing*, to establish a test-taker's level of knowledge and product competence. Adaptive exams look the same as fixed-length exams, but they discover the level of difficulty at which an individual test-taker can correctly answer questions. Test-takers with differing levels of knowledge or ability therefore see different sets of questions; individuals with high levels of knowledge or ability are presented with a smaller set of more difficult questions, whereas individuals with lower levels of knowledge are presented with a larger set of easier questions. Two individuals may answer the same percentage of questions correctly, but the test-taker with a higher knowledge or ability level will score higher because his or her questions are worth more.

Also, the lower-level test-taker will probably answer more questions than his or her more-knowledgeable colleague. This explains why adaptive tests use ranges of values to define the number of questions and the amount of time it takes to complete the test.

Adaptive tests work by evaluating the test-taker's most recent answer. A correct answer leads to a more difficult question (and the test software's estimate of the test-taker's knowledge and ability level is raised). An incorrect answer leads to a less difficult question (and the test software's estimate of the test-taker's knowledge and ability level is lowered). This process continues until the test targets the test-taker's true ability level. The exam ends when the test-taker's level of accuracy meets a statistically acceptable value (in other words, when his or her performance demonstrates an acceptable level of knowledge and ability), or when the maximum number of items has been presented (in which case, the test-taker is almost certain to fail).

Microsoft also introduced a short-form test for its most popular tests. This test delivers 30 questions to its takers, giving them exactly 60 minutes to complete the exam. This type of exam is similar to a fixed-length test, in that it allows readers to jump ahead or return to earlier questions, and to cycle through the questions until the test is done. Microsoft does not use adaptive logic in this test, but claims that statistical analysis of the question pool is such that the 30 questions delivered during a short-form exam conclusively measure a test-taker's knowledge of the subject matter in much the same way as an adaptive test. You can think of the short-form test as a kind of "greatest hits exam" (that is, the most important questions are covered) version of an adaptive exam on the same topic.

Note: *Several test-takers have reported that some of the Microsoft exams can appear as a combination of adaptive and fixed-length questions.*

Microsoft tests can come in any one of these forms. Whatever you encounter, you must take the test in whichever form it appears; you can't choose one form over another. If anything, it pays more to prepare thoroughly for an adaptive exam than for a fixed-length or a short-form exam: The penalties for answering incorrectly are built into the test itself on an adaptive exam, whereas the layout remains the same for a fixed-length or short-form test, no matter how many questions you answer incorrectly.

Tip: The biggest difference between an adaptive test and a fixed-length or short-form test is that on a fixed-length or short-form test, you can revisit questions after you've read them over one or more times. On an adaptive test, you must answer the question when it's presented and will have no opportunities to revisit that question thereafter.

STRATEGIES FOR DIFFERENT TESTING FORMATS

Before you choose a test-taking strategy, you must know if your test is case study based, fixed length, short form, or adaptive. When you begin your exam, you'll know right away if the test is based on case studies. The interface will consist of a tabbed Window that allows you to easily navigate through the sections of the case.

If you are taking a test that is not based on case studies, the software will tell you that the test is adaptive, if in fact the version you're taking is an adaptive test. If your introductory materials fail to mention this, you're probably taking a fixed-length test (50 to 70 questions). If the total number of questions involved is 25 to 30, you're taking a short-form test. Some tests announce themselves by indicating that they will start with a set of adaptive questions, followed by fixed-length questions.

Tip: You'll be able to tell for sure if you are taking an adaptive, fixed-length, or short-form test by the first question. If it includes a checkbox that lets you mark the question for later review, you're taking a fixed-length or short-form test. If the total number of questions is 25 to 30, it's a short-form test; if more than 30, it's a fixed-length test. Adaptive test questions can be visited (and answered) only once, and they include no such checkbox.

The Case Study Exam Strategy

Most test-takers find that the case study type of test used for the design exams (70-219, 70-220, and 70-221) is the most difficult to master. When it comes to studying for a test with case studies, your best bet is to approach each case study as a standalone test. The biggest challenge you'll encounter is that you'll feel that you won't have enough time to get through all of the cases that are presented.

. . . .

Tip: Each case provides a lot of material that you'll need to read and study before you can effectively answer the questions that follow. The trick to taking a case study is to first scan the case study to get the highlights. Make sure you read the overview section of the case so that you understand the context of the problem at hand. Then, quickly move on and scan the questions.

                 As you are scanning the questions, make mental notes to yourself so that you'll remember which sections of the case study you should focus on. Some case studies may provide a fair amount of extra information that you don't really need to answer the questions. The goal with our scanning approach is to avoid having to study and analyze material that is not completely relevant.

. . . .

When studying a case, carefully read the tabbed information. It is important to answer every question. You will be able to toggle back and forth from case to questions, and from question to question within a case testlet. However, once you leave the case and move on, you may not be able to return to it. You may want to take notes while reading useful information so you can refer to them when you tackle the test questions. It's hard to go wrong with this strategy when taking any kind of Microsoft certification test.

The Fixed-Length and Short-Form Exam Strategy

A well-known principle when taking fixed-length or short-form exams is to first read over the entire exam from start to finish while answering only those questions you feel absolutely sure of. On subsequent passes, you can dive into more complex questions more deeply, knowing how many such questions you have left.

Fortunately, the Microsoft exam software for fixed-length and short-form tests makes the multiple-visit approach easy to implement. At the top-left corner of each question is a checkbox that permits you to mark that question for a later visit.

Note: *Marking questions makes review easier, but you can return to any question by clicking the Forward or Back button repeatedly.*

As you read each question, if you answer only those you're sure of and mark for review those that you're not sure of, you can keep working through a decreasing list of questions as you answer the trickier ones in order.

. . . .

Tip: There's at least one potential benefit to reading the exam over completely before answering the trickier questions: Sometimes, information supplied in later questions sheds more light on earlier questions. At other times, information you read in later questions might jog your memory about Windows 2000 Server facts, figures, or behavior that helps you answer earlier questions. Either way, you'll come out ahead if you defer those questions about which you're not absolutely sure.

. . . .

Here are some question-handling strategies that apply to fixed-length and short-form tests. Use them if you have the chance:

➤ When returning to a question after your initial read-through, read every word again—otherwise, your mind can fall quickly into a rut. Sometimes, revisiting a question after turning your attention elsewhere lets you see something you missed, but the strong tendency is to see what you've seen before. Try to avoid that tendency at all costs.

➤ If you return to a question more than twice, try to articulate to yourself what you don't understand about the question, why answers don't appear to make sense, or what appears to be missing. If you chew on the subject awhile, your subconscious might provide the details you lack, or you might notice a "trick" that points to the right answer.

As you work your way through the exam, another counter that Microsoft provides will come in handy—the number of questions completed and questions outstanding. For fixed-length and short-form tests, it's wise to budget your time by making sure that you've completed one-quarter of the questions one-quarter of the way through the exam period, and three-quarters of the questions three-quarters of the way through.

If you're not finished when only five minutes remain, use that time to guess your way through any remaining questions. Remember, guessing is potentially more valuable than not answering, because blank answers are always wrong, but a guess may turn out to be right. If you don't have a clue about any of the remaining questions, pick answers at random, or choose all a's, b's, and so on. The important thing is to submit an exam for scoring that has an answer for every question.

. . . .
Tip: At the very end of your exam period, you're better off guessing than leaving questions unanswered.
. . . .

The Adaptive Exam Strategy

If there's one principle that applies to taking an adaptive test, it could be summed up as "Get it right the first time." You cannot elect to skip a question and move on to the next one when taking an adaptive test, because the testing software uses your answer to the current question to select whatever question it plans to present next. Nor can you return to a question once you've moved on, because the software gives you only one chance to answer the question. You can, however, take notes, because sometimes information supplied in earlier questions will shed more light on later questions.

Also, when you answer a question correctly, you are presented with a more difficult question next, to help the software gauge your level of skill and ability.

When you answer a question incorrectly, you are presented with a less difficult question, and the software lowers its current estimate of your skill and ability. This continues until the program settles into a reasonably accurate estimate of what you know and can do, and takes you on average through somewhere between 15 and 30 questions as you complete the test.

The good news is that if you know your stuff, you'll probably finish most adaptive tests in 30 minutes or so. The bad news is that you must really, really know your stuff to do your best on an adaptive test. That's because some questions are so convoluted, complex, or hard to follow that you're bound to miss one or two, at a minimum, even if you do know your stuff. So the more you know, the better you'll do on an adaptive test, even accounting for the occasionally weird or unfathomable questions that appear on these exams.

. . . .

Tip: Because you can't always tell in advance if a test is fixed-length, short form, or adaptive, you will be best served by preparing for the exam as if it were adaptive. That way, you should be prepared to pass no matter what kind of test you take. But if you do take a fixed-length or short-form test, remember our tips from the preceding section. They should help you improve on what you could do on an adaptive test.

. . . .

If you encounter a question on an adaptive test that you can't answer, you must guess an answer immediately. Because of how the software works, you may suffer for your guess on the next question if you guess right, because you'll get a more difficult question next!

QUESTION-HANDLING STRATEGIES

Based on exams we have taken, some interesting trends have become apparent. For those questions that take only a single answer, usually two or three of the answers will be obviously incorrect, and two of the answers will be plausible— of course, only one can be correct. Unless the answer leaps out at you (if it does, reread the question to look for a trick; sometimes those are the ones you're most likely to get wrong), begin the process of answering by eliminating those answers that are most obviously wrong.

Almost always, at least one answer out of the possible choices for a question can be eliminated immediately because it matches one of these conditions:

➤ The answer does not apply to the situation.

➤ The answer describes a nonexistent issue, an invalid option, or an imaginary state.

After you eliminate all answers that are obviously wrong, you can apply your retained knowledge to eliminate further answers. Look for items that sound correct but refer to actions, commands, or features that are not present or not available in the situation that the question describes.

If you're still faced with a blind guess among two or more potentially correct answers, reread the question. Try to picture how each of the possible remaining answers would alter the situation. Be especially sensitive to terminology; sometimes the choice of words ("remove" instead of "disable") can make the difference between a right answer and a wrong one.

Only when you've exhausted your ability to eliminate answers, but remain unclear about which of the remaining possibilities is correct, should you guess at an answer. An unanswered question offers you no points, but guessing gives you at least some chance of getting a question right; just don't be too hasty when making a blind guess.

Note: If you're taking a fixed-length or a short-form test, you can wait until the last round of reviewing marked questions (just as you're about to run out of time, or out of unanswered questions) before you start making guesses. You will have the same option within each case study testlet (but once you leave a testlet, you may not be allowed to return to it). If you're taking an adaptive test, you'll have to guess to move on to the next question if you can't figure out an answer some other way. Either way, guessing should be your technique of last resort!

Numerous questions assume that the default behavior of a particular utility is in effect. If you know the defaults and understand what they mean, this knowledge will help you cut through many Gordian knots.

MASTERING THE INNER GAME

In the final analysis, knowledge breeds confidence, and confidence breeds success. If you study the materials in this book carefully and review all the practice questions at the end of each chapter, you should become aware of those areas where additional learning and study are required.

After you've worked your way through the book, take the practice exam in the back of the book and the practice exams on the CD-ROM. Be sure to click on the Update button in our CD-ROM's testing engine to download free questions from the Coriolis Web site! Taking tests will provide a reality check and help you identify areas to study further. Make sure you follow up and review materials related to the questions you miss on the practice exams before scheduling a real exam. Only when you've covered that ground and feel comfortable with the whole scope of the practice exams should you set an exam appointment. Only if you score 85 percent or better should you proceed to the real thing (otherwise, obtain some additional practice tests so you can keep trying until you hit this magic number).

. . . .

Tip: If you take a practice exam and don't score at least 85 percent correct, you'll want to practice further. Microsoft provides links to practice exam providers and and also offers self-assessment exams from the Microsoft Certified Professional Web site **www.microsoft.com/trainingandservices/**. You should also check out **ExamCram.com** for downloadable practice questions.

. . . .

Armed with the information in this book and with the determination to augment your knowledge, you should be able to pass the certification exam. However, you need to work at it, or you'll spend the exam fee more than once before you finally pass. If you prepare seriously, you should do well. We are confident that you can do it!

The next section covers the exam requirements for the various Microsoft certifications.

THE MICROSOFT CERTIFIED PROFESSIONAL (MCP) PROGRAM

The MCP Program currently includes the following separate tracks, each of which boasts its own special acronym (as a certification candidate, you need to have a high tolerance for alphabet soup of all kinds):

➤ *MCP (Microsoft Certified Professional)*—This is the least prestigious of all the certification tracks from Microsoft. Passing one of the major Microsoft exams qualifies an individual for the MCP credential. Individuals can demonstrate proficiency with additional Microsoft products by passing additional certification exams.

➤ *MCP+SB (Microsoft Certified Professional + Site Building)*—This certification program is designed for individuals who are planning, building, managing, and maintaining Web sites. Individuals with the MCP+SB credential will have demonstrated the ability to develop Web sites that include multimedia and searchable content and Web sites that connect to and communicate with a back-end database. It requires one MCP exam, plus two of these three exams: "70-055: Designing and Implementing Web Sites with Microsoft FrontPage 98," "70-057: Designing and Implementing Commerce Solutions with Microsoft Site Server, 3.0, Commerce Edition," and "70-152: Designing and Implementing Web Solutions with Microsoft Visual InterDev 6.0."

➤ *MCSE (Microsoft Certified Systems Engineer)*—Anyone who has a current MCSE is warranted to possess a high level of networking expertise including Microsoft operating systems and products. This credential is designed to prepare individuals to plan, implement, maintain, and support information systems, networks, and internetworks built around Microsoft Windows 2000 and its BackOffice family of products.

To obtain an MCSE, an individual must pass four core operating system exams, one core option exam, plus two elective exams. The operating system exams require individuals to prove their competence with desktop and server operating systems and networking/internetworking components.

For Windows NT 4 MCSEs, the Accelerated exam, "70–240: Microsoft Windows 2000 Accelerated Exam for MCPs Certified on Microsoft Windows NT 4.0," is an option. This free exam covers all of the material tested in the Core Four exams. The hitch in this plan is that you can take the test only once. If you fail, you must take all four core exams to recertify. The Core Four exams are: "70–210: Installing, Configuring and Administering Microsoft Windows 2000 Professional," "70–215: Installing, Configuring and Administering Microsoft Windows 2000 Server," "70–216: Implementing and Administering a Microsoft Windows 2000 Network Infrastructure," and "70–217: Implementing and Administering a Microsoft Windows 2000 Directory Services Infrastructure."

The two remaining exams are electives. An elective exam may fall in any number of subject or product areas, primarily BackOffice components. To fulfill the fifth core exam requirement, you can choose from three design exams: "70–219: Designing a Microsoft Windows 2000 Directory Services Infrastructure," "70–220: Designing Security for a Microsoft Windows 2000 Network," or "70–221: Designing a Microsoft Windows 2000 Network Infrastructure." The two design exams that you don't select as your fifth core exam also qualify as electives. If you are on your way to becoming an MCSE and have already taken some exams, visit **www.microsoft.com/mcp/certstep/mcse.htm** for information about how to complete your MCSE certification.

In September 1999, Microsoft announced its Windows 2000 track for MCSE and also announced retirement of Windows NT 4.0 MCSE core exams on 12/31/2000. Individuals who wish to remain certified MCSEs after 12/31/2001 must "upgrade" their certifications on or before 12/31/2001. For more detailed information than is included visit **www.microsoft.com/mcp/certstep/mcse.htm**.

New MCSE candidates must pass seven tests to meet the MCSE requirements. It's not uncommon for the entire process to take a year or so, and many individuals find that they must take a test more than once to pass. The primary goal of the *Exam Prep* series and the *Exam Cram* series, our test preparation books, is to make it possible, given proper study and preparation, to pass all Microsoft certification tests on the first try. Table 1 shows the required and elective exams for the Windows 2000 MCSE certification.

Table 1 MCSE Windows 2000 Requirements

Core

If you have not passed these 3 Windows NT 4 exams	
Exam 70-067	Implementing and Supporting Microsoft Windows NT Server 4.0
Exam 70-068	Implementing and Supporting Microsoft Windows NT Server 4.0 in the Enterprise
Exam 70-073	Microsoft Windows NT Workstation 4.0
then you must take these 4 exams	
Exam 70-210	Installing, Configuring and Administering Microsoft Windows 2000 Professional
Exam 70-215	Installing, Configuring and Administering Microsoft Windows 2000 Server
Exam 70-216	Implementing and Administering a Microsoft Windows 2000 Network Infrastructure
Exam 70-217	Implementing and Administering a Microsoft Windows 2000 Directory Services Infrastructure
If you have already passed exams 70-067, 70-068, and 70-073, you may take this exam	
Exam 70-240	Microsoft Windows 2000 Accelerated Exam for MCPs Certified on Microsoft Windows NT 4.0

5th Core Option

Choose 1 from this group	
Exam 70-219*	Designing a Microsoft Windows 2000 Directory Services Infrastructure
Exam 70-220*	Designing Security for a Microsoft Windows 2000 Network
Exam 70-221*	Designing a Microsoft Windows 2000 Network Infrastructure

Elective

Choose 2 from this group	
Exam 70-019	Designing and Implementing Data Warehouse with Microsoft SQL Server 7.0
Exam 70-219*	Designing a Microsoft Windows 2000 Directory Services Infrastructure
Exam 70-220*	Designing Security for a Microsoft Windows 2000 Network
Exam 70-221*	Designing a Microsoft Windows 2000 Network Infrastructure
Exam 70-222	Migrating from Microsoft Windows NT 4.0 to Microsoft Windows 2000
Exam 70-028	Administering Microsoft SQL Server 7.0
Exam 70-029	Designing and Implementing Databases on Microsoft SQL Server 7.0
Exam 70-080	Implementing and Supporting Microsoft Internet Explorer 5.0 by Using the Internet Explorer Administration Kit
Exam 70-081	Implementing and Supporting Microsoft Exchange Server 5.5
Exam 70-085	Implementing and Supporting Microsoft SNA Server 4.0
Exam 70-086	Implementing and Supporting Microsoft Systems Management Server 2.0
Exam 70-088	Implementing and Supporting Microsoft Proxy Server 2.0

This is not a complete listing—you can still be tested on some earlier versions of these products. However, we have included mainly the most recent versions so that you may test on these versions and thus be certified longer. We have not included any tests that are scheduled to be retired.

* The 5th Core Option exam does not double as an elective.

➤ *MCSD (Microsoft Certified Solution Developer)*—The MCSD credential reflects the skills required to create multi-tier, distributed, and COM-based solutions, in addition to desktop and Internet applications, using new technologies. To obtain an MCSD, an individual must demonstrate the ability to analyze and interpret user requirements; select and integrate products, platforms, tools, and technologies; design and implement code, and customize applications; and perform necessary software tests and quality assurance operations.

To become an MCSD, you must pass a total of four exams: three core exams and one elective exam. Each candidate must choose one of these three desktop application exams—"70-016: Designing and Implementing Desktop Applications with Microsoft Visual C++ 6.0," "70-156: Designing and Implementing Desktop Applications with Microsoft Visual FoxPro 6.0," or "70-176: Designing and Implementing Desktop Applications with Microsoft Visual Basic 6.0"—*plus* one of these three distributed application exams—"70-015: Designing and Implementing Distributed Applications with Microsoft Visual C++ 6.0," "70-155: Designing and Implementing Desktop Applications with Microsoft Visual FoxPro 6.0," or "70-175: Designing and Implementing Desktop Applications with Microsoft Visual Basic 6.0." The third core exam is "70-100: Analyzing Requirements and Defining Solution Architectures." Elective exams cover specific Microsoft applications and languages, including Visual Basic, C++, the Microsoft Foundation Classes, Access, SQL Server, Excel, and more.

➤ *MCDBA (Microsoft Certified Database Administrator)*—The MCDBA credential reflects the skills required to implement and administer Microsoft SQL Server databases. To obtain an MCDBA, an individual must demonstrate the ability to derive physical database designs, develop logical data models, create physical databases, create data services by using Transact-SQL, manage and maintain databases, configure and manage security, monitor and optimize databases, and install and configure Microsoft SQL Server.

To become an MCDBA, you must pass a total of four exams and one elective exam. The required core exams are "70-028: Administering Microsoft SQL Server 7.0," "70-027: Designing and Implementing Databases with Microsoft SQL Server 7.0," and "70-215: Installing, Configuring and Administering Microsoft Windows 2000 Server."

The elective exams that you can choose from cover specific uses of SQL Server and include "70-019: Designing and Implementing Distributed Applications with Visual C++ 6.0," "70-019: Designing and Implementing Data Warehouses with Microsoft SQL Server 7.0 and Microsoft Decision Support Services 1.0," "70-155: Designing and Implementing Distributed

Applications with Visual FoxPro 6.0," "70-175: Designing and Implementing Distributed Applications with Visual Basic 6.0," and two exams that relate to Windows 2000: "70-126: Implementing and Administering Microsoft Windows 2000 Network Infrastructure," and "70-087: Implementing and Supporting Microsoft Internet Information Server 4.0."

If you have taken the three core Windows NT 4 exams on your path to becoming an MCSE, you qualify for the Accelerated exam (it replaces the Network Infrastructure exam requirement). The Accelerated exam covers the objectives of all four of the Windows 2000 core exams. In addition to taking the Accelerated exam, you must take only the two SQL exams—Administering and Database Design. Note that the exam covered by this book is a core requirement for the MCDBA certification. Table 2 shows the requirements for the MCDBA certification.

➤ *MCT (Microsoft Certified Trainer)*—Microsoft Certified Trainers are deemed able to deliver elements of the official Microsoft curriculum, based on technical knowledge and instructional ability. Thus, it is necessary for an individual seeking MCT credentials (which are granted on a course-by-course basis) to pass the related certification exam for a course and complete the official Microsoft training in the subject area, and to demonstrate an ability to teach. MCT candidates must also possess a current MCSE.

This teaching skill criterion may be satisfied by proving that one has already attained training certification from Novell, Banyan, Lotus, the Santa Cruz Operation, or Cisco, or by taking a Microsoft-sanctioned workshop on instruction. Microsoft makes it clear that MCTs are important cogs in the Microsoft training channels. Instructors must be MCTs before Microsoft will allow them to teach in any of its official training channels, including Microsoft's affiliated Certified Technical Education Centers (CTECs) and its online training partner network.

Microsoft has announced that the MCP+I and MCSE+I credentials will not be continued when the MCSE exams for Windows 2000 are in full swing because the skill set for the Internet portion of the program has been included in the new MCSE program. Therefore, details on these tracks are not provided here; go to **www.microsoft.com/trainingandservices/** if you need more information.

Once a Microsoft product becomes obsolete, MCPs typically have to recertify on current versions. (If individuals do not recertify, their certifications become invalid.) Because technology keeps changing and new products continually supplant old ones, this should come as no surprise. This explains why Microsoft has announced that MCSEs have 12 months past the scheduled retirement date for the Windows NT 4 exams to recertify on Windows 2000 topics. (Note that this means taking at least two exams, if not more.)

Table 2   MCDBA Requirements
Core

If you have not passed these 3 Windows NT 4 exams	
Exam 70-067	Implementing and Supporting Microsoft Windows NT Server 4.0
Exam 70-068	Implementing and Supporting Microsoft Windows NT Server 4.0 in the Enterprise
Exam 70-073	Microsoft Windows NT Workstation 4.0
you must take this exam	
Exam 70-215	Installing, Configuring and Administering Microsoft Windows 2000 Server
plus these 2 exams	
Exam 70-028	Administering Microsoft SQL Server 7.0
Exam 70-029	Designing and Implementing Databases with Microsoft SQL Server 7.0

Elective

Choose 1 of the following exams	
Exam 70-015	Designing and Implementing Distributed Applications with Microsoft Visual C++ 6.0
Exam 70-019	Designing and Implementing Data Warehouses with Microsoft SQL Server 7.0
Exam 70-087	Implementing and Supporting Microsoft Internet Information Server 4.0
Exam 70-155	Designing and Implementing Distributed Applications with Microsoft Visual FoxPro 6.0
Exam 70-175	Designing and Implementing Distributed Applications with Microsoft Visual Basic 6.0
Exam 70-216	Implementing and Administering a Microsoft Windows 2000 Network Infrastructure

OR

If you have already passed exams 70-067, 70-068, and 70-073, you may take this exam	
Exam 70-240	Microsoft Windows 2000 Accelerated Exam for MCPs Certified on Microsoft Windows NT 4.0
plus these 2 exams	
Exam 70-028	Administering Microsoft SQL Server 7.0
Exam 70-029	Designing and Implementing Databases with Microsoft SQL Server 7.0

The best place to keep tabs on the MCP Program and its related certifications is on the Web. The URL for the MCP program is **www.microsoft.com/mcp/**. But Microsoft's Web site changes often, so if this URL doesn't work, try using the Search tool on Microsoft's site with either "MCP" or the quoted phrase "Microsoft Certified Professional Program" as a search string. This will help you find the latest and most accurate information about Microsoft's certification programs.

TRACKING MCP STATUS

As soon as you pass any Microsoft exam (except Networking Essentials), you'll attain Microsoft Certified Professional (MCP) status. Microsoft also generates transcripts that indicate which exams you have passed and your corresponding test scores. You can view a copy of your transcript at any time by going to the MCP secured site and selecting Transcript Tool. This tool will allow you to print a copy of your current transcript and confirm your certification status.

Once you pass the necessary set of exams, you'll be certified. Official certification normally takes anywhere from six to eight weeks, so don't expect to get your credentials overnight. When the package for a qualified certification arrives, it includes a Welcome Kit that contains a number of elements:

➤ An MCP, MCSE, or MCSD certificate, suitable for framing.

➤ A license to use the MCP logo, thereby allowing you to use the logo in advertisements, promotions, and documents, and on letterhead, business cards, and so on. Along with the license comes an MCP logo sheet, which includes camera-ready artwork. (Note: Before using any of the artwork, individuals must sign and return a licensing agreement that indicates they'll abide by its terms and conditions.)

➤ A subscription to *Microsoft Certified Professional Magazine*, which provides ongoing data about testing and certification activities, requirements, and changes to the program.

➤ A one-year subscription to the Microsoft Beta Evaluation program. This subscription will get you all beta products from Microsoft for the next year. (This does not include developer products. You must join the MSDN program or become an MCSD to qualify for developer beta products.)

In addition, a Professional Program Membership card and lapel pin will be shipped to you separately from the Welcome Kit.

Many people believe that the benefits of MCP certification go well beyond the perks that Microsoft provides to newly anointed members of this elite group. We're starting to see more job listings that request or require applicants to have an MCP, MCSE, and so on, and many individuals who complete the program can qualify for increases in pay and/or responsibility. As an official recognition of hard work and broad knowledge, one of the MCP credentials is a badge of honor in many IT organizations.

ABOUT THE BOOK

Career opportunities abound for well-prepared Windows 2000 Server administrators. This book is designed as your doorway into Windows 2000 Server installation and administration. If you are new to Windows 2000, this is your ticket to an exciting future. Others who have prior experience with Windows-based network operating systems will find that the book adds depth and breadth to that experience. Also, the book provides the knowledge you need to prepare for Microsoft's certification exam 70-215 "Installing, Configuring, and Administering Microsoft Windows 2000 Server." Passing this exam is a crucial step in becoming a Microsoft Certified Systems Engineer.

Because Windows 2000 Server is an integral part of Windows 2000 networking, it is marvelously scalable and fits into both large and small organizations. It provides the cornerstone on which to build a Windows 2000 network. The success of Windows 2000 Server is reflected in the huge number of software vendors and developers who develop in this environment, or who have switched from other environments to Windows 2000 Server.

When you complete this book, you will be at the threshold of a Windows 2000 Server administration career that can be very fulfilling and challenging. This is a rapidly advancing field that offers ample opportunity for personal growth and for making a contribution to your business or organization. The book is intended to provide you with knowledge that you can apply right away and a sound basis for understanding the changes that you will encounter in the future. It also is intended to give you the hands-on skills you need to be a valued professional in your organization.

The book is filled with real-world projects that cover every aspect of installing, managing, and troubleshooting Windows 2000 Server. The projects are designed to make what you learn come alive through actually performing the tasks. Also, every chapter includes a range of practice questions to help prepare you for the Microsoft certification exam. All of these features are offered to reinforce your learning, so you'll feel confident in the knowledge you have gained from each chapter.

Features

To aid you in fully understanding Windows 2000 Server concepts, there are many features in this book designed to improve its value:

➤ *Chapter objectives*—Each chapter in this book begins with a detailed list of the topics to be mastered within that chapter. This list provides you with a quick reference to the contents of that chapter, as well as a useful study aid.

➤ *Illustrations and tables*—Numerous illustrations of screenshots and components aid you in the visualization of common setup steps, theories, and concepts. In addition, many tables provide details and comparisons of both practical and theoretical information.

➤ *Notes, tips, and warnings*—Notes present additional helpful material related to the subject being described. Tips from the author's experience provide extra information about how to attack a problem, how to set up a Windows 2000 Server for a particular need, or what to do in certain real-world situations. Warnings are included to help you anticipate potential mistakes or problems so you can prevent them from happening.

➤ *Chapter summaries*—Each chapter's text is followed by a summary of the concepts it has introduced. These summaries provide a helpful way to recap and revisit the ideas covered in each chapter.

➤ *Review questions*—End-of-chapter assessment begins with a set of review questions that reinforce the ideas introduced in each chapter. These questions not only ensure that you have mastered the concepts, but are written to help prepare you for the Microsoft certification examination. Answers to these questions are found in Appendix A.

➤ *Real-world projects*—Although it is important to understand the theory behind server and networking technology, nothing can improve upon real-world experience. To this end, along with theoretical explanations, each chapter provides numerous hands-on projects aimed at providing you with real-world implementation experience.

➤ *Sample tests*—Use the sample test and answer key in Chapters 15 and 16 to test yourself. Then, move on to the interactive practice exams found on the CD-ROM. The testing engine offers a variety of testing formats to choose from.

WHERE SHOULD YOU START?

This book is intended to be read in sequence, from beginning to end. Each chapter builds upon those that precede it, to provide a solid understanding of Windows 2000 Server. After completing the chapters, you may find it useful to go back through the book and use the review questions and projects to prepare for the Microsoft certification test for "Installing, Configuring, and Administering Microsoft Windows 2000 Server" (Exam 70-215). Readers are also encouraged to investigate the many pointers to online and printed sources of additional information that are cited throughout this book.

Please share your feedback on the book with us, especially if you have ideas about how we can improve it for future readers. We'll consider everything you say carefully, and we'll respond to all suggestions. Send your questions or comments to us at **learn@examcram.com**. Please remember to include the title of the book in your message; otherwise, we'll be forced to guess which book you're writing about. And we don't like to guess—we want to *know*! Also, be sure to check out the Web pages at **www.examcram.com**, where you'll find information updates, commentary, and certification information. Thanks, and enjoy the book!

SELF-ASSESSMENT

The reason we included a Self-Assessment in this *Exam Prep* book is to help you evaluate your readiness to tackle MCSE certification. It should also help you understand what you need to know to master the topic of this book—namely, Exam 70-215, "Installing, Configuring, and Administering Microsoft Windows 2000 Server." But before you tackle this Self-Assessment, let's talk about concerns you may face when pursuing an MCSE, and what an ideal MCSE candidate might look like.

MCSEs IN THE REAL WORLD

In the next section, we describe an ideal MCSE candidate, knowing full well that only a few real candidates will meet this ideal. In fact, our description of that ideal candidate might seem downright scary, especially with the changes that have been made to the program to support Windows 2000. But take heart: Although the requirements to obtain an MCSE may seem formidable, they are by no means impossible to meet. However, be keenly aware that it does take time, involves some expense, and requires real effort to get through the process.

Increasing numbers of people are attaining Microsoft certifications, so the goal is within reach. You can get all the real-world motivation you need from knowing that many others have gone before, so you will be able to follow in their footsteps. If you're willing to tackle the process seriously and do what it takes to obtain the necessary experience and knowledge, you can take—and pass—all the certification tests involved in obtaining an MCSE. In fact, we've designed *Exam Preps*, the companion *Exam Crams*, *Exam Cram Personal Trainers*, and *Exam Cram Personal Test Centers* to make it as easy on you as possible to prepare for these exams. We've also greatly expanded our Web site, **www.examcram.com**, to provide a host of resources to help you prepare for the complexities of Windows 2000.

The same, of course, is true for other Microsoft certifications, including:

➤ MCSD, which is aimed at software developers and requires one specific exam, two more exams on client and distributed topics, plus a fourth elective exam drawn from a different, but limited, pool of options.

➤ Other Microsoft certifications, whose requirements range from one test (MCP) to several tests (MCP+SB, MCDBA).

THE IDEAL MCSE CANDIDATE

Just to give you some idea of what an ideal MCSE candidate is like, here are some relevant statistics about the background and experience such an individual might have. Don't worry if you don't meet these qualifications, or don't come that close—this is a far from ideal world, and where you fall short is simply where you'll have more work to do.

➤ Academic or professional training in network theory, concepts, and operations. This includes everything from networking media and transmission techniques through network operating systems, services, and applications.

➤ Three-plus years of professional networking experience, including experience with Ethernet, token ring, modems, and other networking media. This must include installation, configuration, upgrade, and troubleshooting experience.

Note: The Windows 2000 MCSE program is much more rigorous than the previous NT MCSE program; therefore, you'll really need some hands-on experience. Some of the exams require you to solve real-world case studies and network design issues, so the more hands-on experience you have, the better.

➤ Two-plus years in a networked environment that includes hands-on experience with Windows 2000 Server, Windows 2000 Professional, Windows NT Server, Windows NT Workstation, and Windows 95 or Windows 98. A solid understanding of each system's architecture, installation, configuration, maintenance, and troubleshooting is also essential.

➤ Knowledge of the various methods for installing Windows 2000, including manual and unattended installations.

➤ A thorough understanding of key networking protocols, addressing, and name resolution, including TCP/IP, IPX/SPX, and NetBEUI.

➤ A thorough understanding of NetBIOS naming, browsing, and file and print services.

➤ Familiarity with key Windows 2000-based TCP/IP-based services, including HTTP (Web servers), DHCP, WINS, DNS, plus familiarity with one or more of the following: Internet Information Server (IIS), Index Server, and Proxy Server.

➤ An understanding of how to implement security for key network data in a Windows 2000 environment.

➤ Working knowledge of NetWare 3.x and 4.x, including IPX/SPX frame formats, NetWare file, print, and directory services, and both Novell and Microsoft client software. Working knowledge of Microsoft's Client Service For NetWare (CSNW), Gateway Service For NetWare (GSNW), the NetWare Migration Tool (NWCONV), and the NetWare Client For Windows (NT, 95, and 98) is essential.

➤ A good working understanding of Active Directory. The more you work with Windows 2000, the more you'll realize that this new operating system is quite different than Windows NT. New technologies like Active Directory have really changed the way that Windows is configured and used. We recommend that you find out as much as you can about Active Directory and acquire as much experience using this technology as possible. The time you take learning about Active Directory will be time very well spent!

Fundamentally, this boils down to a bachelor's degree in computer science, plus three years' experience working in a position involving network design, installation, configuration, and maintenance. We believe that well under half of all certification candidates meet these requirements, and that, in fact, most meet less than half of these requirements—at least, when they begin the certification process. But because all 200,000 people who already have been certified have survived this ordeal, you can survive it too—especially if you heed what our Self-Assessment can tell you about what you already know and what you need to learn.

PUT YOURSELF TO THE TEST

The following series of questions and observations is designed to help you figure out how much work you must do to pursue Microsoft certification and what kinds of resources you may consult on your quest. Be absolutely honest in your answers, or you'll end up wasting money on exams you're not yet ready to take. There are no right or wrong answers, only steps along the path to certification. Only you can decide where you really belong in the broad spectrum of aspiring candidates.

Two things should be clear from the outset, however:

➤ Even a modest background in computer science will be helpful.

➤ Hands-on experience with Microsoft products and technologies is an essential ingredient to certification success.

Educational Background

1. Have you ever taken any computer-related classes? [Yes or No]

   If Yes, proceed to question 2; if No, proceed to question 4.

2. Have you taken any classes on computer operating systems? [Yes or No]

   If Yes, you will probably be able to handle Microsoft's architecture and system component discussions. If you're rusty, brush up on basic operating system concepts, especially virtual memory, multitasking regimes, user mode versus kernel mode operation, and general computer security topics.

   If No, consider some basic reading in this area. We strongly recommend a good general operating systems book, such as *Operating System Concepts, 5th Edition*, by Abraham Silberschatz and Peter Baer Galvin (John Wiley & Sons, 1998, ISBN 0-471-36414-2). If this title doesn't appeal to you, check out reviews for other, similar titles at your favorite online bookstore.

3. Have you taken any networking concepts or technologies classes? [Yes or No]

   If Yes, you will probably be able to handle Microsoft's networking terminology, concepts, and technologies (brace yourself for frequent departures from normal usage). If you're rusty, brush up on basic networking concepts and terminology, especially networking media, transmission types, the OSI Reference Model, and networking technologies such as Ethernet, token ring, FDDI, and WAN links.

   If No, you might want to read one or two books in this topic area. The two best books that we know of are *Computer Networks, 3rd Edition*, by Andrew S. Tanenbaum (Prentice-Hall, 1996, ISBN 0-13-349945-6) and *Computer Networks and Internets, 2nd Edition*, by Douglas E. Comer (Prentice-Hall, 1998, ISBN 0-130-83617-6).

   Skip to the next section, "Hands-on Experience."

4. Have you done any reading on operating systems or networks? [Yes or No]

   If Yes, review the requirements stated in the first paragraphs after questions 2 and 3. If you meet those requirements, move on to the next section. If No, consult the recommended reading for both topics. A strong background will help you prepare for the Microsoft exams better than just about anything else.

Hands-on Experience

The most important key to success on all of the Microsoft tests is hands-on experience, especially with Windows 2000 Server and Professional, plus the many add-on services and BackOffice components around which so many of the Microsoft certification exams revolve. If we leave you with only one realization after taking this Self-Assessment, it should be that there's no substitute for time spent installing, configuring, and using the various Microsoft products upon which you'll be tested repeatedly and in depth.

5. Have you installed, configured, and worked with:

➤ Windows 2000 Server? [Yes or No]

If Yes, make sure you understand basic concepts as covered in Exam 70-215. You should also study the TCP/IP interfaces, utilities, and services for Exam 70-216, plus implementing security features for Exam 70-220.

. . . .

Tip: You can download objectives, practice exams, and other data about Microsoft exams from the Training and Certification page at **www.microsoft.com/trainingandservices/ default/asp?PageID=mcp/**. Use the "Exams" link to obtain specific exam info.

. . . .

If you haven't worked with Windows 2000 Server, you must obtain one or two machines and a copy of Windows 2000 Server. Then, learn the operating system and whatever other software components on which you'll also be tested.

In fact, we recommend that you obtain two computers, each with a network interface, and set up a two-node network on which to practice. With decent Windows 2000-capable computers selling for about $500 to $600 apiece these days, this shouldn't be too much of a financial hardship. You may have to scrounge to come up with the necessary software, but if you scour the Microsoft Web site you can usually find low-cost options to obtain evaluation copies of most of the software that you'll need.

➤ Windows 2000 Professional? [Yes or No]

If Yes, make sure you understand the concepts covered in Exam 70-210.

If No, you will want to obtain a copy of Windows 2000 Professional and learn how to install, configure, and maintain it. You can use *MCSE Windows 2000 Professional Exam Cram* to guide your activities and studies, or work straight from Microsoft's test objectives if you prefer.

. . . .

Tip: For any and all of these Microsoft exams, the Resource Kits for the topics involved are a good study resource. You can purchase softcover Resource Kits from Microsoft Press (search for them at **http://mspress.microsoft.com/**), but they also appear on the TechNet CDs (**www.microsoft.com/technet**). Along with the *Exam Crams* and *Exam Preps*, we believe that Resource Kits are among the best tools you can use to get ready for Microsoft exams.

. . . .

6. For any specific Microsoft product that is not itself an operating system (for example, FrontPage 2000, SQL Server, and so on), have you installed, configured, used, and upgraded this software? [Yes or No]

   If the answer is Yes, skip to the next section. If it's No, you must get some experience. Read on for suggestions on how to do this.

   Experience is a must with any Microsoft product exam, be it something as simple as FrontPage 2000 or as challenging as Exchange Server 5.5 or SQL Server 7.0. For trial copies of other software, search Microsoft's Web site using the name of the product as your search term. Also, search for bundles like "BackOffice" or "Small Business Server."

Tip: If you have the funds, or your employer will pay your way, consider taking a class at a Certified Training and Education Center (CTEC) or at an Authorized Academic Training Partner (AATP). In addition to classroom exposure to the topic of your choice, you get a copy of the software that is the focus of your course, along with a trial version of whatever operating system it needs, with the training materials for that class.

Before you even think about taking any Microsoft exam, make sure you've spent enough time with the related software to understand how it may be installed and configured, how to maintain such an installation, and how to troubleshoot that software when things go wrong. This will help you in the exam, and in real life!

Testing Your Exam-Readiness

Whether you attend a formal class on a specific topic to get ready for an exam or use written materials to study on your own, some preparation for the Microsoft certification exams is essential. At $100 a try, pass or fail, you want to do everything you can to pass on your first try. That's where studying comes in.

We have included a practice exam in this book, so if you don't score that well on the test, you can study more and then tackle the test again. We also have exams that you can take online through the **ExamCram.com** Web site at **www.examcram.com**. If you still don't hit a score of at least 70 percent after these tests, you'll want to investigate the other practice test resources we mention in this section.

For any given subject, consider taking a class if you've tackled self-study materials, taken the test, and failed anyway. The opportunity to interact with an instructor and fellow students can make all the difference in the world, if you can afford that privilege. For information about Microsoft classes, visit the Training and Certification page at **www.microsoft.com/education/ partners/ctec.asp** for Microsoft Certified Education Centers or

www.microsoft.com/aatp/default.htm for Microsoft Authorized Training Providers.

If you can't afford to take a class, visit the Training and Certification page anyway, because it also includes pointers to free practice exams and to Microsoft Certified Professional Approved Study Guides and other self-study tools. And even if you can't afford to spend much at all, you should still invest in some low-cost practice exams from commercial vendors.

7. Have you taken a practice exam on your chosen test subject? [Yes or No]

   If Yes, and you scored 70 percent or better, you're probably ready to tackle the real thing. If your score isn't above that threshold, keep at it until you break that barrier.

   If No, obtain all the free and low-budget practice tests you can find (see the list above) and get to work. Keep at it until you can break the passing threshold comfortably.

Tip: When it comes to assessing your test readiness, there is no better way than to take a good-quality practice exam and pass with a score of 70 percent or better. When we're preparing ourselves, we shoot for 80-plus percent, just to leave room for the "weirdness factor" that sometimes shows up on Microsoft exams.

ASSESSING READINESS FOR EXAM 70-215

In addition to the general exam-readiness information in the previous section, there are several things you can do to prepare for the Installing, Configuring, and Administering Microsoft Windows 2000 Server exam. As you're getting ready for Exam 70-215, visit the Exam Cram Windows 2000 Resource Center at **www.examcram.com/studyresource/w2kresource/**. Another valuable resource is the Exam Cram Insider newsletter. Sign up at **www.examcram.com** or send a blank email message to **subscribe-ec@mars.coriolis.com**. We also suggest that you join an active MCSE mailing list. One of the better ones is managed by Sunbelt Software. Sign up at **www.sunbelt-software.com** (look for the Subscribe To button).

You can also cruise the Web looking for "braindumps" (recollections of test topics and experiences recorded by others) to help you anticipate topics you're likely to encounter on the test. The MCSE mailing list is a good place to ask where the useful braindumps are, or you can check Shawn Gamble's list at **www.commandcentral.com**.

. . . .
Tip: You can't be sure that a braindump's author can provide correct answers. Thus, use the questions to guide your studies, but don't rely on the answers in a braindump to lead you to the truth. Double-check everything you find in any braindump.
. . . .

Microsoft exam mavens also recommend checking the Microsoft Knowledge Base (available on its own CD as part of the TechNet collection, or on the Microsoft Web site at **http://support.microsoft.com/support/**) for "meaningful technical support issues" that relate to your exam's topics. Although we're not sure exactly what the quoted phrase means, we have also noticed some overlap between technical support questions on particular products and troubleshooting questions on the exams for those products.

ONWARD, THROUGH THE FOG!

Once you've assessed your readiness, undertaken the right background studies, obtained the hands-on experience that will help you understand the products and technologies at work, and reviewed the many sources of information to help you prepare for a test, you'll be ready to take a round of practice tests. When your scores come back positive enough to get you through the exam, you're ready to go after the real thing. If you follow our assessment regime, you'll not only know what you need to study, but when you're ready to make a test date at Prometric or VUE. Good luck!

CHAPTER ONE

WINDOWS 2000 ARCHITECTURE

After completing this chapter, you will be able to:

✓ Understand the Windows 2000 architecture and its components

✓ Understand multithreading, multitasking, and multiprocessing

✓ Identify the responsibilities and operation of user mode components

✓ Identify the responsibilities and operation of kernel mode components

✓ Understand the Windows 2000 virtual memory model

✓ Understand and identify the differences in architectures between Windows NT 4.x and Windows 2000

✓ Identify the new features of Windows 2000

Microsoft's long-awaited advanced operating system, Windows 2000, is here. It is designed to replace Windows NT 4.x on both desktop and server computers, and it provides superior performance, flexibility, and security. In this chapter, we'll examine Windows 2000, its new features, its various iterations, and its architecture. We'll also provide a comparison to Windows NT 4.x.

WINDOWS 2000 OVERVIEW

Windows 2000 is the next step in Microsoft's movement toward a single operating system for all computers. It incorporates many of the advances seen in Windows 95/98 and provides superior performance and stability. The performance and stability enhancements of Windows 2000 are the result of its being based on the Windows NT 4.x operating system and architecture. To ensure that it had the customers' best interest in mind, Microsoft asked thousands of end users, industry professionals, and network administrators for their input on improvements they would like to see in Windows 2000. The results are the product you see today.

Windows 2000 is available in three different versions at this time: Professional, Server, and Advanced Server, with a fourth, Datacenter Server, on the way. Windows 2000 Professional is the desktop version of the operating system and replaces Windows NT Workstation 4.0. Windows 2000 Professional is a high-performance, secure operating system for network client computers. It incorporates many of the best features of Windows 95 and 98 including full support for Plug and Play devices, DirectX, and FAT32, and enhances the security, manageability, reliability, and performance of Windows NT Workstation 4.x. The Server edition of Windows 2000, also called Standard Server, is the primary focus of this book and the Microsoft Certification Exam #70-215: Installing, Configuring, and Administering Microsoft Windows 2000 Server. Windows 2000 Standard Server replaces Windows NT 4.0 Server and is designed to provide file, print, and application sharing in a networked environment. It extends the features of Windows 2000 Professional and includes additional features and functions for user and computer management and application sharing as well as operating as a full-fledged Web server. Windows 2000 Server is best suited for small- to medium-sized networks, Web sites, workgroups, and remote office locations. Windows NT 4.0 Enterprise Edition is replaced by Windows 2000 Advanced Server. It provides enhanced support for application and Web services through expanded hardware support, network *load balancing*, and application *fault tolerance* through two-node *clustering*. Finally, the Windows 2000 Datacenter Server product, which is scheduled for release in June of 2000, is a new product in many ways. It does not replace a previous version of Windows NT 4, but expands on the Advanced Server features. Designed for the largest enterprise networks, it will provide 32-node network load balancing and 4-node clustering.

Note: Although the idea of clustering is relatively new to Microsoft operating systems, it is a concept that has been used with mainframe and minicomputers for years. A cluster is a group of computers (individually called cluster nodes) that are configured to operate as if they were a single system. Clusters are used to provide load balancing and fault tolerance on large networks.

THE WINDOWS 2000 ARCHITECTURE

The basic architecture in Windows 2000 is the same as that of Windows NT 4.x. In fact, the architecture has remained fundamentally unchanged since Windows NT version 3.51. However, to increase the availability of the server for user access, enhance the stability of the system, and provide greater efficiency, some changes have been made.

The Windows 2000 architecture is a layered architecture, principally divided into two operating modes: *user mode* and *kernel mode*. Applications reside in user mode, and the operating system resides in kernel mode. Any communication between an application and the hardware must take place in kernel mode. The architecture is also modular in design to provide specialized functionality, performance, and fault tolerance. This means that Windows 2000 is not designed as a single, monolithic application, but rather as a group of smaller programs, each with a specific function that work together. Using this type of design, Microsoft can easily perform updates to the operating system as new technologies emerge or changes are required. Consequently, only those components that need to be updated can be modified rather than updating the entire operating system. Figure 1.1 illustrates the Windows 2000 architecture and its operating modes.

Objects in Windows 2000

Like many operating systems, Windows 2000 uses an object-oriented design. A request for a resource ultimately becomes a request for an *object*. In this environment, an object is a set of associated attributes and their values that define the object as well as a list of related operations that can be performed on the object. Every component of the Windows 2000 operating environment including printers, groups, and server processes is an object. Each object is an independent entity with its own configuration and responsibilities. This is necessary because objects can be shared or accessed by more than one process. The object's identification is a combination of its type and its instance. The

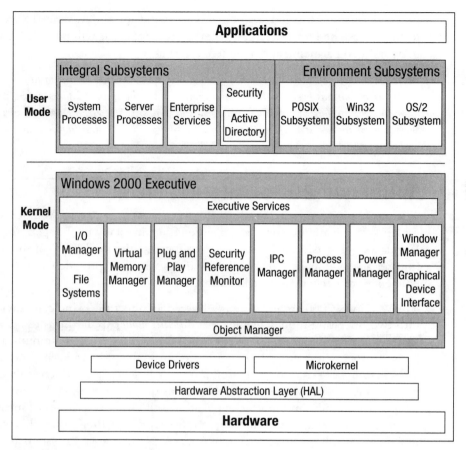

Figure 1.1   The Windows 2000 architecture.

object's *type* is made up of the attributes and services it supports, whereas its *instance* notes which particular entity of the specific type is being referenced. For example, there may be four instances of the file system type, 1 for drive C, 2 for drive D, 3 for drive A, and 4 for the system's CD-ROM drive. When a process requests information from the CD-ROM drive, its request will be to object "file system, 4." Windows 2000 uses the object's identification when verifying whether a requestor has sufficient security assignments to allow access.

Processor Management

One of the most powerful features of Windows 2000 is the way it manages processor utilization. The Windows 2000 processing system design allows applications to be designed with multiple threads that are run concurrently (called *multithreading*), provides the ability for users to efficiently run multiple applications on their computer at the same time (called *multitasking*), and allows the operating system to take full advantage of computers that include more than one microprocessor (called *multiprocessing*).

Discussed throughout this chapter in great detail, the concepts of threads and processes are integral to understanding multithreading, multitasking, and multiprocessing. A *thread* is a set of commands within a program and is the entity to which the operating system grants processor time. A *program* is an executable collection of one or more threads, their code, and other information. When a program is run, a *process* is created in the operating environment and includes memory space and at least one thread. A process is an executable set of commands designed to perform a specific set of steps, allowing access to system resources, such as files and hardware devices. The component of the process in command of the CPU at a particular moment is the thread. The thread runs in the same address space and uses the same system resources provided to its process.

Note: *Although it may seem confusing at first, there are two primary points to remember. A thread is a set of commands that is granted access to the CPU. A process is the operating version of a program and must contain at least one thread.*

Multithreading

As mentioned previously, all programs are made up of at least one thread. In other operating systems (including earlier versions of Windows), processes were able to handle only one thread at a time. If there are multiple functions to be performed, the first thread must be started and completed before the second thread could be started. Processes that are part of Windows 2000 can execute many threads at once, allowing more efficient use of the system; this process is called *multithreading*. As an example, consider the Internet Explorer Web browser. As you type in the URL of a Web site you'd like to visit, one process thread is accepting input from the keyboard and another thread is searching the database of sites you recently visited as you are typing. If the second thread discovers a match, it displays the URL of the match so that you don't have to type in the complete URL.

A thread is actually made up of many components. Each thread has a unique identifier, called its client ID, which is assigned by the operating system. The thread contains the *Registry* settings that represent the current state of the processor while it is executing. The thread is also provided access to the memory storage space used by the subsystems, DLLs, and runtime libraries of the operating system, and is also provided with one memory stack for operating in user mode and another memory stack for operating in kernel mode. A stack is an area of memory reserved for applications to store information on their status. Using separate stacks ensures that the thread is as stable as possible, regardless of the mode in which the thread is run.

Multitasking

In much the same way that many threads can be executed concurrently in multithreading processes, Windows 2000 allows many applications to be run at the same time. This feature is referred to as *multitasking*, even though it is not multitasking in the strictest sense of the word.

If you are familiar with the Intel architecture, you know that processors are only able to perform one function at a time. However, because the operating system manages the processor and the applications running on the system, the user is given the impression that multiple programs are running simultaneously. This is only possible because the number of functions each processor is able to perform in a second has increased dramatically over the years.

Windows 2000 uses a process called *context switching* to achieve multitasking. In a context switching environment, a thread executes until it is forced to wait for available resources or the operating system interrupts its operation. At the point that the thread ceases operation, the operating system saves its context and loads the context of another thread. Once the new thread's context is loaded, it continues execution. This process is repeated indefinitely until there are no more threads to process. Of course, that only happens when the system is powered down.

The operating system's ability to interrupt a thread during its execution is called *preemptive multitasking*. There are two circumstances under which the operating system, specifically the kernel, will preempt (interrupt) the thread's execution: when the thread has run for a predetermined amount of time (a *quantum*) or when a thread with a higher priority requires execution. Windows 2000 allows the administrator to change the quantum length and type for applications and background services through the Control Panel. However, the thread's priority is managed automatically to provide more efficient operation.

Processes and threads in Windows 2000 have 32 possible priority levels. Numbered 0 through 31, the priorities are divided into groups depending on the operating mode of the process: Numbers 0 through 15 are used for user mode processes and numbers 16 through 31 are used for kernel mode processes. The priority of a particular process is assigned by the kernel upon execution. (You can, however, change the priority for a process through the Process tab in Task Manager by right-clicking the process and selecting Set Priority from the pop-up menu.) At the same time, the kernel assigns priority levels for all threads within the process. Known as the base priority level, this acts as the starting point for the kernel when determining the most efficient method of operation. The base priority level for a process serves as a strict starting point and is a single value (e.g., 3). The base priority for a thread, on the other hand, is a range from two levels above to two levels below the priority of the process. A thread whose process's base priority level is 9 will have a range of 7 through 11. Threads also include a priority range called the dynamic priority level, which starts at the base level and moves upward as thread activity increases and downward if it is in a dormant state. The kernel uses the dynamic priority level to change the thread's priority to ensure smooth operation.

Multiprocessing

Although not a concept new to the Windows family of operating systems, Windows 2000 includes support for more processors than ever before. The ability to utilize more than one microprocessor in a computer is called *multiprocessing*. There are two methods for accessing multiple processors, asymmetric and symmetric. In *asymmetric multiprocessing*, the operating system assigns a process to a specific processor, often based on the type of process. For example, application processes run only on CPU1, whereas system processes run only on CPU2. The process is run on the specified processor until it is complete, regardless of the status of the other processor(s) in the system. This means that if CPU2 is bogged down by a particular process, the system may not continue to operate efficiently if other system processes are needed. Although this method of multiprocessing is faster than having a single processor in a computer, it is not the most efficient method of operation. One processor may sit relatively idle while the other churns away.

Symmetric multiprocessing (SMP) operating systems, like Windows 2000, allow any process to be run on any processor, ensuring that the operating system uses all available processor resources. This decreases the overall processing time required for a specific function. To ensure that all waiting threads are granted CPU time, the kernel schedules the processors' time across all waiting threads. Inevitably, there are some threads that automatically run on the same processor each time they are executed, though this is usually limited to kernel mode processes. Windows 2000 processes can also be configured to run only on a specific processor, but this is not recommended.

USER AND KERNEL MODES

As mentioned earlier, the Windows 2000 architecture is divided into two operating modes, user mode and kernel mode. Each component of the architecture functions in one or the other of these modes. The component's responsibility to the operating system and its interaction with the hardware determine whether it operates in user mode or kernel mode.

User Mode

The components that operate in user mode are responsible for the interaction between the user and the operating system and any applications that are run on the computer. User mode components are granted very limited access to the computer's resources. All user mode requests for resources must pass through the processes running in kernel mode, thereby protecting the hardware. This ensures that the hardware in the system is not taken over by a rampant application, thus ensuring higher reliability.

When an application runs on another type of operating system, Windows 95 for example, the application is granted direct access to the hardware when necessary. Many times, the application includes its own device driver to manage the hardware or may avoid the existing driver. In these cases, the application takes control of the hardware and the system locks up and cannot be recovered. By forcing the application through the kernel mode components, access to the hardware is more tightly controlled, and the chances of the system locking completely are minimized.

User mode has two types of components, which are called subsystems: environment subsystems and integral subsystems. Environment subsystems provide Windows 2000 with the ability to run applications written for various operating systems aside from Windows 2000 including those written for earlier versions of Windows (16-bit applications), DOS, OS/2, and POSIX (Portable Operating System Interface for Unix). The environment subsystems emulate the specific operating systems by presenting the application programming interfaces (APIs) that are part of the operating system.

For example, when a POSIX application is run on a Windows 2000 computer and it looks for the *whoareyou* API, the POSIX subsystem provides the API and translates the request. This translation is passed to the Windows 2000 API, which send the request to the appropriate member of Executive Services.

Windows 2000 supports three *environment subsystems*: *Win32*, *OS/2*, and *POSIX*. The Win32 subsystem is responsible for controlling all Windows-based applications and allows Windows 2000 to run Win16 and DOS applications by emulating a DOS environment. The Win32 subsystem is also responsible for all *input/output (I/O)* between other subsystems, ensuring that data is easily exchanged between applications. In addition, the Win32 subsystem has the unique responsibility of managing keyboard and mouse communication. The OS/2 subsystem provides the APIs for a limited number of OS/2 applications; only 16-bit character-based applications are supported. POSIX applications are able to run on Windows 2000 through the use of the POSIX APIs presented by the POSIX subsystem. Many government agencies require POSIX support for their applications and operating systems.

Note: *Those of you who are familiar with the Windows NT 4 architecture will notice some differences in Windows 2000. In particular, the Win16 subsystem has been removed, and its functionality is now included within the Win32 subsystem.*

It is primarily through the use of these various subsystems that Windows 2000 maintains its high degree of reliability. As mentioned previously, unlike applications running on Windows 95/98 and operating systems from other companies, applications do not directly access the hardware interface or device drivers in Windows 2000. Instead, the subsystems access the *Executive Services* (discussed in the section titled "Kernel Mode"), which in turn access the hardware or device drivers. This means that if an application running on a Windows 2000 system becomes unstable, the application can be closed without affecting the rest of the applications running on the computer. In addition, each subsystem is provided a limited address space, and its memory access is limited to virtual memory. Environment subsystems are granted lower priority levels than kernel mode processes and therefore are in control of the processor for less time. This increases the efficiency of the operating system by ensuring that those services that keep the system running are granted the CPU time they need to operate.

Integral subsystems perform various functions that are not related to specific programs, but instead provide access to operating system functions, such as security and network services. For example, the security subsystem manages user authentication, accepts logon requests, monitors user rights and permissions, and tracks resource auditing. The *Active Directory* process operates within the security subsystem. The somewhat misnamed Workstation service is an integral subsystem that provides access to the network redirector and therefore to the network. Many unknowing administrators using Windows NT Server computers have disabled the Workstation service only to find that the system could no longer access the network. The Server service (also an integral subsystem), on the other hand, provides APIs to share resources with the network.

Kernel Mode

Components in user mode are responsible for the application environment and interaction with the user, whereas kernel mode components control the computer's hardware. The kernel mode is a highly protected operating mode in which processes operate in a protected memory area and are granted direct access to the computer's resources and memory. To ensure that the operating system is able to function in the most efficient manner, some kernel mode components are continuously kept in physical memory; they cannot be swapped to the hard drive as part of the paging process.

Because the most important facet of a server is its ability to provide services, the system must maintain a high level of availability. Mediating access to the system's hardware through the kernel mode components increases the chances of the server remaining available.

In addition, the Windows 2000 Executive Services reside in kernel mode. The Executive Services define the interfaces that permit kernel and user mode subsystems to communicate. These services, most of which are discussed in the following section, consist of the following modules:

➤ *File System Manager*—Controls file systems and hard drive activities, including writing, reading, disk repair, drive partitioning, drive configuration, and drive construction.

➤ *Graphics Device Drivers*—Passes graphical instructions created by the gdi32.dll to video and printer drivers that create the software interface to the actual video and printing hardware.

➤ *I/O Manager*—Implements all system I/O via communication with device drivers, regardless of the device involved (printers, hard disks, mice, keyboards).

➤ *Interprocess Communication (IPC) Manager*—Controls application communications with server processes.

➤ *Object Manager*—Manages object naming and security functions. It also allocates system objects, monitors their use, and removes them when they are no longer needed.

➤ *Plug and Play Manager*—Loads, unloads, and configures device drivers for Plug and Play hardware.

➤ *Power Manager*—Monitors and controls power use (mostly used by laptop computers).

➤ *Process Manager*—Creates, tracks, and deletes processes and threads.

➤ *Security Reference Monitor (SRM)*—Verifies the access rights assigned to an object when resource access is requested.

➤ *Virtual Memory Manager (VMM)*—Manages virtual memory space, including physical RAM and paging files.

The following sections discuss the Windows 2000 Executive Services.

The Windows 2000 Executive Services

The Windows 2000 Executive Services are a group of processes that handle most I/O and object management. The only exception is the keyboard and mouse I/O, which is actually handled by the Win32 subsystem. Each component in the Windows 2000 Executive either provides system services or executes internal routines. System services are available to both user mode subsystems and other members of the Windows 2000 Executive. Internal routines are available only to other Executive components.

The I/O Manager handles all input/output functions to and from different devices on the system. The I/O Manager is actually made up of three components: file systems, device drivers, and the *Cache Manager*. Comprised of the necessary drivers for hard drive communication, the network redirector, and the network service, the file systems accept I/O requests and translate the requests into device specific instructions. *Device drivers* are the low-level software components that directly control hardware to accept input or write output. The Cache Manager improves the overall performance of disk drive writes and reads by storing the information in memory. Because disk drives are slower than memory, the Cache Manager accepts the read/write requests from the CPU, stores them in memory, and controls the processes in the background while the CPU focuses on the next task.

The Virtual Memory Manager (VMM) coordinates and controls how Windows 2000 uses *virtual memory*. Virtual memory is the Windows management system that provides private memory address space for each process running on the system. The VMM coordinates the use of a storage area, named the *pagefile*, on the computer's hard drive, where information is moved to and from physical RAM. The process of moving memory to and from the hard drive is called *demand paging*.

With Windows 2000, the Plug and Play features of Windows 95 and 98 are finally available. The Plug and Play system provides a computer's operating system with the ability to detect and configure devices attached to the system. Prior to the introduction of Plug and Play, each interface card in the computer had to be manually configured to use a particular IRQ (interrupt request) and memory address. With the introduction of Windows 95, many devices were able to be configured by the operating system, thereby limiting the number of conflicts between hardware. Plug and Play was not included with Windows NT 4, but was carried over to Windows 98 and now Windows 2000. The Plug and Play Manager is responsible for controlling the Plug and Play process and devices in the computer.

The Security Reference Monitor (SRM) performs one of the most important functions on Windows 2000 Server systems: management and application of the Windows 2000 security system. Working closely with the security subsystem running in user mode, the Security Reference Monitor compares the access rights of the requesting user to the access control list (ACL) of the requested object. If the requesting user has sufficient access rights, the SRM grants the user access to the object.

If you are familiar with the Windows NT 4 architecture, you will notice that the Local Procedure Call Manager has been replaced in the Executive with the Interprocess Communication (IPC) Manager. The IPC Manager coordinates communications between clients and servers. For example, if the Win32 subsystem requests information from the file systems component, the Win32 subsystem acts as the client, whereas the file systems component acts as the server; the IPC Manager coordinates communication between these processes. The IPC Manager performs this function through the use of two components: the *Local Procedure Call (LPC)* facility and the *Remote Procedure Call (RPC)* facility. The LPC facility is utilized when the client and server processes are on the same computer. The RPC facility handles communication between processes on separate computers.

The Windows 2000 Executive's Process Manager handles all areas of operation for processes and threads within the operating system. A process is an executable program or segment of a program designed to perform a specific set of steps. A thread is a set of commands within a process. Each process operating on a computer must have at least one thread, but of course, it may also have more. When the last thread terminates, the process terminates as well. The Process Manager creates processes and terminates them when complete. In addition, it creates threads, stores and retrieves information about the threads as necessary, is able to suspend and resume operation of a thread, and terminates the thread upon completion.

To ensure that Windows 2000 operates in a highly energy efficient manner and handles other areas of power use, specific APIs are included as part of the operating system. Power Management APIs control energy saving features, such as turning off the computer's monitor, when they are invoked. APIs included in this group also work with uninterruptible power supply (UPS) devices to ensure that the system is properly shut down in the event of a power failure. The Windows 2000 Executive's Power Manager is responsible for the operation of the Power Management APIs.

The Window Manager and Graphical Device Interface (GDI) components work together closely and are actually contained in the same Windows 2000 device driver: win32k.sys. The Window Manager is responsible for controlling output to the computer screen and the window displays. It coordinates input received from the keyboard and pointing devices and passes the information to the appropriate application or process. The GDI is accessed by the Window Manager and contains the information and functions needed to create and manipulate graphics on the display.

The Object Manager's sole responsibility is to manage objects that represent operating system resources. In this capacity, the Object Manager is able to create system objects, monitor their use, and delete the objects as necessary. The Windows 2000 Object Manager maintains directory objects, link objects, semaphore and event objects, process and thread objects, port objects, and file objects.

Microkernel

In Windows 2000, only one program component controls the microprocessor: the *microkernel*. The microkernel, also referred to as simply the kernel, manages all I/O with the CPU and synchronizes the operation of all members of the Windows 2000 Executive. If the CPU is considered the brains of the computer's hardware, then the microkernel is the brains of the operating system.

Hardware Abstraction Layer (HAL)

The *HAL* component allows Windows 2000 and its predecessors to be run on both Intel- and Alpha-based hardware platforms. The HAL hides the details of hardware interaction from the rest operating system. The HAL is the Windows 2000 component that contains the hardware specific programs that handle the I/O interfaces, interrupt controllers, and processor controllers of the different platforms. To run on a specific platform, the operating system need only have the correct HAL installed; the rest of the Windows 2000 Executive and operating system can remain as is. This allows Microsoft to maintain a single version of Windows 2000 rather than develop versions for each platform independently.

Class and Device Drivers

As mentioned earlier, device drivers are the low-level software components that control hardware. Device drivers perform translations between the operating system and the hardware. Each device in the computer must have a driver to control it. In some cases, these drivers can be generic, as with industry-standard devices, such as keyboards. Most often, however, the driver for a particular device is unique to that device. For example, a network interface card made by 3Com will use a different driver than a card with the same features made by IBM. The specific commands required to send and receive data from the network are unique to each. For this reason, the device manufacturers are responsible for creating the drivers for their hardware.

Historically, different operating system versions required different versions of the device drivers. When a new operating system was introduced, a new driver was created to support the hardware. As part of their standardization initiative, Microsoft has introduced the *Windows Driver Model (WDM)*. The WDM is designed to allow device manufacturers to create drivers that conform to a consistent standard, which is supported by all Microsoft operating systems. The WDM is supported by Windows 98 and Windows 2000; drivers that are written to the WDM specification will be supported by either operating system.

In addition to eliminating the need for device manufacturers to write multiple versions of device drivers, Microsoft has limited the size and function required of the drivers. This was accomplished by splitting the driver functionality into a *class driver* and a *minidriver.* The class driver portion is written by Microsoft and included with Windows 2000. The minidriver is written by the hardware manufacturer to provide the lowest-level communication with the device. This class driver/minidriver combination provides the greatest levels of flexibility and standardization. In this new configuration, the class driver (the driver portion of the combination) is written to encompass everything needed to control a particular type of device. The device driver remains specific to the hardware installed in the system, but is smaller than versions required for other operating systems.

MEMORY ARCHITECTURE AND MANAGEMENT

To ensure that all applications are provided sufficient memory to operate, Windows 2000 assigns each application a private address space. To manage the address space for each of the applications, Windows 2000 uses an intricate memory management model. This model is based on a linear 32-bit address space and uses a virtual memory management system to coordinate memory use. By using the virtual memory model, users can run more applications concurrently than the physical memory of the system would normally allow. This method of memory management also protects memory resources by preventing situations where one process impinges upon the address space of another.

Note: It is very important to understand the distinction between physical and virtual memory. Physical memory denotes the RAM hardware modules installed in a computer. Virtual memory is the method by which Windows 2000 manages the physical memory and makes it available to applications. In addition, the term virtual memory is sometimes used to refer to the space on the system's hard drive that is used for memory management. However, this area is actually called the pagefile.

Each byte of memory in a Windows 2000 system is assigned a unique address, regardless of whether it is physical memory or virtual memory. The addresses assigned to the physical memory are limited by the amount of RAM in the system. If a computer has 1GB of physical memory, its address space will only include 1GB. Virtual memory, on the other hand, does not have a physical limitation and is therefore limited by the length of the address space. Windows 2000 uses a 32-bit address and is therefore limited to a 4GB address space.

As part of the modular design of Windows 2000, applications are not provided direct access to memory. Both the physical and virtual address space are managed by the Virtual Memory Manager (VMM). When an application uses memory, it makes the request to the VMM and is given the data's address in virtual memory, which is called the virtual address. The VMM presents the entire 4GB virtual address space to an application making a request for memory space.

The 4GB virtual address space is divided into two 2GB sections. The upper half of the virtual address space is reserved for kernel mode threads, whereas the lower half is accessible to both kernel and user mode threads. The virtual address space is further divided so that the lower portion is mapped directly to hardware to provide the fastest access to hardware resources. Windows 2000 splits the remaining virtual address space into a paged and a nonpaged memory pool. Information at addresses in the paged pool can be swapped to disk if necessary. Figure 1.2 illustrates the division of the Windows 2000 virtual address space.

The VMM is a kernel mode component that manages requests from applications for information located at specific memory addresses. To coordinate the data stored in memory, the VMM maintains a memory-mapping table. The memory-mapping table contains the list of virtual addresses being used by each process and the location in physical memory of the data referenced by the virtual addresses. When a thread needs the information stored in memory, it requests the data by using its virtual address. The VMM then locates the data at the corresponding address in physical memory referenced by the mapping table and returns the information to the thread.

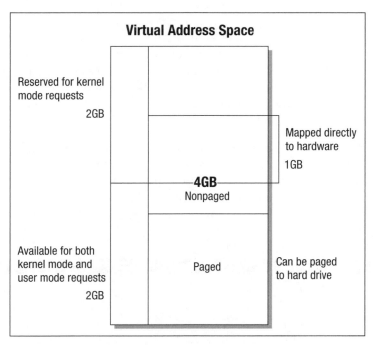

Figure 1.2 The division of the virtual address space.

If necessary, the VMM moves data from the physical memory in the system to a section of the hard drive reserved for use by virtual memory called the *pagefile*. The process of moving information from physical memory to virtual memory on the hard drive is called paging. Each page of memory is 4KB. Windows 2000 will only use paged memory when the physical memory in the computer is full. If the physical memory is full and a thread requests information that is not currently in memory (for example, when a new application is loaded), the VMM moves pages of information currently in physical memory to the pagefile. The VMM then loads the requested data into the recently vacated physical memory.

To identify which pages are in physical memory and which are in the pagefile, the VMM denotes in virtual memory whether the address is for a valid page or an invalid page. Valid pages are currently in physical memory and can be accessed immediately. Invalid pages are stored on disk and are not available to the process. If a thread requests information in an invalid page, the system issues a *page fault* error. However, the thread is still provided access to the information. The VMM traps the page fault, locates the requested pages, loads them into physical memory, and provides the information to the thread. To illustrate this process, refer to Table 1.1. If thread file33 requests memory page PAGE00239, it is returned immediately because it is currently in physical memory. However, if gdi499 requests PAGE20983, a page fault is returned and the VMM fetches the page from the pagefile.

To provide efficient memory management, the VMM performs three specific functions: It chooses which pages to remove from memory, moves pages from disk to memory (called fetching), and places retrieved pages in memory. The VMM will only move information to the pagefile if physical memory is full and a request is made for information not currently in memory. The pages used by a process is called its *working set*.

To determine which pages to swap from physical memory, the VMM uses a first in, first out (FIFO) approach. Information that has been in physical memory for the longest amount of time is the first to be paged out. If a page fault is generated, the VMM references the thread's working set and moves its oldest page back to disk. When fetching information from the pagefile, the VMM uses

Table 1.1   A sample memory-mapping table.

Memory Page	Thread	Address	Age	Status
PAGE18882	net48	AB89DE7	16	Valid
PAGE20983	gdi499	188CF6A	30	Invalid
PAGE00239	file33	BCBE34B	3	Valid
PAGE12309	file136	A289DCE	29	Valid

a retrieval method known as *demand paging with clustering*. Using this method, when the VMM responds to a page fault, it not only retrieves the requested page, but also some pages surrounding it.

The process used to determine where to place retrieved information depends on the current state of the physical memory. If physical memory is not full, it places the retrieved information in the first open page. If memory is full, it moves pages to the pagefile and places the retrieved information in its place. Because most requests are linear and greater than 4KB, this method reduces the number of page faults by anticipating that the next request will be for one of the surrounding pages.

COMPARING WINDOWS 2000 AND WINDOWS NT 4.x ARCHITECTURES

Windows 2000 has a few fundamental differences compared to Windows NT 4; a few of which have already been mentioned. The fact that Windows 2000 supports Plug and Play devices will most likely have the biggest impact on system configurations. The inclusion of the Win16 subsystem in the Win32 subsystem is perhaps the most evident change along with the adjustment in the responsibilities of the LPC Manager and inclusion of the Interprocess Communication Manager. The WDM is supported by Windows 2000 to provide more thorough support for hardware across various Microsoft operating systems. In addition to these modifications, Microsoft has included a number of smaller changes that will impact how people use Windows 2000. The changes outlined in the following sections rely heavily on the changes and additions to the kernel.

Throughout the design phases of Windows 2000, Microsoft polled network administrators the world over in an effort to understand the shortcomings of previous operating systems and address the needs of its customers. Some of the most important changes to Windows 2000 stem from the growth of worldwide networks. Although the Microsoft products have long been recognized as the best in the business, the earlier versions of Windows were written primarily for operation in English and the Roman alphabet. Adjustments were made to these earlier versions to support additional languages and characters, but they did not take into account the nuances of other languages and cultures. Windows 2000, on the other hand, is truly designed with the global network in mind. Every aspect of the operating system, from the kernel to the keyboard interface, is designed to the Unicode specification. Unicode is a standard created by the Unicode Consortium that defines which bytes will represent specific characters. Unicode improves on previous standards of its kind because a single character set is used for all languages. Unicode uses 16 bits for each character, which provides more than 65,000 possible characters in the character set. Every internal component of Windows 2000 uses Unicode characters. In addition, Windows 2000 provides *Native Language Support (NLS)*, which allows administrators to configure a computer with location specific information. The NLS module stores information about the geographic location of the computer and provides the interface appropriate to that area. More than just remembering the language the user speaks, NLS keeps track of the currency settings, date and time formats, and more.

To provide better support for application and database services, Microsoft has introduced the *Enterprise Memory Architecture (EMA)* with Windows 2000 Advanced Server. EMA supports up to 32GB of physical memory that can be addressed by servers with 64-bit processors. Database systems and large data warehouses will be able to take advantage of this expanded capability to efficiently serve the user's needs. Applications must be configured to use the *very large memory (VLM)* APIs of Windows 2000 to take advantage of this specification. Microsoft has also included improved I/O efficiency with support for the *Intelligent I/O Architecture (I2O)*. The I2O standard improves performance by adding a dedicated processor optimized for I/O operations.

From a performance monitoring and tuning standpoint, Windows 2000 includes a number of new performance counters and tools. One of the new tools added to Window 2000 is an enhancement for Web site administrators and Internet Service Providers (ISPs) using *Internet Information Services (IIS)*: the job object. When a Windows system acts as the host for a Web site, there is the potential that a single site might dominate the network and processor functions of the server. A heavily used site or incorrectly designed script could, and has, brought a server to its knees. Windows 2000 includes a *processor accounting* option, configured through IIS, that counts the number of CPU cycles consumed by Web requests (the job object in this case). This allows ISPs to not only charge customers for the amount of hardware time their sites consume, but can also be an early indication of a need to upgrade the server if the load gets too large. Windows 2000 also includes an improvement over IIS's bandwidth throttling called *process throttling*. By enabling process throttling, administrators can specify how much processor time each Web site is able to use, ensuring that one site does not control the hardware.

Finally, overall performance on multiprocessor systems is increased by using a technique called *spin count*. When multiple threads require access to the same resources simultaneously, spin count manages the number of times the thread will attempt to access the resource before waiting.

WINDOWS NT VETERANS' ROUNDUP: WHAT'S NEW IN WINDOWS 2000?

1

In addition to the Windows 2000 components discussed in the previous section, Microsoft has expanded the features and functions of its operating system to make system administration easier, provide better scalability, improve security, increase system availability, and act as the foundation for applications and services.

Administration Features

At the center of the Microsoft administration model is the Active Directory service. Discussed in greater detail in Chapter 2, Active Directory is a centralized, hierarchical organizational directory developed entirely around standards in use on the Internet. Active Directory builds on the concepts used in Windows NT administration and expands the administration model to a global, enterprise level. To truly operate at the enterprise level, Active Directory has eliminated the Primary Domain Controller (PDC)/Backup Domain Controller (BDC) model. A server that participates as a domain controller contains a complete, up-to-date copy of the Active Directory to provide authentication and user services. By using this distributed model, Windows 2000 ensures that network users are able to log on and access the network in the event that a server is unavailable. Another significant benefit of the distributed nature of Active Directory is that users are only required to log on to the network once. Trust relationships, user access, and group access are centrally managed by Active Directory. Regardless of the location of the requested resource, the user need not provide additional logon information.

To provide easy integration with Internet technologies, Active Directory is designed as a native *Lightweight Directory Access Protocol (LDAP)* server. Because it is based on Internet standards and security features, such as *Kerberos v5, Secure Sockets Layer v3, Transport Layer Security* using X.509, certificates, and cross-domain security groups, Active Directory provides a simple, easy to implement security model. In an Active Directory environment, every network resource is included in the Directory and can be managed. This includes not only users and groups, but physical resources, like printers and computers. The Active Directory database can be designed to match the operations of your company and provide secure distributed management capabilities. You can have a manager at a remote office manage user and group configuration for their office without providing access to other areas of the network. In addition, many new applications are being developed using the *Active Directory Service Interface (ADSI)* to take full advantage of the Active Directory, including software running non–Windows systems, such as routers.

Microsoft has also expanded the remote management capabilities of Windows NT 4 with Windows 2000. Using Terminal Services, administrators can connect to and manage remote Windows 2000 computers with as little as a 28.8Kbps modem connection. This applies not only to Windows 2000 Server implementations, but to Windows 2000 Professional computers as well. Terminal Services provides centralized access to applications, so that space on the server rather than space on the local hard drive is used to store application data. Also supported is remote access to applications, whereby the Terminal Server sends only the display information to the client rather than the entire application. The role of the *Microsoft Management Console (MMC)* has been retooled to centralize and unify computer and application monitoring and management. Integrated with Active Directory, the MMC provides administrators with the ability to delegate systems management responsibilities and supplies remote administrators with consoles preconfigured for specific functions.

Repetitive tasks, such as creating standard desktop configurations, can be automated using the *Windows Script Host (WSH)*. Prior to Windows 2000, user interface tasks were difficult, if not impossible, to automate. Using WSH, the administrator can simply provide the script to the user and rest assured that the configuration will be correct. To further ensure standards compatibility, WSH is language independent. Scripts can be written in familiar scripting languages, like JavaScript, and run using the WSH.

Scalability Features

More than ever before, Windows 2000 provides the extensive scalability needed for today's networks. From the smallest workgroup to the largest global network, Windows 2000 Servers get the job done by providing support for the most advanced hardware as well as multiple processors. The Windows 2000 Advanced Server and Datacenter versions support server clustering, which allows for application and network load balancing. Network load balancing provides more efficient utilization of the network by balancing incoming TCP/IP traffic between servers, most often Web servers. Windows 2000 Advanced Server also supports dynamic load balancing for applications that support COM+. With this type of load balancing, COM+ objects are allocated to the Windows 2000 cluster node that has the lowest utilization to provide efficient application services.

Security Features

As mentioned previously, Active Directory in Windows 2000 supports advanced, industry standard security features, such as Kerberos v5. By using Kerberos, users are granted fast, single-logon access to Windows 2000 network resources and other network environments that support the protocol. Kerberos can also be configured to use mutual authentication (a method of authentication that requires both the user and the server prove their identity to each other) and delegated authentication (used to track a user's security access throughout a tiered client-server environment). *IP Security (IPSec)* is yet another industry security standard supported by Windows 2000. IPSec is used to encrypt TCP/IP traffic between systems on a network. The Windows 2000 IPSec module lets administrators enforce encryption between systems without visibility to the user. Another set of security standards that is supported by Windows 2000 is *Public Key Infrastructure (PKI)* and public key applications. These standards are significant because digital signatures, used to verify the authenticity of objects, like email messages, are part of the PKI initiative.

The use of smart cards is expanding rapidly and Windows 2000 provides support for network access based on smart card information. By using smart cards to log on, security administrators are assured, with a high level of confidence, that the system is secure because smart card authentication requires the use of a personal identification number (PIN) in combination with proof-of-possession before access is granted. Support for the *Encrypted File System (EFS)* is also included as part of Windows 2000. EFS provides domainwide file level encryption for data security and recovery. EFS is implemented in addition to the existing access control model and operates as an independent service.

Availability Features

Perhaps the most significant advances over Windows NT 4 are seen in the overall availability of the Windows 2000 Server, that is, the amount of time it is up and running versus being down. The first and most significant of these advances is the reduction in the number of times a server must be rebooted. In the past, when working with Windows NT 4 Server, any addition or change generally required that the system be restarted. With Windows 2000, the number of times you have to reboot has been greatly reduced. Hardware and software configuration is easier and common maintenance tasks no longer require scheduled downtime. Network protocol configuration, such as an IP address change, can be done on the fly without removing the server from service. The file system can be managed and maintained using dynamic storage and PCI (Peripheral Component Interconnect) devices can be configured without interrupting service.

In addition, Microsoft has improved the Backup utility to help prevent data loss. In addition to the standard tape media, the Backup utility allows users to back up data to external hard drives, Zip disks, and recordable CD-ROM drives.

Application and Services Features

The primary function of any network server is to provide services to its clients. File and print services are among the most basic and have been enhanced again in Windows 2000. When using NTFS partitions on a Windows 2000 Server, the file services features have been expanded to include:

➤ *Content indexing*—Provides fast and secure searching for information on a network

➤ *Disk quotas*—Monitors and limits the use of disk space use for specific groups

➤ *Distributed Link Tracking*—Enables client applications to track linked resources that have been moved to another location on the network

➤ *Dynamic Volume Management*—Allows you to change a volume's configuration without taking the system down

➤ *Remote Storage Services*—Monitors available space on the local drive and moves data to remote storage when free space runs low

➤ *Removable Storage Manager*—Manages removable media, such as tapes and CD-ROMs

Windows 2000 includes another advanced file system feature called the *Distributed file system (Dfs)*. Dfs is designed to make locating specific information on the network easier. This is accomplished by grouping related folders into a virtual directory structure. Folders can be linked in Dfs, regardless of their location in the Active Directory.

As mentioned earlier, all network resources are objects of the Windows 2000 Active Directory. This lets devices, like printers and plotters, be shared across domain lines to the entire directory if necessary. It also allows users the ability to quickly locate the most convenient printer for their request. The number of supported printers and their protocols has been increased to more than 2,500, making it easier for organizations to use advanced printing systems, like printer pools. One of the newly supported protocols is the *Internet Printing Protocol (IPP)*. IPP lets you print directly to a URL on the network and instructs Windows 2000 to create printer and print job information in HTML. This document can then be viewed in a Web browser rather than printed to hard copy. Printer management is more dynamic in that local and remote printers can be monitored using System Monitor. Remote printers can also be managed through the MMC from anywhere on the network.

The networking functions of Windows 2000 are also improved over those in Windows NT 4. *Virtual Private Networking (VPN)* has been enhanced to support

1

more secure communication using the *Layer 2 Tunneling Protocol (L2TP)* and the IP Security Protocol mentioned earlier. When a system is configured with multiple network interface cards, referred to as a *multihomed* system, Windows 2000 is able to act as a dynamic gateway or router. The Windows 2000 Server can be configured through a complete set of routing and gateway services tools to provide connectivity between networks with comparatively low additional costs. The *Resource Reservation Protocol (RSVP)* is used by multimedia applications to ensure that the necessary network quality is provided and reserved for transmission, in addition to providing monitoring functions to gauge the impact of such applications. The Windows 2000 RSVP implementation grants or denies service requests based on Active Directory policies and resource availability. Tightly integrated with Active Directory, the *Domain Name System (DNS)* has been identified as the successor to WINS (Windows Internet Naming Service). Working in conjunction with the *Dynamic Host Configuration Protocol (DHCP)* to dynamically update the network's DNS information, Windows 2000 provides an industry standard solution for name resolution.

CHAPTER SUMMARY

Windows 2000 is the latest iteration of Microsoft's powerful Windows operating system. Designed to provide higher performance, increased security, and greater system availability, it is currently available in three versions: Professional, Server, and Advanced Server with a fourth, Datacenter Server, on the way in mid-2000. Windows 2000 Professional is designed for operation on desktop computers and combines the usability features of Windows 98, such as Plug and Play and DirectX support, in addition to enhancing the overall performance of Windows NT Workstation 4.x. Windows 2000 Server, also known as Standard Edition or Standard Server, is the center of Microsoft's network services model. It extends the features of Windows 2000 Professional to provide file, print, and application services to clients on a network. The Advanced Server edition supports more extensive hardware configurations than Standard Server and is the first Windows product to natively support clustering. When Windows 2000 Datacenter Server is introduced, it will further extend the capabilities of Advanced Server with extensive load balancing and clustering support.

The fundamental architecture of Windows 2000 is the same as that of Windows NT 3.51 and 4.x. Many advancements have been made to improve stability and efficiency. Windows 2000 uses a layered architecture divided into two operating modes: user and kernel mode. In addition, the architecture is modular in its design and functionality. Windows 2000 is not a single application, but rather a group of smaller applications, each designed to perform a specific function. Windows 2000 also utilizes an object-oriented design. An object is a collection of information about a resource and a list of operations that can be performed on that object. Every Windows 2000 component is an object; each object is an independent entity with its own configuration and responsibilities. Objects are identified by their type and instance. The object type describes the attributes and services it supports, whereas its instance defines the specific entity being referenced.

Windows 2000 uses advanced processor management techniques to provide the most efficient service possible; they include multithreading, multitasking, and multiprocessing. A thread is a set of commands that is granted access to the processor. A process is an executable group of commands designed to perform specific steps. Windows 2000 supports multithreaded applications, requiring more than one thread be active at a time. During execution, the thread is granted access to the storage space used by the subsystems, DLLs, and runtime libraries of the operating system as well as access to two memory stacks—one for user mode and one for kernel mode. A stack is an area of memory reserved for applications to store information on their status. Windows 2000 also supports context switching (a type of multitasking), which allows multiple programs to be run on the same computer concurrently. Context switching allows a thread to control the CPU for a specific length of time (called the quantum) or until the thread is forced to wait. When the thread ceases execution or is interrupted by the operating system, its context is saved and the kernel loads the context of another waiting thread. Once the new thread's context is loaded, it is executed. The process of the operating system interrupting a thread's execution is called preempting, hence the name preemptive multitasking. The kernel will preempt a thread's execution when the quantum has expired or when a thread of higher priority requires execution. Threads' priorities are automatically adjusted by the kernel to provide efficient operation. Windows 2000 supports multiprocessing, which allows the operating system to take advantage of computers with more than one microprocessor. There are two methods of multitasking: asymmetric and symmetric (used by Windows 2000). SMP allows any process to be run on any processor, which decreases the overall processing time for a specific function. To ensure that all waiting threads are granted CPU time, the kernel schedules the processors' time across all waiting threads.

The Windows 2000 architecture is divided into two operating modes: user and kernel. Components that operate in user mode are responsible for interaction between the user and the operating system. User mode components are granted limited access to the computer's resources and must make all resource requests through components operating in kernel mode. This protects the hardware and applications running on the computer by ensuring that no single process takes complete control of the system. Kernel mode components operate in a protected memory area and are responsible for controlling the computer's hardware. Some kernel mode components are continuously kept in physical memory, increasing the operating efficiency of the system.

The Windows 2000 memory model provides a private address space for each application running on the system. This memory model is based on a 32-bit address space and uses a virtual memory management system to coordinate memory use. The virtual memory model used by Windows 2000 protects memory resources by ensuring that each application remains in its assigned address space. Each byte of memory, either physical or virtual, is assigned a unique address. The addresses assigned to physical memory are limited by the amount of memory in the system, but virtual memory addresses are limited only by the length of the address available—32 bits. This allows for a 4GB virtual address space. Applications are not granted direct access to memory. The VMM is a kernel mode component that manages all memory including memory requests from threads. When a thread makes a request for information in memory, it is provided with the address in the virtual address space. The virtual address space is divided into two 2GB sections. The upper 2GB is reserved for kernel mode threads, whereas the lower area can be used by both user and kernel mode threads. The upper (kernel only) memory area is divided a second time and the lowest portion is mapped directly to hardware for faster memory access. The lower (both kernel and user) virtual memory area is the only portion of memory that can be paged to the system's hard drive. The lower virtual memory area is divided into paged and nonpaged memory pools, however, only information in the paged pool can be transferred to the hard drive. The VMM maintains a memory mapping table that contains the list of virtual memory addresses being used by each process and the physical memory location referenced by the virtual address. If physical memory is full and a thread requests information that is not currently in virtual memory, the VMM swaps pages from memory to the pagefile on the hard drive using a process called paging. Each page represents 4KB of data. A valid page resides in virtual memory, whereas an invalid page is located in the pagefile. When a thread requests an invalid page, the processor returns a page fault error, which is intercepted by the VMM. The VMM then locates the page in the pagefile and moves it back to physical memory for access by the thread. The process of retrieving a page from the pagefile is called fetching. When a page fault is issued, the VMM not only retrieves the requested page but surrounding pages as well to anticipate subsequent requests and prevent another page fault.

The components that operate in user mode are referred to as subsystems and are either environment or integral. Environment subsystems handle the interaction between the user and the operating system including providing support for various types of applications. There are three environment subsystems in Windows 2000: Win32, OS/2, and POSIX. The Win32 subsystem controls all Windows based applications and manages keyboard and mouse I/O as well as all I/O between other subsystems and the kernel mode components. Win32 also provides support for Windows 16-bit applications and DOS applications. The OS/2 subsystem provides support for OS/2 16-bit character based applications. The POSIX subsystem is provided mainly to satisfy a US Government requirement for POSIX support. The POSIX subsystem is limited, and requires some support from the Win32 subsystem for display and communication between applications. Integral subsystems perform various user functions not related to specific programs, such as security authentication and network services. The Active Directory process is part of the security subsystem. The Windows 2000 Workstation and Server services are also considered integral services.

The Windows 2000 components that operate in kernel mode fall into four categories: the Windows 2000 Executive, device drivers, the microkernel, and the HAL. The Windows 2000 Executive is a group of processes that handle I/O (except keyboard and mouse I/O) and object management. System services provided by Executive members are available to components running in both user and kernel mode, whereas internal routines are available only to Windows 2000 Executive components. The Windows 2000 Executive includes the following components:

➤ I/O Manager (made up of file systems, device drivers, and Cache Manager)

➤ IPC Manager

➤ Object Manager

➤ Plug and Play Manager

➤ Power Manager

➤ Process Manager

➤ Security Reference Monitor (SRM)

➤ Virtual Memory Manager (VMM)

➤ Windows Manager and GDI

The microkernel is the Windows 2000 component that manages thread interaction with the CPU and synchronizes the operation of the Windows 2000 Executive members. HAL is the Windows 2000 component that enables the operating system to be run on computers with different platforms (e.g.,

1

Intel and Alpha). The HAL contains hardware specific programs for managing I/O interfaces, interrupt controllers, and processor controllers and is the only component that is fundamentally different between platforms. Device drivers are small software components that control hardware. The WDM allows hardware manufacturers to develop small device drivers that work in conjunction with the class drivers written by Microsoft.

There are a few changes in the architecture of Windows 2000 since Windows NT 4.x. Microsoft has gone to great lengths to ensure that Windows 2000 is able to function as a global network operating system. Significant updates include enhanced memory management using the EMA and more efficient I/O using I2O also improve performance. A number of counters and monitors have been added to Windows 2000 to provide a more accurate picture of the server's operation. Microsoft has expanded the administration features of Windows 2000 with Active Directory, standards-based security using Kerberos, and Terminal Services. Windows 2000 is more scalable than previous versions of Windows in that it supports load balancing, clustering, and multiprocessing. Security is further enhanced by supporting IPSec encryption, smart card authentication, and PKI authentication. The basic design of Windows 2000 provides increased system availability by requiring reboots less often. The Backup utility can be used to recover a system in the event of a catastrophic failure, provided an up-to-date backup is available. Finally, Windows 2000 provides enhanced file, print, and application services using features, such as Dfs, dynamic volume storage, IPP support, VPN L2TP support, and the RSVP protocol. The functionality previously provided by WINS is now provided by the industry standard protocols DHCP and DNS.

REVIEW QUESTIONS

1. Which of the following multiprocessing techniques is used by Windows 2000?

    a. Asymmetric

    b. Context Switching

    c. Symmetric

    d. Demand paging

2. Which of the following Internet standards is used to provide security authentication in Windows 2000 Active Directory?

    a. IPSec

    b. Kerberos

    c. VPN

    d. PKI

3. Which of the following Windows 2000 implementations does not support clustering? [Choose all that apply]

   a. Windows 2000 Professional

   b. Windows 2000 Standard Server

   c. Windows 2000 Advanced Server

   d. Windows 2000 Datacenter Server

4. As part of the modular design of Windows 2000, which of the following terms is used to describe all resources?

   a. Object

   b. Component

   c. Module

   d. Kernel

5. Which of the following Windows 2000 components operates in user mode? [Choose all that apply]

   a. Security Manager

   b. Security subsystem

   c. Security Reference Monitor

   d. Enterprise Services subsystem

6. Place the following pages in the order in which they will be moved to the pagefile.

   a. Page=2387, Age=5

   b. Page=12375, Age=19

   c. Page=6948, Age=21

   d. Page=8749, Age=4

7. The addresses assigned to the physical memory have no limitation except the 32-bit address length.

   a. True

   b. False

8. Which of the following components manages input from a wireless mouse?

   a. Win16 subsystem

   b. Win32 subsystem

   c. I/O Manager

   d. I/O subsystem

9. Which of the following accurately describes the need for the HAL?

    a. The HAL provides a unique interface to each user connected to the computer.

    b. The HAL authenticates user login requests.

    c. The HAL provides hardware specific programs to support multiple platforms.

    d. The HAL provides a method of verifying access rights.

10. Which of the following terms is used to describe the software structure used in the WDM?

    a. Driver/minidriver

    b. Driver/subdriver

    c. Driver/feature

    d. Driver/system

11. Which of the following international standards is used in developing all aspects of Windows 2000 to ensure global use?

    a. ASCII

    b. ANSI

    c. Unicode

    d. ISO

12. Which of the following protocols serves as the native transport for Active Directory?

    a. TCP/IP

    b. IPP

    c. IPSec

    d. LDAP

13. Which of the following new features of Windows 2000 provides extensive remote management features?

    a. MMC

    b. Server Monitor

    c. Terminal Services

    d. IIS

14. Which of the following VMM functions attempts to anticipate requests following a page fault in an effort to prevent additional page faults?

    a. Demand paging with clustering

    b. Paging analysis

    c. FIFO

    d. Pagefile management

15. Which of the following events cause the kernel to preempt a thread's execution? [Choose all that apply]

    a. The thread has returned to a waiting state.

    b. The thread has run the duration of the quantum.

    c. A thread with a higher priority requires service.

    d. The thread is terminated by the Process Manager.

16. In the WDM environment, which of the following is responsible for writing the class driver?

    a. The hardware manufacturer

    b. A third-party developer

    c. The ANSI standards committee

    d. Microsoft

17. Which of the following increases disk drive performance by storing requests in memory and directly managing disk interaction?

    a. File systems

    b. Device drivers

    c. Cache Manager

    d. I/O Manager

18. Which Windows 2000 component interacts directly with system hardware on behalf of applications?

    a. Executive Services

    b. Kernel

    c. Hardware Abstraction Layer (HAL)

    d. none of the above

19. Which of the following Windows 2000 modules can be implemented transparently to users to provide encrypted network communication?

    a. IIP

    b. IPSec

    c. L2TP

    d. DHCP

20. Which of the following describes the role of the Backup Domain Controller in the Active Directory?

   a. The Backup Domain Controller provides user authentication in the event that the Primary Domain Controller is unavailable.

   b. The Backup Domain Controller participates in the Active Directory as a gateway between networks.

   c. The Backup Domain Controller is no longer used in the Active Directory.

   d. The Backup Domain Controller is responsible for application and print services, but not user authentication.

REAL-WORLD PROJECTS

Note: The Windows 2000 System Monitor utility used in this project is covered in detail in Chapter 6. To complete the project, you need a computer running Windows 2000 Server with the Microsoft Management Console and System Monitor installed.

While studying for her Windows 2000 Server exam, Margaret was a little unclear on the concepts of processes and threads. She discussed her dilemma with the other members of her Windows users group. Ken, an MCSE for seven years, worked with her for a while and remembered a trick he learned in one of his first Windows NT Server classes. His instructor said that by using the Performance Monitor, he could easily see the relationship between Windows NT components, like processes and threads, by viewing their counters. Ken explained that with Windows 2000 the System Monitor replaces the Windows NT 4.0 Performance Monitor, but the principles are the same. Margaret left the users group feeling better. She had just installed a copy of Windows 2000 Server on her test system at home and she could test Ken's recommendation immediately. When Margaret returned home, she booted her Windows 2000 system and viewed the Performance counters for the Windows Explorer process and threads.

Project 1.1
To view the Performance counters for the Windows Explorer process and threads, perform the following steps:

1. If you have not already done so, log on to your Windows 2000 Server computer as Administrator or as a user with equivalent access permissions.

2. Select Start|Programs|Administrative Tools.

3. To more efficiently display Start menu options, Windows 2000 may initially hide certain menu items. If Performance is not initially listed in the

Administrative Tools menu, click the down arrows at the bottom of the
menu to display all available icons.

4. Click Performance to start the System Monitor, which is shown in
   Figure 1.3.

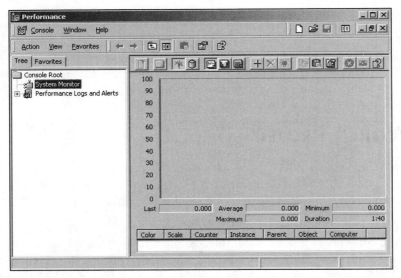

Figure 1.3   The initial screen of the System Monitor Utility.

The System Monitor is used to monitor and graphically represent the
computer's operations. The first screen displays the various performance
counters as a linear graph in real time. In the same way that threads are
identified by their type and their instance, System Monitor counters are
grouped by object and instance. To begin monitoring a particular counter,
you must add it to the chart.

5. Click the Add button (the large plus [+] sign at the top center of the graph
   area). This invokes the Add Counters dialog box shown in Figure 1.4. Note
   that options are included for monitoring counters on remote computers,
   selecting the counter object, selecting the counter, and selecting the
   instance.

6. Click the arrow next to the Performance Object: drop-down box.

7. From the list of available objects, scroll up and select Process.

8. Note that the contents of the Select Counters From List box have changed
   to reflect the types of counters available for processor monitoring. Do not
   change the default option (% Processor Time).

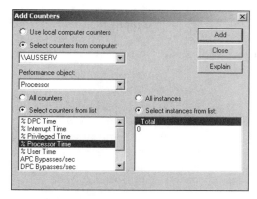

Figure 1.4   The Add Counters dialog box.

9. The Select Instances From List dialog box displays a list of all processes currently running on the system. Select Explorer from the list and click Add. The counter will be added to the graph behind the Add Counters window, and the System Monitor will begin monitoring the counter.

10. At this point you are able to add additional counters to the graph if desired. For now, click Close to return to System Monitor.

11. A line indicating the percentage of processor time being used by the Windows Explorer process will be displayed.

12. To see the effect system operation has on the computer, open three copies of Windows Explorer by selecting it from the Start menu (Start | Programs | Accessories | Windows Explorer).

13. Note how the chart reflects the impact of opening the copies of Windows Explorer.

14. Windows Explorer includes a number of threads that perform specific tasks, such as looking for network resources. To create a clearer picture of how a process affects system performance, you can chart a single thread or set of threads while monitoring the process. Click the Add button to invoke the Add Counters dialog box.

15. Select Thread from the Performance Object: drop-down list.

16. Note that the list of available instances for the Thread counter is exceptionally long. Scroll through the list of instances to locate the Windows Explorer threads. The Windows Explorer threads start with Explorer/0.

17. Select the Explorer/0 thread and click Add. Repeat for other Windows Explorer threads until four or five threads are being monitored (you can do this by selecting a thread and holding the Shift key to highlight multiple threads at once).

18. Click Close.

19. Depending on the stress your system is under, you may not notice a difference in the graph. Return to one of the Windows Explorer windows and navigate through the folder tree.

20. Select Start | Search | For Files or Folders.

21. In the Search For Files Or Folders Named: box, enter "*.txt" and click Search Now.

22. Switch back to the System Monitor and view the activity chart.

CHAPTER TWO

PLANNING FOR INSTALLATION AND DEPLOYMENT

After completing this chapter, you will be able to:

✓ Identify the minimum hardware requirements for running Windows 2000

✓ Locate hardware information on the HCL

✓ Use the Windows 2000 Readiness Analyzer

✓ Develop a plan for implementing Windows 2000 including storage, network services, file systems, and Active Directory

✓ Assess unattended installations of Windows 2000

The first step to ensuring a successful Windows 2000 implementation is planning. Throughout this chapter, we'll explore the system requirements for Windows 2000 Server, the system assessment tool for Windows 2000, and the steps you should take when planning your Windows 2000 Server installation.

WINDOWS 2000 SERVER REQUIREMENTS

As the Windows operating system has grown from Windows 286 to Windows 95 to Windows 2000, the minimum hardware required to run the operating system has increased. With more powerful hardware comes more resource-intensive software and operating systems, which in turn has encouraged manufacturers to develop more powerful hardware, and so on.

Since Windows NT version 4, Microsoft has published a set of minimum hardware requirements (we must emphasize the word *minimum*). For example, Windows NT 4.0 Workstation could, according to the Microsoft specifications, operate on an Intel–based computer running a 486/33MHz processor with 16MB of memory and 110MB of free hard disk space. However, just booting the system with this configuration could take 15 to 20 minutes, and normal operations would be almost impossible. Table 2.1 shows the minimum hardware requirements for Windows 2000 Server.

You may be wondering what it will really take to run Windows 2000 Server. That depends to some extent on what you expect from your server. If there is a hard and fast rule when dealing with Microsoft operating systems, especially the new operating systems, it is this: You can never have too much memory or too much free hard disk space. With this in mind, Table 2.2 outlines the recommended (rather than official) minimum requirements for running Windows 2000 Server. Components not listed either have no upgrade or can function at the technical minimum.

Table 2.1   The minimum hardware requirements for Windows 2000 Server.

Hardware Component	Minimum Specification
Processor	One Intel Pentium 133 processor (or compatible based on HCL)
Memory	128MB RAM
Video	VGA video card and monitor
Keyboard	Any
Mouse	Any
Hard disk	2GB hard disk with 1GB free space
Floppy disk	1.44MB
CD-ROM	Bootable CD-ROM
Network adapter	Any

Table 2.2   Recommended minimum hardware configuration for
Windows 2000 Server.

Hardware Component	Recommendation
Processor	At least one Intel Pentium II 300 (or compatible)
Memory	256MB RAM (PC100 or PC133)
Video	Super VGA video card and monitor that will support at least 800x600 resolution
Hard disk	2GB-3GB free space on a high-speed (7200 rpm) Ultra-IDE, ATA-66, or Ultra-Wide SCSI drive
CD-ROM	Bootable CD-ROM or DVD-ROM operating at least 12x
Network adapter	PCI Fast-Ethernet (100Mbps)

Note: A keyboard, mouse, and network adapter are required for Windows 2000 Server. Although you can install Windows 2000 on a computer without a network adapter, the server installation is designed for connection to other devices. If you are running a computer as a stand-alone desktop, Windows 2000 Professional is best and does not require a network adapter.

The Hardware Compatibility List (HCL)

Whether you are using existing hardware and upgrading to Windows 2000 or buying new hardware to build your server, verify that the hardware is on the *Hardware Compatibility List (HCL)*. Although some in the industry might say that this is just another way for Microsoft to control the industry and limit the type of hardware available to that built only by well-known (and sometimes more expensive) manufacturers, it is actually a matter of testing and reliability. Hardware included on the HCL for Windows 2000 is certified to work in the Windows 2000 environment and is supported by the hardware manufacturer and Microsoft. Microsoft technical support cannot support products that are not certified and included on the HCL. To avoid this problem and make your installation as painless as possible, always verify that all hardware in the computer is included on the HCL.

The HCL is created and managed by the Microsoft *Hardware Quality Labs (HQL)*. The HQL's job is to ensure that hardware is compatible with Microsoft operating systems including Windows NT 4, Windows 98, Windows 2000, and even operating systems still in development, such as Millennium. Before a device can include the Windows logo on its packaging and promotional materials, it must go through the tests defined by the HQL and be certified by Microsoft.

The HQL's home page is located at **www.microsoft.com/hwtest/ default.asp**. It includes information on the certification process, the status of current testing programs, and detailed testing documents for systems, clusters, networking, and SCSI devices. In addition, the page includes a link to the Hardware Compatibility List Web site, discussed later in this section.

The Web site is one of two sources for the information contained in the HCL. The first, and for some the most easily accessible version of the HCL, is located on the Windows 2000 CD in the \Support folder. The hcl.txt file is a plain-text document that lists the hardware on the HCL at the time that the CD was released for production. It is organized into sections based on the type of device. To ensure that devices attached to the computer are compatible, Microsoft tests everything from processors and hard drives to external uninterruptable power supply (UPS) systems and digital cameras. The following section contains an excerpt from the HCL included with Windows 2000 Server.

```
------------------------------------
Display Adapter
------------------------------------
3DFx Voodoo Banshee (AGP)
3DFx Voodoo3 2000 AGP (AGP)
3DFx Voodoo3 2000 PCI (PCI)
3DFx Voodoo3 3000 (AGP)
3DFx Voodoo3 3500 TV AGP (AGP)
3DFx Voodoo3 Compatabale Graphics Adapter (AGP)
3DLabs Inc. 3DLabs Permedia2 Compatable Graphics Adapter (PCI)
Accel Graphics  AccelStar II (PCI)
Accel Graphics  AccelStar II AGP (AGP)
Appian Graphics Jeronimo Pro (PCI)
Asus 3DExplorer 3000 (AGP)
Asus PA 700Pro (AGP)
ATI Technologies, Inc. ATI -264VT2 PCI (PCI)
ATI Technologies, Inc. ATI -264VT3 PCI (PCI)
ATI Technologies, Inc. ATI -264VT4 PCI (PCI)
ATI Technologies, Inc. ATI 3D RAGE II + PCI (PCI)
ATI Technologies, Inc. ATI 3D RAGE II PCI (PCI)
```

To make everyone's life just a little easier, computer manufacturers submit tests not only for individual system devices, such as sound cards and display adapters, but also for complete systems. There are sections near the end of the HCL that are dedicated to single- and multiple-processor servers, desktops, and portables. The tests on these systems are performed using the default configurations provided by the manufacturers. If the computer on which you are installing Windows 2000 has components that were not provided by the system's manufacturer, make sure the additional components are also included on the HCL before proceeding.

2

The HCL is extensive (the HCL included on the CD has more than 28,000 lines) and changes often. As mentioned earlier, the list included on the Windows 2000 installation CD is up-to-date as of the time the disc is released to the public. Because new hardware is continuously released, the HCL on the CD may not be current when you need the information. However, the information contained on the HCL Web site is not only up-to-date, but is a bit easier to navigate and includes more detailed information. Shown in Figure 2.1, the HCL Web site is found at **www.microsoft.com/hcl/default.asp**.

To generate a list of all equipment on the HCL, leave All Products in the Search For The Following: box, select the All Product Categories option from the In The Following Types: drop-down list, and click Go. You will be presented, in groups of 100, with a list of components as shown in Figure 2.2. This list includes the device type, manufacturer, and model of the device. You can also limit your search by populating these fields with specific types of devices or specific manufacturers. As you can see, one major difference between the HCL on the CD and the Web site is that the Web site includes all Microsoft products for which the device could be certified and the certification status. A device that is certified as Windows 2000-compatible, for example, does not meet all of

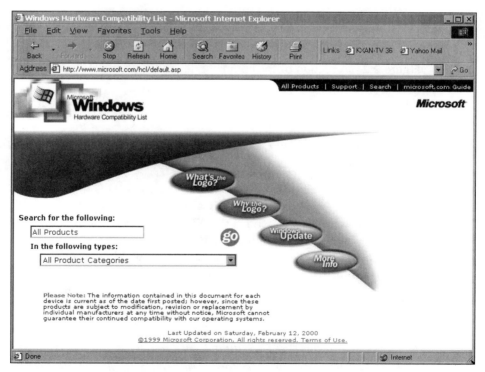

Figure 2.1   The Microsoft Windows Hardware Compatibility List Web site.

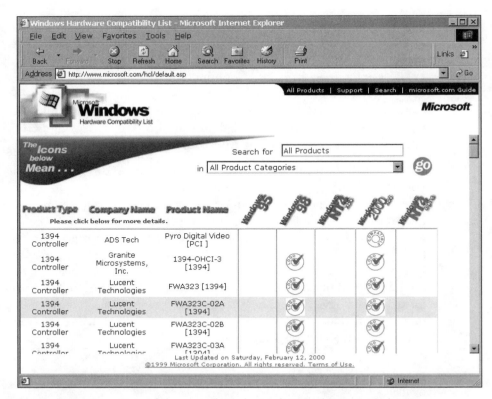

Figure 2.2   A section of the complete device list on the HCL Web site.

the requirements to participate in the Microsoft logo program, but is compatible with Windows.

Note: The icons on the HCL Web page and their meanings are accessed by clicking the "The Icons Below Mean . . ." link.

Another advantage to the HCL listing on the Internet is that additional information on a particular device is accessed by clicking the name of the device. For example, a search for the ATI Rage 128 display device shows that it is "Logo" certified for Windows 98, Windows NT 4 (x86), and Windows 2000 (x86). Clicking the device invokes a new window, which provides the additional information, as shown in Figure 2.3. As you can see, this adapter is "PC99 Compliant," which provides compatibility with the three products listed previously. The displayed information also indicates that the English driver version 6.31.1–CD20C is required for this level of compliance.

Note: When installing Windows 2000 on a system, it's always best to ensure that you have the most recent version of the drivers, which are available from the hardware manu-facturer. At the very least, however, the driver version listed on the Web site is required for

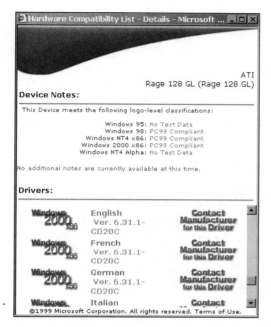

2

Figure 2.3   The HCL information for the ATI Rage 128 display device.

compatibility. Similar to devices not listed on the HCL, devices whose drivers are not compliant are also not supported by Microsoft.

Windows 2000 Server Maximum Hardware Support

Although it may not directly apply to the Windows 2000 Server exam, it is always interesting to know the maximum hardware configuration a Windows operating system supports. There are actually three versions of Windows 2000 Server: Standard Edition, Advanced Server, and the Microsoft Windows Datacenter Server. The features differences between these products are minimal; Advanced Server includes all the functionality of Standard Server with additional support for network load balancing and server clustering, Datacenter Server expands on the features of Advanced Server by adding even more advanced clustering. The biggest differences between the products are the maximum memory and number of processors supported.

Windows 2000 supports *symmetric multiprocessing (SMP)*. Windows 2000 Server supports SMP on up to four processors. In addition, the Standard Edition supports up to 4GB of physical memory. Advanced Server supports up to 8GB of memory and 8-way SMP, whereas Datacenter Server supports an extravagant 32-way SMP and 64GB of physical memory. Even at today's memory prices, that's a lot of memory.

Although these limitations may seem like pie-in-the-sky now, at the rate that technology is advancing, the limits of the operating system's compatibility will be reached in a relatively short amount of time. As previously mentioned, hardware development drives software development, and vice versa. As soon as a manufacturer is able to create and sell a system that will support the maximum configuration for Windows 2000, a new operating system will be released with even higher limitations. Consequently, we are reminded of a Bill Gates quote from the early days of Microsoft: "No one will ever need more than 16MB of memory."

USING THE WINDOWS 2000 READINESS ANALYZER

To help you identify whether all hardware in your system is compatible with Windows 2000, Microsoft has created the *Windows 2000 Readiness Analyzer* tool. This is, in essence, the same tool that runs during the Windows 2000 installation process, but it can be downloaded and run independently to provide you with the opportunity to correct potential issues before installing Windows 2000. The Readiness Analyzer checks your system's configuration and reports potential incompatibilities between the hardware and Windows 2000 by comparing the information in the Registry of the system with known Windows 2000 issues. Unfortunately, the issues identified by the Readiness Analyzer are based on Microsoft and third-party testing and may not be comprehensive. However, this does give you some level of assurance that Windows 2000 will install correctly and not suffer due to preventable hardware issues.

Downloading and Running the Readiness Analyzer

The Windows 2000 Readiness Analyzer is available on the Microsoft Windows 2000 Web site at **www.microsoft.com/windows2000/upgrade/compat/ default.asp** (shown in Figure 2.4). Use of the Readiness Analyzer should be included as part of the overall process of evaluating your existing configuration and its ability to support Windows 2000.

Clicking the Download The Readiness Analyzer button takes you to a download page containing specifications on the system requirements for the Analyzer and the instructions for downloading and running the program. As should be expected, the Readiness Analyzer only runs on Microsoft operating systems that utilize the Registry: Windows 95, Windows 98, Windows NT 3.51, and Windows NT 4. If the system you want to evaluate falls into this category, you can download the appropriate version of the Analyzer by selecting the language from the drop-down list at the top of the window and clicking Next. You will be presented with one last page informing you of the estimated

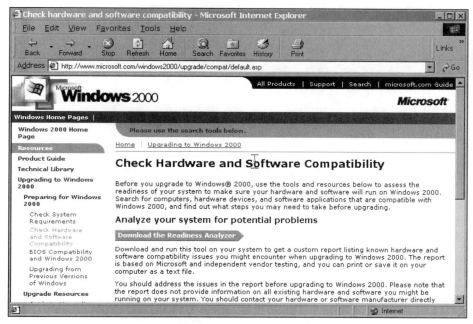

Figure 2.4   The Windows 2000 Software and Hardware Compatibility site.

download time based on your connection speed. Click Download Now to begin the transfer. When prompted, save the file to your local hard drive with the following file name (the default): chkupgrd.exe.

Once the transfer is complete, double-click chkupgrd.exe. The Readiness Analyzer will be started, and you will be asked to confirm the license agreement for the Windows 2000 Readiness Analyzer. To continue, click Yes. The Analyzer will then begin reviewing the configuration of the system on which it is being run. It is important to note that, although the application runs on the Microsoft platforms listed previously, a different type of analysis is done on systems running Windows NT 4 and Windows 98. The analysis of our Windows NT 4.0 Workstation system took less than two minutes and displayed the window shown in Figure 2.5. As you can see, there are two devices in our system that are incompatible with Windows 2000. In most cases, updated device drivers can be downloaded from the Internet to support Windows 2000. However, there may be some instances in which the hardware cannot be made to work with Windows 2000 and must be replaced. Click Finish to complete the evaluation.

The report provided when the Analyzer was run on a Windows 98 computer was much more extensive and included detailed information on potential software incompatibilities as well as identified hardware issues. Regardless of

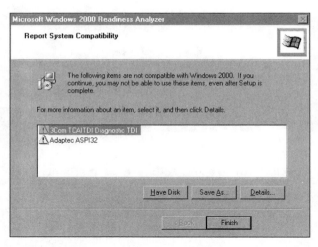

Figure 2.5   The summary report for a Windows NT 4.0 Workstation computer.

which operating system the Analyzer is run on, you are able to save the report file by clicking the Save As button. In addition, the report provides a Print button that allows you to easily create a hard copy of the report.

PLANNING SERVER INSTALLATION

To make your installation of Windows 2000 Server as painless as an installation can be, some planning must take place before the CD is ever inserted in the system. With the added intricacies surrounding the new features of Windows 2000, such as Active Directory and the Distributed file system (Dfs), planning your installation is more important than ever.

There are three analytical and planning functions that have been developed to ensure that the deployment of the Windows 2000 operating system is a success. The first of these is an analysis of the current state of your network and determination of how it matches the business strategies of your company. In many cases, the upgrade to a new server operating system allows you to make changes to the fundamental structure of the organization and the information flow at the same time. The second step involves some projection of where your company is and where it is going. Design decisions made today will have to work for the foreseeable future and perhaps the next two to five years (an eon in the technology age). Finally, a formal, written deployment plan is developed, which includes testing of the new operating system and design, and approval of the test results before implementation. This is perhaps the least-loved implementation requirement of networking professionals the world over; it is also one of the most important. Thorough documentation and testing lets the business units affected by the new design understand how they will be impacted when the change takes place.

Tip: ⋅ ⋅ ⋅ ⋅ ⋅ ⋅ ⋅ ⋅ ⋅ ⋅ ⋅ ⋅ ⋅ ⋅ ⋅

Throughout this process and going forward, adopt a new mantra: "Document, write it down, document" or something equally as exciting. The point is, take the opportunity to get complete documentation of your network and continue to document everything you do.

⋅ ⋅ ⋅ ⋅ ⋅ ⋅ ⋅ ⋅ ⋅ ⋅ ⋅ ⋅ ⋅ ⋅ ⋅

Step 1: Where Are We Now?

This may seem like the easiest step of all and may, in fact, end up being the most difficult. Few network administrators have a complete inventory of the resources attached to their network as well as information on how new or old those resources are. For many companies, as long as there is a computer on every desk and a printer in every department, resources are sufficient. To ensure that all network devices attached to the network are able to effectively and efficiently communicate with the new Windows 2000 Server, a complete inventory should be completed at this stage. This inventory should include the type of resource connected (i.e., computer, printer, scanner, and so on), the hardware configuration of the resource, and the software configuration. In some cases, the only upgrade needed to utilize the new server may be a driver upgrade or a minor change from a standard Ethernet card to a Fast Ethernet card.

Note: This inventory should include not only client-side devices, such as desktop computers, but also other servers on the network, their configurations, and their roles. With the enhanced capabilities of Windows 2000, you may be able to consolidate server functions onto a single system. You may also discover from this information that it will be necessary to upgrade many more of your servers to Windows 2000 than you originally expected.

In addition to completing an inventory of the network resources, a map of the physical network layout is needed. This map should include every device, router, wiring closet, and hub. During the next stages of this analysis, map in hand, you will be able to determine the best place to expand or reconfigure the network, analyze the traffic patterns on the network, and determine the best placement for network devices, such as the Windows 2000 Server. Included on this map should be the network addresses currently being used, which will assist you in determining whether a new addressing scheme is needed and help to facilitate this change when the time comes.

Another potential implementation nightmare can be avoided during this phase of the analysis: surprise connectivity requirements to non-Windows systems or systems outside your network. External connectivity is often well-known and well-documented. However, if you are a recent hire to a company or a consultant, these things invariably pop up only after you've made a complete conversion to the new platform and there's no going back. Just about that time, Bob from Engineering pops his head around the corner and says, "I had a message waiting for me on my system this morning that said my export program to the Unix box at our analyst's site crashed because we couldn't communicate. I guess I forgot to tell you, it runs every Friday. Can you have it fixed by noon?" By performing a thorough and detailed analysis of your network infrastructure and current connectivity, you alleviate this problem and things will go more smoothly.

Analysis of the type of traffic that traverses your network is also necessary. Changes to Windows 2000 have been made that eliminate the need for NetBIOS. Before determining if this is the best path for you to take on your network, you must understand the volume of NetBIOS traffic currently being generated, as well as that from other protocols being used on the network. Traffic volume analysis can also help you determine if this is the best time to consolidate underused existing network segments or split overworked networks into two or more pieces.

The final portion of the analysis of the current state of your network is an accounting of the software running on all workstations and servers. As part of this analysis, indicate which of these applications, if any, generate network traffic and how much.

Once this information has been gathered, categorize the applications and services used on the network by level of need and use. Microsoft recommends using the following categories: *strategic, tactical, legacy,* and *obsolete.* Strategic services and applications are those that are essential to the day-to-day operation of the business and a necessary part of the company's current and future goals. Examples for some companies would be Microsoft Word and Excel, printing services, and accounting programs. Tactical applications are considered worthwhile and needed by the business, but may not be providing the most benefit to the company. An example might be Internet access, which provides employees with the ability to conduct valuable company business remotely. The term *legacy* denotes applications and services that are older and used only by a small group of employees. Legacy applications are usually nearing the end of their usefulness and, if their functions are still required, should be upgraded before they become obsolete. A good example of this is an aging plotter used in drafting. Many legacy resources may not be supported by the newer operating systems, such as Windows 2000. Obsolete applications are those that do not serve their purpose on the network and, from an overall network perspective, are actually a hindrance. During the planning and implementation process, it should be your goal to find a better solution for obsolete applications, encourage users to make the change, and eliminate the obsolete software and services.

Note: Part of the evaluation of a company's current network state is evaluating costs. When getting into this type of analysis, managers and accounting types like to use words like total cost of ownership (TCO) and return on investment (ROI). TCO is determined by identifying areas in which upgrades can be made, assessing the cost of the upgrade, and balancing that against the savings in time, money, and resources. For example, if upgrading a network server costs $5,000, but doing so will save 150 man-hours per month because it is more efficient, and one man-hour costs an average of $15, the server will pay for itself in only 2.2 months. ROI is similar in that it quantifies potential revenue opportunities presented by upgrading. To make this process a tad less confusing, Microsoft has provided a link to a TCO/ROI calculator on its Web site at www.microsoft.com/ ntworkstation/overview/lowestTCO/TCOcalculator.asp.

Step 2: Where Are We Going?

Get out your Tarot cards because this is the point at which a little prognostication comes in handy. You must first review the data you gathered during the first part of the analysis, and be prepared to present your findings to all levels of management. You must then ask questions, such as the following:

➤ Where will this company be in one year? Three years? Five years? Ten years?

➤ Are there plans to consolidate remote resources into a centralized location?

➤ Are there plans to expand geographically through normal growth or acquisitions?

➤ Will you move toward or away from a telecommuting environment?

➤ Will advanced technologies, such as Internet video conferencing, be required for some users? All users? How soon?

Bear in mind that as you ask these questions there may not always be answers, or the answers may be confidential and known only by the President and CEO. But, by asking the questions and gathering as much information as you can, you will be better able to structure your Windows 2000 installation and the network that supports it. Knowing there is a merger in the works within the next 12 months provides you with the opportunity to design the network to include the additional staff and connectivity.

Step 3: Let's Go

The last step in the process is to combine the data you've collected into an implementation plan. This plan should include all levels of information, and the approval process should be defined before proceeding. Many administrators include a broad "executive" review with supporting detailed documentation. When it comes right down to it, the vice president of Human Resources might be on the approval committee, but she may not have the technical background, time, or desire to wade through the technical mumbo-jumbo required for the full rollout plan.

Define the scope of the project specifically and stick to it. If there are many areas that need to be addressed but can be handled separately, divide them into individual projects and proceed in order of necessity. It may come to pass that, although you started out on a Windows 2000 installation project, the wiring in one of the buildings might have to be upgraded to Category 5 cabling and all systems upgraded to 100Mbps Ethernet before you can install Windows 2000. Also as part of the scope, specify those events that constitute a complete project. For example, a Windows 2000 installation project may include upgrading all workstations in accounting to Windows 2000 Professional, installing Advanced Server with clustering, and switching to terminal services for all employees to record the hours they've worked. The project may not be considered complete until the last employee enters his or her time. It is very important to define this at the beginning, so that the project can be measured.

Your implementation plan must include a schedule for thoroughly testing all areas of the upgrade. There will always be that printer in the shipping room that everyone forgets about, but you must make every effort to ensure all devices and software are tested and function properly before the full-blown implementation. Although it may be contrary to your first inclination, test and verify those things you feel will cause the most problems at the outset. This allows you more time to work through the issues and adjust the schedule if necessary. Putting off those things you hate because you know it will not be fun will only lead to delays in the project schedule later in the game.

That said, allow time in your overall schedule for the unexpected. Regardless of how well you plan, there is no way you can foresee and schedule the entire staff of your cabling contractor coming down with the flu. Systems will not always act the way you expect and software that ran fine on one computer may not run the same way on another. Be ready for it, don't get discouraged, and leave time in the schedule.

When things change to the extent that it is necessary to make modifications to the process, update the project plan, set a revised implementation date, and go forward. Be sure to adjust any milestones identified as well and not just the end date of the project. Most importantly, make sure everyone on the project is aware of and understands the nature of the delay. Updating the plan also allows you to evaluate the nature of the delay.

A delay that is caused by a fundamental flaw in the implementation plan will repeat throughout the life of the project. For example, if one key player is assigned many tasks in addition to his or her "normal" job and cannot dedicate the necessary time to the project, delays will be seen in each segment of the project in which he or she is involved. However, if you finish a phase of the project four days behind schedule, a review might remind you that the office was closed for four days due to a blizzard.

PLANNING SERVER STORAGE

The physical layout of your server's storage devices has an effect on its performance and fault tolerance. You must make a determination as to how much storage space is required in the server and, therefore, the number of physical devices, their interface, and the RAID (Redundant Array of Independent Disks) level to use.

In addition to the minimum space required for installing Windows 2000, you must determine the space required for user files, applications, and services. There are many methods for calculating this requirement, and the final number depends on the type of services running on the server, the Active Directory design used on the server, and the amount of space each user is provided for storage.

The decision of which interface to use for your server is a balance between cost and performance. Disk drives with the IDE (integrated device electronics) interface provide large amounts of disk space at a low cost, but at a lower level of performance. The newest, fastest IDE drives available today comply with the *ATA-66* specification. ATA-66 drives have a 66MB/s transfer rate in burst mode. In addition, 7,200 rpm to 10,000 rpm drives are available, which increase the overall performance of the drives. IDE/ATA-66 drives should only be considered for the smallest servers and workstations. However, even these drives do not match the performance provided by drives with the *SCSI* interface.

The most recent iterations of the SCSI specification are Ultra Wide 2 and Ultra 160. Readily available today, Ultra Wide 2 drives operate at no less than 7,200 rpm and have a burst mode transfer rate of 80MB/s. At this time, the fastest SCSI drive available conforms to the Ultra 160 spec, which provides a data transfer rate of 160MB/s—nearly 2.5 times faster than the fastest IDE drive. Of course, this performance comes with a higher price. To illustrate this point, we did an Internet search for comparable hard drives. We found a 20.4GB ATA-66 drive for $209, but the least expensive Ultra Wide 2 drive we could find in a comparable size was 18.3GB for $340.

Note: There are eight different SCSI specifications and not all are entirely compatible. Many of the drives are backward-compatible to previous specifications, but this compatibility means that the devices revert to the lower performance level of the earlier spec. When deciding on the interface type and purchasing drives for your system, be sure that everything you buy conforms to the same standard.

At the top of the hard drive food chain is the *Fibre Channel* interface. This technology is still very new, and it is difficult to make a true comparison with other products. The Fibre Channel specification is designed not around single-disk performance as IDE and SCSI are, but around multiple-disk performance. If the server configuration has five drives or less, you will see no performance improvement over the Ultra 160. However, in environments with large numbers of drives attached to a single system, Fibre Channel provides a significant improvement due to the method it uses to manage data transfer. In fact, unlike any other interface type, Fibre Channel's performance actually increases as more devices are added. For example, with 20 or more devices attached, Fibre Channel provides 100Mbps transfer rates. Fibre Channel also supports increased reliability because of the way it handles error correction and redundancy. Lastly, the Fibre Channel standard supports two unique configuration options: A total of 126 Fibre Channel devices can be attached to a single controller, and the maximum distance between devices can be 10 kilometers when using optical cable.

This technology provides unique opportunities for off-site storage and system configuration. The cost of Fibre Channel drives is not much more than that of Ultra Wide 2 SCSI drives, however, the controllers to support Fibre Channel are expensive. A recent search of major systems manufacturers indicates that a basic Fibre Channel RAID storage system runs anywhere from $5,500 to $18,000 for ten 18GB drives and two-channel controllers.

RAID

RAID (Redundant Array of Independent Disks) was developed to provide fault tolerance and prevent data loss. It does this through various configurations of more than two physical hard drives called levels. The RAID specification defines levels 0 through 5. However, Windows 2000 disk management provides support only for RAID 0 (which provides no fault tolerance), 1, and RAID 5.

RAID 1 is realized when a secondary hard drive acts as a mirror of the primary drive; this is referred to simply as *mirroring*. As data is written to the primary drive, it is also written to the secondary. If the primary drive fails, the data is still available on the secondary drive and can be used until the primary drive is repaired or replaced. Placing the drives on separate hard drive controllers can enhance this configuration. This type of setup is called *duplexing*, which provides an added tier of fault tolerance. In a mirrored configuration, if the hard drive controller fails, the system cannot access the data. But in a duplexed configuration, if the primary controller fails, the secondary controller and secondary drive can continue to provide service to the system.

RAID 5 provides data recovery through the use of data *stripe sets with parity*. To achieve faster performance, RAID 5 writes data to multiple drives at the same time as a stripe. For example, in a three-drive array, a parity stripe would be written to drive 1, with data stripes written to drives 2 and 3. Then, data stripes would be written to drives 1 and 2, with a parity stripe written to disk 3, and so on.

In addition to providing increased read performance over RAID 1, RAID 5 provides enhanced fault tolerance by using parity blocks as the data is written. The information in the parity blocks is calculated by using an algorithm to summarize the data written in the other blocks in the stripe. In the event of a drive failure, the parity information contained in the blocks on the other drives is used to reconstruct the information contained on the lost drive. This can take place while the system is functioning with only minimal impact on performance.

Which RAID Configuration to Use

The determination as to which RAID level to use depends on the number of drives you are planning to include in the system and the performance required of those drives. As mentioned previously, RAID 1 mirrors one drive to another. In effect, you are paying for two drives, but only being able to utilize the storage space on one drive. This type of configuration works well for small systems that require some level of fault tolerance but do not require large amounts of drive space or high performance.

In the vast majority of the servers in production today, RAID 5 is used to provide the most bang for the buck. RAID 5 is more efficient than RAID 1 because it uses parity information to store and reconstruct data. Even in its most basic configuration, you are able to store two drives' data on three drives. This equates to 66 percent usable storage space as opposed to 50 percent in a RAID 1 configuration. In addition, as more drives are added, the percentage of usable space increases, providing consistently greater benefits. However, this advantage is lost when more than seven drives are added to a RAID set. If your server configuration calls for more than seven physical drives, multiple RAID 5 sets should be implemented.

Other Alternatives

As mentioned earlier, Windows 2000 supports RAID 0, 1, and RAID 5 in its disk management structure. This means that the operating system itself manages how data is written to and read from the RAID set. On systems that require high performance from the operating system, removing this management often provides a better option. This is accomplished by using hardware solutions for RAID management. Hardware RAID configurations are often sold as complete sets made up of a specialized RAID drive controller and the specified number of drives. Rather than actively manage data flow to the drives, the operating system hands the data to the RAID controller, which itself handles data management to the drives.

Note: It should also be mentioned that hybrid configurations of RAID 1 and RAID 5 are being utilized to provide the most complete fault tolerance available. Often called RAID 10, this configuration utilizes mirrored RAID sets on separate controllers. In this type of configuration, any single drive failure in the primary RAID set is managed by the primary controller. If multiple drives in the primary RAID set fail or the primary controller fails, the mirror is able to take over and continue providing service. As you can imagine, this type of configuration is expensive and can usually be justified only on those systems requiring nearly 100 percent availability.

Planning Server File Systems

Somewhat like its predecessor, Windows 2000 supports three file systems: FAT16, FAT32, and NTFS. FAT16 is the original file allocation table (FAT) file system that has been used since DOS, FAT32 is an updated version FAT. Windows NT 4 supported FAT, but not FAT32 because FAT32 was released after Windows NT 4. The Windows NT File System (NTFS) was developed for Windows NT 4 and has been continued in Windows 2000. NTFS provides many advantages over FAT including increased security, increased efficiency, greater reliability, and compression.

Similar to Windows NT 4, Windows 2000 provides the ability to install multiple operating systems on a single machine and select the desired operating system when the machine boots. This *dual-boot* configuration is really the only consideration when determining which file system to use on a Windows 2000 computer. The dual-boot feature is generally more of a consideration on Windows 2000 Professional systems than on Windows 2000 Server installations because servers are restricted to one task, whereas workstations may require different configurations for different situations.

Previously, a limitation of Windows NT 4 made it almost necessary to install the operating system on a FAT partition. In the event that Windows NT 4 was installed on an NTFS partition and for some reason the system became unbootable, there was no way to access the files on the partition. Many administrators installed Windows NT 4 on FAT partitions so they could boot from a standard DOS disk and manipulate the files in the Windows NT directories. However, this limitation no longer exists with Windows 2000.

Administrators now have the ability to boot using "safe" mode, which includes NTFS support. In addition, a Recovery Console has been added to the operating system to provide access to the file system when the computer no longer boots. This console is accessed when booting from the startup diskettes or booting from the Windows 2000 CD by choosing the Repair option (R) during Setup and selecting the Recovery Console.

When considering which file system to use, remember that there are many Windows 2000 features that require an NTFS partition, including Active Directory, because of the increased security provided by the file system. Unless there is a solid requirement, such as dual boot with Windows 98, you should always use NTFS.

Planning Distributed File Systems

When network servers were first introduced, there was seldom more than one server per company or location. Connecting users to the server and providing them access to the data they needed was easy. As networks grew, so did the number of servers at each company. Servers took on specialized roles and were dedicated to specific departments. To access data on different servers, users had to log on to each server individually and map a drive letter to the location of the data they needed. To alleviate the confusion caused by multiple logon requirements and data located on multiple servers, Microsoft has included two new features with Windows 2000: Active Directory (which is discussed later in this chapter in the section titled "Planning Active Directory Structures") and the *Distributed file system (Dfs)*.

Dfs allows administrators to create a virtual representation of the data available on network servers and provide increased performance through load balancing and bandwidth management. In addition to providing a single access point for the users to the data they need, the design of Dfs also provides fault tolerance to ensure that users are able to access their data in the event of a failure or planned network outage. Because the security for Dfs relies on NTFS, it is easy to implement and maintain; little additional configuration is required.

Dfs was designed to provide the highest possible level of data availability to users and make it easier for them to access their data. On a large network with many servers, related data can reside on numerous servers, resulting in duplicate or old versions of files, which can cause confusion for users. This is remedied in Dfs by creating a root folder (called the *Dfs root*) and associating with it the locations of related files. For example, at Lycrania, accounting data is stored on three different servers: in the ACCT folder on the LYC1 server, in the PAYROLL folder on the LPRL server, and APAR folder on the PAYABLES server. Using Dfs, the network administrator for Lycrania could create a Dfs root called Accounting through which all users that needed access could reach all files. Rather than logging on to all three servers and locating the appropriate directory, users need only double-click the Accounting share to be granted access.

High data availability is achieved by designing a Dfs structure that includes replicated copies (replicas) of heavily used file shares and limits access across intranet boundaries to reduce network traffic. Network performance is also improved because the users do not interact with the actual file system, only with the Dfs folder structure. A design that includes replicated information allows the administrators to manage downtime while maintaining data availability. Dfs works closely with Active Directory to ensure that users are always granted access to the Dfs tree, even if the Dfs root's server is unavailable. If a Dfs link is configured to identify multiple servers with identical data, Dfs automatically performs load balancing.

Dfs Components and Concepts

There are a number of components and concepts that are unique to Dfs. As mentioned previously, the Dfs root serves as the access point for users to their data. A Dfs root is, in fact, a shared folder that serves as the basis for a Dfs structure. Any shared folder can be a Dfs root. Therefore, it is not necessary to create a new folder to create a Dfs root: An existing folder that is currently being used should be used as the Dfs root for the tree. The server on which the Dfs root resides is called the *host server*. The Dfs root is unique in that it does not contain actual files, but instead contains *Dfs links* to related locations elsewhere on the network. They appear as subfolders in the Dfs root and transparently connect the user to the specified shared folder. As mentioned earlier, a Dfs link can be configured to address multiple (up to 32) identical folders called Dfs shared folders or replicas to provide load balancing and high data availability.

Because it relies so heavily on Active Directory, Dfs implementation is limited to specific Microsoft products. At this time, all Microsoft desktop operating systems, from Windows 95 to Windows 2000 Professional, support Dfs with specialized client software. Windows 95 users must download the Dfs client from the Microsoft Web site, whereas a Dfs client is included with Windows 98, Windows NT 4.0 Server and Workstation (SP3 or later), and Windows 2000 Professional. However, for Windows 98 support of domain-based Dfs servers, a new client must be downloaded. Windows 2000 Server provides full support for Dfs and should serve as the backbone for your Dfs design. Windows NT 4.0 Server must at least have Service Pack 3 installed to host Dfs roots. Unfortunately, Windows NT 4 can only support Dfs roots on stand-alone servers; domain participant servers like domain controllers cannot be host servers.

The Design

Planning the design of your Dfs implementation requires in-depth knowledge of the data on the network servers and how that data is accessed. The first step is to identify collections of folders that can easily be consolidated into a single access point. After that, consider the replication strategy you will use to provide the most current data to all users at all times while limiting network traffic.

PLANNING NETWORK SERVICES

The network services to be used on your network depend entirely on the requirements of your business. Using the information gathered during the first phases of the project, you must determine where network resources, such as printers, are to be placed and the impact those resources will have on network operation. In addition, you must make a decision as to which protocols to use on the network to provide complete connectivity between the client computers, the Windows 2000 Server, and other systems, such as those using Novell NetWare or Unix.

Windows 2000 Protocol Support

Although the details of the various protocols supported by Windows 2000 will be covered in Chapter 8, it is important that we touch on some changes in the standard protocol support for the Microsoft products and discuss protocol considerations for the planning process.

In keeping with the evolving industry-wide acceptance of the TCP/IP protocol suite as the standard, Microsoft has taken a bold step with Windows 2000. The requirement for NetBIOS support has been eliminated, and been replaced by the *Dynamic Domain Name System (DDNS)* protocol. As a result of this move, the *Windows Internet Naming Service (WINS)* is no longer required for name resolution. Aside from giving administrators the ability to standardize on a single protocol suite for all communications, the move to DDNS provides a single source for all name resolution (Internet and intranet), greater security, a higher degree of efficiency, reduced broadcast traffic, and easier support. In addition, DDNS is able to provide resolution over subnet boundaries (something NetBIOS struggled with) and still maintain a dynamic database of names and addresses.

If you are lucky enough to be installing an entirely new network, from servers to workstations, this change is very beneficial. However, when integrating Windows 2000 into an existing network, you must consider whether to include NetBIOS and WINS support on the new server, how long these services will be offered on the Windows 2000 Server, and a plan to update all systems

connecting to the Windows 2000 Server. If you will not be supporting
NetBIOS on your Windows 2000 Server, you must consider the immediate
impact that the server installation will have, the scope of the systems affected by
this decision, and a plan to update the systems to support the Windows 2000
Server without NetBIOS.

*Note: Keep in mind when migrating from WINS to DDNS that there is a chance that
not all computers attached to the network utilize WINS for name resolution. These
systems must be identified and their configuration changed to remove the LMHOSTS
file and configure the DDNS settings.*

Dynamic Domain Name System

DDNS is a more flexible implementation of DNS from the TCP/IP suite. To
effectively replace WINS, it is important that the clients be able to update their
naming information dynamically. DDNS manages this interaction and works
with Active Directory to store zone data. Active Directory is also relied upon to
propagate any database changes throughout the zones on the network, resulting
in faster directory replication than a standard DNS implementation.

Although Microsoft recommends adhering to the TCP/IP-only standard for
network communication, many other protocols are still supported by Windows
2000 to provide connectivity to systems that do not support DDNS. For
connections to computers running older Microsoft or IBM LAN Manager
software, Windows 2000 supports NetBEUI as a transport. NWLink, Microsoft's
implementation of Novell's Internetwork Packet Exchange/Sequenced
Packet Exchange (IPX/SPX) protocol suite, is supported as well to provide
legacy connectivity.

The network services part of your Windows 2000 implementation plan must be
clearly defined and spelled out before proceeding. Because the default name
resolution process has changed from previous Microsoft implementations, the
detailed list of workstations and their configurations is as important in this stage
as any other, if not more. Microsoft recommends not utilizing NetBIOS (if only
Windows 2000 clients are in use) and supporting only protocols in the TCP/IP
suite. Add support for other protocols only as necessary and then on a very
limited basis.

PLANNING ACTIVE DIRECTORY STRUCTURES

Active Directory is the new database in which all network objects are stored
and managed. With Active Directory, every network resource is an object. Users,
groups, printers, organizational roles, and even computers are objects that are
managed independently of each other. Active Directory replaces the Security

Accounts Manager (SAM) database used in Windows NT 3.x and 4.x and provides a hierarchical, distributed database that is scalable to encompass even the largest global corporations. Planning the Active Directory structure for your company is vital to ensuring a successful implementation that will stand the test of time. You must fully understand the role of each type of object in Active Directory and its limitations. Active Directory uses six organizational roles to define the directory and how it functions. From the most detailed to the most general, these organizational roles are organizational units, domains, trees, forests, sites, and the global catalog.

Active Directory Organizational Units (OUs)

The idea behind *Organizational Units (OUs)* is new to Windows 2000, but has been used in other areas of the networking industry for quite some time. The Organizational Unit is the smallest grouping of resources available in the Active Directory: In many companies, multiple OUs combine to create a domain. The OU allows the administrator to group users, groups, printers, file shares, Dfs roots, and other objects into a hierarchical configuration. This provides easier management and the ability to assign users more granular rights than were available in the SAM database. A unique benefit of this configuration is that an administrator can be designated to create and manage all aspects of the OU, but not be granted access to other parts of the domain.

Note: *When designing your Active Directory, create organizational units to the most specific level based on the operation of the business. For example, in a small company, a single Accounting OU can provide the necessary organization and security. However, in a larger company, separate OUs should be created for Accounts Payable, Accounts Receivable, and Payroll.*

Active Directory Domains

The role of domains in Active Directory is a little different than that in SAM. *Domains* define a boundary, also called a partition, between logical groups of objects to provide centralized administration and security. Objects are contained in domains within the Active Directory structure and are defined in the *schema*. The schema literally defines the available object classes and attributes in Active Directory. If you determine that the objects and attributes available in the schema are not sufficient to manage your network, the schema can be extended to include new types of objects or new attributes. To do this, you must obtain a unique root *object identifier (OID)* from the American National Standards Institute (ANSI) for your organization.

As with SAM, Active Directory information must be replicated between servers on the network. However, because Active Directory is a distributed database, there is no master domain controller that manages all database activity and replication. In the Active Directory environment, a server can either be a *domain controller (DC)* or a *member server.* The domain controllers for a partition replicate the partition information amongst themselves and share new information as it is received. Each DC has a read/write copy of their partition of the Active Directory. In addition, trusts between Active Directory domains are created automatically, are two-way, and are transitive. This means that trust relationships are passed down the line, so that if ADOM1 trusts BDOM2 and BDOM2 trusts CDOM3, then ADOM1 automatically trusts CDOM3, and vice versa. Domains in the Active Directory can operate in either *native mode* or *mixed mode.* In mixed mode, the domain partition can be replicated to *downlevel* (Windows NT 3.x or 4.x) backup domain controllers. In native mode (no Windows NT domain controllers present), downlevel replication support is turned off and a true multimaster replication environment is created. In addition, groups can be nested within the domain when operating in native mode.

Note: Native mode is preferrable to mixed mode. Active Directory must limit the options available when communication with Windows NT 3.x and/or 4.x domains is necessary. For best performance, use only native mode. Include plans to either upgrade all servers not able to support Active Directory, or remove those servers from their domain controller role.

Three types of groups exist in Active Directory: domain local groups, global groups, and universal groups. Global groups and universal groups can be granted permissions in any domain, whereas domain local groups can only be granted permissions on member servers and domain controllers. The mode in which the domain is operating also has an effect on the types of objects that can be included in each of the groups. When operating in native mode, domain local groups can contain users, universal groups, and global groups from any domain and other domain local groups from the same domain. In the same mode, global groups can contain users and other global groups from the same domain; universal groups can contain users, other universal groups, and global groups from any domain. In mixed mode, domain local groups can contain users and global groups from any domain, and global groups can contain users from the same domain. Universal groups cannot be created if the domain is operating in mixed mode.

Active Directory Trees

A *tree* is a hierarchical grouping of two or more domains or organizational units in Active Directory; it is a single, continuous namespace where all names descend from the root name. The first domain in the tree is automatically the root of the tree. Each domain or OU created after that point becomes a child of

2

the tree, making a parent–child relationship between the domains. The partitions under the root can also have partitions created below them, making them the parents of the new partitions. This relationship is important because certain configuration settings from the parent are automatically assigned to the child when it is created. The common configuration, global catalog, and schema are passed down from parent to child. Note, however, that this does not apply to accessing resources within the newly created domain. But once the child domain is created, it acts independently and has its own security configurations. As with objects in the SAM database, the domain acts as the barrier between separate security entities. Though a user may have complete access to the parent domain, they are not automatically granted access to the child. This can, of course, be corrected manually to provide a centralized administration structure, but it is not automatic. Figure 2.6 is an example of an Active Directory structure.

Active Directory Forests

As its name implies, a *forest* is an Active Directory configuration made up of more than one tree. Each tree in a forest is created with its own namespace and security. When a forest is created, a transitive trust between the root domains is created, allowing resources to be shared between the trees. When a new tree is added to the forest, it is given the same data as when a child partition is added: common configuration, schema, and global catalog.

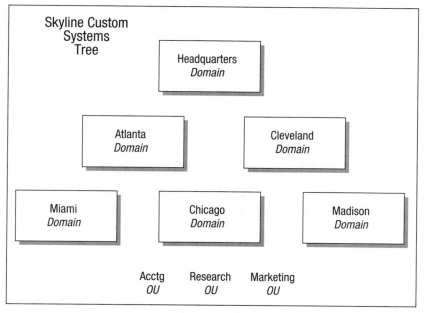

Figure 2.6   The Active Directory structure for Skyline Custom Systems.

Active Directory Sites

Unlike the other organizational roles discussed so far, sites represent the physical location of resources on the network. *Sites* are used to mark the delineation between LANs and WANs to ensure that the network bandwidth required for Active Directory updates is used as efficiently as possible. All servers within a site must share reliable, high-speed network access to be able to actively participate as domain controllers.

The Active Directory Global Catalog

Because all domains, trees, and forests contain separate information, they must be interconnected at another level to enable trust relationships and cross-object access. The *global catalog* is the actual database containing information on all objects that is necessary to provide connectivity between organizational roles. This is important because if you can't locate a global catalog, you can't log on. In the event that you request data that is not in the global catalog, you are provided the object's *distinguished name (DN)*. The object's DN provides you with the information necessary to connect to the object's domain controller and request the resource. When the global catalog returns this type of information, it is called a *referral*.

Creating the Plan

With the information provided and the research on the current and future state of your network, you should be able to design an Active Directory structure for your company. Start at the highest level, meaning the general department or organization level, and base the plan on the operational organization of your company. If you are including Active Directory in an existing Windows NT 3.x or 4.x network, design the domain structure around the new Windows 2000 Server and create a plan to upgrade the existing servers to Windows 2000 Server. To provide the highest performance level, be sure that site configurations are limited to those servers that have reliable, high-speed network access.

ASSESSING UNATTENDED INSTALLATION SCENARIOS

Like earlier versions of the Microsoft operating systems, Windows 2000 affords you the ability to automate the installation process by either using command-line switches at a DOS prompt or window or by providing an answer file for some or all of the questions asked during the installation. Although installing a large number of servers at one time is a daunting task, be absolutely sure you are comfortable with the installation process and are familiar with the options available. We recommend performing a few installations using the normal process first, then perform a few using command-line options, and finally create complete or partial *answer files* for the installation.

There are two different versions of the installation program on the Windows 2000 CD. If you are performing an installation after booting from a DOS, Windows 95, Windows 98, or Windows NT boot disk, use the winnt.exe version of the installation program located on the root folder of the CD. If you are performing an installation through a command-prompt window in Windows 95, Windows 98, or Windows NT, use winnt32.exe. Table 2.3 lists the command-line options for the Windows 2000 installation program.

Table 2.3   Command-line parameters for Windows 2000 Setup.

Version	Parameter	Description
winnt	/a	Enables Accessibility features during the installation.
winnt	/e:[command]	Specifies a command to be run after the installation is complete.
winnt	/r:[folder]	Specifies an additional folder to be copied into the Windows 2000 folder \WINNT. Folder remains after installation is complete. Used to copy drivers and utilities to the server during installation for use later.
winnt	/rx:[folder]	Specifies an additional folder to be copied into the Windows 2000 folder \WINNT. Folder is removed after installation is complete.
winnt	/t:[drive letter]	Specifies partition to which temporary files will be copied during installation. It marks the drive as active and you can install it on another computer (it cannot be a Windows 95 or 98 machine). /syspart and tempdrive must point to same location and Windows 2000 must be installed on primary partition of the secondary hard drive.
winnt	/u:[answer file]	Initiates installation in unattended mode utilizing the answers in the specified file. The /s: parameter must be used in conjunction with /u:.
winnt32	/checkupgradeonly	Performs the Windows 2000 compatibility test on the system. Log report is saved as winnt32.log in the installation directory for Windows NT tests or upgrade.txt in the existing Windows directory for a Windows 95/98 test.
winnt32	/cmd:[command]	Defines a command to be run by the installation program after Setup is complete.

(continued)

Table 2.3 Command-line parameters for Windows 2000 Setup *(continued)*.

Version	Parameter	Description
winnt32	/cmdcons	Can only be used after Windows 2000 is installed. Invokes the Recovery Console at boot to assist in repairing the system.
winnt32	/copydir:[folder name]	Specifies an additional folder to be copied into the Windows 2000 folder \WINNT. Folder remains after installation is complete. Used to copy drivers and utilities to the server during installation for use later.
winnt32	/copysource:[folder name]	Specifies an additional folder to be copied into the Windows 2000 folder \WINNT. Folder is removed after installation is complete.
winnt32	/debug[level:filename]	Specifies creation of a debug file and its location. Level determines what type of messages are recorded in the log. Default is level 2, Warning (the five levels are 0=severe;1=errors; 2=warnings; 3=information; 4=detailed information). Each level includes levels below it.
winnt32	/m:[folder name]	Provides an alternate location containing system files to be used during installation. Setup will check this directory first, then the default directory.
winnt32	/makelocalsource	Specifies all installation files be copied to the local hard drive to ensure they will be available after installation.
winnt32	/noreboot	Does not restart the computer after copying the files so you can run another command.
winnt32	/syspart:[drive letter]	Identifies the partition to which the system startup files will be copied. Must be used with the /tempdrive parameter. It marks the drive as active and you can install it on another computer (it cannot be a Windows 95 or 98 machine). /syspart and tempdrive must point to same location and Windows 2000 must be installed on primary partition of the secondary hard drive.
winnt32	/tempdrive:[drive letter]	Specifies partition to which temporary files will be copied during installation.

(continued)

Table 2.3 Command-line parameters for Windows 2000 Setup *(continued)*.

Version	Parameter	Description
winnt32	/unattend	Instructs Setup to upgrade the current installation of Windows in unattended mode. Setup takes all settings from the current Windows configuration.
winnt32	/unattend:[num:answer file]	Initiates installation in unattended mode using the information in the specified answer file. The num parameter specifies the number of seconds to wait before rebooting after installation and can only be used when running Setup from Windows 2000. Must also use the /s: parameter.
both	/s:[sourcepath]	Specifies the location of the Windows 2000 installation files. Default is the current directory. Must include full path (i.e., x:\i386 or \\server\share\path). Multiple search locations can be specified by providing multiple /s: parameters (for winnt32 only).
both	/udf:[id,UDB_File]	Indicates the uniqueness database file (UDB) to be used when modify the answer file.

Creating a Source Folder for Unattended Installations

Although the installation files provided with Windows 2000 cover many situations, new drivers are always being developed and becoming available, and changes are sometimes necessary. By creating a *source folder*, also called a distribution folder, and adding the updated drivers to be used, you can further streamline your installation. To begin this process, copy the \i386 directory from the installation CD to the volume that is to contain the source folder. After the files are copied, create a subfolder of the correct type under \i386. The contents of this folder are copied to the temporary directory during installation. Table 2.4 lists the four subfolder types the Setup program recognizes.

Table 2.4 Valid folder types for updated drivers.

Folder Name	Description
\$OEM$\$textmode	Folder for installing hardware-dependant drivers, such as SCSI, keyboard, and video. The txtsetup.oem file must also be included in this directory. In addition, all files in this folder must be in the OEMBootFiles section of the answer files.
\$OEM$\$$	Folder for new or updated system files to be copied during the installation process. Subfolders under this directory must match exactly the structure of the Windows 2000 directory.

(continued)

Table 2.4 Valid folder types for updated drivers *(continued)*.

Folder Name	Description
\$OEM$\$1	Folder for files you wish to be copied to the installation drive during setup. Subfolders can be created and will be copied exactly. This folder contains a subfolder called \pnpdrvrs which is used for new or updated Plug and Play device drivers.
\OEM\drive_letter	Folder that specifies files to be copied to the root of the named drive during installation. File names in this folder must be 8.3 at the time of the installation.

After creating the correct folder type, copy the updated drivers and .inf files to their appropriate location under the \i386\OEM folder. Add this line to the answer file being used to identify the location of the drivers to be installed: OEMPnPDriversPath="*Company*", where *Company* is the name of the subfolder you created. Once this is complete, you are ready to begin the installation.

Alternate Answer File Creation Method

Rather than utilize a sample answer file or write one from scratch, you can use the *Setup Manager Wizard* included with the *Windows 2000 Server Resource Kit* and on the Windows 2000 distribution CD. With the *Resource Kit* tools installed (or from the Windows 2000 CD in \support\tools\deploy.cab), run the setupmgr.exe program. You will be asked whether you would like to create a new answer file, create an answer file that duplicates the local computer's configuration, or modify an existing answer file. Select Create A New Answer File and click Next. You will then be asked the type of answer file you are creating: Windows 2000 Unattended Installation, Sysprep Installation, or Remote Installation Services. Choose Windows 2000 Unattended Installation and click Next to continue. The Setup Manager will then go through the various prompts encountered during the installation process and record your responses in the answer file. Once the Setup Manager has completed its query, you will be asked to provide the path and file name for the answer file. After doing so, click Finish to save the file and close the Setup Manager. At that time, the Setup Manager creates a batch file that can be used to automatically launch the installation. The answer file created by the Setup Manager can also be used independently or modified as necessary.

CHAPTER SUMMARY

As with all Microsoft products prior to Windows 2000, the minimum specifications are more stringent than for the previous operating system. In addition, the minimum requirements are somewhat unrealistic for operation in

2

a real-world environment. The recommended configuration for Windows 2000 is a system with at least a Pentium II processor, 300MHz, 256MB RAM, Super VGA video card and monitor, 3GB free hard drive space, a bootable CD-ROM, and a Fast Ethernet adapter. All components in the system must have been tested for the system and be included in the HCL. The HCL is available on the Windows 2000 CD and the Microsoft Web site at **www.microsoft.com/hcl/ default.asp**. The HCL information on the Web site includes all versions of the Windows product since Windows 95 and indicates the level of compliance with the operating system. In addition to appearing on the HCL, the drivers for the hardware must be compliant with Windows 2000. Hardware that is not on the HCL or does not have compliant drivers is not supported by Microsoft.

The Windows 2000 Readiness Analyzer performs a check of the hardware and software on the system to determine whether the computer's existing configuration will support Windows 2000. The Readiness Analyzer is only capable of evaluating systems currently running Microsoft operating systems. The Analyzer can be downloaded from the Microsoft Web site at **www.microsoft.com/windows2000/upgrade/compat/default.asp**. The information presented by the Analyzer and the file name and location are dictated by the operating system currently running on the system.

Planning your Windows 2000 Server installation begins with an evaluation of the current state of the network including the configuration of all workstations, servers, and other network devices. The inventory created at this stage must include all software being run on the devices and any protocols being used. Applications and services fall into four categories: strategic, tactical, legacy, and obsolete. Strategic services are vital to business operations. Tactical applications and services are worthwhile to the business, but may not be providing the most benefit to the company. Legacy services are those nearing the end of their usefulness, and obsolete applications and services not only provide no benefit, but are an actual hindrance to the operation of the network.

The second part of the planning process is determining the course or direction of the network for the next two to five years. This information will help you establish the best design for the network today. After gathering this information, the final step is to develop a plan for implementation, taking into account the information learned from the first two steps. Be sure to include time for slippage and unforeseen circumstances when developing this plan.

The storage design for the servers on your network should be determined based on the requirements of the network and the cost of the equipment. IDE-based drives are the least expensive, but provide the lowest level of performance. SCSI-based drives provide reasonably high performance, but are more expensive. Fibre Channel systems are the most expensive and provide the highest performance level available. Windows 2000 supports two types of fault-tolerant software-controlled RAID: RAID 1 and RAID 5. RAID 1 provides fault tolerance through mirroring and duplexing, whereas RAID 5 provides both increased performance and fault tolerance through disk striping with parity.

Unless there is a requirement to provide access to the file system for another operating system, such as a dual-boot configuration with Windows 98, you should always choose the NTFS file system. NTFS offers a significantly higher security level and many of the features of Windows 2000 require NTFS.

The Distributed file system (Dfs) enhances network operation by providing a method by which the network administrator can consolidate data through a single access point, the Dfs root. The Dfs root can contain links to similar information on other servers to facilitate access to the information for the users on the network. The server on which the Dfs root is stored is called the host server. The design of your Dfs implementation should be based on the operation of your company.

With Windows 2000, Microsoft created a TCP/IP-only communications network by removing NetBIOS. Removing NetBIOS means that the WINS service is also no longer needed. Both NetBIOS and WINS are replaced with the Dynamic Domain Name System (DDNS). Because it is a more advanced version of DNS, it is easily tied to the Internet to provide both internal and external naming functions. To provide legacy connectivity, Windows 2000 supports NetBEUI and NWLink.

Active Directory is one of the most anticipated features of Windows 2000. It is a hierarchical database of all network resources. With Active Directory, all domain controllers (DCs) maintain a fully functional copy of the Active Directory database for the domain, eliminating primary and backup domain controllers. A Windows 2000 computer is either a domain controller or a member server. Active Directory is organized hierarchically from organizational units (OU) to domains to trees to forests. OUs provide a smaller organizational space than the domains used in Windows NT 3.x and 4.x. Domains are much the same as they were in earlier versions of Windows and function as a secure boundary between operational areas. Trees are made up of many domains, and forests are comprised of two or more trees. Though other organizational functions are not physically limited, sites are used to define the physical boundaries between LANs and WANs. Sites are used to efficiently manage replication traffic between servers within a domain or tree. The global catalog contains basic information for searching any object in Active Directory.

To facilitate rapid implementation of Windows 2000, unattended installations are supported. There are two levels of unattended installation: command-line parameters and answer files. The command-line options available depend on the operating system over which you are installing Windows 2000. If you boot to a DOS prompt, you must use winnt.exe. If you run the installation program from a command prompt window within the operating system, you can use winnt32.exe. Answer files can be created manually or by using the Setup Manager Wizard provided with the Windows 2000 CD and the *Windows 2000 Server Resource Kit*.

REVIEW QUESTIONS

1. Which of the following most accurately describes the second phase of the analysis you must perform before installing Windows 2000?

    a. Documenting the plan for implementation and obtaining approval for implementation.

    b. Discussing the future plans for your company and its network.

    c. Creating an inventory of all network devices including servers, workstations, and printers.

    d. Identifying the current status of the network and evaluating its traffic.

2. DDNS is included in which of the following protocol suites?

    a. Windows 2000

    b. NetBIOS

    c. TCP/IP

    d. NWLink (IPX/XPS)

3. In which of the following domain modes are universal groups allowed to contain other universal groups?

    a. Native mode

    b. Passive mode

    c. Active mode

    d. Mixed mode

4. Which of the following is supported only when running Setup in a command prompt window on a Windows 95 system?

    a. /u

    b. /unattend

    c. /s:

    d. /r:

5. During testing, which of the following should you work through and test first?

    a. Situations that will cause the most problems.

    b. Situations that you anticipate will cause some problems.

    c. Situations that you are reasonably, but not quite sure will work.

    d. Situations that you are certain will work.

6. Which of the following items located on packaging or promotional materials indicates that hardware was thoroughly tested and passed certification based on a prefinal release of the operating system?

    a. Logo

    b. Created for Windows 2000

    c. Windows 2000 Compatible

    d. Designed for Windows 2000

7. Which of the following statements does not accurately describe the Readiness Analyzer?

    a. The Readiness Analyzer is available on the Microsoft Web site.

    b. The Readiness Analyzer provides information on the system's current configuration.

    c. The Readiness Analyzer can be run only on computers using a Microsoft operating system.

    d. The Readiness Analyzer provides the same interface and operation regardless of the operating system of the current computer.

8. In an Active Directory configuration, which of the following is used to describe Windows NT 4.x backup domain controllers?

    a. Backward

    b. Downlevel

    c. Downward

    d. Recessive

9. Place the following in their order of maximum hardware support, from smallest to largest.

    a. Windows 2000 Datacenter Server

    b. Windows 2000 Professional

    c. Windows 2000 Advanced Server

    d. Windows 2000 Server

10. When configuring a Dfs link to attach to another domain, which of the following is true today?

    a. Midlevel Dfs links can connect to midlevel Dfs folders in other domains.

    b. Midlevel Dfs links can connect to Dfs roots on other domains.

    c. Midlevel Dfs links can connect to root folders in other domains.

    d. Midlevel Dfs links cannot link to folders in other domains.

11. Which of the following fault-tolerance methods are supported by Windows 2000? [Choose all that apply]

    a. Mirroring

    b. Stripe set with parity

    c. Duplexing

    d. Copying

12. Which of the following is used to describe the server on which a Dfs root share resides?

    a. Host server

    b. Primary server

    c. Main server

    d. Root server

13. Which of the following is responsible for compiling the HCL?

    a. The Microsoft Hardware Quality Labs

    b. The manufacturer's quality control lab

    c. The Microsoft Hardware Compliance Labs

    d. The Harvard College Laboratory

14. Which of the following is used to describe the trust relationships between domains in an Active Directory Tree?

    a. Iterative

    b. Mobile

    c. Suggestive

    d. Transitive

15. For a server operating in a small testing environment, which of the following hard drive interfaces is sufficient?

    a. ANSI

    b. SCSI

c. Fibre Channel

d. IDE

16. Which of the following is used to represent a physical boundary in an Active Directory structure?

   a. Tree

   b. Site

   c. Forest

   d. Domain

17. Which of the following is also referred to as an Active Directory partition?

   a. Tree

   b. Site

   c. Forest

   d. Domain

18. Which of the following is used to describe applications or services that are useful to the organization, but may not be providing the most benefit to the company?

   a. Strategic

   b. Tactical

   c. Legacy

   d. Obsolete

19. Which of the following previously required services is no longer necessary with Windows 2000?

   a. WINS

   b. NetBEUI

   c. NetBIOS

   d. NWLink

20. Which of the following systems cannot support Dfs root shares?

   a. Windows 2000 Advanced Server domain controller

   b. Windows NT 4.0 domain controller

   c. Windows NT 4.0 stand-alone server

   d. Windows 2000 stand-alone server

REAL-WORLD PROJECTS

Upon receiving the evaluation copy of Windows 2000 Server and reading the available literature, Charles Cayhill presented his plans to his supervisor. He was given one of the application servers in the testing lab to install the operating system and put it through its paces. Charles knew the system was currently running Windows NT Server 4.0 and didn't foresee any problems with the upgrade. However, just to be sure, Charles downloaded the Windows 2000 Readiness Analyzer to evaluate the system:

Note: To complete the projects, you will need access to the Internet from your computer and have a copy of the Windows 2000 Server CD-ROM.

Project 2.1
To download the Windows 2000 Readiness Analyzer, perform the following steps:

1. If Internet Explorer is not already running, open it by clicking the icon on the taskbar or by double-clicking the desktop icon.

2. In the Address window, type "**http://www.microsoft.com/ windows2000/upgrade/compat/default.asp**" and press Enter.

3. Click the View A Sample Windows 2000 Readiness Analyzer Tool Report (Text File) link and review its contents. This report is an example of the report generated by the Analyzer.

4. Scroll down to the Hardware section. Note that the Acme M780 monitor may not support Windows 2000.

5. Scroll down to the Program Notes section. Note that a new version of the Zippy Inc. Zip software is required for Windows 2000 and that it can be downloaded from the Zippy site at **www.zippy.abc**.

6. When you have finished reviewing the file, click the Back button on your browser to return to the Hardware and Software Compatibility Web site.

7. Click the Download The Readiness Analyzer link. The Windows 2000 Readiness Analyzer site will be opened. Note that the system requirements for the Analyzer and instructions for download and use are included on this site.

8. Select the appropriate language for the Readiness Analyzer from the drop-down list. The default is the English Language Version, but the program is also available in French, Spanish, German, Italian, Dutch, Swedish, Portuguese (Brazil), Chinese (Simplified), Chinese (Traditional), Korean, Hebrew, Arabic, and Japanese.

9. Click Next. The download Web site will be opened. Note the estimated download time for your connection.

10. Click the Download Now button to continue.

11. When prompted, select Save This Program To Disk and click OK.

12. Locate the folder to which you would like the file to be saved and click Save. Remember the location of the file for the next step.

After downloading, Charles initiated the system analysis and saved the results file for use at a later time.

Project 2.2
To review the launch the Windows 2000 Readiness Analyzer, perform the following steps:

1. After the file has been saved to your hard drive, click Start and select Run.

2. Click Browse and locate the *chkupgrd.exe* file you just downloaded. Select it and click Open.

3. From the Run window, with chkupgrd.exe showing in the Open list, click OK.

4. When prompted, click Yes to accept the license agreement.

5. The analyzer will review the contents of the Registry and perform a check on your system. Depending on the operating system being reviewed, the options available after analysis will be different. On Windows NT systems, the options are Have Disk, Save As, and Details.

6. Click Save As to save the compatibility analysis to the local drive.

7. Click Finish to complete the review.

After finishing the analysis and reviewing the configuration file, Charles was asked to review the hardware configuration for a system his company was considering for purchase. The new system is to be used by the lead design engineer for his company and includes dual-Pentium III processors with Fibre Channel storage and a high-end graphics card (the Voodoo3 Velocity). Although the lead design engineer has no need for a Windows 2000 Server, Charles knows that the same hardware is supported by both Windows 2000 Professional and Windows 2000 Server. He starts by reviewing the HCL included on the Windows 2000 Server CD-ROM:

Project 2.3
To review the Hardware Compatibility List, perform the following steps:

1. Insert the Windows 2000 CD into your drive.

2. If Autorun is enabled on your system, the Windows 2000 upgrade program will execute. When prompted to upgrade to Windows 2000, click No.

3. If the Windows 2000 upgrade program was started, click Exit.

4. Open Windows Explorer by selecting Start | Programs | Windows Explorer.

5. Locate the CD-ROM drive into which you inserted the Windows 2000 CD. Click the CD-ROM icon to open it.

6. Double-click the Support icon to open the \Support folder.

7. From the list of files and folders displayed, double-click HCL. The text-only version of the HCL will be opened. You may be presented with a notice informing you that the file is too large to be opened in Notepad. If so, click Yes to open the file in WordPad.

8. Scroll through the file to the Display Adapter section. Review the list of adapters supported by Windows 2000. Look specifically for the Voodoo3 Velocity by 3Dfx. This card was not supported at the time Windows 2000 was initially released and is not included in the production HCL.

9. Close the HCL text file by selecting File | Close.

Because hardware is continually being updated and tested for compatibility with Windows 2000, Charles knows that just because a card is not listed in the CD-ROM version of the HCL does not mean it is not currently supported by Windows 2000. To check to see if the Voodoo3 Velocity passed compatibility testing since the initial release of the CD-ROM, Charles checked the HCL on the Microsoft Web site; perform the same search on the HCL Web site. Finally, you will review locate and review the sample unattended answer files located on the Microsoft Web site.

Project 2.4
To review the Hardware Compatibility List provided on the Microsoft Web site, perform the following steps:

1. If it is not already open, start Internet Explorer and enter "**http://www.microsoft.com/hcl/default.asp**" in the address window and press Enter. This will take you to the Hardware Compatibility List Web site.

2. In the Search For The Following: window, type in "voodoo3 velocity" and press Enter. This will begin a search of the HCL database for all Microsoft operating systems and display the results shown in Figure 2.7.

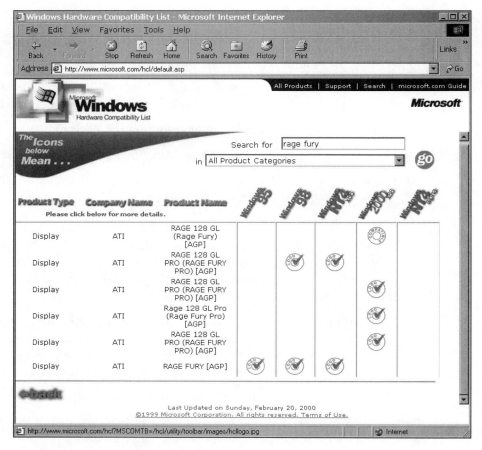

Figure 2.7 The results of the HCL search for *voodoo3 velocity*.

3. Note that the 3Dfx Voodoo3 Velocity is only supported by Windows 2000 and is certified to the Logo level.

4. Click the Voodoo3 Velocity entry (note the color changes when the mouse is over any part of the entry line). The details of the 3Dfx Voodoo3 Velocity testing will be displayed. Note that the display adapter has not been tested for any Windows operating system except Windows 2000 and that it is PC99 Compliant.

5. Close Internet Explorer.

Charles is now ready to proceed. He installs the operating system on the server, tests it thoroughly, and presents his findings to his boss. Charles' boss is impressed with the performance levels and new functionality provided by Windows 2000 and recommends to the board they move forward with the server migration project.

Because his testing report is comprehensive and shows he clearly understands the ins and outs of the operating system, Charles is tasked with upgrading the company's 35 application servers. Knowing it would take an inordinate amount of time to configure each server individually, Charles decides to review the requirements for using unattended installation scripts. After reading through the available information, Charles is ready to write his first script. To get started, he reviews the sample unattended files on the Microsoft Web site and the Windows 2000 Server CD-ROM:

Project 2.5

To locate and review sample unattended answer files, perform the following steps:

1. If it is not already open, open Internet Explorer.

2. Type "**http://www.microsoft.com/TechNet/win2000/dguide/ append-c.asp**" in the Address window and press Enter.

3. Note that this is an online presentation of Appendix C of the Windows 2000 Deployment and Planning Guide, which is part of the *Windows 2000 Server Resource Kit*. The *Resource Kit* is available as part of TechNet or can be purchased separately.

4. Review the information presented with regard to the format that answer files must be in and the keys and values used during an unattended installation.

5. Scroll through the various unattended installation answer files presented. Note that the default answer file (unattend.txt) is provided on the Windows 2000 Server CD in the \i386 directory. This version of the file is rather short, but can be expanded to include information contained in the other files.

6. Note that the samples include everything from a basic Windows 2000 Professional desktop installation to a Windows 2000 Advanced Server Clustering installation. If you determine you would like to use one of these samples, simply highlight its contents and select Edit | Copy. Then paste the contents into a WordPad file and save it with a .txt extension.

Armed with this information, Charles is ready to roll. He is able to upgrade all 35 servers over the course of three weekends by using the unattended answer files he created.

CHAPTER THREE

INSTALLING WINDOWS 2000 SERVER

After completing this chapter, you will be able to:

✓ Understand the various methods of installing Windows 2000 Server

✓ Perform an unattended installation of Windows 2000 Server

✓ Use a Windows 2000 Server CD to install Windows 2000

✓ Install Windows 2000 Server across the network

✓ Upgrade Windows NT 4.0 Server to Windows 2000 Server

✓ Understand the necessity and usefulness of service packs

✓ Troubleshoot Windows 2000 Server installation problems

As mentioned in Chapter 2, the deployment of Windows 2000 Server in an organization requires a lot of planning. Depending on multiple factors, hardware and software prerequisites must be met, and installation decisions must be made regarding the several types and methods of installing Windows 2000 Server. This chapter discusses the decision criteria and provides step-by-step instructions for installing Windows 2000 Server under various circumstances.

INSTALLATION TYPES AND METHODS

One of the first decisions to make when installing Windows 2000 Server is which type of installation you should perform in your organization. Basically, you want to upgrade your servers to Windows 2000 Server if you have an existing centrally managed environment, and you'll be using existing hardware and software. Otherwise, a clean installation is preferred.

You also need to decide whether you want to perform an unattended or attended installation. An *unattended installation* is one in which the installer simply invokes the Windows 2000 Setup program, and the individual settings are entered automatically without any input from the installer. An attended installation is one in which the installer invokes the Windows 2000 Setup program, then manually enters the necessary configuration information throughout the installation. Both types of installations can be performed using a Windows 2000 CD or over a network.

MANAGING AN ATTENDED INSTALLATION OF WINDOWS 2000 SERVER

Attended installations are applicable for both upgrades and clean installations of Windows 2000 Server. If you and your organization choose to perform attended installations of Windows 2000 Server, you simply need access to the Windows 2000 Server Setup files, whether they exist on a CD or on a network.

Note: The hardware requirements for Microsoft Windows 2000 Server are discussed in Chapter 2.

Windows 2000 Installation Procedures

Throughout the installation, Setup displays dialog boxes in which you select and enter specific configuration information. The following sections discuss the Windows 2000 Setup process.

Initial Setup

When the Windows 2000 Setup program is invoked, you are asked whether you want to upgrade to Windows 2000 or perform a clean installation. An upgrade makes many of the following sections in this chapter moot because most of the setup information comes from the existing operating system. If you choose a clean installation, however, you need to customize the installation using the information in the following sections. Also during the initial setup, you need to accept the license agreement.

At this point, a dialog box is displayed and prompts you to create or specify a partition on which you want to install Windows 2000 Server. It provides three choices: Create A Partition From Available Unpartitioned Space, Designate An Existing Partition, or Delete An Existing Partition And Increase Available Unpartitioned Disk Space For The Windows 2000 Partition. You can also choose to format a partition, in which case you are prompted to confirm your choice. The machine reboots when the partition is chosen or formatted.

Note: *Unlike Windows NT 4, partition sizes in Windows 2000 are not limited to 4GB or less.*

Setup then copies the necessary installation files to the computer. When it is finished, Setup reboots the machine automatically.

GUI Portion of Setup

During the GUI portion of Setup, the Setup Wizard is invoked, and the following settings must be defined:

➤ *Administrator account password*—Specify a password. Windows 2000 has a built-in user account called Administrator. Because this account has full control of management tasks for Windows 2000 Server, you should specify a secure password (up to 127 characters) for this account.

➤ *Computer name*—Enter a computer name that is 15 characters or less. (Some languages, such as Chinese, Japanese, and Korean, require more storage space per character; therefore, the length of the computer name in such languages should be 7 characters or less.)

➤ *Licensing mode*—Select your client licensing mode if you are installing. If you are not sure which mode is the correct one to use, choose Per Server because you can change from Per Server to Per Seat one time at no cost.

➤ *Personalization settings*—Provide your name and your organization (optional).

➤ *Regional settings*—Select your preferred accessibility settings, locale, and language (you can select multiple regional settings and languages).

Setup then asks which Windows 2000 Server components you want to install. Table 3.1 presents the available Windows 2000 components and their descriptions.

You must select the components that are appropriate for the server's use. To do so, select the component or service, click Details, and choose the specific components you'd like to install by selecting the checkbox to the left of the items you want to add. After selecting the optional components, Setup prompts you to set the correct date and time. You must also specify whether the system should automatically adjust for Daylight Savings Time.

Table 3.1 Windows 2000 components.

Component	Description
Certificate Server	Allows you to create digital certificates that provide a means of identifying users. It also allows for Layer 2 Tunneling Protocol (L2TP) and encryption of Web data.
Internet Information Services (IIS)	Includes FTP and Web Services, the administrative interface for IIS, common IIS components, and documentation.
Management and Monitoring Tools	Includes tools for monitoring and managing network performance and communications including SNMP (Simple Network Management Protocol).
Message Queuing Services	Supports applications that send messages to queues that control and manage the flow of data to destinations and allows applications to communicate across heterogeneous networks and with temporarily offline computers.
Microsoft Index Server	Enables dynamic full-text searches of data that is stored on Web servers, the computer, or the network.
Microsoft Script Debugger	Used as a stand-alone tool or as an add-on to Internet Explorer. It allows debugging of VBScript and JScript code.
Networking Services	Includes TCP/IP, DHCP (Dynamic Host Configuration Protocol), DNS (Domain Name System), file and print services, and other components needed for a network connection.
Other Network File and Print Services	Enables sharing of files and printers with Macintosh and Unix-based computers.
Remote Installation Services	Enables remote client installation of Windows 2000 Professional over a network.
Remote Storage	Allows the user to use tape media as extensions of NTFS volumes.
Terminal Services	Enables Windows-based clients and terminals to use a virtual Windows 2000 Server desktop session and Windows-based applications.

If Setup detects your network interface cards (NICs), it then prompts you to perform either a typical or a customized installation of Windows 2000 networking components. You can specify networking information (for TCP/IP or other protocols) during Setup, or you can use typical settings, and then make any necessary changes to your networking configuration after installation by using Configure Your Server or other management tools.

Next, you specify the workgroup or domain name to which the server should belong. A domain is a centralized group of computer accounts and resources that share a security database. A workgroup is a basic networking scheme in which resources, administration, and security are distributed throughout the network. The workgroup is designed to enable users to locate network resources within that group. At this point in the installation, select either Workgroup or Domain (choose either a new or existing domain), and provide a workgroup or domain name if it is a new one.

Finally, Setup copies remaining files, configures remaining settings, and reboots. When the machine starts up, so does Windows 2000.

CD-ROM Installation

As its name implies, a CD-ROM-based installation requires the Windows 2000 Server CD. When the CD is inserted into the CD-ROM drive of a server, the Windows 2000 CD splash screen appears (see Figure 3.1). If the machine has an existing version of Windows, you are prompted to upgrade the existing version of Windows to Windows 2000. Choose Yes to this prompt even if you want to perform a clean installation, because you will have the opportunity later to choose whether you want to perform an upgrade or a clean installation.

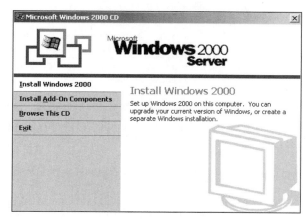

Figure 3.1   The Windows 2000 splash screen.

You can also start the installation by choosing No to the initial upgrade prompt, then choose to install Windows 2000 from the CD splash screen. A third option is to manually run the Setup program using DOS or Windows Explorer. The Setup programs are *winnt.exe* and *winnt32.exe*, both of which can be found in their corresponding source folder (\I386) on the CD. Winnt.exe is a 16-bit Setup program usually used in a DOS or Windows 3.1 environment. Winnt32.exe is a 32-bit version of the Setup program and is used to perform upgrades or new installations to existing installations of Windows 95, Windows 98, Windows NT 4, or Windows 2000. Using this method, you can add additional switches to define how the Setup program should run. The command-line switches for winnt32.exe are shown in Table 3.2, and switches for winnt.exe are shown in Table 3.3.

Table 3.2   Winnt32.exe switches.

Switch	Description
/copydir:*folder_name*	Copies the specified folder within the source directory to the system root directory (\WINNT by default) of the server.
/copysource:*folder_name*	Copies the specified folder within the source directory to the system root directory (\WINNT by default) of the server, then deletes the new folder and its contents when Setup finishes.
/cmd:*command*	Executes a command immediately before Setup is finished.
/cmdcons	Copies additional files to the hard drive that are necessary to load a command-line interface for repair and recovery purposes.
/debug[level]:*file_name*	Creates a debug log at the designated level. By default, it creates C:\winnt32.log at level 2 (the warning level).
/s:*source_path*	Designates the location of the Windows 2000 installation files. To copy files concurrently from multiple servers, use a separate /s switch for each source path.
/syspart:*drive_letter*	Copies Setup startup files to the hard drive and marks the drive as active; requires the use of the /tempdrive switch as well. /syspart and /tempdrive must point to the same partition.
/tempdrive:*drive_letter*	Places temporary files from Setup on the specified drive. Always use /tempdrive and /syspart together.
/unattend[#]:*answer_file*	Invokes an unattended installation using the specified answer file; a number can also be specified to define how many seconds Setup waits between copying the files and rebooting.
/udf:*id,udf_file*	Used with the /unattend switch to define unique parameters for the machine.

Table 3.3   Winnt.exe switches.

Switch	Description
/a	Enables the Windows 2000 accessibility options.
/e:command	Executes a command before the final phase of Setup.
/l:inf_file	Specifies the file name of the setup information (default is dosnet.inf).
/r:folder_name	Specifies an additional folder to be installed.
/rx:folder_name	Specifies an additional folder to be copied.
/s:source_path	Specifies the location of the Windows 2000 Setup files.
/t:temp_drive	Specifies a drive for the temporary files used during Setup.
/u:answer_file	Performs an unattended installation by using an answer file.

3

If your CD-ROM drive is bootable, you can insert the Windows 2000 Server CD and restart your machine (presuming your BIOS is set to boot from the CD-ROM drive). However, if your CD-ROM drive is not bootable, you have the option of using boot disks to start the installation. To create boot disks, you need to use the makeboot.exe command found on the Windows 2000 Server CD (note that you cannot perform an upgrade installation from boot disks, only a new installation). You need four blank, formatted 3.5-inch, 1.44MB floppy disks to perform the following steps:

1. From any machine running Windows or MS-DOS, insert one of the disks into the floppy drive.

2. Insert the Windows 2000 CD into the CD-ROM drive.

3. Assuming the CD-ROM drive is the D: drive, use Start | Run, File Manager or use a command prompt to run the following command:

   ```
   d:\bootdisk\makeboot a:
   ```

   and press Enter.

   Alternately, you can double-click it or execute it from Explorer or File Manager and it will ask for the letter of your floppy drive.

4. Follow the screen prompts to create each of the four setup disks.

Once you have the boot disks, you can place the first disk into the target computer's floppy drive. When you boot the system, the Windows 2000 installation should begin. Setup prompts you to replace the current disk with each of the remaining three disks until the necessary files and drivers have been installed and configured. At that point, you will need the Windows 2000 CD to continue the installation.

Real-World Project 3.1 provides step-by-step instructions for performing a
Windows 2000 Server upgrade using a CD.

Network Installation

To install Windows 2000 Server over the network, a copy of the source files
from the Windows 2000 CD must reside on a share to which you have access.
The subdirectory containing the installation files varies depending on the
architecture of the computer onto which you are installing Windows 2000. For
example, x86-based systems require the files found in the \I386 folder on the
Windows 2000 CD.

Once the source files have been copied to the server, a share must be created.
(You also have the option of sharing the CD-ROM drive.) Users must have
Read access rights to the share as well as NTFS Read permissions, if applicable.
Therefore, unless only specific users need to access the Windows 2000 source
files, the NTFS permissions should be Everyone-Read. This reason for
Everyone-Read is to prevent any accidental deletions or modifications to the
source files, which might cause future installations from this Setup directory not
to work.

To start the network installation (either from within Windows itself or booting
from a DOS network boot disk), you should map a drive to the server's share.
You should then run winnt.exe or winnt32.exe as appropriate. The target
machine merely needs to meet the hardware prerequisites and have a network
connection to the server to perform this installation.

Real-World Project 3.4 provides step-by-step instructions for performing an
unattended installation of Windows 2000 Server over the network.

MANAGING AN UNATTENDED INSTALLATION OF WINDOWS 2000 SERVER

As with Windows NT 4, it is possible to configure an unattended installation so
that an installation can be performed without any user interaction. This
installation method uses an answer file to specify the answers to the information
Windows 2000 Setup needs during the installation process. Fortunately, Microsoft has provided a tool on the Windows 2000 CD in the Support\Tools folder
called Setup Manager to make the creation of the answer file incredibly simple.

Using Setup Manager and Unattended Answer Files

The answer file is a text file that provides answers to installation prompts for
unattended installations. The Windows 2000 Server Setup files contain a sample

answer file called unattend.txt. Any time the /unattend switch is used without specifying an answer file, this default unattend.txt file is used. Its contents are as follows:

```
; Microsoft Windows 2000 Professional, Server, Advanced Server and
; Datacenter
; (c) 1994 - 1999 Microsoft Corporation. All rights reserved.
;
; Sample Unattended Setup Answer File
;
; This file contains information about how to automate the installation
; or upgrade of Windows 2000 Professional and Windows 2000 Server so the
; Setup program runs without requiring user input.
;

[Unattended]
Unattendmode = FullUnattended
OemPreinstall = NO
TargetPath = WINNT
Filesystem = LeaveAlone

[UserData]
FullName = "Your User Name"
OrgName = "Your Organization Name"
ComputerName = "COMPUTER_NAME"

[GuiUnattended]
; Sets the Timezone to the Pacific Northwest
; Sets the Admin Password to NULL
; Turn AutoLogon ON and login once
TimeZone = "004"
AdminPassword = *
AutoLogon = Yes
AutoLogonCount = 1

;For Server installs
[LicenseFilePrintData]
AutoMode = "PerServer"
AutoUsers = "5"

[GuiRunOnce]
; List the programs that you want to launch when the machine is logged
; into for the first time

[Display]
BitsPerPel = 8
```

```
XResolution = 800
YResolution = 600
VRefresh = 70

[Networking]
; When set to YES, setup installs default networking components. The
; components to be set are
; TCP/IP, File and Print Sharing, and the Client for Microsoft Networks.
InstallDefaultComponents = YES

[Identification]
JoinWorkgroup = Workgroup
```

Notice that this answer file consists of sections, parameters, and values for the parameters. Also notice that keys and values are separated by the = sign, and values that have spaces in them have double quotes around them. Although sections can be user-defined, the following is a description of the most common default section headers generated by Setup Manager:

➤ Display

➤ GuiUnattended

➤ Identification

➤ LicenseFilePrintData

➤ NetAdapters

➤ NetClients

➤ NetProtocols

➤ NetServices

➤ Networking

➤ Unattend (required section)

➤ UserData

You should customize the default unattend.txt file for your own environment. Because this is a simple text file, it can be modified using a text editor, such as Notepad or WordPad. To make this process easier, however, Microsoft provides a tool in the Windows 2000 CD called Setup Manager, which is shown in Figure 3.2. Once you install the Support Tools (Real-World Project 3.2 shows you how to install these) and invoke Setup Manager, you are presented with the Windows 2000 Setup Manager Wizard. This wizard can be used to create a new answer file from scratch, modify an existing answer file, or create an answer file based on the configuration on the machine that Setup Manager is running.

Figure 3.2   The Windows 2000 Setup Manager Wizard.

If the Setup Manager Wizard is used to either create a new answer file or modify an existing one, the following options can be selected by the administrator:

➤ Add commands to the "Run Once" section

➤ Configure Internet Explorer (IE) proxy settings (and other IE settings, if you are also using the Internet Explorer Administration Kit)

➤ Configure network settings

➤ Create a distribution folder for the Windows source files

➤ Define computer names (if more than one is specified, a uniqueness database file [UDF] is created)

➤ Designate the installation folder (the default is \WINNT)

➤ Install printers

➤ Set an administrator password

➤ Set display settings

➤ Set telephony settings

➤ Set time zone and regional settings

➤ Set user interaction for the unattended installation

➤ Specify commands to run at the end of Setup

➤ Specify the username and organization name

Real-World Project 3.3 takes you step-by-step through the process of creating a customized answer file using the Setup Manager.

To install Windows 2000 Server in unattended mode from a 16-bit operating system, such as DOS or Windows 3.1, specify the following at the command line:

```
Winnt /u:answer_file
```

To install Windows 2000 Server in unattended mode from a 32-bit operating system, such as Windows 95 or Windows NT, use the following command line instead:

```
Winnt32 /unattend:answer_file
```

To further customize an unattended installation, you can create a UDF, which specifies unique information about a machine, so that the same answer file can be used on multiple machines. For example, the UDF might contain an administrator or server name that varies from installation to installation. Setup Manager automatically creates the UDF, if, while making an answer file, multiple entries for some parameters (such as server name) are specified. The UDF can also be created manually using a standard text editor. Its format is very similar to an answer file; it has section headers, parameters, and values for the parameters.

Creating and Configuring Automated Installation Methods

There are several methods of performing automated (unattended) installations. Depending on the size of your organization and the current technology you have in place, you'll likely choose to run automated installations of Windows 2000 Server using one of the following methods:

➤ Syspart

➤ Sysprep (System Preparation) Tool

➤ SMS (Systems Management Server)

➤ Bootable CD

You can use the Syspart method for clean installations on multiple computers that have dissimilar hardware. Syspart creates a master set of files with the necessary configuration information. These images can then be used on systems with different hardware, and Setup will properly detect the varying hardware but make all other configurations identical to one another. The target server must have two physical hard drives with its primary partition on the target hard drive.

To install Windows 2000 Server using the Syspart method (with winnt32 only), you have to use both the /syspart and the /tempdrive switches in the Setup command. For example, if you want to run an unattended Setup on a machine where its primary partition on the secondary drive is the F: drive, then your Setup command may look like the following:

```
Winnt32 /unattend:unattend.txt /syspart: F: /tempdrive:F: noreboot
```

Note: The /tempdrive switch should be used any time there are multiple hard drives and multiple partitions, so that the user is not prompted for the target partition during the Windows 2000 Setup. It is also a required switch when using the Syspart method of installing Windows 2000.

Sysprep, on the other hand, should be used for complete disk duplications. This method can be used when the target computers have similar hardware including the hardware abstraction layer (HAL) and mass storage device controllers. The disk duplication process is as follows:

1. Install and configure a computer with Windows 2000 Server similar to the way you want the remaining machines to be configured. You can even add applications and customize user settings.

2. Run the System Preparation tool (sysprep.exe) on the master computer.

   You can also use the Setup Manager to create a sysprep.inf file that contains individual computer configuration information.

3. Restart the master computer, and run a third-party disk image duplication tool (such as GHOST) to create a master disk image.

4. Copy this image to other computers.

To run Sysprep immediately after installing Windows 2000, you need to add the required Sysprep files (sysprep.exe and setupcl.exe) in a folder called "Sysprep" under the root directory (under I386, for example). Then you need to add the sysprep.exe command to the [GuiRunOnce] section of the answer file. Once this is done and Setup is invoked, it creates the necessary files that can be used with a third-party image copying tool.

Table 3.4 shows the switches that can be used with Sysprep.

Table 3.4 Sysprep switches.

Switch	Description
-quiet	Runs without user interaction
-pnp	Forces Setup to detect Plug and Play devices on the target machine
-reboot	Restarts the test computer rather than it shutting down
-nosidgen	Does not regenerate the Security Identifier (SID) on the target machine

SMS may be the most efficient method to use to perform centrally managed upgrades of Windows 2000 servers. It is especially helpful when machines are geographically dispersed or when there are bandwidth constraints that mandate upgrades be performed only at certain times of the day. SMS is a separate software package that can be purchased from Microsoft.

Note: SMS cannot be used to perform clean installations of Windows 2000 Server; it can only be used for upgrades.

Finally, a bootable Windows 2000 CD can be used on computers whose basic input/output system (BIOS) allows them to boot from a CD-ROM drive. If you are using this method, you may want to specify this when making your answer file using Setup Manager. If you do, the answer file is saved as winnt.sif on a floppy disk. Setup searches for this file when you boot from the CD.

Insert the floppy disk containing winnt.sif when you invoke Setup from the Windows 2000 Server CD. When Setup begins, the splash screen appears, which allows you to start the installation. While the initial blue "Windows 2000 Setup" screen is being displayed, Setup reads the contents of the winnt.sif file and uses that information to complete the installation.

Note: UDFs cannot be used with the bootable CD method.

UPGRADING TO WINDOWS 2000 SERVER

If you choose to perform an upgrade to your servers, you cannot perform an unattended installation unless you are using SMS to centrally manage the deployment. However, configuration is very simple. The existing user settings, permission settings, and documents are retained. Another benefit of simply upgrading from a previous Windows operating system is that it won't be necessary to reinstall many applications. The following list contains the operating systems that can be upgraded to Windows 2000 Server:

➤ Windows NT 3.51 Server

➤ Windows NT 4.0 Server

➤ Windows NT 4.0 Terminal Server

Note: Windows NT 4.0 Enterprise Edition can only be upgraded to Windows 2000 Advanced Server and Datacenter Server, not Windows 2000 Server.

If you are running another version of a Windows operating system or a version of Windows NT Server earlier than 3.51, you cannot upgrade directly to Windows 2000 Server. You must install Windows NT Server 3.51 or a later version before Windows 2000 Setup can upgrade the server.

When you attempt to upgrade from other versions of Windows, such as Windows 98, Windows 95, or Windows 3.1.1, you will receive a message that you cannot upgrade to Windows 2000 Server (see Figure 3.3).

TIP: When you choose to upgrade your Windows computer using a supported upgrade path, it's wise to first back up the existing drive. You also want to verify that the hardware and applications already installed are compatible with Windows 2000 Server. You can then run Setup and choose to upgrade your current operating system. The Windows system files are automatically installed in the existing system root directory (the default is \WINNT).

WORKING WITH SERVICE PACKS

As with previous Windows NT Server operating systems, you will discover bugs and security holes from time to time. To fix any problems that might occur, Microsoft provides operating system patches and updates, called service packs, as needed. When performing a new Windows NT installation, the operating system has to be installed first, then the service pack can be installed.

Windows 2000 Server, however, supports a technology called *slipstreaming* in which the service pack can be added directly to the Windows 2000 source files. Also, components and applications no longer need to be reinstalled when a service pack is installed using this technology.

TROUBLESHOOTING INSTALLATION PROBLEMS

When installing any product, there is always the possibility of an installation problem. The installation of an entire operating system has several sources of

Figure 3.3   Windows 2000 Setup upgrade error message.

potential problems. The following sections describe some of the most common installation problems and provide solutions you can use to try to resolve them.

Media Errors

If your computer doesn't recognize the Windows 2000 CD, the CD may be scratched or corrupt. Try cleaning the CD or using a different one. You can order a Windows 2000 CD from Microsoft or from various resellers. If the CD is unreadable and a replacement is not available, try installing Windows 2000 over the network, if possible.

Nonsupported CD-ROM Drive

If your BIOS does not allow you to boot from a CD-ROM drive, you may want to create the Windows 2000 boot disks. To do so, use the program called makeboot.exe in Windows 2000. Create and use these disks to start the installation. You should then be able to complete the installation with the CD.

. . . .

Tip: If you have access to a network, you can also copy the source files from the CD to a network share. You can then install Windows 2000 over the network.

. . . .

Insufficient Disk Space

If you do not have the minimum amount of disk space required to install Windows 2000, Setup displays a message informing you that there is insufficient disk space to perform the installation. To resolve this problem, you might want to create a partition using Setup that uses existing free space on the hard drive. You can also delete and format or create partitions as necessary to create a partition that is large enough for installation.

Failure of Dependency Service to Start

If the Dependency service fails to start, invoke the Windows 2000 Setup Wizard, return to the Network Settings page, and verify that you installed the correct protocol and network adapter. Also verify that the network adapter has the proper configuration settings, such as transceiver type, and that the local computer name is unique on the network.

Inability to Connect to the Domain Controller

During the Setup phase of specifying the workgroup or domain name, you may receive a message that the domain name cannot be found. Verify that you are connected to the network and that the domain name you have entered is correct. Also, make sure the NIC and protocol settings are set appropriately. Finally, verify that the DNS server and the domain controller are both online. If everything is correct, properly set, and online, and you still cannot access the domain, choose instead to join a workgroup. Then, once you finish the installation and start Windows, try to join the domain.

You may also encounter this error if the computer name you're trying to use already exists on the network. If you are reinstalling Windows 2000 and using the same computer name, ask the administrator to delete and then re-create the computer account in the domain. Otherwise, try using a different computer name.

Failure of Windows 2000 to Install or Start

If Windows 2000 Server fails to install or start, verify that Windows 2000 is detecting all of the hardware components and that the hardware is on the Hardware Compatibility List (HCL), which can be found at **www.microsoft. com/hcl/**.

If hardware doesn't seem to be the problem, make sure that there isn't any software installed that may be interfering with Windows 2000. If all else fails, try reinstalling Windows 2000.

CHAPTER SUMMARY

This chapter discussed the different types and methods of installing Windows 2000 Server. Upgrading to Windows 2000 from Windows NT 3.51 or Windows NT 4 is a good option if the environment is centrally managed, and you are using existing hardware and software. Upgrades require an attended installation. This chapter discussed the steps necessary to install Windows 2000 using the CD method and over a network.

Also discussed was the power of automated, or unattended, installations when performing clean installations. Setup Manager, which is included on the Windows 2000 CD, makes it very easy to create an answer file to use in an unattended installation. The answer file can automatically answer all of the questions during an unattended installation, and a UDF can customize multiple unattended installations by providing lists of unique information, such as multiple computer names or usernames.

This chapter also explored the various automated installation methods: Syspart, Sysprep, SMS, and bootable CDs.

Finally, slipstreaming, which enables service packs to be installed much easier in Windows 2000 Server than in previous versions of Windows, was mentioned. Slipstreaming allows a service pack to be added directly to the Windows 2000 source files. Also, when adding a service pack, applications and Windows 2000 components no longer need to be reinstalled after a service pack is installed.

REVIEW QUESTIONS

1. Which of the following installation methods can be used for automated upgrades to Windows 2000?

   a. Sysprep

   b. Syspart

   c. SMS

   d. Bootable CD

2. What alternative installation methods can be used if your computer doesn't support bootable CDs? [Choose all that apply]

   a. Setup Manager

   b. Boot disks

   c. Non-bootable CD

   d. Network installation

3. Where should you check to make sure your hardware is compatible with Windows 2000 Server?

   a. **www.internic.net**

   b. **www.microsoft.com**

   c. **www.w3c.com**

   d. **www.hardwarelist.com**

4. Which one of the following statements accurately describes slipstreaming?

   a. A method of adding service packs to Windows 2000 installation files

   b. A network protocol

   c. A Windows Media Technologies component

   d. A method of adding additional drivers to Windows 2000

5. Which of the following winnt32 switches can be used to execute a command before the final stage of Windows 2000 Setup?

   a. /script

   b. /command

   c. /cmd

   d. /c

6. At what point in the Windows 2000 installation do you have the option to set the Administrator name and password?

    a. After the GUI-mode portion of the installation

    b. Before the GUI-mode portion of the installation

    c. During the GUI-mode portion of the installation

    d. During the text-only mode portion of the installation

7. Which of the following are requirements for performing automated installations using Sysprep? [Choose all that apply]

    a. Identical hardware abstraction layers (HALs)

    b. Identical mass storage controllers

    c. Two hard drives

    d. Third-party disk duplication software

8. What does UDF stand for?

    a. Unique database format

    b. Uniqueness database file

    c. Uniqueness data file

    d. Uniqueness database format

9. Which of the following settings are configured in the GUI portion of Setup? [Choose all that apply]

    a. Regional settings

    b. Licensing mode

    c. Organization name

    d. The disk to be partitioned

10. Which of the following files can Setup Manager create? [Choose all that apply]

    a. unattend.txt

    b. unattend.udf

    c. sysprep.inf

    d. remboot.sif

11. SMS cannot be used to perform clean installations of Windows 2000 on servers.

    a. True

    b. False

12. Which of the following operating systems may be upgraded to Windows 2000 Server? [Choose all that apply]

    a. Windows NT 4.0 Workstation

    b. Windows NT 4.0 Server

    c. Windows 98

    d. Windows NT Server 3.51

13. When sharing an installation folder across the network, what permissions should be assigned for the Everyone group?

    a. Write

    b. Read

    c. Install

    d. No Access

14. Which of the following are accurate descriptions for a UDF? [Choose all that apply]

    a. UDFs can be created using a standard text editor.

    b. UDFs can be created using Setup Manager.

    c. UDFs can be created using an unattended answer file.

    d. UDFs can be used as supplements to answer files to specify unique computer names.

15. What is the command used to create Setup boot disks in Windows 2000 Server?

    a. **winnt32 /ox**

    b. **winnt /b**

    c. **winnt32 /b**

    d. **makeboot**

16. The default UDF on the Windows 2000 CD is called unattend.txt.

    a. True

    b. False

17. Which of the following are needed to perform a network installation of Windows 2000 Server? [Choose all that apply]

    a. A network connection

    b. A CD-ROM drive

    c. NetBEUI

    d. A mapped drive to the source files

18. Which switch is used with the System Preparation Tool (sysprep.exe) to make Sysprep run with no user interaction?

    a. –q

    b. /q

    c. –quiet

    d. –pnp

3

19. If you want to install Windows 2000 using a CD, you must add the answer file to a floppy drive and name it what?

    a. winnt.sif

    b. unattend.sif

    c. unattend.txt

    d. answer.txt

20. What components are included in Internet Information Services? [Choose all that apply]

    a. WWW server

    b. FTP server

    c. Gopher server

    d. Administration UI

21. Windows NT 4.0 Workstation can be upgraded to Windows 2000 Server.

    a. True

    b. False

REAL-WORLD PROJECTS

Note: This exercise assumes a test server with Windows NT 4.0 Server. Read the instructions carefully and do not perform this installation on your production machine unless you understand the options presented.

Sarah Jones works for a medium-sized Internet company, which has grown from 120 employees to 1,200 employees in two years. Like its staff, its Internet infrastructure has grown tremendously over the past two years.

The company started out with 6 servers to host its Web site, but because of all the new application and content farms for its Web site, it now has 20 servers. However, the network is a complete mess. Each of the servers contains different types of hardware. The servers also have security holes, have been configured differently, and many of them are running out of hard drive space. Support has been an absolute nightmare for the operations team.

Fortunately, the company has been doing well this year and has decided to buy some new Compaq Proliant servers. These servers have Windows NT 4.0 Server installed.

Sarah has been working on a project to add components for a Windows 2000-compatible infrastructure, such as an Active Directory server and a new domain structure, to the company's existing Internet infrastructure. She is in the final stage of her project, which is installing Windows 2000 on each of the Internet servers. However, the hardware team is two weeks late getting these servers racked and networked.

First thing Monday morning, Sarah's manager walks over to Sarah's desk and sees 20 copies of the Windows 2000 Server CD sitting there, and just shakes her head. According to Sarah's project plan, Sarah only has one day left to perform all 20 installations. Her manager doesn't think she can get it done, but Sarah knows that she can.

Sarah begins by performing a clean installation of Windows 2000 Server on one of the new servers.

Project 3.1

To upgrade Windows NT to Windows 2000 Server, perform the following steps:

1. Insert the Windows 2000 CD into the CD-ROM drive, and choose to install or upgrade to Windows 2000.

2. Setup prompts you to upgrade to Windows 2000 or to perform a clean installation of Windows 2000. Click on Next.

3. This screen offers you the opportunity to view the Directory of Applications. This directory lists Windows 2000 compatible files. Click Next.

4. Setup then copies the necessary installation files to the computer. When it is finished, Setup reboots the machine automatically.

5. After Windows reboots, notice that one of the boot options is Windows 2000 Server Setup. You have five seconds to choose a different operating system; otherwise, Setup automatically continues.

6. The Windows 2000 Server Setup screen appears when Setup begins copying files to the Windows 2000 installation folders on the machine. You are warned that this process takes several minutes to complete. When you finish the installation, the machine reboots automatically.

7. The Windows 2000 Server Upgrade screen appears and Setup starts installing recognized hardware devices. Setup then configures network settings and Windows 2000 components.

8. Setup then performs the Final Tasks, where it installs Start menu items, registers components, saves settings, and removes temporary installation files. Setup reboots the machine one last time.

9. Upon final reboot, Windows starts. At this time, verify that all applications and devices still work correctly.

Next, she installs Setup Manager from the Windows 2000 CD.

Project 3.2
To install Setup Manager, perform the following steps:

1. Insert the Windows 2000 Server CD into the CD-ROM drive. The autorun mechanism opens the CD splash screen and prompts you to upgrade (see Figure 3.4). Click No to close the dialog box, then click Browse This CD on the splash screen.

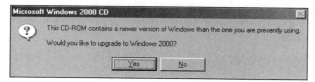

Figure 3.4   Windows 2000 upgrade prompt.

2. Browse to the \support\tools directory, then double-click deploy.cab (see Figure 3.5). From the File menu, choose Edit|Select All. Right-click the selected files, and choose Extract.

Figure 3.5   Extracting deploy.cab.

3. Choose a directory in which these files should be extracted. Click OK.

4. Close the Browse the deploy.cab contents window. Click Exit on the Windows 2000 CD splash screen.

5. Then, use Windows Explorer to browse to the new directory in which you extracted the deploy.cab contents.

6. Double-click on unattend.doc to read more information about unattended Windows 2000 installations.

Sarah then uses Setup Manager to create an unattended file.

Project 3.3
To use Setup Manager to create an answer file and a UDF, perform the following steps:

1. Use Windows Explorer to browse to the directory in which you extracted the deploy.cab files in Project 3.2.

2. Double-click setupmgr.exe.

3. The Setup Manager Wizard launches; click Next.

4. Choose to create a new answer file (default); click Next.

5. Select the Windows 2000 Unattended Installation option (default); click Next.

6. Select Windows 2000 Server; click Next.

7. Select each of the user interaction levels, one by one, to view their description. Choose the Fully Automated answer file type; click Next.

8. Select the checkbox to accept the license agreement; click Next.

9. Enter your name and organization; click Next.

10. Choose the Per Seat licensing mode, but change the number of users to 2000. Click Next.

11. Type **server01** as the name for the computer, click on Add. Type **server02**, and click on Add. Continue in this manner until you have five computer names listed. Click Next.

12. Provide the password for the server's administrator account; click Next.

13. Choose to use the Windows defaults for the server's colors, screen depth, and refresh rate; click Next.

14. Select a Typical network setting; click Next.

15. Select the Windows Server Domain and provide the name of the domain. Then select the Create A Computer Account In The Domain checkbox, and provide the name and password of an administrator account in this domain (see Figure 3.6). Click Next.

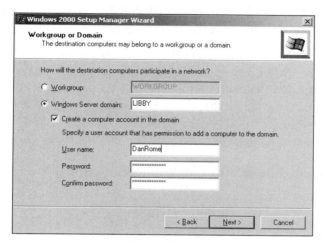

Figure 3.6   Creating a computer account in the domain.

16. Set the time zone; click Next.

17. Select No, Do Not Edit Additional Settings; click Next.

18. Select Yes, Create Or Modify A Distribution Folder; click Next.

19. Choose to create a new distribution folder at C:\w2000 and share it as w2000. Click Next.

20. Choose to install the default mass storage devices (though in Sarah's case, she may point to OEM files on that machine). Click Next.

21. Choose to install the default HAL (though again in Sarah's case, she may point to OEM files on that machine). Click Next.

22. Click Next because there are no commands to be run.

23. Click Next once more because there are no special logos or backgrounds.

24. Click Next again because there are no additional files or folders to be copied.

25. Accept the pathname and answer file name of C:\w2000\unattend.txt. Click Next.

26. Choose to copy the files from CD. Click Next.

27. The Setup files are copied over. Click Next.

28. You receive confirmation that the wizard is complete. Click Finish.

29. Browse to the deploy.cab contents directory, and double-click your newly created answer file and UDF to view them. Close the files when finished.

Upon completion of the answer file and UDF, Sarah verifies that Everyone has Read access to the newly created w2000 share. It is now time to start the installations. She sits at her desk and uses PC-Duo (a third-party remote connectivity tool) to access the machines. One by one, she runs the appropriate installation command.

Project 3.4
To run an unattended installation of Windows, perform the following steps:

1. Map the server's W: drive to the distribution folder.

2. Using DOS, change the current directory to W:\I386

3. Type the following command:

```
winnt32 /unattend:unattend.txt /udf:unattend.udf
```

By lunchtime, Sarah is finished with the installations. She takes a three-hour lunch break and gets back to work around 4:30 to tell her manager she has completed installing Windows 2000.

CHAPTER FOUR

MANAGING RESOURCE ACCESS

After completing this chapter, you will be able to:

✓ Install and configure file and print services

✓ Understand the various methods of installing a printer

✓ Understand the benefits and uses of the Distributed file system (Dfs)

✓ Work with domain-based Dfs

✓ Manage local security on files and folders

✓ Provide access to file shares

✓ Manage Web-based access to files and shares

Virtually all users on a network require access to file and print services. This makes the efficient sharing of files and printers a necessity in an organization. Once the appropriate network services are in place, sharing files, folders, and printers in Windows 2000 is not much different from sharing them in Windows NT 4. The addition of the Computer Management tool and Active Directory, however, provides new features and functionality. This chapter discusses those new features and provides instructions for configuring the file and print services on a Windows 2000 Server. In addition, we examine the *Distributed file system (Dfs)* and show how it can be used to provide an efficient view of network resources for end-users to browse. Finally, this chapter discusses the multiple methods of sharing and accessing network resources.

INSTALLING AND CONFIGURING FILE AND PRINT SERVICES

To make resources available on a network, a server must have the File And Print Sharing service installed. This service is equivalent to the Server service that was required in Windows NT 4. It enables the computer to share folders and printers with other computers on the network. By default, this component is installed and enabled for every connection on Windows 2000 Server. To manually install File and Printer Sharing For Microsoft Networks, perform the following steps:

1. Right-click My Network Places, and choose Properties.

2. Right-click Local Area Connection, and choose Properties.

3. If File And Printer Sharing For Microsoft Networks is not listed, click the Install button, select the service from the list, and follow the prompts. If it is already installed, verify that there is a checkbox next to it to ensure that it is enabled (see Figure 4.1).

If you highlight File And Printer Sharing For Microsoft Networks and click Properties, you will see a Server Optimization tab listing options to optimize your server, as shown in Figure 4.2.

The options are as follows:

➤ *Minimize Memory Used*—Optimize the server for a small number of clients.

➤ *Balance*—Optimize for a mix of file sharing and network applications.

➤ *Maximize Data Throughput For File Sharing*—Optimize the server for file and print services.

➤ *Maximize Data Throughput For Network Applications*—Optimize the server for distributed applications that have their own memory caching (this is the default setting).

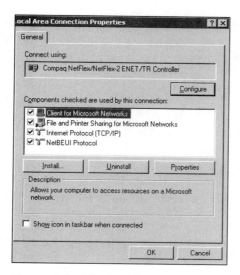

Figure 4.1   The Local Area Connection Properties dialog box.

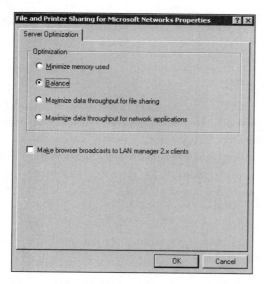

Figure 4.2   The File And Printer Sharing For Microsoft Networks Properties
dialog box.

Also, to enable LAN Manager 2.x clients to browse the network resources,
select the Make Browser Broadcasts To LAN Manager 2.x Clients box. Real-
World Project 4.1 provides step-by-step instructions for optimizing the server
as a file share.

If there are Macintosh machines on the network that need access to the
resources on the server as well, then additional services must be installed. To add
these services, perform the following steps:

1. Open the Control Panel.

2. Double-click Add/Remove Programs.

3. From the left pane, choose Add/Remove Windows components; this
    launches the Windows Components Wizard.

4. Select Other Network File and Print Services and click the Details button.

4. Choose to install File Services For Macintosh and Print Services For
    Macintosh.

The installation of these services also enables the Apple Filing Protocol (AFP)
over TCP/IP and the AppleTalk Protocol, if they are not already installed.

Finally, for NetWare clients, an additional service called File And Print Services
For NetWare can be installed. This service enables Windows 2000 Server to
seamlessly share file and print resources directly with NetWare and compatible
clients.

Working with Printers

In any organization, there are usually several printers to which users on the
network need access. Adding the Printer service to a Windows 2000 Server
machine provides the capability to manage users' access to printers on a
network. However, before installing and configuring this service, the network
administrator must have a firm understanding of Microsoft's printing
terminology as well as the features included with the Windows 2000 Printer
service. Much of the Windows 2000 terminology has changed from
terminology used in Windows NT printing. The following list contains
Windows 2000 terms that provide the essential knowledge needed to work
with printers:

➤ *Logical printer*—The Print service software on the print server.

➤ *Print client*—A computer on a network that initiates a print request.

➤ *Print job*—A file that has been marked to be printed and its corresponding
    print processing commands.

➤ *Print queue*—A series of files waiting to be produced by the printer.

➤ *Print server*—The server that has the printer service installed to manage
    printer access.

➤ *Printer*—The physical hardware that turns a client's soft copy of a file into printed material; formerly referred to as the "print device."

➤ *Printer driver*—The program that enables communications between applications and a specific printer.

➤ *Printer pool*—One logical printer that is set up to send a print job to the first available member of a group of identical physical printers.

➤ *Printer priority*—The printing preference. When several logical printers are set up to send print jobs to one physical printer, an administrator can establish which print jobs take precedence by setting the logical printer priority.

4

In addition to the terminology changes, Windows 2000 has added many enhancements for managing printing services and installing printers. The following are some of the new features:

➤ More than 3,000 printer models are now supported.

➤ Local printers can now be installed and configured automatically using the Windows 2000 Plug and Play capability. Printers connected via a USB (Universal Serial Bus) port, an IEEE 1394 Serial Block Protocol 2 port, or properly configured infrared ports are detected immediately. When a printer is connected to a parallel port, the machine either needs to be rebooted, or the Add/Remove Hardware Wizard or the Add Printer Wizard in the Printers folder can be invoked to detect the printer.

➤ More types of clients, including Windows NT, Windows 95/98, Windows 3.x, Windows for Workgroups, MS-DOS, NetWare, Macintosh, and Unix clients, are supported.

➤ Users can now perform advanced printing tasks even if the printers themselves don't support those features. Users can print multiple pages on one page, print multiple copies of a file, and print pages in the correct order when printers print them in reverse order.

➤ A new user interface makes it easier for administrators and end-users to configure and manage print resources. A Web interface is even available, so that users can view the printer folder and printer queue from within a Web browser.

➤ A new standard TCP/IP port monitor simplifies the installation of TCP/IP printers by automatically detecting the network settings needed to print. This new port monitor also makes installing printers 50 percent faster than with Windows NT 4.

➤ Windows 2000 Server enables administrators to remotely manage and configure printers from any Windows 2000 computer.

➤ Windows 2000 Server provides the capability of publishing printers in the Active Directory to make them easy to find on a network. Publishing printer information to the Active Directory is discussed in more detail later in this section.

➤ Windows 2000 Server System Monitor now includes a Print Queue object, so that administrators can monitor the performance of a local or remote printer.

➤ Administrators can use user permissions and group policies to control access to printers.

➤ Unlike Windows NT 4, all Windows 2000 users (not just administrators) can now modify their own default document settings.

➤ Windows 2000 provides a new printer driver called UniDriver 5.0 and an enhanced 5.0 version of the PostScript printer driver. The UniDriver 5.0 printer driver supports all non-PostScript printers with improved output quality, speed, and compatibility with more devices. The PostScript 5.0 driver provides improved support for postscript printers.

➤ Image Color Management (ICM) 2.0 technology and better halftone and image processing technologies provide better color output quality.

➤ Installing printers and sending print jobs can now be performed over the Internet.

A printer can be connected to any machine on the network, but the printer server makes those printers visible on the network and manages the print requests from client machines. To install a printer from the print server, choose Start | Settings | Printers. Double-click the Add Printer icon to invoke the wizard and add a new printer. Real-World Project 4.3 provides step-by-step instructions for adding and sharing a network printer in Windows 2000 Server.

Publishing printers in Active Directory is an excellent option for managing, finding, and connecting to printers on a network. By default, when you choose to share a printer, that printer is published in the domain as an object in Active Directory. However, if a printer is added and shared on a non-Windows 2000 computer, you must use the Active Directory Users And Computers tool to enter the network path to the printer.

Publishing printers in Active Directory enables Windows-based 32-bit computers to locate the most appropriate printer server for the print job. Attributes for the printers can be set within Active Directory, so that users can search for a printer by feature (such as printing in color), by physical location, or by a combination of features and locations (for example, all color printers on the second floor). Users can save their search criteria for future use, and administrators can create custom searches of which users can take advantage.

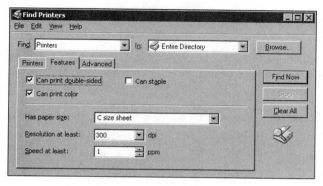

Figure 4.3   The Find Printers tool.

To search for printers, choose Start | Search | For Printers. The initial screen asks for the name of the printer you're searching for. However, as shown in Figure 4.3, you can specify search criteria in the Features tab. The Advanced tab can be used to specify features not listed on the Features tab.

Group policies can be used to define which printers can and cannot be added to Active Directory as well as to provide default printing options or to restrict certain printing options. The Group Policies that are available for defining printing restrictions are:

➤ *Allow Printers To Be Published*—Defines whether printers connected to specific machines can be published to Active Directory.

➤ *Allow Pruning Of Published Printers*—Specifies whether published printers should be removed from the Active Directory when they are no longer available.

➤ *Automatically Publish New Printers In Active Directory*—Allows new printers to be automatically published in Active Directory when they are shared.

➤ *Check Published State*—Defines an additional verification (rather than just at Startup) that all shared printers are published in the Active Directory.

➤ *Computer Location*—Specifies the default location when looking for printers.

➤ *Custom Support URL In The Printer Folder's Left Pane*—Adds a customized Web page link to the left pane of the printer's folder; usually used to point users to a support site.

➤ *Directory Pruning Interval*—Specifies how often the pruning service checks to see if the printer is still online.

➤ *Directory Pruning Priority*—Adjusts the priority of the pruning thread.

➤ *Directory Pruning Retry*—Specifies the number of times the pruning service checks to see if a server is unavailable before finally pruning it.

➤ *Pre-Populate Printer Search Location Text*—Enables pre-populating the location search text field when users search for a printer (for Windows 2000 printers only).

➤ *Printer Browsing*—Announces the presence of shared printers to print browse master servers in the domain.

➤ *Prune Printers That Are Not Automatically Republished*—Defines how to handle the automatic removal of printers when a non-Windows 2000-based printer (or a Windows 2000 printer in another domain) is removed.

➤ *Web-Based Printing*—Determines whether Internet printing is supported on the server.

Assigning appropriate user permissions is also an important aspect of managing printer resources. The following list contains the three levels of printer permissions:

➤ *Manage Documents*—Users can print documents, change document settings and pause, resume, start, restart, and cancel any documents.

➤ *Manage Printer*—Users can add printers, change printer properties, delete printers, set printer sharing, take ownership of print jobs, and change printer permissions.

➤ *Print*—Users can print documents and pause, resume, start, restart, and cancel their own documents. (Default for the Everyone group.)

By default, the Everyone group has Print access only, as shown in Figure 4.4. Print Operators, Server Operators, and Administrators have all three levels of printer permissions. The Creator/Owner has Manage Document permissions.

Internet printing introduces other concerns for managing printer access. For Windows 2000 Server print servers that also run Internet Information Services (IIS), printers can be accessed via the Internet or intranet. A user simply enters the server name along with the printer name as the URL. For example, if the server name of a print server on your intranet is EXXON, and the Hewlett-Packard printer is shared as HP, you can type "**http://exxon/hp**" to manage or print to that HP printer.

When this method of printing is used, security is handled by IIS. The following list contains the types of security that can be used:

➤ *Basic Authentication*—Users are prompted for their usernames and passwords, which are transmitted across the network in clear-text.

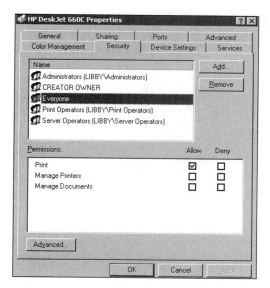

Figure 4.4   Printer Properties, Security tab.

➤ *Digest Authentication*—Usernames and passwords are sent across the network as a hash value.

➤ *Kerberos Authentication*—Windows-based security that is also supported by Internet Explorer

➤ *Microsoft Challenge/Response Authentication*—Also known as integrated Windows authentication, usernames and passwords are automatically submitted and encrypted.

Also, *Secure Sockets Layer (SSL)* can be used on the Web site so that all printing communication, not just names and passwords, is encrypted.

MANAGING FOLDERS AND SHARES

Sharing folders can be performed by selecting Sharing in the Properties of that file or folder. To use the Properties sheet to share a folder, perform the following steps:

1. Right-click the folder, and choose Sharing from the pop-up menu.

2. Choose the Share This Folder radio button, and provide a name for it.

3. Click OK.

You can also share folders by using a Windows 2000 tool called the Computer Management console (shown in Figure 4.5), which is based on the Microsoft Management Console (MMC). It is used to configure and troubleshoot a computer and can be used to create and manage shares.

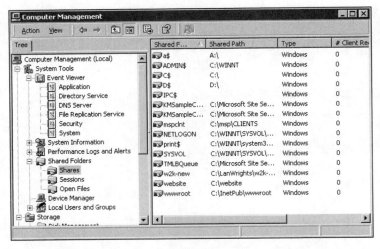

Figure 4.5   The Computer Management console.

Note: In Windows NT 4, you had to use File Manager (winfile.exe) to create a share remotely. However, because the Computer Management console can be used to configure a computer remotely, remote shares can now be easily created in Windows 2000.

To share a folder using the Computer Management console, perform the following steps:

1. Choose Start | Programs | Administrative Tools | Computer Management.

2. In the console tree of the Computer Management console, click Shared Folders under System Tools.

3. Under Shared Folders, right-click Shares, and choose New File Share.

4. When the wizard is invoked, supply the path, share name, and description. Click Next.

5. Choose a permissions type. Click Finish. (Share permissions are discussed in the "Managing Access to Shares" section later in this chapter.)

6. You will receive confirmation that the share has been created and are asked whether you want to create another one. Choose No.

Once a share is available, users access the shares employing one of several methods. The following list contains the most common methods:

➤ *Using My Network Places*—As long as the share has not been defined as a hidden share, users can browse their My Network Places (previously known as Network Neighborhood) to find the server and share name. Also, within My Network Places, you will see an icon called Add Network Place.

Figure 4.6   The Add Network Place Wizard.

Double-clicking on this program invokes a wizard that allows you to specify or browse to a server and share name, as shown in Figure 4.6. Once you create a new network place, that share is available from the root of your local My Network Places.

➤ *Running the UNC*—If a user knows the path to the UNC (Universal Naming Convention) name of the share, he or she can choose Start|Run and type it in. The UNC is usually in the following format: \\server_name\sharename.

➤ *Mapping a network drive*—A user can also assign the share a specific drive letter on their machines. This can be accomplished by choosing Tools|Map Network Drive from the file menu in Windows Explorer. You can also right-click My Computer and choose Map Network Drive. A third method is to use the NET USE command in MS-DOS. For example, to map the UNC of \\slim\mp3 to the F: drive, type the following:

```
NET USE F: \\SLIM\MP3
```

One of the issues with these methods of accessing shares is that users must know the name of the server and the name of the share where the content they want to access resides. Also, if needed documents reside on multiple servers, it becomes quite a hassle to access all of the different paths separately.

To solve this problem, Microsoft introduced Dfs, which can make files and folders that physically sit on different computers look like they reside in one place in the network. This allows shares to be more easily managed and accessed when they reside on multiple machines. For example, if there are technical documents on multiple computers, you can use Dfs to make it appear as though all of the documents reside in a single location. This eliminates the need for users to manually access multiple file servers on the network to find the information they need.

The following terminology is used to describe Dfs concepts. These are terms that you should fully understand before creating and using Dfs in an organization:

➤ *Dfs link*—A link from a Dfs root to a Dfs share or to another Dfs root.

➤ *Dfs root*—A container for files and Dfs links.

➤ *Dfs shared folder*—A network share that is made available via a Dfs structure.

➤ *Dfs topology*—The root, links, and shares organized into a tree structure.

➤ *Host server*—The domain server where the Dfs root resides; it must be a member server or domain controller of the domain.

➤ *Replica*—A folder within a replica set.

➤ *Replica set*—Two or more Dfs roots or Dfs shared folders that participate in replication.

Dfs technology was available in Windows NT 4, but the Dfs administration tool, now called the Dfs Console, has been greatly enhanced in Windows 2000. To start the Dfs Console, choose Start|Programs|Administrative Tools|Distributed File System.

The first decision you need to make when creating a Dfs structure is which one of the Dfs types you want to create: a stand-alone Dfs or a domain-based Dfs.

When you choose to create a new Dfs root, you have the option to choose either one of these types, as shown in Figure 4.7.

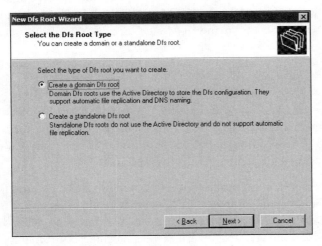

Figure 4.7   The New Dfs Root Wizard.

A Dfs root server stores and retrieves the mappings between the physical and logical shares in what's called the Partition Knowledge Table (PKT). Because a domain-based root automatically publishes its Dfs topology to the Active Directory, the PKT for a domain-based Dfs is stored in the Active Directory. A domain-based Dfs can have multiple levels of Dfs links. The following sections discuss creating each of these types of Dfs roots.

A stand-alone Dfs, however, does not use the Active Directory, so its PKT is stored in the registry of the Dfs root server. Also, a stand-alone Dfs root cannot have root-level shared folders and can only have a one-level-deep hierarchy.

4

Note: Only Windows 98, Windows NT 4 (with Service Pack 3 applied), Windows 98 (with an upgrade applied), and Windows 2000 clients have the necessary Dfs client software to access Dfs resources. Windows 95 clients, however, can download and install Dfs client software free from Microsoft's Web site.

Working with Stand-Alone Dfs

Stand-alone Dfs stores a logical file system topology on a single computer. Therefore, there is no fault tolerance and it does not support automatic file replication.

To install a new stand-alone Dfs tree, follow these steps:

1. Choose Start | Programs | Administrative Tools | Distributed File System.

2. From the Dfs menu, choose Action | New Dfs Root.

3. The wizard is invoked. Click Next to begin.

4. Choose to create a stand-alone Dfs root. Click Next.

5. Enter the server name of the host. Click Next.

6. Choose to either create a new share or use an existing share. If a new share needs to be created, you need to specify the path and the name of the new share. Click Next.

7. Optionally, add a comment for the new root. Click Next.

8. Review your settings for accuracy. Click Finish.

Many times in an organization, it's extremely important that users have uninterrupted access to important files on multiple servers. You can give them this reliability by replicating those files to multiple shares using Dfs. Dfs shared folders can be replicated manually using a stand-alone Dfs. Replication copies the content of one Dfs root to another root share or from one Dfs share to another Dfs share on a different machine.

To replicate a Dfs root from a Dfs link, start the Dfs Console and select New Root Replica from the Dfs Root menu. This invokes the DFS Root Wizard. Once a root share is created, if one of the host servers becomes unavailable, the other Dfs root has a copy of the entire Dfs tree.

To replicate a Dfs share, add the Dfs shared folder to a Dfs link and specify that the folder will participate in replication. Then set the replication policy for that Dfs link's set of Dfs shares. When the files replicate, a copy of the original content is copied to the new share.

Working with Domain-Based Dfs

Domain-based Dfs uses the Active Directory to publish network resources, therefore, it is fault tolerant on an NTFS drive, and is replicated to every participating root server for Dfs. Unlike a stand-alone Dfs, a domain-based Dfs uses the Active Directory to publish network resources and supports automatic file replication.

To install a new Dfs tree, follow these steps:

1. Choose Start | Programs | Administrative Tools | Distributed File System.

2. From the Dfs menu, choose Action | New Dfs Root.

3. The wizard is invoked. Click Next to begin.

4. Choose to create a domain Dfs root. Click Next.

5. Enter the host domain name. Click Next.

6. Enter the server name of the host. Click Next.

7. Choose to either create a new share or use an existing share. If a new share needs to be created, you need to specify the path and the name of the new share. Click Next.

8. Optionally, add a comment for the new root. Click Next.

9. Review your settings for accuracy. Click Finish.

When using domain-based Dfs with the *File Replication Service (FRS)* on an NTFS drive, you can enable Dfs to automatically replicate the content of a Dfs shared folder to the linked shared folders. Once it's enabled, the content between the two shares will consistently be synchronized. By default, FRS synchronizes the content every 15 minutes. To enable automatic replication, use the Replication Policy windows in the Dfs console.

Replicated Dfs links automatically provide the following benefits:

➤ High availability

➤ Prevention of server overload

➤ Easier file services management

However, domain-based Dfs roots rely on replication between multiple Active Directory servers to supply these benefits. Because each Dfs root sends its PKT information to the Active Directory, all other linked Dfs roots must periodically obtain that information from the Active Directory. If the directory becomes unavailable, however, the other Dfs roots are not updated. Therefore, Active Directory replication is necessary to ensure high availability of Dfs root information.

Managing Access to Shares

Within the Computer Management Console Manager, under Shared Folders, in the left pane, you see the following three options:

➤ *Open Files*—Lists all the files on the server that are currently opened by users, and shows permission granted when it was opened, number of locks on it, who accessed it, and what type of connection.

➤ *Sessions*—Lists all users connected to the shares on the server, as well as information about the user, such as files open, connected time, idle time, computer name, type, and whether the user is a guest.

➤ *Shares*—Lists all the shared files and folders on the server, as well as paths, number of connections, type of connection, and comment.

If the File Server For Macintosh service or the Print Server For Macintosh is installed, there may also be a node for Macintosh shares. This allows you to share files and printers with Macintosh clients.

In Windows 2000, there are several shares that are created automatically for administration and system purposes. These shares are hidden, and therefore cannot be seen in My Network Places. However, you can use the Shared Folders snap-in in the Computer Management Console to view them.

The following list contains some of the hidden shares that may be created automatically in Windows 2000 Server:

➤ *ADMIN$*—Points to the system root directory (usually WINNT) and is used by the system during remote administration of the server.

➤ *C$*—Provides Server Operators with the ability to connect to the root directory of the C: drive. If other drive letters are available, those letters are hidden shares as well (for example, D$, E$, and so forth).

➤ *FAX$*—Used by fax clients to temporarily cache files and access cover pages stored on the server.

➤ *IPC$*—Shares the named pipes for use with remote administration and when viewing a server's shared resources.

➤ *NETLOGON*—Used by the Net Logon service to process domain logon requests.

➤ *PRINT$*—Is used for remote administration of printers.

These special shares are not displayed in My Network Places. However, remote users can connect to them using a direct UNC path, a username, and a password that has access to the shares. To protect against unauthorized access, it is highly recommended that the Administrator username be renamed.

Assigning permissions to the folders for a share is also an important aspect of managing file resources. The following list contains the types of access permissions that can be applied to shared folders:

➤ *Change*—Gives the user Read permissions and allows the user to add new files and subdirectories, modify the content of files, and delete subfolders and files.

➤ *Full Control*—Gives the user Read and Change Permissions and allows the user to change NTFS permissions and take ownership of NTFS files and folders.

➤ *Read*—Allows the user to view file names and subfolder names, traverse to subfolders, view the content of the files, and execute program files.

Note: *By default, the Everyone group has all three of these permissions assigned to it.*

Share permissions can be assigned to folders on either FAT or NTFS partitions. If the partition is using NTFS, however, the associated NTFS permissions are used in conjunction with these share permissions (see Chapter 11 for a detailed discussion of NTFS permissions). Basically, a user is given the lesser amount of access. For example, if a user has NTFS Write permissions, but only Read permissions on the share and accesses the share from the network, then he or she has only Read permissions to the files. The interaction between the two types of permissions is discussed in more detail in Chapter 11.

Managing Web-Based Access to Files and Folders

Windows 2000 also provides the capability to make shares available from a Web browser. To create a Web-based share, perform the following steps on a server running IIS:

1. Right-click a folder and choose Properties.

2. Click the Web Sharing tab.

3. Choose which local Web site to share the folder on (usually Default Web Site), and choose to Share this folder.

4. Type an alias for the folder.

5. Choose from the following access permissions:

   ➤ *Directory browsing*—If no default page is specified, a list of the directory's contents is displayed.

   ➤ *Read*—Users can read the content of existing files (this is the default setting).

   ➤ *Script source access*—Users can execute files in this directory.

   ➤ *Write*—Users can create new files and modify the contents of existing files.

6. Choose from the following Application permissions:

   ➤ *Execute (includes scripts)*—Both scripts and executables can run in this directory.

   ➤ *None*—Programs and scripts cannot run in this directory.

   ➤ *Scripts*—Scripts, but not executables, can run in this directory (this is the default setting).

7. Click OK, then click OK again.

Within IIS, a new virtual directory is automatically created. The virtual directory simply points to a local directory on the computer. To access this share from a browser, users can now type "http://<servername>/<sharename>" into a browser.

CHAPTER SUMMARY

This chapter discussed the various methods of managing resource access. We started off by exploring the network services that need to be installed for sharing files, folders, and printers with different types of clients. We then stepped through the process of configuring those network services.

The chapter went on to talk about Windows 2000 printer terminology and concepts. We discussed the many enhancements Windows 2000 has for managing and using printing services. We also discovered that publishing printers to the Active Directory provides an easy way for users to find the most appropriate printers. For example, users can search on certain criteria, such as which building the printer is in or whether the printer prints in color. We also learned about the three levels of printer permissions and which groups possess those permissions:

➤ *Manage Documents*—Print Operators, Server Operators, and Administrators

➤ *Manage Printer*—Print Operators, Server Operators, and Administrators

➤ *Print*—Everyone, Print Operators, Server Operators, and Administrators

We found that printers can now be published and accessed on a Web server. By choosing this method of accessing printers, permissions are managed by IIS.

Next, we reviewed different methods of sharing files and folders including choosing to share a file or folder in its Properties sheet and using the Computer Management console.

We learned about Dfs and how it can be used to publish a logical view of file shares. We then discussed the differences between a stand-alone Dfs and a domain-based Dfs. Basically, a domain-based Dfs provides additional fault tolerance because of its automatic file replication.

We also learned about the three types of access permissions that can be applied to shares:

➤ *Change*—Users can modify content and add new content.

➤ *Full Control*—Users have Read and Change permissions, and they can change NTFS permissions and take ownership of NTFS files and folders.

➤ *Read*—Users can view existing content.

In addition, we discussed how the shares can be managed in the Computer Management console. We talked about the hidden shares that are automatically created in Windows 2000, and we ended the discussion with the topic of Web-based access to files and folders. We learned that it's now very easy to create a local directory in IIS to automatically make a share available through a Web browser.

REVIEW QUESTIONS

1. Which of the following hidden shares provides the named pipes when administering a server remotely?

   a. ADMIN$

   b. IPC$

   c. PRINT$

   d. PIPES$

2. Which of the following benefits does Active Directory provide when publishing network resources? [Choose all that apply]

   a. Provides a secure publication of network resources

   b. Makes it easy for end-users to find information on a network

   c. Provides a simple interface to add network services

   d. Provides an easy interface to create new shares

3. How many printers are supported in Windows 2000?

   a. More than 500

   b. More than 1,000

   c. More than 3,000

   d. More than 6,000

4. Which one of the following statements accurately describes the term *Windows 2000 printer*?

   a. The physical hardware that prints material.

   b. The server that users access to connect to the print device.

   c. The program that enables communication between applications and print jobs.

   d. A computer on a network that initiates a print request.

5. Which of the following IIS authentication schemes sends a user's name and password across a network in clear-text?

   a. Basic Authentication

   b. Microsoft Challenge/Response Authentication

   c. Kerberos Authentication

   d. Digest Authentication

6. Which of the following nodes in the Computer Management console provides a list of users currently connected to the shares on the computer?

   a. Shares

   b. Sessions

   c. Users

   d. Open files

7. Which of the following hidden shares are automatically created when you install Windows 2000 Server? [Choose all that apply]

   a. IPC$

   b. ADMIN$

    c. USERS$

    d. FAX$

8. Which of the following application permissions should be applied if scripts should be executed, but executables should not be?

    a. None

    b. Scripts

    c. Read

    d. Execute

9. Which of the following are methods for accessing a manually created share across a network? [Choose all that apply]

    a. My Network Places

    b. Computer Management console

    c. Map a network drive

    d. Web browser

10. If a Windows 2000 Server is going to be used for file sharing and network applications, which of the following options for Server optimization should be specified?

    a. Maximize memory used

    b. Balance

    c. Maximize data throughput for file sharing

    d. Maximize data throughput for network applications

11. Which of the following definitions most accurately describes the term *printer pool.*

    a. A group of printers

    b. A print service that is set up to send a print job to the first available printer

    c. A list of priorities for which print jobs take precedence over others

    d. A series of files waiting to be produced by the printer

12. A Dfs host server can be a domain controller.

    a. True

    b. False

13. Which of the following are criteria for replicating Dfs content automatically? [Choose all that apply]

    a. FRS

    b. Domain-based Dfs

    c. Stand-alone Dfs

    d. NTFS volume

14. What is the purpose of the Windows 2000 System Monitor's Print Queue object?

    a. Monitors the performance of a local printer

    b. Monitors the performance of a remote printer

    c. Monitors the performance of a local or remote printer

    d. Monitors the performance of a printer queue

15. Which of the following is a group policy that defines how to handle the automatic removal of printers when a non–Windows 2000 printer is no longer available on the network?

    a. Prune printers that are not automatically republished

    b. Allow pruning of published printers

    c. Printer browsing

    d. Directory pruning interval

16. By default, which of the following permissions are given to the Everyone group when a new share is created? [Choose all that apply]

    a. Read

    b. Write

    c. Full Control

    d. None

17. What needs to be installed in order for Macintosh clients to access printers connected to a Windows 2000 Server?

    a. File And Print Sharing Service

    b. Print Services For Macintosh

    c. File Server For Macintosh

    d. Macintosh File And Print Sharing Service

4

18. Which of the following is *not* a permission that you can assign for a Web-based share?

    a. Read

    b. Write

    c. Script source access

    d. Full control

19. Which of the following Windows NT groups can connect to the C$ share of a server? [Choose all that apply]

    a. Backup Operators

    b. Server Operators

    c. Administrators

    d. Everyone

20. Where is the Partition Knowledge Table (PKT) stored on a domain-based Dfs?

    a. Registry

    b. MMC

    c. A Microsoft jet database

    d. Active Directory

21. Dan has Full Control access to an NTFS file share, whereas Libby has Change access to the same file share. Which of the following actions can Dan perform that Libby cannot? [Choose all that apply]

    a. Change data in files

    b. Change NTFS permissions

    c. Take ownership of files

    d. Delete subfolders and files

22. Which of the following are requirements for the use of Distributed file system? [Choose all that apply]

    a. An NTFS partition

    b. File And Print Sharing service

    c. Active Directory

    d. Distributed file system service

23. Which of the following is not a permission type that can be assigned to printers?

   a. Print

   b. Manage Documents

   c. Manage Printer

   d. Manage Print Queue

24. Which of the following terms is used to describe a folder that is automatically replicated to another folder in Dfs?

   a. Dfs link

   b. Replica

   c. Replica set

   d. Replication folder

4

REAL-WORLD PROJECTS

Note: The following exercise assumes a test server with Windows NT 2000 member server with access to an Active Directory. Read the instructions carefully and do not perform this installation on your production machine unless you understand the options presented.

Joe Neal works for a medium-sized 10-year-old corporation whose infrastructure is a complete mess. There are no central file servers, so everyone has programs and documents on various folders throughout the network. When new users join the company, they have a very difficult time finding the information they need.

The company's printers are scattered throughout the network in much the same way. Different departments have their own printers on the network; but, to access the printers, users must know the server name and share name of the printer server.

Because the Information Management department has been blamed for the company's disorganization, the CIO has recently resigned. Joe, however, is interested in becoming CIO of the company, but to do so, he needs to make a major impact on the corporation. He thinks that the recent deployment of Windows 2000 Server offers him the best opportunity. He is going to try to organize all of the file and printer resources into a systematic searchable structure. The current CEO buys into the idea and communicates to all employees that the owners of any material and printers that other employees need to access must be documented and sent to Joe.

Joe gathers all the information sent to him about the file shares throughout the organization. In his research, he learns that all client workstations are either running Windows 98 or Windows 2000 Professional, and that the majority of the software on the file servers apply to both of these operating systems. However, Windows 2000 Server software is also on various file servers, but was meant to be installed only on the test and production servers throughout the company.

Joe also learns that every major department has two black and white printers and two color printers. He organizes this information into the following high-level categories.

➤ Client Software

    ➤ Drivers

    ➤ Utilities

    ➤ Internet and HTML tools

    ➤ Communications software

    ➤ Office suite

    ➤ Operating System Files

    ➤ Miscellaneous

➤ Server Software

    ➤ Drivers

    ➤ Utilities

    ➤ Administration tools

    ➤ BackOffice suite

    ➤ Operating System Files

    ➤ Miscellaneous

➤ Documents

    ➤ Marketing documents

    ➤ Human Resources documents

    ➤ Information Management documents

    ➤ Engineering documents

➤ Printers

   ➤ Marketing printers

   ➤ Human Resources printers

   ➤ Information Management printers

   ➤ Engineering printers

4

Based on this organization, Joe decides to deploy four member servers, each serving as a top-level Dfs root for Client Software, Server Software, Documents, and Printers. Each of the Dfs roots then link to the Dfs roots of their subtopics.

Joe decides to tackle the "Marketing Documents" root first. He starts his quest by installing Windows 2000 Server on a production member server in the domain. He then verifies that File And Print Services has been installed correctly and configures the server to maximize its system resources to be a file server.

Project 4.1
To optimize a Windows 2000 Server for file and print sharing, perform the following steps:

1. Choose Start | Settings | Network and Dial-Up Connections.

2. Right-click LAN, and choose Properties.

3. Verify that the checkbox next to File And Print Sharing For Microsoft Networks is selected.

4. Highlight the File And Print Sharing For Microsoft Networks service, and click Properties.

5. Choose to maximize data throughput for file sharing.

6. Click OK, then click OK again.

Joe talks to the Marketing department about where they keep their documents. In doing so, he discovers that there are various shares throughout the Marketing department's network, and that many of them have redundant or missing information. After doing some file clean up, Joe organizes the files into four types.

➤ Press Releases

➤ Branding and Legal Information

➤ Print Media

➤ Images Library

On four different existing file servers, he creates shares for each of these document types. He knows that there needs to be a Marketing Dfs root with four links. Each of the links are pointers to shares with each of the four document types, as shown in Figure 4.8.

Joe starts the Dfs creation process by creating a share on the new member server that will later act as the Marketing Dfs root.

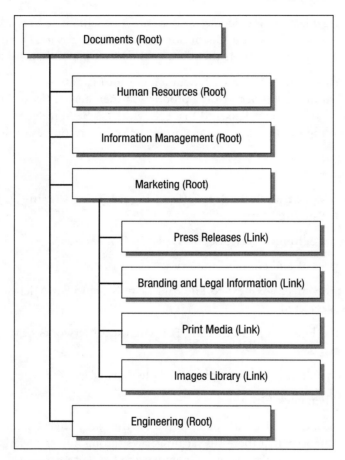

Figure 4.8 A document root tree.

Project 4.2

To create a share on the local file server using the Computer Management console, perform the following steps:

1. Create a new folder called "Marketing Documents" on the C: drive. There should be no content in this directory.

2. Choose Start | Programs | Administrative Tools | Computer Management.

3. In the left pane, double-click Shared Folders to expand its nodes.

4. Double-click Shares.

5. From the file menu, choose Action | New File Share.

6. Browse to the Marketing Documents folder. Click OK.

7. Specify the share name as Marketing Documents and provide a description for them. Click Next.

8. Choose to give Administrators full control, but everyone else Read-only access. Click Finish.

9. When asked whether you'd like to set up another share, choose No.

Because Joe sets up an official file and print server, he connects the Marketing printers to the server, then provided share access to end-users. He knows that when he creates the Marketing Printers Dfs root, he can easily add these shares.

Project 4.3

To set up a printer share on the file and print server, perform these steps:

Note: You do not have to have a physical printer to perform this exercise.

1. Choose Start | Settings | Printers.

2. Double-click Add Printer.

3. The Add Printer Wizard is invoked. Click Next.

4. Choose Local Printer. Click Next.

5. Choose the port through which the printer is connected. Click Next.

6. Choose the manufacturer and model of the printer. Click Next.

7. Specify a standard, but easy to remember printer name, such as Marketing Printer—Color 1. Click Next.

8. Specify the same share name as the printer name. Click Next.

9. Type "Marketing, 3rd floor" for the location, and enter a high-level description of the printer. Click Next.

10. Choose not to create a test page. Click Next.

11. Review the printer settings, and click Next.

12. Right-click the newly created printer icon, and choose Properties.

13. Click the Sharing tab. Make sure that List In Directory is selected. Then click the Additional Drivers button.

14. Select the checkbox next to Windows 95/98, so that Windows 98 clients are able to download the appropriate printer drivers automatically. Click OK.

15. Supply the path to Windows 2000 source files.

16. Click Close.

Joe knows that in order to really make a great impact on the company, he not only needs to share and organize the company's network resources in this manner, but he also needs to provide redundancy for the company network in case any of its servers ever becomes unavailable. Fortunately, there is only one domain in the company, which makes setting up a domain-based Dfs on his production Windows 2000 member server fairly easy.

Project 4.4
To set up a domain-based Dfs, perform these steps:

1. Choose Start | Programs | Administrative Tools | Distributed File System.

2. From the Dfs menu, choose Action | New Dfs Root.

3. The wizard is invoked. Click Next to begin.

4. Choose to create a domain Dfs root. Click Next.

5. Enter the domain name. Click Next.

6. Enter the local server name. Click Next.

7. Choose to use an existing share and, in the dropdown list, choose Marketing Documents. Click Next.

8. Verify the name of the share. Click Next.

9. Review your settings for accuracy. Click Finish.

Joe then starts linking to each of the shared resources on the network. He starts with the Press Releases share he has made earlier on another machine.

Project 4.5
To create a Dfs link, perform these steps:

1. Choose Start | Programs | Administrative Tools | Distributed File System.

2. Highlight the Marketing Documents root.

3. From the file menu, choose Action | Create New Dfs Link.

4. Enter Press Releases for the link name, then specify the UNC of the share corresponding to these documents.

5. Click OK.

6. Perform the same steps for each of the other three links: Branding and Legal Information, Print Media, and Images Library.

Joe performs the same clean up and organization for each of the four high-level roots. Then, he creates one root replica and adds each of the high-level roots (Client Software, Server Software, Documents, and Printers) under one master root called Company Resources.

Users immediately start sending Joe email messages about how easy it now is to find information, and how great it is to be able to find information so quickly. He's bombarded repeatedly with one question: How did you get all of the resources onto one server?

Joe schedules a companywide meeting and explains how Dfs works. He shows the staff that many of the resources are still on their original servers, but now they are easy to find and redundant. The CEO is so impressed that he makes Joe the new CIO of the company.

CHAPTER FIVE

WORKING WITH HARDWARE AND DRIVERS

After completing this chapter, you will be able to:

✓ Explore the Windows 2000 Server hardware environment

✓ Understand the role of Plug and Play

✓ Identify the hardware supported by Windows 2000 Server

✓ Examine the Windows 2000 Server driver classes and structures

✓ Configure hardware devices

✓ Understand hidden and phantom devices

✓ Configure monitors

✓ Handle driver signing options

✓ Update device drivers

✓ Troubleshoot hardware problems

✓ Use the Device Verifier

Windows 2000 Server is designed to run on a wide range of computers, and it supports a larger list of hardware than any other version of Windows. It currently supports thousands of devices and includes additional support for many devices and architectures not previously supported by Windows NT 4, such as *Plug and Play (PnP)* and *Intelligent I/O (I2O)*.

With Windows 2000 Server, Microsoft has listened to the concerns of its users and provided increased reliability, availability, and scalability of the hardware and drivers it supports. What this means in a nutshell is that, in general, a system will not have to be rebooted for each configuration change. The system will also be able to grow as the demands on it increase. In addition, Active Directory extends the interoperability of applications and devices.

Windows 2000 Server provides increased functionality including support for a variety of devices, such as digital audio, still-image devices, video capture, *Digital Versatile Disk (DVD)*, *Universal Serial Bus (USB)*, *IEEE 1394 bus*, *Accelerated Graphics Port (AGP)* graphics, certain multifunction adapters, *uninterruptable power supply (UPS)* service, and *PC Cards*, among others. In many ways, Windows 2000 Server has taken the strengths of both Windows 98 and Windows NT and has incorporated them into this powerful operating system. A key strength taken from Windows 98 is the Plug and Play architecture, which allows Windows 2000 Server to detect new PnP hardware, identify it, and then install the drivers with limited user interaction.

Before you can install Windows 2000 Server, however, you must be certain that you have met the minimum requirements by obtaining the specific hardware and compatible drivers that Windows 2000 Server requires. The operating system also requires a huge amount of system resources and will only accept certain parameters. So, by ensuring that the appropriate system requirements are met, which is vital to the success of your installation or upgrade, you will be able to realize the full strength and power of Windows 2000 Server.

WINDOWS 2000 SERVER HARDWARE ENVIRONMENT

Because of the stringent hardware requirements for Windows 2000, the odds are that there will be systems that are not ready or cannot be upgraded to Windows 2000 Server in their current state. Proper planning prior to the actual installation is vital with Windows 2000 Server. If you are planning to upgrade a Windows NT 4 Server, it is possible that you will need to purchase new hardware prior to the upgrade. By analyzing what you currently have and comparing it to what you need for Windows 2000 Server, you will ensure an easier installation and better performance. In addition, the role the server will play in the organization is important when deciding on hardware requirements.

A server that will host a large database will require different resources than a server that is used for basic file and print services.

It is strongly recommended that you conduct a hardware inventory of all servers and client computers in use in your network. Document all routers, printers, modems, Redundant Array of Inexpensive Disks (RAID) arrays and *Remote Access Service (RAS)* server hardware. Also include Basic Input/Output System (BIOS) settings and the configurations of any peripheral devices, such as printers, scanners, and input devices. The following list provides some of the essential items you should include in your inventory:

➤ Hard drive size

➤ Computer RAM

➤ Processor speed

➤ BIOS

➤ Video card

➤ Network card

➤ Disk controller

➤ Power management

➤ Other items, such as CPU chipset

There are several methods and tools you can employ to conduct this inventory search. One is the trusted pen and paper method for small networks. Or, for a "paperless" approach, Microsoft recommends using Systems Manager Server (SMS) to analyze your network infrastructure. The SMS Hardware Inventory used with the SMS client software collects the hardware inventory and automatically reports the information to SMS. The reasons that SMS is so powerful in accomplishing this task is beyond the scope of this chapter, so suffice it to say that SMS is a robust tool to use.

In addition, Microsoft offers a licensed version of Domain Migrator created by Mission Critical Software, Inc. that will migrate your existing Windows NT Server domains to Windows 2000. The software uses wizards that help model and streamline your network for use with Windows 2000.

Windows 2000 Server also includes the Windows 2000 Readiness Analyzer Tool, which is supplied on the CD. Refer to Chapter 2 for details on the Windows 2000 Readiness Analyzer.

Minimum Requirements and Recommendations

As discussed in Chapter 2, Windows 2000 Server dictates a set of minimum requirements, which defines the absolute lowest level of hardware needed to install Windows 2000 Server. The minimum amount of RAM needed is 128MB and without it Windows 2000 Server will not install.

If you do try to install Windows 2000 Server on a computer with the minimum requirements, you will achieve a successful installation, however, its performance will be sluggish. When you view the Task Manager (press Ctrl+Alt+Delete, then click the Task Manager button) after installation, you will see that the system utilizes most of the memory (even without any applications installed). Figure 5.1 shows the Task Manager and the amount of memory used by Windows 2000 Server. (This particular server is being used as a file and print server with a minimum amount of applications installed.)

The preferred minimum amount of RAM, also mentioned in Chapter 2, is 256MB. In fact, depending on the role the server will play in the network, you may even want to add more. For domain controllers or application servers that provide services to numerous users, 256MB should be thought of as the starting amount of RAM. Windows 2000 Server supports up to 4GB of RAM.

The hard drive partition must have enough free space to accommodate the Setup process. Microsoft literature sets the minimum amount of space needed as 1GB. Other literature suggests that Windows 2000 Server can be installed on 900MB, but why someone would want to cram a server's operating system on

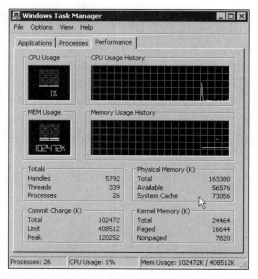

Figure 5.1 Task Manager displaying memory used.

such a limited space is beyond comprehension. Windows 2000 Server actually needs much more space than 1GB, and the need depends on several factors.

If there are components (such as existing user accounts) that must be installed, more hard drive space is needed. If the file system being used is file allocation table (FAT), 100MB to 200MB of additional free space is required. If you are installing across a network, you will need 100MB to 200MB more of free space than if you are installing from a CD. Although there is no set formula for setting a partition size, you should allow for as much space as possible for the operating system. Allowing for an additional 2GB to 4GB of space on the partition is a safe bet, and depending on the applications you are planning to use, you should allow for even more than that. Many items should be considered when trying to factor the space requirements for Windows 2000 Server, such as the size and conditions needed for Active Directory information, logs, pagefile, service packs, and so on. The best advice we can give you is to allow as large a hard drive as you can.

Windows 2000 provides high availability solutions with its Windows 2000 Advanced Server and Datacenter Server products. High availability means that the system is designed to be available 99.9 percent of the time and is able to protect itself from faulty hardware, drivers, and other variables. Use of *cluster services* and *multihomed systems* help to achieve this high percentage of up time.

THE ROLE OF PLUG AND PLAY

Windows 2000 Server includes Plug and Play technology, so that devices can automatically be recognized and detected by the operating system. This helps alleviate the potential for device conflicts.

Plug and Play provides support for a combination of hardware and software and enables the server to recognize and adapt to hardware configurations and changes automatically. There is no need for user intervention or a reboot. Plug and Play installations are made possible through a combination of BIOS, hardware devices, system resources, device drivers, and the operating system. Windows 2000 contains built-in support for thousands of Plug and Play devices including printers, cameras, infrared data ports, DVD, and so on.

Plug and Play support in Windows 2000 Server is different than the Plug and Play support in Windows 95. The Windows 2000 Server Plug and Play does not rely on the Advanced Power Management BIOS or even the Plug and Play BIOS. Both were originally designed for Windows 95. Windows 2000 Server incorporates the newer *Advanced Configuration and Power Interface (ACPI)* specification, which defines a new system board and BIOS interface. ACPI extends Plug and Play to include power management and other configurations, which are under the control of the operating system.

Note: Older versions of ACPI do not support all Plug and Play features for Windows 2000. Obtain the newest version of ACPI to ensure full functionality of Plug and Play.

Windows 2000 Plug and Play is designed for use in business settings, meaning that laptops, workstations, and server computers are the main targets for optimum support. An example of this is the Windows 2000 support of infrared data communications. The system notifies the user if a new infrared device (such as another computer) comes close enough for communication.

Machines that have ACPI system boards are recommended, but computers that do not have an ACPI system board can still use Plug and Play devices, although not all Plug and Play features may be available.

If you install Windows 2000 Server on an ACPI BIOS-based system and have any of the following problems, you will need to obtain a BIOS update from the system manufacturer:

➤ You cannot install Windows 2000 Server because of an ACPI BIOS error.

➤ After you install Windows 2000 Server, power management or Plug and Play functionality is not present.

➤ After you install Windows 2000 Server, power management or Plug and Play is present, but does not function properly.

Microsoft has also developed a "compatibility package" that contains BIOS upgrade information. You can find this information at the Microsoft Web site, **www.microsoft.com**. The following list contains some of the features of Plug and Play in Windows 2000:

➤ Insert and remove Plug and Play devices.

➤ Connect or disconnect from a docking station or network without having to restart the computer.

➤ Add a new monitor or USB keyboard by plugging it in and turning it on.

Note: For a monitor to be supported as Plug and Play in Windows 2000 Server, the monitor, the display adapter, and the display driver must all be Plug and Play; otherwise, the monitor is detected as "Default Monitor." Also, although some devices can be hot-plugged, others (such as internal modems and network adapters) should not be unplugged while the computer is running. Check the hardware documentation to verify the correct installation procedure.

It should be noted that Windows 2000 Server will support Windows NT drivers for the most part, but these drivers generally have no Plug and Play functionality.

Some of the new devices supported by Windows 2000 Server (and Professional) are multiple display support, card services, infrared devices, wireless devices, DirectX 7.0, pluggable PCI, hot-pluggable storage devices, directory enabled networking equipment, and many more. See the section "Windows 2000 Server Driver Classes and Structures" later in this chapter for coverage of these devices.

Similar to Windows 98, Windows 2000 Server offers Plug and Play hardware support that is native to its operating system. When you add Plug and Play hardware to the system, Windows 2000 Server should detect the hardware and install the drivers itself. It allows a user to add hardware dynamically without having to read through manuals or have an extensive knowledge of computer hardware.

When the operating system finds a new piece of PnP hardware, it identifies the hardware and installs the drivers. You also have the options of installing the drivers from the Windows 2000 Server CD, a floppy disk, other CD, or from the Microsoft Windows Update Web site.

When a new device is placed into a Windows 2000 Server machine, the Plug and Play device is detected by a process called *enumeration*. Once detected, the driver is configured and loaded without requiring user input. Resources are then allocated, and other drivers and applications are notified that the new device is available for use. The following list shows the benefits of Plug and Play in Windows 2000 Server:

➤ Automatically allocates resources during enumeration

➤ Contains an automatic installation procedure to ensure that the appropriate drivers are installed and loaded

➤ Dynamically loads, initializes, and unloads drivers

➤ Enumerates devices

➤ Notifies other drivers and applications when a new device is available for use

➤ Provides a consistent driver and bus interface for all devices

➤ Works with power management to handle insertion and removal of devices

When Windows 2000 Server installs a device, it must first have an inventory of all its devices currently residing on the system. This is done during startup either when it communicates with the Plug and Play device directly to allocate the resource settings or from the INF file associated with a non–Plug and Play device.

When you install a new Plug and Play device, allow Windows 2000 Server to detect and configure it. For many Plug and Play cards, you must turn off the computer and insert the device. When you restart the system, Windows 2000 Server will enumerate the device and start the Plug and Play installation automatically. For legacy devices that are not Plug and Play, run the Add/Remove Hardware Wizard found in the Control Panel, and let Windows 2000 Server detect the device.

Non–Plug and Play hardware, including older sound cards, internal modems, and so on, can be installed using the Add/Remove Hardware Wizard. Most vendors supply updated drivers for Windows 2000 Server on their Web sites for older pieces of hardware (or they will eventually). During the installation of Windows 2000 Server, it is recommended that you remove legacy devices, install Windows 2000 Server, and then add the devices through the Add/Remove Hardware Wizard. If two legacy devices are using the same resources prior to the upgrade, this could cause installation problems with Windows 2000 Server. Figure 5.2 shows the Add/Remove Hardware Wizard.

WINDOWS 2000 SERVER HARDWARE SUPPORT

When you install Windows 2000 Server, Windows 2000 Setup automatically checks your hardware and software and reports any potential conflicts. However, it is more prudent to check your hardware against the Windows 2000

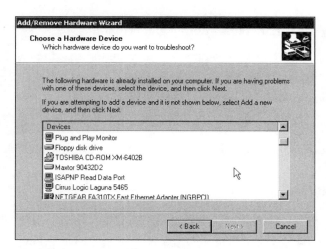

Figure 5.2   The Windows 2000 Add/Remove Hardware Wizard.

Server Hardware Compatibility List (HCL) prior to installation. For more information about the HCL, see Chapter 2.

Other Ways to Check Your System

Windows NT 4 offered a utility called NTHQ (NT Hardware Qualifier), which was a program that produced a detailed report on your system's configuration and could troubleshoot an installation failure due to hardware problems.

Windows 2000 Server has a comparable utility that will scan your system for compatibility and create a report. It is called the Windows 2000 Readiness Analyzer Tool. This utility is discussed in Chapter 2.

5

It is highly recommended that you use this utility (in conjunction with the HCL) before attempting to install Windows 2000 Server. The utility prepares a report, which is found on Windows 95/98 machines at c:\windows\ upgrade.txt or at c:\%systemroot%\winnt32.log on Windows NT machines and lists any complications you may find when you upgrade your system. This utility also identifies which machine will give you problems during the upgrade.

So, what information should you gather prior to installing the operating system? Table 5.1 outlines some of the most common items you should gather information about prior to installation. Each computer is unique, so you should expand on this table and add the components that your system is using.

Table 5.1   Information to gather prior to Windows 2000 Server installation.

Device	Information Needed
BIOS	APM, ACPI, BIOS revision, date, enabled or disabled, settings
Plug and Play	Enabled or disabled in the BIOS
PCI	Type of cards inserted and in which slots
PCMCIA	Type of cards inserted and in which slots
Modem	Internal, external, make, speed, COM port, IRQ, I/O
USB	Devices attached
Sound card	IRQ, I/O, DMA, make, version
Mouse	Make, port (COM, PS/2, or USB)
SCSI controller	Model, chipset, IRQ, bus type
Network card	IRQ, I/O, DMA, make, version, connector type (BNC, twisted pair), bus type
Video	Adapter, chipset, memory, make, version

A few items to note: One type of hardware that is no longer supported is the Microchannel bus. In addition, Alpha is no longer supported; it was dropped by Microsoft in the latter part of 1999. If your system uses a mass storage controller (SCSI, RAID, or Fibre Channel adapter) for the hard drive that is not listed on the HCL, but has a separate driver supplied by the manufacturer for use with Windows 2000 Server, then keep this driver handy during setup. At the early stage of Setup, you will see a line at the bottom of the screen that will prompt you to press F6 to install the drivers for the controller. Further prompts will guide you to supply the driver file for Setup, so that it can access the mass storage controller.

It is also very important to check the HCL for any new technology that your Windows 2000 Server might be required to use (an IEEE 1394 device, for example). Be sure that the brand and make is listed; if not, return the item for one that *is* listed in the HCL.

It is best to check through all of your resources and gather a comprehensive list of the hardware and drivers currently in your network rather than putting the Windows 2000 Server CD into the CD-ROM drive and hoping for the best. Other important files to read before running Setup are read1st.txt and readme.doc. The read1st.txt file provides important preinstallation information on Setup that might pertain to your network's configuration; readme.doc provides important information on hardware, networking, applications, printing, and postinstallation notes.

WINDOWS 2000 SERVER DRIVER CLASSES AND STRUCTURES

Windows 2000 Server uses a newer driver architecture than Windows NT and a somewhat different driver architecture than Windows 98. Windows 2000 Server (and Professional) is designed to simplify the process of installing and configuring devices and drivers. If you are coming from a predominately Windows 98 environment, you will be familiar with the Plug and Play features of Windows 2000 Server. If you are coming from a strong Windows NT background, you will be pleasantly surprised at the ease of use Plug and Play provides.

Because this chapter focuses on hardware and device drivers, let's look at the basic driver and hardware architecture of Windows 2000 to see how the hardware, device drivers, and elements of the operating system interoperate.

Device drivers communicate with the hardware to which they are associated. Software components must communicate with the drivers to enable the hardware to do what the user (via the application) wants it to do. If a user wants the internal modem make a call, he or she uses a software component, generally a graphical user interface tool, where the information is entered (such as a phone number). The software then, when instructed, communicates the commands to the device driver, which in turn instructs the hardware to respond in a particular way. In this case, the modem driver receives the command to dial a certain number. It then opens a port and tells the hardware to begin the dialing process.

The relationship between hardware, drivers, and software components can be thought of as a ring. A design consisting of four rings was developed in the early 1970s on the Multics operating system (after which Unix is patterned). The rings designated different levels of protected privileges, and Intel designed its line of x86 processors around this model using only Rings 0 and 3. Because Windows was first implemented using the Intel processor, Windows adapted the model used by Intel, which used only two of the four rings. Table 5.2 shows how Windows and Unix use the ring pattern.

Stepping beyond this basic ring pattern, Windows 2000 now consists of a very elaborate architecture incorporating how the software interacts with the drivers and ultimately the hardware. It is useful to be familiar with some of the interfaces that are situated between an application and a driver. One of these interfaces is the Registry.

The Registry occupies ring numbers 0 and 3 and interacts with both the user and drivers as well as the operating system, security, application settings, desktop, and user profiles. It is the ultimate and final source for configuration management. Be forewarned: You should not tamper with the Registry unless you have carefully read the help files and instructions and have a current Registry backup. A single change in the Registry could bring your server down and might even require reinstalling the operating system. It is recommended that you use the tools Windows 2000 Server provides to access device drivers to control and communicate with system hardware components.

Much like Windows 98, Windows 2000 Server uses the layered Windows driver architecture called the Windows Driver Model (WDM). The WDM isolates portions of the services required from device drivers, and, in effect, allows all

Table 5.2 Simplified view of the use of the ring pattern by Windows and Unix.

Ring #	Windows	Unix
0	Drivers and critical OS functions	Hardware
1	Not used	Unix kernel
2	Not used	Shell
3	User and OS API calls	User

the specific functions to be accessed from one file. With so many different types of buses that peripherals can be plugged into, such as ISA, MCA, EISA, PCI, and AGP, the WDM allows for a more sophisticated means of accessing hardware, such as loading and unloading drivers dynamically. The layered architecture divides the process of information signaled from the application to the hardware and vice versa.

In addition to Plug and Play, Windows 2000 also supports a new architecture called Intelligent I/O, which is also known as I2O. The I2O SIG (I2O Special Interest Group) is a consortium of computer companies that are working on the development of the I2O architecture. I2O is designed to eliminate I/O (input/output) bottlenecks by using specialized I/O processors (IOP) for interrupt handling, buffering, and data transfer. A separate I2O driver OSM (OS-specific module) then deals with the operating system details and a hardware device module (HDM) to work with the specific device. By dividing the tasks in this manner, I2O decreases the amount of data that needs to be sent over the I/O bus.

The I2O architecture defines a "split driver" model that makes drivers portable across multiple operating systems and host platforms. If an operating system supports the I2O architecture, then the single I2O device driver can be used, regardless of the type of operating system (Windows 2000, Windows 98, Linux, and so on).

Currently, Microsoft dedicates a great deal of resources to certifying drivers to meet the standards it sets for the Windows 2000 operating system (see the section titled "Handling Driver Signing Options" later in this chapter). Manufacturers too are hampered with creating and certifying their devices for each platform. Also, CPU speed is undermined by devices that require a large number of interrupts, which eventually degrades the processors and limits resources that could be used for application processing. I2O relieves pressure on all three fronts by providing manufacturers of operating systems, like Microsoft, with a reliable driver architecture that they can build the operating system around. Now, device manufacturers only need to supply one driver for their device, and the CPU can delegate its resources to other items because the burden of interrupts from the device is handled by the IOP.

Note: As of September 1999, the I2O SIG membership consisted of 90 companies from three continents and 520 nonmember registered developers.

Before breaking away from this discussion of the layered architecture, let's explore how a driver operates with the hardware and with the application. A sample layout is given in Table 5.3, which shows part of the process for interaction with a DVD device in Windows 2000 (these are listed in order).

Table 5.3 Interaction between the software and hardware with a DVD device.

Mode	Item
User mode	DVD playback application software
User mode	DVD file reader
Kernel mode	UDF file system
Kernel mode	DVD-ROM driver
Hardware	DVD drive

As previously mentioned, Windows 2000 supports Plug and Play, and it is optimized for computers with ACPI system boards. There is a variety of devices that are compliant with Plug and Play. The following sections provide details on these devices.

5

USB Devices

A Universal Serial Bus (USB) provides Plug and Play capability for peripheral devices, such as keyboards, mice, and hard drives. Generally, there are two slots on a typical computer for USB devices. USB devices can be used as soon as they are plugged in, which means they are hot pluggable, and the system can use them immediately with no need for a reboot. All USB devices use the same type of I/O connector, which eliminates the need to buy a separate cable for each device. You can also plug multiple USB devices into a single USB port. Table 5.4 shows a list of the different types of USB devices available.

A USB uses a tiered topology and allows you to attach 127 devices to the bus simultaneously. USB currently supports up to five tiers, and each device can be located up to five meters from its hub. An important item to note is that, although you can attach 127 devices, they each need to have their own power supply; otherwise, the number of USB devices you can attach is limited.

Three components make a USB work. The first is the host, also known as the root, root tier, or the root hub. The host is built into the motherboard, or it is installed as an adapter card on the computer's motherboard. If you are thinking of buying a host adapter card, be aware of potential resource conflicts if you have a preinstalled host already on your motherboard. The host controls all traffic on the bus.

Table 5.4 USB devices.

Type	Devices
Input	Keyboards, joysticks, mice (pointing devices)
Storage disk drives	CD-ROM, removable media
Communications	Modems, ISDN adapters, network adapters
Output	Monitors, printers, audio devices
Imaging	Scanners, digital cameras

The second component is the hub. The hub provides a port to attach a device to the bus. Hubs also detect devices that are either bus-powered, which means that they draw their power from the bus, or self-powered, meaning that they can be plugged into the wall. You can take a hub that is self-powered (because it has its own power supply) and plug it into a bus-powered hub. But you cannot connect a bus-powered hub to another bus-powered hub, as the draw for power will be too much.

A bus-powered hub receives its power from the host, which in turn receives its power from the power supply connected to the motherboard. The amount of power that the host provides is a set amount that the device needs. It cannot be divided any further, and the device does not have the ability to accept a larger amount of power, take what it needs, and pass the remaining power on down the line. This is why you cannot have more than one bus-powered hub; there simply is not enough power to facilitate the next unit. In addition, you cannot have a bus-powered hub more than four units downstream from the port because, in this situation, the power flowing downstream slowly loses its integrity until it can no longer meet the minimum requirement for the power supply required by the bus-powered hub. Finally, if you have a bus-powered device that draws more than 100 milliamperes (mA), you cannot connect it to a bus powered hub.

The third component is the device. A USB device is attached to the bus through a port. USB devices can also function as hubs. For example, if you have a USB monitor, and it has ports on it for attaching a mouse and keyboard, then it is a hub as well.

USB supports two data transfer modes: isochronous and asynchronous. An isochronous transfer requires constant bandwidth within certain time constraints. This is due to the requirements of multimedia applications and devices. With isochronous transfer, there is no form of handshaking, and delivery is not guaranteed. Asynchronous transfer, on the other hand, does employ a form of handshaking and guarantees delivery.

Windows 2000 supports configuration of USB devices by using one of two types. The first is hot-pluggable capability in which the hub driver enumerates the device and notifies the system that the device is present. The other is persistent addressing in which the USB device uses descriptors to identify the device, its capabilities, and the protocols it uses. A descriptor contains a Vendor ID (VID) and a Product ID (PID) that tells the computer exactly what to load.

IEEE 1394

The IEEE 1394 (also known as FireWire) is a bus designed for high bandwidth devices. This can include digital camcorders, digital cameras, digital VCRs, and storage devices, and can send data at speeds ranging from 100Mbps to 400Mbps. It provides a high-speed Plug and Play-capable bus and supports both isochronous and asynchronous data transfer. You can connect up to 63 devices to one IEEE 1394 bus and interconnect up to 1,023 buses to form a network of over 64,000 devices with each device having 256 terabytes of addressable memory over the bus.

These numbers are quite impressive. IEEE 1394 devices use a bus cable, which contains two pairs of twisted-pair cabling. There are three interfaces with the cable, a 6-pin connector and cable, a 4-pin connector and cable, and a 6-pin to 4-pin connector and cable. One important note: Windows 2000 only supports IEEE 1394 that is *OHCI (Open Host Controller Interface)*-compliant, so if a device is not OHCI, it will not work with Windows 2000 unless a driver is specifically supplied by the manufacturer. This includes devices that are pre-OHCI, such as Sony's Tin-Tin and TI-lynx. Make sure that the IEEE 1394 device you purchase is supported by Windows 2000 and is on the HCL.

PCI and ISA Devices

The PCI (Peripheral Component Interconnect) bus meets most Plug and Play requirements. Devices that use the PCI bus have a fixed means to identify themselves and set resources. Windows 2000 collects PCI and ISA Plug and Play device resource information from the system BIOS and is able to reassign PCI device resource requirements dynamically. ISA, on the other hand, is different. An ISA (Industry Standard Architecture) bus design allows Plug and Play devices because the specification does not require any change to the ISA buses.

This means that the system takes each ISA device, isolates it, obtains the resource requirements and capabilities, allocates resources to the card, and reserves these resources so that they cannot be assigned to other Plug and Play cards in the computer. PCI devices can be dynamically allocated and changed, whereas ISA devices are fixed once the resources are allocated. When you look at a device's resource setting in Device Manager and see that you cannot change the setting, it is probably due to the fact that the device is an ISA device. Non-Plug and Play ISA devices can coexist with Plug and Play devices in the computer. The information regarding the non-Plug and Play ISA hardware's resources are assigned and stored as static values.

EISA Devices

The EISA (Extended Industry Standard Architecture) is a bus that contains a bus enumerator, which makes these devices accessible to the operating system. Windows 2000 does not reconfigure EISA cards, but instead uses the information gathered from them to determine which resources are used.

DVD

Digital Versatile Disk (DVD) provides storage for audio, video, and computer data. It is most well-known for allowing users to view movies. Playing a movie on DVD can provide a user with a better image quality than a standard TV. DVD can also be used as a storage device and can be cost-effective for storing large data files. The architecture for DVD is complex, and DVD demands a lot from the system. The WDM stream class driver can help because its layered architecture allows for the interconnecting of device drivers to optimize the flow of data.

Digital Audio

Because Windows 2000 supports the USB and the IEEE 1394 bus, it can also support digital audio. Both USB and IEEE 1394 have the bandwidth that digital audio requires. Windows 2000 also uses WDM to handle multiple streams of audio, which means that two applications playing sound can run at the same time, and you will be able to hear both. Windows 2000 can also redirect the audio output to external USB and IEEE 1394 devices, which provide better quality sound.

Still Images and Video Capture

Devices, such as image scanners and digital cameras, are examples of Still Images (STI). These devices work under the WDM, and Windows 2000 supports SCSI, IEEE 1394, USB digital still image, and serial devices. You can access an STI device through the Scanners And Cameras applet in the Control Panel. The Scanners And Cameras icon will appear in the Control Panel when a Plug and Play STI device is detected or if you install the STI device through the Add/Remove Hardware Wizard. Video capture is based on the WDM stream class driver and supports USB and IEEE 1394 cameras as well as PCI and video port analog devices.

Smart Cards

A smart card is a device that is about the size of a credit card and contains an embedded circuit, which stores security information, access levels, passwords, and other information. Windows 2000 has integrated smart card technology, and it is an important part of the system's public key infrastructure security feature. Windows 2000 supports smart cards that are PC/SC (personal computer/smart card) compliant and Plug and Play, but it does not support non-PC/SC compliant cards. A manufacturer might supply a driver for a non-PC/SC for Windows 2000; however, it is recommended that only compliant PC/SC Plug and Play smart cards be used.

PC Card, CardBus, and VL Devices

Windows 2000 supports PC Card products and CardBus, which is a 32–bit version of PC Card. CardBus allows portable computers to run high bandwidth applications. Video Electronics Standards Association (VESA) Local (VL) bus devices are not completely Plug and Play, but they work similarly to ISA devices.

Other Device Types

Many other devices not listed in this chapter can also take advantage of Plug and Play. One of the key elements needed is that the device has to provide a mechanism for identification and configuration. If the device complies with Plug and Play specifications and is designed for Windows 2000, odds are that it will work without a hitch. Some of these devices include IDE (Integrated Device Electronics) controllers, ECPs (extended capabilities ports), and communications ports.

One of the most common ports used for peripheral devices on a computer is the parallel port. If the parallel port is Plug and Play-compliant, it will meet Compatibility and Nibble mode protocols that are defined in IEEE 1284. These modes allow two-way communication between the host and the peripheral device. Devices that connect to the parallel port (such as Zip drives and digital camera disk readers) need the port to be Plug and Play-compliant as well as the device; otherwise, there will be compatibility problems. For example, if an IEEE 1284 printer cable for a new printer is plugged into the back of a Zip drive that is then plugged into the computer's parallel port using a non–IEEE 1284 cable, staff would be in an uproar because they would not be able to print to the new printer.

For a system that is totally Plug and Play, the BIOS must also meet Plug and Play specifications. The recommended BIOS for Windows 2000 Server is one that supports the ACPI standard. By using ACPI and Plug and Play devices, the operating system and BIOS can communicate with each other and share information about the system's resources as well as how the settings should be allocated. This provides a more secure and robust system.

Note: Although Windows 2000 Server is in essence a Windows NT upgrade, you cannot assume that a driver that worked with Windows NT will necessarily work with Windows 2000 Server. Remember to first check the HCL to see if the driver is listed.

Programs that ran in Windows 98 and required direct access to hardware, such as games and antivirus software, will not work in Windows 2000 Server. If versions of these products existed and worked in Windows NT, then the odds are they will function in Windows 2000 Server.

Configuring Hardware Devices

There will be times when you need to access a hardware device to make some changes, troubleshoot, or update your system. Windows 2000 Server creates and maintains a device tree, which is a record of the devices that are currently loaded and is based on the information found in the system's Registry. The device tree is created in RAM each time the system is started or whenever there is a dynamic change in the system's configuration.

The device tree contains device nodes within which are the unique identification codes, the list of required resources (IRQ, memory range), the list of allocated resources, and an indication if the device node is a bus.

To access the information in the device tree, you use the Device Manager. To use the Device Manager, go to the Control Panel, double-click the System applet, click the Hardware tab, then click the Device Manger button. Device Manager contains a representation of the active device tree and lists the system device nodes, which are the actual devices configured in your system.

Device Manager allows you to install or uninstall devices, troubleshoot problems, update drivers, and change the resources that are assigned to the devices. Figure 5.3 shows Device Manager.

The Computer Management Console replaces several tools that were found in Windows NT and is a valuable tool to work with hardware as well as other components in your system. Device Manager can also be accessed from the Computer Management Console. The Computer Management Console is shown in Figure 5.4. It can be found in Administrative Tools.

If a device is Plug and Play, then there are no true default settings because Windows 2000 Server identifies the device and its resource requests and

Figure 5.3   The Device Manager.

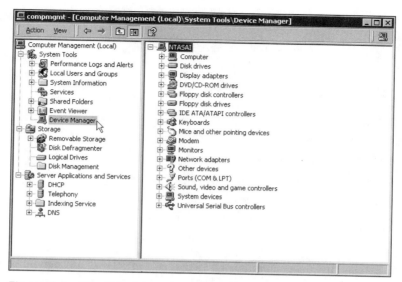

Figure 5.4   The Windows 2000 Computer Management Console.

allocates the settings in reference to the other devices. If one device requests the same settings as another, the system will adjust the settings to accommodate the request. For this reason, it is important that you do not change the resource settings for a Plug and Play device unless absolutely necessary. If you change the resource settings, you will effectively fix the setting for that particular device, and Windows 2000 Server will no longer be able to manipulate the resource if another device requests those settings.

Before you attempt to change a device's resource settings, be aware of the consequences. You can do some real damage to your system and possibly even lose the ability of Plug and Play. Windows 2000 Server does provide the ability to boot into Safe Mode (like Windows 95 and 98). The system can be started in Safe Mode with a minimum number of drivers loaded, which will allow you to make changes or remove a faulty driver.

Make sure that the conflict or problem is a resource conflict and not a missing or incorrect driver. If you did make a change and want to go back to the original settings, you can bring back the original settings by checking the Use Automatic Settings box under the Resources tab of the Device Properties page in Device Manager as shown in Figure 5.5.

If you do need to configure a device manually, then you should first identify a free resource (meaning one that is not already taken by another device). This is done through the System applet in the Control Panel. Select the Hardware tab and click the Device Manager button, then select Resources By Type or

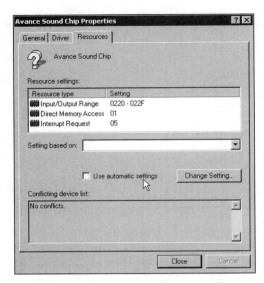

Figure 5.5   Use Automatic Settings box in Device Manager.

Figure 5.6   Device Manager displaying resources by type.

Resources By Connection from the View menu, and expanding the IRQ section. Once you have this information (an example is shown in Figure 5.6), assign the device this resource. Keep in mind as well that a legacy device cannot have its resources dynamically allocated by Windows 2000 Server, and therefore it is best to remove a conflicting legacy device and its drivers and replace it with a device that is compliant with Windows 2000 Server.

A handy technique to use prior to making any device changes is to print the system settings. Doing so establishes a baseline of the devices in your system and their configurations if your modifications do not turn out as expected. This can be very useful when trying to work out a problem when devices have resource conflicts. To print a report, go to Device Manager and click Print. In the Print dialog box, select the type of report that you want, as shown in Figure 5.7.

Let's actually walk through changing a device's resource setting. One more time, a word of caution is needed. You should only change a device's resource settings when absolutely needed. Changing resource settings can cause conflicts and may even potentially cause your system to lose Plug and Play functionality.

Figure 5.8 shows a device that has not been detected and cannot be configured by the operating system. It is an old legacy, non–Plug and Play sound card. Notice the settings Windows 2000 Server does not give in the following Figure 5.9.

Note: Read the instructions carefully and do not perform this on any of your production machines. If you have a legacy device that uses jumpers, you need to make the changes on the actual device's jumpers to match what you have changed using Device Manager.

The following list shows the steps needed to change a device's resource settings.

1. In Device Manager, expand the device class to show the available devices.

2. Double-click the device you want to change, and then click Properties. The Device Properties dialog box is displayed.

3. Click the Resources tab. Notice that the Conflicting Device List shows any conflicting values for resources used by other devices.

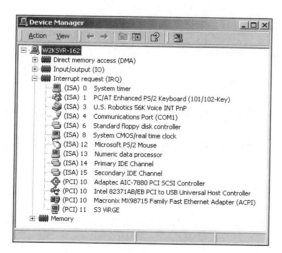

Figure 5.7   The Print dialog box.

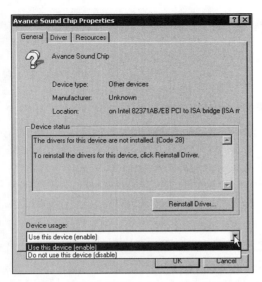

Figure 5.8   Device Manager displaying a device that is not configured.

Figure 5.9   Device Manager displaying the faulty driver's resource settings.

4. In the Resource Type list, select the setting you want to change. Make sure the Use Automatic Settings box is not checked.

5. Click Change Setting. The dialog box for editing the particular setting is displayed. (If a conflict arises, a message will be displayed in the Conflict Information field.)

6. Choose a setting that does not conflict with any other devices, and then click OK.

7. Restart Windows 2000 Server. Then, verify that the settings are correct for the device.

One last note: Windows 2000 Server has the capability to change from uniprocessor support to multiprocessor support through the Device Manager. With Windows NT, you had to use a *Resource Kit* utility named Uptomp, or you had to reinstall the entire operating system.

HIDDEN AND PHANTOM DEVICES

Device Manager does not show all devices by default. Some devices are hidden; for example, some non–Plug and Play devices are hidden. If a device is hidden and is not currently attached to the system, then it is called a phantom device. Viewing hidden devices is relatively easy, whereas viewing phantom devices requires the use of the command prompt (there is no way to distinguish which devices are hidden, phantom, or installed).

To view a hidden device, go to Device Manager | View | Show Hidden Devices. Any devices that are hidden should come into view.

Viewing a phantom device will demand one extra step: You will need to use the command prompt to issue a statement before getting into Device Manager. To do so, perform the following steps:

1. At the command prompt, type

```
set DEVMGR_SHOW_NONPRESENT_DEVICES=1
```

2. Start Device Manager, or

3. At the command prompt, type

```
start devmgmt.msc
```

If you want to set Device Manager to always show phantom devices, then go to the Control Panel, open the System applet, and click the Advanced tab. Then, in the Environment Variables box, type

```
set DEVMGR_SHOW_NONPRESENT_DEVICES=1
```

CONFIGURING MONITORS

With Windows 2000 Server, you can use the Display applet in the Control Panel to configure a variety of settings concerning your display. Items, such as changing the display driver, changing the screen resolution and depth, changing color schemes and text styles, viewing changes to the display before they take effect, configuring display settings for each hardware profile, and configuring multiple monitors (up to nine), are the types of configurations you can modify. This section discusses configuring the display driver.

A superb feature of Windows 2000 Server and Professional is the ability of the system to not allow incompatible display drivers from preventing access to the system. If a display driver fails to load during startup, Windows 2000 Server will use the generic VGA display driver. This ensures that you can start Windows 2000 Server and fix the display driver problem.

You can display, change, configure, or upgrade a display driver in either the Display applet in the Control Panel or through Device Manager. If you purchase a new Plug and Play monitor, you will most likely also receive an adapter. The first step in installing the monitor and adapter is to shut down the Windows 2000 Server. Physically install the adapter and attach the monitor. The system will detect the new monitor during startup and the wizard will guide you through the installation process. After the process is finished, go to Device Manager and click the Monitors node. Double-click the previous monitor, and click the Uninstall button to remove it.

If you need to install a driver, first obtain the driver from the manufacturer (the driver should be supplied on a floppy disk or CD, the Windows 2000 Server CD, or perhaps you can download it from the manufacturer's Web site). Once you have the appropriate driver, follow these steps:

1. Go to Device Manager and expand the Monitors node.

2. Double-click the monitor you need to update; select Properties.

3. Click the Drivers tab.

4. Click the Update Driver button and select the Display A List Of The Known Drivers For This Device So That I Can Choose A Specific Driver option.

5. Select Have Disk, and then click Next. Follow the prompts to install the driver.

If the monitor is not detected, this could mean that either the display adapter or the monitor is not Plug and Play or that it is not compatible with the Plug and Play features of Windows 2000 Server (see the previous section on Plug and

Play). In this case, the monitor will be detected as Default Monitor, and you will need to get an updated driver. If the manufacturer has an updated Windows 2000 INF file that you can install, then follow these steps:

1. Go to Device Manager and expand the Monitors node.

2. Double-click the monitor you need to update.

3. Select Properties, and then click the Drivers tab.

4. Click the Update Driver button.

5. Select the Display A List Of The Known Drivers For This Device So That I Can Choose A Specific Driver option, and click Next.

6. Under Models, choose a driver that is associated with the new monitor or click Have Disk and follow the prompts to install the INF file.

Display monitors are power hungry, and because of this, manufacturers have made attempts to incorporate energy saving features. Through signals from the display adapter, software can place the monitor in standby mode or even turn it off completely, which can reduce the power the monitor needs. Most of the instruction/guide booklets that come with new monitors list the power consumption levels. These features have been available for quite some time.

Windows 2000 Server has a feature called Mode Pruning, which can be used to remove display modes that the monitor cannot support. Mode Pruning compares the graphics modes of the monitor with the adapter, and only the modes that are usable to both will be made available. To enable Mode Pruning, follow these steps:

1. Go to the Control Panel and double-click Display.

2. Click the Settings tab.

3. Click Advanced, and then click the Monitor tab.

4. Select the Hide Modes That This Monitor Cannot Display option.

5. Click Apply.

Figure 5.10 shows the screen where you would select the option of Hide Modes That This Monitor Cannot Display.

HANDLING DRIVER SIGNING OPTIONS

Driver signing has been included in Windows 2000 Server to help promote better driver quality. By using driver signing, a user installing a driver on a Windows 2000 Server or a Windows 98 machine is given notification that the driver has passed all Windows Hardware Quality Labs (WHQL) tests.

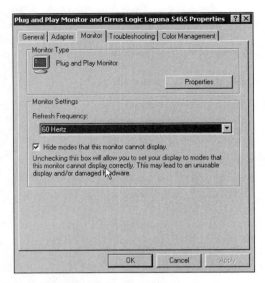

Figure 5.10   Selecting display modes.

Without some form of testing, the operating system could be brought down due to a faulty driver produced by a third party. This was a major problem with Windows NT. The WHQL tests drivers that run on Windows 2000 Server and gives those that pass a digital signature. This signature is associated with the driver and is recognized by Windows 2000 Server. By doing this, the user is assured that the driver is identical to the one that has been tested by Microsoft and found compliant.

Memory leaks were also a constant problem with Windows NT and caused system crashes or the dreaded "Blue Screen Of Death" (BSOD). Many administrators scheduled weekly system reboots to restore the server because of the memory leaks. Most of the time, memory leaks could be traced back to a faulty driver produced by a third party. This is why Microsoft took the initiative to create driver signing and the digital signature verification. Figure 5.11 shows the screen from which you can access driver signing. Anyone who has suffered system crashes associated with memory leaks and BSOD will greatly appreciate the comfort driver signing provides.

Three responses are given with driver signing: Warn, Block, and Ignore. The Warn mode is the default setting. Table 5.5 shows the three different responses and what they mean.

If you are logged on as a member of the Administrators group, you can set as the system default the appropriate setting you want to apply for all users that

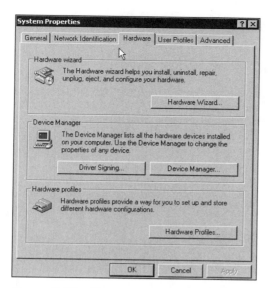

Figure 5.11   Hardware properties, Driver Signing button.

Table 5.5   Three responses of driver signing.

Response	Meaning
Warn	Cautions that the driver has not been signed and provides the option of whether to install it or not.
Block	Prevents all unsigned drivers from being installed.
Ignore	Allows all drivers to be installed, regardless of whether they have been signed.

log on to a particular computer. To set the signature verification options, open the Control Panel and double-click the System applet. Click the Hardware tab, and then click Driver Signing. Under File Signature Verification, click the option for the level of signature verification that you want to set.

Windows 2000 Server also includes Driver Verifier, discussed in the "Driver Verifier" section later in this chapter. This process scans for errors in kernel mode drivers and is able to react to the unstable driver without disrupting the system. Figure 5.12 shows the Code Signing Options window.

UPDATING DEVICE DRIVERS

There will be times when you need to update a device driver, and Windows 2000 Server provides flexible methods to do so. One of these methods is Windows Update, which users of Windows 2000 and Windows 98 have.

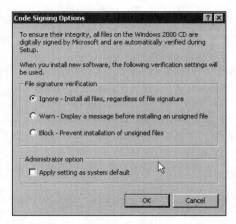

Figure 5.12   Code Signing Options window.

Windows Update allows your computer to install or update drivers from the Windows Update Web site. All drivers and updates on the Web site are WHQL tested and have been digitally signed.

To access this Web site, start at the Microsoft Web site and look for the link for Windows Update. You can also access Windows Update from the link in the Start menu (see Figure 5.13), from Device Manager, or from the Add Printer Wizard. When you access the Windows Update Web site, Microsoft's ActiveX controls compare the drivers installed on your system with the latest updates available. Obviously, if you have disabled ActiveX then you will have to enable it because it must be configured to run on your system for the Update to work.

Windows Update downloads and installs the drivers automatically. Only drivers that have the exact hardware ID as the devices that are installed are offered for download and installation. If there is an exact hardware ID match, Windows

Figure 5.13   Windows Update from the Start menu.

Update checks the driver version to see if the one being offered is more current than the one that is installed. At that point, the updated driver (a CAB file) is downloaded, and the ActiveX control directs the Device Manager to the INF file for installation.

If you would rather have more control updating the driver, instead of allowing Windows Update to do all the work, you can use another method to update the device. To update a driver, perform the following steps:

1. Go to the Control Panel, and double-click the System applet.

2. Select Device Manager.

3. Click the device mode whose driver you want to change.

4. Double-click the driver.

5. Select Properties. Click the Driver tab.

6. Click the Update Driver in the dialog box. This brings up the Upgrade Device Driver Wizard as shown in Figure 5.14.

The wizard asks if you want to search for a better driver and gives you the option of allowing Windows 2000 Server to detect it automatically or search for it yourself. To allow Windows 2000 Server to search for the driver, click the Search For A Suitable Driver For My Device option. Otherwise, click Display A List Of The Known Drivers For This Device So I Can Choose A Specific Driver, and you will have the opportunity to provide the information needed for the new driver.

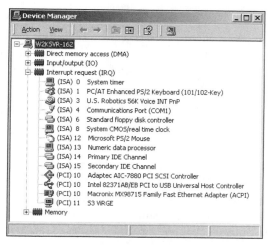

Figure 5.14   Upgrade Device Driver Wizard.

TROUBLESHOOTING HARDWARE PROBLEMS

As a rule, always use hardware and drivers that are digitally signed and on the Windows 2000 Server HCL, and make sure the drivers are updated. An ounce of prevention is indeed worth a pound of cure. Keeping good records is also essential, as well as having a good deal of patience.

A general step to take when trying to work out a problem is to attempt to isolate the problem and repeat the fault. By isolating the situation, you will be able to conduct separate tests that should point you to the resolution. This brings up a second point: Let the problem guide your solution. Try not to force something that may do more harm than good. Suspect the most recent change or addition, and inspect the most common points of failure. Finally, if you get to the point of total frustration, walk away and do something else. You will be surprised at how quickly a solution will come to the surface when you give yourself a chance and some time.

Understanding your system and having good records as to the layout, cabling, previous problems and solutions, upgrades, updates, and the hardware installation dates are vital. Most hardware problems stem from using equipment that is not on the HCL. An example of this is when a machine is upgraded to Windows 2000 Server without consideration of the hardware within it. Windows 2000 Server might be loaded and working fine, but most likely there will be intermittent problems whenever a noncompliant device is activated or when a particular software application needs to interact with a particular device. Without having a record of what is on the machine and what hardware is and is not on the HCL, it becomes quite a daunting task to determine where the problem resides.

There are also times when a piece of hardware that is on the HCL has a physical defect or a defect might surface at a later time. In this case, there is no alternative but to replace the device. Sometimes though, it might be that the device was not properly installed or configured, and it is well worth the effort to open the computer and make sure a device is seated properly.

Windows 2000 Server has several resources for you to use in the event of a hardware problem. You can use the Event Viewer for messages that might pertain to the problem. You can collect information as to the date, time, source, category, event, and other vital data that might help resolve the condition. The Last Known Good Configuration can be used to restore the system configuration to the last known working version, but this will only work if the system has not been logged onto yet. Whenever someone has been logged on, the system records a new Last Known Good Configuration.

Windows 2000 Server, like Windows 98, has a Safe Mode, which will start the system with a minimum amount of drivers loaded. In addition, the Registry can be edited, but this should only be used as a last resort and done by an experienced engineer. The Device Manager can be used to configure, update, or change a device, and if a device was recently updated by Windows Update, you can restore the original files by running Update Wizard Uninstall.

There are technical newsgroups that offer peer support for common computer problems. You can post persistent problems, and others who might have had the same experience will give you some suggestions. The Help file in Windows 2000 Server contains information about online support, and you can find information about newsgroups from Microsoft's Web site.

DRIVER VERIFIER

Driver Verifier is a tool that can isolate and troubleshoot a problem driver in the Windows 2000 Server system. A driver that is poorly written (for example, it may be using an inappropriate version of the WDM) can cause system corruption or failure because these components operate at the kernel level of the operating system. This is yet another reason why only drivers that have been tested and digitally signed should be used with Windows 2000 Server.

Driver Verifier is installed with Windows 2000 Server. You can launch Driver Verifier in two ways. One way is to use the Driver Verifier Manager (verifier.exe), which is located in the %WinDir%\System32 (%WinDir% represents the drive where your Windows files are located; usually, the path is c:\winnt\System32). The other method of launching Driver Verifier is through a Registry edit, but this is potentially very dangerous and should only be done by experienced system engineers.

Certain Registry edits can provide specific functions to resolve a problem, but you should isolate the problem first and research thoroughly the particular Registry edit prior to making any changes. Using the Registry Editor incorrectly can cause serious problems and may result in having to completely reinstall Windows 2000 Server.

TIP: You should back up the Registry before you edit it.

The Driver Verifier provides a fully functional tool with which you can access your system's health, which is why Driver Verifier Manager is the preferred means to activate and use Driver Verifier. It has a command-line interface as well as a graphical user interface. The Driver Status property page gives you an image of the current status of the Driver Verifier, as shown in Figure 5.15.

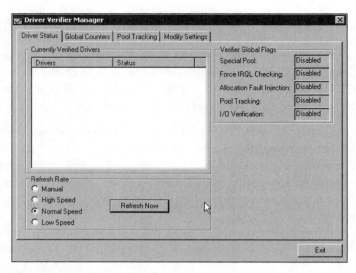

Figure 5.15 Driver Verifier.

Table 5.6 Driver Verifier status.

Status	Meaning
Loaded	The driver is currently loaded and verified.
Unloaded	The driver is not currently loaded, but has been loaded at least once since you restarted the computer.
Never Loaded	The driver was never loaded. This could mean that the driver is corrupt or is missing from the system.

Table 5.6 shows the options that can be listed with Driver Verifier.

You can sort the list of driver names by status or by clicking on the list header. You can also view the current types of verification that are in effect. The status of the drivers is updated automatically, unless you switch to manual refresh mode.

The pool tracking property page allows you to view statistics relating to pool allocations. To view the counters for a specific driver, select the driver name from the box. A driver should share pool allocations with the rest of the system; however, sometimes a poorly written driver will try to allocate more then its share of the pool (most common with legacy devices). The attempt to grab more resources than it is allotted may cause system corruption and instability. By using Driver Verifier, you can allocate all of a driver's pool allocations from a special pool, so that a faulty driver will be redirected to the special pool for its allocations, which will stabilize the system.

Driver Verifier also enables Pool Leakage Detection, which occurs when a driver unloads, but some of its allocations are not freed. Driver Unload Checking is performed to catch drivers that do not clean up resources used (such as look-aside lists, threads, queues, timers, and other resources). Again, this points back to drivers that have poorly written code.

Driver Verifier's Settings page allows you to modify and create Driver Verifier settings. Because any change to the settings will be made to the system Registry, you will have to reboot the computer for the settings to take effect.

You can run Driver Verifier from the command line. Table 5.7 shows some common flags used with Driver Verifier from the command line.

An example of a command line to use Driver Verifier is as follows:

```
C:\verifier /flags 3 /iolevel 2
```

which breaks down to the following:

```
verifier.exe /flags <value> [/iolevel 2]
```

Table 5.8 shows the list of available <value> parameters and their meanings.

Use either 1 or 2 for the /iolevel value. Level 2 verification is stronger than level 1.

Table 5.7   Driver Verifier command-line flags.

Command	Action Performed
verifier.exe /all	Verifies all the drivers in the system.
verifier.exe /volatile /flags <value>	Changes the verifier flags immediately.
verifier.exe /reset	Erases all current Driver Verifier settings.
verifier /query	Dumps the current Driver Verifier status and counters to the standard output.
verifier.exe /log LOG_FILE_NAME [/interval <seconds>]	Logs the Driver Verifier status and counters to a log file (where <seconds> is the period of time you specify).

Table 5.8   Value parameters and their meanings.

Value	Meaning
0	Special pool checking
1	Force IRQL checking
2	Low resources simulation
3	Pool tracking
4	I/O verification

The following command line example provides Pool Tracking and a level 2 verification of the system drivers.

```
C:\verifier /flags 3 /iolevel 2
```

Driver Verifier is a great tool if you must incorporate hardware that is not fully Plug and Play compatible or if you have a legacy driver of some sort. Drivers that are digitally signed should not demonstrate any unusual behavior, but armed with Driver Verifier, you can see for yourself if they do or don't.

Chapter Summary

This chapter explored the power Windows 2000 Server brings to the table in the form of Plug and Play. Plug and Play enables the operating system to dynamically allocate the resources for the hardware and drivers, which is one of the reasons that all hardware used should be listed on the HCL. Plug and Play support simplifies hardware installation and configuration tremendously.

This chapter examined the Windows 2000 Server hardware environment and Plug and Play's role in that environment. It also discussed how to configure hardware devices and provided an introduction to hidden and phantom devices.

Windows 2000 Server driver classes and structures were also discussed. This exploration of drivers included managing driver signing options, updating device drivers, and troubleshooting hardware problems.

Windows 2000 Server supports more devices then any version of Windows NT. This chapter explored how to identify the hardware supported by Windows 2000 Server. It is clear that Microsoft has listened to its customers by increasing the reliability, availability, and scalability of Windows 2000.

Review Questions

1. You have a Windows NT 4.0 Server that you want to upgrade to a Windows 2000 Server. The server has a 4GB hard drive (one partition), 200MHz CPU, 64MB of RAM, and 24x speed CD-ROM drive. All of the hardware is listed on the Windows 2000 Server HCL. What do you need to change in order to have a successful upgrade?

   a. Nothing, all the hardware is listed on the HCL, so no change is needed.

   b. Replace the hard drive with one that has at least 10GB of space.

   c. Replace the 233MHz CPU with one that is at least 500MHz.

   d. Add an additional 64MB of RAM.

2. You have just upgraded your Windows NT 4.0 Server to Windows 2000 Server. You notice that your devices that are Plug and Play are not functioning with all the supported features that they have. What can you do to enable full Plug and Play functionality?

   a. Through Device Manager, edit the properties of each device so that Plug and Play is enabled.

   b. Remove and then reinstall the devices using the Add/Remove Hardware applet in Control Panel.

   c. Check to see if the BIOS is using Advanced Configuration and Power Interface (ACPI), and if not, obtain a BIOS update.

   d. Windows 2000 Server does not support Plug and Play, which is why the devices are not functioning correctly.

3. Which of the following do not meet Windows 2000 Server's minimum requirements for an installation on a new computer? [Choose all that apply]

   a. 128MB of RAM

   b. 8x CD-ROM

   c. 120MHz CPU

   d. 2GB hard drive

4. Which of the following can you use to determine if a two-year-old Windows NT server can be upgraded to Windows 2000 Server? [Choose all that apply]

   a. NTHQ

   b. Windows 2000 Readiness Analyzer

   c. Windows 2000 Server System HAL analyzer

   d. HCL

5. You want to run the Windows 2000 Readiness Analyzer Tool from the command prompt. Which of the following is correct? (The CD-ROM drive is drive d.)

   a. d:\i388>winnt32 /checkupgradeonly

   b. d:\i386>winnt32exe /checkupgradeonly

   c. d:\i386>winnt32 /checkupgrade

   d. d:\i386>winnt32 /checkupgradeonly

6. Your boss has purchased a new PinAmp DF-400 IEEE 1394 board and wants it installed in the new Windows 2000 Server. You followed the installation instructions, but the board doesn't work. What is the most likely cause of this problem?

   a. You used the vendor's installation instructions instead of Windows 2000 Server's Plug and Play capability, which resulted in the board being installed improperly.

   b. The board is not listed on the Windows 2000 Server HCL.

   c. You need to adjust the resource settings through the Registry.

   d. You forgot to write a digital signature on the board.

7. Windows 2000 Server was successfully installed on a machine with 128MB of RAM. The system runs very slowly. What can you do to improve performance?

   a. Increase the amount of RAM to 256MB or more.

   b. Run Windows 2000 Readiness Analyzer to ensure that this machine meets all Windows 2000 Server requirements.

   c. View the HCL for tips on increasing speed.

   d. Increase the speed of the hard drive.

8. Windows 2000 Server can utilize the Plug and Play features of Windows NT 4.0 Server.

   a. True

   b. False

9. Which of the following allow you to view hidden devices in Device Manager?

   a. At the command prompt type:

   ```
   set DEVMGR_SHOW_NONPRESENT_DEVICES=1
   ```

   b. In Device Manager, click the View menu, and then select Show Hidden Devices.

   c. Access the device tree, and select the option to Show Hidden Devices.

   d. Open Explorer, and click the Tools menu, then select Show All Devices.

10. You have a one-year-old Windows NT 4 Server that you want to upgrade to Windows 2000 Server. You make an inventory of the hardware and find that it is all listed on the HCL for Windows 2000 Server. The computer consists of one 350MHz Pentium processor, a 10GB hard drive, ACPI

BIOS, 256MB of RAM, and a 36x CD-ROM. After you install Windows 2000 Server, power management and Plug and Play functionality is not present. What is the problem?

a. When Windows 2000 Server first installs, it fixes all the devices to specific resource settings. You need to go into Device Manager, click Enable Plug And Play from the Tools menu, and reboot the system.

b. When Windows 2000 Server was being installed, you did not select the Enable Plug And Play option during the GUI Setup phase.

c. You need to obtain a BIOS update from the system manufacturer.

d. You should install Windows 2000 Professional first, and then upgrade it to Windows 2000 Server in order to achieve full Plug and Play functionality.

11. During installation, Windows 2000 Server fails to recognize one of your system's SCSI drivers, but you are able to complete the installation. How can you resolve this problem? [Choose all that apply]

a. After installation, add the device through the Add/Remove Hardware applet in the Control Panel.

b. Stop the installation, remove the device, and replace it with one that is on the HCL.

c. After installation, use the Configure Wizard and supply the appropriate driver disks.

d. Stop the installation, and restart the computer. The device will then be found.

12. You have an IEEE 1394 device that does not state whether it is OHCI compliant or not, but the manufacturer supplies a disk and states that the driver will work with Windows 2000 Server. What is the best decision to make in regard to this device?

a. Install the device and the driver.

b. Go to the manufacturer's Web site and confirm that the driver will work with Windows 2000 Server.

c. Do not install the device and driver; purchase another one that is clearly marked that it is OHCI compliant.

d. Install the device and driver, then shut down and restart the machine. If Windows 2000 Server detects and loads the driver, it will work.

13. After moving a new Windows 2000 Server machine that has a Plug and Play network adapter card that is on the HCL, the server cannot connect to the network and you are receiving error messages. What are the most likely causes of this problem? [Choose all that apply]

    a. The cable to the Windows 2000 Server is not properly connected. Check all connections.

    b. The network adapter card is not properly seated.

    c. Plug and Play does not support network adapter cards, so Windows 2000 Server cannot allocate the appropriate resource settings for the card.

    d. Windows 2000 Server assigned a conflicting resource setting for the card.

14. Windows 95, 98, and Windows 2000 Server all share the same specifications for Plug and Play.

    a. True

    b. False

15. Your Windows 2000 Server has been set up and is running with no glitches. You read in a technical journal that a device driver you have has been updated and is available for download. What is the quickest and most reliable way to obtain the new updated driver?

    a. Call the manufacturer and have them send you a disk with the updated driver.

    b. Go to the manufacturer's Web site and download the updated driver.

    c. Use Windows Update and download the updated driver.

    d. Email the manufacturer and request that they send you the updated driver via email.

16. You are the network administrator of a small office, and you do not want users to install unsigned drivers to the Windows 2000 Server or their Windows 2000 Professional machines. What is the best way to do this?

    a. Send each user a memo asking them not to install unsigned drivers.

    b. Set the signature verification option to Block on all computers.

    c. Use Device Manager and under Options select Alert Administrator Of Unsigned Drivers.

    d. Select Ignore under the File Signature Verification in Driver Signing.

17. You need to change a device's resource setting in Windows 2000 Server. What is the best method to use?

a. Use Device Manager, click the device, click Properties, click the Resources tab, and change the setting as needed.

b. Edit the Registry to make the appropriate changes.

c. Use Control Panel, Devices, and double-click the device. Click Properties, and then on the Resources tab to make the changes needed.

d. Reboot the computer, and Windows 2000 Server will offer you a window to make system changes during startup.

18. You have a serial mouse on port COM1 installed with your Windows 2000 Server. You want to change it to a Plug and Play PS/2 mouse. How would you go about this?

a. Plug the new mouse into the PS/2 port. Windows 2000 Server will automatically detect it and you can start to use it.

b. In the Control Panel, double-click Mouse, and on the Hardware tab, click Properties. On the Driver tab, click Update Driver, and follow the prompts.

c. In the Control Panel, double-click Mouse, and on the Hardware tab, click Properties. Change the ports from COM1 to PS/2.

d. Windows 2000 Server does not support PS/2; purchase a USB mouse device.

19. You have recently started to receive error messages with your Windows 2000 Server, but you cannot determine the cause solely from the error message. What options do you have to get more information on a problem? [Choose all that apply]

a. Use the Dr. Watson tool provided with Windows 2000 Server.

b. Check Event Viewer for information that might identify the device or driver causing the problem.

c. Check Service Manager to see if any devices have failed to initialize.

d. Remove any newly installed hardware.

20. You received a STOP boot sector 0x0000007F error message. What can you do to diagnose and resolve this problem? [Choose all that apply]

a. Try removing or replacing newly installed hardware.

b. Restart your computer. At the startup screen, press F8 for Advanced Startup options, and select Last Known Good Configuration.

c. On the Web, search the Microsoft Knowledge Base for stop 0x0000007F and review the recommendations.

d. Check the Event Viewer.

21. You are the network administrator of a Windows NT 4.0 domain with one PDC, 4 BDCs, 50 Windows NT 4.0 Workstations, and 75 Windows 9x clients. You want to produce a reliable report as to what your system has, and what it will take to upgrade your entire network to Windows 2000. What is the best tool to use?

    a. Run Windows 2000 Readiness Analyzer on each computer and keep a record of the results.

    b. Install SMS Server and clients. Use SMS Server to produce a report on your network.

    c. Install GroupWise on one of the servers and have it analyze your network and produce a report.

    d. There is no need to use a tool; Windows 2000 Server and Professional are automatic upgrades to Windows NT and Windows 9x.

REAL-WORLD PROJECTS

Note: This exercise assumes you have a test server with Windows 2000 Server and a test workstation with Windows 2000 Professional. Read the instructions carefully and do not perform this on any of your production machines.

A medium-sized real estate appraisal company has just hired Jeff Smith as its new network administrator. The president of the company is very forward-thinking and has just upgraded all the company's computers to Windows 2000 Server and Windows 2000 Professional workstations. He has hired an outside computer firm to set up, install, and upgrade all the computers in the office. There are, however, some details that still need to be worked out.

Before Jeff can dive into the network administration aspect of his job, the president wants him to work out the kinks and bugs relating to hardware. The president also wants to see how Jeff will respond, as this will serve as a gauge to determine Jeff's competence.

The office consists of three servers running Windows 2000 Server software. One server is a dedicated file and print server, the second runs Internet Information Server and hosts the company's Web site, and the third maintains the company database. There are 20 workstations running Windows 2000 Professional.

The users rely heavily on the file and print server to store their reports, and they also use Zip drives at their workstations to locally store their reports and images. One user who considers herself a "power user" has an internal modem in her machine, which she uses primarily to fax her documents.

The problems the company faces are as follows:

➤ When the employees plugged in their Zip drives, Windows 2000 did not detect them, and they don't have any installation disks to load the drivers.

➤ A power user's internal modem is not functioning. Her computer was upgraded to Windows 2000 Professional, and the modem worked fine for a time, until she installed a network adapter card. The new network card worked, but then the modem wouldn't work at all. She says she has installed and removed the driver over and over, but it still doesn't work, and she insists that she did nothing to the modem when she installed the network adapter card.

➤ The president bought a new monitor for the file and print server, but the colors are not as crisp and detailed as they should be. He checked and found that the server monitor is only using 16 colors in its settings, and he wants it changed to at least High Color 16-bit. He has received a disk from the company that upgraded the system and was told that some kind of "driver" was on it, although he was not really sure what they were saying.

➤ The file and print server is supposed to be a multiprocessor server, but it is currently only running on one processor. The server has two processors. Jeff is to change the server, so that it becomes a multiprocessor server.

➤ Jeff needs to add an additional 128MB of RAM to the file and print server. The company has already purchased the appropriate 128MB DIMM.

Jeff is confident that he can get the jobs done with minimal interference to the staff and their work. Grabbing his toolkit and notepad, he sets off to work.

Project 5.1
To get the Zip drive to function, perform the following steps:

1. Check the cables to and from the Zip drive, and ensure that they are secure and tight.

2. Check that the Zip drive has power (a light should be on the drive).

3. Go to Control Panel and double-click the System applet.

4. Click the Hardware tab, then click Device Manager.

5. Expand the nodes for the ports (COM or LPT).

6. Double-click the port to which the Zip drive is connected.

7. Click Properties; then, on the Port Settings tab, select Enable Legacy Plug And Play Detection checkbox.

8. Click OK.

Once this process was successfully completed, Jeff repeated this process for the remaining workstations. This took him the better part of the afternoon. When he finished, he went to work on the workstation with the problem modem.

Project 5.2

To troubleshoot an internal modem that is not functioning, perform the following steps:

1. Open Control Panel, and double-click the System applet.

2. Click the Hardware tab, and click Device Manager.

3. Expand the node for modems. There should be a yellow question mark or exclamation point beside it.

4. Double-click the modem driver.

5. Read the error message(s).

6. Close all windows and exit Device Manager. Close all open applications and shut down. Turn off the monitor.

7. Disconnect the power cable and the monitor cable.

8. Open the case and locate the internal modem.

Once Jeff found the internal modem, he noticed that it was not secured in the PCI slot; one end was slightly protruding. The user must have pushed it loose when installing the network adapter card. He pushed the modem snuggly into its place and tightened the nut.

9. Close the case, connect the power cable and monitor cable.

10. Turn on the monitor and computer. Log on to the system.

11. Check Device Manager. The modem should not have a yellow question mark beside it. The device should be assigned resource settings in properties.

12. Go to Control Panel and double-click Phone And Modem Options. Use the test feature to ensure that the modem works properly.

Jeff had the user launch Internet Explorer. She was online in a matter of moments and as happy as could be. Jeff then proceeded to the Windows 2000 Server.

Because it was the end of the day, many of the staff had left. Jeff asked the few remaining staff members to log off the network. He shut down the computers that he found left on.

Project 5.3
To update the server's monitor driver, perform the following steps:

1. Open Control Panel; double-click the System applet.

2. Click Hardware, and then click Device Manager.

3. Expand the node for monitor.

4. Double-click the driver.

5. Click the Update Driver button.

6. Select Display A List Of The Known Drivers For This Device So That I Can Choose A Specific Driver, as shown in Figure 5.16.

7. Select Have Disk; click Next.

8. Place the floppy disk with the driver into the floppy disk drive (A:\), and select this as the location for the driver.

9. Windows 2000 Server scans the disk and displays the driver. Click Next.

10. The driver is loaded.

Project 5.4
To change the server from a uniprocessor to a multiprocessor server, perform the following steps:

1. Open Control Panel; double-click the System applet.

2. Choose the Hardware tab, then Device Manager.

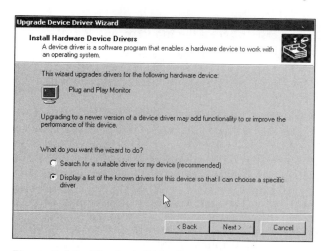

Figure 5.16   The Install Hardware Device Drivers screen.

3. Select the computer node and expand it.

4. Double-click the object located there.

5. Choose the Driver tab; click the Update Driver button.

6. The Upgrade Device Driver Wizard starts. Click the Next button.

7. Select the Display A Known List Of Drivers For This Device So That I Can Choose A Specific Driver. Click Next.

8. In the Select Device Driver page, select Show All Hardware Of This Device Class.

9. Select the appropriate multiprocessor option; click Next.

10. Double-check that the wizard has what you want, and click Next to complete the upgrade process.

Jeff then shut down and rebooted the Windows 2000 Server. He only had one more task to go.

Project 5.5

To upgrading Windows 2000 Server's RAM from 128 MB to 256 MB, perform the following steps:

1. Press Ctrl+Alt+Delete to bring up Task Manager. Make a note of Windows 2000 Server memory usage and total memory.

2. Close all programs, shut down the server, and turn off the power. Turn off the monitor and disconnect the monitor cable from the server. Disconnect the power cable from the server.

3. Open up the server's case to access the motherboard. Read the motherboard instruction book to positively identify where the DIMM slot is located.

4. Carefully insert the additional 128MB DIMM RAM into the available slot.

5. Replace the server's case, and plug the monitor back into the server. Reattach the power cable to the server.

6. Start up the computer. Watch the memory count and be sure that it equals the new amount of memory you just installed.

7. Let Windows 2000 Server load and log on as the administrator.

8. Press Ctrl+Alt+Delete and select Task Manager. View and record the new settings to be sure the new amount of system memory is being applied.

Note: *If you experience any problems at the initial startup of the server, for example, the server does not load or there is a set of loud beeps, remove the extra RAM. The RAM must be identical to the amount that is currently in place.*

What a first day Jeff had, but he felt good that he was able to accomplish all the tasks. He went to the president's office and told him the good news. The president was very happy with Jeff and said that he would make a fine addition to the company.

5

CHAPTER SIX

MANAGING SYSTEM PERFORMANCE, RELIABILITY, AND AVAILABILITY

After completing this chapter, you will be able to:

✓ Use the Task Manager

✓ Use the System Monitor

✓ Record Counter Logs and scan for Alerts

✓ Manage boot options and the boot.ini file

✓ Work with Windows 2000 Backup

✓ Use the Recovery Console

✓ Use IntelliMirror and Remote Installation Service

Performance monitoring and tuning for Windows 2000 can be performed using numerous native tools. In general, Windows 2000 is self-sufficient and self-tuning. However, in some cases, you may find that slight alterations in process priority, active services, or service credentials can improve performance. The primary purpose of performance monitoring is to determine when a system is not upholding the load placed upon it adequately, to locate bottlenecks, and to predict trend load requirements for ongoing system upgrades. In addition to maintaining a high-performance system, you must also manage the reliability of a system along with its availability. Windows 2000 offers many self-healing features as well as many manually initiated repair processes. Windows 2000 also offers intelligent data and OS management through IntelliMirror. This chapter discusses performance monitoring and tuning, system recovery, and IntelliMirror using native Windows 2000 utilities.

MANAGING USE OF SYSTEM RESOURCES

System resources are not network shares or printers, but are the elements of a computer system that enable a system to function. These include memory, drive space, CPU execution, cache, and more. Watching how these elements operate over time can help you understand how to improve performance or allow you to prevent problems. In most cases, monitoring a system is the first step in performance tuning. There are several native Windows 2000 tools that can be used to view how a system is operating.

Task Manager

The Task Manager is a simple tool that provides information on applications, processes, and the general state of the CPU and memory resources. The Task Manager is often the first tool used to obtain a quick peek into the state of a system. When an application fails to respond promptly or the system as a whole becomes sluggish, the Task Manager can present you with the data to determine whether an application or a process is at fault or if just too little RAM is present in the computer.

Launching the Task Manager can be accomplished through at least three methods including:

➤ Entering the Ctrl+Shift+Esc key sequence

➤ Entering the Ctrl+Alt+Del key sequence, and then clicking the Task Manager button on the Security dialog box

➤ Right-clicking over an empty area of the taskbar, and then selecting Task Manager from the pop-up menu

The Task Manager is a dialog box containing three tabs: Applications, Processes, and Performance. The Applications tab (see Figure 6.1) lists all currently active User Mode applications. Beside each listed application, the status of that application is displayed. The possible status states are Running and Not Responding. In some cases, when an application is performing intense internal operations, it is assigned a temporary status of Not Responding. In most cases, if five to ten minutes pass and the status of an application fails to return to Running, you can assume that there really is a problem with the application. On the Applications tab, you have the ability to terminate an active application. Simply select the application from the list of tasks, and then click the End Task button. The system prompts you to confirm the termination. Clicking Yes at this prompt instructs the system to proceed with the termination process. Clicking No at this prompt aborts the termination process.

From the Applications tab, you may also change which application is currently in the foreground. The foreground application is the application that is currently selected and is able to receive mouse and keyboard I/O. This is often indicated by a blue title bar when the default or standard Windows color scheme is in use. A foreground application is also given an execution priority boost of two levels. This is done to improve response time. Without opening Task Manager, you can change the foreground application by simply launching a new application, selecting another application window viewable on the desktop, or selecting another application from the taskbar. From within Task Manager, changing the foreground application is accomplished by selecting the application from the Task list on the Applications tab, and then clicking the Switch To button.

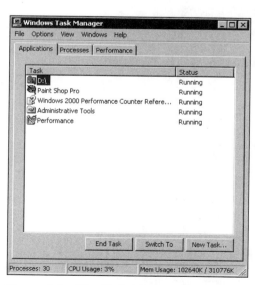

Figure 6.1   The Task Manager's Applications tab.

Another useful function on the Applications tab is the New Task button. This opens a dialog box similar to the Run command from the Start menu. Through the New Task dialog box, you can type in or browse for the path of an executable to launch. Once launched, the new task appears on the Applications tab as a new task.

A final function you may find helpful is the ability to jump to the Processes tab and locate the exact process associated with an active application. This is done by selecting an application, right-clicking on the selected application, and then selecting the Go To Process command. The Task Manager switches to the Processes tab and highlights the main process associated with the previously selected application.

The Processes tab (see Figure 6.2) displays a list of all active processes along with statistics and metrics associated with each process. By default, the Processes tab lists details in addition to the process. These details include the name of process ID (PID), the CPU utilization per second, the total CPU usage time, and the current virtual memory usage. An additional 18 metrics can be selected to be displayed via the Select Columns command from the View menu. Each column of metrics can be sorted by clicking on the column heading name. The first click sorts in descending order, and the second click sorts in ascending order. You should notice a process named System Idle Process. This process is what the system executes when no other processes require access to the CPU. The CPU is actually never idle, but when this process is being executed no real work is being done.

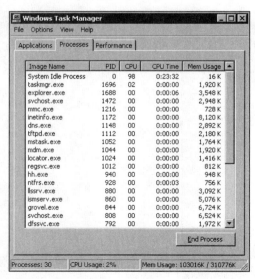

Figure 6.2   The Task Manager's Processes tab.

The Processes tab is the best place to look when attempting to determine which application or process is consuming the CPU's cycles. Simply sort the CPU column in descending order and take note of which process is consuming most of the CPU utilization. If it is any process other than the System Idle Process for more than a few seconds at a time, you have a process that may be operating abnormally. In some cases, you'll want to either adjust the properties of the process or application as advised by the vendor, and in other cases, you'll want to terminate the process. Process termination involves selecting the process, and then clicking the End Process button. The system prompts you to confirm the termination. Clicking Yes at this prompt instructs the system to proceed with the termination process. Clicking No at this prompt aborts the termination process.

As you know, Windows 2000 supports not only Win32 applications, but also DOS and Win16 applications. The NTVDMs (Windows Virtual DOS Machines) created by Windows 2000 to host DOS applications are automatically disassembled when the DOS processes terminate. However, in some cases, a DOS application does not properly terminate and the NTVDM remains. You can manually terminate the NTVDM process by selecting it from the Processes tab and clicking the End Process button. Windows 2000 launches WOWEXEC on top of an NTVDM process to create the environment for Win16 applications. Even when a Win16 application is exited properly, Windows 2000 retains the WOWEXEC environment just in case another Win16 application is launched at a later time. If you run Win16 applications infrequently, it is often a good idea to terminate the Win16 environment manually. On the Processes tab, you'll see WOWEXEC listed as a subelement of an NTVDM process. You can select either WOWEXEC or NTVDM from such a pair, and then click the End Process button to disassemble the Win16 environment. This is also a good method to use to terminate a hung Win16 process without rebooting.

The Processes tab also offers users the ability to change the execution priority of User Mode processes. The execution priority of any application or process initiated by the current user can be altered. Not even administrators have the direct ability to alter Kernel Mode processes' execution priority. To change the execution priority, select a process, and then right-click on the selected process. From the pop-up menu, highlight the Set Priority command. This opens a submenu with the following execution priority options:

➤ *Realtime*—A priority level of 24. This setting is restricted to Administrators.

➤ *High*—A priority level of 13.

➤ *AboveNormal*—A priority level of 10.

➤ *Normal*—A priority level of 8.

➤ *BelowNormal*—A priority level of 6.

➤ *Low*—A priority level of 4.

Once you issue the command to change the priority level of a process, a message is displayed warning you that altering the process execution priorities can render a system unstable. You must then click Yes to proceed or No to abort the priority change process. Even though Windows 2000 has 32 levels (0 through 31) of execution priority and 16 of them are assigned to User Mode processes, only these 6 specific levels can be used to set or change process priorities by users or administrators. The Process Manager and the Microkernel (both located in Kernel Mode) have exclusive access and control over all 32 priority levels.

The Task Manager's Processes tab is the only method available to users and administrators to alter the execution priority of executing processes. However, the Start command utility can be used to launch applications with other than normal execution priority. For a complete listing of the syntax of this command issue **start /?** from a command prompt. The basic syntax to launch an application with a specific execution priority is **start /<*priority-level*> <*program*>** where <*priority-level*> is one of the six levels mentioned earlier (Realtime [for Administrators only], High, AboveNormal, Normal, BelowNormal, or Low). You can also use the Process tab to end a process tree. To do this, right-click a process and select End Process Tree. This stops the process and any related child processes.

The third tab of Task Manager is the Performance Tab (see Figure 6.3). This tab displays information about CPU usage in graphical form and memory usage in both graphical and numerical formats. A thermometer meter and a history graph is displayed for both CPU usage and memory usage. Below the graphs, 12 metrics about the state of memory are displayed:

➤ *Totals: Handles*—The number of system objects in use, such as files, Registry keys, and virtual machines.

➤ *Totals: Threads*—The number of execution threads from all active processes.

➤ *Totals: Processes*—The number of active processes.

➤ *Physical Memory (K): Total*—The size of physical RAM.

➤ *Physical Memory (K): Available*—The amount of unused physical RAM.

➤ *Physical Memory (K): File Cache*—The amount of physical RAM being used for caching files.

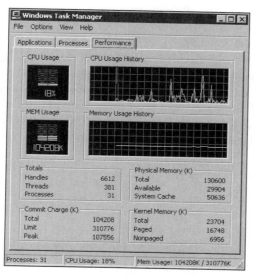

Figure 6.3   The Task Manager's Performance tab.

> *Commit Charge (K): Total*—The total amount of virtual memory allocated to processes or the system.

> *Commit Charge (K): Limit*—The maximum amount of virtual memory on the computer.

> *Commit Charge (K): Peak*—The maximum amount of virtual memory used during the boot session.

> *Kernel Memory (K): Total*—The amount of memory used by the kernel.

> *Kernel Memory (K): Paged*—The amount of total kernel memory that can be saved to a swap file.

> *Kernel Memory (K): Nonpaged*—The amount of kernel memory that always remains in physical RAM.

There are three other controls worth mentioning on this tab. The Show Kernel Times command in the View menu is used to display the portion of CPU usage consumed by Kernel Mode processes in red and consumed by User Mode processes in green. The CPU History command in the View menu is used to display multiple history graphs when two or more CPUs are present in the system. In addition, you can select Update Speed from the View menu to configure update intervals. The available settings are: High, Normal, Low, and Paused.

System Monitor

The System Monitor is the utility within Windows 2000 used to monitor the performance of system and user objects. This updated and improved tool can be used to monitor activity in realtime and record logs of activity for baseline extraction, bottleneck detection, and trending or capacity planning. The System Monitor (see Figure 6.4) is accessed through the Administrative Tools either in the Start menu or the Control Panel as Performance. The System Monitor is actually just one part of the Performance MMC snap-in included with Windows 2000. The second component is Performance Logs And Alerts, which is used to record logs of activity and initiate alerts based on custom thresholds.

The Real-Time Display of Performance is probably the feature of System Monitor that you will be least likely to use. Once you are familiar with System Monitor, most of your work with this tool will be reviewing data stored in recorded logs. You may still use the realtime capabilities to perform quick checks or verifications of alterations or to peek into the ongoing activity of a system, but this will be minimal in comparison to your time spent extracting useful information from recorded data.

The main view of the System Monitor displays the value of measured counters in a graph display by default. Using the toolbar or the System Monitor Properties dialog box, this information can be displayed in a thermometer histogram layout or in a text-only report layout. The toolbar at the top of the display contains the following single-click commands (from left to right):

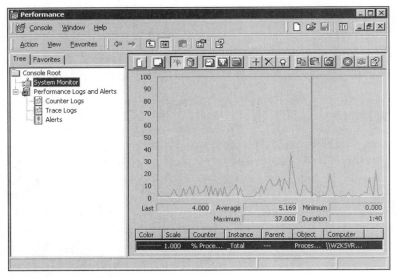

Figure 6.4 The System Monitor in chart view.

➤ *New Counter Set*—Clears the current selection of counters from the display, so a new set can be defined. The existing set of selected counters will be lost unless the console is saved.

➤ *Clear Display*—Clears the displayed measurements and restarts the charting from the left side of the screen. The current set of selected counters is not changed.

➤ *View Current Activity*—Selects realtime as the source for the displayed data.

➤ *View Log File Data*—Used to select the log file from which to pull the displayed data.

➤ *View Chart*—Sets the display to chart mode.

➤ *View Histogram*—Sets the display to histogram mode.

➤ *View Report*—Sets the display to report mode.

➤ *Add*—Adds one or more counters to the display.

➤ *Delete*—Removes the currently selected counter from the display.

➤ *Highlight*—Highlights the chart line of the selected counter.

➤ *Copy Properties*—Copies the current set of selected counters into the clipboard.

➤ *Paste Counter List*—Pastes the set of selected counters in the clipboard onto the display.

➤ *Properties*—Opens the System Monitor Properties dialog box.

➤ *Freeze Display*—A toggle switch used to halt the updating of the displayed activity.

➤ *Update Data*—Each time this button is pressed, performance information for the selected counters is added to the display. This button is only active when manual update is selected via the System Monitor Properties or when the display is frozen.

➤ *Help*—Opens the System Monitor section of the Windows 2000 Help system.

The three modes of display supported by System Monitor offer you various ways of viewing performance data. The chart view displays 100 data points from left to right connected by a line, resulting in a readout similar to a heart monitor. The histogram view (see Figure 6.5) displays either a single (in realtime) or an average (using a log source) value for each counter in a bar graph layout. The report view (see Figure 6.6) displays all the counters in text

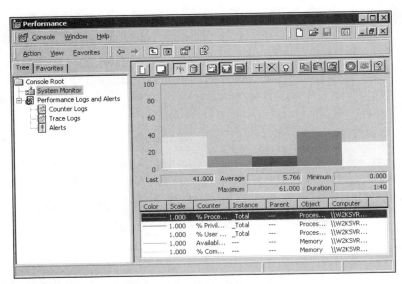

Figure 6.5   The System Monitor in histogram view.

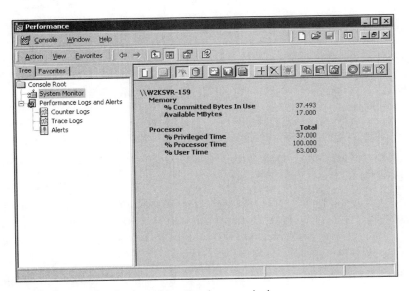

Figure 6.6   The System Monitor in report view.

and numerical format sorted in order by computer, object, and counter context. The report view displays just the last measurement (in realtime) or the average measurement (using a log source).

Below the displayed data area of the graph and histogram views is the legend and the value bar. The legend lists all added or selected counters currently being measured and displayed. The legend lists details, such as the color of the line used for the counter, the scale multiplier, the counter name, its instance, its parent (if applicable), its object, and its computer context; it can also be sorted in ascending or descending order. The value bar lists data relating to the last measurement, average measurement, minimum measurement, maximum measurement, and the graph duration (from left to right) for the selected counter from the legend.

Everything within the Windows 2000 environment is an object, including files, folders, and processes. Every object includes the capability to measure and report performance activity. The System Monitor is the tool created by Microsoft to read and report performance activity for all objects. Each object has a set of counters, and each measures a unique object-specific value related to the operation of that object. In many cases, more than one object of a specific kind will exist within a system. When this occurs, you must indicate which instance of the object to measure. The act of performance monitoring focuses on accessing and reading counters for the desired objects hosted by either the local system or computers accessible via the network. Counters are added to the display area of System Monitor through the Add Counters dialog box (see Figure 6.7).

The Add Counters dialog box is accessed by clicking the Add button (the plus sign) in the toolbar of System Monitor. Counters are selected based on their computer and object context. The process of adding counters is the same no matter which view mode is in use or whether the source of the data is realtime or a log file. The Add Counters dialog box offers the following controls to select counters:

> *Use Local Computer Counters*—This selection defines the computer context as relative. If a console is saved with relative counters, when the console is

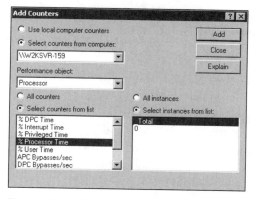

Figure 6.7   The Add Counters dialog box.

used on a different system, the selected counters pull data from that local system instead of the original computer where the console was defined. This selection is often used when creating a performance monitoring profile to be used against several systems on a network.

➤ *Select Counters From Computer*—This selection defines the computer context as absolute. A specific computer is named either by its NetBIOS name, its IP address, or its domain name. You can select a counter from the pull-down list or type one in.

➤ *Performance Object*—This list contains all objects available on the selected computer. Once an object is selected, the counter list is updated to list those counters contained by the selected object.

➤ *All Counters*—This selection is used to add all the counters from the selected object to the display area.

➤ *Select Counters From List*—This area is used to select one or more counters (hold down Shift to select a range or Ctrl to select individual items) to be added to the display area.

➤ *All Instances*—This selection focuses the selected counters on all instances of the selected object.

➤ *Select Instances From List*—This area is used to select one or more instances (hold down Shift to select a range or Ctrl to select individual items) for the selected counter to focus on. When two or more instances are selected, the counter displays the cumulative total from all selected instances of the counter.

The Add button on the Add Counters dialog box is used to add the selected object(s) to the display area. The Close button is used to close the Add Counters dialog box. The Explain button opens a floating window that displays information about the selected counter. This information typically describes what the counter is actually measuring and what the measurements mean.

Useful Counters

There are literally thousands of distinct displayable performance measurements available to you from a single system through the selections of object, counter, and instance. Attempting to view all this data at once is futile. Therefore, you need to focus your attention on smaller areas to look for big picture trends, and then focus on individual subcomponents as you track down a problem. Some of the more common counters to keep a regular watch on and appear most often on certification exams include the following:

➤ *Logical Disk: Current Disk Queue Length*—This counter is used to count the number of disk requests being processed or waiting to be processed by a volume. If this number exceeds two more than the number of spindles contained in the volume, either too much activity is being requested or the hard drive(s) supporting the volume are insufficient for their required tasks. Before assuming a hard drive is the problem, you should also monitor the Physical Disk object version of this counter. If both indicate a lengthy queue, consider upgrading your hard drive(s) and/or drive controller(s). Note that you must enable LogicalDisk counters via the **run** command or command prompt by typing "perfmon –yv". For more information on this, type "perfmon -?" from the command prompt or **run** command.

➤ *Logical Disk: %Disk Time*—This counter is used to measure the percentage of time that the volume is actually busy performing a read or write function. A sustained value of 80% or more over a lengthy period of time (which can mean 15 minutes or 5 hours, depending on the types of services and applications being hosted) and a long Current Disk Queue Length may indicate that the hard drive(s) and/or the drive controller(s) are insufficient for their required tasks.

➤ *Logical Disk: Avg. Disk Bytes/Transfer*—This counter is used to keep track of the average amount of data transferred to or from a volume during each read or write function. If this value remains near 4KB (the size of a memory page), then most of your drive activity is caused by paging. If other memory counters indicate that excessive paging is occurring, you should add more physical RAM to the system. If this value remains very large (more than 1% of your drive capacity), you should consider upgrading the hard drive(s) and/or the drive controller(s).

➤ *Memory: Available Bytes*—This counter is used to measure the total amount of physical RAM not being used by the system or any active process. This value should always remain greater than 4MB. If it falls below 4MB, you should add more physical RAM.

➤ *Memory: Cache Faults/sec*—This counter is used to count the number of times per second a desired memory page is not found in the processor cache and must be pulled from either physical RAM or the paging file. A low level of cache faults is typical, but a consistent high value indicates too little L2 cache. To establish what is normal (and therefore high or low), you must extract a baseline while performing normal system activities. You create a baseline by monitoring system activity during normal operations. In most cases, a value of twice normal is considered high.

6

➤ *Memory: Page Faults/sec*—This counter is used to count the number of times per second a memory page must be pulled from the paging file or from another location in physical RAM. A consistent high value (typically twice normal) indicates too little physical RAM.

➤ *Memory: Pages/sec*—This counter is used to count the number of times per second a memory page must be pulled from the paging file (known as a hard page). A consistent high value indicates too little physical RAM.

➤ *Network Interface: Bytes Total/sec*—This counter is used to measure the amount of data transmitted over a network interface per second. This value includes both inbound and outbound traffic. When this value approaches the maximum throughput for your network interface card (NIC) type, you should consider adding additional interfaces or upgrading your network technology.

➤ *Network Interface: Current Bandwidth*—This counter indicates the size of the current total bandwidth of a network interface. This counter only varies on connections supported by modems or other variable bandwidth devices. If Network Interface: Bytes Total/sec and this value are within 10% of each other, you should consider adding additional interfaces or upgrading your network technology.

➤ *Network Interface: Output Queue Length*—This counter is used to count the number of requests waiting to be processed by the network interface. If this value consistently exceeds two per network interface, you should consider adding additional interfaces or upgrading your network technology.

➤ *Physical Disk: Current Disk Queue Length*—This counter is used to count the number of disk requests being processed or waiting to be processed by a hard drive (or external RAID device). If this number exceeds two more than the number of spindles contained in the hard drive, either too much activity is being requested or the hard drive(s) are insufficient for their required tasks. Before assuming a hard drive is the problem, you should also monitor the Logical Disk object version of this counter (because the problem could be specific to only a single volume and be an issue with virtual memory or a service or application). If both indicate a lengthy queue, consider upgrading your hard drive(s) and/or drive controller(s).

➤ *Physical Disk: %Disk Time*—This counter is used to measure the percentage of time that the hard drive is actually busy performing a read or write function. A sustained value of 80% or more over a lengthy period of time (which can mean 15 minutes or 5 hours, depending on the types of services and applications being hosted) and a long Current Disk Queue Length may indicate that the hard drive(s) and/or the drive controller(s) are insufficient for their required tasks.

➤ *Physical Disk: Avg. Disk Bytes/Transfer*—This counter is used to keep track of the average amount of data transferred to or from a hard drive during each read or write function. If this value remains near 4KB (the size of a memory page), then most of your drive activity is caused by paging. If other memory counters indicate that excessive paging is occurring, you should add more physical RAM to the system. If this value remains very large (more than 1% of your drive capacity), you should consider upgrading the hard drive(s) and/or the drive controller(s).

➤ *Processor: %Processor Time*—This counter is used to keep track of the amount of time the CPU is performing actual work (i.e., not executing the System Idle Process task). A consistent value over 80% may indicate that the CPU(s) is not sufficient for the required tasks. Consider reducing the workload on this system or add additional CPU resources.

➤ *Processor: Interrupts/sec*—This counter is used to count the number of hardware interrupts executed by the CPU per second. If this value exceeds five times your baseline average, you may have a hardware malfunction. The most common culprits of this problem are NICs.

➤ *System: Processor Queue Length*—This counter is used to count the number of threads waiting to be processed by the CPU. If this value exceeds two times the number of CPUs present, then your system is not sufficiently powered to support the required tasks. Consider reducing the workload on this system or add additional CPU resources.

Controlling System Monitor

The layout and display of System Monitor can be customized through the System Monitor Properties dialog box. The General tab (see Figure 6.8) offers the following controls:

➤ *View*—Sets the display view mode to graph, histogram, or report. Set to graph by default.

➤ *Display Elements*—Toggles to display the legend, value bar, and toolbar. All enabled by default.

➤ *Report And Histogram Data*—Sets whether displayed information is the Default (based on type of counters displayed), Current (last measurement only), Average (across all measurements), Minimum (across all measurements), or Maximum (across all measurements). Set to Default by default.

➤ *Appearance*—Sets whether the display area is 3-D or flat. This does little to change its appearance. Set to 3-D by default.

6

Figure 6.8   The System Monitor Properties dialog box, General tab.

➤ *Border*—Sets the border of the display area to none or fixed single. This does little to change its appearance. Set to none by default.

➤ *Update Automatically Every ? Seconds*—Sets the update interval for realtime or the extrapolation interval for log data in seconds. Set to one second by default. Clearing this checkbox sets the display to manual update.

➤ *Allow Duplicate Counter Instances*—Sets whether each instance of an object is treated as a unique entity or not. Enabled by default.

The Source tab (see Figure 6.9) offers the following controls:

➤ *Current Activity*—Sets the source of measured data to realtime.

➤ *Log File*—Sets the source of measured data to a prerecorded log file.

➤ *Time Range*—A button used to extract the time range data from the indicated log file. This button has no function in relation to current activity.

➤ *Slide Bar*—A time range selection bar that indicates the start and stop timestamps included in the selected log file on top and the selected start and stop time stamps below. Clicking and dragging the endpoints of the range shortens or lengthens the selected data range.

The Data tab (see Figure 6.10) offers the following controls:

➤ *Add*—Adds new counters to the display area. Opens the Add Counters dialog box.

➤ *Remove*—Deletes the selected counter from the display area.

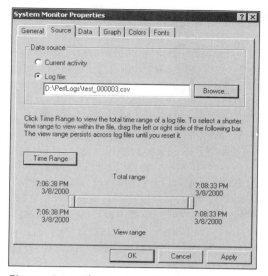

Figure 6.9   The System Monitor Properties dialog box, Source tab.

Figure 6.10   The System Monitor Properties dialog box, Data tab.

➤ *Color*—Sets the graph line color of the selected counter.

➤ *Scale*—Sets the scale multiplier for the selected counter. This item is used to shrink or enlarge a measurement to fit better with the absolute values of other measured counters.

➤ *Width*—Sets the width of the graph line for the selected counter.

➤ *Style*—Sets the line style of the graph line for the selected counter.

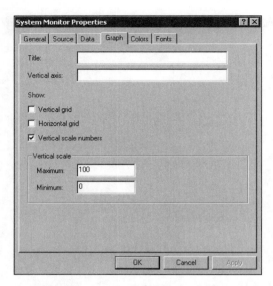

Figure 6.11 The System Monitor Properties dialog box, Graph tab.

The Graph tab (see Figure 6.11) offers the following controls:

➤ *Title*—Defines a title for the System Monitor display area. Blank by default.

➤ *Vertical Axis*—Defines a label for the vertical axis of the display area. Blank by default.

➤ *Vertical Grid*—Toggles to enable vertical line display to a set division of the display area. Disabled by default.

➤ *Horizontal Grid*—Toggles to enable horizontal line display to a set division of the display. Disabled by default.

➤ *Vertical Scale Numbers*—Toggles to enable display numbers on the vertical axis. Enabled by default.

➤ *Maximum*—Sets the uppermost value of the display area. 100 is the default.

➤ *Minimum*—Sets the lowermost value of the display area. 0 is the default.

The Colors tab (see Figure 6.12) is used to define the color schemes used throughout System Monitor.

The Fonts tab (see Figure 6.13) is used to define the fonts used to display numbers and letters throughout System Monitor. Any installed font can be selected along with its style, size, strikeout, or underlined values.

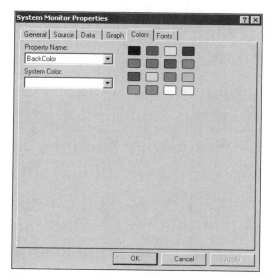

Figure 6.12   The System Monitor Properties dialog box, Colors tab.

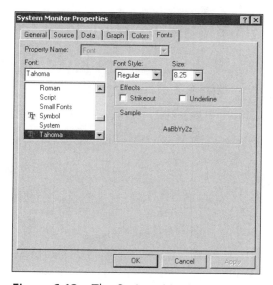

Figure 6.13   The System Monitor Properties dialog box, Fonts tab.

Logging
The real value of the native performance monitoring tools of Windows 2000 is the capability to record logs of performance data. The logging capabilities of Windows 2000 are a separate and distinct service from the System Monitor tool. This service enables logging to occur even when the System Monitor is

not open or in use. Once a log file is created, configured, and started, logging occurs in the background as long as necessary to gather the data you want to capture. Log data can be used to extract baselines, locate bottlenecks, and plan system capacity.

There are two types of logs that can be recorded by Windows 2000: Counter Logs and Trace Logs. Trace Logs require a custom built tool to extract their contents. Windows 2000 does not include such a tool, but details on creating your own tool are contained in the Resource Kit and the Software Development Kit for Windows 2000. The Counter Logs are the logs that can be read by System Monitor.

New Counter Logs can be created when the Counter Logs node, located underneath the Performance Logs and Alerts node of the Performance MMC plug-in (see Figure 6.1), is selected. Issue the New Log Settings command from the Action menu, provide a name for the Counter Log, and then set and define the desired counters and parameters. A Counter Log's dialog box is used to configure every aspect of the log. The General tab (see Figure 6.14) offers the following controls:

➤ *Add*—Adds new counters to the display area. Opens the Add Counters dialog box.

➤ *Remove*—Deletes the selected counter from the display area.

➤ *Interval*—Defines the interval at which measurements are taken and recorded into the log file. Interval is in numerals and has a default value of 15.

➤ *Units*—Sets the units for the interval in seconds, minutes, hours, or days. The default is seconds.

The Log Files tab (see Figure 6.15) offers the following controls:

➤ *Location*—The path to the folder where log files are stored.

➤ *File Name*—The full or prefix name of the log file.

➤ *End File Names With*—A toggle that enables multiple log files to be recorded with file names using sequential or various date layout numbering.

➤ *Start Numbering At*—Defines the sequential value to start with when "nnnnnn" is selected as the file name post-fix.

➤ *Log File Type*—Sets the type of file to be recorded to Binary (the default), Binary Circular File, Text File-CSV (comma delimited), or Text File-TSV (tab delimited). Note that when recorded in a text format, any text editor or data manipulation utility can extract or manipulate data from a log.

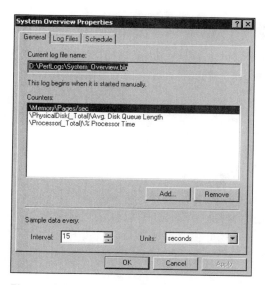

Figure 6.14   A Counter Log's Properties dialog box, General tab.

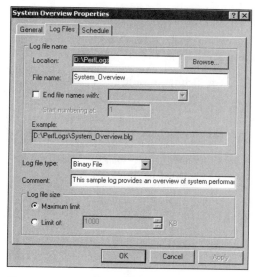

Figure 6.15   A Counter Log's Properties dialog box, Log Files tab.

➤ *Comment*—Used to define a comment for the log file.

➤ *Log File Size*—Used to set the log file size to either a maximum limit (the total amount of drive space available) or a limit in kilobytes.

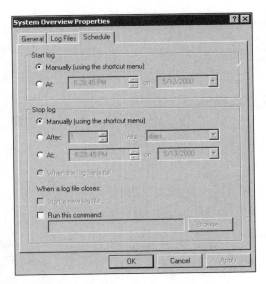

Figure 6.16   A Counter Log's Properties dialog box, Schedule tab.

The Schedule tab (see Figure 6.16) offers the following controls:

➤ *Start Log*—Used to define how a log file is started. Options are manually (or initiated by an alert) or at a specific time and date.

➤ *Stop Log: Manually*—Sets the stop point of a log file to manual.

➤ *Stop Log: After*—Sets the stop point of a log file to a time length.

➤ *Stop Log: At*—Sets the stop point of a log file to a specific date and time.

➤ *Stop Log: When The Log File Is Full*—Sets the stop point of a log file to the point at which the limit defined on the Log Files tab is reached.

➤ *Start A New Log File*—A toggle to enable the automatic creation of a new log file once the current log file is full or scheduled to be closed.

➤ *Run This Command*—Used to define an application or a batch file to launch at the termination of a log file.

A Counter Log can contain any mix of counters from local or remote systems. However, keep in mind that all counters defined within a single Counter Log are subject to the one sampling interval defined on the General tab of that Counter Log's Properties dialog box. To record counters at different intervals, you must define multiple Counter Logs.

A sample Counter Log entitled System Overview is predefined and contains the Memory: Pages/sec, Physical Disk: Avg. Disk Queue Length, and Processor: % Processor Time counters.

Once a Counter Log is defined, it can be started and stopped by issuing the appropriate command from the Action menu when selected. When a Counter Log's icon is green, it is actively recording data. When a Counter Log's icon is red, it is idle and not recording data. Counter Logs continue to record data even when the Performance interface is closed, and automated launches and terminations of Counter Logs occur even when the Performance interface is closed.

After a Counter Log is recorded, you can view its contents by selecting it on the Source tab of the System Monitor's Properties dialog box. When selecting the Time Range to view, keep in mind that the display area only shows 100 data points. If you select a range with more than 100 data points, the data is averaged to 100 points for display purposes. Each displayed point has a vertical line indicating the maximum and minimum values encountered when averaging the data for the displayed point. The original data is not affected by the display interpolation.

6

Alerts

An alert is a monitoring tool used to inform administrators when a specific counter has crossed a custom defined threshold. Alerts are defined on a counter basis and measured only at defined intervals. If a counter's value exceeds the defined threshold at the time of measurement, an alert is triggered. An alert can be used to perform a range of functions or activities once triggered.

New Alerts can be created when the Alerts node, located underneath the Performance Logs and Alerts node of the Performance MMC plug-in (see Figure 6.1), is selected. Issue the New Alert Settings command from the Action menu, provide a name for the Alert, and then set and define the desired counters to watch, their thresholds, and other parameters. An Alert's dialog box is used to configure every aspect of the log. The General tab (see Figure 6.17) offers the following controls:

➤ *Add*—Adds new counters to the list of monitored counters. Opens the Add Counters dialog box.

➤ *Remove*—Deletes the selected counter from the list of monitored counters.

➤ *Alert When The Value Is*—Sets the threshold value and whether the alert occurs when a measured value is over or under the defined threshold. A unique threshold is defined for each counter.

➤ *Interval*—Defines the interval at which measurements are taken and recorded into the log file. Interval is in numerals and has a default value of 15.

➤ *Units*—Sets the units for the interval in seconds, minutes, hours, or days. The default is seconds.

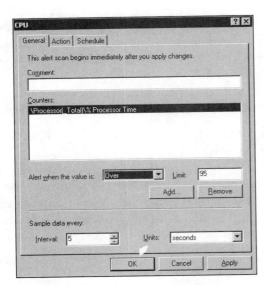

Figure 6.17 An Alert's Properties dialog box, General tab.

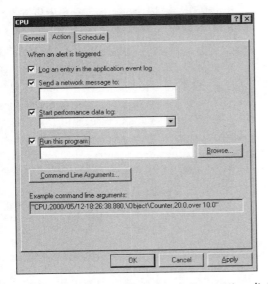

Figure 6.18 A Counter Log's Properties dialog box, Action tab.

The Action tab (see Figure 6.18) offers the following controls:

➤ *Log An Entry In The Application Event Log*—A toggle that enables the recording of an event detail in the Application log when an alert is triggered.

➤ *Send A Network Message To*—A toggle that enables the transmission of a message to a user, computer, or group when an alert is triggered.

➤ *Start Performance Data Log*—A toggle that enables the automatic launching of a selected Counter Log when an alert is triggered.

➤ *Run This Program*—A toggle that enables the automatic launching of a defined program or batch file when an alert is triggered.

➤ *Command Line Arguments*—Used to select which arguments are sent to the listed program as command-line parameter syntax. The available items are single argument string (all items contained within a single set of quotes instead of each individual item contained in a unique set of quotes separated by a space), date/time, measured value, alert name, counter name, limit value, and text message.

The Schedule tab (see Figure 6.19) offers the following controls:

6

➤ *Start Scan*—Used to define how an alert scan is started. Options are manually or at a specific time and date.

➤ *Stop Scan: Manually*—Sets the stop point of an alert scan to manual.

➤ *Stop Scan: After*—Sets the stop point of an alert scan to a time length.

➤ *Stop Scan: At*—Sets the stop point of an alert scan to a specific date and time.

➤ *Start A New Scan*—A toggle to enable the automatic relaunching of the alert scan when the current scan is completed.

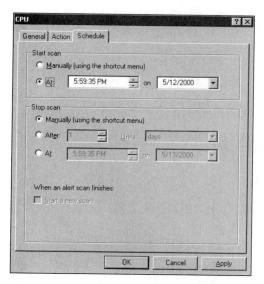

Figure 6.19   A Counter Log's Properties dialog box, Schedule tab.

An Alert can contain any mix of counters from local or remote systems. However, keep in mind that all counters defined within a single Alert are subject to the one sampling interval defined on the General tab of that Alert's Properties dialog box. To test counters at different intervals, you must define multiple Alerts.

Performance Options

Performance Options is a dialog box (see Figure 6.20) where a system is set to be optimized for applications or background services. This dialog box is accessed by clicking on Performance Options on the Advanced tab of the System applet from the Control Panel. A client system should be set to applications. By default, Windows 2000 Professional is set to applications and Windows 2000 Server is set to background services.

Disk Counters

Microsoft chose to enable the Physical Disk counters and not the Logical Disk counters by default on Windows 2000 systems. This is due to the fact that the simple act of gathering the performance data on a logical volume basis causes a measurable effect in the actual performance of those objects. In order to read data on a volume basis for drives via the Logical Disk object, you need to use the Diskperf command to enable those counters. Each time the Diskperf command is used, you must reboot the system for the changes to take effect. The syntax of Diskperf is, diskperf [-y[d|v]] | [-n[d|v]] [*computername*]. The parameters are as follows:

➤ *-Y*—Enables both PhysicalDisk and LogicalDisk objects.

➤ *-YD*—Enables only the PhysicalDisk object.

➤ *-YV*—Enables only the LogicalDisk object.

➤ *-N*—Disables both PhysicalDisk and LogicalDisk objects.

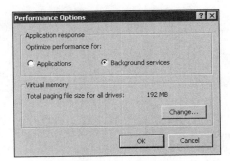

Figure 6.20   The Performance Options dialog box.

➤ *-ND*—Disables only the PhysicalDisk object.

➤ *-NV*—Disables only the LogicalDisk object.

➤ *\\computername*—Performs the object enable/disable on the specified system, which applies to the local system if this item is not included.

RELIABILITY AND RECOVERY

Windows 2000 is a stable and reliable operating system. In most cases, it is self-repairing and able to recover from numerous problems automatically. However, it is still possible for problems to occur that are beyond the operating system's capability to cope. In such cases, several manually initiated solutions can be brought to bear against the issues.

Advanced Boot Options

When you are experiencing difficulty booting Windows 2000, you may want to employ the capabilities of the Advanced Boot Options. These options offer alternative boot methods to aid in circumventing bad drivers or other boot issues. The menu of options is accessed by pressing F8 when the boot menu is displayed. The actual elements found in the Advanced Boot Options menu (see Figure 6.21) varies depending on the services and components installed on the system. The most common elements of this menu are:

➤ *Safe Mode*—Boots Windows 2000 using the minimum drivers and system files. Networking components are not loaded or enabled.

➤ *Safe Mode With Networking*—Boots Windows 2000 using the minimum drivers and system files. Networking components are loaded and enabled, but do not include PCMCIA/PC Card network devices.

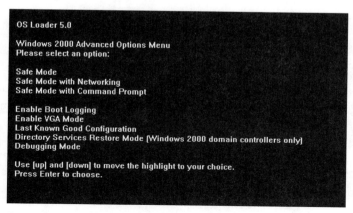

Figure 6.21   The Advanced Boot Options menu.

➤ *Safe Mode With Command Prompt*—Boots Windows 2000 with Safe Mode into a command prompt instead of the standard GUI.

➤ *Enable Boot Logging*—A toggle to enable logging of the boot process into the %systemroot%\Ntbtlog.txt file.

➤ *Enable VGA Mode*—A toggle to enable booting with basic VGA mode video drivers set at 640×480 at 16 colors.

➤ *Last Known Good Configuration*—Boots Windows 2000 using the state of the Registry as saved at the moment of the last successful shutdown.

➤ *Directory Service Restore Mode*—Used to restore Active Directory when damaged before booting into Windows 2000 normally. This option only functions on Windows 2000 domain controllers.

➤ *Debugging Mode*—Boots Windows 2000 normally while transmitting debugging data over a serial cable to another system. Please see the Windows 2000 Resource Kit on using the debugging mode.

boot.ini

The boot menu displayed when a system is booting is created from the data contained in the boot.ini file. This text file can be customized to perform one or more of the Advanced Boot Option selections from the standard boot menu. The boot.ini file is located in the root directory of the system partition. A typical boot.ini file looks like the following:

```
[boot loader]
timeout=30
default=multi(0)disk(0)rdisk(0)partition(4)\W2K
[operating systems]
multi(0)disk(0)rdisk(0)partition(4)\W2K="Microsoft Windows 2000
Professional" /fastdetect
multi(0)disk(0)rdisk(0)partition(3)\Winnt="Microsoft Windows 2000
Server" /fastdetect
C:\="Microsoft Windows"
```

The first section, labeled [boot loader], defines the menu display timeout and the default selection. Items in this first section can be manipulated through the StartUp and Recovery dialog box (accessed on the Advanced tab of the System applet). The second section, labeled [operating systems], defines all the options that will be displayed by the menu. Items in this second section are created when an OS is installed. Each item defines the path to the Startup folder for the OS by using an Advanced RISC Computing (ARC) name.

ARC names define the location of the main operating system files in an absolute context. The syntax of an ARC name is as follows:

➤ *scsi(n)* or *multi(n)*—Defines the type and instance of the drive controller. Multi(n) is used for all drive controller types except for a SCSI controller that does not have onboard BIOS enabled, which is when scsi(n) is used. This element is numbered ordinally (starting with 0).

➤ *disk(n)*—Defines the instance of a SCSI hard drive. This element is only used when scsi(n) is used. It has a default value of 0. This element is numbered ordinally (starting with 0).

➤ *rdisk(n)*—Defines the instance of a hard drive, whether Small Computer System Interface (SCSI) or Advanced Technology Attachment (ATA). This element is only used when multi(n) is used. It has a default value of 0. This element is numbered ordinally (starting with 0).

➤ *partition(n)*—Defines the instance of the partition hosting the boot file for the operating system. This element is numbered cardinally (starting with 1).

➤ *\path*—Defines the path to the operating system's main directory.

The operating system line in the boot.ini file can be customized by adding various command-line parameters. Some of the parameters supported by Windows 2000 are:

➤ */BASEVIDEO*—Used to boot Windows 2000 into basic VGA mode.

➤ */DEBUG*—Used to enable debugging mode.

➤ */SOS*—Used to enable verbose mode (i.e., names of loaded drivers and services are listed on the screen while booting).

➤ */SAFEBOOT:MINIMAL*—Used to boot Windows 2000 with Safe Mode.

➤ */SAFEBOOT:NETWORK*—Used to boot Windows 2000 with Safe Mode With Networking.

➤ */SAFEBOOT:MINIMAL(ALTERNATESHELL)*—Used to boot Windows 2000 with Safe Mode With Command Prompt.

➤ */SAFEBOOT:DSREPAIR*—Used to boot Windows 2000 with Directory Services Restore Mode (domain controllers only).

➤ */BOOTLOG*—Used to enable boot logging.

➤ */NOGUIBOOT*—Used to disable the boot splash screen.

➤ /FASTDETECT—Used to reduce load time by performing a quick
verification of hardware components, rather than a full inspection. That is, it
skips parallel and serial device enumeration.

Startup and Recovery Options

The Startup And Recovery dialog box (see Figure 6.22) is used to alter the
boot menu timeout and the default OS as well as the actions to take in the
event of a STOP error. This dialog box is accessed by clicking Startup And
Recovery on the Advanced tab of the System applet of the Control Panel. The
Default operating system drop-down menu lists all the operating systems
present in the boot.ini file. Selecting an OS from this list elects that OS to be
loaded by default when the timeout expires. The Display List Of Operating
Systems For ? Seconds control is used to define the amount of time offered to
select an alternate OS from the displayed list. This control can be disabled (by
clearing the checkbox), so the default selection is launched automatically.

The bottom portion of this dialog box is used to define how the system
responds when a STOP error occurs. A STOP error occurs when a process
accesses hardware directly (i.e., Windows 2000 Executive was unable to
intercept the action) or when a system level driver performs an illegal
operation. The selections in this area are

➤ Write An Event To The System Log

➤ Send An Administrative Alert

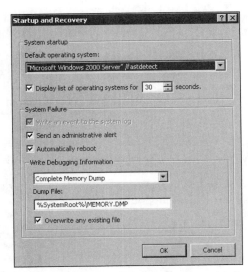

Figure 6.22   The Startup And Recovery dialog box.

➤ Automatically Reboot

➤ Write Debugging Information

Debugging information is a partial or full writing of the memory state to a dump file, %systemroot%\memory.dmp. This data requires specialized tools to extract meaningful information, thus in most cases, will be of little use. A pull-down list allows you to select none, small (64KB), kernel only, or complete memory.

Windows 2000 Backup

Windows 2000 includes a backup utility that offers a simple backup solution for both local and networked data. Windows 2000 Backup works primarily through wizards that guide you through the entire process of performing backups or restorations. However, you can use the tool manually to perform most customized backup operations. Data can be stored on any write-enabled media from tape drives to hard drives to network shares to removable media of any sort. Users can back up any file they own or have read access to. If a user has the Backup Files And Directories user right, he or she can back up every file on the system. The utility is launched from the System Tools section of the Start menu. From the default screen of the tool, you can quickly access the Backup, Restore, and ERD wizards.

When creating a backup, you can include nonfile-based information about the system by selecting the System State element. This captures Active Directory, boot files, COM+ registrations, the Registry, and System Volume configuration information that would otherwise be overlooked. This data is often extremely helpful in restoring a failed system.

Five methods of backup can be performed through this tool:

➤ *Copy Backup*—All selected files are copied to the backup media; the archive bit is not reset.

➤ *Normal Backup*—All selected files are copied to the backup media; the archive bit is reset.

➤ *Daily Backup*—All selected files that have been created or modified within the current day are copied to the backup media; the archive bit is not reset.

➤ *Differential Backup*—All selected files that have been created or modified since the last full or incremental backup are copied to the backup media; the archive bit is not reset.

➤ *Incremental Backup*—All selected files that have been created or modified since the last full or incremental backup are copied to the backup media; the archive bit is reset.

Restoring data is just as easy as backing it up. Just use the Restore tab, select the source of the backup media, and then select the destination. Users can only restore files they own or have read/write access to. Only users with the Restore Files And Directories user right can restore all files on a system.

Recovery Console

The Recovery Console is a command-line tool used to restore a damaged system to a bootable state. It offers limited access to Windows 2000 volumes to manage files and folders, manage services, repair master boot records (MBRs), and even format volumes. The Recovery Console can be installed into Windows 2000 so that it appears as an item on the boot menu, or it can be launched from the four startup boot disks. To launch the Recovery Console, you must log on as Administrator. Commands available through the Recovery Console include **attrib**, **chkdisk**, **copy**, **expand**, and **format**. For a complete list of commands, issue the **help** command from the Recovery Console or consult the *Windows 2000 Server Resource Kit*.

Emergency Repair Process

The four startup boot disks can be used to initiate the Emergency Repair Process (so can the Windows 2000 Server CD). This process can be used to recover from many boot problems including corrupt boot files or damaged volume descriptors. The full process requires an Emergency Repair Disk (ERD) built through the Windows 2000 Backup tool. You may also need the original distribution CD. To initiate the repair process, select R when prompted to select a function to perform when booting from the four startup boot disks or Windows 2000 Server CD. You then need to select one of the two options: fast repair or manual repair. The fast repair option does not require any additional user input or interaction other than providing the ERD and the distribution CD. This option attempts to repair all detected problems with the Registry, system files, the boot volume, and the startup environment. The manual repair option grants you control over selecting the individual repair items and requires user input throughout.

INTELLIMIRROR OVERVIEW

IntelliMirror used in conjunction with Remote Installation Services (RIS) offers a reliable solution within a Windows 2000 network to manage user data, distribute software, control desktop environments, and deploy new or rebuild damaged client systems. IntelliMirror is a collection of capabilities native to Windows 2000 that, when combined, offer very powerful and versatile functions to network administrators. The capabilities of IntelliMirror are divided into three categories:

➤ User Data Management

➤ Software Installation and Maintenance

➤ User Settings Management

User data management grants users access to their data no matter where on the network they are located as well as when they are offline. This element of IntelliMirror relies on the following Windows 2000 components:

➤ Active Directory

➤ Group Policy

➤ Offline Folders

➤ Synchronization Manager

➤ Enhancements to the Windows 2000 shell

➤ Folder Redirection

➤ Disk quotas

Software installation and maintenance maintains a complete set of required applications on all systems. IntelliMirror can distribute software to client systems as well as update, repair, and remove software. This element of IntelliMirror relies on the following Windows 2000 components:

➤ Active Directory

➤ Group Policy

➤ Windows Installer

➤ Add/Remove Programs

➤ Enhancements to the Windows 2000 shell

User settings management maintains a consistent user environment on all computers, both on the network and off. It includes a user's customized desktop as well as enforces environmental restrictions. This element of IntelliMirror relies on the following Windows 2000 components:

➤ Active Directory

➤ Group Policy

➤ Offline Folders

➤ Roaming User Profiles

➤ Enhancements to the Windows 2000 shell

IntelliMirror was designed to function on a Windows 2000 network using Active Directory. Some of its capabilities can be employed on a workgroup or even on a single standalone computer without the need for Active Directory or Group Policy. Keep in mind that once a Group Policy has been applied to a system, the effect on that system remains even when disconnected from the network.

The primary goal of IntelliMirror is to reduce the amount of administrative intervention required to maintain desktop environments for clients. IntelliMirror automates many tasks that are focused on sustaining user data and software as well as controlling the environment. IntelliMirror can also add an additional layer of disaster recovery. When properly configured, every element on a desktop system is duplicated within IntelliMirror. Thus, whether only a single file is deleted, a folder is corrupted, or a whole system is damaged, through IntelliMirror, the client can be returned to full functionality without data loss.

User Data Management

User data is managed based on the domain, site, or OU within which the computer(s) and clients reside. This control is maintained primarily through the use of Group Policies. User data consists primarily of the files contained within a user's home directory and My Documents folder. However, user data also consists of any network share-based resources that the user requires to perform work tasks. IntelliMirror can ensure that both types of data are available to the user no matter where the user is located on the network or even if the user is disconnected from the network.

Through intelligent positioning and mapping of a user's home directory, My Documents folder, and other key desktop and environment folders, a user's personal data can be made available to him or her from any network client. The user home directory is mapped to a network share through the Active Directory Users And Computers interface on the Profiles tab (see Figure 6.23) of a user account's Properties dialog box. Folder Redirection (see Figure 6.24) should be used through Group Policy (found under User Configuration, Windows Settings) to redirect the local folders of Application Data, Desktop, My Documents, and Start Menu to network shares as well. You can also redirect My Pictures, which is by default a subfolder of My Documents. Using both techniques makes a user's data available to the user throughout the network from any client.

To make your data accessible even when offline, you must employ Offline Files. This feature is used to cache local network share resources, so they can be accessed even when you are disconnected from the network. It is important to include the profile folder, the mapped locations defined in Folder Redirection,

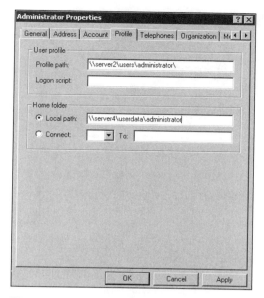

Figure 6.23   The Profile tab of a user account's Properties dialog box.

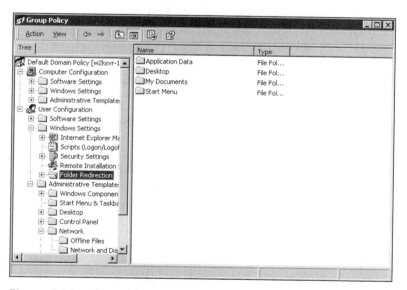

Figure 6.24   The Folder Redirection section of Group Policy.

and any other network shares whose resources are required by the user. Keep in mind that you need enough free drive space to host the files. Offline Files is configured through Group Policy and is located under the Administrative Templates, Network, Offline Files section of either the Computer Configuration or User Configuration (see Figure 6.25).

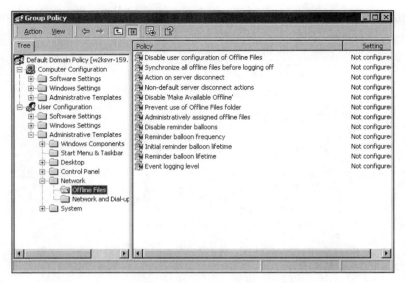

Figure 6.25   The Offline Files section of Group Policy.

Software Installation and Maintenance

Managing software is often the most difficult task to perform on large networks. This is especially true when attempting to deploy new versions or patches to existing software. IntelliMirror can perform a wide range of software management tasks automatically, such as installing new software on demand, deploying patches and updates, removing old software, and offering optional software.

IntelliMirror takes advantage of the Windows Installer tool, which can be employed to create a distribution package known as an MSI file. A distribution package can easily be added to the Software Settings section of Group Policy to distribute the software to all members of the OU. Once an MSI package is added to the Software Settings, a new icon for the software is placed on a user's Start menu. When the user attempts to launch the application for the first time, the system performs the installation (or update, patch, etc.). As soon as the install is complete, the application is launched, and the user is granted control.

IntelliMirror can also offer optional software to users that is installed only when the user specifically asks for it. These offered applications appear in the Add/Remove programs applet. Furthermore, existing MSI packages can be removed. Doing so can result in all instances of that application being removed automatically from all clients, or you can allow each client to decide whether or not to retain the application.

Note: *For information on the Microsoft Installer tool, please see the Windows 2000 Resource Kit.*

User Settings Management

User profiles used with Group Policies enable user desktop environments to be consistent throughout a network, even when a user is offline. User settings management includes retaining the customized desktop, Start menu, and other related items across logon sessions and enforcing access and tool restrictions. Combining both user profiles and Group Policies, a network administrator is able to define a set of environmental controls and be assured that they are enforced across a network automatically.

REMOTE INSTALLATION SERVICE (RIS)

6

IntelliMirror can be combined with RIS to provide a complete disaster recovery solution. RIS is used to install Windows 2000 Professional onto target systems. When RIS is combined with IntelliMirror data, a destroyed client system can be returned to its previous state with no loss of data or control. RIS relies on the following Windows 2000 components:

➤ Active Directory

➤ Group Policy

➤ DHCP

➤ DNS

RIS is used to remotely install Windows 2000 Professional onto new systems using either a DHCP (Pre-Boot Execution Environment) PXE-based remote boot ROM NIC or a RIS boot disk. RIS can also be used to remotely install Windows 2000 Professional over an existing operating system with network capabilities. The capabilities of RIS can be fully automated, so that the only activity required at the target system is to turn it on. RIS does have limitations; specifically, the target computer must meet the following requirements:

➤ Hardware must meet the Windows 2000 Professional system requirements.

➤ All hardware must be HCL compliant.

➤ 1.2GB of hard drive space is required.

➤ A RIS-compatible PCI NIC must be present, which can include:

   ➤ 3Com 3c900 (Combo and TP0), 3c900B (Combo, FL, TPC, TP0), 3c905 (T4 and TX), 3c905B (Combo, TX, FX), 3c905c TX

   ➤ AMD PCNet and Fast PC Net

   ➤ Compaq Netflex 100 (NetIntelligent II), Netflex 110 (NetIntelligent III), Netflex 3

➤ DEC DE 450, DE 500

➤ HP Deskdirect 10/100 TX

➤ Intel Pro 10+, Pro 100+, Pro 100B (including the E100 series)

➤ SMC 8432, SMC 9332, SMC 9432

Note: Before booting a target client with a PXE NIC or a boot disk, be sure to create a DHCP scope for RIS clients.

Installing a client system remotely using RIS typically involves the following steps:

Note: The activities of RIS can be fully automated, so that no user interaction at the client is required.

1. Using either a RIS boot disk or a PXE NIC, boot the target computer.

2. The target computer sends out a DHCP request.

3. The DHCP server sends the address of the RIS server back to the target computer.

4. The user is prompted to press F12 to initiate service and communications with the RIS server.

5. The target computer is verified as a valid recipient of the RIS process.

6. The Client Information Wizard (CIW) is transmitted to the target computer.

7. Logon credentials must be provided to gain access to the network.

8. The available options for installation are listed for a user to select. If only a single option is available, it is started without prompting.

9. A warning is issued that states that the local hard drive will be formatted.

10. The installation is started. Any nonscripted portion of the installation routine results in a user prompt for additional information.

11. After the installation completes, the system is rebooted to Windows 2000 Professional.

12. A user must log on. At this time, all IntelliMirror settings and Group Policies settings applicable to this user and system are applied.

RIS must be installed as an Optional Networking Component through the Network And Dial-Up Connections dialog box or the Add/Remove Programs applet. RIS can only be installed onto a Windows 2000 Server domain controller system. Once installed, RIS is managed through the Active Directory

Users And Computers utility by viewing the Remote Install tab on the Properties dialog box for the domain controller computer. On this tab, the RIS server can be configured to respond to RIS client requests and/or ignore unknown client requests. A list of current RIS clients can be displayed. The Advanced Settings button opens another dialog box where configuration elements are configured, such as:

➤ Client computer name generation parameters

➤ Within what OU the computer account should be created

➤ Create new installation images

➤ Associate an automated script with an installation image

➤ Delete installation images

➤ Manage tools installed onto client systems (OEM use only)

RIS boot floppies can be built using the rbfg.exe tool. This tool must be launched manually from the Run command or from a command prompt. It is located in the %systemroot%\system32\reminst and \RemoteInstall\Admin\ i386 folders on the system where RIS is installed. After launching the tool, the simple GUI interface is displayed (see Figure 6.26). Select the floppy drive letter, insert a floppy disk into the drive, and then click Create Disk.

The Remote Installation Services Group Policy is used to grant or deny access to various installation capabilities. These include Automatic Setup, Custom Setup, Restart Setup, and Tools access (see Figure 6.27). The RIS section of Group Policy is located under User Configuration, Windows Settings.

To grant users access to an installation image, simply grant them Read & Execute, List Folder Contents, and Read permissions to an image's template

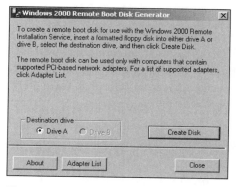

Figure 6.26   The Remote Boot Disk Generator tool.

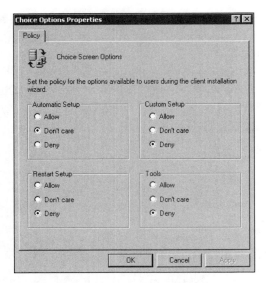

Figure 6.27   The RIS Group Policy.

folder and contents. The template directory is found in a path, such as
\RemoteInstall\Setup\English\Images\<<image name>>\i386\templates.

Custom unattend.txt files can be associated with RIS installation images. In
fact, multiple answer files can be associated with each image, so the user can
select from them. Fully customized RIS images can be created using the
RIPrep tool. Such images are extracted from a sample system that can include
software and configuration. However, Windows 2000 Professional must be
installed onto drive C: along with all installed software, and the target system for
such an image must have the same core hardware components as the original
sample system.

CHAPTER SUMMARY

Windows 2000 includes native tools to perform system monitoring, system
repair, and the automation of data distribution and management. All these tools
are designed to maintain a high-performance network that adequately supports
any type of activity. Quick recovery and data integrity are important to any
network administrator.

The Task Manager is used to obtain a quick view on the state of a system. It
offers views of active applications and processes as well as the means to
terminate problematic software. Through the Task Manager, you can manipulate
the execution priorities of processes.

The System Monitor is used to monitor activity in realtime and record logs of activity for baseline extraction, bottleneck detection, and trending or capacity planning. The System Monitor can extract performance data from any and all objects within the Windows 2000 environment from local and remote systems. Data can be displayed in various layouts from both realtime and log-based sources. Performance Logs can be used to collect data in the background while normal operations are going on. Log files can be used within System Monitor as well as third-party or custom tools. Alerts are used to inform administrators when operational parameters have exceeded expected limits.

Windows 2000 offers several reliability and recovery options to ensure the ability to boot as well as the stability of a system. The Advanced Boot Options are used to bypass damaged drivers or boot into a reduced environment, so that changes can be afforded. The boot.ini file is used to construct the boot menu. The contents of this file can be edited to alter the common startup parameters using command-line syntax. The Startup and Recovery Options is used to define the default OS and how the system should handle STOP errors. Windows 2000 Backup can be used to back up user data, system data, and even the System State, which includes Active Directory, boot files, COM+ registrations, the Registry, and System Volume configuration information, which would otherwise be overlooked. The Recovery Console is an advanced troubleshooting tool that can be used in some cases to restore a severely damaged system to a functioning state. It is a command-line–only interface that grants limited access to Windows 2000 volumes (and therefore files) and services. The Emergency Repair Process is a tool that can repair damaged boot and startup files.

IntelliMirror is a combination or integration of native Windows 2000 components and capabilities into an automated solution to manage user data, software deployment, and user environments. It combines features of Active Directory and Group Policy to reduce the amount of administrative intervention required throughout a network. It basically stores user data on network shares, caches network resources locally, offers automated software distribution (including patching, upgrading, and removal), sustains custom user desktop environments, and enforces access and environmental controls over clients both online and offline.

The RIS can be used to fully automate the deployment of Windows 2000 Professional clients. When used with IntelliMirror, a client can be re-created or rebuilt without losing any data.

REVIEW QUESTIONS

1. Task Manager can be used to view which of the following types of information? [Choose all that apply]

   a. CPU utilization

   b. Kernel Mode process consumption of CPU resources

   c. Total number of active processes

   d. Percentage of CPU consumption per second per process

2. Within System Monitor, all objects have the same measurable and readable counters.

   a. True

   b. False

3. When System Monitor is closed, what performance-related activities can still function in the background? [Choose all that apply]

   a. Timed launching of log files

   b. Realtime graphing of performance data

   c. Scanning for alerts

   d. Alteration of a counter's scale

4. Which of the following are true of Counter logs? [Choose all that apply]

   a. Only record data based on objects.

   b. All counters within a single log are measured upon the same interval.

   c. Can be recorded in text format.

   d. All counters must be from the same system.

5. Which object is not enabled or present on Windows 2000 systems for performance monitoring by default?

   a. System

   b. Logical Disk

   c. Processes

   d. Redirector

6. A problem exists if a queue counter consistently has a measured value of how many more than the number of elements or components in the object?

   a. 1

   b. 2

   c. 3

   d. 6

7. When the _____ counter consistently has a measured value of 4KB, you can assume that most drive activity is caused by paging.

   a. Logical Disk: Avg. Disk Bytes/Transfer

   b. Memory: Page Faults/sec

   c. Memory: Available bytes

   d. Logical Disk: % Utilization

6

8. The System Monitor can only display how many data points within its display from left to right?

   a. 10

   b. 50

   c. 100

   d. 256

9. At what sustained level or above does the Processor: % Processor Time counter indicate a possible problem?

   a. 5

   b. 50

   c. 75

   d. 80

10. Which of the following can be performed when an alert is triggered? [Choose all that apply]

   a. A message is sent to the Administrator.

   b. The system is rebooted.

   c. A Counter Log is started.

   d. An event detail is written to the Application Log.

11. Using Task Manager or the Start command, which execution priority(ies) cannot be employed by typical users? [Choose all that apply]

    a. 24

    b. 10

    c. 6

    d. 3

12. Windows 2000 Professional's Performance Options are preset to what?

    a. Applications

    b. Background services

    c. Peer Web Services

    d. Workgroup authentication

13. Which of the following Advanced Boot Options will not allow network access over PC card NICs? [Choose all that apply]

    a. Safe Mode With Networking

    b. Safe Mode With Command Prompt

    c. Enable VGA Mode Boot

    d. Last Known Good Configuration

14. Which ARC name appearing in a boot.ini file would indicate the correct partition for Windows 2000 Server if it was installed onto the only partition on the third SCSI hard drive connected to the onboard BIOS-enabled drive controller?

    a. multi(0)disk(0)rdisk(2)partition(1)

    b. multi(0)disk(0)rdisk(3)partition(1)

    c. multi(1)disk(0)rdisk(2)partition(1)

    d. scsi(0)disk(2)rdisk(0)partition(1)

15. Which types of backups performed by the Windows 2000 Backup tool do not reset the archive bit? [Choose all that apply]

    a. Copy

    b. Normal

    c. Daily

    d. Differential

16. The Recovery Console is a command-line interface that grants limited access to manage files and folders, manage services, repair MBRs, and even format volumes.

    a. True

    b. False

17. IntelliMirror can be used to perform which of the following activities? [Choose all that apply]

    a. Grant user access to data anywhere on the network or while offline.

    b. Deploy software.

    c. Retain a consistent user interface even on various clients.

    d. Control access to elements of the OS, such as Registry editing.

18. IntelliMirror can serve as a disaster recovery solution by providing a means by which all user data can be restored in the event of a failure.

    a. True

    b. False

19. Which of the following must be configured to grant a user access to his or her personal data and general network resources anywhere on the network and when offline? [Choose all that apply]

    a. Folder Redirection

    b. Home directory definition

    c. Software distribution

    d. Offline files

20. RIS can only be installed onto a Windows 2000 Server domain controller, but it can be used to deploy both Windows 2000 Professional and Windows 2000 Server.

    a. True

    b. False

REAL-WORLD PROJECTS

Project 6.1
To use System Monitor to watch performance in realtime, perform the following steps:

1. Launch the Performance Utility from the Administrative Tools menu. Administrative Tools is found either in the Start menu

(Start | Programs | Administrative Tools) or in the Control Panel (Start | Settings | Control Panel).

2. Select the System Monitor node in the left pane of the MMC Performance snap-in console.

3. Click the plus sign to open the Add Counter dialog box.

4. Select Use Local Computer Counters.

5. Select the Processor object.

6. Select the % Processor Time counter.

7. Click Explain. Read the text about the selected counter.

8. Click Add.

9. Select the Memory object.

10. Select the Available Mbytes counter.

11. Read the text about the selected counter.

12. Click Add.

13. Click Close.

14. Launch and close an application three times to force higher CPU and memory activity.

15. Notice how the readings displayed through the System Monitor reflect your activities on the system.

16. Close the Performance tool by issuing the **exit** command from the Console menu.

Project 6.2
To create and configure a Counter Log, perform the following steps:

1. Launch the Performance Utility from the Administrative Tools menu. Administrative Tools is found either in the Start menu (Start | Programs | Administrative Tools) or in the Control Panel (Start | Settings | Control Panel).

2. Expand the Performance Logs And Alerts node in the left pane of the MMC Performance snap-in console.

3. Select the Counter Logs node.

4. Issue the **new log settings** command from the Action menu.

5. Enter a name for the new Counter Log, such as "CPUdaily".

6. Click OK. The Properties dialog box for the new Counter Log is displayed.

7. On the General tab, click Add. The Select Counters dialog box opens.

8. Select Use Local Computer Counters.

9. Select the Processor object.

10. Select the % Processor Time counter.

11. Click Add.

12. Click Close.

13. Change the interval to 10 seconds.

14. Select the Log Files tab.

15. Select the Limit Of radio button, and set the limit to 10KB.

16. Select the Schedule tab.

17. Set the time to 2 minutes from the current time.

18. Select the When The Log File Is Full radio button.

19. Click OK.

20. Watch the counter log name's icon. It eventually turns green (when the time defined in Step 17 occurs). It then performs measurements until 10KB of data is recorded. Do not start the next project until the icon turns red again.

Project 6.3
To view data from a Counter Log, perform the following steps:

1. Select the System Monitor.

2. Click Properties (the one with a notepad and a pointing finger). The System Monitor Properties dialog box is displayed.

3. Select the Source tab.

4. Select the Log File radio button.

5. Click Browse to locate and select the log file created in Project 6.2.

6. Click Time Range.

7. Click and drag the front and/or end points of the slider bar to select a region.

8. Click the Data tab.

9. Click Add. The Add Counters dialog box appears.

10. Select Use Local Computer Counters.

11. Select the Processor object.

12. Select the % Processor Time counter.

13. Click Add.

14. Click Close.

15. Click OK.

16. The recorded log data is displayed for the selected counter within the selected time range. You can return to the Source tab to alter the time range.

17. Close the Performance tool by issuing the **exit** command from the Console menu.

Project 6.4
To create an Alert object, perform the following steps:

1. Launch the Performance Utility from the Administrative Tools menu. Administrative Tools is found either in the Start menu (Start | Programs | Administrative Tools) or in the Control Panel (Start | Settings | Control Panel).

2. Expand the Performance Logs and Alerts node in the left pane of the MMC Performance snap-in console.

3. Select the Alerts node.

4. Issue the New Alert Settings command from the Action menu.

5. Type in a name for the new Alert, such as "CPUdaily".

6. Click OK. The Properties dialog box for the new Alert is displayed.

7. On the General tab, click Add. The Select Counters dialog box is displayed.

8. Select Use Local Computer Counters.

9. Select the Processor object.

10. Select the % Processor Time counter.

11. Click Add.

12. Click Close.

13. Select Over from the Alert When The Value Is drop-down list.

14. Set a limit of 60.

15. Select the Action tab.

16. Select the Send A Network Message To checkbox.

17. Type in your username in the field.

18. Select the Schedule tab.

19. Select the After radio button under Stop scan.

20. Set the time and date to 30 minutes.

21. Click OK.

22. Close the Performance tool by issuing the Exit command from the Console menu.

23. Launch and close an application several times until an alert message is displayed.

24. Click OK on the message.

Project 6.5
To install RIS, perform the following steps:

1. Log onto a Windows 2000 Server domain controller as Administrator (or an account with administrative privileges).

2. Open the Add/Remove Programs applet from the Control Panel (Start | Settings | Control Panel).

3. Click Add/Remove Windows Components. The Windows Components Wizard is displayed.

4. Locate and select the Remote Installation Services checkbox.

5. Click Next.

6. When prompted, provide the original distribution CD for Windows 2000 Server or the path to a network share of the files.

7. When a message is displayed that the install is complete, click Finish.

8. When prompted, reboot your computer.

9. After the reboot, log in as Administrator (or an account with administrative privileges).

10. Open Configure Your Server from the Administrative Tools.

11. Click Finish Setup. The Add/Remove Programs applet is displayed.

12. Click Configure on the Configure Remote Installation Services area (it will be highlighted). The Remote Installation Services Setup Wizard is launched.

13. Click Next.

14. Provide a path where the RIS installation images will be stored. This must be a nonsystem drive formatted with NTFS. Be sure the drive has sufficient space, typically 2GB or more is adequate.

15. Click Next.

16. Select the Respond To Client Computers Requesting Service checkbox.

17. Click Next.

18. Provide the path to the distribution CD for Windows 2000 Professional or the path to a network share of the files.

19. Click Next.

20. Provide a name for the folder that will host the RIS installation images.

21. Click Next.

22. Provide a description of the RIS installation image currently being created.

23. Click Next.

24. Review the outline of the defined settings.

25. Click Finish to accept and apply the settings.

26. RIS is configured and an installation image is created; the progress of this activity is displayed.

27. When the window indicates that the process is complete, click Done.

28. Close the Add/Remove Programs applet (and Control Panel if open).

29. Close the Configure Your Server dialog box.

Project 6.6
To create a custom RIS installation image, perform the following steps:

1. On a target computer, install Windows 2000 Professional using RIS (the default or original RIS image created in Project 6.5 can be used). This computer and OS installation is referred to as the sample system.

2. Install any additional applications and Windows 2000 components. Perform all desired configuration or environmental changes.

3. From the sample system, launch RIPrep from the **run** command using a Universal Naming Convention (UNC) name, such as "\\\<RISservername>\ Reminst\Admin\I386\RIPrep". The RIPrep wizard is launched.

4. Click Next.

5. Type in the name of the Windows 2000 Server where RIS is installed.

6. Click Next.

7. Provide a name for the storage folder where this custom image will be created.

8. Click Next.

9. Provide a description and help text for the RIS installation image.

10. Click Next.

11. A list of any running applications or services is displayed. Stop any listed service or application before continuing.

12. Click Next.

13. Review the displayed settings.

14. Click Next.

15. Click Next again.

16. The RIS image is built and stored on the RIS host system. The workstation is then shut down.

Project 6.7
To enable Folder Redirection, perform the following steps:

1. Open the Active Directory Users And Computers utility from Administrative Tools menu.

2. Select the domain or Organizational Unit (OU) for which to configure folder redirection.

3. Issue the **properties** command from the Action menu.

4. Select the Group Policy tab.

5. Select a listed Group Policy for this container.

6. Click Edit.

Note: To add a new Group Policy, instead of editing an existing Group Policy, click New.

7. Expand the User Configuration section.

8. Expand the Windows Settings section under User Configuration.

9. Expand the Folder Redirection section.

10. Select Application Data in the right pane.

11. Issue the **properties** command from the Action menu.

12. Select the Target tab.

13. Select either Basic or Advanced:

   ➤ *Basic*—Provides a UNC path for the network share to store this folder for all users.

   ➤ *Advanced*—Uses the Add button to associate a UNC path for each unique user or group.

14. Select the Settings tab.

15. Don't make any changes to the default settings.

16. Click OK.

17. Repeat Steps 10 through 16 for the Desktop, My Documents, and Start Menu items.

18. Close the Group Policy editor.

19. Click OK on the container's Properties dialog box.

20. Close the Active Directory Users And Computers tool.

CHAPTER SEVEN

MANAGING STORAGE

After completing this chapter, you will be able to:

✓ Understand Windows 2000 storage architecture

✓ Create user profiles and understand storage issues

✓ Work with data compression

✓ Work with data encryption

✓ Manage disk quotas

✓ Troubleshoot disk problems and failures and use Disk Defragmenter

Data storage is vital in today's workplace, from small companies to large enterprises. An office can be crippled for days if data has not been stored properly and access to it cannot be obtained. Management of data was a key issue for Microsoft when designing Windows 2000. The importance of this issue resulted in many new features that make managing and storing data much more secure and robust.

Proper data and storage management ensures that your system will run more effectively. The tools provided with Windows 2000 allow network administrators to make the most of available disk space and gain better control of the operating system, software applications, and data files.

The Removable Storage and Remote Storage consoles within the Computer Management administrative tool are two new key features of Windows 2000. They address the matter of data management and storage and provide new, powerful features to the operating system. In addition, not only does Windows 2000 include many of the useful features found in Windows NT 4, but it also offers several more. The use of data compression creates extra storage space on the volumes, whereas data encryption ensures that unauthorized users cannot view data. Disk quotas enable network administrators to maintain control over how much disk space users have access to.

WINDOWS 2000 STORAGE ARCHITECTURE

There have been significant changes to the storage architecture of Windows 2000. One of the main factors addressed regarding storage architecture in Windows 2000 had to do with storage space required in large enterprises. The growth of data has been exponential, and the demand for additional storage space has pushed many systems and applications to their limits. The Windows 2000 architecture is designed to meet these demands, is scalable, and provides fault tolerance for mission-critical applications. The Removable Storage and Remote Storage consoles are two features designed with these factors in mind.

Removable Storage

Removable Storage provides management features for removable storage media and robotic storage libraries. Simply put, media is a piece of hardware that stores data. Media can be an 8mm tape, a magnetic disk, an optical disk, a CD-ROM, or many other forms of storage. Most media has a single side, which can only be used one way. Some types of media, such as a magneto-optical disk, have two sides. Each side can be used, but only one side can be accessed at a time, much like a cassette tape for your stereo.

Removable Storage assigns each media a unique ID, called a *logical identifier*. Applications that request data to be placed on the specific media call the media's ID to Removable Storage, and Removable Storage communicates with the driver. If the media begins to fail, Removable Storage is able to replace the media with another. Because Removable Storage is able to use the same ID with another media, the application does not know that the media has been changed.

Removable Storage provides Windows 2000 with information on various types of devices and installs the appropriate drivers. Removable Storage has taken over functions that were previously the responsibility of the device manufacturer or independent software vendor (ISV) who needed to provide support for the device. Removable Storage allows providers of storage applications to concentrate on user features, rather than hardware issues.

Prior to Removable Storage, a vendor who developed a backup program needed to include access to drivers and programming methods to account for the various types of backup media available, for example, 8mm tape drives, Digital Audio Tape (DAT), Digital Linear Tape (DLT), Digital Versatile Disk (DVD), and so forth. So, not only did the program have to address all the features it was expected to have, such as backup and restore, but it also had to function with the equipment the customer was using. Because it is very difficult to write, update, and troubleshoot code for a seemingly unending supply of backup media, many vendors simply provided a list of specific devices that their software would support. If you bought a new system and configured it with the hardware required, all worked well, but for the majority of systems, most equipment was already purchased, installed, and running other mission-critical applications. Problems arose when a new backup software package was installed and could not locate the existing backup media because it was not supported.

Removable Storage provides the low-level services that act on the requests made by applications. Removable Storage mounts and dismounts media, cleans drives, adds and removes media, keeps a library inventory, accesses media and library attributes, and enables or disables libraries, drives, and media. Figures 7.1 and 7.2 show a graphical representation of device access before Windows 2000 and with Windows 2000 and Removable Storage.

Removable Storage addresses the complexities of configuring software to work with a variety of backup media. Removable Storage uses *media pools* to organize the media. A media pool is a group of devices. Media pools are used to control access to the media, share media across applications, and group media by its use. Removable Storage mounts a tape when needed by the backup application, and applications can use Removable Storage to identify and keep track of the tapes they use. Figure 7.3 shows the Removable Storage console from within the Computer Management utility.

7

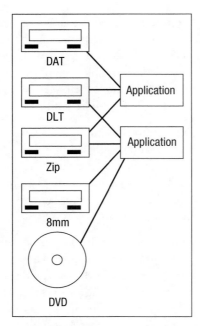

Figure 7.1 Access to devices prior to Windows 2000 and Removable Storage.

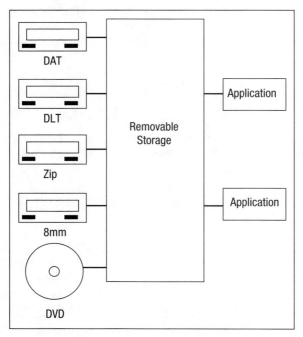

Figure 7.2 Access to devices with Windows 2000 and Removable Storage.

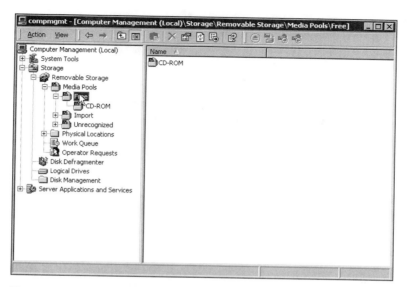

Figure 7.3   The Removable Storage console.

A media pool is a collection of devices that share some common attributes. There are two classes of media pools: system and application. System pools hold media not currently in use by an application. System pools have three categories: free, unrecognized, and import. Free pools are devices that can be freely shared among applications, but contain no data. An application is able to draw media from the free pool if required and can return it when no longer needed. The unrecognized pool is media that Removable Storage does not recognize. If data is written on a device that is in the unrecognized pool, Removable Storage cannot catalog or read it, although the application using the device might be able to do so. Import pools are new media that have been added to a library.

The second class of media pools is application pools. Application pools are created and controlled by applications or by the Removable Storage console to group media. Grouping the media is important if more than one application is sharing the media because permissions can be assigned to the shared media. Figure 7.4 shows a sample system pool.

Removable Storage relies on Plug and Play to tell it which devices have been attached to the system, which is why it is important for these device to be supported by Windows 2000 Plug and Play. Removable Storage goes through the list of drives that are attached to the system to detect which ones are attached inside the robotic library and which ones are standalone drive libraries. For the most part, Removable Storage can perform this process automatically.

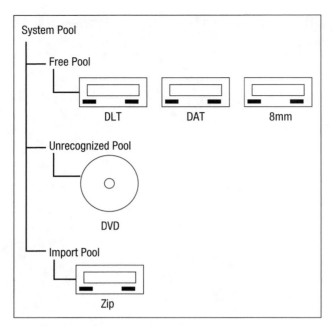

Figure 7.4   Sample System Pool.

There are times, however, when manual configuration is required. When installing a client application that is aware of Removable Storage, the application performs its configuration and setup during installation and is assigned to the free pool. Most applications draw media from the Free Pool. There are many drive and robotic libraries available, but Windows 2000 does not support all of them. You should check the Hardware Compatibility List (HCL) to ensure that Windows 2000 supports the device prior to your purchase.

Windows 2000 Removable Storage media can be classified as being in one of two locations: a *library* or an *offline media physical location*. A library is simply the media device or devices and can consist of many different types of data storage devices. A CD-ROM that is used to write data to a CD is considered a form of library called a standalone library. The other major type of library is the robotic library, which can hold many tapes or disks and can automate many processes.

A library can contain several items, as well as just one device to store data. The devices have certain features in common, such as a slot. A slot is the storage location in the library that holds media, such as a tape. A slot looks similar to the floppy drive on a PC, only it is usually wider and sometimes longer, depending on the type of media used. Slots can be organized into a collection called a magazine.

A drive is also a part of the library. A drive is a device that can read and write to a tape or cartridge. A good example of a drive is the Iomega Zip drive. This drive can read and write to the Zip cartridge that is inserted into it. Libraries also have transports, which move the tape from its slot to the drive and then back again. Bar code readers, insert/eject ports, and doors are also part of the library. Removable Storage treats all libraries in the same manner, so that its program interface is consistent and easier to read. Libraries that only have one form of media, such as a CD-ROM, are treated by Removable Storage as a library with one drive and an insert/eject port.

The offline media physical location is where Removable Storage lists media that is not in a library. This refers to media that is stored in a safe, on a shelf, or in a cabinet. It also refers to media that is stored in a different physical location, such as a different building. When media is removed from an online library, Removable Storage classifies it as being offline. Likewise, if it is placed back in the online library, its status changes to being online again.

The Removable Storage database keeps track of all the media components by storing the status of the system components and maintaining the media inventories. It includes information on the configuration and state of the library, media, pool configuration and contents, library work list, and operator requests. In essence, it stores all the properties of the objects that Removable Storage manages. The database is used only by Removable Storage and cannot be accessed by applications or administrators.

It is important to back up the Removable Storage database because the information not only lists the devices and libraries, but also the applications installed and the methods the applications use with Removable Storage. Therefore, it is vital to maintain a regular backup of the Removable Storage database. The default location of the Removable Storage database is %SystemRoot%\System32\ntmsdata.

Removable Storage provides a snap-in interface that allows administrators to add, view, and modify objects, as well as insert and eject media, dismount and mount media, check status information, and perform inventories. This snap-in can be run by typing the following line at the command prompt:

```
Ntmsmgr.msc
```

Or you can find the snap-in underneath the Storage node in the Computer Management snap-in.

REMOTE STORAGE

Remote Storage is a storage management application that migrates data from the primary storage area to a secondary storage area. Remote Storage was created to grade and rank data; therefore, because it is hierarchical, the data is stored in the most cost-effective method possible. Data that is accessed frequently is stored on high-performance, high-quality media, whereas data that is accessed infrequently is stored on less expensive media. In simpler terms, the data that is used most often is kept in local storage, whereas data that is used less frequently is transferred to remote storage.

The network administrator sets guidelines that Remote Storage follows to determine how it manages the data. The first guideline the network administrator sets is the desired free space. This tells Remote Storage how much free space is to be kept on the managed volume. The second guideline set is for file selection criteria. This allows Remote Storage to determine which data is eligible for movement to remote storage.

Remote Storage manages files that are stored locally and remotely based on the guidelines established by the network administrator. This process is transparent to the user. In a nutshell, Remote Storage identifies, tags, and premigrates rarely used files from the local drive to the remote drive. When a file has not been used for a specified time in this premigrated state and desired free space is less than what is indicated on the guidelines, Remote Storage removes this file from the local disk and places it on the remote drive. A placeholder is left on the local drive and to the user, it appears as though the file is still there. However, placeholders viewed in Windows Explorer are visually different than normal files. If the user opens the file that has been moved to a remote drive, Remote Storage retrieves the file from the remote location and moves it back to the local drive. Table 7.1 provides a summary of Remote Storage.

There are certain circumstances that can cause a noticeable delay in the transfer from a remote storage location to the local drive. One delay may be caused by the speed of the network to the device storing and accessing the file. Another

Table 7.1   Remote Storage in Windows 2000.

Item	Description
Placeholder	Has a system-defined attribute that contains information so the file can be retrieved from a remote storage location.
File size of the placeholder	The size of a placeholder is zero bytes.
Disk quotas	Based on file size and are not changed by Removable Storage. Therefore, files sent to a remote storage location do not decrease the disk quota allotment.

Note: Disk quotas are discussed in the "Managing Disk Quotas" section later in this chapter.

delay may be caused by the availability of the device in Remote Storage, because the device may be stored offline. If the media needs to be mounted prior to the file being accessed, there will be a delay in the user's ability to access the file. A notification can be configured so a message is issued to the user if the recall is going to take some time to complete.

If a user renames a placeholder, Remote Storage recalls the file content and copies it to the new file. The new file resides on the local drive. Regardless of where the data is stored, Remote Storage retrieves the data from the storage location and provides it to the user requesting the data. Remote Storage is limited to a single media type (so it cannot be used in a mixed media configuration), but supports all tapes that Removable Storage supports, such as 4mm, 8mm, and DLT. Remote Storage can manage as much data as the storage pool allows.

7

USER PROFILES AND STORAGE ISSUES

On computers running Windows 2000, a user profile is automatically created when a user first logs on to a computer. The profile that is created maintains the desktop settings for the user on the local computer, and at each logon, the desktop is restored. User profiles are the desktop settings for each user's work environment on the local PC. There are three different types of profiles, as shown in Table 7.2.

There are advantages to using user profiles. One advantage is that more than one user can use the same computer. When a user logs off, his or her settings are saved and when the user logs on again, his or her personal desktop settings are restored. The previous user's changes do not affect the new user's settings. The next advantage is that profiles can be stored on the server, so it does not

Table 7.2   Different types of user profiles.

Type	Defination
Local User Profile	Created the first time a user logs on to a Windows 2000 PC. It is stored in C:\Documents and Settings*username*. Changes made to the profile are saved on the local PC.
Roaming User Profile	Created by the network administrator and saved on the server. It is accessed from the server and copied to the workstation the user logs on to. Changes made to the profile are saved on the server.
Mandatory User Profile	A roaming profile that cannot be changed by users. It can be set for users or groups.

Note: When a new user profile is created on a machine, the ntuser.dat file is created for the user, and the common program groups are displayed on the desktop. The ntuser.dat file overrides the current Registry settings for the local machine.

matter where a user logs in; his or her settings are loaded to the computer the user is using. This type of setup is called a roaming user profile.

Mandatory user profiles are an ideal tool to use to reduce administrative overhead. They provide a standard user configuration and allow you to set up the desktop settings that are most productive for you and your company's needs. An administrator can create a default profile that is appropriate for a user's given task and limit the applications that can be run. For example, temporary employees hired to do only data entry can log in on arrival, open a specific application, enter data, close the application, and then log out at the end of their shift. There is no need for them to use other applications, so their user profile does not provide access to other installed programs.

In addition, any changes made to the desktop by a user with a mandatory profile are not saved when the user logs out. Upon logging back in, the user is given the mandatory desktop as specified by the administrator. This ensures a uniform company desktop environment, as well as reduces troubleshooting overhead. For example, if a user makes changes to the desktop and then encounters problems during that logon session, the administrator can request that the user log off and then log back on. With the mandatory profile back in place, the administrator can determine if the problem was a result of a change on the user's part or if it was unrelated.

Table 7.3 shows the relationship between common tasks performed with user profiles in Windows NT 4 and Windows 2000 Server. Access to most common tasks has been moved from Windows NT 4 Administrative Tools | User Manager to Windows 2000's Active Directory Users And Computers utility.

Every user profile begins as a copy of the Default User, which is the default user profile that is stored on each computer that is running Windows 2000. The ntuser.dat file that is created contains the various configuration settings and is the Registry portion of the user profile.

Table 7.3   User profiles in Windows NT 4 and Windows 2000 Server.

Task	Windows NT 4	Windows 2000 Server
Add a path to a user profile	Administrative Tools|User Manager	Active Directory Users And Computers|Users
View contents of user profile	Winnt\Profiles*Username*	Documents And Settings*Username*
Copy a user profile	System utility	System Properties, User Profiles
Home directory path	Administrative Tools|User Manager	Active Directory Users And Computers|Users
Logon script	Administrative Tools|User Manager	Active Directory Users And Computers|Group Policy

Roaming user profiles are stored on the server; therefore, any user can log on from any workstation (running Window NT or Windows 2000) to a Windows 2000 domain and be provided with his or her user profile. When a user logs in, the profile and user are authenticated by the Directory Service. After authentication is complete, the settings and documents that are stored on the server are copied to the workstation. Windows 9x profiles can be stored on the server as a separate profile.

Active Directory is used to assign the location of user profiles on the server. You enter the user profile path in the user's domain account where you want the profile to be stored on the server. When the user logs on for the first time after this adjustment, the profile is copied to the server from the workstation where the user is logging on. When the user logs off, the profile is saved to the local workstation as well as the server. The next time the user logs in, the profile at the local workstation is compared to the profile on the server, and if the server has a newer profile, it is copied to the workstation. If the profiles are the same, the local profile is used.

Note: See Project 7.4 in the "Real-World Projects" section later in this chapter for information on how to set up roaming user profiles.

If the server is not available, the locally cached profile is used. If the user has not logged on to the computer before and a local profile for the user is not stored on the computer, a message is displayed and the default profile is created. If the user profile is not available at logon, it is not updated when the user logs off in the event that the server comes back online while the user is currently logged on.

If there are no roaming profiles created the first time a user logs on, a user profile is created using the user's name. The contents of Default User are then copied to the new user's profile folder. Any changes made by the user during the current session are saved as the user's own user profile.

Storage Issues

Windows 2000 utilizes two types of configurations of disk structures for disk storage: basic and dynamic. Basic disk is similar to the structure used in Windows NT and is the default setup used by Windows 2000. You can use both basic and dynamic disks on the same computer with any combination of FAT16, FAT32, or NTFS. The only catch is that all volumes on a disk must be either basic or dynamic.

The basic disk is the disk that contains the primary partitions, extensions, and logical drives. This structure has not changed since MS-DOS was used as the operating system of choice. MS-DOS, Windows 9x, and Windows NT operating systems can access a basic disk. The basic disk, set up by default in

Windows 2000, allows users to work with a familiar environment and use troubleshooting methods and tools they currently have, especially if upgrading from a Windows NT environment.

Basic disks support basic volumes, which include primary partitions, logical drives within extended partitions, volumes, and striped sets (as created with Windows NT). Windows 2000 supports mirrored and RAID 5 (striped sets with parity) volumes only on dynamic disks that run on Windows 2000 Server.

In the Windows NT environment, Disk Administrator is used to work with disks—to format them, create mirrors and volumes, and so forth. Disk Administrator is no longer found in Windows 2000; it has been replaced by the Disk Management Microsoft Management Console (MMC) snap-in. It is very easy to add and use this utility. Disk Management allows you to work with both dynamic and basic disks. MMC is covered in Chapter 10. Figure 7.5 shows the Disk Management window.

You can use many of the same tools when working with basic disks in Windows 2000 as you did in Windows NT. There are two improvements over Windows NT's Disk Administrator: You no longer need to commit changes to save them, and you do not need to reboot the computer for changes to take effect. Changes are implemented immediately, without any form of confirmation.

A dynamic disk is a disk that has been upgraded by Disk Management and does not use partitions or logical drives. Instead, there are dynamic volumes, which

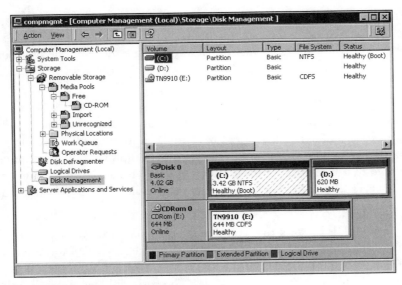

Figure 7.5 Disk Management window.

can only be accessed by Windows 2000 and are not supported on portable computers or removable media. Disks that use Universal Serial Bus (USB) or FireWire interfaces are also not supported. The dynamic volume that is created can support simple, spanned, and striped volume types as well as fault-tolerant types, such as mirrored disks or RAID 5. However, the system volume and the boot volume cannot be part of a spanned or extended volume.

If you have a basic disk and you upgrade it to a dynamic disk, you will not be able to extend it. The reason for this is that the basic disk, even after conversion, is still linked to the partition table and must match the listings there. Extending a volume increases the size, but because dynamic disks do not report to the partition table, an error will occur when the partition table looks for the disk of a certain size and finds differences. For this reason, a basic disk that has been upgraded cannot be extended as a dynamic disk. The only way around this extension problem is to go to the upgraded volume (which cannot be the system or boot volume), save the data on the volume somewhere else, delete the volume, and re-create it as a dynamic volume. Table 7.4 shows some of the differences between the basic disk and dynamic disk features.

Table 7.5 shows some of the similarities between basic and dynamic disks.

Table 7.4   Basic disk and dynamic disk features.

Basic	Dynamic
Primary partition	Simple volume
System and boot partitions	System and boot volumes
Active partition	Volume partition
Extended partition	Volume and unallocated space
Logical drive	Simple volume
Volume set	Spanned volume
Stripe set	Striped volume

Table 7.5   Similarities between basic and dynamic disks.

Task	Basic	Dynamic
Check capacity, free space, status	x	x
View size, drive letter, label, type, file system	x	x
Create drive letter assignments for volumes, partitions, CD-ROM	x	x
Create disk sharing, security arrangements	x	x
Upgrade to dynamic, revert to basic	x	x

Note: Upgrading a basic disk to a dynamic disk does not result in data loss. Reverting from dynamic to basic does require that data be backed up or it will be lost.

Legacy arrangements are still supported by Disk Management in Windows 2000. Disk Management supports striped sets that were created in Windows NT on a basic disk; however, you cannot create new ones because multiple disk storage systems need to use the fuller functionality of dynamic disks. One additional feature that Windows 2000 provides that Windows NT did not is support for FAT32. Windows 2000 adapted FAT32, which was introduced with Windows 95 OEM Service Release (OSR) 2. To troubleshoot a volume that is formatted in FAT32, you need to use a tool that recognizes this file format and is designed for Windows 2000.

WORKING WITH DATA COMPRESSION

Windows 2000 supports compression on individual files and folders as well as NTFS volumes. You can have compressed files in folders that are not compressed and compressed folders containing files that are not compressed. The files and folders that are compressed on an NTFS volume can be accessed and read by a Windows application in their current state. You do not have to use a program to decompress the files or folder first. Data compression frees up disk space for more data or files.

When you access a compressed file or folder, the file or folder is automatically decompressed when the file is read and recompressed when it is either saved or closed. There is no need for an additional mechanism or application to facilitate this process.

Files and folders on an NTFS volume reside in one of two states: compressed or not compressed. The compression state of the folder is exclusive to the state of the files it contains, meaning that a folder's state does not affect the file's state. A folder that is compressed can have files that are not. This situation can happen when you copy a file that was not compressed into a compressed folder or if you selectively decompress a file within a compressed folder.

To compress or decompress a file or folder is relatively easy. You can use Windows Explorer or a command-line utility called Compact. You are able to set the compression state for a folder and the individual files that reside in the folder. This gives the user the advantage of being able to selectively choose which files to compress. In addition, if you have Read and Write permissions, you are not only able to change the state of compression locally, but are also able to do it across the network. Figure 7.6 shows the dialog box from which data compression can be set.

It is also possible to compress an NTFS volume with data compression. To do so, open My Computer and right-click the drive. Select Properties | General, and then check the Compress Drive To Save Disk Space checkbox to compress the entire drive, as shown in Figure 7.7.

Figure 7.6   Advanced Attributes dialog box.

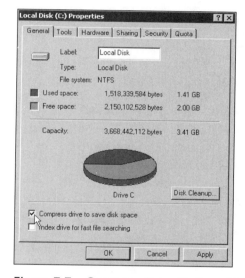

Figure 7.7   Compress Drive To Save Disk Space checkbox.

The Compact program is a command-line utility that enables the user to compress a folder or file from the command prompt (generally, the C:\ prompt). The Compact program also shows the current state of a folder or file; that is, whether it is compressed or not. There are basically two reasons to use the command-line utility instead of the graphical user interface.

The first reason is that you can create a batch script to run the command. With a batch script, a user can compress a file simply by clicking on an icon on the desktop. The second reason to use the command-line utility is that Compact forces the operation to complete even if the system fails during the procedure. This provides added protection against the operation hanging in the middle of the process, causing possible corruption of the file or folder.

Moving a compressed file locally to a file or folder on an NTFS volume results in the file remaining compressed. A file keeps its compression state regardless of the state of the new folder it is moved to. Copying a file or folder either locally or across the network causes a change in the compression state of the file or folder being copied. The state of each file or folder is controlled by the compression attribute of the volume to which it is being copied.

To illustrate this, an uncompressed file named, for example, Report2.doc is moved from the folder C:\Work Files\December (which is not compressed) to D:\Work Files\January, which is a compressed folder (the folder January is compressed). Both volumes are NTFS. The file Report2.doc remains in its uncompressed state after the move. Therefore, after the move, the file retains its compression state regardless of the state of the target folder. Figure 7.8 shows this in a graphical form.

Copying a compressed file is a different story. Copying a compressed file from a compressed folder to an uncompressed folder results in the file being decompressed. Let's work with the previous example again, but with some changes to the compression states of the file and folders. A compressed file, C:\Work Files\December\Report2.doc, is copied from the folder December (which is compressed) to a new folder located at D:\Work Files\January, which is not compressed. Both are NTFS volumes. The file Report2.doc does not remain in its compressed state after the copy; it changes to the state of its new parent folder and, therefore, is decompressed. Figure 7.9 shows this in a graphical form.

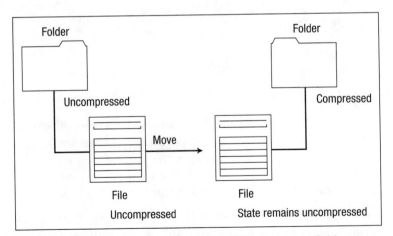

Figure 7.8   Moving an uncompressed file between folders.

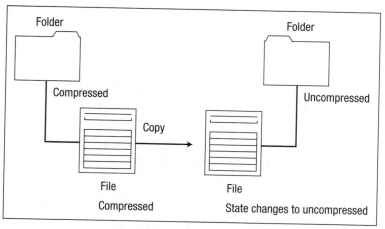

Figure 7.9 Copying a compressed file between folders.

Copying a compressed file in a compressed folder to an uncompressed file (with the same name) in a compressed folder also results in a change. In this case, the file being copied takes on the attribute of the file in the target folder, regardless of the compression state of the folder.

Hopefully you are not confused yet because there is more. The previous examples assume that the drives are NTFS volumes, but what happens in a mixed mode where NTFS coexists with one or more different flavors of FAT? When you move or copy a file between a FAT folder to an NTFS folder, the file always assumes the attributes of the NTFS folder. However, because Windows 2000 only supports compression on NTFS volumes, any compressed files that are transferred from a Windows 2000 NTFS volume to a folder on a FAT volume (Windows 9x or a floppy drive) are decompressed automatically.

Windows 2000 can work with NTFS for compressing and decompressing a file or folder. However, the file or folder loses its compression if it is transferred to a FAT volume.

Compressed Files on a Nearly Full Disk

Think about this interesting scenario: What if you have a disk (or volume) that is almost full, and you want to add more compressed files? For example, you have 5MB of space left on your disk and your compressed file only needs 3MB of space, but an error message appears that indicates that there is not enough disk space to write the file. How can this be? Mathematically, the file should be able to fit in the remaining space.

NTFS allocates spaced based on the uncompressed size of the file, and if the uncompressed size of the file exceeds the remaining space available on the drive, an error message appears. In this case, the best solution would be to move the file to another volume, and then make room in the current volume by backing up rarely used files or folders to a storage device and deleting them from the volume or freeing space on the volume by moving other files off the drive.

Windows 2000 uses a 3-byte minimum search for its NTFS compression rather than the 2-byte minimum used by DoubleSpace, which helps boost performance for NTFS compression. NTFS offers realtime access to a file by accessing a compressed file, decompressing it when opened, and then compressing it when closed. However, the benefits to the user for realtime access mean that there is performance degradation when copying files across the network. When copying across the network, a compressed file is decompressed, copied, and then recompressed as a new file in its new location, even when it is copied on the same drive. On networks, this might affect bandwidth and speed as a file is copied to another drive on the network. Although, in general, the degradation and speed loss is not noticeable, a Windows 2000 Server with plenty of write traffic could see a hit on its performance when using data compression. A network administrator should weigh the costs and benefits before implementing compression on a heavily used network server.

Note: NTFS only supports compression for cluster sizes up to 4KB. Anything over 4KB in cluster size will not have compression available.

WORKING WITH DATA ENCRYPTION

Security has come to the forefront of many IT departments. As data becomes a more and more precious commodity, the appeal to hijack sensitive data by unscrupulous people grows in proportion. As more workers carry laptops and take their company's sensitive data on the road with them, it becomes easier for someone to seize an unattended laptop. Oddly enough, the person stealing the laptop may not be taking it for its resale value, but instead, for the data that is on its hard drive.

Even though Windows 2000 uses NTFS, which can secure folders and files and lock permissions, there are ways of getting around the security that NTFS provides. One way around NTFS is during the initial boot sequence. Standard boot procedure has the computer read the floppy disk during the boot sequence prior to reading the hard drive. This feature allows the option of installing a repair disk or a boot disk in the event of a system failure. However, this also leaves a machine wide open to attack. By putting in a specialized floppy disk, the computer boots off the floppy and the user gains access to the file system using a tool that bypasses the system security and reads Windows

NTFS disk structures. If someone is determined to get at the data, he or she will eventually do so.

These issues were taken seriously by Microsoft and solutions were incorporated into Windows 2000 using the Encrypting File System (EFS), which works only on NTFS volumes. EFS is basically data encryption with more enhanced features. It is based on symmetric key encryption in conjunction with public key encryption. A user is issued a digital certificate with a public and private key pair that is used for EFS. Each file is encrypted using a randomly generated key, independent of the public/private key pair. This form of randomly generated key encryption provides a more secure environment, which makes it harder to run attacks that try to determine a key.

To encrypt files, use Windows Explorer, My Computer, or a command prompt. EFS allows a user to start encrypting files right away. In fact, the user will not notice any change. EFS sets up the key pair for the file encryption for the user automatically, eliminating administrative efforts. The file encryption (and decryption) is supported either through the entire directory or on a per file basis. When encrypting a directory, all files and subdirectories that are marked are automatically encrypted, and each file has a unique key.

To encrypt a file, open Windows Explorer, and select the file or folder to encrypt. Right-click the file or folder, select Properties, and then click the Advanced button. This displays the Advanced Attributes window as shown in Figure 7.10.

Select the Encrypt Contents To Secure Data checkbox, and then click OK. You are presented with a Confirm Attribute Changes dialog box, as shown in Figure 7.11.

Figure 7.10   Advanced Attributes window.

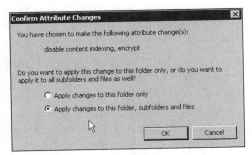

Figure 7.11 Confirm Attribute Changes dialog box.

Note: *If the file is compressed, you cannot encrypt it without removing the compression.*

Select the desired option, and then click OK. The files and folders selected are now encrypted.

You can encrypt files from the command prompt using the Cipher tool, which provides a rich set of features to choose from. Table 7.6 shows some useful command-line tools.

The following is an example of a command-line procedure for encrypting a file.

```
c:\cipher /e myresume.doc
```

To decrypt the file, type

```
c:\cipher /d myresume.doc
```

To encrypt an entire directory:

```
c:\cipher /e "My Documents"
```

To encrypt all files that have "personal" in their name:

```
c:\cipher /e /s *personal*
```

Table 7.6 Command-line tools used with EFS.

Command	Action
cipher	Tool used to encrypt/decrypt files or directories.
/e	Encrypts the specified file.
/d	Decrypts the specified file.
/s: *dir*	Encrypts/decrypts all files in the directory and subdirectory.
/i	Continues encryption/decryption even if errors occur.
/q	Reports only important information.

To see if a file is encrypted or not, the user can check the properties of the file and look for the encrypted attribute in Windows Explorer. Because encryption is transparent to the user, he or she can simply work with the file as usual—opening, closing, editing, and saving. If other users try to open the file, they will receive an "Access Denied" message because they do not own the key to open the file. Figure 7.12 shows what happens when another user tries to open an encrypted file.

As you can see, Notepad opens to a blank form, and an error message is generated. If you click OK on the error message, you will able to use the blank form created by Notepad. However, it will not be the file that you tried to open.

To open an encrypted file, the user does not need to run a specific application to decrypt it. EFS automatically detects if the file is encrypted, and if so, decrypts the file using the key stored in the system's key store. Key storage is based on the CryptoAPI architecture, which is the interface for cryptographic operations and enables users to store keys on secure devices, such as smart cards. Figure 7.13 shows a file listed in Windows Explorer that has been encrypted.

Recovery Agent

Whenever a file is encrypted, there is always the chance that it cannot be read again. The owner of an encryption key who, for example, is planning to leave the company might, if disgruntled, encrypt all files and shared files that he or she has access to. To ensure access to all encrypted files, EFS is designed to be used only when a recovery agent is available.

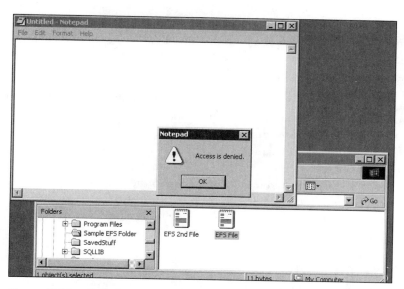

Figure 7.12 Failed attempt to access an encrypted file.

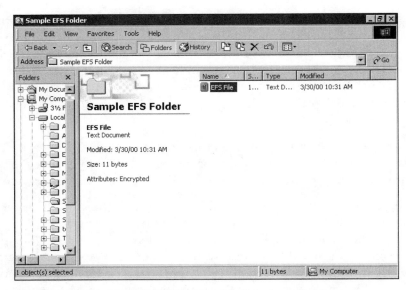

Figure 7.13   An encrypted file listed in Windows Explorer.

EFS recovery policy is implemented as part of the overall Windows 2000 security system, and is either a part of the domain or the local workstation if it is a standalone unit. The recovery policy is integrated with the domain/local security policy. The EFS Policy User interface allows the recovery agents to back up recovery keys, generate recovery keys, and perform other management functions.

Windows 2000 has incorporated an ingenious way to ensure that encrypted data can be recovered. The Windows 2000 security infrastructure requires that data recovery keys are created or EFS is not enabled. This is done automatically, and the user does not need to intervene by setting up data recovery keys. Only the keys that are randomly generated by EFS can be recovered using data recovery.

If a user forgets a key or if an employee leaves the company and the company wants to recover files and data that the employee encrypted, the file is sent to a recovery agent. The agent imports the file on a secure machine (it can be sent to the agent via email, for example), and the network administrator or designated recovery agent uses a command-line tool to decrypt the file. The recovery agent then sends the file, in plain text format, back to the user. A recovery agent is issued a certificate with public and private keys that are used for recovery operations. The recovery agent is the highest-level administrator account. Recovery can only occur on the computer where the recovery key is located.

EFS Architecture

EFS uses a public key scheme in conjunction with symmetric key encryption to encrypt data. The key is generated by an algorithm and is set to a certain length. The key is used to encrypt the file and is then itself encrypted and stored in a special field called the Data Decryption Field (DDF). The encryption information is then connected to the file. A recovery key is created and stored in a recovery field called the Data Recovery Field (DRF). Because the recovery portion is not expected to be used often, it can be stored on a more secure device, such as a smart card or a tape, which can be removed from the system.

You can remove the recovery key from the system by using the Certificate Export Wizard. Log on as the administrator, and then use the Certificate Export Wizard to export the certificate and private key to a removable medium, such as a floppy disk. The wizard creates a .pfx file on the floppy disk, and you can then remove the floppy. Next, to delete the private key from the computer, check the Delete The Private Key If The Export Is Successful checkbox from the Export File Format page of the wizard. This deletes the key from the computer. Then, copy the .pfx file on the floppy to another floppy disk. Store one floppy disk onsite in a secure location (such as a safe) and the other disk offsite.

There are four main components of EFS in the Windows 2000 operating system. The first component is the EFS driver. This driver sits on top of NTFS and communicates with EFS to request encryption keys, DDFs, DRFs, or other management services. It then passes the information on to the EFS file system runtime library (FSRTL) to perform the requested operation (write, read, open, and so on). This is all transparent to the user.

The FSRTL is the second component of EFS. FSRTL is a module within the EFS driver that handles the operations, such as read, write, open, encrypt, decrypt, recover, and append. Although FSRTL is part of the EFS driver, the two never communicate directly because they both use NTFS to communicate with each other.

The third component of EFS is the EFS Service. The EFS Service is part of the operating system's security subsystem, and it uses the Local Procedure Call (LPC) communication port to communicate with the EFS driver. It interfaces with CryptoAPI to provide encryption keys and create DDFs and DRFs. EFS uses the DESX encryption algorithm for key generation and file encryption operations.

EFS Service also provides support for Win32 Application Programming Interfaces (APIs), the fourth component of EFS. Win32 APIS provide programming connections for encrypting, decrypting, recovering, importing, and exporting files. This section is a simplified explanation of the architecture. You should consult materials detailing the architecture of EFS for the exact methods of the encryption process.

Encrypting Files and Folders

It is recommended that you encrypt a folder instead of individual files. The main reason for this is ease of use. If a folder is encrypted, the files are automatically encrypted, and the files remain encrypted during and after editing. But this only works if the application doing the editing leaves the file in the same folder. Some applications place the edited file in the Temp folder and leave it as plain text. This defeats the purpose of encrypting the file to begin with. An application such as Microsoft Word uses the folder in which the file is located for temporary and backup files, and therefore, you are assured that as long as the folder is encrypted, all the files in that folder, temporary or not, are also encrypted.

Encrypting a directory ensures that all files and subdirectories are encrypted. This is useful when a user wants to specify an entire directory as encrypted and copy encrypted files to it. The directory list can still be viewed and worked with, however, the files cannot be opened unless the user has the appropriate key.

If you copied an encrypted file from one file system to another, it would lose its encryption, which means that the copy function decrypts the file and leaves it decrypted. Copying a file to another encrypted folder encrypts the file. Moving a file will not change its attributes (meaning that if it was not encrypted, it remains so even if the new folder is encrypted). However, this only takes place within NTFS volumes. If a file is encrypted, most likely the user wants it to remain so after a move or a copy. The way to ensure this is to use the Export Encrypted File and Import Encrypted File features. These guarantee that the encrypted file remains encrypted, even if sent to non-NTFS volumes. Table 7.7 lists the status of files when moved, copied, or renamed.

Certificates are issued to users when they encrypt files. You can view the certificates using the Certificate Console, which is a snap-in to the MMC. Likewise, the recovery agent is also given a certificate for recovery. This too can be viewed in the Certificate Console for the recovery agent.

Table 7.7 Moving, copying, or renaming an encrypted file.

Task	Status
Changing the name	Remains encrypted.
Move	Remains encrypted if the target volume is Windows 2000 NTFS; otherwise the file is decrypted.
Copy	Remains encrypted if the target volume is Windows 2000 NTFS; otherwise the file is decrypted.

Note: When an encrypted file is sent to the destination, EFS decrypts the file and sends it as plain text. When it reaches the destination, it will then be re-encrypted if the target drive supports EFS.

Some final notes: Do not encrypt files when logged on as the local or domain administrator. Because the administrator is the default recovery agent, the recovery key is assigned to the administrator's account. If you encrypt a folder as the administrator, you will, in effect, have both keys, and the effectiveness of EFS recovery is compromised. It is always best to allow users to encrypt the files.

You can encrypt any number of files and folders, but you cannot encrypt files or folders in the system root folder (generally C:\Winnt\). Because these files need to be accessed during system startup, the keys needed to decrypt the files during startup are not made available. This results in the operating system not being able to read the files it needs to start, which renders the system unavailable.

Note: You must have write access to a file to encrypt it.

MANAGING DISK QUOTAS

Disk quotas allow the network administrator to assign a certain amount of disk space to each user in the network and to enable a warning to the network administrator if users meet or come close to their allotted amount. Disk quotas enable the operating system to quantify the usage of each individual user, so that one or two users do not manipulate the system by commandeering space on the server.

When enabling disk quotas, there are two values that need to be set. The first is the disk quota limit, which specifies the amount of space a user can use. You, as the network administrator, define the disk quota limit. For example, if you want to limit each user to 30MB of space, you would set the disk quota limit to 30MB. A user cannot exceed the space limitation that is set. Disk quotas can also generate an event log when the user is either close to the space limit or exceeds it. A user is charged against the disk quota every time he or she copies or saves a new file to the volume. A charge also takes place if a user takes ownership of a file.

The second value that needs to be set is the disk quota warning level, which issues a warning to users when they are close to the limit. Using the previous example, you set the disk quota limit at 30MB, so set the quota warning level at 25MB. By issuing a warning, the user knows that it is time to either remove some files or move some files to another location.

It is possible to set a disk quota limit and allow the user to exceed the limit. You use this feature when you want to track users' space usage, but not limit them from using space on the drive. It is also possible to log an event whenever a user exceeds the amount of space that was allotted. For example, when a user downloads images from the Internet and stores them in his or her personal folder on the server, thinking that the server has an unlimited amount of free space. Left unchecked, this folder can easily become quite large and take up space needed by other applications and users. By having an event logged when the user has exceeded his or her allotted space, the network administrator is notified and by examining the log, can take the appropriate action.

Let's look at how this works. When you select the Log Event When A User Exceeds Their Quota Limit option, an event is written to the Windows system log. After notification that a user has exceeded the quota limit, this event can be viewed by the network administrator. If the Log Event When A User Exceeds Their Warning Level option is selected, an event is written to the system log, which tells the network administrator that a user has exceeded the warning level. Event Viewer can view system logs and users are not notified of the logs. The Event Viewer only shows the date and time that the infraction occurred; it does not keep statistics or information about the users after the infraction.

You can enable disk quotas on local volumes as well as network volumes; however, the volumes must be formatted with Windows 2000 NTFS and be shared from the root directory. To enable disk quotas, right-click the drive letter or icon, select Properties, and then select the Quota tab, shown in Figure 7.14.

When you first enable disk quotas on a volume, the usage on the volume is monitored from the time it is first enabled. Existing volume users do not have disk quotas applied until you set them. Another important item to note is that file compression does not affect disk quota limits. If a user has only 2MB of space left and wants to add a file that is 1.5MB compressed, but is 3MB

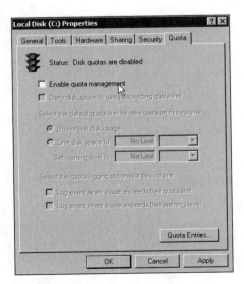

Figure 7.14   Quota tab.

decompressed, he or she is not able to do so because the disk quota system looks at the actual decompressed size of the file and not the compressed size.

As noted previously, disk quotas can be applied to a Windows 2000 operating system with NTFS-formatted drives. A Windows NT 4 system that has NTFS-formatted drives and is upgraded to Windows 2000 is also supported because the setup feature of Windows 2000 converts the NTFS to the updated version. Disk quotas are based on the ownership of the files, so as long as the system (i.e., NTFS) is able to distinguish the owner of the file, disk quotas work. However, for volumes that are formatted with FAT or FAT32, disk quotas will not be able to function. The reason for this is FAT and FAT32 volumes are owned by the system, and individual users cannot own files on FAT or FAT32 volumes as they can with NTFS.

As discussed in the previous paragraphs, disk quotas can be set on a local workstation and a server. The benefit for setting disk quotas on a workstation is that if a workstation has multiple users, each user is assigned a certain amount of space that protects the system from abuse or manipulation by someone storing too much data on it.

Disk quotas can be used for remote users as well, which is a strength of Windows 2000. The remote computer volume must be formatted with NTFS and shared. The network administrator can enable disk quotas on the remote computer, and the computer becomes a part of the disk quota management.

Let's get into the nitty-gritty of what happens when disk quotas are enabled. If disk quotas are enabled on a volume that already has users and files, Windows 2000 calculates the disk space being used by the users who have copied, saved, moved, or taken ownership of a file up to that point. The disk quota limit and warning level are then applied to each user based on these calculations and tracking begins. If a user has not copied, saved, or taken ownership of any files prior to the time disk quotas were enabled, he or she starts with a fresh account.

In the NTFS system, the usage information is stored by the user's SID (security identifier), not the user account name. Therefore, when a user's account name is entered in the Quota Entries window, the domain controller must match the account name with the SID.

One important issue to consider is if a user other than the administrator installed Windows 2000 on the computer. In this case, the space used by Windows 2000 is applied against the user who installed the operating system. Therefore, either the administrator should perform all installations and additions of components, or the user who installed Windows 2000 should be given a higher quota limit based on the space that Windows 2000 takes or given no limit at all. If the network administrator installed Windows 2000 on the computer, there is no problem because the administrator cannot be denied disk space on a volume even if he or she exceeds the set limit.

So what happens when users exceed their disk space allotment? If you selected the Deny Disk Space To Users Exceeding Quota Limit checkbox, then users receive an "insufficient disk space" error on their screen. They are not able to write data to the volume until they have freed up space to do so. This is comparable to using floppy disks. Once you meet or try to exceed the amount of space a floppy can handle (1.44MB), an error message is displayed stating that there is not enough space available, and you have to either remove some files or use a higher capacity device.

Each application determines how it notifies the user that the volume is full and that the user cannot write to the disk. To the application, it appears that the volume is full and there is no more room to write to (as with the floppy example). The application then notifies the user in whatever way it is programmed to handle an error.

Deleting a user from a volume where disk quotas are in place can be tricky. The first step is to remove all the files owned by that user from the volume or change the ownership of all the files. The second step is to delete the user's disk quota limits and warnings from the Quota Entries window.

TROUBLESHOOTING DISK PROBLEMS AND FAILURES AND USING DISK DEFRAGMENTER

Disk drives can and will fail. Sometimes there are warnings, such as intermittent problems that lead up to the disk failure; other times there are no warnings—for instance, you turn on the PC and the disk drive does not work. An external power surge can wipe out the internal components of a computer that does not have a surge protector, and sometimes even a surge protector is not enough. The internal power supply can also malfunction, sending a surge through the computer that wipes out everything.

Although no computer is fail proof, there are preventative actions you can take and combining these actions with strategic planning can make a computer running Windows 2000 more resilient. Developing plans and procedures for recovering from failures before they occur can minimize damage and time lost.

When your PC boots (starts) there are two sectors that are critical: the Master Boot Record (MBR) and the boot sector. Both contain executable code and the data required to run the code. The MBR is the most vital structure on the disk and is created when the disk is first partitioned. The MBR contains code that allows the computer to boot Windows 2000 (and Windows 9x and

Windows NT for that matter). The MBR contains the master boot code, the disk signature, and the partition table.

The master boot code scans the partition table for the active partition. Even if you have used Disk Management to upgrade your disks to dynamic disks, the master boot code is still able to obtain the information it needs to function correctly. The master boot code finds the starting sector of the active partition, loads a copy of the boot sector from the active partition into memory, and then transfers control to the boot sector, which launches its executable code.

After the master boot code finishes, the MBR scans the partition table. This is a fixed, standard layout that is independent of the operating system. Each table entry is 16 bytes long with a maximum of four entries, meaning that there can be a total of only four partitions per disk. The first field in the partition table is the Boot Indicator Field. This field indicates whether the partition is the active partition. The next field is the System ID Field, which defines the type of file system (FAT16, FAT32, or NTFS). The System ID Field also identifies the extended partitions, if any. Windows 2000 uses the System ID Field to determine the system drivers to load during setup.

If the master boot code cannot complete its functions, one of the following error messages will appear:

```
Invalid partition table.
Error loading operating system.
Missing operating system.
```

If one of these errors occurs, it could be because the active partition was not found during the master boot code's scan. This happens if the wrong partition is identified as the active partition. The way to correct this problem is to use the MS-DOS startup disk, and then use the Fdisk tool to select and set the active partition.

Warning!   Be forewarned—you should have experience working with Fdisk before you attempt to make changes to your system. It is possible that your system could be unusable if Fdisk is handled incorrectly.

An error message, such as those listed previously, could be the result of the MBR becoming corrupt. There are a number of ways this could happen: through human error, a virus, or some other factor. Generally, however, a virus (more often than not) corrupts the MBR by altering it in some fashion. A virus can infect and alter the MBR causing the system to become unusable. The virus generally alters the system and is started when the master boot code is activated by the BIOS, which is before the operating system is loaded. The virus can copy the MBR to another location and use its own MBR, so that it appears that the computer is running normally. Other viruses move the MBR to a sector where it can be overwritten, and thus render the system unusable.

To restore the MBR, you can use Recovery Console. Once you have logged on, at the command prompt type

```
fixmbr
```

Recovery Console notifies you that this operation may cause data to be inaccessible on the hard drive (but without the MBR, it is inaccessible anyway) and asks if you want to proceed. If you do, Fixmbr overwrites the master boot code and leaves the partition table intact. So, if it was the MBR that was corrupted (by a virus for example), this resolves the problem. However, if the problem lies in a number of other factors, the result is limited.

Fdisk /mbr is a command that can be run from the MS-DOS prompt and works in a similar fashion to the Recovery Console's Fixmbr. The process with Fdisk /mbr is to rewrite the MBR to the hard drive. For older viruses, this works well; however, new viruses are able to immediately reinfect the system because they have the properties of file infector (which are viruses that infect files) and MBR viruses. Therefore, Fdisk /mbr is limited in its ability.

It is possible to create a backup of the MBR using the DiskProbe tool that is available for Windows 2000 and Windows NT. There are also third-party MS-DOS based MBR backup tools.

Boot Sector

The boot sector is located at the first sector (sector 1) of each volume. It is used to start your computer and operating system and contains vital code, including information that the file system uses to access the volume. The boot sector is first created when the volume is formatted. For Windows 2000, the boot sector on the active partition loads and starts the NTLDR file (which is short for NT Loader, and is the file that loads the Windows NT kernel), which proceeds to load the operating system.

Boot sector viruses, such as MBR viruses, are also activated before the operating system is loaded and are activated during the phase of the master boot code. Some boot sector viruses change the boot sector with their own code and allow the system to appear as if it is running normally. Others relocate the boot sector, making access impossible or not allowing the system to start.

If the boot sector cannot find NTLDR, Windows 2000 cannot start. This happens if NTLDR is moved, deleted, renamed, or is altered in some way. If

NTLDR is corrupted or if the boot sector is corrupted, you can use the Emergency Repair Disk (ERD) to repair these problems. The ERD is discussed in the "Emergency Repair Disk" section later in this chapter.

To replace the boot sector, you can use a backup created with DiskProbe and restore it with this tool. However, for NTFS volumes, there is another alternative. When an NTFS volume is created (or reformatted), NTFS duplicates the boot sector and either places it at the end of the volume (Windows 2000 and Windows NT 4) or at the logical center (Windows NT 3.51 and earlier). You can use DiskProbe to locate and then copy this sector to the beginning of the volume. There are also third-party MS-DOS–based tools that locate and copy the boot sector to the primary boot sector on the volume.

Disk difficulties can stem from a number of problems, and there are tools you can use to troubleshoot them. DiskProbe is one such tool. It can be used to examine and change information on individual disk sectors. Another tool, DiskMap can be used to display the layout of partitions and logical volumes. Neither tool, however, can be used when the system is using dynamic disks. DiskProbe can be found on the Windows 2000 Setup CD in the \support\tools folder. DiskMap is part of the Resource Kit tools in the *Windows 2000 Server Resource Kit* CD. As with Fdisk, be very cautious when using these tools. There is another important tool that is provided with the installation of Windows 2000—Disk Defragmenter, which we cover in the following section.

Disk Defragmenter

Disk file systems become fragmented over time and with heavy use. The operating system saves a file in the first available space on the disk without concern as to whether it can fit into one section. This causes fragmentation on the disk, which can slow or degrade disk performance.

Windows 2000 includes a tool to defragment the hard drive, appropriately named Disk Defragmenter. If a disk is fragmented, the disk heads jump back and forth across the disk area while reading a file, which slows performance. The Disk Defragmenter consolidates the files spread out over the drive and groups them more efficiently, so the operating system can quickly locate and read them. It is recommended that you defragment (or analyze) your hard drives once a month to check on the health of your hard drives.

To use Disk Defragmenter, log on as the Administrator (or have Administrator rights). Select Start | Programs | Accessories | System Tools | Disk Defragmenter. The Disk Defragmenter window opens, as shown in Figure 7.15.

The drives for your system are listed in the window. Disk Defragmenter can defragment NTFS, FAT16, and FAT32 volumes. Analyze the drive by selecting

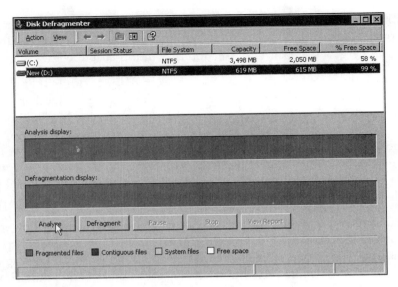

Figure 7.15   Disk Defragmenter window.

the drive and clicking the Analyze button. A pop-up window displays the progress of the analysis, and once complete, gives you the option to view a report, defragment the drive, or close the window. Project 7.3 in the "Real-World Projects" section later in this chapter provides instruction using Disk Defragmenter.

It is best to defragment a hard drive when there is minimal or no other use of the server (or PC) that it resides on. When files are being accessed, moved, or used during the defragmentation process, the hard drive will suffer performance degradation. Also, keep in mind when creating the schedule to run Disk Defragmenter that the more heavily used a PC or server is, the more the hard drive becomes fragmented. So a heavily used server should be checked more often than a rarely used workstation.

Before installing a new application, Disk Defragmenter should be run so larger blocks of free space are made available. You should also run Disk Defragmenter when a computer begins to run slower than usual or when access to network files or services are not as quick as they used to be. Defragmenting the drive often speeds up performance and access times.

Emergency Repair Disk (ERD)
In the event that Windows 2000 does not start up, you have the option of using the ERD. Most Windows NT administrators know this procedure well. The ERD is created during the initial installation or through a NT Backup option. An ERD should be made after a successful installation and the computer is

working well. This way, you are sure that the files backed up onto the ERD are solid. If the system fails, you can start the system using the Windows 2000 Setup CD, and insert the ERD when prompted. The ERD is not a replacement for system backups; it does not include data, programs, or the Registry; it simply contains the files needed to restore the system. The ERD makes basic system repairs to the system files, boot sector, and the startup environment. Table 7.8 shows the files that are copied to the floppy disk when the ERD is created.

Warning! Windows 2000's ERD does not include a copy of the Registry files. This is different than Windows NT, which had a copy of the Registry stored on the ERD. The backup files for the Registry for Windows 2000 are located in the %SystemRoot%\Repair folder. These files are from the original installation of Windows 2000 and do not reflect changes that were made to the system since the time of installation.

When you start the recovery process, you are given two repair options: Manual and Fast. The Manual Repair feature allows the administrator to repair specific system files, boot sector problems, and other startup difficulties. It is recommended for advanced users only. Manual Repair does not check the Registry files. There are three items to choose from with Manual Repair:

➤ *Inspect Startup Environment*—Checks and verifies that the Windows 2000 files in the system partition are correct. If any files, such as Ntdetect.com, boot.ini, or NTLDR are missing or corrupt, Repair replaces them with those from the Windows 2000 Setup CD.

➤ *Verify Windows 2000 System Files*—Uses Checksum to verify that each installed file is good and matches the files that were installed from the Windows 2000 Setup CD. If a file does not match, a message is presented stating this fact and asks if you want to replace the file. This procedure also checks that startup files, such as NTLDR and Ntoskrnl.exe, are present and valid.

Table 7.8   Contents of the ERD created by Windows 2000.

File	Contents
Autoexec.nt	A copy of the %SystemRoot%\System32\Autoexec.nt, which is used to start up the MS-DOS environment.
Config.nt	A copy of the %SystemRoot%\System32\Config.nt, which is used to start up the MS-DOS environment.
Setup.log	A log of which files were installed files and Cyclic Redundancy Check (CRC) information for use during the repair process. This file contains the read-only, system, and hidden attributes.

Note: You should create a new ERD after every service pack, system date change, or updated driver is installed.

➤ *Inspect Boot Sector*—Verifies that the boot sector on the system partition still references NTLDR. The repair process can only replace the boot sector for the system partition on the first hard disk.

The other option is Fast Repair, which is the easier of the two options to use and does not require user input. If this option is selected, the emergency repair process attempts to repair the problems relating to the system. Fast Repair also checks the Registry files, if they are accessible. The three options that are included with Manual Repair are automatically checked during Fast Repair.

Windows 2000 also provides an alternative to using the emergency repair process and the ERD: the Recovery Console. The Recovery Console is a text-mode command interpreter that is separate from the Windows 2000 command prompt. It allows the administrator to gain access to the hard drive of a computer running Windows 2000. Windows 2000 does not have to be started to run Recovery Console. It allows limited access to NTFS and FAT (both FAT16 and FAT32) without starting the GUI, and it can repair the MBR. Recovery Console is covered in detail in Chapter 6.

To check the disk for corruption, you can use Chkdsk; however, this tool cannot correct errors if there are open files, so be sure that all files are closed prior to running it. If a file is open, Chkdsk offers to check the volume automatically the next time the computer is started.

Disk problems can occur that do not involve the MBR, partition table, or boot sector, and Windows 2000 may not have the tools to troubleshoot these other problems. However, you generally get some sort of error message, such as a stop message, when a disk problem occurs. If you write down the stop message, including the numbers, you can look up the message and number using the Microsoft TechNet CDs or at the Microsoft Web site.

A computer contracts most MBR viruses or boot sector viruses from an infected floppy disk, but a virus can be picked up in any number of ways (e.g., a Trojan horse residing in an application, a rogue Web site, email, and so on). Windows 2000 can contain MBR or boot sector viruses, but only if it has started up. If the virus disables the system before Windows 2000 can start up, then other methods must be used to get the system up and running again. Windows 2000 protects itself from these viruses by only accessing physical disks through protected-mode disk drivers. Because the viruses in these cases need the BIOS to replicate and function, they're not able to do so under the Windows 2000 protected-mode disk drivers because Windows 2000 does not use the BIOS mechanism that the viruses depend on.

If you come across an MBR or boot sector virus, the first step is to obtain a well-known commercial antivirus program designed for Windows 2000. The antivirus software most likely has a boot disk that scans for MBR or boot sector viruses, eliminates them, and if possible, restores the MBR or boot sector if it can find them on the disk (to where the virus moved them). Being able to restore your system after a virus attack is more than worth the cost of the software. Scan all hard disks and floppy disks with the antivirus software and update it regularly.

Windows 2000 provides an antivirus tool called AVBoot. It is located on the Windows 2000 Setup CD in the folder \Valueadd\3rdparty\Ca_antiv or in \Valueadd\Ca_antiv. Figure 7.16 shows the window with the files.

To use the program, insert a clean floppy disk (3.5" high density), use Windows Explorer to find Makedisk.bat on the Windows 2000 Setup CD, and then double-click the file. A screen similar to the one in Figure 7.17 will appear.

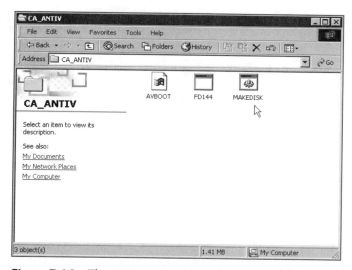

Figure 7.16   The AVBoot program folder located on the Windows 2000 Setup CD.

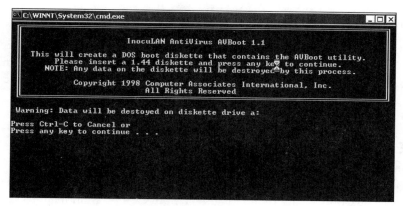

Figure 7.17   Starting Makedisk.bat.

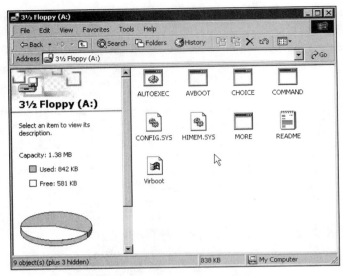

Figure 7.18   Contents of the AVBoot disk.

This file makes a startup disk that contains AVBoot. Figure 7.18 shows the contents of the disk.

Complementary metal-oxide semiconductor (CMOS) problems occur when something changes or happens to the basic devices of the computer, which include RAM, video, storage, and so on. If you swap slot positions between an Industry Standard Architecture Video Graphics Array (ISA VGA) card and an ISA internal modem, you may get a CMOS error. To correct CMOS errors, enter the CMOS utility at startup. The way to do so is usually stated on the screen when an error occurs. The computer uses the CMOS Checksum to see if any values have been changed (by ways other than CMOS). If the Checksum is not correct, the computer will not start. You then need to correct the configuration to get CMOS working again. It is a good idea to write down (or print) the CMOS information prior to a problem occurring.

If the computer uses SCSI adapters, make sure that the adapters are listed on the Windows 2000 HCL and updated drivers for Windows 2000 are available. Finally, always make sure cables and connections are secure. A disk that cannot be accessed during startup might simply not be properly plugged in!

CHAPTER SUMMARY

There are many new techniques for managing data and storage with Windows 2000. These include data compression, encryption, removable storage, remote storage, disk quotas, and disk defragmentation. Compression helps to save on disk space usage. Encryption helps to keep data secure. Removable and remote storage help manage data availability. Finally, disk quotas ensure that no one user overruns the available system storage, whereas disk defragmentation helps to improve disk efficiency.

Properly managing data and storage ensures that your system runs more effectively as well as having made the most efficient use of disk space. The tools provided with Windows 2000 allow the network administrator better control of the operating system as well as offer fuller functionality. By managing data using the tools mentioned in this chapter, you ensure that your data is accessible in the most efficient manner possible.

REVIEW QUESTIONS

1. Julie was moved to a different department in the same company, and the network administrator wants to remove her account from the disk quotas that are placed on the volume her former department uses. He opens the Quota Entries window and tries to remove Julie but cannot. What must be done first?

   a. The user account must first be deleted, and then it can be removed from the Quota Entries window.

   b. The network administrator must remove all of Julie's files from the volume (moving them to another volume or tape, deleting them if she no longer needs them, or transferring ownership to another person). Then he will be able to remove Julie from the Quota Entries window.

   c. The network administrator must go to the command prompt and type "C:\Diskquotas remove /Julie \w\p".

   d. Windows 2000 Server automatically removes her account once it is notified that she is in another department.

2. Administrator Bob wants to assign mandatory user profiles to users on the network. He edits the path in each user account to be \\server\ share*username*, but users are able to make changes to their user profiles and the changes are restored each session. What did Bob forget to do?

   a. Users can make changes to user profiles and if they have the appropriate permissions, they can save their changes. Bob needs to reassign the users' permissions.

   b. The path in the users' accounts should read *server**localshare**username*.man.

c. Bob needs to change the NDS permissions for each user.

d. The Ntuser.dat file needs to be changed to Ntuser.man, and the path needs to be edited to read *server**share**username*.man.

3. A user wants to encrypt a file that is compressed, but is not able to. What is wrong?

   a. The user does not belong to the Administrators group, and therefore cannot encrypt files.

   b. The file must be decompressed first, and then it can be encrypted.

   c. Only a recovery agent can encrypt compressed files.

   d. The file does not belong to a folder that is encrypted.

4. The new network administrator wants to use disk quotas and goes to a Windows 98 machine, right-clicks the drive, and then selects Properties. However, the Quota tab is not listed. Why is this?

   a. Disk quotas are only supported by Windows 2000 NTFS. Windows 98 uses the FAT file system.

   b. The network administrator must first enable disk quotas by selecting Control Panel | System | Enable Disk Quotas.

   c. Disk quotas can only be viewed from the command prompt in Windows 98.

   d. The network administrator does not have the appropriate permissions to enable disk quotas.

5. Windows 2000 can display alternate colors for compressed files and folders.

   a. True

   b. False

6. A user has a disk quota set at 50MB and has already used 47MB. She wants to save a compressed file that is 2MB. When she tries to save the file, she gets an error message that the disk is full. What is the problem?

   a. By adding a 2MB file, she will have surpassed the warning limit for the disk's quota, and that is why it does not allow her to add the new file.

   b. There are invisible files that are taking up space that she cannot see. She should select Tools | View All Files in Windows Explorer to see all files that are taking up disk space.

   c. The disk drive is corrupt, and she should contact the network administrator.

   d. Disk quotas use a file's actual size, not its compressed size when determining the amount of space a file will use.

7. Sally moves an uncompressed file that is located in a folder on her Windows 2000 Professional hard drive to the Windows 2000 Server's compressed "work storage" folder. All volumes are NTFS. What happens to the file during the transfer?

   a. The file changes its attributes to the new parent folder and is automatically compressed.

   b. An error message appears on Sally's computer stating that the file is in an incompatible state and needs to be changed to a compatible one.

   c. The file retains its attributes and remains uncompressed.

   d. The server's folder changes its attributes and becomes decompressed.

8. A user wants to encrypt his folder and the files it contains and does so following the network administrator's instructions. However, after going through the process, he can still open, close, save, and edit the files without any notification or delay while the file is in use. He feels that the files (and folder) are not encrypted. How can he be assured that they are? [Choose all that apply]

   a. Check the folder and files attributes using Windows Explorer.

   b. He is correct; his folder and files are not encrypted. It is the network administrator who must set up encryption first on his directory before he can use encryption.

   c. His folder is encrypted, but the files are not. He must go through and encrypt each individual file.

   d. The network administrator can log on as a user and demonstrate that the files cannot be opened by other users.

9. Jeff needs to copy a file from his workstation to the network server, but he is confused as to what happens to the file's compression state. His workstation's folders and files are not compressed, and he knows that the target folder on the server is compressed. He would prefer that the file be compressed on the server. All volumes are NTFS. What is the best solution?

   a. Contact the network administrator and ask to have the folder on the server changed to a decompressed state so that he can copy the file, and then change it back to a compressed state, which compresses the file.

   b. Copy the file to the network server's folder.

   c. Compress the file, copy it to the server's folder, and then ask the network administrator to decompress the file for him.

   d. Compress the file, copy it to the server's folder, and then decompress the file on his workstation.

10. Name the areas where roaming user profiles can be stored. [Choose all that apply]

    a. In a local Windows 2000 Professional workstation's cache

    b. In the NDS tree (using the RPC protocol)

    c. On the Windows 2000 Server

    d. In a Linux workstation's cache

11. Randy is using a Windows 98 workstation and needs to access a file on the Windows 2000 Server in his company. He opens the folder and notices that the file is compressed. He is happy about this because it is a large file and he is running out of room on his computer. He copies the file to his workstation without any problems, but when he uses Windows Explorer to see if the file is in its targeted location, he notices that the file is twice the size it was on the server and no longer has the compressed attribute. What happened?

    a. Randy copied the file instead of moving it. Moving a file retains its compression state, whereas copying a file causes it to take on the state of the destination folder.

    b. Randy did not have the appropriate permissions to copy the file, which is why the file lost its compressed state.

    c. His Windows 98 workstation is using FAT16 instead of FAT32, which is not compatible with Windows 2000 Server's FAT64 and is why the file lost its compressed state.

    d. His Windows 98 workstation is using a version of FAT, and the Windows 2000 Server is using NTFS. Whenever a file is transferred from NTFS to FAT, the compression state is lost because Windows 2000 only supports compression on NTFS volumes.

12. Joe is a new system administrator and realizes that he needs to defragment the server's hard drive, but is not sure how often he should do it. What is the recommended time frame that Joe should use to check if the server's hard drive needs defragmentation?

    a. He does not need to do anything. Windows 2000 automatically notifies him when he should defragment the hard drive by default.

    b. He should check the hard disk and defragment it once a month or more if the server is highly used.

    c. He should check the hard disk and defragment it every other month.

    d. He should check the hard disk and defragment it twice a year.

13. Patty loses her private key and can no longer access her encrypted files. What options does she have?

    a. She should inform the network administrator, who can then recover the files with the recovery agent.

    b. She should search for her private key in the %SystemRoot%\user profile\key storage file. This is the location in which private keys are stored.

    c. There is nothing she or anyone else can do, and she will have to delete the files.

    d. Microsoft Support online provides a universal master key that unlocks all encrypted files.

14. Bill has just received a warning that he is nearing the limit of disk space that he has been assigned. What is the best method for him to use to free up disk space?

    a. Go through all of his folders and delete the ones he does not use often or that he can re-create if needed.

    b. Compress his folders and the files they contain.

    c. Contact the network administrator and ask for more disk space.

    d. Move folders and files that are rarely used to a backup medium, such as a tape.

15. You are running out of disk space on a volume and want to compress some folders and files to free up space. What is the best method to use when selecting which files and folders to compress?

    a. Compress files and folders that are used often.

    b. Compress files and folders that are not used often.

16. Maria is the network administrator for a medium-size company. The network server is a heavily used file and print server with many large folders and files stored on it. Maria wants to free up space on the server, so she compresses the majority of the folders. Now users are complaining that it is taking much longer to retrieve their files. Why is this?

    a. Maria forgot to select the Optimize Disk Performance checkbox when compressing the files.

    b. Data that is compressed takes longer to access than data that is not compressed.

    c. The users need to compress the folders on their workstations, so the file transfer is from compressed folder to compressed folder, which makes for faster access time.

    d. After the next system backup, the access time will be back to normal.

17. You have encrypted files, but suspect someone is stealing them from the company and is able to read them. The recovery agent is a trusted source. How else could the files be stolen and read?

    a. The thief has a special cracking tool that is able to determine the key.

    b. The thief is copying the file to his or her own encrypted directory, allowing access.

    c. Only the network administrator is able to do this, so he or she must be guilty.

    d. The folder is not encrypted, so when the file is edited, it is stored as plain text in a temp file. The thief is taking this file.

18. Joe is an experienced Windows NT 4.0 Server administrator. He has just upgraded one of his servers to Windows 2000 Server. He is looking for Disk Administrator and selects Start | Programs | Administrative Tools, but cannot find it. What must Joe do?

    a. Joe must use the Disk Management MMC snap-in.

    b. Disk Administrator has been moved and is now found under System Tools in Control Panel.

    c. Disk Administrator has been replaced by Disk Management, which is a third-party add on.

    d. Something went wrong with the installation. Joe should reinstall Windows 2000 Server.

19. Susan has a Windows 2000 Server with one hard drive and one partition formatted as FAT16. She wants to convert the hard drive from a basic disk to dynamic disk, but she is not able to. Why is this? [Choose all that apply]

    a. Dynamic disks only support striped sets.

    b. She needs to use NTFS as the file system.

    c. You cannot upgrade a volume that is the system or boot volume.

    d. The workstations are Windows 98, so the server knows that these systems cannot access a dynamic disk and does not permit the upgrade.

20. You have a disk quota management procedure in place, and the settings allow users to exceed their disk limits. A user did exceed his or her disk limit, and you noticed the event in Event Viewer, but no other messages have been left since. Why is this?

    a. Event Viewer logs the date and time of the infraction, but does not keep statistics or information about the user's disk usage.

    b. Since exceeding the limit, the user must not be saving files on their volume, but instead must be saving them on floppy disks, so there is no additional information to track.

c. You must assign a log file in the user's profile to keep track of the information.

d. Event Viewer must be instructed to keep this information. Select Tools | Logs | Advanced, and then select Keep Disk Quota Statistics.

21. A user with a roaming profile stored on a Windows 2000 Server asks if he is able to log on to several machines simultaneously. What should your response be?

a. No. Roaming profiles can only be used at one machine at a time because the profile is stored at the server, which can only be accessed by one machine. If he tries to log on multiple times, the default profile from the local machine is used.

b. If the roaming profile is created with an additional file, multi.dat, then the user can log on to several machines simultaneously.

c. Yes. But the user should not make changes to his profile while doing this.

d. No. The user will need to have a multiroaming profile, which is only available on Windows 2000 Advanced Server.

REAL-WORLD PROJECTS

Note: This exercise assumes you have a test server with Windows 2000 Server and a test workstation with Windows 2000 Professional. Read the instructions carefully and do not perform this on any of your production machines.

Sam is a network administrator and has just set up his new Windows 2000 Server and Windows 2000 Professional clients. He has been working with the new system for about one month and feels confident that critical company functions and software are working within established parameters.

He decides that it is time to tackle more advanced issues and sets his sights on establishing disk quotas, compressing certain archived folders, and defragmenting the Windows 2000 Server's hard drive. Sam also has an employee suggestion box, and much to his surprise, it contained a good suggestion. (Sam tossed the other suggestions into the trash.) The suggestion stated that users were tired of coming back to their workspace and finding that someone had completely altered their desktop settings. They wanted to have their desktop settings applied whenever and wherever they logged on.

Sam took his ideas to the CTO and was heartened by her response. She was pleased that Sam was working so well and that he continued to make performance adjustments to the network. She wondered if he would be able to make the compressed folders more visibly noticeable when viewed with Windows Explorer, and he responded with a confident "Yes." Sam left her office and went straight to work.

Project 7.1
To set disk quota amounts, perform the following steps:

Note: This only works on volumes that are formatted with NTFS, and you must be a member of the Administrators group or the Quota tab will not appear.

1. Open My Computer by double-clicking the desktop icon.

2. Right-click the disk drive (usually C:).

3. Select Properties.

4. Click the Quota tab.

5. Select the Enable Quota Management checkbox (the other options will become available, as shown in Figure 7.19).

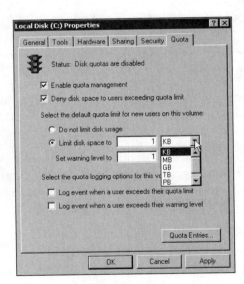

Figure 7.19   Quota tab options.

6. Check that the Deny Disk Space To Users Exceeding Quota Limit checkbox is selected (it is selected by default when you select Enable Quota Management). This option does not allow users to exceed the amount of disk space you assign.

7. Click the Limit Disk Space To option, and assign the amount of 30MB. Set the Set Warning Level to 25MB.

8. Select the logging options, and click Log Event When A User Exceeds Their Quota Limit and Log Event When A User Exceeds Their Warning Level. This informs the administrator when a user passes his or her warning limit and quota limit.

9. Click the Quota Entries button. This takes you to the Quota Entries For *Local Disk* window (where *Local Disk* is the name of the current disk), as shown in Figure 7.20.

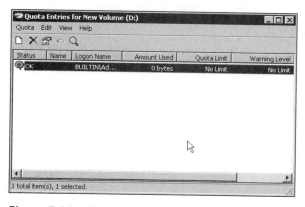

Figure 7.20   Quota Entries For *Local Disk* window.

10. Select Quota|New Quota Entry as shown in Figure 7.21.

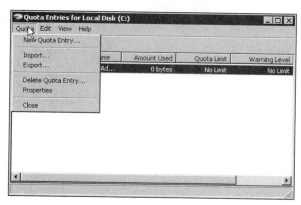

Figure 7.21   New Quota entry.

11. Click the name of the user(s) to add. Click the Add button.

12. The Add New Entry pop-up window appears. Click OK.

13. Click the Limit Disk Space To option, and assign the amount of 30MB. Set the Set Warning Level to 25MB.

14. Repeat this process for each additional user. When finished, click OK. You can view the entries in the Quota Entries For Local Disk window. Close the window.

Project 7.2
To set the compression state, perform the following steps:

1. Start Windows Explorer.

2. Right-click the folder you want to compress. An example is given in Figure 7.22. Note the file size of 2.47MB and that the attribute is Normal.

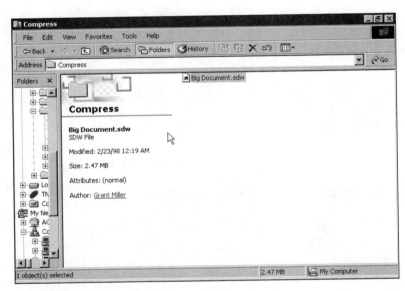

Figure 7.22   A file prior to being compressed.

3. Select Properties | General Tab.

4. Click Advanced.

5. In the Advanced Attributes box, check the Compress Contents To Save Disk Space checkbox, and then click OK.

6. Click OK to exit Properties.

7. Windows 2000 displays the Confirm Attribute Changes dialog box. This box gives you the option of either compressing the folder only or compressing the folder and its subfolders and files.

8. Select Apply Changes To This Folder, Subfolders And Files, and click OK.

9. To view the new attribute of the compressed folder, select the folder in Windows Explorer. An example is given in Figure 7.23. Note that the attribute has changed; the file size is still listed as 2.47MB.

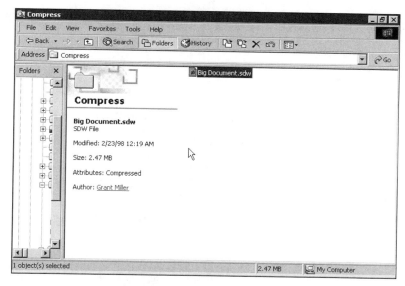

Figure 7.23 Windows Explorer displays the new attribute of the compressed file.

10. To view the properties and the compressed size of the file, right-click the file. Select Properties | General | Advanced. The file's properties are given with the new size of the compressed file, as shown in Figure 7.24.

Figure 7.24   The Properties window gives the file's new compressed size.

Project 7.3

To defragment the hard drive, perform the following steps:

1. Select Start | Programs | Accessories.

2. Select System Tools | Disk Defragmenter.

3. The Disk Defragmenter window opens.

4. Select the volume and click the Analyze button. The volume is analyzed and a graphical Analysis Display report is displayed.

Note: If your drive is not badly fragmented, you may receive a You Do Not Need To Defragment This Drive Now error. If this is the case, you may not need to continue with this exercise.

5. A pop-up window informs you that the analysis is complete. It gives a recommendation (defragment the volume or not) and options to View Report, Defragment, or close.

6. Click the View Report button.

7. Review the information given in the report. You can print or save the report if desired.

8. Click the Defragment button. The system begins the defragmentation process.

9. After defragmentation is complete, a graphical Defragmentation Display is shown with the results, as shown in Figure 7.25.

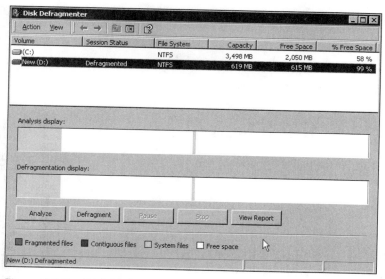

Figure 7.25   Disk Defragmenter's defragmentation display.

10. A pop-up window appears stating that defragmentation is complete and offers you a view of the defragmentation report. Click Yes. A report similar to the one shown in Figure 7.26 is displayed.

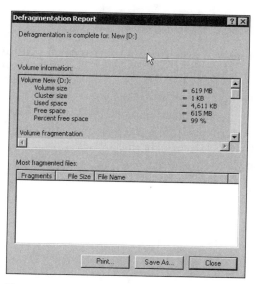

Figure 7.26   Disk Defragmenter's Defragmentation Report.

Project 7.4

To create a roaming user profile, perform the following steps:

1. Open Windows Explorer. Create a folder named "userprofiles".

2. Share the new folder. Close Windows Explorer.

3. Select Start | Programs | Administrative Tools.

4. Open Active Directory Users And Computers.

5. In the details pane, right-click the user account you want to create the profile for.

6. Click Properties.

7. Click the Profile tab.

8. Type the path information for the profile path, for example, *server*\userprofiles*username*.

Note: You need to create a folder named userprofiles and share it if one does not exist already. If your server is called NTServer, then the path is \\NTServer\userprofiles\username. The username refers to the user's network name and provides an alternative to typing each user's name individually.

9. Click OK.

The next time the user logs on, the local profile is copied to the server.

Optional: To create a mandatory user profile, perform the following steps:

1. Open Windows Explorer. Create a folder named userprofiles.

2. Share the new folder.

3. Find and rename Ntuser.dat to Ntuser.man in the user's profile and make sure the file is available in that user's folder.

4. Close Windows Explorer.

5. Select Start | Programs | Administrative Tools.

6. Open Active Directory Users And Computers.

7. In the details pane, right-click the user account you want to create the profile for.

8. Click Properties.

9. Click the Profile tab.

10. Type the path information for the profile path, for example, *server*\\userprofiles*username*.man.

11. Click OK. The next time the user logs on, the user has the mandatory profile.

Project 7.5

To change the display color for compressed folders, perform the following steps:

1. Open Windows Explorer.

2. From the menu selections in Windows Explorer, select Tools.

3. Select Folder Options.

4. Click the View tab.

5. Select the Display Compressed Files And Folders With Alternate Color checkbox.

6. Click OK. The compressed names of the files and folders should now be in a different color than noncompressed files and folders. The compressed names of the files and folders will be colored blue (similar to a hyperlink) if the system colors have not been changed from the default.

7

CHAPTER EIGHT

NETWORKING WINDOWS 2000 SERVER

After completing this chapter, you will be able to:

✓ Understand the Windows 2000 network architecture and how it fits into the Windows 2000 architecture

✓ Understand the function of the OSI model and its layers

✓ Understand the role of border layers and identify the border layers employed by the Windows 2000 network architecture

✓ Understand, install, and identify the network protocols used by Windows 2000

✓ Understand IP addresses, subnet masks, and dotted-decimal notation

✓ Understand the Windows 2000 network services including DHCP and DNS

✓ Understand virtual networks and how they are implemented and supported by Windows 2000

✓ Identify network components and their roles

✓ Understand the routing process and the protocols used by Windows 2000

Like many other components, the Windows 2000 network architecture and functionality are based on previous versions of Windows. With Windows 2000, however, Microsoft has moved to incorporate native support for industry standard protocols and operation, giving it greater interoperability than other versions of Windows. In adopting these standards, Microsoft has moved away from many familiar protocols, such as NetBEUI and NetBIOS. In addition, many of the central components of Windows NT have been updated to support these protocols.

WINDOWS 2000 NETWORK ARCHITECTURE

As discussed in Chapter 1, the overall Windows 2000 network architecture follows a layered model. The Windows 2000 architecture specifies two types of layers: functional and boundary. A functional layer consists of various software components that perform similar tasks. For example, the component Windows 2000 uses to communicate with another Windows 2000 computer is similar to the component that Windows 2000 uses to communicate with a Macintosh computer. Both components are part of the same functional layer in the architecture. To standardize interaction between components, Windows 2000 uses what are known as *boundary layers*. A boundary layer is a software component that serves as a connection point between layers. Boundary layers define the specifications to which all components must be written to ensure that communication takes place. By using the boundary layer method, device manufacturers, protocol developers, and application programmers need only include functionality to the nearest boundary layer, rather than through all levels of the model.

For example, a programmer working on an accounting system does not have to write code to communicate with every available network card and across the network to print. Instead, the program is written to communicate with the boundary layer, reducing the amount of code that must be written. The layering process also ensures that all applications use the same process for communicating throughout the model and across the network.

As shown in Figure 8.1, the Windows 2000 network architecture consists of three main component layers divided by two boundary layers. The topmost layer of the architecture includes the network services components and application programming interfaces. Between the top layer and the next layer is the Transport Driver Interface (TDI) boundary layer. Below the TDI boundary is the Network Device Interface Specification (NDIS) boundary layer, followed by the network protocol layer. At the bottom of the architecture is the layer that includes the network adapter cards and their drivers. Each of these layers and their components are discussed in detail in later sections of this chapter.

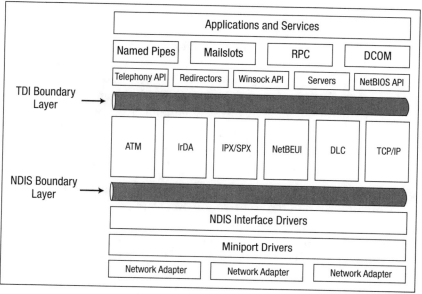

Figure 8.1   The Windows 2000 network architecture.

The Open Systems Interconnection (OSI) Model: Standard for Layered Architectures

The idea of a layered architecture is not new to the computing world. In fact, all of today's network architectures are, at least to some degree, based on a standard that was first introduced in 1978: the OSI model. Understanding how the model is constructed makes it easier to understand other layered network architectures, like the one used in Windows 2000.

Note: It is important to note that the OSI model is a theoretical model. No network architecture developed since its introduction follows its design exactly. That being said, it is an invaluable tool for understanding the ins and outs of network communication and provides the basis for many computing models.

The OSI model was created on the basis that for network communication to take place, specific steps needed to happen in a specific order. Each of the steps between the application on one computer and the application on another computer is basically the same. Further, these steps can be standardized so that applications on one computer can rely on the mechanisms of the model for data delivery to the applications on another computer.

There are seven layers in the OSI model, which was developed to provide an international network communication standard. When creating the OSI model, the International Organization for Standardization (ISO) used a basic set of guidelines to ensure the broadest coverage within the standard. The first of these principles was that each layer's function be decided with the final goal of defining internationally standardized protocols. Each layer was also defined for a specific function, and delineation between layers was only specified when an additional level of abstraction was needed. When a boundary between layers was needed, it was to be defined as to minimize the amount of information transferred between interfaces. Finally, enough layers were defined to separate distinct functions, but as few as possible to keep the architecture from becoming unmanageable. As daunting as this task may seem with these guidelines, the ISO was successful and the OSI model was born.

The layers of the OSI model are (from the top down): Application, Presentation, Session, Transport, Network, Data Link, and Physical. As mentioned earlier, each layer is responsible for a specific segment of end-to-end network communication; each layer relies on the services of the layer below and provides services to the layer above. The responsibilities of the layers of the OSI model are as follows.

➤ *Application*—Provides the access point to the network for applications and processes running on the computer. It is at this level that all user-mode processes function and user-generated commands are initiated.

➤ *Presentation*—Acts as the translator between the application running on the computer and the network. The software running at the Presentation layer converts the requests received from the Application layer into commands in the format specified by the network being used. This includes conversions, such as changes in character-code sets and bit order reversal. In addition, the Presentation layer is able to employ compression and encryption to provide more efficient and secure transmission.

➤ *Session*—Facilitates communication between processes on the sending and receiving systems. The sending Session layer process marks each message it sends to the Transport layer to identify where the message starts and ends, which ensures the receiving process does not communicate a message to the upper layers prematurely. The Session layer makes use of acknowledgment messages to synchronize transmission between sender and receiver. Specialized network functions, such as secure resource access and user authentication, are also handled at the Session layer.

➤ *Transport*—Ensures all messages are delivered to the upper layers in order and without duplication or error and creates and maintains a virtual circuit session between the processes. To facilitate this, the Transport layer uses acknowledgments to ensure reliable message delivery and limits the flow of messages from the sending system if the receiving system's buffers are full.

Because the lower layers in the communication path may require smaller messages than the Transport layer, it is also able to divide messages received from the Session layer into segments before passing them along. When this occurs, the Transport layer includes sequence information in each segment, which it utilizes to ensure messages are sent to the upper layers in the correct order.

Note: The Transport layer and all layers above it are considered end-to-end layers. The software at these layers does not consider the mechanics of the lower layers or the method for transmission between the systems. Instead, the software components at these layers on one system communicate directly with their counterparts on the other system. For example, if a CEO of a company wants to speak with the CEO of another company, one may ask his assistant to get his counterpart on the line. From that point until he speaks with his counterpart, the CEO is not aware of the things going on to make the conversation possible, only that he is able to communicate with his friend in the same position in another company.

➤ *Network*—Coordinates communication beyond the subnet to which the computer is connected, including deciding on the path the data takes based on current network conditions and the priority of the service being used. This process is known as routing. As part of this routing function, the Network layer moves the data frames to a router if the frame's destination address is not on the local subnet. The Network layer is also responsible for resolving a computer's logical address to its physical network adapter address. In determining the best path for the data to take and controlling the flow of data on the network, the Network layer is provided the ability to fragment and reassemble frames. The Network layer can also instruct a specific computer to cease sending frames if a router is overloaded or, if the a router is busy, it can instruct the computer to use a different router.

➤ *Data Link*—Ensures error-free transmission of data frames between computers over the Physical layer through mechanisms such as frame flow control and sequencing, frame acknowledgment and error detection, creation and management of virtual links between the communicating devices based on network adapter addresses, media access control and management, and review of all received frames to determine whether they should be passed to the higher layers. The Data Link layer is further subdivided into the *Media Access Control (MAC)* and the *Logical Link Control (LLC)* sublayers. The MAC sublayer provides hardware addressing information for communication with network interface cards across the network. The LLC sublayer provides error correction and flow control of network data.

➤ *Physical*—Controls how raw data is sent and received over the physical network medium (called data encoding). Data encoding determines which signal represents a binary 1 or 0, how the sending computer structures the data, and how the receiving computer recognizes the beginning of a package of data. Also, it specifies whether data is transmitted using optical or electrical signals and whether the signaling method used is analog (broadband) or digital (baseband).

It is important to remember that the OSI model is a guideline, not a set of hard and fast rules. Although many protocol suites and architectures include components that function at each layer, it is not a requirement. Some network protocols, for example, may not need error checking or acknowledgments and so may not include Transport layer components. Figure 8.2 expands on Figure 8.1 and maps the Windows 2000 network architecture to the OSI model.

The Network Services and Programming Interface Functional Layer

At the top of the Windows 2000 network architecture, this layer is comprised of the software components that provide network services to users and applications. These components are divided into two categories: services and application programming interfaces (APIs). There are two primary services that operate in this area: the server service and the workstation service.

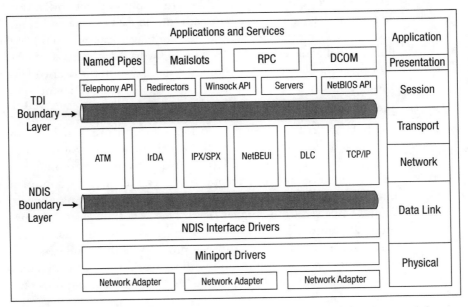

Figure 8.2 The Windows 2000 network architecture and the OSI model.

As mentioned in Chapter 2, both the server and workstation service are used on Windows 2000 computers communicating on a network, regardless of the version of the operating system on the computer. Many network administrators have made the mistake of turning off the workstation service on a Windows NT or 2000 Server, simply because of its name, only to find that the server can no longer function on the network without it.

As mentioned in Chapter 1, network services, such as workstation and server, are implemented as part of the integral subsystem and operate in user mode. In fact, both the workstation and server service consist of two components, one that operates in user mode, and one that operates as part of the file system in kernel mode. The server service is responsible for fulfilling requests for the computer's resources. These requests may come from other computers on the network or other processes on the same computer. The server service components are the Service Control Manager utility and a file system driver. The Service Control Manager operates in user mode and initiates all services and coordinates communication with the file system driver. The server service file system driver operates in kernel mode below the I/O Manager and works with the other file system drivers and with the lower levels of the network architecture to fulfill service commands, such as read and write.

As the complementary architecture component to the server service, the workstation service manages the process of requesting resources. Like the server service, the workstation service is made up of two components, the user-mode interface and the Windows 2000 redirector, which is a file system driver and part of the I/O Manager. Upon receipt from another user-mode component or application, the workstation service user interface forwards the request to the I/O Manager. The I/O Manager then handles the request by accessing the appropriate file system driver. In the event that the request is for a network resource, the I/O Manager uses the Windows 2000 redirector to complete the request. The redirector accepts requests for network resources from the workstation service user-mode interface and forwards them to other components of the network architecture for fulfillment.

To illustrate: If a user-mode process requests a file from the local hard drive, the workstation service forwards the request to the I/O Manager, which uses the NTFS file system component. On the other hand, if the process requests a file located on another computer on the network, the workstation service sends the request to the I/O Manager, which uses the Windows 2000 redirector to access the appropriate network resource.

The Windows 2000 redirector is an important part of the overall network architecture. The redirector allows communication between Windows 2000 computers and computers running Windows 95/98, Windows for Workgroups,

8

LAN Manager, LAN Server, and other computers using the Common Internet File System (CIFS), which is discussed in the section titled "Interprocess Communication (IPC) Components" later in this chapter. Because the redirector is implemented as a file system component, the I/O Manager is able to access network resources and local resources using the same method. This also allows the redirector to coexist with other redirectors, allowing access to other types of networks, such as Novell NetWare or Unix. In addition, because it operates as part of the kernel, the redirector is able to directly call other kernel-mode components, such as the Cache Manager and Security Reference Monitor.

Resource Access Components

There are two additional components of the Windows 2000 network architecture that are used to provide access to network resources: the Multiple Uniform Naming Convention Provider and the Multi-Provider Router (MPR). The Universal Naming Convention (UNC) is used to identify specific network servers and the resources available on those servers. UNC names begin with two backward slashes and the name of the server to be accessed. From that point, the name of the shared resource and subsequent fields are separated by backward slashes. For example, the UNC for the MYFILES folder on the DDRIVE share on the AUSSERV server would be \\AUSSERV\DDRIVE\MYFILES.

The Multiple UNC Provider (MUP) allows multiple redirectors on a Windows 2000 system access to UNC resources. The MUP does this by freeing the applications from maintaining their own UNC provider lists. If there are multiple redirectors on the computer, the MUP acts as an arbitrator to determine which redirector to use when a request is made. UNC-defined requests from applications are received by the I/O Manager and passed to the MUP. If the UNC has been accessed recently, the MUP directs the request to the previously used redirector. If the UNC is not in the MUP listing, the MUP sends the name of each of the UNC providers to determine the location of the resource and the provider that is able to process the request. The workstation service of Windows 2000 relies on the MUP and is a prerequisite for operation.

The MPR operates in a similar fashion to the MUP, but is used to determine the appropriate redirector for Win32 Network (WNet) API commands. Not all applications use UNC names to identify network resources. Some network vendors may choose to use different interfaces for communicating with their redirector. The MPR intercepts non-UNC commands and forwards the requests to the appropriate redirector based on the information provided by the network vendor.

Interprocess Communication (IPC) Components

Controlled by the IPC Manager discussed in Chapter 1, the IPC components provide bidirectional communication between clients and servers. The IPC mechanism is used to allow concurrently running tasks to communicate among themselves, regardless of whether the tasks are running on the same computer or on different computers. This includes distributed processes that operate on different microprocessors on the same computer and distributed client/server applications.

Distributed client/server applications divide the processing requirements between the client computer and the more powerful server. The client-side portion of the application may include a simple user interface and the programming necessary to accept input from the user. Once the information is obtained from the user, the client-side application passes the processing responsibilities to the server to ensure faster, more efficient processing. There are many ways to implement this type of distributed processing and Windows 2000 supports a number of Interprocess Communication mechanisms.

The first of these is the CIFS. CIFS is an enhanced version of the Server Message Block (SMB) protocol that has been submitted for review as an Internet standard. CIFS is a native protocol of Windows 2000 that enables file sharing between computers across corporate intranets and the Internet. The CIFS standard defines the commands used to exchange information between computers. To do this, the redirector packages the request for a remote file into the CIFS structure that is sent over the network. In addition, the redirector manages network communication by sending CIFS messages to the protocol stack. These messages provide information for connection establishment and teardown, file manipulation, namespace utilization, printing, and other miscellaneous messages to use mailslots and named pipes (discussed later in this section).

CIFS is supported by all Microsoft operating systems including Windows for Workgroups, Windows 95, 98, NT, and 2000, and Microsoft OS/2 LAN Manager. In addition, because it is based on accepted standards, it is also supported by Unix, VMS, DEC Pathworks, LAN Manager for Unix, 3Com 3+Open, MS-Net, Macintosh, and IBM LAN Server systems. As part of Windows 2000, CIFS is used to maintain file integrity and provide concurrent use of a single file. CIFS allows multiple clients to access the same file concurrently by controlling file sharing and file locking, even when concurrent connections span the Internet. File integrity is ensured by using an aggressive file caching method. When a file is used by a computer, it is stored in a cache buffer. This buffer must be cleared after the first computer is finished using it to ensure the next computer uses the most up-to-date version of the file. Only one copy of the file is active at any time, preventing corruption of the file.

CIFS also provides tuning mechanisms that allow the protocol to be configured for optimal use over slow links like dial-up connections. When used to access

8

files on NTFS partitions, CIFS allows for greater security than other file manipulation protocols. In addition to allowing anonymous transfers, CIFS supports secure file transfer and authenticated file access. Finally, CIFS is optimized for use on global networks by supporting Unicode file names and globally significant names. By using the Distributed file system (Dfs) and CIFS, users can create a local representation of the global network so that files can be easily accessed, regardless of their location.

*Note: For more information on CIFS and its status as an Internet Standard, refer to the Microsoft Developer Network Web Workshop on CIFS at **http://msdn.microsoft.com/ workshop/networking/cifs/**. CIFS 1.0 has been submitted as an Internet-Draft document as a protocol specification to the Internet Engineering Task Force (IETF). Internet-Draft is the first step to acceptance by the IETF as a standard. Microsoft is currently working to have CIFS accepted as an Internet RFC, the final step to standardization.*

The second IPC component is the Remote Procedure Call (RPC). The Windows 2000 RPC implementation is a communication technique that is compatible with the Open Group's Distributed Computing Environment (DCE) specification and is compatible with other DCE systems such as Linux and Unix. RPC mechanisms are used in Windows 2000 to facilitate communication between client and server applications. The Windows 2000 RPC implementation differs from other RPC implementations because it relies on other IPC processes to establish and manage communications between the applications. Because RPC utilizes the other IPC components for communication, applications can exist on different computers and truly function in the distributed client/server model.

Like many other Windows 2000 components, RPC uses an object-oriented structure that defines specific functions that are managed by different programs or drivers. The Windows 2000 RPC performs these functions through components called dynamic link libraries (DLLs). The Windows 2000 RPC is made up of the RPC APIs, Network Data Representation (NDR) marshalling, the RPC Stub, and the datagram, local, and connection-oriented runtime components. The RPC APIs are responsible for registering servers, name resolution, connection establishment, endpoint resolution, and security. NDR marshalling is responsible for packaging and unpackaging parameters into the NDR format. A stub is a specially compiled library that is referenced by an application. The RPC stub is generated by the Microsoft Interface Description Language for each communication interface. The runtime components provide communication paths for three different scenarios: communication between processes on the local computer, network communication using connectionless protocols (also called datagram protocols) such as UDP, and network communication using connection-oriented protocols (session protocols) such as TCP.

The component object model (COM) is Microsoft's object-oriented programming model that defines how objects within an application interact with each other or with objects in another application. An object is a software component designed to perform a set of related functions to support an application. To provide this functionality between applications on different computers, Microsoft enhanced COM to create the distributed component object model (DCOM). The DCOM model is used by application programmers to create a client/server application that supports distributed processing. Each object in DCOM provides a specific function, such as sorting and database searches. A set of functions is combined to create an interface, which provides an access point to applications requiring the object's services. Because an object can contain more than one interface, the object responds to an application's request with a pointer to the correct interface. By utilizing the distributed component object model, programmers are able to utilize an easy-to-use mechanism for integrating applications on a network. The model provides a more easily configurable interface than other IPC components and allows the programmer to tightly control security features like domain authentication, remotely start applications, or integrate ActiveX Web browser applications.

8

The final IPC components are referred to as named pipes and mailslots. Like the workstation and server services, named pipes and mailslots are implemented as file system drivers. These high-level interprocess communication mechanisms are used both by networked computers and local processes.

Named pipes and mailslots rely on CIFS to provide connectivity to other computers on the network. A pipe is a reserved section of memory that is used by one process to pass information to another. In the Windows 2000 environment, named pipes provide reliable, connection-oriented messaging between client/server applications. Microsoft's WNet API implementation of named pipes is based on the OS/2 API and provides backward compatibility with Microsoft LAN Manager and its applications. With Windows 2000, Microsoft has enhanced named pipes with a feature called impersonation to provide greater security. Using impersonation, the server changes its security identity to that of the client, thereby limiting the permissions to those granted to the client, rather than those of the server itself.

Mailslots perform a function similar to named pipes. Named pipes provide reliable, connection-oriented communication, whereas the mailslots used by Windows 2000 are connectionless communication mechanisms. Because they are connectionless, mailslots are most often used by broadcasts to locate computers and services on the network. Delivery of this type of broadcast message is not guaranteed, but the messages are received the majority of the time. Microsoft has chosen to incorporate second-class mailslots to provide this service. A first-class mailslot is a connection-oriented, guaranteed-delivery messaging process. Because connection-oriented messaging is handled by named pipes, first-class mailslots are not supported by Windows 2000.

Application Programming Interfaces (APIs)

An API is a specific set of programming routines designed to request and carry out lower-level services provided by the operating system. Applications are written to utilize specific APIs for specific functions. By relying on existing Windows 2000 APIs for functions like network access, application developers are able to minimize development time. In addition, because Microsoft creates the APIs used in Windows 2000, applications written to the API specification are the most likely to run successfully and the least likely to cause problems. On the other hand, applications not in compliance with the API specification may not work correctly.

The Windows 2000 network architecture includes five main APIs: WNet, Telephony, Messaging, NetBIOS, and Winsock.

➤ *WNet API*—Provides the Windows networking (WNet) interface to applications requiring network interaction. Win32 applications are created using the WNet API specification and are therefore able to interact with the underlying network and communicate with other computers across the network, regardless of the type of network. As mentioned earlier, the Multi-Provider Router is used to determine the appropriate redirector for Win32 commands sent using the WNet API.

➤ *Telephony API (TAPI)*—Lets programmers develop applications that take advantage of the wide variety of features and services available over telephone networks. TAPI not only supports data transmission over telephone networks, but voice as well. It includes support for a large range of connection types and management techniques as well as call management functions, such as call waiting and voicemail.

➤ *Messaging API (MAPI)*—Provides applications with the ability to work with various messaging services. Messaging applications like Microsoft Outlook use MAPI to communicate with different message service providers like Microsoft Fax. MAPI is an industry standard that is fully supported by applications outside the Microsoft product line.

➤ *NetBIOS API*—Provides support for legacy applications and services. NetBIOS is a standard API that is used to develop client/server applications. Included as part of the Microsoft network architecture since its inception, the NetBIOS API is used primarily to identify computers on the network and to facilitate communication between those computers. The NetBIOS API is able to utilize three main protocols for transport: NetBEUI Frame (NBF), NetBIOS over TCP/IP (NetBT), and NWLink NetBIOS

(NWNBLink). NBF was the first protocol designed for NetBIOS use and is best suited for small networks. NBF has no functionality at the Network layer of the OSI model and therefore cannot be routed. NetBT provides a routable, industry standard method for transporting NetBIOS. NetBT utilizes the transport services of the TCP/IP protocol suite, the industry standard, which is used on the Internet for communication. NWNBLink provides the same services as NetBT, but uses the NWLink protocol for transport instead of TCP/IP. Both TCP/IP and NWLink are discussed in the "Windows 2000 Network Protocols and Services" section later in this chapter.

➤ *Winsock API*—Provides applications access to the transport protocols at the lower levels of the network architecture. Versions of Winsock prior to Windows 2000 were able to function only with specific protocols. This has changed and the Windows 2000 Winsock implementation is protocol independent. Like many other Windows 2000 components, Winsock is based on an industry standard, specifically the Sockets API, which is used for datagram- and session-based communication over TCP/IP, NetBIOS, NWLink, and AppleTalk. Winsock supports both connectionless and connection-oriented communication. Because it is based on an accepted industry standard, the Winsock API provides a familiar interface to programmers familiar with Unix or other operating systems that use Sockets.

Windows 2000 supports both Winsock 1.1 and Winsock 2.0. Like the NetBIOS API, Winsock 1.1 support is included to ensure that legacy applications operate successfully. The Winsock 2.0 interface is compatible with the Windows Open Systems Architecture (WOSA) and includes improvements over Winsock 1.1, like enhanced name resolution using different methods (Domain Name System, Novell Directory Services, and X.500), multimedia enhancements like Quality of Service (QoS), and multipoint and multicast communications.

As mentioned previously, Winsock 2.0 supports a multimedia enhancement known as Quality of Service, or QoS. QoS is a new development that came about because many network types, like Ethernet, use connectionless transmission, which does not guarantee that all packets will reach their destination, or, if they do, that they will arrive in the correct order. To work around this issue, protocols like TCP/IP were developed, which ensured data integrity through mechanisms like retransmission of missing packets and reassembly of packets received out of order.

This process works well for basic applications, such as email and file transfer, but new applications, like streaming video and audio, must be sure that data packets arrive on time, every time, in order. Connection-oriented networks, on the other hand, ensure that data packets reach their destination intact and in order. In addition, connection-oriented networks support multiple connections between each computer and provide the ability to specify levels of service for each connection. For example, the level of service for a computer's connection to a database server may be set for connectionless transmission using retransmission, whereas its connection to a video conferencing server is set to provide fast, guaranteed delivery. Microsoft provides this support in Windows 2000 through Winsock 2.0, the Generic Quality of Service (GQoS) API, and the Resource Reservation Signaling Protocol (RSVP).

Transport Driver Interface (TDI) Boundary Layer

Below the APIs and services lies the Transport Driver Interface (TDI) boundary layer. The TDI provides the standard interface for communication between services and network transport protocols. TDI is unique in the network architecture in that it is not represented in the operating system by a driver, but is merely a specification for passing data between two functional layers. The TDI defines the call mechanisms and functions by which the transport protocols and clients communicate.

Note: *Though it is a standard and part of the Windows 2000 network architecture, some legacy protocols and APIs do not directly interface with the TDI. NetBEUI, for example, does not interface with the TDI. To provide support for these applications, Windows 2000 includes emulator modules. Emulator modules provide the access points the legacy applications expect and convert the information received into the format specified by the TDI.*

The Network Protocols Functional Layer

Discussed in greater detail in the "Windows 2000 Network Protocols and Services" section of this chapter, a protocol is a specification to standardize data packet creation and transmission, which allows computers to communicate. Data packets move down the protocol stack on the sending computer, across the network medium, and up the protocol stack on the receiving computer. Windows 2000 includes support for seven network protocols: TCP/IP, ATM, IPX/SPX, NetBEUI, AppleTalk, DLC, and IrDA. Each protocol is best suited for a specific network environment.

➤ Being the most widely accepted industry standard protocol suite, TCP/IP is the default protocol of Windows 2000.

➤ Asynchronous Transfer Mode (ATM) is a connection-oriented, guaranteed delivery protocol that is best used for video conferencing, voice, and high-volume/high-reliability data communication.

➤ The Internetwork Packet Exchange/Sequenced Packet Exchange (IPX/SPX) protocol suite is supported by Windows 2000 through NWLink and is best suited for networks on which both Windows 2000 and Novell NetWare servers reside.

➤ The NetBIOS Extended User Interface (NetBEUI) was developed for small networks and is included with Windows 2000 to support Windows NT Workstations.

➤ The AppleTalk protocol suite was developed by Apple Computer Corporation and provides interconnectivity with Apple Macintosh computers.

➤ The Data Link Control (DLC) protocol was developed for IBM mainframe computers and was later adopted by Hewlett-Packard for communication with network attached printers; it is included with Windows 2000 to provide printer connectivity.

➤ Infrared Data Association (IrDA) is a protocol suite that encompasses a set of bidirectional, short-range, high-speed, wireless protocols used for communication with personal digital assistants (PDAs), digital cameras, and some printers.

8

The Network Device Interface Specification (NDIS) Boundary Layer

NDIS defines the network driver architecture used in Windows 2000. NDIS allows network protocols, such as AppleTalk and NWLink, to interface with the network adapter and communicate over the network medium. To operate in Windows 2000, network adapter drivers must be written to the NDIS specification.

Like other portions of the network architecture, the NDIS layer isolates the network adapter from most software components and allows upper-layer protocol components to operate independent of the network adapter. This design provides the ability to include more than one network adapter in a computer and to have more than one protocol operate over a single adapter. Through NDIS, an unlimited number of network adapters can be installed in a computer, and an unlimited number of protocols can be bound to one adapter. NDIS is implemented as part of the network architecture through a driver called the NDIS wrapper because it surrounds all NDIS device drivers. The NDIS wrapper is the component that provides the interface between the protocols and the NDIS device drivers.

To provide comprehensive support, Windows 2000 NDIS includes separate interfaces for connectionless and connection-oriented protocols. Prior to Windows 2000, NDIS included a single interface designed for connectionless protocols. One of the new features of Windows 2000 is the inclusion of an NDIS interface called CoNDIS for connection-oriented protocols like ATM. Connection-oriented protocols communicate by creating a dedicated connection between the sending and receiving computers. Called a virtual circuit (VC), this connection ensures that all data is sent in sequence. Virtual circuits are created and maintained by a call manager, which is part of the NDIS interface.

In addition to adding support for connection-oriented protocols, the Windows 2000 implementation of NDIS provides new features not available in earlier versions of Windows. The Wake-On-LAN feature, for example, is new to Windows 2000 and is used to "wake-up" computers when a network event, such as a remote access request, occurs. To save energy, computers are able to shut down specific functions and "sleep." If supported by the network adapter, the Wake-On-LAN feature of NDIS wakes up the computer when it is accessed over the network by a previously registered packet or a magic packet, or when a connection event, like plugging, in a network cable occurs.

Windows 2000 NDIS also includes support for network Plug and Play, which uses software to configure and manage compatible hardware devices with little user intervention. Because many protocols used today include a media sensing function, NDIS also provides this support. Media sense is the ability of the network adapter to report to the protocol when it is or is not physically connected to the network medium.

Finally, the Windows 2000 NDIS implementation provides for offloading specific TCP/IP tasks from the Transport layer of the protocol stack onto the network adapter itself. To do this, the transport driver queries the adapter to determine whether it can perform TCP/IP tasks. If so, NDIS allows for offloading checksum calculation, packet segmentation, fast packet forwarding, and IPSec authentication and payload encapsulation. To ensure the data received is identical to the data sent, a checksum calculation is performed, and its value is added to the packet before transmission. The sending and receiving computers use the same calculation to determine the value of the checksum; if they match, transmission was successful.

Because not all networks have the same packet size specifications, the size of the packet is usually determined at the Transport layer and the message from upper-layer processes is divided into segments. This segmentation can also be performed by a network adapter that supports TCP/IP task offloading. When a computer is equipped with a multiport network adapter, NDIS can rely on the adapter to forward packets from one interface port to the other without passing the packet back to the CPU, thereby increasing overall network speed and reducing the work of the processor. As you learned in Chapter 1, Windows 2000 supports the IPSec security standard, which handles authentication and encryption at the packet processing layer on IP networks. Offloading all of these functions to the network adapter ensures that the CPU uses its processing time efficiently and increases network performance.

NDIS Drivers

To fulfill its role as the interface between the protocols and the network adapters, NDIS uses two types of drivers: intermediate and miniport. There are two types of intermediate drivers, the LAN Emulation Intermediate driver and filter drivers, which operate between the protocol stack and the miniport drivers. The LAN Emulation Intermediate driver is used to translate messages from connectionless transport protocols into the connection-oriented format used by the network. This allows the protocols to operate as if communicating over a LAN and provides the reliability of a connection-oriented network like ATM. In fact, only ATM is able to take advantage of this feature at this time, but because the network architecture is modular, a new network technology could easily be implemented using the same functionality. When special tasks, such as encryption, packet tracing, and compression are required of NDIS, a filter driver is used. Because it is an intermediate driver, packets are passed through the filter driver before moving on to the protocols in the upper layers. Windows 2000 services like QoS and network load balancing rely on specific NDIS filter drivers.

Closest to the actual network adapter hardware, miniport drivers connect to adapters and provide the link to the upper layers of the network architecture. The miniport drivers include the hardware specific commands necessary to manage sending and receiving data over the network adapter or other hardware device. The miniport driver is the only component of the network architecture that the hardware manufacturer is required to produce. However, if additional functionality is desired, a hardware manufacturer can create an intermediate driver.

The Network Adapter Cards Functional Layer

The lowest layer of the network architecture is the functional layer encompassing the network adapter cards and other physical devices. Devices operating at this layer are responsible for placing data on and removing data from the network medium. Because the entire architecture is modular, the specific operation of devices at this level is not defined as part of the architecture. From traditional networks, like Ethernet and Token Ring to ATM and infrared, the design of the Windows 2000 network architecture allows for virtually any networking device or medium.

WINDOWS 2000 NETWORK PROTOCOLS AND SERVICES

Windows 2000 relies on a number of specifications and software components to communicate with other computers across a network. The following sections will review the Windows 2000 network protocols and the primary network services. When reviewing the network services and protocols, remember that the network architecture is modular and easily supports additions or deletions. If a protocol is not listed in this section, it does not mean that Windows 2000 will not support it. The architecture allows for future development of protocols and services.

Windows 2000 Network Protocols

In its simplest definition, a protocol is a set of rules that governs interaction and communication. This applies as much to the world of international diplomacy as it does to computer networking. When visiting China, diplomatic protocol defines how you should behave when greeting your host, whether or not to shake hands, and the language used to communicate. Networked devices must also follow similar rules to ensure that the receiver understands the message sent. Networking protocol specifications define how messages are structured, how large a single message can be, what to do when a message is lost or damaged in transit, and how to determine who is authorized to act on a message. As you'll see in the next sections, the protocols supported by Windows 2000 run the gamut from simple protocols designed for workgroups to large, complex protocol suites. A protocol suite is a group of related protocols that are implemented as one unit. Many protocols and protocol suites include functionality that spans multiple layers of the OSI model.

Note: Many of the protocols listed in this section are extensive and complex. TCP/IP and ATM are both detailed enough to warrant books of their own. In fact, Microsoft has a separate exam just for networking with TCP/IP. The discussion here will provide you with sufficient information to install, configure, and manage the protocols in a real-world environment. More information on these protocols can be obtained through Microsoft TechNet, the Microsoft Web site, and other Web connected resources like the IETF.

The Transmission Control Protocol/Internet Protocol (TCP/IP) Suite

As its name implies, the TCP/IP protocol suite is used as the primary protocol of the Internet. However, TCP/IP predates the Internet as we know it by two decades. Designed in 1969 as the transport protocol for an experimental government network called ARPANet, TCP/IP has grown from two very basic protocols to an all-encompassing international network communication standard. The growth and acceptance of TCP/IP has been paralleled and sometimes driven by the expansion and metamorphosis of the original ARPANet into today's Internet.

Note: ARPANet was developed by the Department of Defense's (DoD) Advanced Research Project Agency (ARPA), sometimes called DARPA, to connect mainframe computers at government installations and research facilities across the country. No one ever considered the possibility that one day the Defense Department's research network, which was used to send top-secret military information, would eventually become the network children use to send letters to Santa.

To ensure efficient operation, the TCP/IP protocol suite uses many individual protocols, each of which performs a specific function. For example, one protocol handles name resolution, whereas another verifies network connectivity, and a third is used for email transport. This modular design has helped ensure that TCP/IP not only survived the wild world of networking longer than any other protocol, but also steadily grew in popularity to reach its status of de facto communication standard. As new technologies came into vogue and computers were used for different tasks, TCP/IP was able to add and change components and still maintain its primary goal, which was to provide communication between network devices, particularly those connected to disparate internetworks.

8

TCP/IP Structure

The TCP/IP protocol suite is unique in many ways. One is that it predates the OSI model by nearly a decade and therefore does not follow it exactly. Instead, TCP/IP follows a four-layer theoretical model called the DARPA model. As shown in Figure 8.3, the DARPA model divides network functions along some of the same lines as the OSI model, but it also groups the lower layer and upper layer together into larger, more general specifications. The DARPA model is comprised of the Application, Host-to-Host Transport, Internetwork, and Network Interface layers.

At the top of the TCP/IP architecture is the Application layer. The DARPA Application layer nearly encompasses the top three layers of the OSI model—Application, Presentation, and part of Session. Protocols that operate at this layer are responsible for providing local applications access to the other protocols in the TCP/IP suite. Most new protocols are developed to operate in the Application layer. In fact, the protocol that is used to display Web pages on the Internet, the Hypertext Transport Protocol (HTTP), is an Application layer protocol. Other well-known Application layer protocols are the Routing Information Protocol (RIP), the File Transfer Protocol (FTP), the Domain Name System (DNS), and the Simple Mail Transfer Protocol (SMTP). The Winsock and NetBIOS APIs also operate at the Application layer.

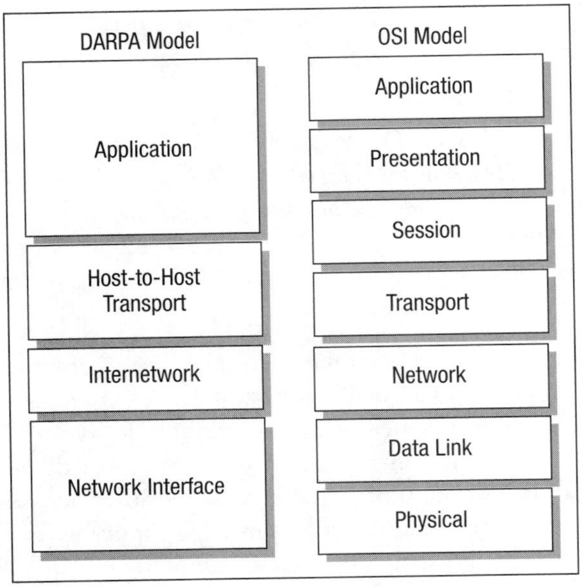

Figure 8.3   TCP/IP's DARPA model as compared to the OSI model.

Below the Application layer is the Host-to-Host Transport layer, generally referred to as simply the Transport layer. Performing the same functions as the lower portion of the OSI Session layer and all of the OSI Transport layer, the TCP/IP Transport layer provides protocols on the Application layer with connectionless and connection-oriented communication services. There are two protocols that operate at this layer and provide communication services to Application layer protocols: User Datagram Protocol (UDP) and Transmission Control Protocol (TCP). Connectionless services, also called datagram services, are provided by the UDP. Because it does not guarantee data delivery, UDP is used when a single packet's worth of data is transferred, when the overhead required by connection-oriented protocols is considered detrimental, or when the Application layer protocols ensure reliable delivery through their own mechanisms. The TCP is used to provide connection-oriented (session) communication services to protocols operating at the Application layer. TCP is responsible for establishing and managing communication sessions to ensure reliable data delivery. To do this, TCP utilizes packet sequencing, acknowledgment of packet delivery, and packet recovery mechanisms in the event that a packet is lost during transmission.

The protocols at the Internetwork layer handle packaging data for transmission, addressing packets once they are created, and routing packets from source to destination across the internetwork. The primary protocol that operates at this layer is the Internet Protocol (IP). A routable protocol, IP handles packet addressing, fragmentation, reassembly, and routing. The Internet Group Management Protocol (IGMP) is used to control specialized broadcast groups called IP multicast groups. The Address Resolution Protocol (ARP) is responsible for resolving the computer's Internet layer address to its Network Interface layer address. (The address resolution process is discussed more thoroughly in the "IP Addresses" section later in this chapter.) To provide diagnostic functions and error reporting, the Internet layer protocol Internet Control Message Protocol (ICMP) is used.

Note: The Internet layer of the TCP/IP model does not take advantage of packet sequencing or acknowledgments to provide reliable delivery. The TCP/IP protocol suite was designed under the assumption that the components of the Network Interface layer and Internet layer could not guarantee packet delivery. Because of this, the protocol's designers opted to perform this function at the Transport layer.

The lowest layer of the DARPA model is the Network Interface, or Network Access, layer. There are no TCP/IP protocols defined that operate at this layer. Rather, the TCP/IP model relies on the network interface card to place packets on and retrieve packets from the network medium. By design, TCP/IP is able to communicate over many different types of networks. The Network Interface layer of the TCP/IP model includes the functionality of the Data Link and Physical layers of the OSI model.

Primary TCP/IP Protocols

As mentioned earlier, the TCP/IP protocol suite is made up of many protocols, each of which provides a specific function. In fact, there are more than one hundred protocols that make up the entire protocol suite. Many of the protocols are no longer used and even more are not utilized by Windows 2000. There are six protocols that operate below the Application layer as the core of the Windows 2000 TCP/IP implementation: IP, ICMP, ARP, IGMP, UDP, and TCP. In addition, there are numerous Application layer protocols that provide essential services to Windows 2000. For the purpose of this discussion, we will review FTP, Telnet, RIP, and HTTP.

➤ *IP*—Provides datagram (connectionless) communication services for the protocol suite. Like other connectionless protocols, IP does not guarantee packet delivery, but makes a "best effort" to ensure that the data packet reaches its destination. IP is als o responsible for managing logical address assignments, packet fragmentation, and reassembly. Packet fragmentation takes place when a transmitted packet is too large for a network in the communication path. This is most often seen on networks that include mixed technologies, like Frame Relay and Ethernet. An IP packet is made up of two primary parts, the IP header and the IP payload. The payload is comprised of the data handed to IP by the upper-layer protocol and is considered a whole unit. The IP header is attached to the payload and is comprised of fields for the source IP address, the destination IP address, identification, protocol, checksum, and Time-to-Live (TTL). The source and destination IP address fields specify the devices sending and receiving the packet. A unique identification number is assigned to each datagram and is placed in the identification field. In addition, if the packet is fragmented at any point during transmission, the identification field is used to label each fragment of the packet. The protocol field lets the receiving device know to which upper-layer protocol the information in the packet is destined. As mentioned earlier, the checksum is used as a basic measurement of whether transmission is successful. The Time-to-Live field specifies the number of networks the packet is allowed to travel through before being discarded. The TTL is established when the packet is created; each time the packet passes through a router, the router decreases the TTL by at least one. When a router receives a packet with a TTL set to zero, it discards the packet.

➤ *ICMP*—Provides troubleshooting mechanisms and error reporting for packets that cannot be delivered. ICMP does not provide reliability for IP communication, but rather reports errors to provide feedback on specific conditions. ICMP reports the status of transmission with five primary messages: echo request, echo reply, redirect, source quench, and destination unreachable. Echo request messages are sent to verify connectivity to a specific system; if received, the queried system sends echo reply messages. The PING troubleshooting utility uses ICMP echo requests to probe the network for a destination host to determine connectivity. Redirect messages are used by routers to identify a better route if one is available. Routers use source quench messages to inform a sending host that its packets are being dropped due to network congestion; the sending host then reduces its transmission rate. A destination unreachable message is sent to inform the sending host that the datagram cannot be delivered to its destination. ICMP expands on these messages to provide more specific information if available.

➤ *ARP*—Because not all connections between client and server computers are direct wired and dedicated, it is necessary to assign an address to networked devices. On an Ethernet network, for example, hosts are identified by a physical (MAC) address that is part of the Data Link layer. Communication at the Physical layer uses the destination's physical address to specify the intended receiver. IP does not have exposure to the station's physical address on its own; it uses logical, Network layer addresses to identify networked computers. ARP is used to take a station's IP address and determine its physical address before the packet is passed to the Network Interface layer. ARP is the last TCP/IP protocol to add data to a packet on the sending computer.

➤ *IGMP*—TCP/IP does utilize broadcasts except in special situations. By denying this feature, TCP/IP networks are able to operate more efficiently than those that rely on broadcasts. However, there are some instances in which IP messages must be sent to multiple hosts at the same time. To do this, TCP/IP uses IGMP and specially configured groups of systems called IP multicast groups or host groups. Each member of the multicast group is configured to listen for IP traffic destined for a specific multicast address. When a multicast is required, the sending computer places the group's multicast address in the destination IP field and all members of the group process the packet.

➤ *UDP*—The TCP/IP suite's connectionless datagram protocol, UDP, is used by applications that do not require guaranteed data delivery or applications for which the need for speed outweighs the need for delivery confirmation. UDP uses a port assignment to specify the location for sending messages. When an application sends a message to another computer using UDP, it must not only specify the destination host's IP address, but the receiving process's UDP port assignment as well. Many IP services and applications have preassigned ports to prevent confusion and ensure that all services are able to communicate. Preassigned ports are referred to as well-known ports. For example, the Trivial File Transfer Protocol (TFTP), a "lite" version of the FTP protocol, uses UDP for transport and uses port 69.

➤ *TCP*—Provides the connection-oriented communication services not provided by UDP. TCP establishes a connection between the sending and receiving systems and ensures that the data reaches its destination. Before being passed to IP, each data segment is assigned a sequence number. The receiving computer must acknowledge receipt of each sequence number by sending an acknowledgment message called an ACK within a specified period. If the sending device does not receive a response within the specified time, it resends the segment. For sequence number acknowledgment to operate effectively, the client and server must make each other aware of the first sequence number they are going to use. This is done using a method called the three-way handshake. The handshake is initiated by the client sending a segment to the server with its initial sequence number and the size of a buffer called the window on the client, which is used to store incoming messages. The server replies with a segment containing its chosen initial sequence number, an acknowledgment of the client's sequence number, and the window size of its receiving buffer. Finally, the client sends a segment acknowledging the server's sequence number. Like UDP, TCP uses port assignments to identify the upper-layer processes involved in the communication. TCP ports below 1024 are well-known ports and are assigned to specific TCP/IP functions.

8

Note: Although TCP and UDP both use ports to identify processes, and many of the well-known port assignments are the same, TCP ports and UDP ports are different. The default port assignment for a process using TCP may not necessarily be the same for an identical process using UDP. Refer to the "TCP/IP Resources" section later in this chapter for more information on well-known TCP and UDP ports.

➤ *FTP*—One of the oldest members of the TCP/IP protocol suite, FTP is an Application layer protocol that provides file transfer and manipulation services. Though it relies primarily on TCP for transport, FTP is able to use UDP as the situation dictates. FTP uses port 20 for the data transfer and port 21 as a control port. FTP is an example of a process that has been assigned the same port numbers for both TCP and UDP.

➤ *RIP*—RIP works in conjunction with IP to provide information to routers on the network. On its own, IP does not have a mechanism for dynamically notifying other routers of changes in the network topology. If the structure of the network changes, the routing tables on each router must be updated manually. RIP was developed to provide a dynamic method for handling network topology changes. Using RIP, each router on the network periodically sends the information in its routing tables to the routers to which it is connected. When a router receives the routing update from another router, it checks the information in its routing table and makes updates as necessary. This ensures that all routers on the network have an accurate picture of the network to use when determining the best path to the destination.

➤ *HTTP*—From a technical perspective, IP is the protocol of the Internet. But from a consumer prospective, HTTP has greater exposure. HTTP was specifically designed as the transport for the Hypertext Markup Language (HTML), the language in which most Web pages are written. Different variations of HTTP provide for secure transmission and enhanced performance.

IP Addresses

The part of TCP/IP that confuses people most often is also one of the most important to understand—IP addressing. As you know, IP manages the computer's logical address and is responsible for adding the IP address of the destination computer to the segment before it is sent across the network. Each network device using TCP/IP has a unique IP address. A computer's IP address is referred to as a *logical address* because it has no dependence on a Data Link layer address, such as an Ethernet MAC address. In addition, logical addresses can be manually assigned or adjusted, whereas physical addresses generally cannot.

An IP address is a single address that is divided to represent the network to which a device is attached and its host identifier on that network. This distinction is possible because, although it is a single string, the address is actually divided into two segments, the network ID and the host ID. The network ID portion of the address is used by IP when a segment is sent on the network. By comparing its own network ID with the network ID of the destination, IP is able to determine whether the destination is on the same network. If the network IDs match, it means the destination is on the same network and IP can send the segment directly to the destination computer. If the network IDs do not match, then IP forwards the segment to the nearest router for transmission across the internetwork.

The source and destination IP address fields of the IP header are 32-bits long, providing support for 32-bit addresses. Because 32 bits are difficult to work with as a single unit, IP addresses are generally divided into four 8-bit parts called octets. To further simplify representation, each octet is then represented by a decimal number with a value between 0 and 255. Dots are placed between the octets to clearly define each octet's boundaries. This method for representing IP addresses is called dotted-decimal notation.

Each octet's value is determined by converting the binary 1s and 0s to decimal notation. A binary number's decimal value is calculated by adding the value of the spots occupied by 1s. If the octet contains all 0s, the value is 0; if the octet contains all 1s, the value is 255. Decimal values for the binary positions are assigned from right to left, which can cause some confusion. The decimal value for each bit is (from the right) 1, 2, 4, 8, 16, 32, 64, 128. For example, an octet containing 10000000 has a decimal value of 128 (128+0+0+0+0+0+0+0). The value for 11010010 is 210 (128+64+0+16+0+0+2+0), and the value for 00101001 is 41 (32+8+1). Table 8.1 lists some sample IP addresses and their binary representation.

Note: *It is very important to understand how decimal values are calculated. Microsoft has provided a tool for converting binary to decimal and vice versa. The calculator included with every version of Windows can operate as a scientific calculator and easily perform the conversion. To use the calculator, select View | Scientific. Then enter the decimal number you wish to have represented in binary, and click the Bin radio button. The conversion works the other way as well. Enter a string of binary 1s and 0s, and click the Dec radio button. When operating in binary mode, be sure the Byte option is selected. Remember, though, the calculator will not be available when you take the exam.*

When the issue of developing an addressing model for the ARPANet was first discussed, the designers were confident that a 32-bit address was sufficient to provide addressing for the foreseeable future. As things developed, it became clear that a flat, 32-bit address space was not as efficient or easy to manage as it

Table 8.1 Binary values for sample IP addresses.

Dotted-Decimal Format	Binary Format
128.34.223.8	10000000 00100010 11011111 00001000
7.125.67.43	00000111 01111101 01000011 00101011
250.99.101.1	11111010 01100011 01100101 00000001
96.58.155.228	01100000 00111010 10011011 11100100

could be, and it was decided to divide the available addresses into five groups called classes to accommodate different sized networks. An address's class identifies which address bits represent the network ID, and which represent the host ID. As an extension of this, the class also defines the maximum number of hosts that can be connected to the network. The top three classes were designed for specific types of networks, A for very large networks, B for medium to large networks, and C for smaller networks.

A class A address uses the first octet for the network ID and the last three octets for the host ID. This provides support for up to 16,777,214 hosts (256×256×256–2). The high–order bit (the one farthest left) is always 0 for class A addresses, meaning the maximum value of the first octet is 127. In fact, addresses starting with 127 are reserved for loopback testing, so class A addresses are identified as addresses beginning with 1 through 126. This also means that there are only 126 class A networks defined. As you can imagine, these addresses were assigned to large global corporations long ago.

Class B addresses use the first two octets for the network ID and the last two octets for the host ID, providing 16,384 networks and 65,534 hosts per network. The two high–order bits are always set to 1 0, meaning that class B addresses start with octets numbered from 128 through 191.

Class C addresses were designed for use on small networks and utilize the first three octets to denote the network ID and the last octet for the host ID. This configuration means that there are 2,097,152 possible networks with 254 hosts per network. As you might imagine, there are many networks that are too large for a single class C address, but too small to fully utilize a class B address. This did cause problems and was remedied by adjusting the class restrictions in special circumstances. The value of the first octet of a class C address is 192 through 223 because the three high–order bits on class C addresses are always set to 1 1 0.

Class D and class E addresses are defined, but cannot be used for normal network communication. Class D addresses are reserved for multicasts and are specified by the four high–order bits being set to 1 1 1 0. Unlike addresses in classes A, B, and C, all of the remaining bits are used to define the multicast address. An address with the four high–order bits set to 1 1 1 1 is a Class E address. Class E addresses are experimental and reserved for future technologies.

Subnet Masks

Although the IP address class structure clearly defines the delineation between an address's network ID and host ID, most TCP/IP implementations are not configured by providing the network's class. A different mechanism is needed at the bottom layers of the network architecture to provide this function. To do this, IP uses subnet masks. A subnet mask acts as a template against which the IP address is compared to determine which bits represent the network ID and which represent the host ID. Working from the high-order bit, the network ID is indicated by a 1 in the subnet mask. For example, the subnet mask for class A addresses is 11111111.00000000.00000000.00000000, or 255.0.0.0. Subnet masks are also represented with a /X after the address, where X represents the number of bits in the subnet mask. For example, 156.24.0.0/16 indicates a 16-bit subnet mask, or a class B mask.

As mentioned previously, the IP address class structure did not always provide for the most efficient use of network addresses. If a class A network was implemented with a single network and more than 16 million hosts, network communication would be impossible. To provide better structure to network addresses, subnet masks were allowed to go beyond the class structure and specify the subnet mask to the bit level. A subnet mask is a 32-bit number that identifies the host ID portion of an IP address. For example, if a network administrator was assigned a class B address, but had no more than 1,200 hosts per network, he could use a subnet mask of 11111111.11111111.11111000. 00000000 (255.255.248.0). This subnet mask provides for up to 2,046 hosts per network and 30 subnets.

TCP/IP Resources

Although this coverage only scratches the surface of the configuration options available with the Windows 2000 TCP/IP implementation, it is sufficient for the purpose of this book. You should be familiar with the TCP/IP components and their use in the real world. More information on the TCP/IP protocol suite, well-known TCP and UDP ports, subnet masks, and other TCP/IP topics is available on the Web at the following URLs.

➤ *www.microsoft.com/windows2000/default.asp*—Search for TCP/IP, UDP Port, or subnet mask.

➤ *www.microsoft.com/WINDOWS2000/library/resources/reskit/ samplechapters/cnbb/cnbb_tcp_kscb.asp*—This excerpt from the Windows 2000 Resource Kit covers the TCP/IP Architecture.

➤ *www.iana.org*—The Internet Assigned Numbers Authority (IANA) is responsible for managing port assignments and other TCP/IP services, like DNS. The site includes a link to a text document listing all well-known TCP and UDP ports.

➤ *www.ietf.org*—The IETF is responsible for the TCP/IP protocol suite itself. Potential standards must be accepted by the IETF before being considered a part of the TCP/IP suite.

➤ *www.arin.net*—The American Registry for Internet Numbers (ARIN) Web site provides information on IP addressing and includes a detailed reference library.

Asynchronous Transfer Mode (ATM)

ATM is a high-speed, connection-oriented protocol that is ideally suited for high-bandwidth applications, like video conferencing and data communication. ATM is most often implemented over fiber-optic network media to provide the highest reliability and speed. ATM is able to provide high-speed communication by using a fixed-length data cell. Because all cells that cross the network are the same size, 53 bytes, network devices do not waste processing power determining the size of each data packet. ATM uses connection-oriented communication over a switched network topology. An endpoint on the ATM network establishes a virtual circuit with another endpoint prior to any data being sent. During the establishment process, the endpoint also negotiates a QoS contract for the connection. The QoS contract defines parameters, such as the maximum allowable delay, the amount of bandwidth to be used, and other parameters supported by the virtual circuit. The QoS contract extends the length of the virtual circuit from one endpoint to the other.

ATM is unique in that it acts as both a transport mechanism for protocols like TCP/IP and as a network service transported by other networking technologies such as xDSL (variants of Digital Subscriber Line technologies). IP over ATM is supported by Windows 2000 to provide transport for IP packets over ATM networks. ATM compensates for IP's unreliability through its own connection-oriented structure. Working with TCP/IP's ARP, the ATMARP server manages a database of IP and ATM addresses, enabling IP communication over the ATM network. xDSL is a fairly new networking standard that is able to provide high-speed communication over standard telephone lines. Windows 2000 supports sending ATM cells over xDSL connections. Because xDSL is a high-speed networking implementation, Windows 2000 is able to continue to utilize the ATM QoS and reliability features.

IPX/SPX (NWLink)

The IPX/SPX protocol suite was developed by Novell for its NetWare product. Based on the Xerox Network System (XNS), IPX/SPX is a comprehensive protocol suite that provides services at all layers of the OSI model. IPX is a connectionless Transport layer protocol, whereas SPX provides a connection-oriented service. NWLink is the Microsoft implementation of Novell's

IPX/SPX protocol suite. It is included with Windows 2000 to provide connectivity to NetWare networks.

NetBEUI

NetBEUI was originally developed by IBM as an enhancement to NetBIOS. IBM designed NetBEUI to provide network access for small workgroups using LAN Manager products. Microsoft adopted NetBEUI early on and has relied on its networking mechanisms ever since. Until Windows 2000, NetBEUI was the default protocol used by all Windows products. It is included with Windows 2000 to provide support for legacy workstations and applications.

NetBEUI provides both connectionless and connection-oriented services depending on the requesting application's requirements. The biggest drawback to NetBEUI, and the issue that eventually led to its demise, is that it was designed specifically for use on small, workgroup networks. In this environment, NetBEUI is fast and reliable. However, NetBEUI was not designed to be transmitted between internetworks and therefore has no functionality at the Network layer of the OSI model. This means that NetBEUI traffic cannot be routed between networks. This being the case, if two computers running only NetBEUI require connectivity across network boundaries, the networks would have to be opened to each other completely, potentially flooding the network with erroneous traffic.

8

AppleTalk

The AppleTalk protocol suite was developed by Apple Computer for communication with Macintosh computers. Windows 2000 supports the AppleTalk protocol to allow Macintosh computers access to Windows 2000 systems.

DLC

Another protocol originally developed by IBM, DLC was designed for communication with IBM mainframe computers. However, DLC was never intended as a primary protocol between computers in a client/server environment. In addition to providing a method for communication with IBM mainframe systems, Hewlett-Packard utilizes DLC for communication with network connected printers. It is for this role, more than mainframe access, that Windows 2000 provides native DLC support.

IrDA

The IrDA is a standards group focused on utilizing point-to-point wireless infrared for network communication. Windows 2000 includes support for the IrDA standards for communication with portable computers, digital cameras, PDAs, and printers. The IrDA standards provide support for Winsock applications to utilize IrDA as well as IrTran-P (a method for transmitting images over infrared connections). For more information on the IrDA, its standards, and general information on infrared communication, go the to IrDA Web site at **www.irda.org**.

Installing Windows 2000 Protocols

Windows 2000 uses the TCP/IP protocol suite as its native transport and therefore it is the default protocol loaded during the installation process. After installation, the procedure for installing Windows 2000 protocols is the same, regardless of the protocol. All areas of the Windows 2000 network connection are controlled through the My Network Places applet. To add a protocol or service, right-click the My Network Places icon and select Properties, or double-click the Network And Dial-Up Connections icon in the Control Panel. Depending on the configuration of the computer, a window similar to the one shown in Figure 8.4 will be displayed. If the computer includes a modem or other type of network connection, a separate icon will be displayed for that connection.

Right-click the Local Area Connection icon and select Properties from the menu. This invokes the Local Area Connection Properties window, which displays the network components currently installed in the computer. If you are familiar with Windows NT 4, you will notice a change in the network configuration options. With Windows 2000, Microsoft has returned to using a single configuration window for all components associated with a particular connection, rather than a separate configuration tab for Protocols, Adapters, and Services. To install a new protocol (or other network component), click Install. Select Protocol from the Select Network Component Type window and click Add, as shown in Figure 8.5.

The options displayed in the next window depend on the protocols currently installed on the system. On a computer that only has TCP/IP installed, for example, the Select Network Protocol window will include AppleTalk, DLC, NetBEUI, and NWLink IPX/SPX Compatible Transport Protocol. IrDA is

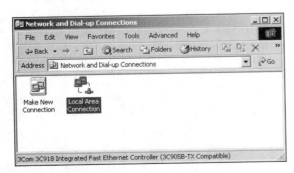

Figure 8.4   The network options for a Windows 2000 computer.

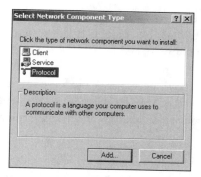

Figure 8.5   Adding a Windows 2000 protocol.

available only if an infrared communication adapter is installed in the computer and is recognized by Windows 2000. To install a particular protocol on the computer, select it from the Select Network Protocol window and click OK. Windows 2000 installs the protocol and returns you to the Local Area Connection Properties window. Click Close to complete the installation.

One of the most important advances of Windows 2000 over Windows NT 4 is the reduction in the number of reboots required during configuration. In Windows NT, the system would need to be restarted before the new protocol could be used. However, with Windows 2000, that is no longer the case, and the protocol can be utilized immediately.

Windows 2000 Network Services

Many Windows 2000 network components have been included to enhance operation, secure the network, and ease administration. Many of these services are based on TCP/IP protocols and are accepted industry standards. Some, like Dynamic DNS (DDNS), are enhancements to industry standards to provide the services expected with Windows networks. Throughout this section of the chapter, we'll explore some of the network services available with Windows 2000, their installation, and their operation.

Dynamic Host Configuration Protocol (DHCP)

The DHCP is a TCP/IP protocol and standard that is used to automatically configure computers on a network. Each device connected to a TCP/IP network must be assigned a unique IP address and configured with the correct subnet mask, router address, and the IP addresses of servers on the network. Because these settings can be configured manually, the opportunity exists for users or administrators to incorrectly configure systems, resulting in duplicate IP addresses and invalid subnet masks or other settings. The results of these errors can be anything from the inability to communicate outside the local subnet to complete transmission failure.

DHCP was developed to automate setting the IP configuration for devices on the network. On a network using DHCP, settings such as IP address, subnet mask, router, and DNS server are centrally managed by a DHCP server to ensure that all devices are correctly configured. In addition, DHCP can be used to effectively manage a limited number of IP addresses, called a scope, available on a network. Like other Windows products, Windows 2000 can utilize the services of DHCP servers for configuration; Windows 2000 Servers are also able to act as DHCP servers.

A DHCP server is a specially configured computer that provides configuration services to requesting clients based on the information in its DHCP database. The DHCP database contains a pool of valid IP addresses to be automatically assigned to clients and a list of reserved IP addresses, which are manually assigned. This set of addresses is called the DHCP scope. In addition, the database includes IP settings for all computers on the network and the length of time each client is allowed to keep its IP address. The length of time a client is assigned an address is called the lease. Because only the IP address is a required DHCP field, the other settings, including subnet mask, are called DHCP options.

The first time a DHCP client connects to a network, it must obtain an IP address from a DHCP server. When it connects, it searches for a server by broadcasting a special packet called DHCPDiscover. This packet is easily identifiable because unlike other IP packets on the network, the source IP address is 0.0.0.0. When the DHCP server receives a DHCPDiscover packet, it responds with a DHCPOffer packet containing an available IP address and other DHCP options. When the client receives the DHCPOffer, it responds by broadcasting a DHCPRequest packet that includes the IP address and indication of acceptance of the address. If the request is validated by the server and accepted, it sends a DHCPAck acknowledgment packet, which indicates the client can use the address and complete initialization. If the requested address is no longer available or cannot be used for any reason, the server sends a DHCPNak (negative acknowledgment) packet and the client must restart the lease process from DHCPDiscover.

Note: To ensure that all clients are serviced as quickly as possible, many networks include multiple DHCP servers. If a client receives more than one DHCPOffer, it accepts the first valid offer it receives.

There are also other DHCP packet types used by the client before and during a lease. The DHCPDecline packet is sent by the client if the configuration in the DHCPOffer appears to be invalid. Once sent, the client begins the lease process anew. If the client is being removed from the network (that is, a user issues an

ipconfig/release command), it may send a DHCPRelease packet to the server to release the IP address and cancel the remaining lease. The DHCPInform packet, a new message type supported by Windows 2000, is used by computers on the network to obtain DHCP option configurations from the server, but not IP addresses. DHCP is not supported in previous Microsoft DHCP implementations and may not be supported by third-party DHCP servers.

During the lease, the client passes through six specific states: Initializing, Selecting, Requesting, Binding, Renewing, and Rebinding. The states are identified by the packets sent by the client and the action taken on the packets received.

1. The client is in Initializing state when it does not yet have an IP address or if the DHCPRequest is denied. The DHCPDiscover packet is sent during this state and has a source IP address of 0.0.0.0 and a destination address of 255.255.255.255 and is sent by UDP from port 68 to port 67. DHCPDiscover includes the media access address of the computer so that communication can take place.

2. During Selecting, the client chooses a DHCPOffer from those received. The DHCPOffer sent by the server includes the offered IP address, the corresponding subnet mask, and the duration of the lease. As the client waits for a DHCPOffer response, it will retry at 2, 4, 8, and 16 seconds, plus a random interval between 0 and 1,000 milliseconds. If no offer is received, the client waits five minutes, then sends a DHCPDiscover every five minutes. The DHCPOffer is sent to the client's media access address (destination), includes the server's IP address (source), and is also sent from UDP port 68 to UDP port 67.

3. The client moves into the Requesting state after receiving a DHCPOffer from a server. At this point, the client has determined the IP address it wants to use and broadcasts the DHCPRequest to all servers. If sent during a new lease, the DHCPRequest broadcast is sent to all servers, but includes the address of the server that sent the DHCPOffer in the data portion of the packet. The specified server responds to the request and all other outstanding offers are revoked by the other servers.

   The client also enters the Requesting state upon startup if it has previously used a leased IP address. In this case, the client broadcasts a DHCPRequest for its previous address to all DHCPServers. The DHCPServer that is able to fulfill the request responds with a DHCPAck or DHCPNak. If a DHCPAck is received, the client proceeds to the Binding state. If a DHCPNak is received, the client returns to Initializing and begins the complete DHCP process.

8

Note: Although the DHCPRequest packet contains the address the client would like to use, it is sent as a broadcast because the IP address has not yet been assigned to the client.

4. Upon receipt of the DHCPAck, the client enters the Binding state. The DHCPAck contains the complete details of the lease including the agreed upon IP address and any DHCP options. The client uses the information included in the packet to complete TCP/IP initialization and begin communicating on the network. The IP address is assigned to the client until the lease expires or it is released by the client.

5. Although DHCP is designed so that client computers can easily use different addresses each time they are powered on, it is still preferable for the client to keep the same IP address as often as possible. A client attempts to renew its address after 50 percent of the lease has expired. To do this, it sends a DHCPRequest to the server that owns the lease. Except under unusual circumstances, the server automatically responds with a DHCPAck containing the IP address, new lease information, and DHCP options. Packets sent during the Renewing state are sent directly to and from the client and server; no broadcasts are used.

6. In the event that the client cannot communicate with the server from which the lease was obtained, and 87.5 percent of the lease has expired, the client will broadcast DHCPRequests for its current IP address to any DHCP server. Any available server can respond with a DHCPAck, which allows the client to continue to use the same address on a new lease, or a DHCPNak. If a DHCPNak is received, the client must discontinue using the current IP address and start the process from scratch.

A Windows 2000 Server can be configured to provide DHCP services. Like many network services, the DHCP service can be installed through one of two methods: the Add/Remove Programs applet in the Control Panel or the Configure Your Server administrative tool. To install the DHCP services through the Control Panel, open the Add/Remove Programs applet and click the Add/Remove Windows Components icon. A list of all Windows 2000 components is displayed with those installed indicated by checkmarks. As shown in Figure 8.6, select the Networking Services option, and click Details.

Click the box next to Dynamic Host Configuration Protocol (DHCP) to select it for installation. Click OK to return to the components list. Click Next to continue. The next steps you will take depend on the components currently installed on the system. Certain components, like Terminal Services, include verification steps before continuing. Click Next until the Configuring Components dialog box appears. After configuring the DHCP component, the Completed The Windows Components Wizard dialog box appears. Click Finish

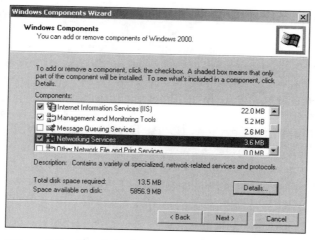

Figure 8.6   The list of Windows 2000 components available through the Add/Remove Programs applet.

to conclude the installation, and click Close to exit the Add/Remove Programs applet. Like other Windows 2000 networking components, DHCP is immediately ready to use without restarting the computer.

DHCP is configured through its own applet located in the Start | Administrative Tools menu. As shown in Figure 8.7, the first step to perform before using the DHCP server is to add a scope. A scope is the list of addresses and their subnet masks. Windows 2000 also supports a specialized DHCP grouping called a

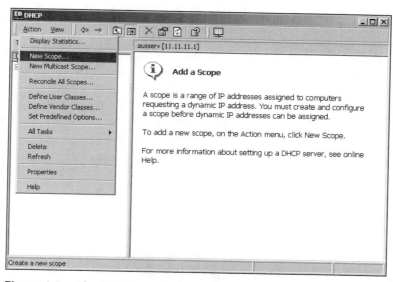

Figure 8.7   The DHCP configuration and management applet.

superscope. This is a set of related scopes that is used to support multiple, logical IP subnets. After configuring the scope of unique IP addresses, you can configure the DHCP options that are identical for all leases including DNS server addresses, DNS domain name, and other server addresses. Once configuration is complete, client computers can request addresses from the server and automatically configure their IP network settings.

Windows 2000 Naming Services (DNS, DDNS, and WINS)

The Windows operating systems have always relied on logical computer names for network communication. Based initially on the IBM LAN Manager model and NetBEUI, Microsoft has expanded its computer naming features in Windows 2000 to include industry standards and continues to support legacy systems.

DNS is the standard naming system used on the Internet. Part of the TCP/IP protocol suite, it associates simple language names to IP addresses, for example, the Web site name www.microsoft.com to 207.46.130.45 (only one of their many addresses). One of a Windows 2000 Server's many possible roles is that of a DNS server. In fact, Windows 2000 relies completely on DNS for name resolution.

DNS is a hierarchically organized, distributed system that contains various data host data including hostname, domain name, and IP address. The hierarchical organization of DNS takes place initially at the domain name level. If you spend time on the Internet, you are already familiar with domains, though you may not know it.

The Internet Domain Name System is managed by the Name Registration Authority (NRA). This NRA is responsible for maintaining the top-level domains and ensuring unique names are assigned to each requesting company or individual. The top-level domains are org (nonprofit organizations), gov (nonmilitary government organizations), mil (military government organizations), net (backbone networks and internet organizations), edu (schools, universities, and education related organizations), com (commercial organizations), num (phone numbers), arpa (reverse DNS), and two-letter country codes, such as au (Australia), fi (Finland), and jp (Japan). As you can probably deduce, the Internet site names you are familiar with fit into this organization based on their use. Below the top-level domains, the NRA assigns the names and maintains the master database to ensure duplicates are not created and traffic is directed to the correct site. Like IP addresses, domain names read from right to left from the top-level domain and become more specific as the address progresses. For example, joesnetgarage.com.lu identifies the domain name assigned to Joe's Network Garage (a for-profit corporation) in Luxembourg. The domain administrator at Joe's Network Garage is then responsible for assigning specific computers' IP addresses to their names and ensuring the information is correctly propagated to the Internet. If Joe's Network uses three Internet connected computers, one for Web access, one for FTP access, and one for news access, the administrator might assign 155.21.86.111 to www.joesnetgarage.com.lu, 155.21.86.233 to ftp.joesnetgarage.com.lu, and 155.21.93.12 to nntp.joesnetgarage.com.lu. A computer's complete address (www.joesnetgarage.com.lu, for example) identifies its exact location in the DNS structure and is referred to as its fully qualified domain name (FQDN).

When a computer needs to resolve a name to an IP address, it uses a query process dictated by the type of computer making the query. There are two basic types of DNS queries: those initiated by a client, known as a resolver in DNS lingo, to a server (specifically a name server), and those between name servers. Recursive queries are generally initiated by client systems and force a server to respond to a request, regardless of whether the request succeeded or failed. During a recursive query, if a name server cannot resolve the request, it must contact other DNS servers in an attempt for resolution. An iterative query is generally initiated by a name server and requires that the requested name server provide the best information possible based on the information available. If the queried server is not able to answer the request, it merely sends a negative response.

Perhaps the biggest drawback to the traditional DNS system is the fact that each administrator is responsible for updating their DNS entries manually; no automated update capability existed until recently. As mentioned earlier, Windows 2000 relies primarily on DNS to resolve not only names of Internet computers, but those on the local network as well. Because computers' names are continuously changing and they are constantly being turned on and off, it is impossible for a network administrator to manually update the DNS database effectively. To alleviate this issue and still comply with the industry standard, Microsoft has introduced the Dynamic Update using the Dynamic Domain Name System (DDNS) protocol. DDNS is a new protocol that has been submitted to the IETF for consideration under RFC 2136. This standard provides a method for dynamically updating the database through the *update* message type. Using update messages, the DHCP client process on every Windows 2000 computer attempts to register itself with the DNS server and update its records. To ensure complete registration, all Windows 2000 computers run the DHCP process whether they are DHCP clients or not. During automatic registration with the DNS server, if a duplicate host name is discovered, the first name is automatically deleted and the new name and IP address are added to the database.

Prior to Windows 2000, Microsoft relied on the Windows Internet Naming Service (WINS). WINS uses the NetBIOS naming convention to identify computers on the network and works in much the same way as DNS. However, WINS was designed to operate on small workgroup networks and does not scale well to the global network. However, by design, WINS automatically keeps track of the name and address associations for all devices connected to the network and requires little configuration to do so.

To maintain standards compatibility, Microsoft recommends not installing the Windows 2000 WINS components unless absolutely necessary. If there are computers currently on the network that rely on WINS for name resolution, such as Windows NT, 95, and 98 systems, explore the steps necessary to decommission WINS. If the Windows 2000 Server is attached to a network with only Windows 2000 systems, there is no need to load WINS at all.

If it is necessary to transition from WINS to DNS, it is possible to configure the services to work together to provide an easier migration. WINS and DNS are both part of the new TCP/IP environment in Windows 2000 and therefore integrate rather well. For example, Windows 2000 DNS includes the Use WINS Forward Lookup to assist the DNS server in resolving local hostnames. It does this by checking the WINS database in the event that a recursive query cannot be resolved by the DNS server itself.

Because it is relied upon so heavily, DNS is included in the standard installation configuration of Windows 2000. However, there may be circumstances that would preclude DNS from being installed. DNS and other Windows 2000 services can be installed and configured through the Configure Your Server utility. Open this utility by selecting Start | Programs | Administrative Tools | Configure Your Server. As shown in Figure 8.8, this utility is, in essence, a one-stop configuration shop for your Windows 2000 Server. DNS is a network service and is located under the Networking section. Click the down arrow next to Networking to display the complete list of services.

Click DNS to proceed with the installation. You will be presented with links on the right-hand side of the screen that allow you to learn more about DNS, set up DNS, or open a glossary link about IP addresses. Click Set Up DNS to proceed. If DNS is already installed, you will be sent directly to the configuration window. If DNS is not yet installed, Windows 2000 will automatically install it for you before continuing. You may be prompted to provide the Windows 2000 CD as the installation continues. Once installation is complete, click Next to proceed to the DNS configuration window shown in Figure 8.9. Click the Manage DNS link to launch the DNS configuration utility. The DNS configuration and management utility is actually a Microsoft Management Console (MMC) plug-in and works on the same basis as the DHCP manager and other MMC utilities.

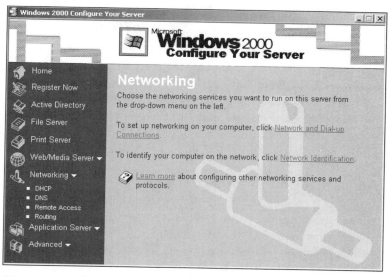

Figure 8.8   The Windows 2000 Configure Your Server utility.

8

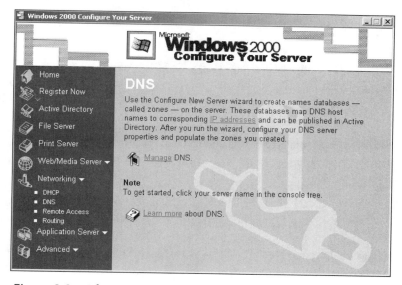

Figure 8.9   After installing DNS, a link is provided to Manage DNS.

Internet Authentication Service (IAS)

Another new service provided with Windows 2000, the IAS, is Microsoft's implementation of the industry standard Remote Authentication Dial-In User Service (RADIUS). Using the RADIUS protocol, IAS provides centralized authentication, authorization, auditing, and accounting (known as AAAA) for remote network connections, like VPN and dial-up. RADIUS's centralized design allows for simplified administration and single logon access to the network for remote connections. Because the IAS RADIUS server is integrated with Windows 2000, it works with the Active Directory during authentication and when network resources are accessed to grant or deny access. IAS works in conjunction with the Remote Access Service (RAS) to provide secure access over standard dial-up and VPN connections. IAS is installed through the Add/Remove Windows Components applet in the Network Services group. After installation, it is managed through its own MMC plug-in, accessed through Start | Programs | Administrative Tools | Internet Authentication Service.

QoS Admission Control Service (ACS)

Operating as part of the QoS component of Windows 2000, the QoS Admission Control Service is used to manage the network bandwidth and resources on particular network subnets. QoS ACS is also installed through the Add/Remove Windows Components applet. Once installed, QoS ACS can be configured to manage network traffic over a particular subnet. To do this, both the sending and receiving devices must support QoS, though they are not both required to be Windows 2000 systems. The QoS ACS is able to control subnet utilization based on policies, which means they can be applied to both users and groups.

Windows 2000 Network Services Resources

Because the Windows 2000 network services are based on industry standard protocols and services, extensive information is available. Refer to the following Web sites for more information on the services and their configuration:

➤ *www.microsoft.com/technet*—TechNet includes detailed articles on all Windows 2000 services and their implementation.

➤ *www.ietf.org*—Includes complete information on all Internet standards. Refer to RFCs 2131 and 2132 for information on DHCP; 1034, 1035, and 2136 for DNS and Dynamic Update; 2138 and 2139 for RADIUS; and 2211 and 2212 for QoS. Also review the information on the Resource Allocation Protocol (RAP) at **www.ietf.org/html.charters/rap-charter.html**.

WORKING WITH VIRTUAL PRIVATE NETWORKS (VPNs)

The term *VPN* is used to refer to a secure remote connection to a local network that is made over an insecure public network like the Internet. Prior to the introduction of VPNs, remote users requiring network access had to dial in to the local network or connect through a permanent dedicated connection, like a leased 56Kbps or T1 line. With pure dial in connections, mobile remote users usually have to pay heavy long distance charges for access to the network just to do their jobs. Toll-free 800 numbers are an option, but are also very expensive. For remote offices, even the lowest cost dedicated lines are expensive, both for the monthly surcharge and the additional equipment required on both ends of the connection. VPNs give the users and administrators the ability to utilize the low-cost options available for connecting to the Internet and still maintain high security standards. Figure 8.10 shows an example of different types of connections available using virtual private networking.

VPN Components

To create a virtual connection over a public network, specific components must be available. At one end of the VPN connection is the VPN server, which accepts connections from VPN clients and authenticates their request for access

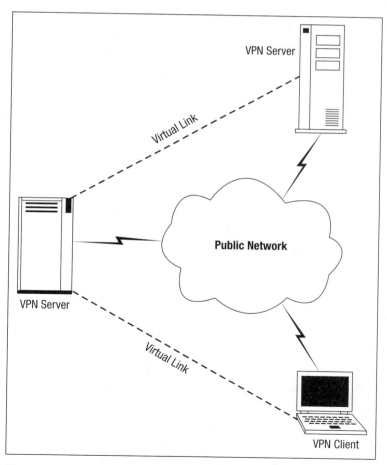

Figure 8.10   Example of virtual private network connections.

to the local network. As illustrated in Figure 8.10, VPN servers can provide connectivity to both client workstations and other VPN servers. When the VPN connection is made between servers or routers, the VPN is used to extend the network to incorporate multiple devices on both sides of the connection, rather than one device as seen in a standard point-to-point dial-up scenario.

A VPN client initiates the connection to the server. Computers running most of the more recent Windows operating systems (Windows 95 through Windows NT 4) can function as a VPN client when attaching to a Windows 2000 computer acting as the VPN server. In addition, any non-Microsoft computer using the Point-to-Point Tunneling Protocol (PPTP) can connect to a Windows 2000 VPN server as a client. A router-to-router connection can be established between two Windows 2000 computers and between a Windows 2000 computer and a Windows NT 4 computer running the Routing and Remote Access Service (RRAS).

The term *tunnel* is used to refer to the virtual connection between the VPN client and the VPN server. Specifically, the tunnel is the portion of the link over which data is encapsulated for transmission. A VPN connection is created when the data sent through the tunnel is encrypted for secure transmission. It is possible to create a tunnel and transmit data between the client and server without employing encryption, but this is technically not a virtual *private* network connection. Protocols like PPTP, mentioned earlier, are referred to as tunneling protocols. These protocols are used to encapsulate, encrypt, and transmit the data. In addition to PPTP, Windows 2000 supports the Layer Two Tunneling Protocol (L2TP), which utilizes IPSec (IP Security).

To act as a VPN server, the RRAS must be installed. Once installed, the VPN service can be configured to accept incoming connections from clients. Because VPN encapsulates data into either PPTP or L2TP, VPN connections can use any Windows 2000 protocol. Because most VPN tunnels are created over the Internet, however, TCP/IP is most often used. After installation, RRAS is configured like other network services, through the MMC and its own plug-in.

Addressing and Routing

Because VPN tunnels are extensions of the local network, it is important to understand how addressing and routing are implemented over VPN. When a connection is established, the server assigns an IP address to the client and changes the client's default route setting to route all traffic through the VPN server. This takes place whether the connection is client/server or router-to-router.

When a dial-up connection is created, the server allocates two IP addresses, one for the dial-up connection itself (using PPP) for communication over the Internet, and one address for use on the internal network. The VPN server then manages the translation between the intranet address and the Internet address. To devices on the internal network, the client appears as if it is directly connected to the network. All information destined for the VPN client is routed to the address assigned and managed by the VPN server.

As you've learned, the default route is the path specified for traffic to follow if the destination device is not on the local subnet. When a VPN is created, this route must be updated to direct all traffic to the VPN server. For a point-to-point connection where the client is not connected to another network, this configuration is fine. However, if the client computer is connected to another network or an ISP, completely changing the default route may not be a good idea. When this occurs, the VPN software keeps the existing default route, but assigns it a higher metric, so that the preferred path is through the VPN connection. If the VPN server is not able to provide a path to a particular destination, the original default route is used.

Router-to-router connections must also take into account routing and addressing. In actuality, the addresses are not generally changed when router-to-router connections are created because the routers are assumed to have static addresses. Router-to-router VPN connections fall into one of two categories: temporary or persistent. A temporary connection is created through most dial-up connections, whereas a persistent connection is used with leased lines or special dial-up connections not meant to be taken down. The type of routing used between the networks depends on the type of connection established between the routers. For temporary connections between small networks, manual static routing or auto-updated static routing is best. For larger networks and persistent connections, the VPN connection should use and recognize the routing protocols used on the network.

Using VPNs with Advanced Networking Devices

To ensure that their Internet connections are as secure and functional as possible, many networks employ advanced networking devices, like firewalls and network address translators (NATs). When a VPN connection is established through these devices, however, some caveats apply. Keep the following issues in mind when implementing a VPN connection through one or both of these devices.

A firewall is a device that examines all traffic to and from a given network and grants or denies access based on information in its configuration database. The most common firewalls in use today are employed when connecting private networks to public networks, like the Internet. For connecting to the Internet, firewalls are configured to use IP filtering. Because Internet traffic relies on IP for transport, the firewall can be configured to allow specific IP addresses access to the Internet, but deny access to all other addresses. When a VPN server is introduced into a network using a firewall for Internet access, there are two configuration options: placing the VPN server between the firewall and the Internet, and placing the VPN server behind the firewall. Figure 8.11 illustrates both configurations.

When placed between the firewall and the Internet, the VPN server must be configured with packet filters to specify that only VPN traffic is accepted. It is very important that the filters be applied to the Internet connected network adapter and not the adapter connecting the VPN server to the intranet. Because data received from the VPN server must still pass through the firewall, administrators can specify network access parameters for VPN clients as they do for other Internet-based clients.

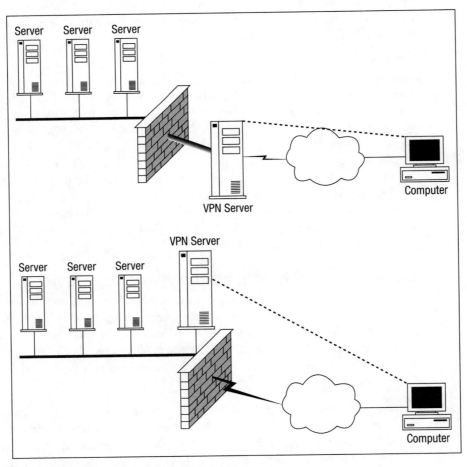

Figure 8.11   Two VPN/firewall combinations.

More often, the VPN server is placed behind the firewall to provide the highest level of security. In this configuration, the VPN server is managed in the same manner as other Internet accessible resources, like FTP servers and Web servers. For this configuration to work, the firewall must be configured to allow tunnel maintenance information and tunneled data through to the VPN server. Once the firewall has been configured, the VPN server functions as if using a direct connection to the client.

NATs are used to provide IP address conversion between the intranet and the Internet. A NAT is a specially configured router that is most often used on small networks to provide Internet connectivity. The IETF has specified a range of IP addresses designated as private, which means they can be assigned to computers that do not require registered Internet access. These addresses are 10.0.0.0/8 (class A), 172.16.0.0/16 (class B), and 192.168.0.0/24 (class C). Many companies do not provide Web services, but require Web access. These companies have no requirement for registered IP addresses and are prime candidates for using private IP addresses. Network address translators are used by companies like this to convert the private addresses used on the local network into an IP address or group of addresses as specified by their ISP. To facilitate communication through a NAT and VPN server, a NAT editor must monitor tunnel creation and ensure the integrity of the connection. RRAS includes an editor, which is loaded automatically, that performs this function.

BASIC ROUTING AND PROTOCOL MANAGEMENT

As mentioned earlier, when Windows 2000 network architecture components receive a request for a resource on another computer, the information is sent down from the Application layer through the OSI model, across the network media, and up through the OSI model on the receiving computer. When the network is comprised of a single segment, this communication is simple; placing the data on the network media is sufficient to provide communication with the destination system. Unfortunately, most networks in use today consist of more than a group of computers connected to a single segment. The process of directing data between network segments is called routing.

The term network is used to generically describe a combination of individual components that provide a method for computers to communicate. Each of the components of a network falls into one of the following routing function groups as defined by the International Standards Organization (ISO): end system, intermediate system, router (both hardware and software), network, and internetwork. From a routing perspective, an end system (also called a host) is a network device that does not have the ability to forward packets between network segments. An intermediate system, on the other hand, is a device that has the ability to forward packets from one segment to another. This name applies to all forwarding devices, regardless of the OSI layer at which the forwarding takes place; bridges, routers, and switches are all intermediate systems. Routers are intermediate systems that operate at the network layer of the OSI model to connect networks via a common protocol. The term hardware router indicates a networking device whose sole function is to route packets. Hardware routers are designed to perform this task as efficiently as possible and do not generally include support for other functionality. Conversely, software routers are not dedicated routers, but rather systems that provide routing services in addition to their other services. By its technical routing definition, a network is a portion of the networking infrastructure that is delineated by a Network layer intermediate system and is assigned the same network layer information. Network devices that operate below the network layer are included in the definition of the network. Figure 8.12 illustrates a network that includes devices operating below the Network layer. An internetwork is, quite simply, a collection of two or more networks connected by routers.

Note: *Routing products from companies, like Cisco and Bay Networks, are examples of hardware routers. A Windows 2000 computer configured for routing is a software router.*

As mentioned earlier in this chapter, network device addresses are made up of two fields: the host address and the network address. The host address, also called the host ID or node ID, can be either the physical address of the host's network interface card or a logical address assigned by an administrator. Whether the physical address or a logical address is used depends on the protocol. The network address, or network ID, identifies the specific network within the internetwork to which the host is attached. When a host begins communication, it compares its own network ID with the network ID of the destination to determine whether the destination is on the same network. If the destination host is on another network, the source sends the data to a router for traversal across the network to the destination host. The term internetwork address refers to the combination of the host and network addresses. For example, if the host with logical address BIGSYS is connected to network GEORGIA, its internetwork address would be GEORGIA.BIGSYS.

Note: *The dotted-decimal representation of a device's IP address, including the subnet mask, is its internetwork address. The subnet mask is required to differentiate between the host ID and its network ID. For example, a device's host ID might be 0.0.25.112 and its network ID 156.86.0.0 resulting in an internetwork address of 156.86.25.112.*

When a packet is sent, it contains fields for a source internetwork address, a destination internetwork address, and a hop count. The hop count field defines the length of time the packet is allowed to traverse the network. A new packet

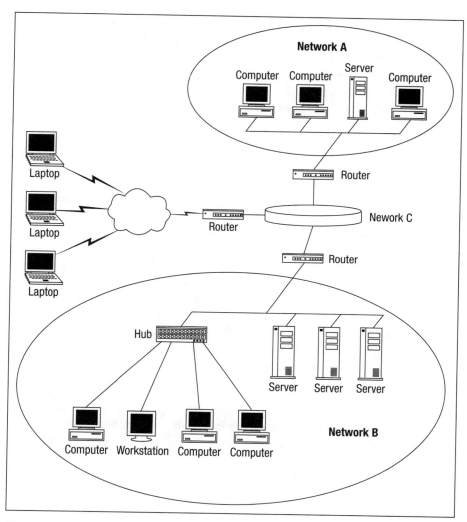

Figure 8.12   A sample network including lower layer networking devices.

may be assigned a hop count of 12, for example. As a router processes the packet for transmission across the network, it reduces the value of the hop count by 1 and includes the new hop count in the packet when it is sent to the next router. When the packet's hop count reaches 0, the packet is discarded.

Routing Fundamentals

The process of moving data from the source host to the destination host requires that the protocol make a determination as to where the packet's next step is. This determination process is divided into two categories: host routing and router routing. As you might imagine, host routing takes place on the sending host when data is to be sent to another system. As the host prepares to send data, it examines the network ID of the destination and sends the packets either directly to the destination host (if the network IDs are the same) or to a router. Router routing is similar to host routing, but describes the process the router uses to determine whether to send the packet to another router or directly to the destination host.

If a host uses a routable protocol, the first step in the host routing process is determining the internetwork address of the destination. The method for obtaining the destination internetwork address depends on the exact protocol being used, most often broadcasts or directory lookup through services like DNS. Once it has obtained the destination internetwork address, the host's protocol compares the network ID portion of the destination address with its own to determine the destination's location in the internetwork. If the destination is on the same subnet as the source host, the source communicates directly with the destination by directing data to the destination's physical address. This communication method is called direct delivery. It is important to remember that network hosts have two addresses: physical and internetwork. With some protocols, the physical address is used as part of the internetwork address, but they are separate fields in the structure of a packet. In the direct delivery model, the packet's destination physical address and destination internetwork address identify the same system.

The other side of the host routing coin is seen when the destination's internetwork address indicates the destination host is on a different subnet than the source. In this scenario, the packet cannot be delivered directly to the destination, so the source host forwards the packet to an intermediate router. Because the lowest communication layers support only direct communication, the source host sets the packet's destination physical address to that of the router and sets its destination internetwork address field to the address of the ultimate destination system.

For indirect host routing to work, the source host must determine to which router the packets should be directed. It does this by either determining the first hop on the path to the destination host or by discovering the complete path through the network the packet will take. If a host uses first hop routing, it sends the data to the specified router, which then uses the router routing techniques discussed in the "Routing Tables" section to direct the traffic to the destination. Protocols that use the first hop indirect delivery method are able to select the first hop by using one of the following processes.

➤ *Default route*—From the host's perspective, the simplest solution by far. The host's default route identifies the router to which all traffic addressed to a destination for which no other host or network route exists. For example, the network at a company's remote office most likely only needs one connection outside the local network—the link to the corporate network. Computers on the remote network are configured to send all external traffic through the corporate connection. This catch-all path is called the default route.

➤ *Host routing table*—A static list of networks known to the host and the address of the router serves as the next hop to the network. Depending on the protocol, the routing table may also include fields for the cost of the route (in terms of throughput) or the current state of the route. In its most basic configuration, the host routing table can be a simple text file stored on the host device. This works well in small environments in which the state of the network seldom changes. However, each time a change is made to the architecture of the network, each table must be updated manually.

➤ *Dynamically updated host routing table*—Certain protocol suites, such as TCP/IP, provide the ability to dynamically update host routing tables. The Windows 2000 TCP/IP implementation supports this function through ICMP messages. When a router identifies a better path, it sends an ICMP message to the host, updating the host's routing table. Although this provides a similar function to the RIP, it is not the same and operates independently.

➤ *Eavesdropping*—Another next hop determination method available to some protocols is the ability to listen to traffic generated by other computers on the network to determine the next hop.

➤ *Network query*—As a last resort, a host without a routing table or specified default route can determine the physical address of the first hop router by sending queries to all routers on the network. To do this, the host sends a broadcast or multicast transmission requesting the best path to a specific subnet. The routers respond with information regarding their path to the subnet in question and the host makes the determination for the best router to choose for the first hop.

The second method available to hosts for determining the router that packets should be directed for transmission to their destination is to determine the complete path through the network to the destination. In addition to defining the first hop the packets will take, a host in this environment goes through a route discovery process that gives it a clear picture of the network. Armed with this information, the host includes the exact steps the intermediate routers are to take to deliver the information in the packet's Network layer header. This routing method is called source routing because the source host makes the route determination and includes it in the packets as they are sent. Because the route is already specified, intermediate routers on source routing networks are little more than packet shufflers. They read the information provided in the Network layer by the source host and direct the traffic as instructed.

8

Of the two host routing methods, source routing is implemented far less often. The source host must determine the path for each communication session, which increases the traffic on the network and requires additional processing by the source host. There are two source routing implementations, however, which might be encountered at some point. IP source routing is used in testing environments when it is necessary to specify the path data takes through the network. The Token Ring network architecture also uses source routing, but it is not truly routing because it is handled at the Data Link layer.

When the source host uses first hop routing to send data to determine the first step for the data, the router uses router routing processes, similar to host routing processes, to determine the next step for the data. If the destination network ID indicates a subnet to which the router is directly connected, it sends the packets directly to the destination host's physical address. If not, the router consults its routing tables and forwards the packet to the next hop toward the destination. Each router along the path repeats this process until the destination network is reached.

Routing Tables

As mentioned earlier, a routing table is a list of network destinations used by both hosts and routers to facilitate communication across an internetwork. The location of the routing table and its contents is dictated by the protocol being used. For example, IP routing tables are used by both hosts and routers and include different fields than IPX routing tables, which are only used by routers. In addition to the default route described previously, routing tables include network routes and host routes. As its name implies, a network route describes the path to a network, whereas a host route identifies the path to a specific internetwork address. Most routing tables are comprised only of network routes and possibly a default route, but host routes can be added for load balancing or to create a specific path between devices.

To provide useful information to routers, routing tables include specific fields. Though a specific protocol may not utilize all the fields described, most routing tables include fields for network ID, next hop, route cost, TTL, and interface field. The network ID field is network route or host route being defined. Next hop, also called the forwarding address, identifies the next router in the path. The information in the route cost field is used to determine the best path through the network if more than one path exists. Also called a metric, the cost of the route can be measured as the number of hops between the host and the destination, the amount of time it takes a packet to reach the destination network (called delay), the throughput of the link, and the reliability of the link. The TTL or lifetime of the route indicates the length of time the route is kept in the routing table. The interface field is a port number (or other identifier) used when forwarding packets to the network ID. Routers continuously exchange information on the state of the network and available routes. Routes for networks not directly connected to the router are learned from other routers and maintained in the routing table. Because all networks are not directly connected, a router may not be aware of a network failure if an update is not received. By specifying a lifetime for the route, the routing table is able to discard routes that may no longer be active. When one router receives a routing information update from another router, it resets the TTL for the route and communication continues. If the TTL expires without an update being received, the router assumes the route is no longer available.

Updating Routing Tables

Routing tables can be maintained and updated through one of two methods: static routing and dynamic routing. Static routing tables are maintained by hand and are useful in smaller network environments or when specific paths must always be taken. Because they do not rely on information from other routers, using static routing tables reduces broadcast traffic on the network and ensures efficient router operation. A router is configured with only the specific routes needed for hosts on its network to communicate. This can also be used to provide a more secure network environment. For example, on a large network with many subnets, the computers on the design team's network may be the only systems allowed to access the data warehouse servers on a different network. If a router on the data warehouse network is configured with a single static route to the design team's network, the servers will be unable to communicate with computers anywhere else on the network.

The downsides to static routing are that it is not fault tolerant and does not scale well to larger networks. The reason for both drawbacks is the same: manual configuration. As a network grows, more and more time must be dedicated to router maintenance to ensure that communication between all subnets is possible. In addition, if a communication link or router fails, each router and host on the network must be updated either with a different path or by removal of the destination altogether. On a network of any size, it is possible that the problem could be fixed before all the routers are updated.

Dynamic routing allows for automatic routing table maintenance using routing protocols. These protocols can use both periodic and on-demand messages to hosts and routers of the state of the network. Because dynamic routing is automatic, it is easy to configure and provides fault tolerance to the network. If a failure occurs, the involved routers provide the information to the other routers on the network; they are then able to determine if an alternate path exists to the destination. In addition, dynamic routing scales well to large networks including the global Internet.

8

Routing Protocols

All major protocol suites including IPX/SPX and TCP/IP encompass a method for updating network information between devices. In fact, each protocol suite has two separate protocols that can be used for dynamic routing. IP uses the RIP and Open Shortest Path First (OSPF); IPX has its own version of RIP and the NetWare Link Services Protocol (NLSP). RIP functions the same way for both IP and IPX; OSPF and NLSP are also very similar. These protocol groups utilize different methods for monitoring the state of the network and updating other devices. The processes used by the protocols to sense and adapt to changing network conditions is very important as it affects overall performance. The routing protocols define which method is used for the exchange of routing information, how often it is exchanged, and how quickly the network recovers from a failure.

When a portion of an internetwork fails, it must reconfigure itself to adjust to the failure and accurately represent the new topology. The state of network stability in which all routers have an accurate picture of network configuration is called *convergence*. After a failure, the reconvergence time is important because data can potentially be sent down paths that no longer exist and might be lost or corrupted.

The RIP is a distance vector protocol, meaning it measures routes based on their distance from the router, generally by hop. A route with three routers between source and destination is preferred over a route with five routers. Both IP and IPX use RIP to periodically advertise the information in the routing table to other routers on the network. To ensure that all routers have the most accurate, most up-to-date routing information, RIP broadcasts the entire contents of the routing table down each interface on the router. Receiving routers accept the information in the broadcast and calculate their routing table accordingly. RIP is useful because it is easy to implement and automatic. However, on large networks, the overhead created by periodic RIP broadcasts has a detrimental impact on network performance. The default configuration specifies full-table transmission every 30 seconds. If RIP were used on the Internet today, no other traffic would have access to the network. Perhaps the biggest consideration, however, is that RIP networks are slow to converge. Because RIP uses broadcasts, the messages are not acknowledged and a broadcasting router may supply invalid information until a failed route's TTL expires.

Link state routing protocols, on the other hand, provide a much lower convergence time. This is because link state protocols monitor the state of the network and send updates when its topology changes. Rather than periodically broadcasting their routing tables, link state routers send unicast or multicast messages that contain only information on the attached networks and their state. If a network segment occurs, the routers on both sides send an update and the network reconverges quickly. OSPF and NLSP are link state protocols that fit well onto larger networks because they utilize smaller routing tables and low overhead. However, the calculations required for link state routing are extensive and therefore equipment is more expensive than for distance-vector routing. Link state routing also requires a higher level of understanding for design and troubleshooting. Although you are essentially able to plug a RIP router into a network and have it work immediately, link state routers require a certain level of planning and configuration before becoming operational, much less optimally efficient.

CHAPTER SUMMARY

Like other components, the Windows 2000 network architecture is layered, providing easier integration and development for hardware and software vendors. At the top of the network architecture is the component layer made up of network services and API components. Under this layer is the TDI boundary layer, followed by the network protocol layer. Between the network protocol layer and the lowest functional layer is the NDIS layer. The lowest functional layer contains the components that manage the network adapter cards.

The OSI model is a theoretical, seven-layer model for network communication developed by the ISO. The top layer is Application, which provides the interface to the user and acts as the access point to the network for processes and applications. Next is the Presentation layer, responsible for converting the binary data received from the network into the language required by the application. Third from the top is the Session layer, which manages connections between applications on the sending and receiving computers. The Transport layer follows and ensures all messages are delivered to the upper layers intact and complete. The Network layer coordinates communication between computers and handles addressing. The Data Link layer ensures error-free communication between computers. The lowest layer of the OSI model is the Physical layer, which controls how data is sent over the physical network medium.

In the Windows 2000 architecture, the API and services layer contains the workstation and server services, redirectors, and file systems. The Multiple Uniform Naming Convention and Multi-Provider components allow multiple redirectors to be loaded on a system and also determine the appropriate redirector to Win32 Network (WNet) commands. IPC components provide bidirectional communication between clients and servers and are integral to the client/server functionality of Windows 2000. The CIFS is the native file sharing protocol for Windows 2000 and defines the commands used to exchange information between computers. RPC components are responsible for registering servers, name resolution, connection establishment, endpoint resolution, and security on the Windows 2000 computer. DCOM is Microsoft's distributed programming module for creating client/server applications. Named pipes and mailslots provide dedicated connection points for communication network communication. Windows 2000 supports many APIs that carry out low-level services for the operating system. The primary Windows 2000 APIs are WNet, TAPI, MAPI, NetBIOS, and Winsock.

The TDI boundary layer provides the standard interface for communication between services and network transport protocols. TDI is not represented by a software component in the operating system, but is a standard to which components on either side must comply. The network protocols functional layer specifies packet creation and transmission. Window 2000 includes support for seven network protocols: TCP/IP, ATM, IPX/SPX, NetBEUI, AppleTalk, DLC, and IrDA. The NDIS boundary layer defines the network driver architecture used in Windows 2000 and allows upper-layer protocol components to operate independently of network adapters. This allows Windows 2000 computers to have unlimited network adapters installed and have an unlimited number of protocols bound to a single adapter. The NDIS layer is designed to allow network device manufacturers the least amount of programming necessary by dividing the driver specifications into intermediate and miniport. Miniport drivers are the components that actually communicate with the network hardware.

With Windows 2000, Microsoft has moved to native support for many industry standard protocols and services. TCP/IP is the default protocol suite for Windows 2000 and the protocol of the Internet. TCP/IP uses a layered structure and is divided into many protocols, each with a specific task. The DARPA model consists of only four layers: Application, Host-to-Host Transport, Internetwork, and Network Interface. The primary protocol of the TCP/IP suite, IP, provides datagram communication and is responsible for addressing. ICMP provides troubleshooting assistance by returning error messages for packets that cannot be delivered. ARP associates IP addresses to physical addresses. IGMP groups computers so that multicasts can be used to communicate with many devices at the same time. UDP is a connectionless transport protocol, whereas TCP is a connection-oriented protocol. TCP uses the three-way handshake to establish communication between the devices and determine the packets' beginning sequence numbers. FTP provides file transfer and manipulation services. RIP is used by routers to exchange routing information. HTTP is used to transmit documents written in HTML, usually Web pages.

IP addresses are 32-bit logical addresses represented in decimal format that uniquely identify the device on the network. Addresses are divided into five classes (A, B, C, D and E), three of which (A, B, and C) can be used for network devices. The network ID portion of the IP address is denoted by using a subnet mask. From left to right, the binary digits set to 1 represent the network ID with the remainder of the digits representing the host ID. Subnet masks can be divided along octet boundaries or at any point in the address. Subnet masks can be written in either decimal format (255.255.255.0) or as an indication of the bits in the mask (/24).

ATM is a high-speed, connection-oriented protocol that is well suited for real-time applications, such as video conferencing. NWLink is Microsoft's implementation of the IPX/SPX protocol suite and is mostly used for communication with Novell NetWare systems. NetBEUI is provided for legacy computer and application support. The AppleTalk protocol is supported by Windows 2000 to provide access to Apple Macintosh computers. DLC was originally designed for communication with IBM mainframe computers, but is mostly used now with Hewlett-Packard printers. IrDA is a group of point-to-point infrared protocols used for wireless networking.

The DHCP service is used to automatically configure IP addresses and other settings for devices on the network. Windows 2000 can act as either a DHCP server or a client. The DHCP server provides addresses with their corresponding subnet masks from a database of available addresses called a scope. The client leases the IP address from the server for a specific length of time. When the lease is 50 percent complete, the client requests the same address from the server. If the server or address is not available at that time, the client sends a general DHCPRequest for the same address to all servers. If no server is able to acknowledge the request, the client must start the lease process from the DHCPDiscover process once again.

Windows 2000 relies on the industry standard DNS for name resolution. DNS is a hierarchically organized, distributed system that uniquely identifies computers on the Internet. The top-level domains are managed by the NRA and are organized by function and country. The top-level domains are org, gov, mil, net, edu, com, num, arpa, and two-letter country codes, such as jp, fi, and au. DNS is a static system that requires manual configuration of each domain. To provide support in Windows 2000, DNS has been expanded to include dynamic updates to the database.

The IAS uses RADIUS to provide centralized authentication, authorization, auditing, and accounting for remote network connections, like VPN and dial-up. The QoS ACS is used to manage network traffic and resources used by computers and applications.

VPNs provide secure remote connections over insecure, public networks like the Internet. VPN connections are created either between clients and servers or between two VPN servers. This allows support for both mobile, dial-in users and remote office networks. A tunnel is the portion of the connection between client and server over which the data is encrypted for transmission. Windows 2000 supports both the PPTP and L2TP VPN protocols. Because the protocols are encrypted through the tunnel, addressing and routing are handled differently than with normal connections. In addition, firewalls and NATs must be configured to support VPNs.

For devices to communicate across network segments, routers must be employed to move the data from one segment to the next. The ISO defines network components as end system, intermediate system, router, network, and internetwork. An internetwork is a collection of interconnected networks. A device's internetwork address describes its precise location on the internetwork and is a combination of its network ID and host ID. When a data packet is sent from a host system, the host first looks at the destination network ID to determine whether the packet can be directly sent to the destination computer or has to be routed. If it must be routed, the host determines the device to which it should send the packet to ensure it gets to its destination. On some networks, the source host specifies the exact path the packet should take through the network. On most, however, the source determines the next hop to which the packet will be sent, and relies on other networking devices to deliver the data to the destination. The source either makes this determination based on its configuration by listening to the network for clues or by querying the routers on the network. Routing tables contain destination network addresses, the next hop to reach the destination, the cost of the route, and the TTL of the route. Routing tables are either maintained manually (static) or dynamically. Static routing is best suited for small networks whose topology seldom changes, whereas dynamic routing scales well to larger networks. Routing protocols use either distance-vector or link state algorithms to maintain their routing tables and update other routers on the network. Distance-vector protocols, like RIP, use periodic broadcasts to provide information to other routers, whereas link state protocols send messages only when there is a topology change.

REVIEW QUESTIONS

1. Which of the following networking devices translate private IP addresses to public IP addresses for communication over the Internet?

   a. VPNs

   b. Router

   c. NAT

   d. Bridge

2. Which of the following is the binary representation of 137?

   a. 01100111

   b. 10010001

   c. 10110001

   d. 10001001

3. Which of the following are provided with Windows 2000 to support legacy Windows applications? [Choose all that apply]

   a. NWLink

   b. NetBEUI

   c. DLC

   d. NetBIOS service

4. In the TCP/IP protocol suite, which of the following best describes the role of ARP?

   a. Associates computer names to physical addresses

   b. Associates computer names to IP addresses

   c. Associates IP addresses to physical addresses

   d. Associates IP addresses to upper-layer protocols

5. Which of the following is used by Windows 2000 to ensure file integrity?

   a. FTP

   b. UNC

   c. RPC

   d. CIFS

6. Which of the following represents a Class B subnet mask? [Choose all that apply]

   a. 255.255.0.0

   b. /16

   c. /18

   d. 255.255.255.0

7. Which of the following addresses is used to direct all host traffic not specified in the routing table?

   a. Primary route

   b. Host route

   c. Default route

   d. Network route

8. Which of the following resource access components provides support for multiple redirectors on a single computer?

   a. UNC

   b. MUP

   c. IPC

   d. MPR

9. Which of the following is the link state protocol for TCP/IP?

   a. OSPF

   b. RIP

   c. NLSP

   d. DHCP

10. Which of the following services includes the Windows 2000 VPN components?

    a. RRAS

    b. RADIUS

    c. DHCP

    d. Workstation

11. Which of the following IPC components is used for broadcast messaging?

    a. Mailslots

    b. TCP ports

    c. Named pipes

    d. NetBIOS

12. Which of the following protocols is Microsoft's implementation of another networking company's primary protocol?

    a. TCP/IP

    b. AppleTalk

    c. NetBIOS

    d. NWLink

13. The DHCPOffer packet uses which of the following address combinations?

    a. Source IP address/destination IP address

    b. Source physical address/destination physical address

    c. Source physical address/destination IP address

    d. Source IP address/destination physical address

14. Which of the following DHCP packets is sent by the client when the lease is no longer required?

   a. DHCPDecline

   b. DHCPReject

   c. DHCPInform

   d. DHCPRelease

15. Which of the following APIs is used to implement Quality of Service?

   a. WNet

   b. TAPI

   c. Winsock

   d. MAPI

16. To support remote dial-up connections, which Windows 2000 service uses the RADIUS standards?

   a. IAS

   b. VPN

   c. ACS

   d. TCP

17. At which layer of the OSI model does the TCP protocol operate?

   a. Transport

   b. Network

   c. Session

   d. Data Link

18. Which of the following describes the first step in the lease renewal process?

   a. When the lease term is complete, the client sends a DHCPDiscover packet.

   b. When the lease is 50 percent complete, the client sends a DHCPRequest to the server from which the lease was obtained.

   c. When the lease is 87.5 percent complete, the server sends a DHCPRenew packet to the client.

   d. When the lease is 50 percent complete, the server sends a DHCPOffer to the client.

19. Which layer of the OSI model creates a virtual circuit between sending and receiving processes?

   a. Application

b. Session

c. Transport

d. Presentation

20. Which of the following NDIS features initializes the computer when a signal is received from another computer?

a. IPSec

b. Wake-on-LAN

c. CoNDIS

d. TCP offloading

21. What are networks on which the sending host dictates the route data takes across the network called?

a. Source routing

b. Host routing

c. Router routing

d. Dynamic routing

22. Which of the following protocols uses the NDIS LAN Emulation intermediate driver?

a. IPX

b. TCP

c. ATM

d. NetBEUI

23. Which of the following components of the Windows 2000 architecture is not represented by a software component and represents the interface between services and protocols?

a. TDI boundary layer

b. NDIS boundary layer

c. WNet boundary layer

d. DHCP boundary layer

24. Which of the following network architecture components provides communication paths between processes running on the same computer?

a. RPC

b. DCOM

c. CIFS

d. NDR

25. Which of the following is the default service used by Windows 2000 for name resolution?

    a. WINS

    b. DHCP

    c. DNS

    d. IGMP

26. Which of the following protocols are used by Windows 2000 to create private, tunneled connections? [Choose all that apply]

    a. PPTP

    b. WinTunnel

    c. Winsock

    d. L2TP

27. Which of the following is included in a routing table entry to assist the router in determining the best path for the data?

    a. Interface

    b. Metric

    c. Default route

    d. TTL

28. Which of the following most accurately describes UDP?

    a. Provides connectionless datagram transport

    b. Ensures reliable packet delivery

    c. Provides encryption and encapsulation for VPN connections

    d. Provides configuration services

REAL-WORLD PROJECTS

Note: To complete the projects, you will need access to a Windows 2000 Server with TCP/IP installed and have a copy of the Windows 2000 Server CD.

After weeks of proposals and meetings, the project was approved. Jason's proposal to the Executives was a zero administration initiative incorporating many of the Windows 2000 features. There was some skepticism from management with regard to relying so heavily on new technologies and Jason was forced to extend his testing schedule by nearly three weeks. The first step in the project was to get a DHCP server configured and prepared for testing. Jason was given a Windows 2000 Server that had previously been used for other testing. He knew the installation was solid, but was not entirely sure of the protocol configuration on the system. Knowing that many test systems in his organization were not assigned permanent IP addresses, but that a DHCP server needed to have the same address all the time, he booted the system and checked its TCP/IP configuration.

Project 8.1
To review a computer's TCP/IP settings, perform the following steps:

1. Open the Properties for My Network Places by right-clicking the icon and selecting Properties from the menu.

2. Right-click the Local Area Connection icon and again select Properties, invoking the Properties applet.

3. In the window, the list of installed components is displayed. Components that have a checkmark are configured to function on the displayed network adapter. Scroll through the list of components, select Internet Protocol (TCP/IP), and click Properties.

4. In order to provide network services like DHCP and DNS, most Windows 2000 Server systems require specific IP addresses rather than relying on automatically assigned addresses from other servers. Ensure that the Use The Following IP Address checkbox is selected and verify that the IP address and subnet mask are configured for the server.

5. Note that it is through this window that the default gateway and DNS servers are configured. Check these settings, and click Advanced to review additional settings.

6. Through the Advanced TCP/IP Settings window, you are able to configure multiple IP addresses on a network adapter, provide additional information on DNS servers and their operation, configure WINS, and manage specialized settings like IP security and TCP/IP filtering. In the majority of cases, these settings will not need to be changed. Click OK to return to the TCP/IP Properties window, then click OK again to return to the Local Area Connection Properties window. Click OK a third time to complete the configuration.

While reviewing the TCP/IP configuration, it occurred to Jason that the DHCP service may not currently be installed on the system. A quick check of the Start menu confirmed his suspicions as there was no entry under the Administrative Tools menu. Before testing could begin, Jason had to install the DHCP service.

Project 8.2
To install the DHCP service, perform the following steps:

1. Select Start | Programs | Administrative Tools | Configure Your Server.

2. The Configure Your Server utility provides a single location for installing and configuring many Windows 2000 components. To install the DHCP service, click the Networking link as shown in Figure 8.13, and then click the DHCP link.

3. The DHCP configuration window is displayed next, which provides a description of the service with links to information on related topics like IP addresses, a link to Learn More About DHCP, and a link to launch the Windows Component wizard. Click Start to begin the installation.

4. From the list of available network components, select Networking Services and click Details.

5. A list of the supported Windows 2000 network components is displayed. Click the box next to Dynamic Host Configuration Protocol (DHCP) and ensure that the checkbox is selected before clicking OK. Click OK.

6. From the initial list of Windows components, click Next to continue.

7. You may be presented with additional configuration windows verifying the current setup of your server. Continue to click Next until the Configuring

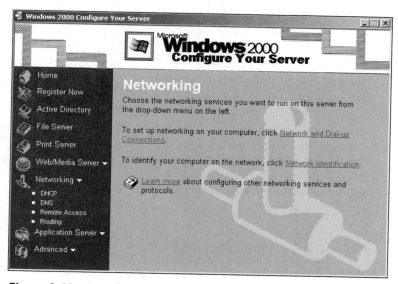

Figure 8.13   Installing and configuring the DHCP service.

Components window is presented. You may be asked to provide the Windows 2000 CD during the configuration phase. If so, insert the CD, and click OK.

8. Once configuration is complete, click Finish to end the session.

Jason returned immediately to the Configuring Your Server utility. Moving on, Jason was now ready to configure the DHCP server.

Project 8.3
To configure the DHCP server, perform the following steps:

1. After installing the DHCP server, you will be returned to the Configuring Your Server utility. The Next button in the bottom-right corner of the window begins the configuration process. Although this button is available before the service is installed, clicking it invokes a message reminding you that you have to install a DHCP server before continuing. However, you are now ready to proceed. Click Next.

2. The presented window again provides links to learn more about the tools and services being used: Manage DHCP and Open The DHCP Manager. At this point, clicking either the Manage DHCP or the Open The DHCP Manager link has the same result. Click Open The DHCP Manager.

3. The MMC is started with the DHCP plug-in already loaded. The left side of the window lists all DHCP servers. The right side displays the servers' configuration. Click the icon for the server you are working on.

4. After a moment's processing, you are presented with a dialog reminder in the right pane stating that you must add a scope before using DHCP. Click the Action menu and select New Scope to start the New Scope Wizard.

5. Click Next to continue.

6. The next dialog box is used to assign a name and description for the scope. Because many scopes can be configured on a single server, it is important to name the scopes in such a way that their roles are easy to identify. For example, specifying one scope for the Accounting department and a different scope for the Engineering department allows you to easily manage the network and makes migration of one department to another server or network easier. Enter a name and description for the scope you are creating ("Test Scope" for example) and click Next.

7. The next dialog box asks to specify the range of IP addresses for use by the scope. In addition, you must specify the subnet mask that accompanies the IP address. Note that Windows 2000 DHCP supports subnet mask

configuration in both decimal and bit-notation format. Click the arrows next to the Length window and the decimal value of the subnet mask changes accordingly. Enter the beginning and ending range of IP addresses to be used by DHCP (for example, 192.168.0.1 through 192.168.0.254), adjust the subnet mask (255.255.255.0), and click Next.

8. If there are systems that currently have static IP addresses within the range specified, you can configure DHCP to skip assigning the address in the next dialog box. If it is a single system's address that should be excluded from the assignment, enter it in the Start IP Address field, and click Add. If a range of addresses should be excluded, enter the beginning and ending IP addresses in the fields, and click Add.

9. Click Next to continue.

10. The next window is used to specify the lease duration. Most address leases are measured in days (the default is 8 days, 0 hours, and 0 minutes), but the lease duration can be configured down to the minute level. Set your preferred lease duration, and click Next to continue.

11. You are then provided the opportunity to configure additional settings for DHCP clients accessing the scope. For testing purposes, this is not necessary now, but take the opportunity to review these settings at a later date. Refer to Microsoft TechNet for information on the many configuration options available. Click Next to continue.

12. Click Finish to complete the scope configuration and return to the DHCP Manager.

13. After exiting the configuration program, one additional step is necessary before the scope can be used by clients. Right-click the recently created scope and select Activate from the menu. Once activated, the DHCP server is prepared to provide IP addresses to requesting clients.

8

CHAPTER NINE

MANAGING NETWORK INTEROPERABILITY

After completing this chapter, you will be able to:

✓ Understand the different systems with which Windows 2000 can interoperate

✓ Manage multiple protocols on Windows 2000 systems

✓ Explain the uses of SNMP

✓ Know how Novell NetWare and Windows 2000 interoperate

✓ Understand how Macintosh clients can share information with Windows 2000

✓ Detail the Unix and SNA utilities supported by Windows 2000

Wouldn't it be nice if everyone's networks were designed from the ground up with only a single protocol, a single server type, and the same clients throughout an organization? Well, for most, this is a pipe dream. Most administrators not only have to support multiple systems, but also interoperate them.

End users don't care that Unix servers use a different protocol than Windows 2000 Servers. Or that their user account on the NetWare server is different than the one on the Windows 2000 Server. All they care about is why they have to use different applications when dealing with different operating systems; why they have a Windows 2000 system and a dumb IBM terminal on their desks; and why their Windows 2000 password has expired and the NetWare one has not, forcing them to remember two passwords.

Administrators can make it easier for users to deal with some of these issues. Many of the more popular operating systems today have tools available to make the interoperation between the different operating systems less painful. Windows 2000 is no exception.

In this chapter, we examine some of the most common utilities and tools available to administrators for interconnecting Windows 2000 networks with Novell NetWare, Apple Macintosh, Unix, and SNA based systems. Remember that most of the tools covered in this chapter are available from Microsoft, but are not the only ones available.

WINDOWS 2000 INTEROPERABILITY OVERVIEW

In today's computing world, interoperability among different operating systems is essential and becoming easier to achieve. One of the benefits of the Internet is that it uses a standard set of protocols in Transport Control Protocol/Internet Protocol (TCP/IP). Almost every system on the planet now supports TCP/IP in one form or another. As more and more systems take full advantage of TCP/IP, interoperating them will become easier and easier. Eventually, the system you use at work or at home will be able to communicate seamlessly with any other system regardless of the operating system or hardware configuration.

Until that day comes, however, administrators must learn to live with the plethora of systems in use today. Many older legacy systems still exist and still use legacy protocols. These include Novell NetWare 4.x and earlier with its IPX/SPX protocol, Apple Macintosh with its AppleTalk protocol, and Windows NT with its NetBEUI protocol.

MANAGING MULTIPLE PROTOCOLS AND NETWORK SERVICE ARCHITECTURES

As stated previously, Windows 2000 systems must communicate with other systems using different protocols and services. Imagine the following scenario.

You are leading a company meeting. There are four other company employees in the meeting from four subsidiaries in different parts of the world: one from Germany, one from France, one from Japan, and one from China. Five languages are spoken by the five attendees (yourself included), which are English, German, French, Japanese, and Chinese. There are two ways that communication among the five of you can take place.

The first way is that one of the attendees (say you for example) must speak all five languages. All communication must go through you. This means that if the German employee wants to speak to the Japanese employee, he or she must communicate with you in German, and you must translate the messages into Japanese. Complex, isn't it?

The second method is to choose a common language (English, for example) and have a translator be present for each language spoken. These translators must be fluent in the language they are translating as well as English.

Now let's compare this scenario to the matter at hand. The first method, the one where you must do all the translating uses different protocols to communicate between the different systems. If your system is a Windows 2000 system that must communicate with a NetWare system, a Macintosh system, a Unix system, and an IBM mainframe system, then it must be able to communicate using the native protocols of these systems: IPX/SPX, AppleTalk, TCP/IP, and SNA.

One of the drawbacks of this method is that although your system may be able to communicate using all these protocols, it does not know which system "speaks" which language. You therefore must specify an order, known as the binding order, for the order in which the protocols must be tried. Let's say that you use the following binding order: TCP/IP, IPX/SPX, AppleTalk, NetBEUI, and SNA. If your system needs to communicate with an IBM mainframe, it will first send a message to the mainframe using the first protocol on its binding order, TCP/IP. When TCP/IP times out, it will try the next, IPX/SPX, and so on. Finally, it will try the SNA protocol and succeed. As you can see, this is not very efficient. What is the solution? Minimize the effects by controlling the binding order properly. If TCP/IP is the most commonly used protocol, place it

9

at the top of the list. Follow this rule for all protocols used. If a system is removed and the protocol is no longer needed, remove the protocol from the binding order.

This rule can also be applied to installing gateways on your Windows 2000 system. By definition, a gateway is a device that provides translation between nonsimilar networks. If the Unix system needs to communicate with the NetWare server, it sends your Windows 2000 system the request using TCP/IP. Your system translates the request to IPX/SPX and sends the message to the NetWare server. The same process is repeated for the response. As you can imagine, this is extremely process intensive and can cause severe bottlenecks on your Windows 2000 Server.

FUNCTIONS OF SNMP AND OTHER NETWORK MANAGEMENT PROTOCOLS

As computer networks become more complex, the task of managing all the network devices becomes increasingly difficult. For this reason, several protocols have been developed for the management of network equipment. One of the more popular protocols today is known as Simple Network Management Protocol (SNMP). SNMP allows you to communicate between SNMP-enabled devices (also known as SNMP Agents) and a central Network Management System (NMS) or SNMP Manager.

Although SNMP was developed to be used with TCP/IP-based networks, it has been adapted to also work with IPX-based networks. SNMP can be used to communicate status information with many different devices. These devices include:

➤ Novell NetWare systems

➤ Printers

➤ Rack-mounted modem systems

➤ Routers

➤ Smart hubs and switches

➤ Uninterruptable power supplies

➤ Unix-based systems

➤ Windows 2000 systems

➤ Windows NT systems

Each device participating in SNMP has a specialized database associated with it. This database is known as management information base (MIB). The MIB defines what information is to be collected about the device in question. For example, a MIB associated with a workstation may collect information, such as the name of the computer, the login name, the location, or the operating system version. Another MIB (associated with a rack–mounted modem system) may supply the same information as that of the computer, but also include such data as the voltage being supplied from the power supply, the RPM of the cooling fans, or the phone number of the person logged into modem number 12.

An SNMP agent installed on a device collects the hardware and software information as defined by the MIB and forwards that information to the SNMP Manager. On a Windows 2000 system, for example, the SNMP Agent and the SNMP service are one and the same.

You can write your own MIB, as long as you understand the format. As you can see in the following code, a MIB file is a simple text file that can be modified to fit with a specific agent. The MIB that follows is a portion of the nntp.mib file that is located in the %systemroot%\system32\inetsrv folder. It is divided into two sections. The first section identifies the MIB, whereas the second section defines the objects (or data) that is read by the agent.

9

```
NntpServer-MIB DEFINITIONS ::= BEGIN
IMPORTS
enterprises,
OBJECT-TYPE,
Counter
FROM RFC1155-SMI
 internetServer
 FROM InternetServer-MIB;
-- microsoft OBJECT IDENTIFIER ::= { enterprises 311 }
-- software OBJECT IDENTIFIER ::= { microsoft 1 }
-- internetServer OBJECT IDENTIFIER ::= { software 7 }
 nntpServer OBJECT IDENTIFIER ::= { internetServer 6 }
 nntpStatistics OBJECT IDENTIFIER ::= { nntpServer 1 }
-- NNTP Server Statistics
 totalBytesSentHighWord OBJECT-TYPE
SYNTAX Counter
ACCESS read-only
STATUS mandatory
DESCRIPTION
 "This is the high 32-bits of the total number of
 of BYTEs sent by the NNTP Server"
 ::= { nntpStatistics 1 }
```

```
totalBytesSentLowWord OBJECT-TYPE
SYNTAX Counter
ACCESS read-only
STATUS mandatory
DESCRIPTION
 "This is the low 32-bits of the total number of
 of BYTEs sent by the NNTP Server"
 ::= { nntpStatistics 2 }
```

Each of the bits of information that can be retrieved by the MIB are defined using the following values:

➤ The Object type

➤ The syntax

➤ The read/write permissions

➤ The status

➤ A description for the counter object

SNMP Communication

User Datagram Protocol (UDP) is used for all IP communication between the SNMP Monitor and the Agents. As you will recall, UDP uses connectionless communication, hence is faster than Transport Control Protocol (TCP), which uses a connection-based communication method. There are two types of messages that are communicated between the Agents and the Monitor: SNMP messages and SNMP traps.

SNMP messages are used to transfer information between the SNMP Monitor and Agents, whereas SNMP traps are used as alerts. If an event based on a specified criterion occurs, the Agent sends a trap message to the SNMP Monitor. There are currently four SNMP messages:

➤ Get

➤ Get-Next

➤ Get-Bulk

➤ Set

The SNMP trap is known as a notify message. The following sections define each of the messages.

Get

Get is the most basic of SNMP messages. It is initiated by the SNMP Monitor and requests information about a specific SNMP counter. For example, a simple Get message using the NNTP MIB shown earlier gets the total number of bytes sent by the NNTP server.

Get-Next

The Get-Next message requests the next logical information collected by the SNMP Agent. It is normally used for collections (such as multiple IP addresses bound to a single interface).

Get-Bulk

The Get-Bulk message allows the Agent to send as much information as is allowed in the message. It minimizes the amount of communication that takes place between the Monitor and the Agent. Message requests such as this normally occur when the SNMP Monitor refreshes its stored information about an SNMP Agent.

Set

Assuming that the write permission exists on a specific counter, the Set message is used to set the value as desired. Some counters will be read-only, such as the number of bytes sent by the NNTP server. Others, such as the location of the SNMP device might be read/write. This allows an administrator to remotely modify some information about the device.

Notify

Notify is the only message type that is transmitted to the SNMP Monitor by the Agent without the Monitor requesting the information. This type of message is used when a defined criterion is met, such as when the system is rebooted or a service has stopped responding. It is usually up to the SNMP Monitor to decide what action needs to be taken (if any) to correct the problem.

SNMP Communities

At first glance, it appears as though no security exists in SNMP. Fortunately, this is not the case. SNMP uses SNMP Communities for setting its permissions. An SNMP Community can be compared to a password. Usually, two communities exist. The first is usually referred to as *public* and is the read-only community. Any SNMP Monitor that is aware of that community name can get information from the SNMP Agent, but cannot set any read/write information. The second community type is the read/write community, usually referred to as *private*. Any Monitor that has this community name can set the values of any read/write specified properties.

If you don't care if others can read information about your SNMP devices, then leave the public community as is. If, however, that information must be kept secret, you should change both the public and private communities to names that are not easily guessed. These should then be treated as a regular password and be kept secret.

Note: Try to specify different names for the public and private communities. You may find that the need arises to grant one SNMP Monitor read-only access and another read/ write. By setting different community names, this is made easy.

NOVELL NETWARE INTEGRATION

Before Microsoft's Windows NT (and subsequently Windows 2000) was available, the market leader in the Network Operating System (NOS) arena was Novell. Several years ago, Novell, with its NetWare NOS, controlled a majority of the PC Network market.

When Microsoft released Windows NT, it knew that the only way organizations would migrate from Novell NetWare to Windows NT was if the two could interoperate. With this in mind, Microsoft created its own version of Novell's protocol, IPX/SPX; the Microsoft version is called NWLink. Upon hearing the previous statement, many anti-Microsoft people might state that they are not surprised that Microsoft "stole" the protocol. This, however, is not the reason for Microsoft's creation of its own version. The reason for this is simple. As stated previously, Novell had a stronghold of the market at the time and did not want to let Microsoft take some of its market share. Novell therefore would not share its IPX/SPX code with Microsoft. It is for this reason that to this day, the best software for connecting Windows NT/2000 and NetWare comes from Novell.

Microsoft, on the other hand, needed to share some of its APIs with developers, so that developers could produce applications for Windows NT/2000. Novell therefore had both the Microsoft APIs and its own IPX/SPX. It only makes sense that Novell would build the best tools using this technology.

It is important for you to know the NetWare integration tools that are available for Windows 2000 Server. These components are

➤ NWLink IPX/SPX/NetBIOS Compatible Transport Protocol (NWLink)

➤ Gateway Service For NetWare (GSNW)

➤ Services For NetWare

Each of these components is discussed in the following sections.

NWLink IPX/SPX/NetBIOS Compatible Transport Protocol (NWLink)

IPX/SPX is the default protocol in NetWare servers through version 4.x. With version 5.0, Novell moved to a true TCP/IP server. As you will see in the GSNW section, if NetWare 5.x servers interoperate on the network, TCP/IP should be used. Microsoft has changed the name assigned to this protocol several times, but NWLink is its current name.

If your system is connecting with Novell NetWare 4.x servers or earlier, this is the protocol that should be installed on the server that will perform the communication. Although TCP/IP is available for NetWare 4.x or earlier, it is not a full implementation and interoperability problems might occur.

GSNW

In Windows NT Workstation, Client Services For NetWare (CSNW) was used to connect the Windows NT Workstations to NetWare servers. In Windows NT Server and Windows 2000 Server, the component used to make this connection is known as Gateway (and Client) Service For NetWare (GSNW).

9

GSNW allows the Windows 2000 Server to connect with NetWare servers running in either of its two modes. With NetWare 3.1x and earlier, the directory that stored all user and group information used a flat file system (much like Windows NT). This directory structure had some major limitations and was known as the Bindery. With NetWare 4.x, Novell introduced the Novell Directory Service (NDS). NDS was far superior to the Bindery and used a hierarchical structure (Windows 2000's Active Directory uses a similar structure). Because both methods existed when Microsoft released GSNW, it supports both methods.

When connecting to a NetWare server running the Bindery (NetWare 3.1x or earlier) or Bindery-emulation (NetWare 4.x and later), all that is needed to make the connection is the name of the server. With NDS, however, the NDS tree and Context are needed.

One of the major strengths (and weakness as you will soon see) of GSNW is its ability to connect all the Windows clients to the NetWare servers without installing any additional protocols and/or software on the clients. Because all the Windows clients can communicate with the Windows 2000 Server and the Windows 2000 Server can communicate with the NetWare servers through GSNW, the Windows 2000 Server can act as a gateway between the two networks. The Windows 2000 Server converts the Server Message Block (SMB) used by the Windows systems to the NetWare Core Protocol (NCP) used in NetWare networks.

As mentioned previously, GSNW has a couple of weaknesses. The first deals with security and the second with performance. When the Windows 2000 Server connects to the NetWare server through GSNW, it uses an account that is created on the NetWare server to get all file and printer information. Because this account is usually a Supervisor (in NetWare 3.x and earlier) or Admin (in NetWare 4.x and later), any files and printers shared with the Windows clients is granted the security level assigned to the share. To allow users to have different security levels to access the data, multiple shares must be created.

The second drawback is that of performance. When a Windows client makes a request for information stored on a NetWare server, it is up to the Windows 2000 Server to go get that information (converting from SMB to NCP and back to SMB) and send it to the client. Now, imagine what would happen to the performance if 10, 50, or 100 clients make a request. As you can see, GSNW quickly becomes a major bottleneck. For this reason, GSNW is recommended in either low traffic level situations or during a migration from NetWare to Windows 2000.

Tip: If the NetWare server being communicated with is TCP/IP, then TCP/IP is used and no conversion of protocols is required. This greatly increases GSNW's performance.

Services for NetWare

Microsoft has a product available that greatly increases interoperability between Novell NetWare and Windows 2000. This product is sold independently of Windows 2000 and is known as Services For NetWare.

Services for NetWare includes the following utilities:

➤ Microsoft Directory Synchronization Services

➤ File Migration Utility

➤ File And Print Services For NetWare (FPSN)

The following sections explain each of these utilities.

Microsoft Directory Synchronization Services

The Microsoft Directory Synchronization Services provides two-way synchronization between Windows 2000's Active Directory and NetWare's NDS and it provides one-way synchronization with Netware's 3.x binderies. Any object that is created or modified in one of the Directory services is automatically created or modified on the other. For example, if a user is created in Active Directory, the Directory Synchronization Services automatically creates the same user object in NDS. If the password is then modified in NDS, the Directory Synchronization Services updates the user object in the Active Directory to reflect the password change.

This greatly reduces the overall cost of maintaining two distinct directory services and their subsequent operating costs.

Note: *Novell also provides a similar utility known as Novell NDS for Windows NT/2000.*

File Migration Utility

The file migration utility allows an administrator to move entire directory structures from NetWare servers to Windows 2000 Servers. This file migration utility copies all files and maintains the directory structure and all object security. If your organization is migrating from NetWare to Windows 2000, this tool is a must. It is the quickest, most reliable way of moving the data and security to Windows 2000 systems.

File And Print Services For NetWare (FPSN)

FPSN does the opposite of what GSNW does. GSNW allows Windows 2000 clients to connect to file and printer information on NetWare servers, whereas FPSN allows NetWare servers and clients to connect to Windows 2000 Servers. The Windows 2000 Server emulates NetWare servers and appears as such to the clients. It does this so well, in fact, that a Windows 2000 Server running FPSN actually appears as a NetWare server to another Windows 2000 Server running GSNW.

Once FPSN is installed, you can create NetWare shares using the following procedure:

1. Select Start|Run.

2. In the Open field, type "MMC" and click OK.

3. Choose the Add/Remove snap-in option from the Console menu.

4. Click Add.

5. Select the Shared Folders snap-in, and click the Add Button.

6. Click Close.

7. Click OK.

8. Choose the Save As option from the Console menu.

9. Enter a name for the new MMC, and click Save.

Once the MMC application is created, the following steps need to be completed to create a new NetWare share:

1. Run the Shared Folder MMC snap-in.

2. Right-click Shares, and choose the New File Share option.

3. Ensure that the Novell NetWare checkbox is selected.

4. Enter a Share description for the Novell NetWare share.

5. Click Next.

6. Click Finish.

APPLETALK NETWORK INTEGRATION

Many organizations still have a large number of Apple Macintosh systems. In the past, Apple had AppleShare servers available for sale. These allowed a Macintosh network to share files and printers. One of the drawbacks of these servers was their cost as compared to Intel-based solutions.

Microsoft realized early on that if its operating system supported the Macintosh clients, more of the AppleShare business would come its way. Microsoft approached Apple about licensing its software to run on (at the time) Windows NT. Apple agreed and Services for the Macintosh was born.

It is important to realize that the code used to share files and printers between a Windows 2000 network and Macintosh systems is based on the original AppleShare code. For this reason, Macintosh systems see the Windows 2000 systems as just another Macintosh server. As far as they are concerned, the server they are communicating with is a Macintosh.

Services for Macintosh consist of two different components:

➤ File Server For Macintosh (FSM)

➤ Print Server For Macintosh (PSM)

Both services rely on the AppleTalk protocol. Therefore, before we delve into these services, let's discuss the protocol itself.

Understanding AppleTalk

In the same way that Microsoft has its own transport protocol in NetBEUI and Novell has its with IPX, Apple uses its own protocol known as AppleTalk. Macintosh systems have one of three network transports that you might run into: Ethernet, LocalTalk, and Token Ring. AppleTalk communicating over each of these three media types is known as EtherTalk, LocalTalk, and TokenTalk. Although you might run into LocalTalk (requiring a LocalTalk adapter to be installed in your system) or TokenTalk (requiring a Token Ring adapter in the server), EtherTalk is by far the most common flavor of AppleTalk you will encounter.

Both File and Print Server For Macintosh require that AppleTalk be installed. This is done automatically when one of the services is installed. One of the other prerequisites for the file service is that at least one volume be formatted using NTFS. Because of the different file system structures between MacOS and Windows, only NTFS can emulate the MacOS file structure.

Each AppleTalk network is assigned a number between 0 and 65534. This number can either be assigned by the administrator or by the first device that is installed on the network.

Similar to the way that TCP/IP systems are known as *nodes*, AppleTalk systems are also known as nodes. Every node on the AppleTalk network must have a unique number. This number is either assigned manually to each system or automatically. An AppleTalk network can have up to 253 nodes.

Also, multiple nodes can be grouped together (much in the same way as TCP/IP subnets). Normally, *zones* are used to group systems and resources that are close to one another, such as departments, building floor, or offices. Zones are similar to resource domains in TCP/IP. Using this configuration, when a Macintosh user looks for resources using the Macintosh Chooser (similar to Network Neighborhood), only close resources appear.

Routers are used to connect the different zones. Unlike TCP/IP networks, these routers are usually servers (such as Windows 2000). Most TCP/IP routers, however, can also route AppleTalk (such as Cisco routers, assuming that they have the AppleTalk software installed). Another benefit of installing AppleTalk is the ability to route AppleTalk traffic or accept RAS calls from remote Macintosh clients.

File Server For Macintosh

In the Macintosh world, a shared volume on a remote server is known as a Macintosh-Accessible Volume (MAV). These are synonymous with a Share in the Windows-based world.

There are some restrictions when creating MAVs that you need to be aware of. The first, and most important, is that MAVs cannot be nested within other MAVs. This means that if you create a MAV at C:\Documents, you will not be able to create one at C:\Documents\Macintosh. If you do, the error shown in Figure 9.1 appears. For this reason, Microsoft recommends that you start creating MAVs at the lowest point in the folder tree hierarchy.

Figure 9.1 Error attempting to create nested MAVs.

Creating MAVs

Creating MAVs is not as simple as creating a shared folder, but is not a difficult task if you are aware of the steps. If you were to simply share a folder using Windows Explorer, that folder would only be available to Windows-based clients. The Macintosh clients would not see any of the shared folders. To create the shared folders, you need to use the Share Folder MMC snap-in. This utility is installed on the hard drive, but is not configured as a Management Console by default. If Macintosh clients are prevalent on your network, you might consider creating a tool for it as follows:

1. Select Start | Run.

2. In the Open field, type "MMC" and click OK.

3. Choose the Add/Remove snap-in option from the Console menu.

4. Click Add.

5. Select the Shared Folders snap-in, and click the Add Button.

6. Click Close.

7. Click OK.

8. Choose the Save As option from the Console menu.

9. Enter a name for the new MMC, and click Save.

Once the MMC application is created, the following steps need to be completed to create a new MAV:

1. Run the Shared Folder MMC snap-in.

2. Right-click Shares, and choose the New File Share option. The Shared Folder wizard runs as shown in Figure 9.2.

3. Ensure that the Apple Macintosh checkbox is selected.

4. Enter a Share description for the MAV.

5. Enter a name for the MAV in the Macintosh Share Name field.

Figure 9.2   The Shared Folder wizard.

6. Click Next.

7. Click Finish.

Notice that the Shared Folder MMC snap-in displays both the Windows Shares and the Macintosh MAVs (see Figure 9.3).

One final item that needs to be covered with MAVs is permissions. MacOS uses permissions that are very different than the ones used in Windows 2000,

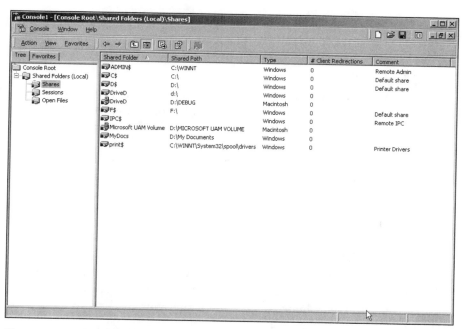

Figure 9.3   The Shared Folder MMC snap-in.

Table 9.1 MacOS permissions versus Windows 2000 permissions.

MacOS Permission	Windows 2000 Equivalent
None	No Access.
Read Only	Read and List Folder Contents.
Write Only	Write Only. Items can be created but not read or listed.
Read/Write	Full Control.
Can't Rename, Move, Or Delete This Item	Modify.

and they can only be applied at the folder level, not the file level. Table 9.1 illustrates the MacOS permissions and their Windows 2000 equivalents.

The MacFile Utility

Windows 2000 also ships with a command-line utility that allows you to administer FSM Servers, MAVs, users, and files. This application is the MacFile.exe utility. Although MacFile appears to be a single application, it is, in fact, four distinct utilities in one. It contains

➤ MacFile Server

➤ MacFile Volume

➤ MacFile Directory

➤ MacFile Forkize

Each of these components is covered in the following sections.

MacFile Server

The MacFile Server command is used to manage FSM servers. Tasks include controlling the login messages, the number of sessions allowed, and whether guests can log in. MacFile Server uses the following syntax:

```
macfile server [/server:\\computername] [/maxsessions:number |
unlimited] [/loginmessage:message]
```

Table 9.2 lists the switches and their descriptions (as described in the Windows 2000 Help).

MacFile Volume

MacFile Volume is used to control MAV. Using this tool, an administrator can create or delete MAVs and configure MAVs that are currently installed on the server. MacFile Volume uses the following syntax:

Table 9.2   The MacFile Server command-line switches.

Switch	Description
/server:\\computername	Specifies the server on which to change parameters. If omitted, the operation is performed on the local computer.
/maxsessions:[number	unlimited]	Specifies the maximum number of users who can simultaneously use File and Print Servers for Macintosh. If omitted, the maxsessions setting for the server remains unchanged.
/loginmessage:message	Changes the message Macintosh users see when logging on to the File Server for Macintosh server. To remove an existing logon message, include the /loginmessage parameter, but leave the message variable blank. If omitted, the loginmessage message for the server remains unchanged from the previous setting. The maximum number of characters for the logon message is 199.

```
macfile volume {/add | /set}[/server:\\computername] /name:volumename
/path:directory [/readonly:[true | false]] [/guestsallowed:[true |
false]] [/password:password] [/maxusers:number | unlimited] {/remove}
```

Note: The /remove parameter can only be used with the /server and /name parameters.

Table 9.3 lists the switches and their descriptions (as described in the Windows 2000 Help).

Table 9.3   The MacFile Volume command-line switches.

Switch	Description
/add	Adds a volume using the specified settings.
/set	Changes a volume using the specified settings.
/server:\\computername	Specifies the server on which to add, change, or remove a volume. If omitted, the operation is performed on the local computer.
/name:volumename	Specifies the volume name to be added, changed, or removed. This parameter is required.
/path:directory	Specifies the path to the root directory of the volume to be created. This parameter is valid and required only when adding a volume.
/readonly:[true	false]	Specifies users cannot change files in the volume. Use true or false to change the current setting of the volume. If omitted when adding a volume, changes to files are allowed. If omitted when changing a volume, the read-only setting for the volume remains unchanged.

(continued)

9

Table 9.3 The MacFile Volume command-line switches *(continued)*.

Switch	Description
/guestsallowed:[true | false]	Specifies whether users logging on as guests can use the volume. If omitted when adding a volume, guests can use the volume. If omitted when changing a volume, the guests allowed setting for the volume remains unchanged.
/password:password	Specifies a password required to access the volume. If omitted when adding a volume, no password is created. If omitted when changing a volume, the password remains unchanged.
/maxusers:number | unlimited	Specifies the maximum number of users who can simultaneously use files on the volume. If omitted when adding a volume, an unlimited number of users can use the volume. If omitted when changing a volume, the maxusers value remains unchanged.
/remove	Removes the specified volume.

MacFile Directory

The MacFile Directory MacFile is used to control the users and groups assigned to the MAV. It can also be used to set MacOS–like permissions on these MAVs. The MacFile Directory uses the following syntax:

```
macfile directory [/server:\\computername] /path:directory
[/owner:ownername] [/group:groupname] [/permissions:permissions]
```

Table 9.4 lists the switches and their descriptions (as described in the Windows 2000 Help).

Table 9.4 The MacFile Directory command-line switches.

Switch	Description
/server:\\computername	Specifies the server on which to change a directory. If omitted, the operation is performed on the local computer.
/path:directory	Specifies the path to the directory to be changed on the Macintosh-accessible volume. The directory must exist; MacFile Directory does not create directories. This parameter is required.
/owner:ownername	Changes the owner of the directory. If omitted, the owner remains unchanged.
/group:groupname	Specifies or changes the Macintosh primary group associated with the directory. If omitted, the primary group remains unchanged.
/permissions:permissions	Sets permissions on the directory for the owner, primary group, and world (everyone). An 11-digit number is used to set permissions. The number 1 grants permission; 0 revokes permission (for example, 11111011000). The position of the digit determines which permission is set; see Table 9.5. If omitted, permissions remain unchanged.

Table 9.5 MacFile Directory permissions.

Position	Permission
1	OwnerSeeFiles
2	OwnerSeeFolders
3	OwnerMakeChanges
4	GroupSeeFiles
5	GroupSeeFolders
6	GroupMakeChanges
7	WorldSeeFiles
8	WorldSeeFolder
9	WorldMakeChanges
10	Can't rename, move, or delete the folder
11	Apply permissions to the current folder and all subfolders

Table 9.5 lists the MacFile Directory permissions.

MacFile Forkize

The last component of the MacFile utility is the Forkize. It allows an administrator to modify the type for a file. It also allows one to combine the data and resource forks of a file. It is a rarely used component of the MacFile utility. The MacFile Forkize uses the following syntax:

```
macfile forkize [/server:\\computername] [/creator:creatorname]
[/type:typename] [/datafork:filepath] [/resourcefork:filepath]
/targetfile:filepath
```

Table 9.6 lists the switches and their descriptions (as described in the Windows 2000 Help).

Table 9.6 The MacFile Forksize command-line switches.

Switch	Description
/server:\\computername	Specifies the server on which to join files. If omitted, the operation is performed on the local computer.
/creator:creatorname	Specifies the creator of the file. The Macintosh Finder uses the creator parameter to determine the application that created the file.
/type:typename	Specifies the type of file. The Macintosh Finder uses file type to determine the file type within the application that created the file.
/datafork:filepath	Specifies the location of the data fork that is to be joined. You can specify a remote path.

(continued)

Table 9.6   The MacFile Forkize command-line switches *(continued)*.

Switch	Description
/resourcefork:filepath	Specifies the location of the resource fork that is to be joined. You can specify a remote path.
/targetfile:filepath	Specifies the location of the file created by joining a data fork and a resource fork or specifies the location of the file whose type or creator you are changing. The file must be on the specified server.

Print Server for Macintosh

You can use the Print Server for Macintosh in one of two ways. First, any Windows 2000 printer can be captured and shared with the Macintosh clients. Second, it allows you to capture a Macintosh-based printer and share it with your Windows 2000 clients. This second method allows you to print to a Macintosh printer without having to install the AppleTalk protocol on each of the client systems. Instead, the systems communicate with the PSM Server using their default protocol and print to that server.

Note: *When you share a Windows-based printer with Macintosh clients, they see the printer as a generic laser printer running PostScript Level 1 at 300 dpi.*

Unlike FSM's client permissions, PSM does not allow you to control permissions on a per user basis. Instead, you need to create a dedicated user account that will be used to connect to PSM to print. Once this account is created, configure the PSM service to use that account as follows:

1. Select Start | Programs | Administrative Tools | Computer Management.

2. Navigate to the Services container.

3. Double-click the Print Server For Macintosh service.

4. Select the Log On tab.

5. Choose the This Account radio button.

6. Enter the name of the account (or browse to it by clicking the Browse button).

7. Enter and confirm the password assigned to this account.

8. Click OK.

9. Right-click the Print Server For Macintosh service, and choose the Restart option from the pop-up menu.

Sharing a Printer

The process of sharing a printer with your Macintosh clients can be slightly different than sharing it with Windows clients. If the printer is already connected to the Windows 2000 Server, all that needs to be done is for you to share the printer as you would any other printer.

If, however, a new printer is to be created, start the Add Printer Wizard as usual. Instead of selecting the existing port to connect the printer to, notice that a new port type (AppleTalk Printing Devices) exists, as shown in Figure 9.4. Once this port is selected, an AppleTalk Printing Devices browser window appears (see Figure 9.5). Navigate to the desired printer, select it, and click OK.

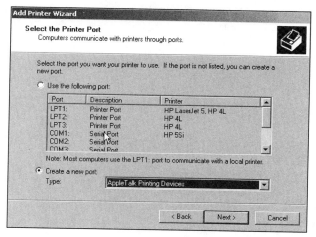

Figure 9.4   The New AppleTalk printing device port.

Figure 9.5   The AppleTalk Printing Devices browser window.

ADVANCED WINDOWS NETWORKING SERVICES

A couple of different integration tools and utilities are available as add-on products from Microsoft. These products enable an administrator to interoperate Windows 2000 with Unix systems and IBM mainframe systems. This section introduces these tools.

Unix Network Integration

Unix has always been one of the most popular NOSs around. With Linux gaining in popularity, it is becoming more and more common for Windows 2000 systems to share information with Unix systems.

Linux has a product known as Samba, which allows a Linux system to share information with a Windows 2000 system. Likewise, Microsoft offers an add-on utility known as Windows Services for Unix version 2.0 (SFU).

Part of the problem of sharing information between the two radically different operating systems is that they use such a different method for sharing files. Windows 2000 uses Common Internet File System (CIFS) to share files, whereas Unix uses Network File System (NFS).

Windows Services for Unix version 2.0 allows for the following:

➤ Synchronization of account information between the two systems

➤ Sharing of network resources (files and printers)

➤ Support for graphical and command-line based administration of local and remote systems

➤ Use of some Unix tools on the Windows 2000 System

Table 9.7 lists some of the more common Unix commands supported by Windows Services for Unix.

Table 9.7   Unix commands supported by SFU.

Command	Description
cat	Concatenates and displays a file
chmod	Changes the permissions of files and directories
chown	Changes the owner of files and directories
cp	Copies files or directories
grep	Searches files for specified patterns and displays the results
ln	Creates a hard link between files
ls	Lists the directory listing (similar to the DOS dir command)
mkdir	Creates a directory

(continued)

Table 9.7   Unix commands supported by SFU *(continued)*.

Command	Description
more	Lists a file, one page at a time
mv	Moves files or directories
rmdir	Deletes a directory
wc	Counts the number of lines, words, or characters in a specified file
vi	A basic text editor

Internetworking with SNA Hosts

Mainframes are still part of the networks in many large organizations. One of the most popular mainframe systems is the IBM mainframe, which is based on the SNA protocol.

Microsoft provides a separate application to support the interoperation between Windows 2000 and IBM mainframes. This tool is part of its BackOffice product. In previous versions of BackOffice this utility was known as SNA Server. It is now known as Host Integration Server 2000.

Similar to GSNW, Host Integration Server 2000 acts as a gateway between the Windows 2000 systems and the SNA server (known as the SNA host). The SNA clients (the Windows 2000 systems) can print to printers on the SNA host, transfer files, and access the SNA host using terminal services.

9

CHAPTER SUMMARY

In this chapter, we discussed some of the protocols, services, and utilities available with Windows 2000 to allow for communication between different operating systems.

We explained how SNMP can be used to collect information about different types of systems including servers, switches, and routers. There are two types of messages used with SNMP: SNMP messages and SNMP traps. SNMP messages consist of one of four commands (Get, Get-Next, Get-Bulk, and Set), whereas SNMP traps use the Notify command. SNMP uses different communities for authentication; there are usually two different communities, a public one (used for read-only situations) and a private one (used for read/write situations).

Microsoft has included with Windows 2000 the capability for a single Windows 2000 Server to act as a gateway into the NetWare network. Although this allows you to easily configure all clients to access NetWare resources without installing any extra software on them, this method is not recommended as a solution but rather as either a temporary connection or a migration tool. Also available from Microsoft are tools, such as the File Migration Utility to help migrate files from

NetWare to Windows 2000 while maintaining structure and security; the File and Print services to allow NetWare clients to connect to the Windows 2000 Server; and Directory Synchronization to connect Active Directory and NDS.

Windows 2000 can act as an AppleShare server. This allows you to share Windows 2000 files and printers with your Macintosh clients and Macintosh printers with your Windows 2000 client. As far as the Macintosh clients are concerned, the Windows 2000 client is just another Macintosh.

REVIEW QUESTIONS

1. When communicating between a Windows 2000 system and a Novell NetWare server using GSNW, which configurations of NetWare are supported? [Choose all that apply]

    a. Bindery

    b. Active Directory

    c. NDS

    d. Universal Directory Service

2. For the AppleTalk protocol, what is its equivalent to TCP/IP's domain?

    a. Collection

    b. Cell

    c. Zone

    d. Node

3. Which protocol is *not* available on the Windows 2000 installation CD?

    a. NWLink IPX/SPX/NetBIOS Compatible Transport Protocol

    b. TCP/IP

    c. AppleTalk

    d. SNA

4. Which of the following is not a benefit of GSNW?

    a. The quickest way for multiple Windows 2000 systems to access a NetWare server printer

    b. Only a single NetWare user license is used

    c. The most efficient way for multiple Windows 2000 systems to access a NetWare server

    d. The quickest way to connect multiple Windows 2000 systems to a NetWare server file share

5. Which of the following is a requirement before FSM and PSM can be installed?

    a. TCP/IP must be installed.

    b. The Microsoft Client for the Macintosh must be installed on each Macintosh client.

    c. AppleTalk must be installed.

    d. NetBEUI must be installed.

6. TCP/IP is the protocol most commonly used with GSNW.

    a. True

    b. False

7. What term does AppleTalk use to define the systems on its network?

    a. Host

    b. Node

    c. System

    d. MacNoid

8. Which of the following is the Apple implementation of AppleTalk that uses the Ethernet media?

    a. AppleEther

    b. EtherTalk

    c. LocalTalk

    d. TokenTalk

9. Which of the following is *not* a feature of the MacFile utility?

    a. Directory

    b. Volume

    c. Forksize

    d. Server

10. Which of the following devices can be managed using SNMP (assuming that they are SNMP-compliant)? [Choose all that apply]

    a. Server

    b. Router

    c. Hub

    d. Stereo

9

11. Which of the following protocols is used most often with GSNW?

    a. TCP/IP

    b. SNMP

    c. NWLink

    d. AppleTalk

12. Which of the following are requirements of GSNW when used as a client? [Choose all that apply]

    a. NWLink IPX/SPX/NetBIOS Compatible Transport Protocol

    b. NTFS

    c. An account on the NetWare server

    d. Ethernet

13. The MIB in SNMP is defined as what?

    a. Men in black

    b. Multiple internet block

    c. Management information base

    d. Media information block

14. Which of the following is the Apple implementation of AppleTalk that uses the Token Ring media?

    a. RingTalk

    b. EtherTalk

    c. LocalTalk

    d. TokenTalk

15. Which file system does Unix normally use?

    a. NFS

    b. CIFS

    c. NDS

    d. SFT

16. Which file system does Windows 2000 use to share files?

    a. NFS

    b. CIFS

    c. NDS

    d. SFT

17. Windows 2000 ships with both Gateway Services For NetWare and Client Services For NetWare.

    a. True

    b. False

18. Which of the following is the Apple implementation of AppleTalk that uses the LocalTalk media?

    a. AppleTalk

    b. EtherTalk

    c. LocalTalk

    d. TokenTalk

19. GSNW allows Novell NetWare clients to connect to file and printer resources on a Windows 2000 system.

    a. True

    b. False

9

REAL-WORLD PROJECTS

Your current organization uses Windows 2000 Servers and clients. Another company has just been acquired by your organization. The newly acquired company uses Novell NetWare servers as its file and print servers. Both networks have been relocated to a central location.

Some of the data located on the NetWare servers needs to be made available on your network.

Project 9.1

To install the NWLink IPX/SPX/NetBIOS Compatible Transport Protocol, perform the following steps:

1. Right-click My Network Places, and choose Properties from the pop-up menu.

2. Right-click the Local Area Network icon that you would like the protocol installed on, and choose Properties from the pop-up menu.

3. Click Install.

4. Select the Protocol option, and click Add.

5. Choose the NWLink IPX/SPX/NetBIOS Compatible Transport Protocol option, and click OK.

6. Click OK to complete the installation.

Project 9.2
To install Gateway Services For NetWare, perform the following steps:

1. Right-click My Network Places, and choose Properties from the pop-up menu.

2. Right-click the Local Area Network icon that you would like the gateway installed on, and choose Properties from the pop-up menu.

3. Click Install.

4. Select the Client option, and click Add.

5. Choose the Gateway (And Client) Services For NetWare, and click OK.

6. When the Select NetWare Logon dialog box appears, choose the connection method. If you are connecting to NetWare 3.x or earlier, choose the Preferred Server radio button, and enter the name of the server. If you are connecting to NetWare 4.x or later server running NDS, choose the Default Tree And Context radio button, and enter the Tree and Context.

7. Click OK.

8. Click OK to complete the installation.

Your organization is working on a project and has hired some graphic designers to assist with it. The graphic designers use Apple Macintosh computers and need access to both files and printers on the Windows 2000 network. It is up to you to install the correct services on your server to accomplish this.

Project 9.3
To install File Services For Macintosh, perform the following steps:

1. Select Start|Settings|Control Panel.

2. Double-click Add/Remove Programs.

3. Click Add/Remove Windows Components.

4. Click Next.

5. Navigate to the Other Network File And Print Services option, select it, and click Details.

6. Select the File Services For Macintosh checkbox, and click OK.

7. Click Next.

8. Click Finish.

Project 9.4
To install Print Services For Macintosh, perform the following steps:

1. Select Start | Settings | Control Panel.

2. Double-click Add/Remote Programs.

3. Click Add/Remove Windows Components.

4. Click Next.

5. Navigate to the Other Network File And Print Services option, select it, and click Details.

6. Select the Print Services For Macintosh checkbox, and click OK.

7. Click Next.

8. Click Finish.

Project 9.5
To view the network binding order, perform the following steps:

1. Select Start | Settings | Network And Dial-Up Connections.

2. Select Advanced | Advanced Settings. This reveals the Advanced Settings dialog box where bindings are managed (see Figure 9.6).

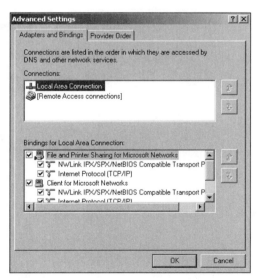

Figure 9.6   The Advanced Settings dialog box.

3. Select a connection from the connection box.

4. Notice the contents of the lower field where installed services and protocols are listed in their binding order. Also notice the items closer to the top of the list are bound in priority to those listed lower on the list. Finally, notice the checkbox beside each item that allows you to disable that service or protocol.

5. Click Cancel.

6. Select File | Close.

CHAPTER TEN

ADVANCED WINDOWS 2000 NETWORK SERVICES

After completing this chapter, you will be able to:

✓ Describe the components that make up the Internet Information Services

✓ Know how to create and modify Web sites using the IIS snap-in

✓ Explain what the IIS Administration Web site is used for

✓ Configure a server to accept both dial-up and virtual private networking connections

✓ Manage inbound connections for Remote Access Server

✓ Explain the differences between Remote Administration and Application Server modes in Terminal Services

✓ Install applications to be used in Application Server mode

This chapter covers three advanced networking components of Windows 2000—Internet Information Services (IIS), Remote Access Service (RAS), and Terminal Services. These components are not necessarily components that every Windows 2000 installation requires (unlike, say, TCP/IP); however, you should understand these advanced networking concepts.

Internet Information Services (IIS) is a suite of protocols that allows a Windows 2000 Server to act as several different Internet servers. Some of these servers include email (using Simple Mail Transfer Protocol), file transfer (using File Transfer Protocol), Internet newsgroups (using Network News Transfer Protocol), and Web servers (using Hypertext Transfer Protocol).

Remote Access Service (RAS) is part of the Routing And Remote Access Services (RRAS) suite of protocols for Windows 2000. The RRAS protocols allow an administrator to connect clients to the network through either a direct dial-up connection (RAS) or a secure Internet connection (virtual private networking).

Although Terminal Services are available for Windows NT (in the Windows NT Terminal Server Edition), Windows 2000 allows the services to be installed and uninstalled. This gives administrators greater flexibility in how a server performs. Two configuration modes are available—Remote Administration and Application Server. Remote Administration mode allows two administrators to perform administrative tasks on the server as if they were accessing it locally, whereas the Application Server mode allows users to use the processing power of the server to run their applications. To convert from Remote Administration mode to Application Server mode, run the Add/Remove Windows Components Wizard, and choose the Application Server Mode radio button.

MANAGING SERVER-BASED WEB SITES WITH IIS

Microsoft markets Windows 2000 as an *Internet server*. What this means to organizations is that Windows 2000 is designed to work seamlessly with both Internet and intranet infrastructures. One of the best Internet features built into Windows 2000 is known as Internet Information Services (IIS). In previous versions of Windows, IIS was only the Internet Web server component and was known as the Internet Information Server. IIS has come a long way since its initial version 1 release. Some of the features included in IIS version 5 with Windows 2000 include:

➤ *File Transfer Protocol (FTP) Server*—FTP is the industry standard protocol used to transfer information between two systems on the Internet. The systems do not need to run the same operating systems. For example, a Windows 98 system can transfer files from a Windows 2000 system over the Internet just as easily as it can from a system running Linux as its operating system.

➤ *FrontPage 2000 Server Extensions*—Microsoft offers a Web site authoring application known as FrontPage 2000. This application is available as either a standalone application or as one of the applications in the Office 2000 Premium suite of applications. Some of FrontPage's specialized features require a component to be executed on the server. These features can include search pages, counters, and other specialized components. These components will not run properly unless the Web server supports the FrontPage 2000 Server Extensions. When this option is installed, all Web sites hosted on the server can support FrontPage 2000 developed Web sites. However, you have the option of disabling the extensions on a per Web site basis.

➤ *Internet Information Services Snap-In*—As described in the "Working with the MMC" section later in this chapter, IIS predominantly uses the Microsoft Management Console (MMC) for its administration. When you install IIS, the snap-in used to manage IIS is also installed.

➤ *Internet Services Manager (HTML)*—Like some earlier versions, IIS allows an administrator to configure and control IIS over the Internet. This is done using the HTML version of the Internet Services Manager (ISM). The Internet Services Manager is the application used to configure the Internet Information Server in previous versions of IIS. The ISM allows the administrator to perform nearly all the same tasks that he or she could perform using the IIS snap-in. Because the ISM utility is used over the Internet, however, you must take care to secure the connection between the management station and the server itself.

➤ *Network News Transfer Protocol (NNTP)*—This feature is new to Windows 2000 and was not available as a component from Microsoft in the past. If NNTP was needed with Windows NT, either Exchange Server or a third-party tool had to be installed. By installing the NNTP service, the Windows 2000 Server becomes a Usenet or NNTP server. As with FTP, this server can now operate with any other server using the same protocol, regardless of the operating system.

➤ *Simple Mail Transfer Protocol (SMTP)*—One of the key protocols used to send mail over the Internet, SMTP is used when one server is sending a message to another. This protocol is not used by client systems to pick up delivered messages; that task is assigned to either the Post Office Protocol version 3 (POP3) or Internet Message Access Protocol version 4 (IMAP4). As with NNTP, this feature was not available as a built-in feature in previous versions of Windows. Instead, either Exchange Server or a third-party utility must be installed on a Windows NT system to add this functionality.

10

Note: Microsoft's new messaging and collaboration server—Exchange 2000—requires both the NNTP and SMTP services to be installed. Unlike previous versions of Exchange Server, which installed these components, Exchange 2000 uses the Windows 2000 versions of these services.

➤ *World Wide Web Server*—At the heart of IIS is the World Wide Web Server. This service is what allows a Windows 2000 Server to become a Web site hosting server. This allows your organization to use Windows 2000 as a very robust and reliable platform for hosting your Internet and intranet Web sites.

. . . .
Tip: Differentiating the Internet Information Server of previous Windows NT operating systems and the Internet Information Services of Windows 2000 is important. The Windows NT version is usually on the Web server itself (although the FTP server is sometimes bundled in the definition), whereas the Windows 2000 version is an entire suite of tools and services that are to be used on the Internet.
. . . .

Installing IIS

IIS is installed by default when Windows 2000 is installed. The administrator can choose to not install the IIS components by customizing the setup. Not all Windows 2000 Servers need to be configured as Web servers. In fact, most organizations have dedicated servers that are only used to host Internet or intranet Web sites. The first portion of this section assumes that IIS was not installed during the setup process (or that it was uninstalled at a later date).

Because Windows 2000's native networking protocol is Transmission Control Protocol/Internet Protocol (TCP/IP), and TCP/IP uses the industry standard Domain Name System (DNS) for its name resolution, configuring it to work properly with IIS is much simpler than with Windows NT. We will, however, cover some of the prerequisites that must be in place before IIS is installed and configured.

First, you must recognize that a user can access a remote server running as a Web server in three ways:

➤ **http://FQDN**—Where *FQDN* is the fully qualified domain name (for example, **www.microsoft.com**).

➤ **http://ip_address**—Where *ip_address* is the TCP/IP address that is assigned to the system. If the server is to be accessed from the Internet, the TCP/IP address must be a valid address that belongs to the organization, or the server must be behind a router that can use Address Translation to convert the invalid internal address to a valid external address. This address method is normally used when no name resolution services exist on the network.

➤ **http://computer_name**—Where *computer_name* is the NetBIOS name for the server. This method is normally only used when accessing a server that is internal to an organization. External systems have to use either the FQDN method or the TCP/IP address method.

Although IIS works on a system in which an IP address is dynamically assigned, a statically assigned IP address is the preferred choice. This is especially true when the system is to be accessed from the Internet. The Internet relies on DNS to resolve IP addresses to FQDN. If the IP address of a Web site changes (this can occur if the system is rebooted or if the lease of the assigned IP address expires) and the DNS is not updated to reflect the change (this assumes that Dynamic DNS is not running), then a client on the Internet might attempt to contact the Web server using the old address, which is no longer valid. This could cause your Internet Web sites to be unavailable to the Internet. In many organizations, this could mean a major loss of income. Obviously, this is something that organizations and administrators would like to avoid. Therefore, assigning a static address is the best way to configure your server.

If a Web site is to be published on the Internet for clients and employees to access, then an FQDN is desired. People tend to remember an FQDN over a TCP/IP address. For example, if we asked you to tell us the domain used by Microsoft on the Internet, you would most likely say that it is **www.microsoft.com**. However, if we asked you to tell us Microsoft's Web server's TCP/IP address, you most likely wouldn't know that one of them is 207.46.131.45. Computers use IP addresses, whereas people use FQDNs. Therefore, a method is needed to translate between the two. The method is the Domain Name Service (also known as the Domain Name System). For your organization to be accessible via its domain name (for example, **www.mycompany.com**), then the relationship between the FQDN and its IP address must be listed in a DNS server on the Internet. Larger organizations tend to host their own DNS servers, whereas smaller enterprises use other organizations' DNS servers. The most common DNS servers used (if you do not host your own) are those of your Internet Service Provider (ISP). ISPs are set up to host multiple domains in their DNS servers.

10

TIP: Before your organization can have a presence on the Internet, its domain name must be registered. Many companies offer to register domains for you. One of the most popular domain registration services is offered by Network Solutions. Network Solutions used to be known as InterNIC (actually, it was always known as Network Solutions, but referred to as InterNIC), and it was the only way to register many of the top-level domains, including .com, .net, and .org. Network Solutions can be contacted at **www.networksolutions.com**. A list of all accredited domain registrar sites can be found at **www.internic.net**.

After the prerequisites are met, you are ready to install IIS. To do so, perform the following steps:

1. Click Start | Settings | Control Panel.

2. Double-click Add/Remove Programs.

3. Click Add/Remove Windows Components. The Windows Components Wizard appears, as shown in Figure 10.1.

4. Select Internet Information Services (IIS), and click Details.

5. Select the desired subcomponents to be installed with IIS (see Figure 10.2), and click OK when done.

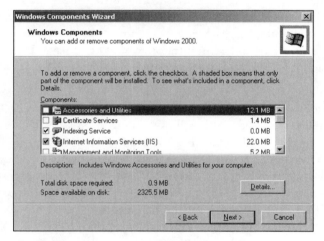

Figure 10.1   The Windows Components Wizard.

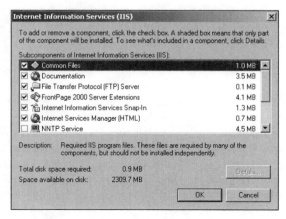

Figure 10.2   The IIS subcomponents menu.

6. Click Next.

7. At this point, the Windows Components Wizard installs IIS. You might be asked to provide the Windows 2000 Server CD-ROM for the installation to continue. Click Finish when done.

8. Click Close to close the Add/Remove Programs applet.

Working with the MMC

As mentioned, IIS uses an MMC snap-in to configure and control the Internet Information Services, as shown in Figure 10.3. The best (and usually quickest) way to configure and control IIS is to use the snap-in for all IIS configuration changes rather than some of the other available methods. This, however, might not always be possible. Therefore, the HTML version of the administration console is covered later in this chapter.

Creating a Custom Management Console

The Internet Information Services snap-in is installed in the Administrative Tools menu, from which you can configure custom MMC consoles. If, for example, you need to modify users and groups and then grant them access to

10

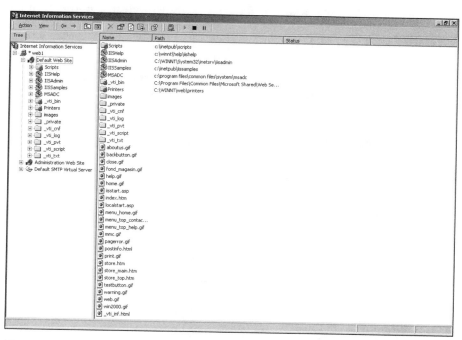

Figure 10.3   The Internet Information Services snap-in.

the Internet server, creating a custom Management Console might make sense. To configure a customized Management Console, use the following steps:

1. Select Start|Run.

2. Type **mmc** in the Open text box.

3. Click OK.

4. Select Add/Remove Snap-In on the Console menu.

5. Click Add.

6. Select the Internet Information Services snap-in in the Add Standalone Snap-In window (refer to Figure 10.4), and click Add.

7. Repeat Step 6 to add any other desired snap-ins.

8. Click Close to close the Add Standalone Snap-In window.

9. Click OK to close the Add/Remove Snap-In window.

10. Select Save on the Console menu.

11. Enter a name for the newly created Management Console, and click Save. Note that the new Management Console is created in the Administrative Tools menu by default.

Configuring IIS Using the Snap-In

As mentioned, most of the configuration changes made to IIS are done using the Internet Information Services snap-in (also known as the Internet Services Manager, or ISM). The ISM snap-in can be accessed by selecting

Figure 10.4   The Add Standalone Snap-In window.

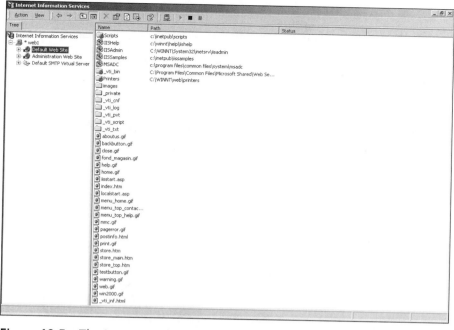

Figure 10.5   The Internet Information Services snap-in.

Start | Programs | Administrative Tools | Internet Services Manager and is
displayed in Figure 10.5.

You should understand that IIS is a huge product. Unfortunately, you cannot
gain a complete understanding of IIS in a few pages. In fact, several books are
dedicated to using IIS to create and maintain Internet sites. Because of this, we
only cover some of the basic tasks that can be performed using the IIS snap-in
here. Namely, the next few sections cover:

➤ Creating a new Web site

➤ Creating a new virtual directory

➤ Modifying Web site permissions

➤ Changing a home directory

➤ Changing default documents

➤ Controlling Web site performance

Creating a New Web Site

To create a new Web site, follow these steps:

1. Select Start | Programs | Administrative Tools | Internet Services Manager.

2. Navigate to and expand the desired server.

3. Right-click the server, and choose New | New Web Site. The Web Site Creation Wizard appears.

4. Click Next.

5. Enter a description for the new Web site, and click Next.

6. Select the IP address to be used with the Web site, the port, and the Host Header (if any). Then, click Next.

7. Enter a path to indicate the storage location for the Web site files, and click Next.

8. Select the desired permissions for the new Web site, and click Next.

9. Click Finish.

Creating a New Virtual Directory

To create a new virtual directory, follow these steps:

1. Select Start | Programs | Administrative Tools | Internet Services Manager.

2. Navigate to and expand the desired server.

Host Headers

A single computer can support multiple Web sites in two ways—by using multiple TCP/IP addresses or Host Headers.

If multiple TCP/IP addresses are assigned to the same physical (or different) network card on a single server, then each IP address can be dedicated to a Web site. As you might imagine, an organization hosting multiple Web sites would quickly run out of TCP/IP addresses. Therefore, this method only works in situations in which a small number of Web sites are hosted on a single system. For this reason, Host Headers were developed.

With Host Headers, the same TCP/IP address is assigned to multiple Web sites, but the Host Header value is different. This allows a Web server to differentiate among Web sites. For example, let's say you have two different Web sites—**www.companyA.com** and **www.companyB.com**—but you only have a single TCP/IP address. You could set the Host Header of the first Web site to **www.companyA.com** and the Host Header of the second Web site to **www.companyB.com**. When a client tries to contact **www.companyB.com**, their browser (assuming it is less than a couple years old) not only contacts the server via the TCP/IP address, but it also passes a Host Header of **www.companyB.com**. This notifies the Web server that the second Web site is the desired site.

3. Right-click the Web site where the new virtual directory is to be created, and choose Virtual Directory. The Virtual Directory Creation Wizard appears.

4. Click Next.

5. Enter an alias for the virtual directory, and click Next.

Note: An alias is the name that will be added to a URL to access the virtual directory. This directory can exist on the same system or a remote system from the main Web site. To access the virtual directory, enter "URL: www.mycompany.com/alias/".

6. Enter a location for the folder where the files are to be stored, and click Next.

7. Choose the desired permissions, and click Next.

8. Click Finish.

Modifying Web Site Permissions

To modify Web site permissions, follow these steps:

1. Select Start | Programs | Administrative Tools | Internet Services Manager.

2. Navigate to and expand the desired server.

3. Right-click the desired Web site, and choose the All Tasks | Permissions Wizard option on the pop-up menu. The Permissions Wizard appears.

4. Click Next to start the wizard.

5. Choose either the Inherit All Security Settings or Select New Security Settings From A Template option by selecting the appropriate radio button, and click Next.

6. If you selected the Select New Security Settings From A Template option in Step 5, choose the desired template, and click Next.

7. Choose the desired option for directory and file permissions (see Figure 10.6), and click Next.

8. Verify the settings to be applied, and click Next.

9. Click Finish to complete the wizard.

Changing a Home Directory

To change the home directory, follow these steps:

1. Select Start | Programs | Administrative Tools | Internet Services Manager.

2. Navigate to and expand the desired server.

10

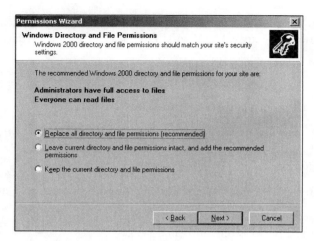

Figure 10.6 Selecting the desired directory and file permissions settings.

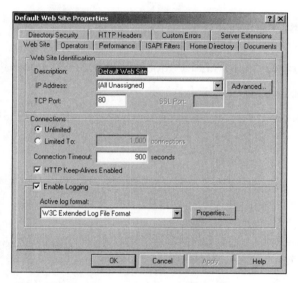

Figure 10.7 The Web Site Properties pages.

3. Right-click the desired Web site, and choose the Properties option on the pop-up menu. Figure 10.7 illustrates the various options available when configuring a Web site.

4. Select the Home Directory tab.

5. Choose one of the three options—A Directory Located On This Computer, A Share Located On Another Computer, or A Redirection To A URL:

➤ If the A Directory Located On This Computer option is selected, enter a local path to the directory, and click OK.

➤ If the A Share Located On Another Computer option is selected, enter the location to the share using the *\\server\share* format, and click OK.

➤ If the A Redirection To A URL option is selected, enter the desired URL using the *http://server* format, and click OK.

Changing Default Documents

A default document is loaded by a Web server when no document is requested. This arrangement allows a user to enter a URL (**http://www.company.com**) without knowing that the document to be loaded is the index.htm file. To change the default document setting, follow these steps:

1. Select Start | Programs | Administrative Tools | Internet Services Manager.

2. Navigate to and expand the desired server.

3. Right-click the desired Web site, and choose the Properties option on the pop-up menu.

4. Select the Documents tab.

5. To add a default document, click Add, enter the name of the default document (for example, index.htm), and click OK.

6. To remove a default document association, highlight the default document to be removed, and click Remove.

7. Click OK when done.

10

. . . .

Tip: You can control the order in which IIS checks for default documents. To do this, select the default document association that you want modified, and click the Up arrow to move it up or the Down arrow to move it down. IIS attempts the default documents (until it finds a valid one) by starting from the top of the list and moving downwards.

. . . .

Controlling Web Site Performance

To control Web site performance, follow these steps:

1. Select Start | Programs | Administrative Tools | Internet Services Manager.

2. Navigate to and expand the desired server.

3. Right-click the desired Web site, and choose Properties on the pop-up menu.

4. Select the Performance tab.

5. You can tune your Web site according to the number of hits you expect it to experience per day by moving the slider control to the desired option.

6. Another option is known as *Bandwidth Throttling*. This option is enabled by checking the Enable Bandwidth Throttling checkbox and entering a value. The value limits the amount of the available network traffic to the Web site.

7. The final option is known as *Process Throttling* and controls how much of the CPU is to be used as a maximum on the server. Enable this option by checking the Enable Process Throttling checkbox and entering a value.

8. Click OK when done.

Configuring IIS Using the HTML Internet Services Manager

The ISM is a full-featured interface used to control IIS. It offers a lot of administrative functionality, as discussed in the following sections.

Verifying the Administrative Web Site Port

After the ISM (HTML) is installed, it is automatically configured with a specialized port (this port is randomly assigned a number between 2000 and 9999). Before you can access IIS through HTML, you need to know what this port is. This port is known as the *Administrative Web Site port*. To verify the Administrative Web Site port, follow these steps:

1. Select Start | Programs | Administrative Tools | Internet Services Manager.

2. Expand the server for which you want to find the Administrative Web Site port.

3. Right-click Administrative Web Site, and choose the Properties option on the pop-up menu.

4. Ensure that the Web Site tab is selected. Note the number in the TCP Port field. This is the Administrative Web Site port (see Figure 10.8).

5. Click OK.

Limiting Access to Local Machines

Another feature of the Administrative Web Site is that it limits access to the local machine (the system on which the Administrative Web Site is installed). If the Administrative Web Site is to be accessed by systems other than the local system, then the following steps need to be completed:

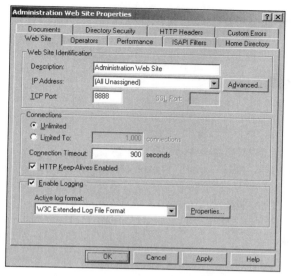

Figure 10.8   The Administrative Web Site port number.

1. Select Start | Programs | Administrative Tools | Internet Services Manager.

2. Expand the server for which you want to find the Administrative Web Site port.

3. Right-click Administrative Web Site, and choose the Properties option from the pop-up menu.

4. Select the Directory Security tab.

5. Click Edit in the Anonymous Access And Authentication Control section.

6. Note that only the Integrated Windows Authentication method is selected by default. Be careful in enabling other authentication methods, because they can introduce weaknesses into your Internet infrastructure. Click OK.

7. Click Edit in the IP Address And Domain Name Restrictions section. The IP Address And Domain Name Restrictions window appears, as shown in Figure 10.9.

8. Select either the Granted Access or the Denied Access radio button, click Add, and enter the appropriate computer, group of computers, or domain name.

Warning: Although granting or denying access based on the domain name seems like a good option, it is very expensive in processing cycles. Every time the Administrative Web Site is accessed, the Web server has to perform a reverse lookup to confirm that the originating computer is in the correct domain.

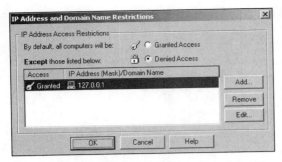

Figure 10.9   The IP Address And Domain Name Restrictions window.

Note: *If the Granted Access radio button is selected, then the addresses listed in the Except Those Listed Below section are denied access. However, if the Denied Access radio button is selected, the addresses listed in the Except Those Listed Below section are granted access.*

9. Click OK on the IP Address And Domain Name Restrictions window.

10. Click OK on the Administration Web Site Properties window.

Starting the Administrative Web Site

After the Administrative Web Site port number is known, it can be accessed using the server's FQDN, IP address, or name. The address takes on one of the following forms (assuming that the Administrative Web Site port is *8888*):

➤ http://FQDN:8888/

➤ http://IP_Address:8888/

➤ http://Computer_Name:8888/

To start the Administrative Web Site, follow these steps:

1. Start Internet Explorer (Start | Programs | Internet Explorer).

2. In the Address field, enter "http://*yourserver:8888/*", and press Enter.

3. Depending on your authentication method, you might be asked to supply logon credentials. Also, if you are not using secure connections, a warning appears. If such a warning appears, click OK.

4. The Internet Services Manager (HTML) appears, as shown in Figure 10.10.

5. On the main page, you can create a new Web site, delete or rename an existing site, or view a site's properties by clicking the New, Delete, Rename, or Properties links.

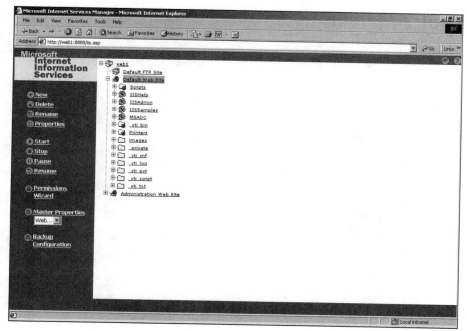

Figure 10.10   The Internet Services Manager (HTML).

6. Click the Default Web Site link in the right pane. The Properties pages appear. Note that the links in the left portion of the window (see Figure 10.11) match the tabs in the Properties dialog box displayed in the snap-in (as shown earlier in Figure 10.7).

7. Close Internet Explorer when done.

Indexing Server Content

Windows 2000 automatically installs the Indexing Service. This service is used by Windows 2000 to not only index and catalog the data stored in the Web sites, but also the data stored on the system.

Warning!	Although the Indexing Service is installed when Windows 2000 is installed, it is set to start manually. This means that it will not start unless you or another service forces it to start. The reason the service is not running by default is that indexing your system can be very processor-intensive if large amounts of data reside on your system. Use caution when enabling this service.

The Indexing Service allows your organization to create Web pages that will search a wide range of data files that are to be shared with the Internet. These

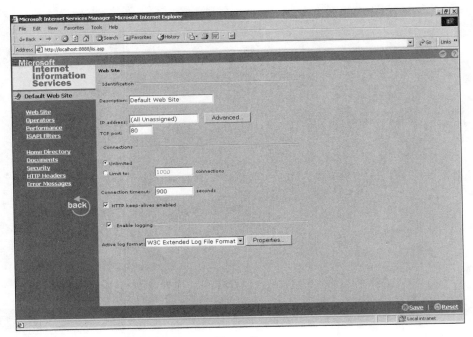

Figure 10.11   The Web Site property options.

pages can be custom created or can be created using FrontPage 2000's search forms (assuming that the Web involved is FrontPage enabled). Windows 2000 also ships with a snap-in that can be used to search for information on both the system and the Web server. This snap-in, unfortunately does not have a dedicated utility. To use the Indexing Service snap-in, follow these steps:

1. Select Start|Run.
2. Type "MMC" in the Open field.
3. Click OK.
4. Select Add/Remove Snap-In on the Console menu.
5. Click Add.
6. Select the Indexing Service snap-in, and click Add.
7. Choose to index either the local system or a remote system, and click Finish.
8. Click Close.
9. Click OK.
10. The Indexing Service snap-in displays, as shown in Figure 10.12. Save the snap-in if so desired.

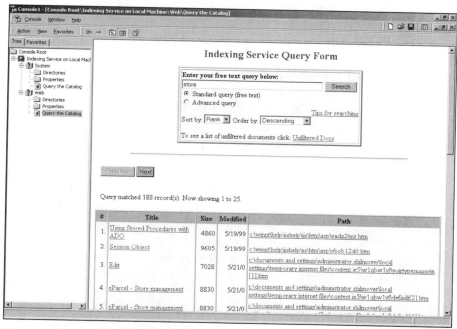

Figure 10.12   The Indexing Service snap-in.

After the Indexing Service is started and the snap-in is launched, you can search for keywords in documents by expanding the Indexing Service node, highlighting the Web site and choosing the Query The Catalog option from the pane on the right, entering keywords, and clicking Search. Not only that, but the snap-in can be used to re-index specific directories (by right-clicking on the desired directory and choosing the All Tasks | Rescan option) and to add other directories that are not indexed by default.

Tip: When indexing a large number of documents, ensure that enough time is given for all the documents to be indexed. This assumes that the Indexing Service is started for the first time.

Troubleshooting IIS

When you experience problems with IIS, you might have difficulty knowing for sure what is causing problems. Therefore, to prepare for troubleshooting IIS, you need to be aware of a few common configuration issues that can cause IIS to stop functioning correctly. This section covers the following common issues:

➤ Incorrect permissions

➤ Missing files

> ➤ Problems with multiple Web sites

> ➤ Wrong port number

Incorrect Permissions

Perhaps the most common problem encountered regarding accessing IIS is due to incorrect permission settings. This makes perfect sense when you remember the following:

> ➤ IIS uses different authentication schemes for granting access to the server itself.

> ➤ IIS uses permissions that are assigned through the IIS snap-in.

> ➤ If a Web site's data exists on an NTFS partition, IIS uses NTFS permissions as well.

With pervious versions of IIS, solving permissions problems could be a long and tedious process. An administrator needed to use the trial-and-error method to find a solution to the problem. However, with IIS version 5's Permissions Wizard, this task is much simpler.

To help troubleshoot permissions problems, check the Security Summary screen in the Permissions Wizard (see Figure 10.13). This is done by right-clicking the Web site in ISM and selecting All Tasks | Permissions Wizard from the pop-up menu. This one screen can solve many permissions-based problems, because it does most of the work for you.

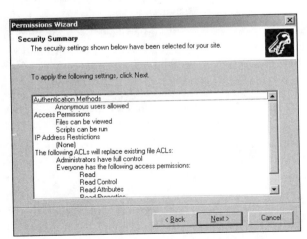

Figure 10.13   The Permissions Wizard's Security Summary screen.

Missing Files

Although standards abound on the Internet, there are still many ways to perform the same tasks. For example, the following list of files are all valid names for the default document of a Web site (these are names that are actually used, rather than made up for this example):

- default.htm
- default.html
- default.asp
- index.htm
- index.html
- index.asp

As you can see, a simple mistake in the default document name (default.htm versus default.html) can make a Web server return an error message to the client. If you attempt to access a Web site and receive an error message, try to access it again using the full path. For example, if **www.mycompany.com** fails, try **www.mycompany.com/index.htm**. This simple test lets you know if an access error message stems from the path or from the file the server is looking for.

10

Problems with Multiple Web Sites

One of the most common problems related to hosting multiple Web sites on a single computer with a single IP address is that administrators tend to forget about Host Headers. Creating multiple Web sites is easy; it's trying to start the subsequently created sites that causes the problems. If you attempt to start a Web site without first setting its Host Header information, you will get the error message shown in Figure 10.14.

The error message shown in Figure 10.14 is misleading. The reason the second site failed to start is simple. The first site uses a TCP/IP port of 80 (the default port for HTTP) with no Host Header. The second site is also attempting to use

Figure 10.14   An error that displays after unsuccessfully attempting to start a second Web site on the same system.

port 80 with no Host Header. Obviously, this cannot take place because the server would have no way of differentiating between the two sites. By setting a Host Header to the second Web site, both Web sites can start with no error messages.

Wrong Port Number

Many people do not realize that when they enter a URL in their browser, it communicates on a dedicated port to the server. The port for HTTP is port 80. The reason most people do not know this is that the browser indicates this data automatically. What really happens when you enter **http://www.company.com** in your browser is that it sends **http://www.company.com:80** to the server. The server then knows that the service watching port 80 is to get the request. That service happens to be the Web server.

If an administrator sets a different port number to a Web site, the client will still attempt to access the site using port 80 (unless a different port is specified). To fix this problem, assign a Host Header to the Web site, assign it a different IP address, or specify the different port number in the browser request.

WORKING WITH REMOTE ACCESS

Windows NT has been able to perform multiprotocol routing and remote access since version 3.51 Service Pack 2 (albeit using separate services). With later Service Pack revisions for Windows NT 4, Microsoft introduced the Routing And Remote Access Service (RRAS). This service includes not only the routing protocols (Routing Information Protocol [RIP] for IP and RIP for Internetwork Packet Exchange [IPX]), but also remote access protocols (such as Point-to-Point Protocol [PPP]). With Windows 2000, the following features are supported with RRAS:

➤ AppleTalk routing

➤ Demand-dial routing

➤ Internet Authentication Service (IAS)

➤ Internet Control Message Protocol (ICMP) router discovery

➤ Internet Group Management Protocol (IGMP)

➤ Layer 2 Tunneling Protocol (L2TP) over IP Security (IPSec)

➤ Network Address Translation (NAT)

➤ Open Shortest Path First (OSPF) for IP

➤ Remote Authentication Dial-In User Service (RADIUS) client

➤ RIP version 2 for IP

This section concentrates on the remote access portion of RRAS.

RAS Overview

Windows 2000's RAS allows clients to connect to an organization's network and/or to the Internet. With previous versions of Windows, the only built-in option was to connect to a modem (or modem pool) that was physically attached to the server. The client could then communicate on the network using Point-to-Point Protocol (PPP) or across the Internet via the RAS server (assuming that this option was enabled). Service Packs added the option to enable virtual private networking (VPN) with Windows NT. This allowed users to connect to an organization's network securely from the Internet.

When a client connects to a RAS server, the client can either be granted access to the RAS server only (local access) or to the RAS server and the network. Much like with Windows NT, Windows 2000's RAS allows for two types of connections—dial-up and VPN.

With dial-up connections, a client dials into a modem that is connected to the server, is authenticated by the server, and is then granted the appropriate access. With VPN access, the client first connects to the Internet (using their Internet Service Provider). They then initiate a second connection to the VPN server. The VPN server creates a secure *tunnel* between itself and the client. All data that is now passed between the two is encrypted, and the client acts as if it is a local system.

10

Installing and Configuring RAS

Unlike many other services in Windows 2000, RRAS is installed by default. However, it is also disabled by default. If you check the Routing And Remote Access Service, you will notice that it is disabled. You will not be able to start the service, because the options are grayed out. To enable RRAS, follow these steps:

1. Select Start | Programs | Administrative Tools | Routing And Remote Access.

2. Right-click the server on which RRAS is to be enabled, and choose the Configure And Enable Routing And Remote Access option.

3. When the Routing And Remote Access Server Setup Wizard appears, click Next.

4. Choose the configuration that best fits your needs (Internet Connection Server, Remote Access Server, VPN Server, or Network Router) or choose the Manually Configured Server option:

   ➤ If you choose the Internet Connection Server option, click Next, and proceed to Step 5.

   ➤ If you choose the Remote Access Server option, click Next, and skip to Step 7.

   ➤ If you choose the VPN Server option, click Next, and skip to Step 11.

   ➤ If you choose the Network Router option, click Next, and skip to Step 16.

   ➤ If you choose the Manually Configured Server option, click Next, and skip to Step 18.

5. Select to either configure the server for Internet Connection Sharing or to set it up as a router with network address translators (NAT), and click Next.

6. Choose the Internet connection to use, click Next, and skip to Step 18.

7. Verify that the required protocols are installed on the server, and click Next.

8. Choose a network connection to use and click Next.

9. Select an IP address assignment method and click Next.

10. Choose whether RADIUS is to be used (this should only be used if you are maintaining multiple RAS servers), click Next, and skip to Step 18.

11. Verify that the required protocols are installed on the server, and click Next.

12. Select the Internet connection to use, and click Next.

13. Choose the network connection to use, and click Next.

14. Select an IP address assignment method and click Next.

15. Choose whether RADIUS is to be used (this should only be used if you are maintaining multiple RAS servers), click Next, and skip to Step 18.

16. Verify that the required protocols are installed on the server, and click Next.

17. Choose whether demand-dial connections are supported, then click Next.

18. Click Finish.

19. Click Yes to start the Routing And Remote Access Service.

Managing Inbound Connections

Controlling inbound connections to a RAS server is a fairly simple process. The task of controlling these connections can be divided into two sections— controlling users before they connect and controlling users after they connect.

Controlling Dial-In Access to a Server

To control a user's dial-in access to a RAS server, follow these steps:

1. Display the Dial-In tab in the desired user's properties page (see Figure 10.15).

2. Choose whether the user's permission is set to allow, deny, or set by the policy (covered in the next section).

3. Choose a callback feature (if any).

4. Click OK.

Managing a Currently Connected User

After a user is connected, the connection can be viewed and controlled using the Routing And Remote Access utility (refer to Figure 10.16). To manage a currently connected user, follow these steps:

1. Select Start | Programs | Administrative Tools | Routing And Remote Access.

2. Navigate to Remote Access Clients.

10

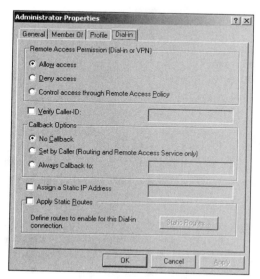

Figure 10.15   The Dial-In Properties page.

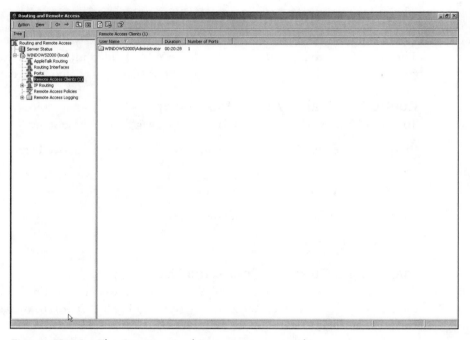

Figure 10.16 The Routing And Remote Access utility.

3. To find the status of the connected user, right-click the user, and choose the Status option on the pop-up menu.

4. To disconnect a connected user, right-click the user, and choose the Disconnect option on the pop-up menu.

5. To send a message to a connected user, right-click the user, and choose the Send Message option on the pop-up menu. Enter the message to be sent, and click OK.

Working with Remote Access Policies

With Windows 2000, RRAS becomes an extremely powerful, yet flexible way of connecting users to an organization's network. Part of RRAS's strength comes from *remote access policies*.

Remote access policies allow you to set different conditions under which access is either granted or denied. This allows you to configure a large number of users at the same time and to allow various levels of access based on client configuration. Some of the conditions that can be set include:

➤ Friendly name for the RADIUS client

➤ IP address of the RADIUS client

➤ Manufacturer of the RADIUS proxy or NAS

➤ Phone number dialed by user

➤ Phone number from which calls originate

➤ Protocol to be used

➤ Time periods and days of week during which a user is allowed to connect

➤ Tunneling protocols to be used

➤ Type of physical port used by NAT

➤ Type of service a user has requested

➤ Windows groups that a user belongs to

To establish a new remote access policy, perform the following steps:

1. From within the Routing And Remote Access tool, expand the server node in the left pane.

2. Right-click Remote Access Policies and select New Remote Access Policy.

3. Give the new policy a name, then add any attributes you would like to define for the policy.

4. When you've added the desired attributes, click Next on the Add Remote Access Policy wizard.

5. Select either the Grant Remote Access Permission or Deny Remote Access Permission radio button and click Next.

6. From the final screen of the wizard, you can either edit the remote access profile or click Finish.

10

Managing Remote Access Profiles

After a user is authorized and connected to the network, a remote access profile can be applied. A remote access profile controls some of the properties assigned to a connection. Namely, these properties can include:

➤ Idle disconnect time

➤ Maximum session length

➤ Day and time limits

➤ Dial-in media

➤ Encryption

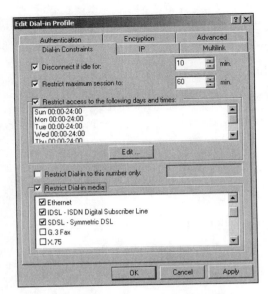

Figure 10.17 The Edit Dial-In Profile properties page.

The remote access profiles can be accessed when modifying the remote access policy. To edit the profile, right click the policy, select Properties, and click the Edit Profile button. Figure 10.17 illustrates some of the properties available for remote access profiles.

WORKING WITH TERMINAL SERVICES

One of the major downsides to Windows NT is the administrator's inability to control and configure remote servers. With Windows NT, third-party utilities are generally needed to allow for this administration task to be completed. Another limitation of previous versions of Windows is that Windows did not act as a true application server.

A company known as Citrix provided a solution for Windows NT. This solution, named MetaFrame, allowed Windows NT systems to be remotely controlled and to act as true application servers. Later in Windows NT's lifespan, Microsoft released Windows NT Terminal Server Edition (Windows NT TSE). This version included a limited version of MetaFrame to allow for some added remote administration functionality.

With Windows 2000, Microsoft includes new sets of services that give administrators more remote control over their servers as well as the ability to allow servers to operate as applications servers. These new services are known as Terminal Services. Terminal Services is accessible by clients running all versions of Windows; MS-DOS clients are not supported.

Before we look at how Terminal Services are installed and configured, you need to understand what they really are. In a nutshell, Terminal Services allow for all client applications, storage, and processing to occur on the server. Instead of physically sitting in front of the Windows 2000 Server and working on the system, a user simply opens a terminal window (similar to a Telnet session). The user sees a Windows 2000 Logon screen (as shown in Figure 10.18). When users enter their credentials and are logged onto the system, they are actually running sessions on the server, not on their client machines. Currently, several client platforms can be used to access the server in this way. These include Windows CE-based devices, client computers, and Windows Terminals.

After a client is connected to a Terminal Server, all keystrokes and mouse movements on the client are converted to commands and sent to the server. The server then interprets the commands as though they are executed on a session running on the server. In essence, this allows a client to double-click an application installed on the server to execute the application.

Technically, any system that can have the client portion of Terminal Services installed and a TCP/IP connection can connect to the server. The TCP/IP connection can include access through the Internet, virtual private networking (VPN), remote access, and wireless.

10

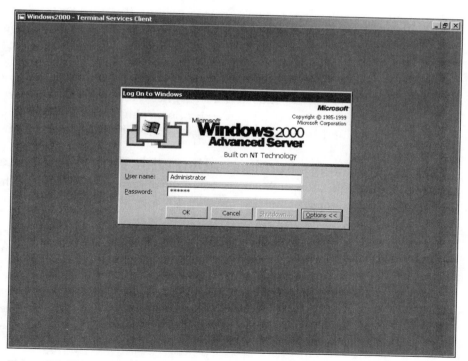

Figure 10.18   Logging onto a system using Terminal Services.

Terminals

Although Unix systems have been using terminals to access servers for years, it has only been recently that Windows has been able to do the same. The reason for this is simple. The Unix terminals were known as *dumb terminals*, because they really did not have any logic in them. They simply connected to the server based on a configuration set by the administrator. The problem with connecting such terminals to Windows is that all the rich functionality of Windows that most people take for granted (such as a mouse and a graphical user interface), could not be displayed on one of these dumb terminals.

Recently, a new breed of terminals has come on the market. Although most of these terminals do not have hard drives installed in them, they do have a color display, a keyboard, a mouse, and a network adapter. This allows them to connect to a central server (the server hosting Terminal Services) and execute all the available applications and utilities installed on the server. Windows terminals, or *WinTerms*, are cheaper than full-blown PCs and are cheaper to operate and maintain (they require minimal configuration and no obsolete hardware, because the applications rely on server hardware).

Unlike previous versions of Windows NT, where a different version of the operating system needed to be installed to activate Terminal Services (in Windows NT 4 Terminal Server Edition), Terminal Services are built into Windows 2000. They can be installed and uninstalled without completely reinstalling the software. As described in the following sections, Terminal Services can simply be installed or uninstalled in the same way as most other Windows 2000 services. After Terminal Services are installed, you can set them up to operate in one of two modes—Remote Administration and Application Server. Both of these configurations are covered in the following sections.

Remote Server Administration with Terminal Services

Finally, administrators of Windows-based servers can remotely control their servers without purchasing and installing third-party software. Once Terminal Services are installed in Remote Administration mode, any task that can be performed while physically sitting in front of the system can be performed from any system on the network that can connect to the server and is running the Terminal Services client software.

Note: With Terminal Services installed in Remote Administration mode, an administrator can perform any task that can be performed while physically sitting in front of the system. This, of course, excludes any physical changes to the system, such as inserting/ejecting floppy and CD-ROM disks, removing tapes, or other physical system changes.

If you will only be administering the Windows 2000 Server (not running applications remotely on it), make sure that you only install Terminal Services as Remote Server Administration. The overhead involved in running applications remotely is considerable higher than the overhead of just the Remote Server Administration.

To install Remote Server Administration, follow these steps:

1. Select Start | Settings | Control Panel.

2. Double-click Add/Remove Programs.

3. Click Add/Remove Windows Components.

4. When the Windows Components Wizard appears, check the Terminal Services checkbox, and click Next.

5. Select the Remote Administration Mode radio button, and click Next (see Figure 10.19).

6. You might be required to provide the Windows 2000 Server CD-ROM. When the setup completes, click Finish.

7. Click Yes to restart the system.

Sharing Applications in Terminal Services

You need to understand exactly what an application server is. First off, client licensing for applications is required. This is done through the Terminal Services Client Creator administrative tool. Many people think that if they install application files on a server, map a network drive to the client, and execute the

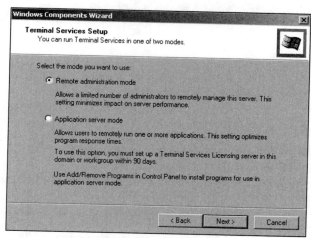

Figure 10.19   Installing Terminal Services in Remote Administration mode.

application, then the server is acting as an application server. This is, in fact, false. What makes this interesting is that Microsoft wanted us to believe that this was the case with some of the earlier versions of Windows NT. This was because Windows NT was not a true application server. A true application server can be defined as follows: A server that stores the application files and data in memory and executes the application in its memory, not the client's. The client simply receives the results of the application's execution.

To install Terminal Services in the Application Server mode, follow these steps:

1. Select Start | Settings | Control Panel.

2. Double-click Add/Remove Programs.

3. Click Add/Remove Windows Components.

4. When the Windows Components Wizard appears, check the Terminal Services checkbox, and click Next.

5. Select the Application Server Mode radio button, and click Next (see Figure 10.20).

6. Choose the desired permissions configuration (either Windows 2000 users or Windows NT Terminal 4 users), and click Next.

7. A list of applications that might not be compatible appears. Note the applications, and click Next.

8. The Terminal Services components are installed. You might be required to provide the Windows 2000 Server CD-ROM.

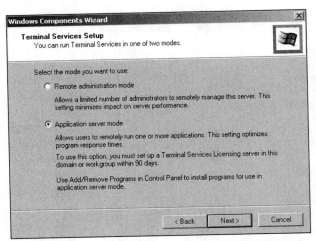

Figure 10.20   Installing Terminal Services in Application Server mode.

9. When the setup completes, click Finish.

10. Click Yes to reboot the server.

Configuring Applications for Terminal Services

After Terminal Services are installed in Application Server mode, all the administrator has to do is reinstall applications that are to be executed using Terminal Services. You will notice that any application left running in the Terminal Server session will still be running when the user logs into the session again. This looks and feels more like a true client system.

For example, if you run Microsoft Outlook for your email and you go for lunch, you most likely lock the workstation. When you return from lunch, you simply unlock the workstation and Outlook is still running. What's more, if any new email has arrived for you, Outlook has picked it up. Similarly, any scheduled tasks or appointments will appear. The same would be true with the Terminal Server session.

When a Terminal Server is in the Remote Administration mode, any applications running on the server when the session is closed are automatically terminated. It is therefore easy to see why the Application Server mode uses considerably more resources than the Remote Administration mode.

10

CHAPTER SUMMARY

This chapter introduced you to some of the new features and services available with the Internet Information Service, including SMTP, NNTP, FTP, and Web sites. You learned how to create multiple Web sites on a single server and control the amount of bandwidth allowed for each site.

Windows 2000 ships with the Routing And Remote Access Service. This service allows the Windows 2000 Server to accept dial-up and VPN connections as well as enables Windows 2000 Server to act as a router and perform Network Address Translation. This chapter describes the steps involved in configuring RRAS and controlling users and connections.

Finally, the chapter covers the modes in which Terminal Services can operate—Remote Administration and Application Server. The differences between the two modes are explained as well as their benefits and drawbacks.

REVIEW QUESTIONS

1. Which of the following is not an IIS service?

   a. SMTP

   b. SNMP

   c. NNTP

   d. FTP

2. Which of the following is a valid configuration of SiteA and SiteB on the same system?

   a. Both SiteA and Site B use port 80.

   b. Both SiteA and SiteB use the same Host Header.

   c. SiteA and SiteB use the same Host Headers and the same port numbers.

   d. SiteA and SiteB use different port numbers and Host Headers.

3. Which of the following is the easiest method to use for configuring Web site permissions?

   a. Rights Wizard

   b. Windows Explorer

   c. Permissions Wizard

   d. Command line

4. The Internet Services Manager (HTML) can be used to restart the Web services.

   a. True

   b. False

5. Which port does the Administration Web Site use?

   a. 80

   b. 81

   c. 8080

   d. A random port assigned during setup

6. The Application Server mode of Terminal Services does not use any more processing power than the Administration mode.

   a. True

   b. False

7. How many administrators can connect to a system running Terminal Services in Remote Administration mode?

    a. 1

    b. 2

    c. 4

    d. 8

8. Which of the following are remote policy properties that can be set? [Choose all that apply]

    a. Time periods and days of week during which user is allowed connect

    b. Operating system to be used by client

    c. Protocol to be used

    d. Phone number dialed by user

9. Which of the following is not an option when configuring RRAS?

    a. Internet Connection Server

    b. Remote Access Server

    c. Gateway Server

    d. VPN Server

10. Once Terminal Services are installed, they cannot be uninstalled.

    a. True

    b. False

11. IIS requires a static IP address before it can be installed.

    a. True

    b. False

12. Which clients are supported for connecting into Terminal Services? [Choose all that apply]

    a. MS-DOS

    b. Windows 3.1

    c. Windows 98

    d. Windows 2000

10

13. Once Terminal Services are configured to operate in the Remote Administration mode, how can they be converted to the Application Server mode?

    a. Run the Add/Remove Windows Components Wizard, and choose the Application Server Mode radio button.

    b. In the Terminal Services Configuration Application, click the Convert button.

    c. Uninstall Terminal Services, reboot the system, and reinstall Terminal Services.

    d. This cannot be done.

14. Terminal Services running in Application Server mode is compatible with 100 percent of applications.

    a. True

    b. False

15. Which TCP/IP port is used by a default Web server?

    a. 21

    b. 25

    c. 80

    d. 110

REAL-WORLD PROJECTS

Your organization is currently running its corporate Web site on a Windows 2000 system. Two new products are being launched by your organization at the same time, and management wants individual sites to be set up for each of the new products.

An outside firm has created the Web sites, and all Domain Name Service entries are controlled by your organization's ISP. The two domains are **www.reallycoolproduct.com** and **www.equallycoolproduct.com**. You are limited in that no extra IP addresses exist and because all available resources were pumped into the two products. Therefore, you must work with what is at hand.

Project 10.1
To install the www.reallycoolproduct.com Web site, perform the following steps:

1. Select Start | Programs | Administrative Tools | Internet Services Manager.

2. Right-click the Web server, and choose the New | Web Site option.

3. When the Web Site Create Wizard appears, click Next.

4. Enter a description for the site, such as "The Web site for the really cool product".

5. Click Next.

6. In the Host Header For This Site field, enter "www.reallycoolproduct.com".

7. Click Next.

8. Enter the path to where the files for the Web site are to reside. For example, enter "C:\InetPub\reallycoolproduct".

9. Click Next.

10. Ensure that the Read and Run scripts checkboxes are checked, and click Next.

11. Click Finish.

12. Right-click the newly created Web site, and choose Start on the pop-up menu.

13. Right-click the Web site, and choose Properties on the pop-up menu.

14. Select the Performance tab.

15. Check the Enable Bandwidth Throttling checkbox, and enter a value of 256 in the Maximum Network Use field.

16. Check the Enable Process Throttling checkbox, and enter a value of 15 in the Maximum CPU Use field.

17. Select the Home Directory tab.

18. Ensure that the Index This Resource checkbox is checked.

19. Select the Documents tab.

20. Click Add.

21. Enter "index.htm", and click OK.

22. Move the index.htm entry to the top of the list.

23. Select the Custom Errors tab.

24. Highlight error 400, and click Edit Properties.

25. Browse to the file corresponding to the error level as given to you by the Web site designer.

26. Click OK.

10

27. Repeat steps 23 through 26 for all other error levels.

28. Click OK.

Project 10.2
To install the www.equallycoolproduct.com Web site, perform the following steps:

1. Select Start | Programs | Administrative Tools | Internet Services Manager.

2. Right-click the Web server, and choose New | Web Site.

3. When the Web Site Create Wizard appears, click Next.

4. Enter a description for the site, such as "The Web site for the equally cool product".

5. Click Next.

6. In the Host Header For This Site field, enter "www.equallycoolproduct.com".

7. Click Next.

8. Enter the path to where the files for this Web site are to reside. For example, enter "C:\InetPub\equallycoolproduct".

9. Click Next.

10. Ensure that the Read and Run scripts checkboxes are checked, and click Next.

11. Click Finish.

12. Right-click the newly created Web site, and choose Start on the pop-up menu.

13. Right-click the Web site, and choose Properties on the pop-up menu.

14. Select the Performance tab.

15. Check the Enable Bandwidth Throttling checkbox, and enter a value of 384 in the Maximum Network Use field.

16. Check the Enable Process Throttling checkbox, and enter a value of 25 in the Maximum CPU Use field.

17. Select the Home Directory tab.

18. Ensure that the Index This Resource checkbox is checked.

19. Select the Documents tab.

20. Click Add.

21. Enter "index.htm", and click OK.

22. Move the index.htm entry to the top of the list.

23. Select the Custom Errors tab.

24. Highlight error 400, and click Edit Properties.

25. Browse to the file corresponding to the error level as given to you by the Web site designer.

26. Click OK.

27. Repeat steps 23 through 26 for all other error levels.

28. Click OK.

You did such a great job configuring the Web sites that management has decided to give you another project. A Windows 2000 Server was installed with Terminal Services. You must create and install the client software on 150 systems.

Project 10.3
To install and create the Terminal Server client floppy disks and install the client, perform the following steps:

10

1. Select Start|Programs|Administrative Tools|Terminal Server Client Creator.

2. Choose the Terminal Services For 32-bit x86 Windows option, and click OK.

3. Insert the first floppy disk, and click OK.

4. Insert the second floppy disk, and click OK.

5. At the client machine, insert floppy disk 1, and run the Setup.exe file.

6. When the Terminal Services Client Setup screen appears, click Continue.

7. Enter your name and the name of your organization.

8. Click OK.

9. Confirm your name and organization name, and click OK

10. Click the I Agree button.

11. Click the large button on the left to install the Terminal Services Client software.

12. Click Yes to instruct the setup program to configure the Terminal Services Client software so that it works with all users on the system.

13. Click OK when done.

After you completed 80 systems, someone approached you and asked you why you are installing the client using floppy disks rather than over the network. You decide to install the last 70 systems over the network.

Project 10.4
To create a share for the Terminal Server Client software and install the client, perform the following steps:

1. Select Start|Run.

2. Type "C:\Winnt\system32\clients", and click OK.

3. Highlight the TSClient directory.

4. Right-click the directory, and choose Sharing on the pop-up menu.

5. Click Share This Folder.

6. Click OK.

7. At the client machine, select Start|Run.

8. Type "*server**TSClient*".

9. Double-click the Win32 folder.

10. Double-click the Disks folder.

11. Double-click the Disk1 folder.

12. Double-click Setup.

13. When the Terminal Services Client Setup screen appears, click Continue.

14. Enter your name and the name of your organization.

15. Click OK.

16. Confirm your name and organization name, and click OK.

17. Click the I Agree button.

18. Click the large button on the left to install the Terminal Services Client software.

19. Click Yes to inform the setup program to configure the Terminal Services Client software so that it works with all users on the system.

20. Click OK when done.

21. Repeat this process for any other client computers.

You have just been informed that a former employee can still access the network by dialing into the RAS server. It is up to you to stop the ex-employee from gaining access without changing the password or deleting the account.

Project 10.5

To disable RAS access to an ex-employee, perform the following steps:

1. Select Start | Programs | Administrative Tools | Active Directory Users And Groups.

2. Locate the ex-employee's account.

3. Right-click the account, and choose Properties on the pop-up menu.

4. Select the Dial-In tab.

5. Select the Deny Access radio button.

6. Click OK.

10

CHAPTER ELEVEN

MANAGING WINDOWS 2000 SERVER SECURITY

After completing this chapter, you will be able to:

✓ Implement, configure, and manage security using the Group Policy in Windows 2000

✓ Implement, configure, and manage Local Security Policy in Windows 2000

✓ Implement, configure, and manage security using the Security Configuration tools

✓ Implement, configure, and manage security using NTFS

✓ Implement, configure, and manage auditing

✓ Encrypt data on a hard drive using Encrypting File System (EFS)

In a secure network, the administrator's objective is to prevent unauthorized access to information and damage (either unintentional or malicious) to data and systems. However, this must be accomplished in such a way that legitimate users still have access to resources that they need to do their work. Windows 2000 provides several tools with which to secure various components of a server. They include

➤ *Auditing*—Allows the administrator to monitor what users are doing on a server.

➤ *Encrypt and decrypt files and folders*—Prevents access to data from unauthorized users.

➤ *NTFS permissions*—Restricts the access users have to files and folders.

➤ *Policies*—Manages what users may or may not do within the network and on their own machines.

All of these security tools are discussed in this chapter.

USING POLICIES TO MANAGE SYSTEM AND NETWORK SECURITY

When you initially encounter policies, they may seem a bit complicated. Three reasons for this complexity are

➤ Policies permeate Windows 2000; you will find them everywhere from RAS to rights to restrictions on passwords.

➤ Policies have different names; for example, there are Local Security Policies, Domain Security Policies, and Group Policies. To make matters worse, Group Policies have very little to do with groups. In fact, Group Policies are applied to Active Directory *containers*.

➤ As with many Windows applications, there are several different ways to achieve the same result when it comes to policies. Until you become familiar with the interface and the logic behind policies, the policy creation process can be a little confusing.

However, keep the following in mind when you feel as though your mind is swimming in what seems like hundreds of policies.

Active Directory is like a skeleton for a network; it gives the network structure and form. A policy is like a heart (with a brain), beating away in the background. Policies, if used correctly, will keep the computers in your network running smoothly. They do, however, require careful planning. This chapter will help you understand how they work and give you the basic information you need to configure them.

Of course, the question you are probably asking is, "What is a policy?" A dictionary definition of the word policy is: "Prudent conduct, sagacity; course of general plan of action to be adopted by a government, party, or person." As you can see, policies are considered to be synonymous with wisdom and good judgment. From a Windows 2000 perspective, you need to consider what happens when you configure a computer. Some settings can only be configured for the computer as a whole, whereas others can be different for each user who logs on to that computer.

The *Registry* is a database that contains settings that have been configured for the computer and all the users who have logged on to that computer. Many of these settings are configured during installation or through the Control Panel applets. Some settings are stored in folders in a user's profile. Some settings can be configured by one of the Administration Tools. When you use one of these tools, you are in effect configuring the Registry. But this still does not explain why you need policies for some settings and not for others.

It is one thing to sit at a single computer and configure it to your heart's content; it is an entirely different matter to configure 10, 20, hundreds, even thousands of computers, and then have to do it all again when you need to change a setting or restore the settings for a user. Ultimately, a policy is there to provide a plan of action, so that you can change the settings on multiple computers easily. The two types of policies that exist in Windows 2000 are:

11

➤ *Group Policy*—Designed for desktop change and configuration management within Windows 2000 domains. A Group Policy is really part of a very large technology called Microsoft IntelliMirror (the other components are Active Directory, Synchronization Manager, Offline files, and Remote Installation Services).

In this chapter, however, focus is on the policies and the parts of policies that are used to configure *security* settings for computers. These include what a user's desktop and Start menu look like, and what a user may or may not do on a computer, as well as the more traditional security issues, such as password settings and user rights, for example.

➤ *Local Policy*—Contains local configuration settings specific to a computer. The user environment would be very unfriendly if Microsoft made you use a policy to configure your desktop, for example. When you are configuring a single computer (and you are normally sitting at that computer), there are tools that you can use to easily change the configuration—which are easier and safer than modifying the Registry directly.

Consequently, the Local Policy tools provided contain only a subset of the settings available for configuration in Group Policy. Also some actions, such as automatically distributing software, are not of much use from a Local Policy viewpoint, so would not be available to be configured locally. However, there are still some settings that need to be configured and for which there is not a tool with dialog boxes and wizards. Rather than expecting you to edit the Registry directly, these settings have been made available to you by means of a policy called a Local Policy. As an administrator, you are, of course, able to configure the Local Policy on a remote computer.

Group Policy

Setting up and configuring individual computers is time consuming. In Windows 2000, the Group Policy provides administrators with a way of controlling configuration settings for users and computers from a central location. Configuration options include what appears on a user's desktop and menus, running scripts, automatically installing software, and redirecting folders to name just a few. The Group Policy allows administrators to establish particular requirements for a user or computer and have those requirements continually enforced. This results in a lower total cost of ownership by enforcing these settings centrally rather than on a user-by-user basis. The Group Policy name, however, is a little confusing because you apply a policy to a container in Active Directory and not to a group. In Windows 2000, the Group Policy replaces the Windows NT System Policy.

The Group Policy has the following features:

➤ It can be applied to sites, domains, and organizational units (SDOUs).

➤ By default, it is applied to all the child OUs too.

➤ By default, it affects all the users and computers in a particular SDOU.

➤ To fine-tune which users and computers are affected, the administrator can use security groups.

➤ Unlike Windows NT 4, Registry settings are removed when the Group Policy Object is removed.

Group Policy Objects

Technically, a *Group Policy Object (GPO)* is a virtual storage location for the Group Policy settings. The contents of the GPO are stored in two locations.

➤ *Group Policy Container*—An Active Directory object. It stores version and status information.

➤ *Group Policy Template*—A folder hierarchy in the SYSVOL folder on a domain controller. It stores policy information.

Note: You can think of a GPO as a set of configuration settings that are applied as a unit.

Applying the Group Policy

A GPO is always associated with the following Active Directory objects: a site, a domain, or an organizational unit. Multiple SDOUs can be associated with one GPO, and multiple GPOs can be associated with one SDOU. By default, each SDOU inherits GPOs from its parent. Any settings configured locally are applied first; then the GPOs are applied in the following order: site, domain, OU. In other words, the GPO closest to the user or computer is applied last.

For example, take a look at Figure 11.1; the Marketing OU has two GPOs applied to it (GPO3 and GPO4), whereas GPO4 has also been applied to the Sales OU. Look at how user accounts in the Sales OU inherit GPOs when the default inheritance settings are unchanged: GPO1 will be applied to each user account first followed by GPO2. GPO2 will override settings common to both policies. Finally, GPO4 is applied, overriding any settings common to all three policies. The default inheritance can be changed.

A *site* GPO affects all the domains in a site, but is stored in only one domain (the root domain of the forest by default). You must therefore consider the traffic that will be generated because each computer will need to contact a domain controller in the domain that contains the site GPO. In some cases, it may be better to create identical GPOs for each domain, rather than one for the site.

Note: You must be a member of the Enterprise Admins group to create a site GPO.

11

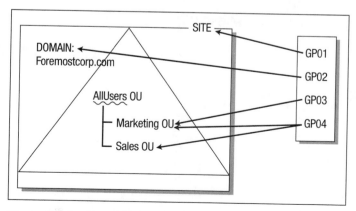

Figure 11.1   How GPOs are applied in Active Directory.

Creating and Managing GPOs

When you open Administration Tools from the Start Menu, you will not see a tool for creating and managing Group Policies. However, Windows 2000 provides two ways to work with group policies.

To use the first method, open Active Directory Users And Computers from the Start | Programs | Administrative Tools menu (to use the Active Directory Administrative Tools, the Netlogon service must be started). Right-click a domain name or an OU, and select Properties from the resulting menu. Select the Group Policy tab. From this dialog box (shown in Figure 11.2), you can create new policies (the New button), associate other GPOs with the current container (the Add button), and modify existing GPOs (the Edit button). You can also select users to whom the policy will apply. This first method is the easier method.

Note: *This method will work for domain and OU Group Policies. To manage GPOs linked to a site, open Active Directory Sites And Services, select the site name, and configure the properties as discussed in the previous paragraph.*

To use the second method, open the Microsoft Management Console (MMC) by selecting Start | Run and type "MMC", then click OK. From within the MMC, select Console | Add/Remove Snap-In. Click Add, and choose Group Policy. Then click Browse. Select Local Computer or one of the following tabs: Domain/OUs, Site, Computer, or All. This method allows you to select the extensions you want to include in the GPO that you are creating.

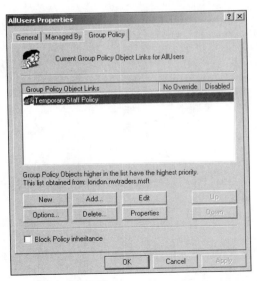

Figure 11.2 Working with Group Policy objects in Active Directory.

The following Group Policy extensions are available:

➤ *Administrative templates (computers and users)*—Controls Registry settings, desktop appearance, and system services.

➤ *Folder redirection (users only)*—Folders, such as My Documents, can be stored on a network location, rather than on the local drive.

➤ *Internet Explorer maintenance*—Provides administrative functions for Internet Explorer.

➤ *Remote installation services*—A service for deploying Windows 2000 Professional.

➤ *Scripts (logon/logoff and startup/shutdown)*—Allows administrators to specify scripts to run when a computer starts up and shuts down and when a user logs on and off.

➤ *Security settings*—Allows creation of account, local, public key, and IP security policies.

➤ *Software installation (computers and users)*—Enables administrators to manage how software is installed and managed.

Bear in mind that this list does not map directly to what you see on the screen when you edit a GPO (see Figure 11.3). Several headings have to be expanded to make these settings visible. Extensions refer to the fact that .dll files are used to implement certain parts of policies. Several policy extension .dll files are located on the client computers.

11

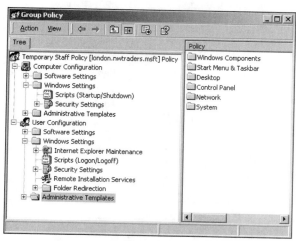

Figure 11.3 Configuring a GPO.

When editing a GPO, the two main categories are Computer Configuration and User Configuration. Each has the following folders: Software Settings, Windows Settings, and Administrative Templates. The subfolders may differ for each category as not all settings are applicable to both computers and users. We won't discuss all of these settings; however, Table 11.1 describes the default contents of a GPO.

To configure a setting, expand the folders until the setting you want to configure is displayed in the details pane. Double-click the setting. For administrative template settings, choose from the following options (see Figure 11.4):

➤ *Not Configured*—Ignore this setting.

➤ *Enabled*—Implement this setting.

➤ *Disabled*—Do not implement/remove this setting. If this setting had been previously enabled, it will be removed from the Registry.

Table 11.1 Summary of the folders within a GPO.

Category	Folder	Subfolder
Computer configuration	Software setting	Software installation
	Windows settings	Scripts
		Security settings
	Administrative templates	Windows components
	System	
	Network	
User configuration	Software setting	Software installation
	Windows settings	Internet Explorer maintenance
		Scripts
		Security settings
		Remote Installation Services (RIS)
		Folder redirection
	Administrative templates	Windows components
	System	
	Network	
	Printers	
	Start menu and Taskbar	
	Desktop	
	Control Panel	

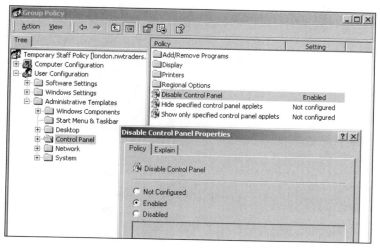

Figure 11.4   Configuring administrative template settings in a GPO.

Modifying Default Inheritance

By default, child containers inherit Group Policy settings from parent containers. Also, by default, all the policies are applied to all the objects in those containers. You can change these inheritance patterns as summarized in Table 11.2.

11

Table 11.2   Different ways to change the default inheritance of Group Policy.

Configuration Setting	To What You Apply It	Description of Effect
Processing order for multiple GPOs	The GPOs associated with a single container	GPOs are processed from top to bottom as listed on the Group Policy tab in the SDOU's properties.
No Override	A GPO (at the parent SDOU level)	This prevents a child container from blocking or overriding settings defined by a policy higher up in the hierarchy. If several GPOs are configured with No Override, the highest GPO in the hierarchy takes precedence.
Block Inheritance	A child SDOU	This blocks all policies from parent containers except those for which No Override has been configured.
Filtering scope of a GPO: Apply Group Policy: Allow or Deny	Security Group (or a user)	Ensures that the policy is applied only to members of the specified security group. By choosing the Deny option, you can ensure that a particular policy is not applied to specific groups.

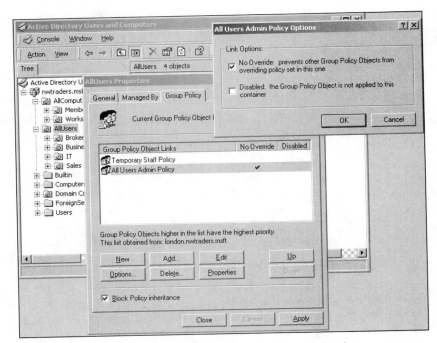

Figure 11.5 The All Users Admin Policy Options dialog box.

To configure the processing order and No Override option, as displayed in Figure 11.5, right-click the SDOU. Choose Properties, and select the Group Policy tab. Use the Up or Down buttons to change the order. To enable No Override, select the GPO, click Options, and select No Override.

To change the order in which GPOs are applied to an organizational unit, use the Up and Down buttons on the AllUsers Properties dialog box (see Figure 11.5). To block inheritance of GPOs from parent containers, select the Block Policy Inheritance checkbox. To configure the Block Inheritance, right-click the SDOU. Choose Properties, and select the Group Policy tab. Select the Block Policy inheritance checkbox.

When you filter the scope of a GPO, you are essentially specifying which security groups a policy should or should not apply. To do this, right-click the SDOU. Choose Properties, and select the Group Policy tab. Select the GPO, and click the Properties button. The Properties dialog box for the GPO opens. Select the Security tab (see Figure 11.6).

If you want a GPO to apply to a specific group, add the group, and then assign the Allow Read (must be set for the policy to be applied) and Allow Apply Group Policy to that group. Remember to clear the checkboxes for the Authenticated Users because all user accounts are members of this group.

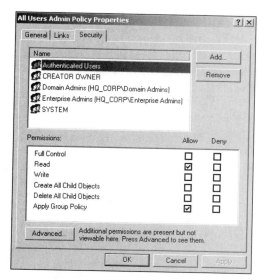

Figure 11.6   The Security tab.

You can add and remove groups from the list. If you want to apply the GPO to a group, select the Allow Read and Allow Apply Group Policy permissions for the group. If you do not want the policy to apply to the group, select Deny Apply Group Policy. Remember that all users are members of the Authenticated Users group. You should remove this group from the list or clear its checkboxes if you want the GPO to apply only to another group that you have specified. Do not check Deny for the Authenticated Users group because this will mean that the policy will not be applied to any of the users within the container. The Deny permission always takes precedence over Allow.

Permission Settings for GPOs

The default permissions assigned to a GPO are listed in Table 11.3

Table 11.3   Default permissions assigned to a GPO.

Group or User Account	Permissions
Authenticated Users	Read
	Apply Group Policy
Creator/Owner	None
Domain Admins	Read
Enterprise Admins	Write
System	Create all child objects
	Delete all child objects

11

You can assign permissions for the GPO to groups and users. Remember that permissions are cumulative for users who belong to multiple groups with the exception of Deny, which overrides the Allow permission. The permissions to apply for the most common situations are as follows:

➤ To have a GPO apply to a security group (that is, to filter the GPO), give them Read and Apply Group Policy permissions.

➤ To allow a security group to control all aspects of a GPO, give them Read and Write permissions.

To see the full list of permissions, click the Advanced button on the Security tab in the Properties dialog box for the GPO.

Disabling and Removing GPOs

You can disable the user settings, the computer settings, or the entire GPO. If a GPO contains only user settings, you can improve performance by disabling the computer settings in the GPO. The converse is also true: That is, you can disable the user settings for GPOs that contain only computer configurations. On the Group Policy tab, select the GPO, and click Properties. Select the General tab, as shown in Figure 11.7, and then select the appropriate checkbox.

You can disable a GPO if you do not want it to apply to a container. This would normally be a temporary measure because the GPO will still be linked to the container. On the Group Policy tab, select the GPO, and double-click the Disabled column to the right of the policy's name. A check will be placed in this column.

Figure 11.7 Disabling user or computer configuration settings for a GPO.

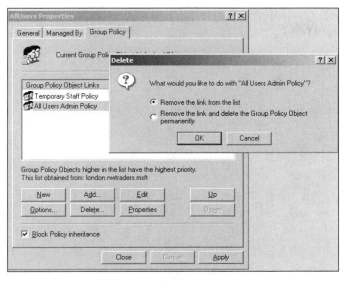

Figure 11.8   Deleting the link between a GPO and a container.

If you want to break the link between a GPO and a container, on the Group Policy tab, select the desired GPO, click the Delete button, and choose Remove The Link From The List, as seen in Figure 11.8.

Processing Group Policy Settings

The Group Policy can configure settings that are associated with the computer and settings that are associated with the user logging on. It is sometimes possible to configure the same setting in the Computer Configuration and User Configuration sections of the policies. It is important to understand the order in which these are applied because settings applied last could override earlier ones. The Group Policy settings are processed in the following sequence:

1. The computer starts.

2. Computer Configuration settings are processed.

3. Startup scripts run.

4. All settings that affect the computer are processed before the user is presented with a logon screen.

5. The user logs on.

6. The user configuration settings are processed.

7. Logon scripts run.

Some actions, such as software installation and folder redirection, occur only when the computer is turned on or when the user logs on. These actions could have unpredictable results if they occurred while the user was logged on.

Windows 2000 periodically refreshes the Group Policy settings. By default, on client computers (including member servers), this happens every 90 minutes with a randomized offset of up to 30 minutes. On domain controllers, the default period is five minutes. Although the default values can be changed, you cannot schedule a specific time to apply the GPO to a client computer.

Security Policies

Security policies refer to either the Local Security Policy or to the configuration of the Security subfolders within a GPO. To understand the difference between these, examine the kind of settings that can be configured for Security Policies. These are described in Table 11.4 and shown in Figure 11.9.

These security settings can be configured either through the Local Security Policy of a particular computer or by choosing the Security subfolders, which are available in both the Computer Configuration and User Configuration settings of Group Policy. Normally, you would use GPOs in a network that is using Active Directory because it would be easier to manage these settings centrally. However,

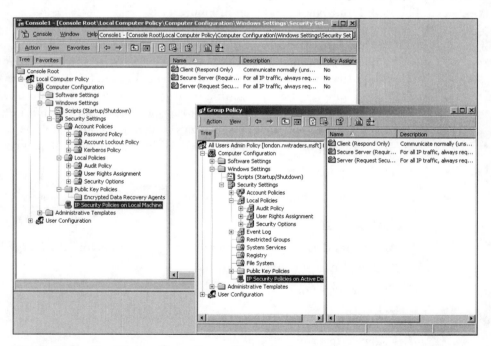

Figure 11.9   Security configuration settings via Local Computer Policy and Group Policy.

Table 11.4 Security settings available in a Local Security Policy and Group Policy.

Setting	Description	In a Local Security Policy	In Group Policy
Account policies[1]	Password restrictions and lockout settings Kerberos settings	✓	✓
Local policies[2]	Auditing policies User rights Security options	✓	✓
Event log	Settings for system, application, and security logs		✓
Restricted group	Use this to enforce membership of important groups.[3]		✓
System services	Configure security and startup settings for services.		✓
Registry	Configure security on Registry keys (none configured by default).		✓
File system	Configure NTFS permissions for local files (none configured by default).		✓
Public key policies	Encrypted data recovery agents Domain roots, enterprise trusts Trusted Certificate Authorities Automatic Certificate Request Settings	✓	✓
IPSec policies	*Client (responds only)*—Client will use secure communications if the server requests it. *Server (requires security)*—The server will only use secure communication if the client requests it. *Secure server (requests security)*—Secure channel mandatory for any communications.	✓	✓

1. Account policies can only be configured for the domain. They are not processed if you configure them at the OU level (even though they are available). Account policies are discussed in the next chapter.

2. Local policies and Local Security Policy are not the same thing. Local policy settings can be configured in the Local Security Policy or via Group Policy.

3. For example, if you define the Administrators group as a restricted group, you must also specify the group's members in the policy. If a user is added to the Administrators group (in the normal way) and the user is not defined as a member in the policy, the user will be removed the next time the policy is applied. Conversely, if a user who has been defined as a member of the restricted group is missing, that user will be added to the group.

you can still configure many of these settings locally on a particular machine. In a small workgroup-type network that is not using Active Directory, the only way to configure security settings is locally for each machine.

11

What happens if security settings have been configured in a GPO and locally for the same computer? The rule for GPOs still stands for security policies: Local settings are applied first, followed by any GPO settings for site, domain, and OU.

As mentioned previously, there are several ways of accomplishing the same result. This is particularly true for security policies. Table 11.5 describes various methods for opening different security policies.

Local Policies

You can configure a Local Policy for all Windows 2000 computers. The Local Security Policy tool displays the settings configured locally as well as the effective settings. If GPOs have also been used, the effective settings may differ from the locally configured settings. Remember the following rule: The local settings are applied first, then any site GPOs, then domain GPOs, and finally GPOs linked to the OUs in which the computer and user accounts have been placed.

System Policies

Group Policy is only available in Windows 2000 domains, that is, when Active Directory is being used. Group Policy does *not* provide client support for Windows NT 4 or Windows 95/98 clients.

Windows NT 4 uses System Policies to centrally manage computer and user settings. In a Windows NT 4 domain, there can be only one policy configured per domain. In this policy, you can configure settings for particular users, the

Table 11.5   Different ways of opening various policies.

Method 1	Method 2	Notes
Administrative Tools →Domain Security Policy	Active Directory Users and Computers →*DomainName* →Default Domain Policy GPO →Computer Configuration →Windows settings →Security Settings	Each domain has a default security policy that is applied to all users and computers within that domain. You can either modify this default policy or create additional policies.
Administrative Tools →Domain Controllers Security Policy	Active Directory Users and Computers →Domain Controllers OU →Default Domain Controller Policy GPO →Computer Configuration →Windows Settings →Security Settings	This is a Local Security Policy that is applied to each of the domain controller computers in that domain.
Administrative Tools →Local Security Policy	MMC + Group Policy snap-in for Local Computer →Computer Configuration →Windows Settings →Security Settings	A Local Security Policy exists for each Windows 2000 computer, whether it is in a domain or a workgroup.

default user, and groups of users. Settings can also be configured for particular computers and the default computer. An important difference between System Policy and Group Policy is that System Policy changes the Registry. In other words, the changes made by System Policy are not removed when the policy is removed.

You can configure a Windows 2000 domain to use System Policy. However, you would need to install the System Policy Editor tool (poledit.exe) from the Windows 2000 CD because it is not available by default. The Group Policy can also coexist with the System Policy. This situation may result during migration from Windows NT 4 to a Windows 2000 environment. However, using both kinds of policies does complicate matters.

By default, Windows 2000 computers do not use System Policy. However, you can enable it through an option within the Group Policy. If you do enable the System Policy, be prepared for some surprises because the System Policy and Group Policy are not processed in the same order. The order is as follows: The computer starts, the GPO computer configuration is applied, and then the user logs on. The System Policy (both user and computer settings) is then applied. Finally, the User Configuration settings of the GPO are applied. This means that the computer settings of the System Policy can overwrite GPO settings, whereas the GPO user settings can override user settings from the System Policy. If you are confused, imagine this in a real-world situation with many computers.

11

Further complications result when computer accounts are in a Windows NT 4 domain, and user accounts are in a Windows 2000 domain, and vice versa.

➤ If the computer account is in a Windows NT 4 domain, and the user account is in a Windows 2000 domain, both Windows NT 4 clients and Windows 2000 clients receive only the Computer Policy.

➤ If the computer account is in a Windows 2000 domain, and the user account is in a Windows NT 4 domain, then the Windows NT 4 client receives the Group Policy. A Windows 2000 computer gets Group Policy, and no policy is applied to the user unless System Policy has been enabled for Group Policy.

➤ If a Windows 2000 user or computer account is a member of a Windows NT 4 domain, the computer or user receives the System Policy.

Using Predefined Security Templates

Windows 2000 comes with several predefined security templates (see Figure 11.10). When you upgrade a Windows NT 4 computer to Windows 2000, the security settings will not be the same as those on a computer on which you performed a clean installation of Windows 2000 on NTFS. You can use the Basic*nn* templates to bring an upgraded computer to the same level as that of a cleanly installed one. This changes the security settings on a Windows 2000 Professional computer to the default security settings. In particular, users are no longer members of the Power Users group and, consequently, the Users group has less restrictive security. This is not considered a secure configuration. The remaining templates provide increased security on Windows 2000 computers. You cannot use a security template to define settings for computers formatted with the FAT file system; the computer to which a template applies must be formatted with NTFS.

To load the templates, run the MMC, then add the Security Templates snap-in. You can use the templates as they are or modify copies of them to create your own custom templates. To make a copy of an existing template, right-click it, choose Save As, and then give it a new name. Template files use a file type of .inf. A template can then be applied to computers either via the Local Policy or via GPOs.

Analyzing Security

You can analyze the security settings on a particular machine. This is something you can do at regular intervals to ensure that the security settings have not changed over time. Analysis can also be used to review what-if scenarios while you are developing and refining security policies.

Windows 2000 provides a tool that can perform a security analysis on a computer or configure a computer, so that the settings match those of a particular template. To use this tool, you must first create a template file (.inf) containing the settings you ultimately would like a group of computers to have.

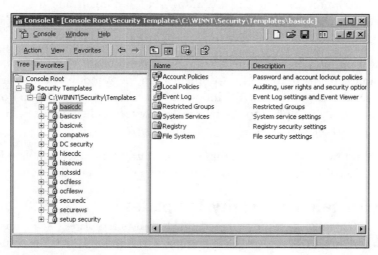

Figure 11.10 Security templates available for Windows 2000 computers.

You then use the tool to compare the security settings of a particular local computer with those contained in the template file. You must specify a database file (.sdb) to store the comparison information.

To analyze security, add the Security Configuration And Analysis snap-in to an MMC console. After adding the snap-in, the details pane gives instructions for setting up the database, as displayed in Figure 11.11. After you have configured the database details, apply the template and perform the analysis. Any discrepancies between the local computer and the template are marked with a red flag, whereas consistent settings are marked with a green check. Settings that have neither a flag nor a check were not configured in the original template. Once a database has been created, it can be used repeatedly to analyze or configure computers.

Using the Security Configuration Toolset

If you need to configure many computers or want to schedule a task that periodically analyzes important computers within your network, you can use secedit.exe, a command-line utility. Secedit can also be used to force a computer to receive an updated Group Policy.

The **secedit** command can take the following parameters:

➤ *Analyze*—Performs an analysis.

➤ *Configure*—Configures a computer to conform to some standard.

11

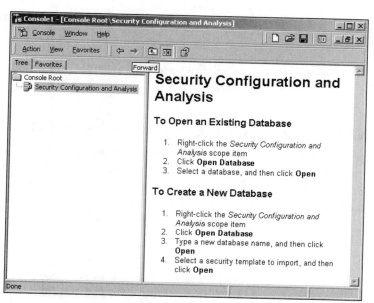

Figure 11.11   Using the Security Configuration And Analysis snap-in.

➤ */Export*—Exports the security settings from a computer.

➤ */Refreshpolicy*—Refreshes policies.

➤ */Validate*—Validates the syntax of a security template.

The following parameters require that you specify either a database (with the /db parameter) or a template (with the /cfg parameter):

➤ */Areas*—Allows you to configure or export specific sections of the security settings. Valid area names are: SecurityPolicy, Group_mgmt, User_rights, Regkeys, Filestore, and Services.

➤ */Enforce*—Forces a refresh of the computer's policy settings, even if there have been no changes to the policy since the last time it propagated.

➤ */RefreshPolicy machine_policy*—Causes a Group Policy propagation event. Group Policy will check for changes since the last propagation event and apply them to the computer.

➤ */Validate*—Verifies the syntax of a template created using Security Templates snap-in.

➤ */Verbose or /Quiet*—Provides either a detail log or no log when used with the previous parameters.

Example
If you wanted to change the user rights and security policy settings on a computer using a database called WSTypeOne and log the output to a file with the same name, you could use the following command:

```
Secedit /configure /db WSTypeOne.sdb /areas user_rights securitypolicy
/log c:\winnt\security\logs\WSTypeOne.log
```

UNDERSTANDING NTFS FILE SYSTEM SECURITY

A file system determines the way in which files are stored on a hard drive. From a user's perspective, it controls how the files can be named and what attributes can be configured for a file. In addition, the file system has mechanisms for keeping track of file details, writing the file's contents to the drive, and retrieving the file's contents. These mechanisms and attributes are different for different file systems.

Windows 2000 supports three file systems: FAT16, FAT32, and NTFS. Of these, NTFS is the only one that provides security features. In fact, there are several types of security features that are available only on NTFS: permissions, auditing, and Encrypting File System (EFS). Permissions, which are covered in this section, deal with what users may do to files and folders. Auditing, covered in the "Auditing Windows 2000 Server" section of this chapter, concerns monitoring users' actions when they are accessing files. EFS provides encryption for files and is also covered later in this chapter.

NTFS comes with *standard permissions* and *special access permissions*. A standard permission is a set of preconfigured special access permissions. Standard permissions are normally suitable for most situations. However, there may be times when you need to fine-tune permissions, and for those situations, you use the special access permissions.

In addition to the standard and special access permissions, NTFS also distinguishes between folder and file permissions. *Folder permissions* are applied to folders and determine what users may do within the folder, for example, list the names of files, add files, or delete files. *File permissions* are applied to files and determine what a user may do to a file, for example, read the contents, execute the file, modify the contents, or delete the file.

Special access permissions may differ slightly for folders and files. To understand which permissions are encompassed by standard permissions, you need to know what special access permissions are available. Table 11.6 lists the 13 special access permissions.

Note: When two permissions are listed separated by a slash, the first refers to a folder permission and the second to a file permission.

11

Most of the standard permissions that follow—with the exception of List folder contents—can be applied to files or folders. The actions permitted differ slightly for a folder and file in some cases as described in Table 11.6.

Table 11.6 Special access permissions.

Special Access Permission	Effect on a Folder	Effect on a File
List Folder / Read Data	View the contents of the folder, that is, the names of files and subfolders.	View the contents of a file, that is, the data in a file.
Traverse Folder / Execute File	Move through folders to reach files and folders. This would be used to allow users to traverse folders for which they do not have permissions.	Run programs.
Create Files / Write Data	Create or add files to folder.	Modify the contents of a file.
Create Folders / Append Data	Create new subfolders.	Append (add) to an existing file. Cannot modify existing data.

(continued)

Table 11.6 Special access permissions (continued).

Special Access Permission	Effect on a Folder	Effect on a File
Delete Subfolders and Files	Delete a folder or a file even if not granted the Delete permission.	Not applicable to files.
Delete	Delete a folder or a file.	Delete a folder or a file.
Read Attributes	View attributes, such as read-only, hidden, archive, and system.	View attributes such as Read-only, hidden, archive, and system.
Write Attributes	Modify attributes.	Modify attributes.
Read Extended Attributes	View additional attributes. Extended attributes are defined by the application and may vary.	View additional attributes. Extended attributes are defined by the application and may vary.
Write Extended Attributes	Modify extended attributes.	Modify extended attributes.
Read Permissions	View which permissions have been granted to users.	View which permissions have been granted to users.
Change Permissions	Change the setting for the permissions listed in this table. This allows users to change permissions without having the Full Control permission.	Change the setting for the permissions listed in this table. This allows users to change permissions without having the Full Control permission.
Take Ownership	Allow a user to become the owner of a file or folder.	

➤ *Full Control*—All the special permissions.

➤ *List folder contents*—List folder. This permission can only be applied to folders.

➤ *Modify*—Read and Write standard permissions plus Delete, Delete subfolders and files.

➤ *Read*—List folder/Read Data, Read Attributes, Read Permissions, Read Extended attributes.

➤ *Read & Execute*—Read standard permission plus Traverse folder/Execute file.

➤ *Write*—Read standard permission plus Create files/Write Data, Create folders/Append data, Write attributes, Write extended attributes.

Viewing and Setting Permissions

To see what permissions have been set for a folder or file, use Windows Explorer to locate the folder or file. Right-click it, and select Properties. Click the Security tab. As shown in Figure 11.12, the Name box displays which groups (or users) have been granted (or denied) access. To see what permissions

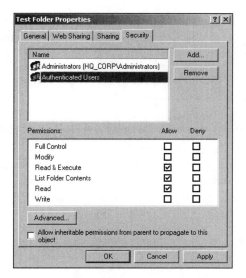

Figure 11.12   The Properties dialog box of a file or folder displays the permission settings.

a particular group has, click that group. The Permissions box now displays which permissions have been set for the highlighted group. If the checkboxes for the permissions are gray, it means that those permissions have been inherited from a parent folder or the root of the volume.

You can add or remove groups or users in the Name box. Select each user or group, then in the Permissions box, allow or deny any of the standard permissions listed by selecting the appropriate checkbox.

Note: Only administrators, users with the Full Control permission, users with the Change permission special access permission, and owners of files and folders can change permission settings.

Securing a Windows NTFS Volume

By default, a volume formatted with NTFS assigns the Full Control permission to the Everyone group for the root of the volume. Also by default, permissions in a parent folder propagate to subfolders. This means that, unless you change these default settings, every user who can access the volume will have Full Control over all the folders and files in that volume. This is obviously not desirable because it compromises the security benefits provided by NTFS.

First, remove the Everyone group from the list of permitted users for that drive and all its subfolders. Next, give the Administrators group Full Control. It is also a good idea to give System (a special user account) Full Control of folders that are used by the system account. The system account is normally used to run services on a server. If, after modifying permissions, you discover that some services are not working, it may be that you unknowingly removed some necessary permissions from the system account.

Next, you need to decide which other groups need access. As a rule, it is better to assign permissions to groups rather than individual users; this makes it much simpler to keep track of who has what permissions. If you would like to give all the users on your system read access (for example) to a folder, assign Allow Read to the Authenticated Users group. In most cases, it is more secure to use the Authenticated Users group rather than the Everyone group when assigning permissions. Authenticated Users have been granted access by the computer or a domain controller and are legitimate users. Everyone means exactly that: Everyone, regardless of how they gained access to the resource.

Note: Windows 2000 assigns permissions to the system folders (normally, the \WINNT folder and its subfolders). These permissions should not be changed. Doing so may make the operating system inoperable.

Unless applications specifically require it, do not assign Write permissions to folders with executable files in them. Normally, Read And Execute permission is sufficient. This prevents users from accidentally (or deliberately) deleting files and also prevents virus infections.

If the checkboxes for permissions are grayed out, they have been inherited from a parent folder and cannot be modified directly. To change these permissions, you can do one of the following:

➤ Modify the permissions of the parent.

➤ Choose the opposite permission. For example, check Deny if the grayed permission is Allow. This may not work in some instances, such as with the Everyone or Authenticated Users groups.

➤ Clear the Allow inheritable permissions from parent to propagate to this object checkbox.

Using Special Access Permissions

Although you will probably use standard permissions most of the time, there are times when they don't give you exactly what you require. In these cases, use the special access permissions. To assign special access permissions, open the Security tab of the Properties dialog box for the file or folder. Click the Advanced button to open the Access Control Settings dialog box (see Figure 11.13).

Next, either add or select the desired user or group and click the View/Edit button to display the Permission entry dialog box and specify to which objects

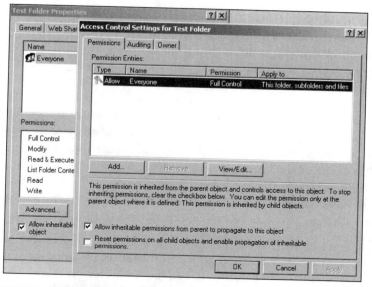

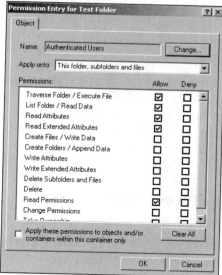

Figure 11.13   The Access Control Settings and Permission Entry dialog boxes used to assign special access permissions.

these permissions should apply (for example, the default is This Folder, Subfolders And Files). To change this setting, select an option from the Apply Onto pop-up menu. Select or clear the desired checkboxes for the desired permissions. Click OK to accept your changes.

Take Ownership Permission

The Take Ownership special access permission requires additional discussion. To understand how this permission works, consider the following. If Joe creates a file, he is the owner of that file; as such, he has the equivalent of Full Control over the file. Joe creates a file that has confidential information in it. He decides that he does not want anyone else to access his file and denies access to this file for all other users including administrators. Joe breaks a leg on a skiing trip and is away from work for several weeks. His manager urgently needs information from this file and is unable to access it. As the administrator, you can take ownership of the file and change the permissions, so that the manager can use the file. Alternatively, as the administrator, you can assign Joe's manager the Take Ownership special access permission for that file. The manager then takes ownership, changes the permissions, and reads the file.

It is important to note that the administrator or manager has to *take ownership* of the file. You can never make someone an owner or give someone else ownership of a file. It will be very clear to Joe on his return that the file now has a new owner. If, as in this case, the action was legitimate, there is no reason for concern. On the other hand, if another user had somehow managed to take ownership of the file, he or she would not be able to give that ownership back to Joe, so the breach of security would be very clear.

Why did these users need to take ownership of the file in the first place? Because they had been denied all access, they could not change the permissions. The only way to change the permissions is to take ownership of the file. By default, the administrator can always take ownership of any file or folder. But not even the administrator can explicitly change that ownership to another user; the administrator can only assign the Take Ownership permission to another user.

Which Permissions Take Precedence?

There are three rules to bear in mind when working with NTFS permissions:

➤ *Permissions are cumulative*—If a user belongs to several groups, all of which have been assigned permissions to a particular folder or file, by adding up the permissions assigned to each group, you can determine the effective permission for that user. In other words, the least restrictive permissions apply.

➤ *Deny always overrides Allow*—This is the only exception to the preceding rule. If a user has the Allow Read permission from group A, but Deny Read permission from group B, he or she will not be able to read the file. In general, try to avoid using Deny. If you do not want a user or group to access a file or folder, just remove their names from the list displayed in Figure 11.12. In particular, do not Deny access to the Everyone group. Because every user is a member of the Everyone group, no one will be able to access that file or folder, irrespective of other permissions assigned to them.

➤ *File permissions override folder permissions*—If you assign Read to a folder and Modify to a single file within that folder to a user, that user will be able to change that one file, but only view the contents of other files within that folder.

Permission Inheritance

As previously mentioned, permissions assigned to a folder are, by default, propagated to all the subfolders and files within those folders. This holds true for existing files and files that are created at a later time. It is much simpler to keep track of permissions assigned to folders rather than to files. It is also simpler to assign permissions to a few top level folders and allow the permissions to propagate. And, this is what you should aim for. But, of course, this may not be practical all the time.

To prevent a child from inheriting the permissions from a parent, do the following: Open the Security tab of the Properties dialog box for the file or folder. The Allow Inheritable Permissions From Parent To Propagate To This Object checkbox is available in two places, but each provides the same function. You can either use the checkbox on the Security tab (refer to Figure 11.12), or click the Advanced button to open the Access Control Settings dialog box (refer to Figure 11.13). Once you clear the checkbox, the folder, which is no longer inheriting from the parent, in turn becomes a parent to any subfolders and files. You will be prompted as to which permissions this new parent folder should have (see Figure 11.14).

11

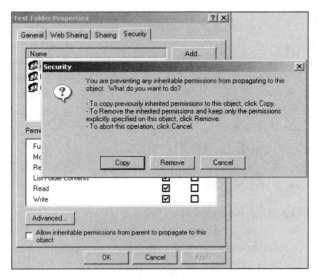

Figure 11.14   When you specify that a particular folder should no longer inherit its permissions from its parent, you must select which permissions the particular folder should get.

Note: The Access Control Settings dialog box can also be used to reset permissions on all child objects and enable propagation of inheritable permissions.

Special Access Permissions

When you set special access permissions, you have additional control over how they are inherited. In the Permission Entry dialog box (shown earlier in Figure 11.13), the Apply These Permissions To Objects And/Or Containers is cleared by default. This means that the configured permissions will be applied to all subsequent files and folders that are created. If this option is enabled, the permissions will not apply to subsequent files and folders that are created, and only apply to the files and folders that are already present.

Copying and Moving Files

What happens to permissions assigned to files when you move them or copy them? First, the destination must be NTFS. The FAT file systems do not support permissions, so your files will lose all their permissions if you move or copy them to a FAT formatted volume.

If you are moving or copying them to NTFS volumes, the rules are as follows:

➤ If a new file is created in the process, the file inherits the permissions of the target folder.

➤ If a new file is not created in the process, the file retains its original permissions.

So, when is a new file created and when not? The answer to this question is as follows:

➤ If you copy a file, a new file is always created.

➤ If you move a file within the same volume or partition, a new file is not created. NTFS just changes some pointers to the file, but does not actually write a new file to the drive.

➤ If you move a file to a different volume or partition, a new file is indeed created. In this case, the file is first copied to its new location, and then deleted from its original location.

You can think of a change in partition or volume as a change in drive letter. For example, if you move a file from drive C: to drive E:, you have moved the file to a different partition, and the file will inherit its permissions from the folder on drive E:. On the other hand, if you move a file from one folder to another folder on drive C:, the file will not take on the permissions of the target folder, but will retain its original permissions.

Combining NTFS and Share Permissions

To access a folder on another computer, the folder must first be shared. When you share a folder, you can also assign share permissions to it. Share permissions are simpler than Windows NTFS and have the following characteristics:

➤ Share permissions can only be applied to folders; there are no file permissions. This means that the permissions for files are determined entirely by the permissions configured for the shared folder.

➤ There are only three permissions that you can either Allow or Deny:

  ➤ *Change*—All Read permissions plus create and delete files as well as modify the contents of files.

  ➤ *Full Control*—Allows full control over the object.

  ➤ *Read*—View names of folders and files and their contents.

➤ If a user belongs to several groups for which share permissions have been defined, the effective share permissions for that share are cumulative. This is the same for NTFS.

When you share files that are on a Windows NTFS volume, the effective permissions that users receive are a combination of the share and the NTFS permissions. This is how it works:

➤ First, determine what the cumulative share permissions are for a particular user.

➤ Next, determine what the cumulative NTFS permissions are for the user.

➤ The effective permissions for the user will be the most restrictive of the preceding permissions.

Given this principle, it makes sense to assign Full Control to Authenticated Users for a share. You can then control the access with NTFS permissions. If you make changes to both permissions, it can be difficult to troubleshoot, as the next example shows.

The employee handbook is available in a shared folder, which resides on a Windows NTFS volume.

The NTFS permission settings are:

➤ *Administrators*—Allow Full Control

➤ *HBEditors group*—Allow Standard Read and Write permissions

11

The share permissions are:

➤ *Authenticated Users*—Allow Read

➤ *HRDept group*—Allow Change

➤ *TempStaff group*—Deny Full Control

If users, who are members of the HBEditors group, access the handbook via the share, they will get a cumulative NTFS permission of Standard Read and Write permissions. Their cumulative share permissions are Read (they are members of Authenticated User). Thus, their effective permissions for accessing the share are Read (the most restrictive).

On the other hand, users who are members of the HBEditors and HRDept groups will get a cumulative NTFS permission of Standard Read and Write permissions. Their cumulative share permissions are Read + Change. Thus, their effective permissions for accessing the share are Read + Write (the most restrictive of the available permissions).

A user who is a member of the TempStaff group will be denied access to the share (even if that user was a member of the Administrators group, too). A user working at the computer on which the folder resides and is not a member of HBEditors or Administrators will also not have access to the folder.

AUDITING WINDOWS 2000 SERVER

Windows 2000 allows you to track actions performed by users and the operating system. This tracking process is called *auditing*. The actions are called *events*. Once you have decided which events and which aspects of those events you want to audit, you configure a security policy. The audited events are then written to the security log on the computer where the events occurred. Use Event Viewer to view the security logs.

The entry in the event log contains the following information:

➤ The name of the user performing the action

➤ The event (that is the action) and when it occurred

➤ Whether the action was successful or failed

➤ Additional information, for example, the name of computer that the user was using at the time

Events That Can Be Audited

You can use auditing to monitor who is logging on to the network, which users are accessing particular files, printer usage, who has modified security settings, and so on.

The following events can be audited:

➤ *Account logon*—When a user logs on, the username and password are checked. This process is called *authentication*. If a user logs onto a local computer, the event is recorded on that computer. If a user logs onto a domain, the authenticating domain controller records the event.

➤ *Account management*—Adding, removing, and modifying user or group accounts. This includes password changes.

➤ *Directory service access*—When a user accesses an object in the Active Directory. You must also configure additional settings for the specific objects within the Active Directory.

➤ *Logon*—A user logs on or off a computer or makes or breaks a network connection to a computer. This event is recorded by the computer being accessed.

➤ *Object access*—A user accesses a file, folder, or printer. You must configure additional settings in the Properties dialog box for the particular objects you want to audit.

➤ *Policy change*—Changes made to account policies, auditing policies, and user rights.

➤ *Privilege use*—A user exercises a particular right; an administrator takes ownership of a file.

➤ *Process tracking*—An application performs an action. Normally, this is only useful to programmers.

➤ *System*—A user restarts or shuts down a computer. Also, an action that affects the security log itself.

Planning Auditing

The kind of auditing you can do falls into several categories. On one hand, you should always audit basic security events, such as logons. On the other hand, you may decide to audit very specific events to check up on a situation. You may also periodically audit some events, just to keep an eye on matters. Remember that there is not much use in having piles of event logs that you never look at.

Planning an audit policy involves considering the following:

➤ *Which computers to audit*—Actions performed on a computer are stored in that computer's security logs.

➤ *Which events to audit*—Do not audit too many types of events. Apart from the fact that this makes it difficult for you to wade through a very full log, it places an overhead on the system.

➤ *Whether you will audit success or failure*—Frequently, you monitor success when you want to count numbers; for example, to determine printer usage or the number of people accessing a file. You often monitor failure to check for attempts at unauthorized access.

➤ *Decide whether you need to track trends of system usage*—If you decide to do this, you will need to archive the security logs.

➤ *Review the security logs frequently*—Somebody may be busy trying to hack into your system, and unless you look at the logs, you will never know. Information is only recorded in the logs, so you will not be alerted.

Configuring Auditing

To audit a single computer, use the Local Security Policy. You can also configure the audit settings in a security template, and then apply the template to the local computer. To apply a policy to all the computers in a SDOU, use the Group Policy.

Note: *You must be a member of the Administrators group to configure auditing.*

To configure an audit policy for the local computer, do the following: From Administrative Tools, choose Local Security Policy. Expand Security Settings, then expand Local Policies. Click Audit Policies. Figure 11.15 shows the details pane displaying the events that can be audited and their current settings. Double-click an audit event, and then select Success or Failure or both. If you want to audit access to a resource object (for example, a file or a printer), you need to take some additional steps, which are explained in the next section.

Auditing Resources

To audit resources, such as printers as well as files and folders on NTFS volumes, you need to do the following: Enable Audit Object Access in the Security Policy. Use Windows Explorer to locate the resource. Right-click it, and choose Properties. On the Security tab, click Advanced. Select the Auditing tab. For each user, group, or computer that you add, select which operations are to be audited for success and failure as shown in Figure 11.16.

Viewing Security Logs

To view the security logs, do the following: From Administrative Tools, choose Event Viewer. In the console tree, click Security Log. You can now scroll through the log entries. If there are many entries, use the Filter and Find commands on the View menu to limit what is displayed or to search the logs.

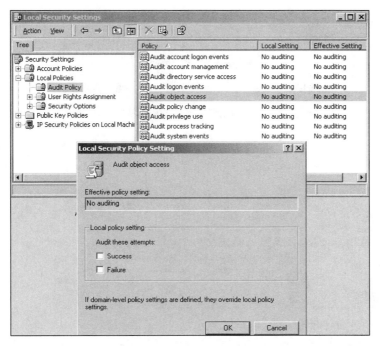

Figure 11.15   Configuring an audit policy for the local machine.

11

USING THE ENCRYPTING FILE SYSTEM (EFS)

The Encrypting File System (EFS) provides file level encryption for files on
Windows 2000 NTFS volumes. Although EFS uses public/private key
technology, it is transparent to the user as well as applications and very easy to
use. *Transparent* means that the user does not have to do anything explicit to
make the keys work. Only the original user who encrypted the file and
designated recovery agents can decrypt the file. This is true even if the
ownership of the file changes. Files remain encrypted when moved or copied
within NTFS volumes or when they are backed up.

Although you can encrypt a single file, it is usually easier to enable encryption
for a folder. This does not mean that the folder itself is encrypted. However, all
the files within that folder are automatically encrypted.

➤ To encrypt a file or folder, open the Properties dialog box for the file. On the
General tab, click Advanced, and then click Encrypt contents to secure data.

➤ You do not have to do anything special when you want to use an encrypted
file. EFS transparently locates the private key in a user certificate and uses it
to decrypt the file on the fly.

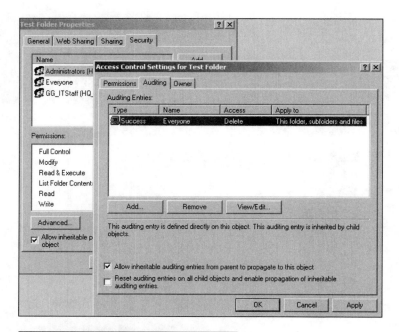

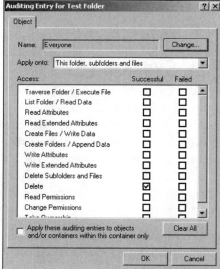

Figure 11.16   Configuring auditing for a folder.

➤ If you later want to remove the encryption, just clear the Encrypt Contents To Secure Data checkbox.

Note: EFS uses standard 56-bit encryption. North American users can obtain 128-bit encryption by ordering the Enhanced CryptoPak from Microsoft. Files using 128-bit encryption cannot be decrypted on a system using 56-bit encryption.

Recovery agents (usually an administrator) can decrypt the file if necessary. This means that there will not be any data loss due to a user no longer being available or losing his or her private key. To recover an encrypted file, send the file to the Recovery Agent's computer, which contains the agent's private key. To decrypt the file, the agent clears the Encrypt Contents To Secure Data checkbox in the file's Properties dialog box.

Important notes on encryption:

➤ Encryption and compression are mutually exclusive. This means that you cannot encrypt compressed files or compress encrypted files.

➤ You need NTFS to use encryption (and compression). If a file is copied to a partition using a different file system, the encryption will be removed.

➤ You cannot share an encrypted file. Only the owner (and the Recovery Agent) can access an encrypted file.

Cipher Command

You can also use cipher.exe if you require more EFS functionality than Explorer gives you. If you use the cipher command without parameters, it displays the status of the file or folder. The parameters are described in Table 11.7. The syntax for the command is as follows (all the parameters are optional):

```
Cipher  /e  /d  /s:foldername  /I  /f  /q /h /k  pathname
```

11

CHAPTER SUMMARY

To secure a computer and the data on it, you can use the Group Policy to configure security settings on many computers or for many users. You can also use the Local Policy to configure security settings on a single computer. You can use the System Policy to configure security settings for non–Windows 2000 client computers.

In addition, you can use the following tools to analyze security configurations: NTFS permissions to restrict access to files and folders, EFS to encrypt files on the fly, and auditing to monitor access, attempts at access, and other activities on a particular computer.

The easiest way to create and work with GPOs is via Active Directory Users And Computers. Select the Properties of the SDOU, and click the Group Policy tab. You can also load the Group Policy snap-in to the MMC.

REVIEW QUESTIONS

1. A Group Policy Object can be linked to which of the following? [Choose all that apply]

   a. A site

   b. A domain

   c. An organizational unit

   d. A security group

2. How can you improve performance when using GPOs?

   a. Use many GPOs with only a few settings configured in each.

   b. Assign the same GPO to many different organizational units.

   c. Disable Computer Configuration in a GPO that only has User Configuration settings configured.

   d. Use groups to filter the users to which the GPO applies.

3. You remove a GPO from an organizational unit that contains computers. What happens to the computer settings that were configured via the GPO?

   a. The computers retain all the GPO settings. The administrator will have to remove them.

   b. The settings for all the computers are completely cleared. Nothing will be configured on the computers.

   c. The computer settings are unaffected. The GPO has only been removed from the OU, not the computers.

   d. The GPO settings are removed from the computers. The computers will revert to settings configured manually on the computers.

4. Which of the following methods allow you to change the default inheritance for GPOs? [Choose all that apply]

   a. You can specify the Block Inheritance option for a GPO.

   b. You can specify the Block Inheritance option of an organizational unit.

   c. You can specify the Block Inheritance option for a Security Group.

   d. You can specify the No Override option for a GPO.

   e. You can specify the No Override option of an organizational unit.

   f. You can specify the No Override option of a Security Group.

   g. You can use Deny Apply Group Policy for a GPO.

   h. You can use Deny Apply Group Policy for an organizational unit.

   i. You can use Deny Apply Group Policy for a Security Group.

5. What happens when you configure the Block Inheritance option when using Group Policy?

   a. It prevents all GPOs from the parent containers applying to a particular organizational unit.

   b. It prevents a particular GPO linked to a single parent container from applying to all the child containers.

   c. It prevents all GPOs in the forest from being applied to a Security Group.

   d. It prevents a particular GPO linked to multiple parent containers from applying to all the child containers.

6. Which statement is true about Group Policies?

   a. The administrator can edit the Registry to schedule specific times when GPOs should be applied to computers and users.

   b. You can force a GPO propagation event to refresh the settings on a computer.

   c. By default, a GPO is refreshed automatically every 30 minutes on domain controller.

   d. By default, a GPO is refreshed automatically every 30 minutes on a client computer.

11

7. What is the correct order in which security policies are applied?

   a. Site policies first, then domain policies, then OU policies with the Local Security Policy last.

   b. Domain policies first, then site policies, then OU policies with the Local Security Policy last.

   c. Site policies first, then the Local Security Policy, then domain policies with OU policies last.

   d. The Local Security Policy first, then site policies, then domain policies, with OU policies last.

8. What is the correct default processing order for applying settings from Group Policy?

   a. The computer starts, and the startup scripts run. The user logs on. Logon scripts run, and the user's settings are configured. The remaining settings for the computer are configured.

   b. The computer starts, and the user logs on. Startup scripts run, then logon scripts. The settings for the computer are configured, then the settings for the user are configured.

   c. The computer starts, the computer policy is applied, and startup scripts run. The user logs on, the user policy is applied, and logon scripts run.

   d. The computer starts, and the user logs on. The settings for the computer are configured, then the settings for the user are configured. Startup scripts run, then logon scripts.

9. What is the command-line utility that can be used to configure the security settings of a computer?

   a. cipher.exe

   b. cfgsec.exe

   c. security.exe

   d. secedit.exe

10. For which one of the following can predefined security templates not be used?

   a. To bring computers that were upgraded from Windows NT 4 to the same level as cleanly installed Windows 2000 computers.

   b. To provide increased security for computers using the FAT file system.

   c. To configure Windows 2000 computers with a security level compatible with that of Windows NT 4.

   d. To configure Windows NT 4 computers with a security level compatible with that of Windows 2000.

11. An important difference between Windows 2000 Group Policy and Windows NT 4 System Policy is that:

   a. If a GPO is removed, the configuration settings specified by the GPO are also removed from the computers' Registry. System Policy changes to the Registry persist after the System Policy has been removed from the domain.

   b. Group Policy can configure settings for users and computers. System Policy can only configure settings for the user.

   c. Group policy processes the computer configuration before the user logs on. System Policy processes the computer configuration after the user has logged on.

   d. Group Policy cannot be applied to Windows NT 4 clients.

12. Select the types of permissions that you can configure on NTFS. [Choose all that apply]

   a. General Permissions

   b. Standard Permissions

   c. Specialized Permissions

   d. Special Access Permissions

13. Which security features does NTFS provide? [Choose all that apply]

    a. Encryption of data being sent across the network from one machine to another.

    b. Auditing.

    c. A file encryption mechanism that prompts the user for a password each time the file is used.

    d. A standard permission called Modify & Delete.

14. Terry works for a training company and prepares a schedule for each month. The schedule files are in a folder called Schedules. Terry does not want other users to view the file she is currently working on because the information may not be correct. However, she wants other users to be able to view the names and contents of the completed files only. Also, other users should not be able to make any changes to the files or add their own files to the Schedules folder. What permissions should you assign to the Schedules Folder? [Choose all that apply]

    a. Deny Full Control for the Everyone Group.

    b. Deny Read (special access permission) for the Domain Users group.

    c. Allow Terry Full Control.

    d. Allow Read (standard permission) for the Authenticated Users group.

    e. Allow Read and Write (standard permissions) for the Users Group.

15. Terry copies a file from the Schedule folder to another folder called Archives on the same partition. What permissions does the file have in the Archives folder?

    a. The file will inherit the permissions set for the Archives folder.

    b. The file will retain the permissions it had in the Schedule folder.

    c. The file will lose all its permissions.

    d. The file will acquire the default permissions assigned to Terry's user account.

16. Terry realizes that she would rather move old files from the Schedule folder to the Archives folder on the same partition. What permissions will the files have in the Archives folder?

    a. The file will inherit the permissions set for the Archives folder.

    b. The file will retain the permissions it had in the Schedule folder.

    c. The file will lose all its permissions.

    d. The file will acquire the default permissions assigned to Terry's user account.

11

17. You have assigned the following permissions to the AccData folder:

    ➤ Authenticated Users group: Allow Standard Read Permission

    ➤ AccDept group: Allow standard Read and Write permissions

    ➤ TempStaff group: Deny Full Control

    ➤ Administrators group: Allow Full Control

    Tom, a temporary staff member, is in the TempStaff group. What access will he have to the files the AccData folder?

    a. He will only be able to view the names of files and the contents of the files.

    b. He will have Full Control over all the files.

    c. He will have no access.

    d. He will only be able to view some files and make changes to those files.

18. You create a share for the AccData folder in Question 17, so that users can access the data via the network. You give the share the following permissions:

    ➤ Authenticated Users group: Read

    ➤ Administrators group: Full Control

    ➤ Everyone: Deny Full Control

    What permissions do you have as an administrator when you access the AccData folder via the network?

    a. You will only be able to view the names of files and the contents of the files.

    b. You will have Full Control over all the files.

    c. You will have no access.

    d. You will only be able to view some files and make changes to those files.

19. Sharon wants to find out how many users are reading the employee handbook, which is contained in a file called Handbook.doc. She opens the Properties dialog box for the file, and navigates to the Auditing tab, but finds that she is unable to configure the auditing. What is the reason for this?

    a. Only Enterprise Admins can configure auditing on a Windows 2000 server.

    b. She must restart her computer before she can configure auditing.

    c. She needs to enable Audit Object Access in the Audit Policy of the Local Security Policy.

    d. She has not configured Event Viewer to use a security log.

20. Maria wants to encrypt a file containing sensitive salary information. The technology that she will be using to do this is:

    a. EFS

    b. NTFS

    c. TCP

    d. IPSec

REAL-WORLD PROJECTS

Note: This exercise assumes you have two test servers with Windows 2000 Server. One should be configured as a domain controller, the other as a member server. Be sure to set up the Active Directory group and user accounts described in the following paragraphs to successfully complete this exercise. Read the instructions carefully, and do not perform this on any of your production machines.

Foremost Corp. is a medium-sized company that offers a range of stock market related services. They host a Web site for subscriber clients and offer an email list service to which clients can subscribe to get a daily market report. Several Windows 2000 member servers are used for IIS, Exchange, and SQL. The SQL databases contain subscriber, customer, and accounting information. In addition to the member servers, the company has two domain controllers and has implemented Active Directory. All the client workstations are running Windows 2000 Professional.

The Active Directory structure for the company is a single domain called ForemostCorp.com. The following organizational units have been created: AllComputers, which contains MemberServers and Workstations; AllUsers which contains IT, Business, Sales, and Brokers. All drives have been formatted using NTFS.

Apart from the default groups, the following security groups have been added: GG_IT, GG_Business, GG_Sales, GG_Brokers, GG_Managers, GG_Executives, and GG_TempStaff.

In addition, the following user accounts exist: Alan, Tracy, Barry, and George.

Eleanor is one of the network administrators and has just received her task list from her manager for the day. The following describe and explain the tasks she must perform.

11

Configure a security policy that will apply to all the computers in the ForemostCorp domain. For legal purposes, display a message warning unauthorized users. This message must be displayed whenever someone tries to log on.

Project 11.1
To configure a domain security policy that will apply to all the computers, follow these steps:

1. Select Start | Programs | Administrative Tools | Domain Security Policy.

2. Expand the following in the order listed: Windows Settings, Security Settings, Local Policies, and Security Options.

3. In the details pane, double-click Message Text For Users Attempting To Log On. Select the Define this policy setting checkbox. In the text box type "No unauthorized access to Foremost Corp's computers and network".

4. In the details pane, double-click Message Title For Users Attempting To Log On. Select the Define This Policy Setting checkbox. In the text box type "Foremost Corporation".

5. Select Restricted Groups (under Security settings). Right-click Restricted groups, click Add Group, then Browse. Select the Administrators group in the details pane. Click Add, click OK, and click OK again.

6. Right-click the Administrators group, click Security. Then click Add (for Members of this group) and Browse. Select the Domain Admins group. Click Add, click OK, click OK again, and click OK one last time.

Make sure that the Administrators group on all computers contains only the Domain Admins group. Every now and then others get added as a temporary measure, and we always forget to take them out. This will also restore the Domain Admins to the local Administrators group if they have been removed for some reason. Ensure that only Administrators can log on locally to the member servers.

Project 11.2
To create and configure the GPO for the MemberServers OU, follow these steps:

1. Navigate as follows: Administrative Tools | Active Directory Users And Computers, ForemostCorp.com, AllComputers, MemberServers.

2. Right-click the MemberServers OU, select Properties, click the Group Policy tab, and click New to create a GPO called Member Server Security Policy.

3. Make sure that the Member Server Security Policy is selected, and then click Edit.

4. Expand the following: Computer Configuration, Security Settings, Local Policies, and User Rights.

5. Double-click Log On Locally in the details pane.

6. Click Define These Policy Settings.

7. Click Add, Browse, and select Administrators, click Add.

8. Close Group Policy.

9. On the Group Policy tab, click Member Server Security Policy, and then click Options. Select the No Override checkbox.

10. Click OK to exit the Properties.

Project 11.3

To create and configure a GPO for the AllUsers OU that only applies to the TempStaff group, follow these steps:

1. In the console of Active Directory Users And Computers, right-click the AllUsers OU, select Properties, click the Group Policy tab, and create a GPO called Temporary Staff Policy. Create a second GPO for the AllUsers OU called All Users Admin Policy.

2. Select the Temporary Staff Policy, and then click Edit.

3. Expand the following: User Configuration, Administrative Templates, System, and Logon/Logoff.

4. In the details pane, double-click Disable Change Password. Click Enabled and OK. Close Group Policy.

5. On the Group Policy tab, select the Temporary Staff Policy, and then click Properties.

6. Select Disable computer configuration settings.

7. On the Security tab, clear the checkmark for Apply Group Policy Permission from all the listed users and groups.

8. Add the TempStaff group, and select the Allow checkboxes for Read and for Apply Group Policy Permissions. Click OK.

The Vice President thinks we should remove Control Panel for all users except those in the IT department (of course). Let's give it a try—we can always put it back later if things do not work out.

11

Project 11.4
To configure a GPO that applies to AllUsers except the ITUsers OU, follow these steps:

1. On the Group Policy tab, select the All Users Admin Policy, and then click Edit.

2. Expand the following: User Configuration, Administrative Templates, and Control Panel. Click Control Panel.

3. In the details pane, double-click Disable Control Panel. Click Enabled and OK.

4. Close Group Policy. Click OK to close AllUsers Properties.

5. In the console tree, right-click the ITUsers OU, and choose Properties. On the Group Policy tab, select the Block Inheritance checkbox, and then click OK.

6. Close Active Directory Users And Computers.

Alan (the manager for the brokers) has some spreadsheet files that he wants to share with his staff. He only wants the brokers to have access to the files. He wants complete control over the files, and his assistant, Tracy, must be able to modify the files, whereas the rest of his staff should only be able to read the files. Please set this up for him on his machine.

Project 11.5
To configure NTFS and share permissions, follow these steps:

1. From the server, use Windows Explorer to navigate to the root of a drive formatted with NTFS, for example C:.

2. Right-click C:, choose Properties, and select the Security tab.

3. Remove Everyone from the list. Add Alan's user account and allow him Full Control. Close the Properties dialog box.

4. Create a new folder on the C: drive.

5. Right-click the folder, choose Properties, and select the Security tab.

6. Add Tracy's user account and allow her Read and Write.

7. Add the GG_Brokers and allow them Read.

8. Click the Sharing tab. Share the folder with a share name of Stats.

9. Click the Permissions button.

10. Remove the Everyone Group.

11. Add the Authenticated Users and allow them Full Control.

12. Click OK as needed to close all the dialog boxes.

Barry has asked for assistance with some files that he needs to use. The files were created by George, who has left the company, and Barry cannot change the permissions on the files.

Project 11.6
To take ownership of files, follow these steps:

1. Make sure you are logged on to the domain controller using an administrator account. Use Windows Explorer to navigate to George's files.

2. Right-click the file Barry needs to use, and select Properties.

3. On the Security tab, click the Advanced button.

4. Click the Owner tab. In the list, click Administrators, and then click Apply. Notice that the new owner is the Administrators group. Click OK.

5. Add Barry and allow Full Control for the file.

11

CHAPTER TWELVE

MANAGING USERS
AND ACCOUNTS

After completing this chapter, you will be able to:

✓ Describe Windows 2000 authentication protocols and access controls

✓ Implement, configure, and troubleshoot Windows 2000 accounts

✓ Describe Active Directory concepts

✓ Implement domains and trusts

✓ Implement, configure, and troubleshoot Windows 2000 account policies

E ach user who logs onto a network should have a user account. This account verifies the user's identity to computers in the network when the user wants to access a resource (for example, a file) from another computer. Once the user's identity has been verified, the user will have access to the resource according to the permissions attached to the resource object.

This chapter explores many aspects of user and account management. We begin with an examination of the different protocols Windows 2000 can use to perform the verification process. We then step through the process of creating and configuring accounts.

We'll also provide an introduction to some Active Directory concepts and issues. In a Windows 2000 domain, accounts are created in Active Directory, and it is therefore necessary to have some understanding of how Active Directory works.

Finally, we explore account policies, which are used to control passwords, account lockouts, and Kerberos settings for the domain.

WINDOWS 2000 AUTHENTICATION AND ACCESS CONTROLS

Authentication is the process by which different parties identify each other. For example, when you want to sit for an exam, you may be asked to produce some form of photographic ID; or if an unmarked car pulls you over, you may ask the plainclothes policeman to produce his ID before presenting your own to him.

Authentication and authorization are not the same thing. *Authorization* provides access control, for example, when you are asked for your ticket before entering a cinema. If you have a valid ticket, you will be allowed in; if you do not, you will have no access to the cinema. The ticket does not provide any information regarding your identity. On the other hand, a driver's license can be used for authentication (proof of your identity) and authorization (allows you to drive the class of vehicle specified).

In computer terms, authorization describes the mechanisms to control access, for example, by using rights and NTFS permissions. Once a user has been authenticated and can access an object, the permissions or rights attached to that object determine the type and extent of access. NTFS permissions were described in Chapters 4 and 11.

Likewise, authentication describes the method used by computer systems to verify the identities of the parties involved when, for example, a user logs on to a network or if a service on one computer needs to contact another computer. The client must present some credentials to verify its identity. In some cases, the client may also require the destination computer to present credentials proving that the destination computer really is who it says it is. This is referred to as *mutual authentication*.

Windows 2000 supports two authentication protocols, which are discussed in detail in the next few sections.

➤ Kerberos version 5

➤ NTLM (NT LAN Manager)

Windows 2000 Logon and Authentication Services

How does Windows 2000 decide which authentication method it will use? Kerberos is the preferred method, which means that it is what Windows 2000 will first attempt to use. If it does not work, NTLM will be used. Table 12.1 describes how the various types of logons and authentication mechanisms are related.

Kerberos and Strong Authentication

Kerberos is a standard industry protocol, which provides a mechanism for a user and a server to identify each other or for two servers to provide mutual identification before opening a network connection between them.

Because network traffic is not secure by default, Kerberos encrypts parts of the authentication messages that pass between the two parties involved in a very particular way. This prevents a third party from viewing passwords, nabbing a message and using it to impersonate one of the original parties, or implementing many of the other ways unscrupulous people have dreamt up to obtain access to resources to which they have not officially been granted access.

12

Table 12.1   Different authentication mechanisms for Windows 2000 logons.

Authenication Mechanism	Logon Method
Kerberos	Users logging on to a Windows 2000 domain from a Windows 2000 computer using a password.
	Default for authenticating to services across the network.
Kerberos + Certificates	Users logging on to a Windows 2000 domain from a Windows 2000 computer using a smart card.
NTLM	Users logging on to a Windows 2000 domain from a non-Windows 2000 computer (that is, Windows NT, 9X, 3.11).
	Users logging on to a Windows NT 4 domain from any type of Windows computer.
	Users logging on to a Windows 2000 computer locally. This only occurs on computers running Windows 2000 Professional or on member server computers.

A shared secret, known only to the two parties involved, forms the cornerstone of Kerberos. What do we mean by a shared secret? Well, if Carl and Sue agree on a special code word and do not tell anyone else about it, they have a shared secret. If Carl sends Sue an email, he could include the secret word in his message and thus indicate that he, and not someone else sitting at his machine, sent the email. But, because such messages are sent as plain text, this is not secure.

Taking this one step further, Carl could use the code word as a password to encrypt part of the message, and only Sue could decrypt it because she is the only other person who knows the password. To prevent someone from stealing a message and replaying it later, the encrypted part of the message could include Sue's IP address and a time stamp. Part of the verification process is to ensure that a newly received message does not have a time stamp that is earlier or equal to that of the last one received. By default, Kerberos is configured to allow a maximum difference of five minutes between the clocks of the two parties. For this reason, clock synchronization within Windows 2000 domains is very important.

The password used by Sue and Carl is called a *symmetric key* because the same password is used to encrypt and decrypt information. We refer to these special passwords as *keys* because they are used to lock or unlock (encrypt or decrypt) messages. The user (the human being) does not need to know what the key actually consists of because it is often a complicated algorithm. Client software uses the key on the user's behalf.

How are these secrets, or keys, managed to provide authentication credentials? This brings us to the Key Distribution Center (KDC), an important Kerberos service, which runs on each domain controller as part of Active Directory. The KDC can obtain password and account information from Active Directory, and it also issues Kerberos tickets. Tickets are the partially encrypted messages containing identifying information.

When a user logs onto a Windows 2000 domain, authentication gets only a little more complicated than it was for Sue and Carl. Let's now consider Ulrich (the user) who wants to take a ride on the SpaceRide (a service) in a theme park (the domain). With Kerberos now guarding the gate, security is tight. Ulrich presents his password via Kerberos to the KDC. If the password is correct the KDC issues Ulrich a ticket that he can use during the rest of his visit to the park. This ticket is sometimes called a user ticket or a Ticket Granting Ticket (TGT). It contains a symmetric key, a copy of which is kept by the KDC. Once Ulrich receives his TGT, he uses his password to decode it and memorizes the key it contains. This key is known only to the KDC and Ulrich.

Ulrich now wanders around the park for and looks at what's available. He decides he wants to try the SpaceRide, so he goes to the Ticket Granting Service (TGS) booth and presents his TGT. The TGS verifies that he is Ulrich (with the key known only to them) and issues him a session ticket. The session ticket contains a specially encoded section for the SpaceRide and, in essence, provides Ulrich with a new key that only he and the SpaceRide knows. Ulrich again memorizes everything verbatim, even the bits he cannot decode. Before Ulrich can get on the SpaceRide, he must present the session ticket information to the SpaceRide.

The decoded ticket contents authenticate Ulrich to the SpaceRide. If Ulrich needs to, he can also verify that the SpaceRide is indeed the real one. Ulrich can now access the SpaceRide according to the permissions granted to him by the park administrator. If Ulrich then wants to try another ride, he must go back to the TGS, present the TGT again, and, if everything checks out, he will be issued a different session ticket. What happens if he wants a second ride on SpaceRide? Provided his first ticket has not expired, he can recall the details from memory and reuse the ticket.

In essence, this is what happens within a Windows 2000 domain, with one fundamental difference: Although a user (the human) supplies the password when logging on, all that ticket requesting business is carried out by the client software running on the Windows 2000 computer. When a ticket is issued, it is cached on the user's computer in a nonpaged part of RAM. And, luckily for the user, he or she can remain blissfully unaware and uninvolved with the authentication mechanics. In a Windows 2000 domain, a user logs onto the domain by supplying a username and password to a domain controller (DC). The KDC, which is available on all DCs, issues a TGT to the user's computer. Each time the user wants to connect to a service within the network, the user's computer requests the appropriate session ticket from the KDC.

12

The use of smart cards for logging on introduces an additional component called *certificates* to the logon process. A smart card resembles a credit card. The magnetic strip holds a certificate and the user's private key. Public and private keys always work in pairs and are mathematically generated. Public keys refer to special algorithms that anyone can use to encrypt information, but only the user with the matching private key can decrypt the information. The pair of keys are asymmetrical: One key encodes the data and the other decodes it. Public keys often go hand in hand with certificates, which are digitally signed statements that verify the identity of the user.

This brings us to the Public Key Infrastructure (PKI). The word infrastructure is self-explanatory. A key is an algorithm that encrypts and decrypts data. A public key is one of a pair and can be used by anyone to encrypt information. A certificate binds the public key to a user, computer, or service that holds the private key. Certificates can be revoked if need be. The PKI is the system of services used to issue and manage certificates and public/private keys. When a smart card (rather than a password) is used during logon, Kerberos uses certificates to authenticate the user.

Note: Smart card logons are not the only services to use certificates and public/private keys. In fact, EFS (Encrypting File System), authentication, secure communications with Web servers, email encryption, and digital signatures are just a few other services that can use the PKI.

Just as you are prompted for your PIN when using an ATM machine, you must enter a PIN when using a smart card. By entering the correct PIN, you indicate that you are really the designated owner of the smart card. Any encoded information that needs to be sent to your machine can be encrypted with your public key (available via the PKI). The matching private key (stored on the smart card) is then used to decode the message. Because your computer (with the smart card) is the only one with the matching key, no one else can decode the message. It is important to understand that the PIN is not the user's private key. The PIN is really a key to unlock the private key (similar to a lock box used by realty agents). Software on the user's machine retrieves the private key when it is needed.

Tip: Although you can use several settings within account policies to configure ticket settings, it is recommended that you have a much more detailed understanding of Kerberos before changing the default settings.

Windows NT Challenge-Response Authentication

Remember that authentication is a method to identify a user. In most cases, the user needs to supply a username and password, which have to be transmitted across the network to the appropriate authority. There are many different ways to accomplish this; for example, Kerberos uses shared secrets (symmetric keys). *Challenge-response authentication* uses a simpler method to encrypt a password.

When a user logs on with a password, the last thing anyone who is concerned about security would want is for the password to remain in clear text. A simple encryption scheme would simply encode the password the same way each time. This of course means that someone lurking with a packet sniffer could just extract the encrypted password and "replay" it without knowing the actual password.

The Challenge-Response Authentication Protocol (CHAP) ensures that the encrypted form of the password is different each time a user logs on. A simple

CHAP mechanism works as follows: Jenna logs on and types in a password at the local computer. Jenna's computer then sends a message, which in essence says, "I am looking for a computer that authenticates users" out on the network. The authenticating computer sends a randomly generated series of characters (called a challenge) to Jenna's computer. Jenna's computer encrypts both the challenge characters and Jenna's password and returns the result to the authenticating computer. The authenticating computer decrypts the information it receives and removes the challenge characters—the remaining characters form Jenna's password. The challenge is different every time, so there is no point in capturing the packet containing the password and trying to impersonate the user by replaying it. To improve security, challenge-response mechanisms may use complicated algorithms as part of the challenge.

MSCHAP is an implementation of CHAP, which is used by Windows computers when they connect via a dial-up connection to an authenticating computer.

LAN Manager Authentication

In Windows 2000, NTLM authentication is used when pre-Windows 2000 clients or servers are present in a Windows 2000 domain. When you switch a domain from mixed mode to native mode, NTLM is disabled. Recall from Table 12.1 that NTLM is also used when logging on locally to Windows 2000 member servers or Professional computers. NTLM is a less secure protocol than Kerberos when used for network authentication and would not be very efficient in very large networks for the reasons described in the following paragraphs.

12

NTLM authentication uses a Microsoft implementation of CHAP. It encrypts the password differently each time, preventing unauthorized impersonation. It also authenticates the user to the domain controller. Because this protocol was developed before the Internet was as ubiquitous as it is nowadays, it expected only valid servers to be available on the network and consequently does not provide a way to authenticate the server to the client computer. From a modern perspective, this is not ideal because we now have to deal with intranets, extranets, the Internet, and the possibility of having many unknown users accessing our networks. Kerberos, in contrast, provides for mutual authentication of client and server.

NTLM is not as efficient within larger networks, particularly if wide area network (WAN) links are involved. Each time a user accesses a server, the server must verify the user's identity with a domain controller. Only after the server has satisfactorily identified the client can the client computer establish a connection with the server. With Kerberos, the client computer obtains a session ticket that can be used repeatedly to access a particular server. The communication also occurs only between the client and the server via the session ticket. The server does not have to contact a domain controller to verify the user's identity.

UNDERSTANDING WINDOWS 2000 ACCOUNT TYPES

Logon, login, userid, logon name, username, and account are all synonyms for the same thing. In the Windows 2000 environment, we tend to use the terms user logon and account. An account allows the user to be authenticated and to be effective, should be combined with a password.

In a Windows 2000 network, there are two types of accounts: user accounts and computer accounts. User accounts, in turn, can be divided into two types as well: local accounts and domain accounts.

Note: It is important to understand that each Windows 2000 computer has a user accounts database.

Let's consider a workgroup situation first. Figure 12.1 shows a peer-to-peer network with three Windows 2000 Professional computers. Each computer has a local user account database. These databases are independent of each other and are managed by a user(s) with administrator privileges on that computer. If Patrick wants to log onto his machine as Pat, the administrator of the machine must create an account called Pat in the local accounts database of PC1. When user Pat tries to access a file, which is stored on Suzi's machine, he is denied access because there is no Pat user account in the local accounts database on PC2. Suzi (or the administrator) would need to create another account with username Pat in the local accounts database on PC2.

Within a workgroup, the following occurs:

➤ Each machine is administered locally and independently of other computers.

➤ Local user accounts can only access resources on the machine on which they were created.

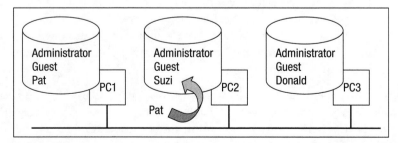

Figure 12.1   Windows 2000 Professional computers in a workgroup; each computer has an independent accounts database.

➤ Multiple user accounts need to be created if users need to access resources on computers other than their own.

In contrast to a workgroup is a Windows 2000 domain, which results when at least one Windows 2000 Server has been promoted to a DC. A DC is a Windows 2000 Server running Active Directory. The user account information is stored in the Active Directory, and all computers and users within the domain have access to Active Directory. Within a domain the following occurs:

➤ User accounts are administered centrally within Active Directory. Windows 2000 client computers can also be managed centrally.

➤ A single user account is used to access all resources within the network.

Note: Users logging on from Windows 2000 Professional or Windows NT 4 Workstation computers still have access to the local accounts database. At logon, these users can choose to log on to the local computer or into the domain. If they log onto the local computer, they will not have rights within the domain and will only have access to resources on the local computer. If they log onto the domain, they will be able to access domain resources, but may have very limited rights on their own computers.

If you are using Windows 2000 Professional or Windows NT Workstation computers within a Windows 2000 domain, you will also need to create *computer accounts* for these computers. Windows 2000 or Windows NT member servers also require computer accounts. (Note that Windows 9x machines do not require computer accounts.) Computer accounts do not require passwords because a computer does not log onto the domain, only users do. However, computer accounts provide an additional level of security. Only users working at computers with valid computer accounts can log onto the domain.

User Logon Names

It is important to have a naming convention for user accounts because names need to be unique within certain boundaries. A naming convention describes how a user logon name is allocated and what happens when duplicates result. For example, you may decide that user logon names will consist of a user's first name and the first initial of the last name. Furthermore, to avoid duplicates, all names will have a number at the end. This means that Sharon Robinson may have SharonR01 as a user logon name, whereas Sharon Riley could be SharonR02.

User logon names can have a maximum of 20 characters and may be a combination of letters of the alphabet, numbers, and other characters (including spaces). User logon names may not contain the following characters: < > [ ] / \ | , ; : "? * + =. When you create the account, you can use a mix of uppercase and lowercase characters, but the user logon name itself is not case sensitive. This means that you can type the name in all lowercase letters when you log on. User logon names need to be unique within the local accounts database. For a Windows 2000 domain, user logon names must be unique within the forest.

Passwords

All accounts should have passwords. Users often do not appreciate the importance of this requirement, thinking that the work they do is not particularly confidential. However, poor password practices put the entire network at risk. Each small break in security can become a stepping stone to other parts of the network.

Windows 2000 allows a maximum of 128 characters for a password. Educate users to use strong passwords. Passwords should not consist of the user's name or a simple word. Use a combination of lowercase and uppercase characters, some numbers, and other characters. As the administrator, you can also specify a minimum password length.

Note: Although user logon names are not case sensitive, passwords are case sensitive.

You must decide whether you, as administrator, will control passwords or whether the users will control them. In most cases, users supply their own passwords, but you may want to control the passwords for certain accounts, for example, for temporary workers. In general, it is not a good idea to allow multiple users to use a single account. Security is usually compromised if the password becomes common knowledge and there is less accountability. Even if you audit the actions of the user account, you may not know who was using the account at a certain time.

Tip: If more than one user is using a particular account, for example, the Guest account, you should ensure that users cannot change the password.

Working with Local Accounts

Local user accounts can only be created on Windows 2000 Professional or member server computers. They should only be used in a workgroup environment or if Windows 2000 Server has been installed as a standalone server. Local accounts have fewer properties than domain accounts.

To create accounts within the local accounts database for a computer, select Start | Programs | Administrative Tools | Computer Management, and then select System Tools | Local Users And Groups. Right-click the Users container, and choose New User from the pop-up menu. Figure 12.2 displays the screen presented next.

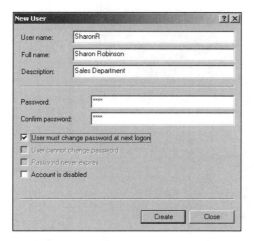

Figure 12.2   Creating a new local user account.

In the User Name field, type a user logon name, for example, SharonR. In the Full Name field, enter the user's full name, for example, Sharon Robinson. The Description field allows to you to enter additional information, for example, the department. Type in the password (which will not be displayed) twice, once in the Password field and again in the Confirm Password field. Select the password options that you want to apply to this account. Click Create to create the account.

Tip: You can create several accounts if necessary. Once you have finished, click Close.

12

Working with Domain Accounts

To create domain accounts, use Active Directory Users And Computers. Expand the domain name if necessary. As shown in Figure 12.3, you will be presented with several default *containers*: Users, Computers, and Builtin.

Note: The containers Users, Computers, and Builtin are not organizational units (OUs). They cannot contain other OUs, nor can Group Policy be applied to them. These containers are used to hold existing accounts when a Windows NT domain is upgraded to Windows 2000. Although you can create accounts within in these containers, it is not recommended, even for very small networks. Remember that networks tend to grow, so always plan for a bigger picture than the one you are currently looking at.

Instead of creating accounts in the default containers, you should create OUs. For a small network, create a single OU for the user accounts. It's very easy to move accounts to other OUs within the domain at a later stage. Larger networks may require a great deal of planning and thought when it comes to

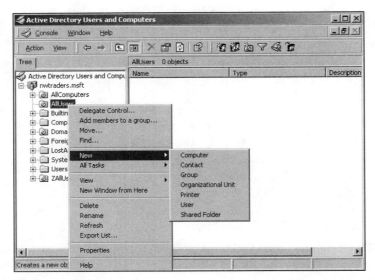

Figure 12.3 Creating domain user accounts using Active Directory Users And Computers.

creating domains and OUs. To create an OU, right-click the domain name (or an existing OU), and then choose New | Organizational Unit. Type in a name and click OK.

To create user accounts within the OU, right-click the OU, and choose New | User. Windows 2000 uses a wizard to create a domain account. The first screen just deals with the various names you need to provide for the account. The second screen allows you to set the password details. As shown in Figure 12.4, there are several additional name fields (or attributes) on the first screen; these are described in Table 12.2.

Table 12.2 Domain user account attributes.

Attribute	Description	Uniqueness Restriction
First Name, Last Name, Initials	These names are primarily used during searches. They do not have to be unique. Either the first name or last name must be specified. The initials are optional.	No restrictions.
Full Name	This defaults to the First and Last names, but can be changed. This name is displayed within Active Directory as the user's account name. It is a required entry.	The Full Name must be unique within the container (OU) in which the account is created.

(continued)

Table 12.2 Domain user account attributes *(continued)*.

Attribute	Description	Uniqueness Restriction
User Logon Name	This is the name the user uses to log on. The User Logon name together with the suffix (the domain name) is referred to as the User Principal Name (UPN). It is a required entry.	The UPN (the user logon name + the domain name) must be unique within the forest.
User Logon Name (pre-Windows 2000)	This name is used by users logging on from non-Windows 2000 computers, that is, from Windows NT or 9x computers. It is a required entry.	Pre-Windows 2000 logon names must be unique within the domain.

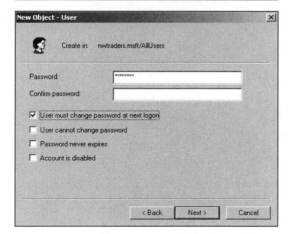

12

Figure 12.4   The first two screens presented by the wizard when creating new domain user accounts.

Once you have specified the name information, click Next. Type in the password (which will not be displayed) twice, once in the Password field, and again in the Confirm Password field. Select the password options that you want to apply to this account. In most cases, you should enable User Must Change Password At Next Logon because the first password that you give a user is not secure (for one thing, you know what it is!). Click Next to display a summary of your choices, and then click Finish to create the account.

Configuring Account Properties

Once the account has been created, you can set various options for it. Right-click the account and choose Properties. A dialog box with several tabs opens. Some of the tabs are used to specify address, telephone, and company information. The following tabs are all related to Terminal Services and Remote Access Server (RAS): Sessions, Remote Control, Terminal Services Profile, Environment, and Dial-in. But several other tabs are also important when creating user accounts.

To change settings that you selected when you created the account, select the Account tab. On this tab, as shown in Figure 12.5, you can change logon name and password settings. You can also specify a date when an account should expire. On the specified date, the account will automatically be disabled. This is very useful for temporary accounts or in academic environments, where you do not want students to use accounts after the academic year has ended.

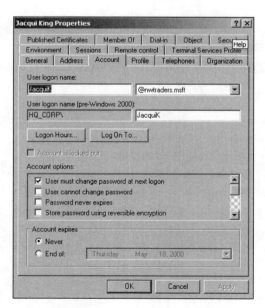

Figure 12.5 Configuring settings on the Account tab for a domain user account.

Two buttons on this tab need further discussion: Logon Hours and Log On To. The Logon Hours button is used to specify times during which a user may log onto the network. By default, users can log on 24 hours a day 7 days a week, but you may need to restrict access for certain users or in high security networks. Use the Log On To button to specify the names of computers from which users may log onto the network. Again, you may need to use this setting in high security networks or educational environments.

The Member Of tab is used to specify to which groups a user belongs. Rights and permissions should be assigned to groups rather than to an individual user because this makes the administrative load easier.

Configuring Profile and Home Folder Properties

The Profile tab is used to assign a home folder and a path for a user's profile, as displayed in Figure 12.6. A home folder is a folder, normally on a server, that has been allocated to a specific user. Each user has his or her own home folder. Users normally store documents within their home folders. There are a variety of reasons you may want to assign a home folder: Users may have insufficient disk space on their local machines; the disks on a server are backed up regularly; and users may need to access their files while logged onto different machines.

A profile consists of all the settings and configuration options that a user has selected for the desktop, for example, the startup menu or the display. The first

12

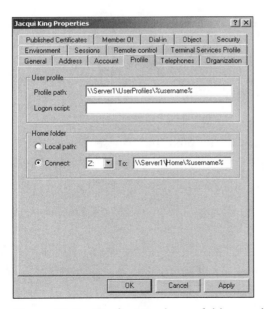

Figure 12.6   Configuring home folders and profile locations for domain user accounts.

time a user logs onto a Windows 2000 computer, Windows 2000 uses default configuration settings to create a profile for that user. Provided the user has not been restricted, he or she is able to customize a variety of settings. These changes are then saved back to the personal profile. This means that the next time a user logs onto that machine, the customized profile will be loaded, and the user would not have to reconfigure the computer again. This also means that several users could use one computer, and each could have his or her own independent settings.

If users work at different machines, they would need to configure their desired settings at each machine. To allow users to have the same profile, irrespective of which Windows 2000 computer they are working at, you could create a roaming profile. To do this, create a share (called UserProfiles, for example) on a server. On the Profile tab for the selected user account, type the following in the profile path box: "\\ServerName\UserProfiles\%username%".

Notice the use of the variable %username%. You could just use the user's account name, but using the variable provides for greater flexibility. Windows 2000 automatically replaces the variable with the user's account name. However, the benefit of using %username%, rather than actually typing the user's name, is that if you copy this account, %username% is automatically replaced with the name of the new account.

Disabling Accounts

You can disable an account if you wish to make it temporarily unavailable. You could, for example, do this if someone is going to be away for a long period of time. This is preferable to deleting the account and re-creating it later. To disable an account, right-click the account name, and choose Disable from the pop-up menu. A red cross will be included in the icon next to the account.

Copying Accounts

To copy an account, right-click the account, and choose Copy. Enter logon name and password information on the screens provided by the wizard.

The properties from the following tabs are copied to the new account:

➤ Account tab except the logon name and password information specified when copying the account.

➤ Member of tab. The new account will automatically have all the rights and permissions assigned to those groups.

➤ Profile tab (with appropriately modified entries for the paths).

➤ Address tab except Street Address.

➤ Organization tab except Title.

The following properties are *not* copied:

➤ General tab properties

➤ Telephones tab properties

➤ Dial-in tab properties

➤ All the properties on tabs relating to Terminal services: Environment, Sessions, Remote Control, and Terminal Services Profile

➤ All rights and permissions assigned explicitly to a user account

Template Accounts

A template account acts like a blueprint for new accounts. It is just a normal user account for which you have configured group membership, logon hours, and so on, but the account is never actually used by a user. You could, for example, create a template for Helpdesk staff or for students enrolled for Physics 101. Normally, you disable the template account to prevent unscrupulous users from using it.

When you need to create a new user who needs the same settings as those in the template, you simply copy the template account, specifying the settings that are unique to that user. Remember to clear the Account Is Disabled checkbox.

When you create template accounts, it is a good idea to start them with the same character or word. This groups them together, so that it is easier to find them and work with them. Some administrators start all template account names with an underscore, for example, _Sales Staff Template. This groups all the templates at the top of the displayed list in Active Directory Users And Computers. If you prefer them to be at the end, use something like Z_Sales Staff Template.

12

Working with Computer Accounts

To create computer accounts, use Active Directory Users And Computers. Expand the domain name if necessary, right-click the OU in which you wish to create the account, and choose New | Computer. Type the name that has been assigned to the computer.

Note: Computer names must be unique within the forest.

For additional security, you can also specify which user(s) or group(s) may join this computer to the domain.

If you are creating a computer account for a Windows NT computer, you must select the Allow Pre-Windows 2000 Computers To Use This Account checkbox.

TROUBLESHOOTING ACCOUNT PROBLEMS

Once users start using the accounts that you have created for them, they will inevitably run into some problems. The following list contains some of the most common problems and how to deal with them.

➤ The user cannot log on and is receiving messages that the username or password is invalid. The most common reason for this that the Caps Lock key is on. Remember that passwords are case sensitive (but logon names are not).

➤ If you have configured passwords to expire periodically, users frequently ignore the messages warning them to change their passwords. Once D-day has come and gone, their original passwords no longer work. In this case, reset the password in Active Directory Users And Computers. Normally, you would specify a very simple password and enable User Must Change Password At Next Logon. Warn the users that they will need to come up with a different password.

➤ If you have created special user accounts that are used by some services, for example, Exchange or SQL server, care must be taken when configuring the password options. Make sure that the User Must Change Password At Next Logon checkbox is clear and Password Never Expires is checked. If you fail to do so, the services that use these accounts may stop working.

➤ Accounts could be disabled if they were configured to expire on a certain date, or you forgot to clear the Disable checkbox when copying them. Look in the Active Directory Users And Computers listing to see whether the account has been disabled.

ACTIVE DIRECTORY CONCEPTS AND ISSUES

A domain in Windows 2000 groups computers, users, and other objects and forms a boundary with respect to security. More about the security issues throughout the rest of this chapter—for now, let's focus on the objects within a domain.

Among many other features, Windows 2000 has been designed for scalability. This means that it should work well even when there are many users and computers within a domain. This also means that Windows 2000 and the administrator(s) need to be able to keep track of all the objects and their properties. A good place to keep a list of the objects and their details is in a directory; for example, a telephone directory allows you to locate a name and corresponding telephone number easily.

A directory that lists objects is useful, but can we improve on this idea? With a computer we can make the directory "active"; in other words, we can provide service components that can replicate and distribute data, make the information usable, and enforce security, for example. Once we combine a directory with these service components we have a *Directory Service*. Many networking operating systems use a directory service. Active Directory is the directory service used by Windows 2000 domains.

Terms and Concepts

By introducing a Directory Service, there are a whole host of new terms and concepts, which need to be defined.

Namespace

When you want to find a phone number for a particular person, you need to select the correct directory. You could choose the directory in which numbers are listed for a particular city or an internal company telephone list. Each of these directories corresponds to a particular *namespace*. A namespace is a bounded area in which a given name can be resolved. The internal company list only contains employee information, whereas the city directory has a much larger namespace. Active Directory is primarily a namespace. It is a bounded area (which only references objects within it) and in fact, resolves the name of an object to the object itself (in very much the same way that NTFS resolves a file name to the actual file on the disk). The namespaces used by Active Directory correspond to those used for Internet domain names.

Objects and Containers

Active Directory contains objects, for example, users, computers, groups, and containers. Containers are special objects; they can contain other objects, and do not represent something tangible.

12

Distinguished Name

Every object in Active Directory has a distinguished name (DN), which describes exactly where that object is located and what its name is. The DN for Larry Ferguson in the ABCCorp.com domain would look like this:

DC=COM, DC=ABCCorp, CN=Users, CN=Larry Ferguson

where DC stands for domain component and CN for common name.

When you refer to an object, you do not always use the full DN. Instead, you make use of the relative distinguished name (RDN) of the object, in other words, just the name of the object. So Larry Ferguson is the RDN for Larry, and Users is the RDN for the container in which user Larry has been created. An RDN is that part of the DN that is an attribute of the object itself.

Domains, Domain Trees, and Forests

A domain, as mentioned earlier, forms a *security* boundary. This means that security policies and administrative rights applied in one domain do not affect another domain. A single domain, however, does not necessarily form the namespace boundary for Active Directory because Active Directory can contain more than one domain.

Although domains form security boundaries, they do not have to correspond to physical boundaries. A domain can span WAN connections, so it is possible to have multiple LANs within one domain. Conversely, it is possible to have several domains within one local area network (LAN). Each domain requires one or more DCs.

You would need multiple domains for the following:

➤ Different password policy requirements

➤ Different Internet domain names

➤ Decentralized administrative control

A *trust* is a relationship established between two domains to enables users from one domain to be authenticated by another domain and to access resources in the other domain. In Windows 2000, all trusts are two way and transitive. If a two-way trust exists between domain A and domain B, it means that domain A trusts domain B, and domain B trusts domain A. Transitive trusts mean that if domain A trusts domain B, which in turn trusts domain C, then domain A also trusts domain C (see Figure 12.7).

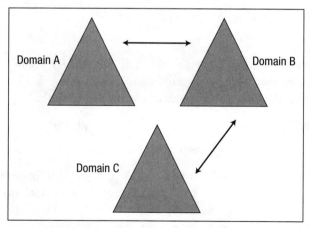

Figure 12.7 How transitive trusts work in Windows 2000.

A *domain tree* consists of a hierarchical arrangement of domains that share a contiguous namespace. Domains in a tree automatically use two-way transitive trusts.

A *forest* is group of trees that do not share a contiguous namespace. Each tree has its own namespace. The first tree created is called the root tree and forest name. The root tree contains the configuration and schema for the forest.

All the trees (and hence all the domains) in a forest have

➤ A common configuration

➤ A common schema

➤ A single Global Catalog

➤ Two-way transitive trust relationships with each other

Active Directory allows you—in fact, encourages you—to use DNS-like names for its domains. If you have registered an Internet domain name, for example, munntrade.com, you can name your single Active Directory domain munntrade.com, as displayed in Figure 12.8. The munntrade.com domain would be the forest domain. Note that there is *no* need to create one Active Directory domain called com with a child domain called munntrade.

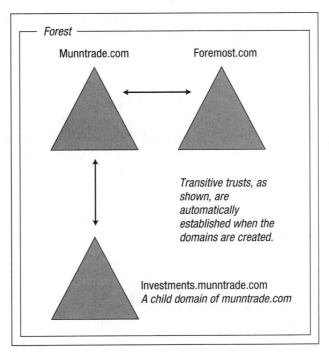

Figure 12.8   Domains and trees within a forest.

However, if your company grows or acquires a new subsidiary and you decide to place its users and computers in a subdomain of your current Active Directory domain, the new domain could be called investments.munntrade.com.

Your fast-growing company then acquires yet another business concern, which already has a registered Internet domain name of Foremost.com, and you decide that you do not wish to change it. You could create a new tree within the same forest, as in Figure 12.8. This new domain would then be the root domain for a new tree within the forest (but it will not be the forest root domain—that honor belongs to munntrade.com).

Organizational Units

Active Directory allows you to create containers within a domain. These containers are called OUs, and they can be nested if necessary. You can create user and computer accounts within an OU and apply different policies to them. In many cases, OUs may provide a good alternative to creating separate domains. Remember that you should create OUs for administrative reasons—the resulting structure does not have to match the reporting structure of the business, but it must be logical from a network administrative view point.

Active Directory Sites

A site contains one or more well-connected networks (or IP subnets). Site and domain boundaries are not related. Domains are a component of the logical structure of Active Directory, whereas sites are created as a result of the physical structure of the network. You should designate different networks to be in different sites in order to optimize logon and replication traffic across WAN links.

The Global Catalog

Each forest has one *Global Catalog*, although it may have several Global Catalog servers. The Global Catalog is used to locate objects within the forest. As an analogy, consider a large company with many branches in different cities. Each branch holds detailed records about its own employees. The company publishes a company employee directory. This directory contains only a subset of the information pertaining to each employee—just the name, position, telephone number, and office location, but it contains these details for all employees in the entire company. Similarly, a Global Catalog contains a subset of the attributes for objects within the entire Active Directory forest. The detailed information for each object, however, is held in the domain in which the object was created.

Windows Domain Types and Models

The directory database in Windows NT 4 imposed a limit on the domain size. As a result, large organizations would have needed several domains to accommodate all their users and computers. The recommended domain model was to put the user accounts in domains by themselves (called account domains) and all the computers in separate domains (called resource domains). This also allowed different administrators to be responsible for different resources.

These multidomain models required two-way trusts to be configured between all the account domains and one-way trusts to be configured between all the account domains and the resource domains. Keeping track of and managing trusts in a large organization ended up being a complex task.

In Windows 2000, Active Directory does not impose restrictions on its size and has, in fact, been designed to scale well. In many cases, it may be possible to do away with all the domains and use a single domain with appropriate OUs. However, if you need separate domain names or security policies, you will need to create more than one domain.

Managing Trust Relationships

Trusts are automatically established between:

➤ Adjacent domains within a tree, that is, between parent and child domains

➤ The forest root domain and the root domain of each tree within the forest

Because these trusts are transitive and two-way, users can log on from any domain within the forest and could access resources throughout the domain, provided they have the correct permissions. Authentication requests follow the trust paths. For example, in Figure 12.9, a user with an account in domain 3 logs on at a computer located in domain 5. The request is passed up the one tree, across to the other tree, and down that tree.

12

Explicit Trusts

Apart from the trusts described previously, which are automatically created, it is possible to manually create an explicit trust. There are two kinds of explicit trusts: shortcut and external trusts.

Shortcut trusts can be created between any two domains within the forest. A shortcut trust could be created, as shown in Figure 12.9, to shorten the authentication path. Although you explicitly need to create these shortcut trusts, they are still transitive. Note that transitive trusts only exist between domains within the same forest.

External trusts are created to domains outside of a Windows 2000 forest, and unlike the shortcut trusts, are nontransitive and one-way. To create a two-way trust, create two one-way trusts. If you wish to establish a two-way trust between two forests, you must explicitly create them. This is also true for trusts between a Windows NT domain and a Windows 2000 domain.

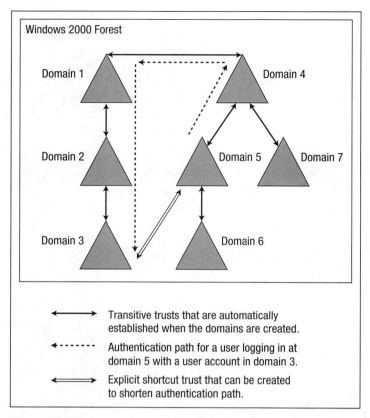

Figure 12.9 Trust paths used for authentication and creating a shortcut.

Interoperating with Windows NT Domains

Trusts can exist between Windows 2000 and Windows NT domains. These trusts are created in two ways. They are either created explicitly by the administrator or are preserved during an extended upgrade process. All trust relationships between Windows 2000 and Windows NT domains are nontransitive and one-way. A two-way trust consists of two one-way trusts.

USING ACCOUNT POLICIES

Account Policies provide additional controls for the following:

➤ Password restrictions

➤ Lockout settings

➤ Kerberos settings

Account policies are a subset of Security Policies and were described in the previous chapter. Recall that you could configure security settings either through the Local Security Policy of a particular computer or by choosing the Security subfolders, which are available in both the Computer Configuration and User Configuration folders in Group Policy.

Windows 2000 Account Policy Model

You configure a local Account Policy for each computer in a workgroup environment. In a Windows 2000 domain, use Group Policy to configure an account policy. It is important to note that, although it appears as if you can configure different Account Policies to apply to different OUs, the Account Policy settings are not processed at the OU level.

Note: Account policy settings are only processed at the domain level.

The fact that you can only configure Account Policies at the domain level must be taken into consideration when planning your Active Directory structure. If you, for example, require different password settings for different users, you may need to have different domains. Alternatively, some creative use of policy override and inheritance settings could solve the problem too. Also, remember that Group Policy can be configured to apply to security groups (and users).

Implementing Account Policies

To implement Account Policies, configure security settings either through the Local Security Policy of a particular computer or by choosing the Security subfolder, which is available in the Computer Configuration folder in Group Policy as shown in Figure 12.10.

12

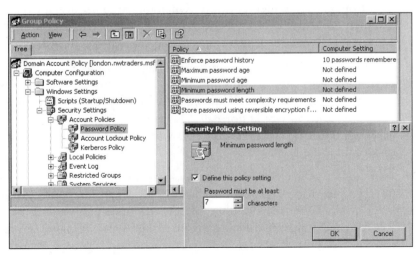

Figure 12.10   Configuring Account Policies for a domain.

Configuring Account Policies

There are three subpolicies under Account Policies you can configure:
Password, Account Lockout, and Kerberos.

Password Policies

The following restrictions can be imposed upon passwords:

➤ *Minimum password length*—The minimum number of characters that a
password must contain. By default, Windows 2000 allows blank passwords,
so this should always be changed. Passwords should normally be at least six
characters long. The longer the password, the more difficult it is to crack.
Remember that this is the minimum length, so users can use longer
passwords if they wish.

➤ *Maximum password age*—The maximum number of days that a user may use
the same password. You can specify any value from 0 through 999. In high
security networks, you may wish to use a value as low as 30 days; if security
is less important, the values of 90 through 180 days (3 through 6 months)
may be good values. Users will be warned that their passwords are about to
expire. However, they often ignore these messages, so you need to ensure
that they are educated about strong passwords and that they must change
them periodically. A value of zero specifies that passwords do not expire. In
general, leaving zero as a value is not a good idea because passwords do
become compromised over time. By forcing regular changes to the
passwords, the network's security is improved.

➤ *Minimum password age*—The minimum number of days that a user must keep
a password before they can change it. You may wish to use this to prevent
users from changing their password (when forced to because it has expired),
and then immediately changing it back to the original one. However, you can
prevent this by enforcing a password history as discussed next.

➤ *Enforce password history*—The number of passwords the system remembers,
preventing users from reusing the same password immediately or repeatedly
using two or three favorite passwords. If you have configured a Maximum
Password Age, you would normally also configure a value to enforce the
password history. If set to zero, the password history is not enforced. The
maximum value is 24.

➤ *Passwords must meet complexity requirements*—If you have installed a password
filter, you can force passwords to meet the filter's requirements. For example,
Windows NT 4's password filter (passfilt.dll) forces passwords to be at least
six characters long; prevents users from using their own name or logon
name as a password; and forces a strong password using a combination of
mixed case, symbols, and numbers.

➤ *Store password using reversible encryption for all users in the domain*—Stored passwords are normally encrypted. If reversible encryption is enabled, passwords can be recovered in an emergency. However, remember that if a user forgets his or her password, the administrator can just reset it—this is not an emergency!

Account Lockout Policies

The following settings can be configured for lockouts:

➤ *Account lockout threshold*—The number of logon attempts that a user can make using the wrong password. This is a mechanism used to thwart hackers. You can use any value from 0 through 999. A value of zero (the default) specifies no lockout. Do not make the value too low as users do forget passwords or make mistakes while entering passwords. Values ranging from 6 through 15 are frequently used.

➤ *Account lockout duration*—The duration for which the locked out account will remain locked out. If a value of zero is specified, the account remains locked out until unlocked by an administrator. To unlock an account, open the Properties dialog box for the user in Active Directory Users And Computers. Click the Account tab and clear the Account Is Locked Out checkbox.

➤ *Reset account lockout threshold after*—The number of minutes for which the lockout threshold is maintained after the last bad logon. An example will better illustrate this setting: Let's say that the Account Lockout Threshold has been set to 6, and the Reset Account Lockout Threshold after has been set to 10 minutes. Jane attempts to log on with an old password and fails. She makes four unsuccessful attempts at logging on, and then stops to answer the phone. The lockout "timer" then starts its countdown from 10 minutes. If Jane returns to her computer before the 10 minutes are up, she will only have two more attempts at logging on before her account is locked out. On the other hand, if Jane returns after the 10 minutes have elapsed, the lockout threshold will have been reset back to 6. The lockout threshold is also reset if the logon is successful.

12

Kerberos Policies

Kerberos version 5 is the primary authentication mechanism used by Windows 2000 in an Active Directory domain. As described earlier, Kerberos uses tickets to verify the identity of users and network services. Although several configuration settings are provided under the Kerberos Policies section, only administrators who have a comprehensive understanding of Kerberos should make modifications to these settings. Fortunately the default settings work just fine in most cases, as a detailed discussion of these settings is beyond the scope of this book.

Managing Account Policies

Managing account policies for a domain is relatively straightforward because you can frequently configure a single policy for the entire domain.

If you have created only a single account policy, it is a good idea to configure it with the No Override option, as discussed in Chapter 11. Because Account Policies are only applied at the domain level, you cannot configure these settings at the OU level. If you have not selected the No Override option, it is possible to Block the Inheritance at the OU level. If there is no other Account Policy, a situation may result, for example, where users have no restrictions imposed with respect to their passwords.

If you want user accounts in some OUs to have stricter password settings than users in other OUs, you can create two Account Policies, for example, Strict Account Policy and Not So Strict Account Policy. Configure Strict Account Policy with No Override—this one will be applied to all users and must be applied first. Configure Not So Strict Account Policy, and enable Block the Inheritance for those OUs to which you do not want it to apply. This policy is applied second, overwriting all the settings applied by the Strict Policy, but only for those OUs that are not blocking inheritance. Make sure that the Account Policies are listed in the correct order on the Group Policy tab for the domain.

Troubleshooting Account Policies

The following list describes some problems that may occur with Account Policies.

➤ Domain Account Policies always override the settings for a policy that has been configured locally for a Windows 2000 Professional or member server computer.

➤ Account Policies are only applied at the domain level, even though Windows 2000 allows you to configure these settings in a policy applied at an OU level. However, Account Policies applied at the OU level are ignored.

➤ Recall from Chapter 11 that when you block inheritance for sites, domains, and organizational units (SDOUs), you have blocked *all* policies applied to parent containers. To prevent the block from applying to an Account Policy, select the No Override checkbox for the policy.

CHAPTER SUMMARY

Authentication is the process by which servers and users verify each other's identities. Windows 2000 supports the following authentication protocols for users logging on to local computers or into the network: Kerberos version 5, Kerberos plus certificates, and NTLM.

Authorization, on the other hand, controls the access that users have to resources within the network. In Windows 2000 this is achieved by means of NTFS and assigning rights to users through security policies.

Windows 2000 uses computer accounts for all Windows 2000 and Windows NT computers. This prevents unauthorized computers from participating in the domain. Two types of user accounts exist on Windows 2000 computers: local user accounts and domain user accounts.

Active Directory is the directory service used by Windows 2000 domains. To implement Active Directory, at least one Windows 2000 server must be promoted to a DC.

Active Directory uses a hierarchical tree structure, which contains objects and all the attributes (properties) for each object. Some of the object and components are described in the following list.

➤ A *domain* is a security boundary, which means that security policies and administrative rights applied within one domain do not apply in another domain. Each domain has its own password policies.

➤ A *trust* is a relationship between two domains that enables users from one domain to access resources in another domain. In Windows 2000 all trusts are two-way and transitive and are automatically established between two adjacent domains.

➤ A *domain tree* contains domains that share a contiguous namespace.

➤ A *forest* can contain more than one domain tree. Each tree in a forest uses its own namespace, that is, the namespaces of the all the trees are not contiguous. All domains in a forest share a common schema, configuration, and Global Catalog. Each forest has a single forest root domain, which is the first domain that is installed in the forest.

➤ *OUs* are containers within a domain and are used for administrative purposes to group objects. OUs can be nested, forming a tree structure within a domain.

Account Policies are only processed at the domain level. You can configure more than one Account Policy for a domain, but take care when assigning the order. The last policy applied can override settings configured in an earlier applied policy. You can configure the following settings in an Account Policy: password policies, account lockout policies, and Kerberos policies.

12

REVIEW QUESTIONS

1. What is the preferred authentication protocol for Windows 2000 computers in a Windows 2000 domain?

   a. NTLM

   b. MSCHAP

   c. Kerberos

   d. Certificates

2. When would NTLM authentication be used? [Choose all that apply]

   a. A user logging onto a Windows NT 4 domain from a Windows 2000 computer.

   b. A user logging on locally to a Windows 2000 member server computer.

   c. A user logging onto a Windows 2000 domain from a Windows 2000 Professional computer.

   d. A user logging onto a Windows 2000 domain from a Windows 98 computer.

3. When a user logs onto a Windows 2000 domain with a password, what does Kerberos use to encrypt authentication information?

   a. Public keys

   b. EFS

   c. Certificates

   d. A symmetric secret key

4. What does Kerberos use to authenticate servers and users to each other?

   a. Private coupons

   b. Access tokens

   c. Session tickets

   d. Smart cards

5. To make Windows 2000 use Active Directory, you must:

   a. Install the Active Directory service on a domain controller using Active Directory Domains and Sites.

   b. Promote at least one Windows 2000 server to a domain controller.

    c. Select the Enable Active Directory checkbox in Active Directory Users And Computers.

    d. Make sure that all the computers in the network are using Windows 2000.

6. Which features are provided by Active Directory? [Choose all that apply]

    a. A single user logon can be used to access all resources in the network.

    b. User accounts must be configured on every Windows 2000 computer that users want to access.

    c. Users do not *need* to supply a password at logon because Active Directory keeps track of encryption keys. Passwords are configured to provide an additional level of security.

    d. Windows 2000 can authenticate users who are using smart cards.

7. There are two types of user accounts that can be used with Windows 2000 computers: local and domain user accounts. Which statements are correct about local user accounts? [Choose all that apply]

    a. Local user accounts can be created in Active Directory.

    b. Local user accounts can be used to access resources throughout the network.

    c. Local user accounts can only access resources on the machine on which they were created.

    d. You can use one of the System Tools in Computer Management to create local user accounts.

    e. When you use a local user account to log onto a computer, the Kerberos protocol is used for authentication.

8. When you create accounts within Active Directory, you should do which of the following?

    a. Create all the user accounts in the container called Users.

    b. Create organizational units to hold accounts.

    c. Make the logon names very complicated to prevent hackers from gaining unauthorized access.

    d. Use Active Directory Sites And Services to create user accounts.

12

9. You are about to create the following three new user accounts in Active Directory. All the accounts will be created in the Sales OU and use MunnTrade.com as the suffix. You have written down the details for each account as follows:

	First account	Second account	Third account
First Name	Sally	Sally	SalesTemp
Initials	H		
Last Name	Jellybean	Jellybean	
Full Name	Sally Jellybean	Sally Jellybean	SalesTemp
User logon name	SallyJ	SallyJ1	SalesTemp
Pre-windows logon name	SallyJ	SallyJ1	SalesTemp1

[Choose all that apply]

a. You will not be able to create the second account because you must specify a value for the initials.

b. You will be able to create the third account because you need to specify either a First Name or a Last Name.

c. You will not be able to create the second account because the Full Name must be unique within the Sales OU.

d. You will not be able to create the third account because the User logon name and pre-Windows logon name must be the same name.

10. You are creating user accounts. How can you configure the settings for the accounts?

a. Use the Log On To button on the Account tab to specify which hours users may log onto the network.

b. Use the Group Members tab to assign the user account to a group.

c. Use the Profile tab to configure a home folder location for the user.

d. You can disable an account when you create it. You can then configure an expiry date on which the account will automatically become enabled.

11. You would create a roaming profile when:

a. You want to configure the same profile for all the users who work on one computer.

b. You want to configure independent profiles for different users who all work on the same computer.

c. Users who use a portable computer to log onto the network need roaming profiles.

d. You want users to receive the same profile, irrespective of the computer from which they log on.

12. When you copy an existing user account, some settings are not copied to the new account. Choose all the settings that are *not* copied to the new account.

    a. Dial-in settings

    b. All the settings on the tabs related to Terminal services

    c. The settings on the Profile tab

    d. Group membership

13. You are creating a template account that you want to use in the future to create new users for the Marketing Department. You want to configure as many settings as possible, so that when you copy the template account to create a new user, you'll need to supply or modify as few as possible. What could you do to make the template efficient to use?

    a. Make sure the account is disabled.

    b. Configure a complicated password because this password will be used for all new accounts created using the template account.

    c. Use the variable %username% when configuring home folders.

    d. Do not enter a password for the template account because you will then be prompted to enter a new password when you use it to create a new account.

14. Choose the one correct statement for Computer accounts.

    a. Computer account names must be unique within the forest.

    b. Computer accounts are needed for all computers that join the domain.

    c. Computer accounts are only needed for Windows 2000 server computers.

    d. To create computer accounts, you use Active Directory Domains And Trusts.

15. What is Active Directory?

    a. A tree-like structure, representing the physical cabling of your network

    b. A replacement for Internet domain names

    c. A DNS name

    d. The directory service used by Windows 2000 domains

16. What is a distinguished name, as used in Active Directory?

    a. A distinguished name identifies important Windows 2000 servers with specialized roles, like a Global Catalog server, to Active Directory.

    b. Every object in Active Directory has a distinguished name, which describes exactly where that object is located and what its name is.

c. Only special objects, such as servers and administrator accounts, have a distinguished name for improved security. This name can only be used by Windows 2000 administrators.

d. A distinguished name is a hidden name that is only used by Active Directory during replication between domain controllers.

17. Which statement is not true about trees and forests?

a. Each tree forms a contiguous namespace, but the namespaces for all the trees within a forest are not contiguous.

b. A two-way transitive trust is automatically created between the roots of two trees in a forest.

c. All trees in a forest share a common schema.

d. There is one Global Catalog per forest.

18. Your expert services have been requested in designing the Active Directory structure for a company. Which one of the following do you *not* need to consider?

a. You may need to use more than one domain if a large company has divisions that have registered different Internet domain names.

b. In a forest containing more than one domain tree, you can configure shortcut trusts to shorten authentication paths.

c. The physical network infrastructure will affect how many domains you need to configure. Each network separated by a WAN link will require a separate domain.

d. Placing user accounts in OUs makes it easier to manage them. You can easily move accounts to a different OU within the domain.

19. Which (one) statement is true about account lockout settings?

a. The administrator can lock out an account at any time.

b. To unlock an account, the administrator can use Active Directory Users And Computers.

c. If the Account lockout duration setting is set to 10, it means the user has 10 minutes from first attempting to log on to enter the correct password. If the user has not supplied the correct password within 10 minutes, he or she will be locked out.

d. If the Account Lockout threshold has a value of zero, it means that the account will remain locked out until reset by the administrator.

20. You are designing an Active Directory structure for a company with 150 employees. It has been decided that, except for employees in Research and Development (R&D), all users must use a password of at least six characters and must be forced to change it every three months. The CEO has insisted that all the R&D users must use passwords that are at least 10 characters long and expire every month. How can you configure your Active Directory structure to accommodate this demand and also make it efficient to administer?

    a. Create two forests, each containing one domain. Place the R&D users in the one domain and the remaining users in the second domain. Configure and apply separate Account Policies for each forest. Because two-way transitive trusts are automatically created between two Windows 2000 forests, you do not have to configure any trusts.

    b. Create one domain, create OUs for each department, and place the users in appropriate OUs. Create two account policies called All Users Account Policy and RD Account Policy, respectively. Configure the RD Account Policy with the appropriate password settings. Configure the Users Account Policy with the appropriate password settings. Apply the RD Account Policy to the R&D OU only. Apply the All Users Account Policy to all the other OUs.

    c. Create one forest with two domain trees. Place the R&D users in a single domain in one tree. For each of the remaining departments, create separate domains in the second tree, and place the remaining users in the appropriate domains. Create two Account Policies called All Users Account Policy and RD Account Policy, respectively. Configure the RD Account Policy with the appropriate password settings. Configure the Users Account Policy with the appropriate password settings. Apply the RD Account Policy to the domain tree containing the R&D users. Apply the All Users Account Policy to the other domain tree. Create an explicit two-way trust between the two trees, so that you can easily administer both trees.

    d. Create one domain, create OUs for each department, and place the users in appropriate OUs. At the domain level, create and apply two Account Policies called All Users Account Policy and RD Account Policy, respectively. Make sure that the RD Account Policy is applied before the All Users Account Policy. Configure the RD Account Policy with the appropriate password settings and ensure No Override is enabled. Configure the Users Account Policy with the appropriate password settings and ensure that the No Override checkbox is cleared. For the R&D OU, ensure Block Inheritance is checked.

12

REAL-WORLD PROJECTS

Note: This exercise assumes you have one test server with Windows 2000 Server configured as a domain controller and a Windows 2000 Professional computer. Read the instructions carefully, and do not perform these projects on any of your production machines. The names used in these exercises are examples; use the names of your test servers in the place of specific references in the steps that follow.

Munn Trading Corporation is a small import/export company that has recently upgraded its network to Windows 2000. A legacy accounting and inventory system has been replaced by a SQL server database and a Visual Basic application. The company has two DCs and has implemented Active Directory for security reasons. Because there are currently only about 50 employees, SQL server has been installed on the one DC. All the client workstations are running Windows 2000 Professional. The servers are called Munn1 and Munn2.

Lee is a one-man IT department and has installed the DCs using a single domain called MunnTrading.com. Although this is a small company, Lee is preparing for expansion and has created two OUs called AllComputers and AllStaff. The owner of the business has asked him to implement certain restrictions on some accounts. Today, Lee is preparing to create user and computer accounts for the staff. He also wants to configure an Account Policy. He has made a list of his activities for the day.

➤ Decide on a naming convention and assign logon names to all users.

➤ Create a new "working" administrator account with a strong password. Rename the Administrator account (to improve security) and give it a strong password. Store the details for the renamed account in the company safe.

➤ Create a normal user account for the administrator. This account will be used by the administrator when doing non–network–related activities, like working with email, writing up reports, and so on.

➤ Create the following security global groups: GGSales, GGWarehouse, GGAdmin, GGManagers, and GGTemps.

➤ Create template accounts for Sales, Warehouse, Admin, and Temporary staff as follows. All documents created by users are to be stored on a server, so that they can be backed up regularly. Temporary staff may only log on during working hours. The Warehouse staff tend to used different computers placed at strategic locations in the warehouse, so they need roaming profiles. Put the home and profile folders on Munn1, as SQL Server has been installed on Munn2. Table 12.3 summarizes this information.

Table 12.3   Details for template accounts.

Template	Groups	Home Folder	Profile Location
Sales	GGSales	\\Munn1\Home\%username%	
Warehouse	GGWarehouse	\\Munn1\Home\%username%	\\Munn1\Profiles\%username%
Admin	GGAdmin	\\Munn1\Home\%username%	
Temporary	GGAdmin GGTemps	\\Munn1\Home\%username%	

Note: Logon hours for Temporary are Monday – Friday, 7:00 A.M. – 7:00 P.M.

➤ Modify the Default Domain Group Policy to include the following Account Policy specifications:

> ➤ Minimum password length: 6 characters
>
> ➤ Maximum password age: 120 days
>
> ➤ Enforce password history: 10 passwords to be remembered
>
> ➤ Account lockout threshold: 8 attempts
>
> ➤ Account lockout duration: indefinite—must be reset by administrator
>
> ➤ Reset account lockout threshold after: 1 hour

Project 12.1

To prepare a naming convention and assign logon names, perform the following steps:

1. Because this is a small company, Lee decides that logon names will consist of the first name and the first initial of the last name. If a duplicate name results, subsequent names will use an additional letter from the last name. For example, Joe Smith will have JoeS as his logon name, and Joe Summers will use JoeSu.

2. Lee decides to rename the current administrator account to Godzilla and gives it the following password: MdG;jsVBc++ .

3. His own working administrator account will be called LeeAdmin with the password BtDtGtts; (this is not as bad as it looks—the letters stand for Been There, Done That, Got The Tee Shirt). Note that the semicolon (;) is part of the password. He will create the account in the Users container because he does not want any policies that he may apply to the AllUsers OU to apply to this account.

4. His normal user account for day-to-day work will be LeeA, and he decides to use a password of Space3Mate. Because this is an account just like all the other staff members will have, it will be created in the AllUsers OU.

12

Project 12.2

To create the "working" administrator account, perform the following steps:

1. Log onto one of the DCs using the default Administrator account. Open Active Directory Users And Computers and expand MunnTrade.com. Right-click the Users container, and choose New | User.

2. Enter the following information on the first screen presented by the wizard.

    First Name: Lee

    Last Name: Admin

    Full Name: Lee Admin

    User Logon Name: LeeAdmin@MunnTrade.com

    User Logon Name (pre-Windows 2000): LeeAdmin

3. On the second screen, type the password "BtDtGtts;" twice, and make sure the User Must Change Password At Next Logon checkbox is cleared. Click Next, and then click Finish.

4. Right-click the account for LeeAdmin, select Properties, and then click the Member Of tab. Click Add, select the Domain Admins group, click Add, and then click OK.

5. Click OK to close the properties for LeeAdmin.

6. If necessary, scroll up to the Administrator account. Right-click the Administrator account, and click Reset Password.

7. Type the new password "MdG;jsVBc++" twice and make sure that the User Must Change Password At Next Logon checkbox is cleared.

8. Right-click the Administrator account, and click Rename. Type "Godzilla" and press Enter. In the dialog box presented, type the following information: User Logon Name: "Godzilla"; User Logon Name (pre-Windows 2000): "Godzilla", making sure the Munntrade.com domain is selected. Click OK.

Project 12.3

To test the new Admin account and create the normal user account for the administrator, perform the following steps:

1. Check that the LeeAdmin account works by logging off and logging on with the LeeAdmin account.

2. Open Active Directory Users And Computers and expand MunnTrade.com.

3. Right-click the AllUsers OU, and choose New | User.

4. Enter the following information on the first screen presented by the wizard.

First Name: Lee

Last Name: Andrews

Full Name: Lee Andrews

User Logon Name: LeeA@MunnTrade.com

User Logon Name (pre-Windows 2000): LeeA

5. On the second screen, type the password "Space3Mate" twice, and leave the checkbox for User Must Change Password At Next Logon cleared. Click Next, and then click Finish.

6. You will not be able to test this new account while working at the DC because normal users do not have the right to log on locally at a DC (by default). You need to go to one of the Windows 2000 Professional computers and test the account.

While logged on as LeeA, Lee loads a list of all the current employees into his spreadsheet program and assigns logon names to all the users. There are only two duplicates, and they are easily dealt with in terms of the naming convention. He prints out the list, so that he can refer to it later when he creates the accounts.

Because the new administrator account is now functional, Lee writes the details for the original administrator's account on a piece of paper, places it in an envelope, and asks the owner of the company to put the sealed envelope in the company safe.

Project 12.4
To create global security groups, perform the following steps:

1. At one of the DCs, log on using the LeeAdmin account.

2. Open Active Directory Users And Computers and expand MunnTrade.com.

3. Right-click the AllUsersOU, and choose New | Group.

4. For Group Name, type "GGSales", and then make sure Global and Security are selected. Click OK.

5. Repeat step 4 for the other groups: GGWarehouse, GGAdmin, GGManagers, and GGTemps.

12

Project 12.5
To create a share for the home folders and profiles, perform the following steps:

1. Make sure you are logged onto Munn1 with the LeeAdmin account.

2. Open Explorer and create a folder on an NTFS volume with sufficient space. Call the folder Home Folders. Leave the default permissions or assign Allow Full Control NTFS permissions to Authenticated Users.

3. Right-click Home Folders, and click Sharing. Type "Home" for the share name; click Permissions, remove the Everyone group, and give Authenticated Users Full Control.

4. Repeat the previous steps for the Profiles folder.

Project 12.6
To create template accounts, perform the following steps:

1. Make sure you are logged onto one of the domain controllers with the LeeAdmin account.

2. If necessary, Open Active Directory Users And Computers and expand MunnTrade.com.

3. Right-click the AllUsersOU, and choose New | User.

4. Enter the following information on the first screen presented by the wizard.

   First Name: Z_Sales

   Last Name: Template

   Full Name: Z_Sales Template

   User Logon Name: Z_SalesT@MunnTrade.com

   User Logon Name (pre-Windows 2000): Z_SalesT

5. On the second screen, type a strong password twice, and select the Account Disabled checkbox. Click Next, and then click Finish. Note the red cross.

6. Right-click the Z_Sales Template account, click Properties, and then click the Profile tab.

7. Click Connect, accept the Z: drive, and type "\\Munn1\Home\%username%" in the box for the Home Folder.

8. Because all the template accounts need to have the Home Folder entry, it is quicker to create the remaining template accounts by copying the Z_Sales Template account than is to repeat steps 3 through 7 for each new template.

9. For each of the remaining template accounts (Warehouse, Admin, and Temps), do the following: right-click Z_Sales Template, and choose Copy. Enter the appropriate information for the various names and for the password. Ensure that the account is disabled.

Project 12.7
To configure the template accounts, perform the following steps:

1. If necessary, Open Active Directory Users And Computers and expand MunnTrade.com and the AllUsers OU.

2. Right-click the Z_Sales Template, and choose Properties. On the General tab, type "Sales Department" for a Description. Click the Member Of tab. Click Add, select the GGSales group, and click Add. No other configurations are currently needed, so click OK to close the Properties dialog box.

3. Right-click the Z_Admin Template, and choose Properties. On the General tab, type "Administration Department" for a Description. Click the Member Of tab. Click Add, select the GGAdmin group, and click Add. No other configurations are currently needed, so click OK to close the Properties dialog box.

4. Right-click the Z_Warehouse Template, and choose Properties. On the General tab, type "Warehouse Department" for a Description. Click the Member Of tab. Click Add, select the GGWarehouse group, and click Add. Select the Profile tab, and for the Profile Path type "\\Munn1\ Profiles\%username%". No other configurations are currently needed, so click OK to close the Properties dialog box.

5. Right-click the Z_Temps Template, and choose Properties. On the General tab, for Description type "Temps" for Administration Department. Click the Member Of tab. Click Add, select the GGAdmin and GGTemps groups, and click Add. Select the Account tab, and click the Logon Hours Button. These users may only log on between 7:00 A.M. and 7:00 P.M., so drag the mouse over the times when they are not allowed to log on, and click Logon Denied. No other configurations are currently needed, so click OK to close the Properties dialog box.

Project 12.8
To create user accounts, perform the following steps:

1. If necessary, Open Active Directory Users And Computers and expand MunnTrade.com and the AllUsers OU.

12

2. Create an account for Neil Smith in the Warehouse department as follows: Right-click the Z_Warehouse Template account, and choose Copy. Enter Neil's information on the first screen presented by the wizard. Click Next, and enter a password for Neil. Clear the Account Is Disabled checkbox, and check the User Must Change Password At Next Logon checkbox. Click Next, and click Finish.

Lee repeats step 2 for each name on his list of employees that he printed out earlier.

Project 12.9
To create an Account Policy, perform the following steps:

1. If necessary, Open Active Directory Users And Computers and expand MunnTrade.com.

2. Right-click the name of the domain (MunnTrade.com), select Properties, and then click the Group Policy tab. Click New, type "Munn Trading Account Policy", and press Enter.

3. Make sure Munn Trading Account Policy is selected, and click Edit. Navigate to Computer Configuration | Windows Settings | Security Settings | Account Policies | Password Policy.

4. Double-click the following options listed, and for each, select Define This Policy Setting And Configure with the values shown.

   ➤ Minimum password length: 6 characters

   ➤ Maximum password age: 120 days

   ➤ Enforce password history: 10 passwords remembered

5. Click Account Lockout Policy in the tree pane, and configure the following options in the details pane.

   ➤ Account lockout threshold: 8 invalid attempts

   ➤ Account lockout duration: 0 minutes

   ➤ Reset account lockout threshold after: 30 minutes

6. Close the Group Policy window. To make the policy more efficient, disable the User Configuration portion of the policy. Make sure that the Munn Trading Account Policy is selected, and then click Properties. On the General tab, select the Disable User Configuration settings. Click OK to close the properties dialog box. Click Close.

7. At a Windows 2000 Professional computer, log on with your LeeA account, and test the password policy options that you have set.

CHAPTER THIRTEEN

AUTOMATING ADMINISTRATIVE TASKS

After completing this chapter, you will be able to:

✓ Understand why an operating system needs task automation

✓ Configure and schedule tasks using the Windows 2000 Task Scheduler

✓ Explain the historical development of the Scheduler service

✓ Explain the historical development of Windows Script Host

✓ Use Windows Script Host with different scripting engines

✓ Explain the proper techniques for using logon scripts in an Active Directory environment

✓ Understand the difference between MS-DOS batch files and scripts

✓ Detail the advantages and disadvantages of using batch files versus scripts

✓ Test and troubleshoot scripts using the Microsoft Script Debugger

This chapter discusses the Windows 2000 task automation features that are used to schedule and automate administrative tasks. We will take a brief look at how task automation was handled in previous versions of Windows NT and show how this facility has been improved in Windows 2000.

Next, we'll explore the Windows Script Host (WSH), a facility that allows the administrator to create scripts in the Windows environment. Then we'll explain how scripting can be used to control various system functions and compare the use of scripts versus batch files in user logon scripts.

Before we launch into a discussion of Task Scheduler—the tool used to schedule system tasks—we will explain this tool's significance. Once you understand the importance of this tool, we'll explore its use in the Windows 2000 environment.

WINDOWS 2000 AND TASK AUTOMATION

Windows 2000 has several new features that support the automation of administrative tasks. Included in these features is Task Scheduler, which is a much improved version of the Scheduler service that was included with previous versions of Windows. In addition, the WSH is now included as a part of the operating system. Previously, WSH was only available by download from the Microsoft Web site.

Microsoft has also included more command-line versions of the tools used to manage various operating system functions and services, such as the Dynamic Host Configuration Protocol (DHCP) and Domain Name System (DNS), as well as user and group management. By making command-line versions of these previously GUI-only tools available, Microsoft has made it possible to script many of the administrative tasks in Windows 2000. In addition, the interface to Active Directory is easily scriptable, so that the management of Active Directory objects can also be automated. Along with the addition of improved Task Scheduling and a solid scripting environment, Microsoft has made it much easier to automate administrative tasks in the Windows 2000 environment.

TASK SCHEDULER

Every operating system is able to run jobs interactively with a user at the keyboard directing operations in real time. Most server operating systems are able to handle typical server type programs, such as databases and email, which run continuously as a service. Most operating systems that are used in medium to large environments provide a method of running *batch* jobs. Batch jobs are programs or processes that can be run unattended without—or with a minimum of—user intervention. Usually, these types of jobs perform system or disk-intensive tasks that are best run before or after normal business hours. An example of these types of jobs are sorts, database defrags, and database merges.

In addition, most of these same operating systems provide some type of job control language that can be used to automate the running of jobs or administrative tasks. For example, in the IBM world, the midrange systems use Operator Control Language (OCL), whereas the big systems use Job Control Language (JCL). These languages work with a job scheduler function, so that the system administrator can use them to schedule and run jobs or tasks at specific times using specific resources.

For a server operating system to be taken seriously as an enterprise class operating system, it needs to have some kind of Scheduler service, so programs and tasks can be scheduled to run at assigned times without any user intervention. Although previous versions of Windows NT attempted to provide a scheduling service using a set of hastily assembled utilities, Windows 2000 has included Task Scheduler, which makes scheduling tasks much easier and more reliable.

Overview

Task Scheduler is similar to the Scheduler service that was used in previous versions of Windows NT. The Scheduler service was a background service that you could use to schedule tasks to run unattended on a Windows NT system. In these earlier versions of Windows NT, you would use the AT (automated task) command from the command line to interact with the Scheduler service. The AT command was used to schedule programs, batch files, or scripts to run at a scheduled time. If you had access to the *Windows NT Server Resource Kit*, a utility included on the CD called WINAT simplified scheduling tasks by presenting the configuration options via a GUI interface.

It seemed at times that the Scheduler service was an afterthought in the design of previous versions of Windows. The Scheduler service was not enabled upon installation and had to be configured manually. The command-line interface program, AT, was very poor with limited and confusing command switches. Even the optional program WINAT, which was included with the *Windows NT Server Resource Kit*, was not very intuitive. To make matters worse, there was very little documentation to support the service, and what little documentation was available was very poor. Although a skilled system administrator could get things working after a certain amount of experimentation and tinkering, it was obvious that this service was not a well thought out solution.

Fortunately, this service has been corrected in Windows 2000. The Windows 2000 Task Scheduler is a far more robust tool, and it is implemented more

13

seamlessly with the operating system. The background service that works with Task Scheduler is enabled by default and configured to run as a service with Local System rights. Task Scheduler is installed with the basic Windows 2000 installation and provides a GUI interface that is intuitive and easy to use. In addition, Task Scheduler is well documented in the Windows 2000 Help files.

Task Scheduler allows you to schedule a program, script, or batch file to run at a scheduled time. It enables scheduling events to run once, daily, weekly, or monthly. In addition, it allows you to schedule an event to run at system startup or user logon. The tasks that you create using Task Scheduler can be saved as .job files. These files can be placed on other computers to run the scheduled task there. This allows system administrators to preconfigure system maintenance tasks for client machines in a central location and place them on their client machines. The preconfigured task will then run as scheduled.

The job files are saved from the task entries in the Scheduled Tasks folder. By sharing this folder, these files are visible to other users on the network by browsing using the Network Neighborhood application. The job files can also be distributed via email or placed on the user machines using a utility, such as Systems Management Server (SMS).

Additionally, Task Scheduler can be manipulated by developers using common programming languages or even via scripting. Task Scheduler is a COM-based object, so the application programming interfaces (APIs) are fully documented. This not only allows tasks to be scheduled programmatically, it also allows developers to build scheduling into their applications using Task Scheduler objects.

Scheduling Tasks Using the **AT** Command

For those system administrators that have used previous versions of Windows NT, tasks can also be scheduled in Task Scheduler using the **AT** command. By using the **AT** command, you can list or schedule tasks to be run at predetermined times, just as you can via the Task Scheduler GUI. The advantage of scheduling tasks via the **AT** command is that it can be easily scripted.

*Note: The tasks that are created using the **AT** command do not generate .job files. All task configuration information created via the **AT** command is stored in the Registry.*

The command-line options available for the **AT** command are as follows:

```
AT [\\computername] [ [id] [/DELETE] | /DELETE [/YES]]
AT [\\computername] time [/INTERACTIVE]
    [ /EVERY:date[,...] | /NEXT:date[,...]] "command"
```

The following information can be viewed in Windows 2000 Server by running **C:\>AT /?** at the command prompt.

➤ *\\computername*—Specifies a remote computer. Commands are scheduled on the local computer if this parameter is omitted.

➤ *id*—Is an identification number assigned to a scheduled command.

➤ */delete*—Cancels a scheduled command. If id is omitted, all the scheduled commands on the computer are canceled.

➤ */yes*—Used with the cancel all jobs command when no further confirmation is desired.

➤ *time*—Specifies the time when a command is to run.

➤ */interactive*—Allows the job to interact with the desktop of the user who is logged on at the time the job runs.

➤ */every:date[,...]*—Runs the command on each specified day(s) of the week or month. If the date is omitted, the current day of the month is assumed.

➤ */next:date[,...]*—Runs the specified command on the next occurrence of the day (for example, next Thursday). If the date is omitted, the current day of the month is assumed.

➤ *"command"*—Specifies the Windows 2000 command or batch program to be run.

When specifying a program or batch file to run, always specify the entire path beginning with the drive letter. If you are running a program or batch file on a remote computer, you must specify the Universal Naming Convention (UNC) notation (in the form of \\servername\sharename) for the server and share name, rather than a remote drive letter. In addition, the **AT** command does not automatically load the command interpreter. Unless the task that you are scheduling is an executable (.exe) file, you must precede the command with cmd /c; for example:

```
Cmd /c go.bat > c:\go.log
```

When entering the date and the time that you want the task to occur, remember to specify the time as *hours:minutes* in 24-hour notation (00:00 [midnight] through 23:59). Days can be entered as M-F, or you can specify the numeric day of the month. In addition, you do not have to use sequential days. As long as each entry is separated with commas, you can specify nonsequential days, such as:

M,W,F, or 1,4,7,14,20,

For example, if you wanted to schedule a batch file that would perform certain clean up duties on your system, such as deleting *.tmp files at regular intervals during the week, you would use the **AT** command with the following command-line options.

```
C:\>at 12:00 /every:m,w,f c:\wsh\cleanup.bat
```

This command would tell Task Scheduler to run the batch file *cleanup.bat* every Monday, Wednesday, and Friday at noon, presumably while you are at lunch. When the **AT** command is entered at the command line without any parameters, you will receive a list of scheduled tasks:

```
C:\>ATStatus ID Day     Time      Command Line1   Each M W F    12:00 PM
c:\wsh\cleanup.bat2   Each 1 5 9   12:00 AM
c:\test\status.bat
3   Each 1 15 31  3:00 AM
c:\test\computepay.bat
```

The Status ID is used when you want to delete a single job. Normally, if you use the /delete command switch with the **AT** command, all of the scheduled jobs are deleted. If you just want to delete a single job, specify the Status ID of the job on the command line:

```
C:\>AT 3 /delete
```

When scheduling tasks using the **AT** command, you must be a member of the Local Administrators group. The scheduled job can run while someone who has fewer rights is logged on, or the system can be logged off, but the user who performs the initial scheduling has to have the proper rights.

All programs and batch files that are run using the **AT** command are run as background processes, unless you specify the */Interactive switch*. When the interactive switch is specified, any prompts generated during the execution of the task are displayed to whatever user is logged on to the system at that time.

When you run tasks without the interactive switch, these tasks are run as background processes, so there is no output displayed. If you want to write the output of the task to a log, you need to use the escape symbol and the redirection symbol:

```
C:\>at 03:00 /every:01,15,31 c:\test\computepay.bat ^>c:\log.bat
```

Note: Using the escape character with the redirection symbol to direct the output of the scheduled task to a file was never documented in previous versions of Windows NT. This and other tips are available in the Windows 2000 Help files.

Under Windows 2000, the Scheduler service runs in the security context of the Local System account. This account might not have the authority to run tasks created using the **AT** command. The account that is used to control tasks created by the **AT** command can be changed using Task Scheduler. To change the account that is used by the **AT** command:

1. Select Start | Settings | Control Panel.

Note: Task Scheduler can also be accessed through the Start | Administrative Tools menu.

2. Double-click the Scheduled Tasks folder. The Scheduled Tasks window opens (see Figure 13.1).

3. From the System menu, click Advanced, and then select AT Service Account.

4. Select the This Account radio button, and then type in the name of the account that you would like to use for tasks created by the **AT** command.

5. Type in the password, and then type it in again to confirm.

6. Click OK to save.

As you can see in Figure 13.1, the tasks that were created using the **AT** command are listed by Task Scheduler. By default, all tasks created using the **AT** command are displayed in the Scheduled Tasks window. You can tell which tasks were scheduled via the **AT** command by the Task name. The **AT** command scheduled tasks always have the name of AT *Status ID*. In Figure 13.1, the tasks have a Status ID of 1 through 4, so the task names are AT1 through AT4.

When using Task Scheduler, you can display the tasks; however, if you make any modifications to the tasks, such as changing the schedule or path name, you will

13

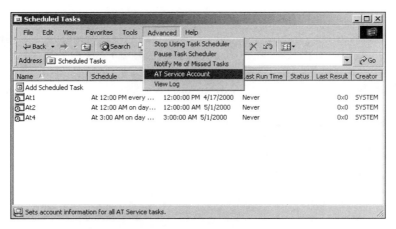

Figure 13.1   The Scheduled Tasks window.

be unable to view or modify the task using the **AT** command. In addition, any tasks that are created using Task Scheduler cannot be viewed or modified using the **AT** command. This is because Task Scheduler adds additional information to the task and saves it in a .job file, not in the Registry where the **AT** command stores its tasks. Once a task has been modified using Task Scheduler, it cannot be used with the **AT** command again.

Scheduling Tasks Using Task Scheduler

Task Scheduler can be thought of as a GUI version of the **AT** command; however, it adds many additional features. Using Task Scheduler you can add, modify, delete, disable, or stop any scheduled tasks. You also can view tasks that are scheduled to run on remote computers. In addition, for problem determination purposes, you can view a log file that lists the past scheduled tasks, or you can select the option so that you will be notified if any scheduled task fails to run.

Task Scheduler is controlled by the Scheduled Task Wizard. The wizard allows you to create a task, schedule it to run at the desired time(s), control how it runs, or change the schedule as needed. The wizard is started by double-clicking on the Add Scheduled Tasks prompt. You can also add tasks by dragging and dropping batch files, programs, or scripts from the desktop or Windows Explorer on to the Scheduled Tasks window.

As mentioned earlier in the chapter, the Task Scheduler service runs in the security context of the local system account. This account usually does not have the authority to run most system tasks, so as part of the task setup, you will be prompted for the account that you want to use to run the task. Using the appropriate account allows you to configure each task to be run with just the right amount of security and no more.

However, because of the way that Windows 2000 handles the security associated with .job files, when you move a .job file to a different system, you will have to reenter the security account that you want to run the task under. This is because the security system is responsible for storing the account credentials, and that information cannot be transferred between systems.

Using the Scheduled Task Wizard

You can use the Scheduled Task Wizard to schedule a batch file that adds new users to the Active Directory database. In this case, because it is going to add a large number of users, the following example schedules the task to run after normal business hours when not much is happening on the network. To set up a task using the Scheduled Task Wizard, perform the following steps.

1. Select Start | Settings | Control Panel.

2. Double-click the Scheduled Tasks folder. The Scheduled Tasks window opens.

3. Double-click Add Scheduled Task. The Scheduled Task Wizard starts (see Figure 13.2). Click Next.

4. The Scheduled Task Wizard displays a list of applications that it has found on your system. You can either select one of these programs, or click Browse to select one that is not listed. Click Browse.

5. The Select Program To Schedule window appears. From this window, you can navigate to the program, batch, or script file that you want to run. Navigate to the desired file. Click Open to continue.

6. The Scheduled Task Wizard prompts you to type in a name for the task. Type in "Add new users to AD". Next, you need to select how often you want to perform this task. There are selections for:

   ➤ Daily

   ➤ Weekly

   ➤ Monthly

   ➤ One Time Only

   ➤ When My Computer Starts

   ➤ When I Log On

7. Select the One Time Only radio button (see Figure 13.3) to run this batch file once. Click Next.

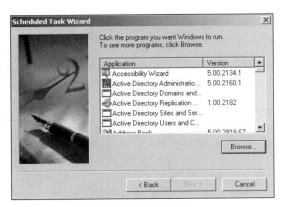

Figure 13.2   The Scheduled Task Wizard.

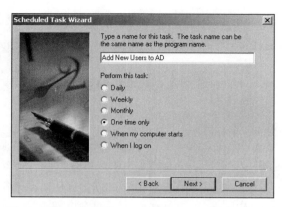

Figure 13.3   Adding new users and selecting the frequency of the scheduled task.

8. Options to set the time and the date for the task are displayed on this screen. Leave the date as is, and set the start time to 11:59 P.M. Click Next.

9. Enter the name of an account that has the proper authority to run the batch file, and enter the appropriate password. Because this batch file has to access Active Directory objects, it needs administrative access. Enter an account with Administrator rights in the format *domain\userid*. Type in the password twice, and then click Next.

10. You'll receive a summary of the options that you selected to schedule this task. Review the options. If any need to be changed, click Back to return to the previous screens. Click on Finish to complete scheduling the task. However, if you want to look at the advanced properties that are available, select the Open Advanced Properties For This Task When I Click Finish checkbox. Click Finish.

11. The advanced properties window opens for this task. On this screen, you can change any of the options that you have already configured, or you can select some new options. There are four tabs:

   ➤ *Task*—The options available on this tab were previously selected as you worked your way through the wizard. They can be changed on this tab if any are incorrect.

   ➤ *Schedule*—The schedule was previously selected using the wizard. However, there are many additional scheduling options available from this tab (see Figure 13.4). For example, you can show multiple schedules, or you can add additional times when you want the task to run. By selecting the Advanced button, you are presented with more scheduling options, such as running the task for a specified length of time, repeating the task every x minutes or hours, and scheduling a stop time for the task.

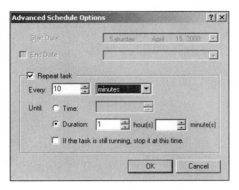

Figure 13.4 Advanced Schedule Options.

➤ *Settings*—The Settings tab allows you to stop the task after it has been running for a specified length of time. It also allows you to specify that the task is only to be started if the computer has been idle for a certain length of time or to stop the task if the computer is no longer idle. In addition, this tab contains settings useful for running tasks on laptop computers. Included are options to not start the task if the computer is running on batteries, stop the task if the computer goes into battery mode, or wake the computer to run the task (see Figure 13.5).

➤ *Security*—The Security tab allows you to specify the permissions that specific users and groups have for this task. You can prevent users from changing the schedule of a task or deleting it by limiting their permissions.

12. Click OK to save the task when you are finished.

13

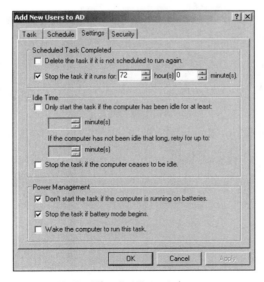

Figure 13.5 The Settings tab.

Working with Tasks

The GUI interface of the Task Scheduler tool makes it very easy to work with tasks. After the task has been entered, you can run it immediately, end it, or delete it. In addition, at any time after you have scheduled a task, you can use Task Scheduler to modify any of the settings.

To change a scheduled task:

1. Select Start | Settings | Control Panel.

2. Double-click the Scheduled Tasks folder. The Scheduled Tasks window opens.

3. Double-click the task that you want to modify. The Scheduled Task properties window appears.

The properties window has the same four tabs that were described for the advanced properties window in the previous section. Make any needed changes, and then select OK to save them.

The task can also be manipulated in other ways. From the Scheduled Tasks window, right-click the task that you want to work with. From the pop-up menu, you have the options to:

➤ Run the task immediately.

➤ End the task if it is already running.

➤ Cut or copy the task to the system clipboard.

➤ Delete the task.

➤ Rename the task.

➤ Configure the properties of the task.

Saving Tasks As Job Files

The tasks listed in the Task Scheduler window can be saved to a folder and copied or mailed to other machines to run as scheduled.

To copy a task to another folder or machine:

1. Select Start | Settings | Control Panel.

2. Double-click the Scheduled Tasks folder. The Scheduled Tasks window opens.

3. Select the task that you want to copy.

4. From the System menu, click Edit, and then select Copy To Folder.

5. The Browse For Folder window appears.

From here, you can select any folder on the same machine or another machine to copy the task object to. If you have the proper permissions and the Scheduled Tasks folder on another machine is shared, you can copy the task object directly to it. Because the task is just another object, it can be copied, moved, and deleted in the same way as any other object in Active Directory.

Viewing Tasks on Remote Computers

If you have administrative rights on remote computers, you can view their scheduled tasks (if the folder is shared). To view the Scheduled Tasks on a remote computer:

1. Double-click My Network Places.

2. Double-click either Entire Network or Computers Near Me, whichever is appropriate.

3. A network folder opens. Search for the remote computer in the folder.

4. Double-click the remote computer that you want to view.

5. A list of shared folders on the remote computer appears.

6. Double-click the Scheduled Tasks folder.

Troubleshooting Problems with Task Scheduler

Most problems with Task Scheduler are caused by insufficient permissions on the target machine to run the desired task, a typo in the configuration, or an incorrectly coded batch file or script. The event log is one of the best diagnostic tools to use to look at the target machine to see if the task actually ran and to see if any errors occurred.

Another source of diagnostic information is found in the Task Scheduler window. When the tasks are viewed in the Details view, each task entry has a status column that indicates the status of the task. The status indicators displayed are as follows:

➤ *Blank*—Either the task is not currently running, or it ran successfully.

➤ *Could Not Start*—The task failed to start.

➤ *Missed*—The time window was missed.

➤ *Running*—The task is running now.

13

The Task Scheduler program has two options that can be turned on, which can assist you in diagnosing problems. The first is the Task Scheduler log. The log shows

- When Task Scheduler was started
- When Task Scheduler was shut down
- What tasks were run
- The Exit code of the task

The exit code of the task is probably the most important part of the log. Most programs that complete successfully have an exit code of zero. If you receive a nonzero exit code and the task did not complete successfully, it might warrant further investigation. The documentation for most programs contains a list of exit codes and their meanings. To view the Task Scheduler log:

1. Select Start | Settings | Control Panel.
2. Double-click the Scheduled Tasks folder. The Scheduled Tasks window opens.
3. From the System menu, click Advanced, and then select View Log.
4. The Task Scheduler log is opened in a Notepad session (see Figure 13.6).

Task Scheduler logs information into the file sequentially, so you will have to scroll down to the bottom of the file to see the most recent entries.

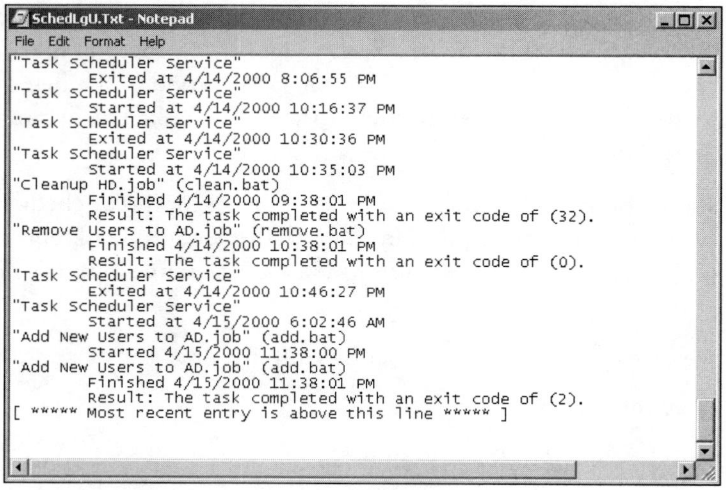

```
SchedLgU.Txt - Notepad
File  Edit  Format  Help
"Task Scheduler Service"
	Exited at 4/14/2000 8:06:55 PM
"Task Scheduler Service"
	Started at 4/14/2000 10:16:37 PM
"Task Scheduler Service"
	Exited at 4/14/2000 10:30:36 PM
"Task Scheduler Service"
	Started at 4/14/2000 10:35:03 PM
"Cleanup HD.job" (clean.bat)
	Finished 4/14/2000 09:38:01 PM
	Result: The task completed with an exit code of (32).
"Remove Users to AD.job" (remove.bat)
	Finished 4/14/2000 10:38:01 PM
	Result: The task completed with an exit code of (0).
"Task Scheduler Service"
	Exited at 4/14/2000 10:46:27 PM
"Task Scheduler Service"
	Started at 4/15/2000 6:02:46 AM
"Add New Users to AD.job" (add.bat)
	Started 4/15/2000 11:38:00 PM
"Add New Users to AD.job" (add.bat)
	Finished 4/15/2000 11:38:01 PM
	Result: The task completed with an exit code of (2).
[ ***** Most recent entry is above this line ***** ]
```

Figure 13.6 The Task Scheduler Log.

In Figure 13.6, you can see that various tasks have been run with different exit codes. This type of information can point you in the direction of a problem with a scheduled task. The default size of the log is 32KB, and it will wrap around when it reaches its maximum size. The name of the file is schedlgu.txt, and it is stored in the \WINNT folder.

The Notify Me Of Missed Tasks option can also be of assistance. When this option is selected, the administrator is notified whenever a scheduled task does not run for whatever reason. To turn on the Notify option, perform the following steps.

1. Select Start | Settings | Control Panel.

2. Double-click the Scheduled Tasks folder. The Scheduled Tasks window opens.

3. From the System menu, click Advanced, and then select Notify Me of Missed Tasks.

When this option is turned on, the user who configured it receives the system message shown in Figure 13.7 whenever a task is missed.

A missed task is a task that was scheduled at a specific time, but could not run because the computer and/or Task Scheduler service was not operational. The missed task notification occurs after the computer or Task Scheduler service is restarted and Task Scheduler notices that the current time exceeds the next run time of a task. When this happens, a system message is sent to the user and an entry is inserted into the Task Scheduler log.

13

Best Practices

Because of its added flexibility, it is best to always use Task Scheduler for scheduling tasks versus using the **AT** command. Using Task Scheduler is advantageous because it provides a log of every scheduled task and can notify the system administrator if a scheduled task does not run.

The following list contains some additional tips for using Task Scheduler.

➤ Remember to schedule resource intensive tasks for times when the system workload is light.

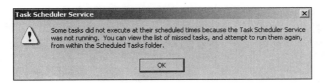

Figure 13.7 Missed task notification.

➤ Make sure that the time and date of the system are correct, so that the task is performed at the correct time.

➤ Turn on the option to be notified if the scheduled tasks do not run.

➤ To track important tasks, use redirection to send output to a log file.

➤ Under Windows 2000, all passwords except for the Administrator password have an expiration date. If you are scheduling recurring tasks, either remember to regularly change the password of the account that you are using to schedule these tasks, or use the administrator account to schedule them.

WINDOWS SCRIPT HOST (WSH)

Earlier in the chapter, it was noted that in order for an operating system to be considered an enterprise class system, it had to provide the proper functionality to automate jobs and administrative tasks. Most operating systems provide some sort of sophisticated job control language that enables the system administrator to automate lengthy and repetitive tasks.

The job control language used in previous versions of Windows NT was the batch language, which was included with various versions of MS-DOS. Although the MS-DOS batch language is small and fast, it is very limited in the tasks that it can perform, and it is not a true scripting language. In addition, it never included any debugging tools, so bugs within batch files were usually very difficult to find.

Microsoft has attempted to remedy the shortcomings of the batch language by including the WSH application in Windows 2000. WSH is part of the operating system in both Windows 2000 and Windows 98. The version of WSH that is available for Windows 95 and Windows NT clients is currently the 5.0 version. The newer 5.1 version is included with Windows 2000. The new version contains a few new features including more command-line options and a script debugger.

WSH allows you to run scripts supported by various scripting engines. WSH is not a scripting application per se, however, it provides an interface to the operating system, so that various scripting engines can be plugged into it. The scripting engines themselves are COM objects and support all of the objects that other languages for the Windows platform support including ActiveX objects. The WSH application has minimal memory requirements and is ideal for both interactive and noninteractive scripting needs, such as logon scripting and administrative scripting.

Microsoft includes two scripting engines with WSH, a VBScript engine and a JScript engine. VBScript is a subset of Microsoft's Visual Basic product. Anyone who is familiar with Visual Basic or Visual Basic for Applications (VBA) should be able to create VBScripts without any problems. JScript is Microsoft's version of the JavaScript language. Again, there are enough similarities between these languages that a good Java programmer should be able to create decent JScripts. There are also several third-party plug-in scripting engines available; some are freeware, whereas others are commercial products. The most popular add on scripting engines are for Perl, but there are also engines available for REXX, Kix, XLNT, and other languages.

The scripting engine used is decided at runtime. When a scripting engine is installed for use with WSH, because it is a COM object, it is registered with the operating system. When an object is registered, information about it is inserted into the Registry. The information in the Registry allows WSH to decide which scripting engine to use with the code that is to be run. It does this by examining the command line and reading the extension on the script file. For example, if the script file extension is .vbs, WSH will look in the Registry to find an entry that corresponds to the .vbs extension. The information in the Registry will tell WSH to use the VBScript scripting engine with file names ending with .vbs.

The scripting engine that you use with Windows 2000 is mostly a matter of preference. If you have a background in Visual Basic, obviously, it will be best to use the VBScript engine. However, if you are crazy for Java, use the JScript engine. The capabilities of each scripting language for administrative tasks are very similar, so the decision should be based on which language you and your company are most comfortable with.

CScript

13

There are two versions of the WSH included with Windows 2000. The first is the command-line version, CScript.exe. This version is normally used when you need to run scripts in the background without any user intervention. All parameters that are to be used are entered on the command line. CScript uses the following syntax:

```
cscript [script name] [wsh parameters] [script parameters]
```

The CScript parameters include

➤ *Script name*—This is the name of the script file that will be run; it includes any necessary path information. Example: *c:\scripts\logon.vbs*

Note: *The script file name must include the extension, so that WSH can identify which scripting engine to use.*

➤ *Windows Script Host parameters*—These are the command-line switches that tell WSH how to run the script. WSH parameters are always preceded by two slashes (//), so that it can differentiate its parameters from the parameters of your script.

➤ *Script parameters*—These are the command-line parameters that are passed to the script. Script parameters are always preceded by one slash (/).

The command-line options for CScript are as follows (this information can be viewed by typing "C:\cscript.exe /?" at the command prompt).

➤ *//B*—Batch mode; suppresses script errors and prompts from displaying

➤ *//D*—Enables Active Debugging

➤ *//E:engine*—Uses engine for executing script

➤ *//H:CScript*—Changes the default script host to CScript.exe

➤ *//H:WScript*—Changes the default script host to WScript.exe (default)

➤ *//I*—Interactive mode (default, opposite of //B)

➤ *//Job:xxxx*—Executes a WSH job

➤ *//Logo*—Displays logo (default)

➤ *//Nologo*—Prevents logo display; no banner will be shown at execution time

➤ *//S*—Saves current command-line options for this user

➤ *//T:nn*—Time out in seconds; maximum time a script is permitted to run

➤ *//X*—Executes script in debugger

➤ *//U*—Uses Unicode for redirected I/O from the console

Let's look at a few of these command-line options in more detail.

The //B option should be used for running scripts unattended. Note that if you use this parameter, you do not have to specify a logo parameter. The opposite of this option is the //I option, which is the interactive mode. This is the mode that you should run your scripts in while writing and testing them, so that you will receive all error messages and warnings and will have more control over the script.

The //E:engine parameter is new to Windows 2000. This parameter allows you to specify which scripting engine to use with the script. Normally, this parameter is not used. However, it might be necessary to use this option in the future as more third-party scripting engines become available and file name extensions used to differentiate the different script engines become more limited.

Another new feature in the version of WSH included with Windows 2000 is the //D and the //X parameters. The //D parameter enables the script debugger, whereas the //X parameter is used to actually execute the script in the debugger. The script debugger is used to trace logic errors in your scripts. We will cover the debugger in the "Script Debugging" section later in this chapter.

The two //H parameters are used to set the default script application. These options allow you to double-click a script file from the desktop or within My Computer or Windows Explorer and automatically start the script engine. The default is to start the script file in WScript.

The //T parameter allows you to configure the script timeout in seconds, which is the length of time that the script can run before it is automatically ended. This is a good option to use when running scripts unattended because it allows a script that is caught in an infinite loop to be ended before it can do any damage.

WScript

The second version of WSH included with Windows 2000 is WScript.exe. WScript is the Windows GUI version of WSH. WScript also has several command-line parameters that can be configured (see Figure 13.8). To display them, type "wscript /?".

Because WScript is a Windows program, you can also control some of the options from its properties page. To get to the properties page, type "wscript". From the properties page, you can configure the option for script timeout and indicate whether or not to display the WSH logo when running a script.

13

WSH Files

WSH also allows you to configure script parameters using a .wsh file. This file is similar in concept to the .pif files, which have been used with Windows for years. To create a .wsh file:

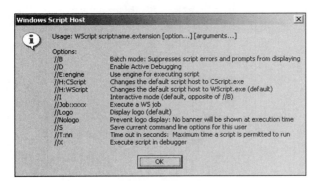

Figure 13.8 WScript command-line parameters.

1. From Windows Explorer or My Computer, right-click a .js or .vbs file. The pop-up menu appears.

2. Select Properties. A properties page appears, which is similar to other properties pages with one exception, there is a Script tab.

3. Configure the Script properties, and then click Apply or OK to save.

After you click Apply or OK, a .wsh file is created (with default settings unless specified otherwise) with the same name as the script. This file contains the properties that you configured earlier. The .wsh files allow you to have a unique configuration for each script that you run. In addition, you can create multiple .wsh files with different names for a script file, so that the script uses different settings depending on which .wsh file is used. The following is an example of a typical .wsh file.

```
[ScriptFile]
Path=c:\wsh\test.wsh
[Options]
Timeout=6
DisplayLogo=1
BatchMode=0
```

The .wsh files can be used with either version of WSH. To run a .wsh file from the command line type

```
C:\>cscript scriptname
```

Or, to run the script using the WScript version, just double-click the script file icon.

If you have a large number of small scripts that you need to keep track of, you can organize these files by making use of another feature of the .wsh files. Using the job id parameter, you can incorporate all of your scripts into one file and separate them by giving each routine a different job name. For example:

```
<package><job id="HelloWorldvbs"><script language="VBScript">
     Wscript.Echo "Hello World from VBS"
</Script>
</Job>

<job id="HelloWorldjs">
<script language="JScript">
     Wscript.Echo "Hello World from JScript"
</Script>
```

```
</Job>
```

```
</package>
```

To call the VBScript version, you would use the following command line:

```
Cscript //Job:HelloWorldvbs Scripts.wsf
```

Using WSH

WSH and its associated scripting engines are similar to most modern programming languages in that they rely on the use of objects. WSH and the scripting engines come with a set of objects that are used to provide functionality. However, the objects that are provided with WSH can be used with any of the scripting languages that are used with WSH.

Some of the most common WSH objects are

➤ *WScript*—This object provides information about the current script and any arguments associated with it.

➤ *WshArguments*—This object is used to access the command-line options.

➤ *WshCollection*—This object is used as a repository for other objects.

➤ *WshEnvironment*—This object is used to work with the environment variables.

➤ *WshNetwork*—This object is used to access the network; it allows you to map drives and attach printers.

➤ *WshShortcut*—This object is used to work with Windows shortcuts.

➤ *WshShell*—This object is used to work with and manipulate the Windows Shell. It includes the Windows desktop, Start Menu folders, and shortcuts. This object can also be used to work with the Windows Registry.

➤ *WshSpecialFolders*—This object is used to work with the Windows folders including the Desktop and Start menu folders.

➤ *WshUrlShortcut*—This object is used to work with Internet shortcuts.

➤ *FileSystemObject*—This object is used to work with files and folders.

Now that you know what objects you have to work with, let's put them to use in the obligatory first script to print out Hello World.

```
//The old standard Hello World Program
//written in JScript
```

```
//
    Wscript.Echo "Hello World from JScript";
```

This example was written in JScript. There is not much to it as you can see. As a matter of fact, you could use the same code in VBScript, the only difference would be the comment delimiters and the lack of the line ending character. In the sample code, one of the WSH objects was used. Again, it can be used with any of the scripting languages.

Note also the differences between running a program using the command–line version of CScript versus the GUI version of WScript. The CScript version displays the text in the command window, whereas the WScript version displays the output from the program in a window (see Figure 13.9).

Now let's get a little more involved with coding. Let's use VBScript this time with the FileSystemObject to see how much free space you have on the C: drive. You will have to use the FileSystemObject with the Drives object to get to the free space information. First, you need to create an instance of the FileSystemObject:

```
' Instantiate a FileSystemObject
set fs=Wscript.CreateObject("Scripting.FileSystemObject")
```

Once you have your object, you need to use it to pull data out of the Drives object:

```
' get data from specified drive
set Disk=fs.drives("c:")
```

You can then send the information to the screen.

```
' display drive info
Wscript.echo("Free Space = " & disk.availablespace)
```

Let's look at the completed script:

```
'Quick and dirty script to find freespace on a drive
dim fs, disk
```

Figure 13.9   Output from WScript.

```
' Instantiate a FileSystemObject
set fs = createObject("Scripting.FileSystemObject")
' get data from specified drive
set disk=fs.drives ("c:")
' display drive info
Wscript.echo "Free Space = " & (disk.FreeSpace)
```

Using WSH with Active Directory

Now that Windows 2000 domains are controlled by Active Directory, the average system administrator will most likely be supporting far more users. Because the theoretical maximum of 40,000 objects that could be stored in a Windows NT 4 domain has now been increased to anywhere from 2 through 16 million objects in Active Directory, things can get out of hand pretty quickly.

To handle that many objects, the system administrator needs to find other ways to perform common tasks and will probably try to automate as many common tasks as possible. This is where the WSH comes in. The system administrator can create scripts to handle a lot of the repetitive tasks performed in a network, such as adding or removing users, moving users between organizational units or domains, and setting and resetting passwords.

Active Directory has been designed to have an open interface, so that common scripting tools can be used to manipulate and control the Active Directory objects. The two most common ways to interface with Active Directory programmatically are via the Lightweight Directory Access Protocol (LDAP) and the Active Directory Service Interface (ADSI). Using WSH, the administrator can create scripts that leverage either or both of these interfaces to automate common tasks.

13

For example, let's look at an example of how to work with Active Directory. When working with Active Directory, you first have to bind to the container that you want to work with. This is accomplished by using GetObject with the distinguished name of your organizational unit.

```
set oU =GetObject("LDAP://CN=Accounting,DC=sasnak,DC=com")
```

After you have accomplished this, it is easy to just select an object and an attribute, and set it to whatever value you want.

```
oUser.PAssword = "password"
```

After the value has been changed, you need to write the changes back to the directory, and then clear the local object cache.

```
oUser.SetInfo
Set oUser = nothing
```

The following VBScript is a basic example of how to change an attribute of an object in Active Directory. In this example, the name of an organizational unit is taken from the command line, and then the password field of all the users in that OU is reset to "password":

```
'set Password to "password"
' this script gets the OU name from the command
' line and sets the password of all users in that
' OU to "password"

Dim oArgs
Set oArgs=Wscript.Argument
'get Organization Unit from command line
'
set oU =GetObject("LDAP://CN=" & oArgs(0) &",DC=sasnak,DC=com")
for each oUser in oU
    wscript.echo(oUser.name)
    oUser.PAssword = "password"
    oUser.SetInfo
    Set oUser = nothing
Next
```

Although this is a very simple example of the scripting interface of Active Directory, it is used to show the possibilities of integrating scripting into your work with Active Directory.

Script Debugging

Even the best of us do not write error-free scripts all the time. One of the most important parts of learning to write scripts is learning how to fix broken scripts. Scripts can be afflicted with a variety of errors, and it is the creator's responsibility to maintain the scripts appropriately.

The most common type of scripting error is a *syntax error.* A syntax error occurs when the scripting code does not follow the spelling or formatting rules of the scripting language. Syntax errors are the most common errors, especially for beginners. Typical examples are misspelled words or missing parameters. Most commands have to be spelled out with just the right number of parameters in exactly the right order.

Another type of error includes *runtime errors.* Runtime errors are only discovered when you actually run the code. Typical causes of runtime errors are improper use of commands or use of variables that are not properly initialized.

In addition, *logic errors* can occur. Logic errors are generally the most difficult to find because everything seems to work well, but for some reason two and two now equals six! The other types of errors generate error codes, whereas a logic error might go unnoticed for years. Typically, the only way to find most logic errors is to crawl through the code checking each line carefully. However, the best way to find logic errors is by using a debugging program.

Microsoft has supplied Script Debugger in Windows 2000, which is a utility that can be used to debug both VBScript and JScript code. Unfortunately, because the Script Debugger and these scripting languages were originally designed for use with Internet Explorer, there are some limitations when using it for scripting. Fortunately, there are some workarounds.

Because of the way the Script Debugger was originally designed, the WScript object is not supported in Internet Explorer, so it isn't supported within the debugger. Instead, you will have to use the alert() function, which uses the same basic syntax.

After you have added the necessary changes to your scripts, you can load them into the Script Debugger. The easiest way to do this is via the command line:

```
Cscript resetpassword.vbs /Users //d //x
```

The previous line opens the main window for the debugger. Even with some of the previously mentioned limitation, the Microsoft Script Debugger (see Figure 13.10) does a fairly good job of debugging scripts. It includes all of the standard features of debuggers including breakpoints and single stepping, and it even allows you to step over functions. The help file for the debugger is very extensive, and you should spend some time reviewing it before your first debugging session.

13

Even though there are numerous third-party scripting languages available for the Windows NT platform, a major problem is that there is no guarantee that

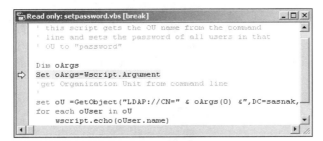

Figure 13.10   The Microsoft Script Debugger.

the runtime files needed for the scripts are installed on every machine where they are needed. Now that Microsoft has made WSH part of the operating system, system administrators are able to write scripts that can be used throughout the enterprise because they can be assured that the scripts will be able to run on all machines.

BEST PRACTICES

This section contains a few brief guidelines to help you decide to script or not to script.

When to use a script:

➤ When the task is repetitive

➤ When the task will take a long time to run with very little user input

➤ When the task has to be performed the same way every time

When not to use a script:

➤ When the task will vary in execution each time it is performed

➤ When the task takes just a few minutes to run

➤ When the task is only to be performed once

LOGON SCRIPTS

Logon scripts are short scripts that contain commands, executable programs, or both, which execute each time a user logs in. Logon scripts are a method of automating the configuration of a user's work environment. They can include functions as simple as displaying a banner page with the current company news or attaching the user session to various network resources, such as file shares or printers. In addition, a logon script can run any executable program or call another script.

In this section, we will start by examining the history of logon scripts, and then look at how they are implemented in the Windows 2000 environment. We will then work with some sample logon scripts written in various scripting languages.

History and Overview

Logon scripts, in one form or another, have existed for years on just about every computer platform from mainframes to the PC. There has always been a common need to automatically configure a user session without user or administrator intervention.

A logon script allows you to either standardize the setup of various users or supply a custom setup for certain users. The way you use a script depends on which logon script the user is assigned. Typically, a logon script is written in whichever command language is available on the platform.

Using logon scripts, the system administrator is able to centralize control over application and data locations. By defining drive mappings via the logon script instead of letting the user attempt to do it, the administrator is assured that all users are working with an identical configuration. Because logon scripts can be applied to a large number of users, the administrator can easily make changes to the configuration by just changing a script instead of having to visit each individual desktop.

Logon scripts can also be used for various system maintenance activities. An administrator can add routines to delete the files in temporary directories, run disk utilities in the background, and perform various other activities. The logon script can also be used to install applications or apply updates to existing applications.

Logon scripts can be assigned to a user, a group of users, or all of the users in an organizational unit, site, or domain. There can be different logon scripts for different departments or locations. If you are using one of the more full-featured batch languages for your logon scripts, you can have the script perform a different set of tasks, depending on which group the user is assigned to.

The logon scripts in previous versions of Windows NT were simply the standard MS-DOS–like batch files, which have been used on the Microsoft operating system platforms for years and years. The MS-DOS–based command language has remained very limited, even with the extra functionality that Microsoft added to the command set for the Windows NT 4 platform.

13

Unfortunately, although Microsoft has added a few new features to the batch language for Windows 2000, they are not significant. The MS-DOS batch language still does not provide a decent method of performing looping or decent support for variables, and the error handling is minimal at best. In addition, there is no facility for debugging or troubleshooting completed scripts.

Let's face it, the various versions of Windows were designed for the typical user who is used to interfacing with a computer via a GUI interface, instead of for the hard-core command-line junkies.

Note: *Evidence that the Windows operating system was designed for the typical user is shown in the way Microsoft has arranged the desktop menus in Windows 2000; the Command Prompt is an "Accessory" not an "Administrative Tool."*

Now that we have thoroughly dissuaded you from using the MS-DOS batch language, we can say that for most logon scripts, using a programming language like VBScript or JScript is overkill. Even though a standard batch language does not easily support looping and basic programming structures, for most logon scripts, these items are not needed.

The typical logon script is used to map network drives, maybe set up an environment variable or two, and possibly display the network news of the day. Usually, these tasks can be easily handled using the standard batch language.

How Logon Scripts Work

Logon scripts are created by the system administrator to customize the network environment to the users' needs. In Windows 2000, logon scripts are stored in the SYSVOL, which is the share that is automatically replicated among all of the domain controllers. This is a big improvement from the previous versions of Windows NT, where the system administrator had to place the scripts in the logon share, and then had to manually configure the replication pattern for the network. This older method was error-prone, and the replication mechanism was infamous for replication failures that did not present any errors.

After the logon script is stored in SYSVOL, the system administrator assigns the script to one or more users. This can be accomplished either by configuring the user object or by applying the script via a Group Policy. When the user logs on to the domain, the script runs and performs whatever tasks the system administrator has coded in it.

In its very basic form, a logon script is nothing more that a text file containing a set of commands. You can include commands from the batch language, or you can call any other application that is available. The logon script can also be used to map network drives and set environment variables. Although a logon script is typically a batch file (.bat or .cmd extension), an executable program can also be used.

Environment Variables

The MS-DOS batch language does not support variables in the normal sense. Logon scripts use objects called *system* and *user environment variables*. System and user environment variables are used by Windows 2000 as repositories of information that can be used to find programs, allocate memory space, and control various programs. These strings can contain information, such as drive, path, file name, or memory size. For example, the TEMP environment variable specifies the location where programs place temporary files.

User environment variables are unique to each user. They can be set by the user, the system administrator, or by an application program. However, system environment variables are set by Windows 2000 and can only be set or changed by the administrator. To view and change environment variables, perform the following steps.

1. Select Start | Settings | Control Panel.

2. In the Control Panel, double-click the System icon. The System Properties window appears.

3. Select the Advanced tab.

4. Click the Environment Variables button. A window like the one shown in Figure 13.11 appears.

If you have the appropriate permissions, from this window you can add, change, and delete the desired environment variables. When you click OK, Windows 2000 will save the variables in the Registry for you.

Environment variables can also be set using the **set** command. The **set** command can be used from the command line or in a script to display, configure, or remove environment variables. The syntax of the command is

```
SET    [variable=[string]]
```

When the **set** command is typed by itself, it displays all of the defined variables, as shown in the following example.

```
C:\>Set
ALLUSERSPROFILE=C:\Documents and Settings\All UsersAPPDATA=C:\Documents
```

13

Figure 13.11   Environment Variables.

```
and Settings\Administrator.WINDOWS-WRKN306\Application Data
CommonProgramFiles=C:\Program Files\Common Files
COMPUTERNAME=WINDOWS-WRKN306
ComSpec=C:\WINNT\system32\cmd.exe
HOMEDRIVE=C:
HOMEPATH=\
LOGONSERVER=\\WINDOWS-WRKN306
NUMBER_OF_PROCESSORS=1
OS=Windows_NT
Os2LibPath=C:\WINNT\system32\os2\dll;
Path=C:\WINNT\system32;C:\WINNT;C:\WINNT\System32\Wbem;C:\Program
Files\Resource Kit\;C:\Program Files\Support
Tools\;C:\windows;c:\windows\command;c:\srvtools;
PATHEXT=.COM;.EXE;.BAT;.CMD;.VBS;.VBE;.JS;.JSE;.WSF;.WSH
PROCESSOR_ARCHITECTURE=x86
PROCESSOR_IDENTIFIER=x86 Family 6 Model 5 Stepping 0, GenuineIntel
PROCESSOR_LEVEL=6
PROCESSOR_REVISION=0500
ProgramFiles=C:\Program Files
PROMPT=$P$G
SystemDrive=C:
SystemRoot=C:\WINNT
TEMP=C:\DOCUME~1\ADMINI~1.WIN\LOCALS~1\Temp
TMP=C:\DOCUME~1\ADMINI~1.WIN\LOCALS~1\Temp
USERDNSDOMAIN=sasnak.com
USERDOMAIN=SASNAK
USERNAME=Administrator
USERPROFILE=C:\Documents and Settings\Administrator.WINDOWS-WRKN306
windir=C:\WINNT
```

To add a new variable value to the environment, specify values for both the variable and the string:

```
SET    Tempvariable=whatever
```

Windows 2000 adds the specified variable value to the environment and associates the string with that variable. If the variable already exists in the environment, the new string value replaces the old string value. If you use the **set** command with only a variable name and the equal sign, the variable will be cleared.

With logon scripts, you can use the environment variables similar to the way you would use variables in a regular language. However, because you are limited to using a string, you cannot use variables for any mathematical calculations, and you have to be careful to not use the name of a variable that is already in use.

When using an environment variable in a script, the format %*variable*% with percent signs surrounding the name must be used. The percent signs are used to tell the script file to replace the variable name with a value. The following example uses variables in a script:

```
@echo off
set sysadminname=Joeecho.
Echo %sysadminname% welcomes you to the %USERDOMAIN%
domain!C:\>ShowMeJoe welcomes you to the Sasnak domain!
```

Several variables are very useful in logon scripts. They are as follows:

➤ *%COMPUTERNAME%*—The name of the computer on which the script is running.

➤ *%HOMEDRIVE%*—The user's local workstation drive letter connected to the user's home directory.

➤ *%HOMEPATH%*—The full path of the user's home directory.

➤ *%LOGONSERVER%*—The domain controller that processed the user's last network logon.

➤ *%OS%*—The operating system of the user's workstation.

➤ *%USERDOMAIN%*—The domain to which the user logged on.

➤ *%USERNAME%*—The user.

Script Commands

13

A logon script can be created with a simple text editor. The average logon script can be created in a few minutes with little effort. There is a basic set of commands provided for use with batch files and logon scripts. The following sections contain a selection of some of the commands that are useful for logon scripts.

Call

The syntax for the **call** command is as follows:

```
call [drive:][path] filename [batch-parameters]
call :label [arguments]
```

The **call** command is used to call other scripts from the script that is running. After the processing of the second script has been completed, control is returned to the first script, as shown in the following code listings (Listings 13.1, 13.2, and 13.3).

Listing 13.1   FirstScript.bat.

```
@echo off
echo We start here
call SecondScript.bat
echo I'm back!
```

Listing 13.2   SecondScript.bat.

```
@echo off
echo Welcome to the Second Script!
Echo Go back now
```

Listing 13.3   Running FirstScript.bat.

```
C:\>Firstscript
We start here
Welcome to the Second Script!
Go back now
I'm Back
```

A new feature in Windows 2000 provides the capability of using the **call** command to jump to a label in the file. The processing continues with the first statement after the label and proceeds until it reaches the end of the file. Control is then returned to the statement after the initial call statement and processing continue (Listing 13.4). This new feature allows you to keep everything in one file and simulates calling a subroutine. The output is shown in Listing 13.5.

Listing 13.4   Jumping to a label in FirstScript.bat.

```
@echo off
echo We start here
call :Second
echo I'm back!
Goto :EOF
:Second
echo Welcome to the Subroutine!
Echo Go back now
```

Listing 13.5   Running FirstScript.bat.

```
C:\>Firstscript
We start here
Welcome to the Subroutine!
Go back now
I'm Back
```

Echo

The syntax for the **echo** command is as follows:

```
echo [on | off] [message]
```

The **echo** command is used for two purposes: to turn off the echoing of commands to the screen and to display a message on the screen. The **echo** command's default is to echo all commands to the screen when you run a script. To turn this feature off, insert the *@echo off* command as the first line of your script. The @ sign prevents the **echo** command from being displayed. To display a message, use the format: *echo Your message here*. To display a blank line, use echo with a period: *echo.* See the previous script for examples.

Setlocal/Endlocal

The syntax for the **setlocal** and **endlocal** commands is as follows:

```
Setlocal
Endlocal
```

The **setlocal** and **endlocal** commands are used together to localize environment variables. This means that whatever environment variables are set after the invocation of the **setlocal** command will either be returned to their previous values if they existed before the **setlocal** command, or destroyed if they were newly created, when the script reaches the **endlocal** command. If the **endlocal** command is omitted, it will be implicitly enforced at the end of the script.

For

The syntax for the **for** command is as follows:

```
for %%variable in (set) do command [command-parameters]
```

The **for** command is used to increment through a set, creating a form of pseudolooping. The **for** command performs the operation specified by the **do** command while files or text strings exist in the group specified by the **set** option. Each time the **for** command is incremented, the file name or string being read will be contained in the %%variable. This script file is another way of performing a directory command:

```
Rem Display_bat
For %%z in (*.bat) do @echo %%z
```

13

```
D:\>display_bat
add.bat
do.bat
dx.bat
```

*Note: When using **for** in a batch file, the variable is used in the format %%z. When used from the command line, it is %z.*

Goto

The syntax for the **goto** command is as follows:

```
goto label
```

The **goto** command is used to direct execution to a line with the specified label. A new feature in Windows 2000 is the :EOF (end of file) feature. When the line **goto :EOF** is encountered in a script, the script will terminate, even though the EOF label is not in the file. An example of this feature in use is in the script file that was used to demonstrate the **call** command.

If

The syntax for the **if** command is as follows:

```
if [not] errorlevel number command [else expression]
if [not] string1==string2 command [else expression]
if [not] exist filename command [else expression]
```

The **if** command is a standard programming construct that is used in most programming languages. The **if** command allows you to execute different parts of a logon script, depending on whether or not a condition is satisfied. In the example code, if the first string is equal to the second string, "Yes" will be echoed to the screen; if they are not equal, "No" will be echoed.

```
Rem Sample if demo script
rem
If string1==string2 (echo Yes) else echo No
```

The three most common scenarios for using the **if** command are

➤ *If errorlevel*—If a utility program returns an errorlevel, the **if** command can be placed on the line after the program. It then checks for whether there is a specific errorlevel or no specific errorlevel.

➤ *If x==x*—This is the most common usage for the **if** command. It does a comparison and performs a command, depending on the results of the comparison.

➤ *If exist*—This option checks whether a file exists and takes the appropriate action.

Rem

The syntax for the **rem** command is as follows:

```
rem [comment]
```

The **rem** command is used to insert comments into scripts. It is good practice to fully comment your script files, so that others that may need to maintain them will understand what you have done. In addition, if you have not looked at a script file in a long time and something breaks, you might not remember what you were trying to do without proper comments to jog your memory.

Net use

The syntax for the **net use** command is as follows:

```
NET USE [devicename | *] [\\computername\sharename[\volume]] [password |
*]] [/user:[domainname\]username] [[/delete] | [/persistent:{yes | no}]]
```

The **net use** command has a variety of uses. The most common use within a logon script is to map a drive letter to a shared folder or a volume. A typical example is

```
Rem Example of Net Use
Net Use e: \\sasnak\Accounts
Net Use f: \\sasnak\d$
```

Remember that the **for, goto,** and **if** commands are used to allow conditional processing of the commands in the logon script. For example, the **if** command carries out a command based on the results of a condition. The other batch commands are used to control input and output and call other scripts.

Now that the basic principles of logon scripts have been provided, let's put one together in Listing 13.6 using some of the commands that you have learned.

Listing 13.6 Typical example of a logon script.

```
@echo off
echo.
Echo    Welcome to the World of Windows 2000!
Echo.
Call :Message
Rem Map network drives, delete any connections first
Net use /d /y
```

13

```
Rem  map network drives
Net use g: %logonserver%\accounting
Net use h: %logonserver%\d$
Echo.
Echo. ****  Hello %USERNAME%! Welcome to the %USERDOMAIN% Domain!
Echo.
Echo.
Goto :EOF
:Message
rem display system message
echo. ****                                        ****
echo. **** The network will be down over the weekend ****
echo. **** Please save your work and shutdown      ****
echo. **** promptly at 5 PM on Friday.             ****
echo. ****                                        ****
```

The previous code is a typical example of a logon script. It performs various actions, such as displaying any network news, and uses the new *goto :EOF* feature of the **call** command. In addition, the **net use** command is used to map to a share and a network drive using system environment variables. Then more variables are used for a friendly greeting.

The following output of the logon script is what the user would see, based on this example.

```
Welcome to the World of Windows 2000! ****
**** **** The network will be down over the weekend **** ****
Please save your work and shutdown
**** **** promptly at 5 PM on Friday.                 ****
 ****                                      ****


You have these remote connections:    H:\\WINDOWS-WRKN306\d$
Continuing will cancel the connections.
The command completed successfully.
The command completed successfully.


  ****  Hello Administrator! Welcome to the SASNAK Domain!
```

After you have created a suitable logon script, you have to save it, and then assign it to a user. In the Windows 2000 Active Directory environment, all logon scripts are saved to the SYSVOL. This allows the scripts to be automatically replicated to all of the domain controllers.

Assigning Logon Scripts

There are two ways to assign a logon script to a user, via Group Policy, which only applies to Windows 2000 clients; and by configuring the user profile, which works with all clients. Windows 2000 is very flexible in that there are five script types that are supported. They are

➤ *Legacy Logon Scripts*—These are the same type of logon scripts that were used in previous versions of Windows NT. They are assigned in the user object in a similar fashion to the way they were assigned in Window NT 4. Legacy logon scripts can be used with Windows 2000 clients, Windows NT clients, or Windows 9x clients. They are the only way to use logon scripts with non-Windows 2000 clients because the other scripts are assigned via Group policy and are only supported on Windows 2000 clients.

➤ *Group Policy Startup Scripts*—This is a new feature. These scripts run when the client machine is started.

➤ *Group Policy Shutdown Scripts*—This is a new feature. These scripts run when the client machine is being shut down. This type of script is handy for automatically deleting the contents of the Temp folder. Sometimes sensitive material is copied to the temp folder inadvertently.

➤ *Group Policy Logon Scripts*—These are the same type of user logon scripts that were used in previous versions of Windows NT. The difference is that they are assigned via Group Policies.

➤ *Group Policy Logoff Scripts*—This is a new feature. These scripts allow you to assign a script that runs when the user logs off the network. They can be used for various cleanup tasks (especially security related), to unmap drives, or release various resources.

13

To assign a logon script using the user profile:

1. Select Start | Programs | Administrative Tools | Active Directory Users And Computers.

2. In the console tree, double-click the container of the user account that you wish to add the logon script to.

3. Locate the user object in the right pane of the console, then double-click it to open the User Properties window.

4. In the User Properties window, select the Profile tab (see Figure 13.12).

5. In the Login Script field of the Profile window, enter the path and the name for the logon script (\winnt\sysvol\sasnak.com\scripts\logon.cmd).

6. Click OK to save.

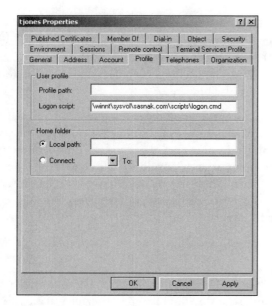

Figure 13.12 User Properties Profile tab.

7. Log on as the user that the script was assigned to, and check that the script functions correctly.

Although assigning a logon script to a user profile will work with all clients, it can be quite tedious to assign scripts to a large number of users. In addition, large batches of scripts can be a nightmare to manage if the logon script names change frequently. The best solution is to assign logon scripts via Group Policy. This allows all changes to be performed in one place. When assigning scripts using a Group Policy, you have the option of also assigning a logoff script. Unfortunately, Group Policies can only be used with Windows 2000 clients. To assign a logon script using Group Policies:

1. Open the appropriate Group Policy console for the users that you want to apply the policy to.

2. Click the User Configuration icon, and then click the Windows settings folder.

3. Click the Scripts (Logon/Logoff) icon.

4. In the right pane of the console window, double-click the Logon icon.

5. The Logon Properties window opens. Click Add. The Add a Script window appears.

6. In the Add a Script window, you can either type in the name of the logon script, or you can click Browse to locate it. Type the script name. Click OK.

7. Click OK again to close the Properties window.

8. Log on as the user that the script was assigned to, and check that the script functions correctly.

The procedures to assign Group Policy Startup and Shutdown scripts are similar. They are also assigned via the Group Policy console.

Note: *On a Windows 2000 client, the logon scripts run in the background, so you will not see them execute as you would on a pre-Windows 2000 client. However, this setting can be changed via Group Policy.*

Group Policy Shutdown Scripts

Startup and shutdown scripts are new features in Windows 2000. Startup and shutdown scripts are assigned to a computer versus the logon and logoff scripts, which are assigned to users. The startup and shutdown scripts are useful for making customizations to the computer that are not user specific.

A good example of a where a Group Policy Shutdown script is useful is on a mail or a database server, where background services must be stopped before the system can shut down.

Anyone who has had the opportunity to work with Exchange Server knows that if you select shutdown or restart without stopping the Exchange services first, you can be assured of a long wait while the services are stopped by the system. Most system administrators create a batch file with an icon on the desktop, so that they can click it to stop the services and restart the system. Unfortunately, most of us forget to click the icon from time to time, usually when we are in a hurry and can least afford the long wait for everything to stop on its own.

13

The following logoff script can be used to stop the Exchange services:

```
rem Exchange Server Shutdown Script
rem Stop Microsoft Exchange Services
rem
rem
echo Stopping Services
net stop MSExchangePCMTA
net stop MSExchangeFB
net stop MSExchangeDX
net stop MSExchangeIMC
net stop MSExchangeMTA
net stop MSExchangeIS
net stop MSExchangeDS
net stop MSExchangeSA
```

Note: The previous code is a typical example of the services running on an Exchange Server. The actual number and sequence of services will depend on your individual configuration.

There are two ways to assign this logoff script. The first is to apply it to the Exchange Server using a Local Group Policy. However, if you have more than two Exchange Servers in your enterprise, it is more efficient to create an organizational unit for your Exchange Servers, place all of the Exchange Servers in the organizational unit, and apply the policy to that OU.

Although Exchange Server was used as an example, this method can be used with any server that has services that take a long time to shut down.

Using WSH for Logon Scripts

WSH and its various languages can be used to create very sophisticated logon scripts. The majority of limitations that affect the MS-DOS–based batch language supplied with Windows 2000 are nonexistent in the programming languages that are supplied with WSH. Earlier in the chapter, we examined WSH and saw how easily it can be used to automate miscellaneous tasks.

The following code contains the logon script that was previously created in the MS-DOS batch language and is now converted to VBScript.

```
' This script shows how to perform the same functions
' as the previously shown logon.cmd in VBScript
Dim network
Set network = Wscript.CreateObject("wscript.Network")
Set shell = Wscript.CreateObject("Wscript.Shell")
set env = shell.environment
'create network environment and shell objects, the shell object will be
'used for popup messages
'
shell.Popup " Welcome to the World of Windows 2000!    "& _
"The network will be down over the weekend "&_
"Please save your work and shutdown "&_
"promptly at 5 PM on Friday."
'

'
network.MapNetworkDrive "G:", "\\" & "logonserver" & "\accounting"
network.MapNetworkDrive "H:", "\\" & "logonserver" & "\d$"
```

The past few sections have provided a basic overview of some of the most commonly used commands in logon scripts. We did not attempt to show all of the different permutations that are available for each command.

Logon scripts are not required. They just provide an additional method for the system administrator to automate the setup and configuration of the user environment.

Best Practices

Here are some additional tips for using logon scripts:

➤ Assign logon scripts via Group Policy whenever possible. Managing and keeping track of what users have been assigned which script will be easier.

➤ Use Logoff scripts for those applications that are slow to shut down. Exchange Server is a good example.

➤ Document your scripts! Use as many comments as necessary to explain what you are trying to do. No one wants to have to maintain old scripts that cannot be understood.

CHAPTER SUMMARY

This chapter explored how to automate repetitive tasks in Windows 2000. It is important to remember that although scripting can be a real time saver, it does not have to be used for every task. You should always take into account the time it will take to develop and debug a script to perform a task. There will be times when it will take longer to create the script than it does to manually perform the task.

We have looked at how to use logon scripts to automate user configurations and various other tasks in Windows 2000. It is important to remember that you don't have to use a sophisticated language to create a logon script when all you need to do is map a couple of drives. The MS-DOS batch language is very small and very fast. It also takes very few lines of code to perform many tasks. Not all situations will require the complex looping and data structures that can be supplied by the more sophisticated scripting languages.

When scheduling tasks, use an account that has the proper rights to support the task. This can minimize the amount of damage that can occur if the task should have a catastrophic error, but it also can prevent an unauthorized process from gaining too much access to your network.

13

REVIEW QUESTIONS

1. Which versions of Windows use the **AT** command to schedule tasks? [Choose all that apply]

   a. Windows 3.11

   b. Windows NT 4

   c. Windows 2000

   d. Windows 98

2. Where is scheduled task data created using the **AT** command stored?

   a. A .job file

   b. A .tsk file

   c. %windir%

   d. Registry

3. Where is scheduled task data created using the Windows 2000 Task Scheduler stored?

   a. A .job file

   b. A .tsk file

   c. %windir%

   d. Registry

4. Tasks that are scheduled using the **AT** command can be viewed and modified using Task Scheduler.

   a. True

   b. False

5. Which group must you be a member of to schedule tasks using the **AT** command?

   a. Power Users

   b. Server Operators

   c. Backup Operators

   d. Administrators

6. Which group must you be a member of to schedule tasks using Task Scheduler?

   a. Power Users

   b. Server Operators

   c. Whatever group has sufficient permissions to complete the task

   d. Administrators

7. Which tools can be used to diagnose problems with Task Scheduling? [Choose all that apply]

   a. PerfMon

   b. Task Scheduler Log

   c. Notify Me Of Missed Tasks option

   d. None of the above

8. What does the Task Scheduler log show? [Choose all that apply]

   a. Missed tasks

   b. When the task was started

   c. Exit code from tasks

   d. The next time that the task is scheduled

9. Which scripting engines are included in Windows 2000 WSH? [Choose all that apply]

   a. JavaScript

   b. VBScript

   c. JScript

   d. VBAScript

10. How do you determine which scripting engine to use with WSH? [Choose all that apply]

    a. Script file name extension

    b. Command-line switch

    c. Batch file

    d. Registry setting

11. WSH supplies a set of objects that can be used with scripting languages other than VBScript.

    a. True

    b. False

12. WSH can be used with Active Directory via what interface? [Choose all that apply]

    a. ADSI

    b. Kerberos

    c. LDAP

    d. ADPI

13

13. All attributes in Active Directory can be changed via scripting except for passwords.

    a. True

    b. False

14. What are the common types of scripting errors? [Choose all that apply]

    a. Syntax

    b. Logic

    c. Overflow

    d. Runtime

15. The Microsoft Script Debugger was designed especially for use with WSH.

    a. True

    b. False

16. In Windows 2000, Logon scripts, by default, are stored in the NETLOGON share.

    a. True

    b. False

17. Using scripts is always recommended over using batch files created using the MS-DOS batch language.

    a. True

    b. False

18. The enhancements added to the MS-DOS batch language in Windows 2000 makes it equal to most scripting languages.

    a. True

    b. False

19. Logon scripts and batch files are created using the Microsoft Script Editor.

    a. True

    b. False

20. What types of scripts are supported in Windows 2000? [Choose all that apply]

    a. Logon Scripts

    b. Group Policy Logon and Logoff Scripts

    c. Group Policy Scheduled Scripts

    d. Logoff Scripts

21. Logon Scripts are required in Windows 2000.

     a. True

     b. False

22. What commands and utilities can be used to schedule tasks in Windows 2000? [Choose all that apply]

     a. WinAt

     b. **AT**

     c. Task Scheduler

     d. Task Manager

23. What is the advantage of using the **AT** command instead of Task Scheduler?

     a. Smaller

     b. Faster

     c. Ease of use

     d. Can be scripted

24. Which command line is in the correct format to schedule go.bat to run unattended?

     a. AT 12:00 go.bat

     b. AT 12:00 cmd /c go.bat

     c. AT 12:00 cmd /c c:\go.bat

     d. AT 12:00 /I cmd /c go.bat

13

REAL-WORLD PROJECTS

Note: This exercise assumes you have two test servers, one with Windows 2000 Server and the other with Windows NT 4. Read the instructions carefully, and do not perform these projects on any of your production machines.

A medium-sized architectural firm has contracted with Jeff Smith to complete the migration of its network from Windows NT 4 to Windows 2000. A previous consultant upgraded all of the domain controllers to Windows 2000, but the company that she worked for went bankrupt, so she had to leave before she could complete some of the follow-up tasks that were requested.

The office consists of three servers with only two currently running Windows 2000 Server software. One server is a dedicated print server that is still running a previous version of Windows NT; the second server has been upgraded to

Windows 2000 Server and runs Exchange Server. The third server has been upgraded to Windows 2000 and is the domain controller. There are 250 workstations running various versions of Windows.

The tasks that were not completed are as follows:

➤ The database administrator has a sort job that he needs to run during nonbusiness hours. Currently, he has to dial in to the system and start the job manually; he needs a way to automate this task. If possible, he would like to run it around midnight when there are no users on the system. He has everything set up in a batch file, and because it is a new product, the product needs to be able to interface with Active Directory.

➤ The architectural firm purchased a smaller company, and it wants the new users to be given userids on the network. A list of user names has been dumped to a space-delimited file.

➤ The existing print server does not support Windows 2000, so it will have to be replaced with a new one. All of the printers will have to be moved to the new server.

➤ Because of some changes on the network, users will have to be mapped to some new drive shares. Currently, users are not using logon scripts, but it seems like a good time to introduce these.

Jeff is confident that he can get the jobs done with minimal interference to the staff members and their work. Grabbing his command reference and notepad, he sets off to work.

Project 13.1
To automate the sort job, perform the following steps:

1. Select Start | Settings | Control Panel.

2. Double-click the Scheduled Tasks folder. The Scheduled Tasks window opens.

3. Double-click Add Scheduled Task. The Scheduled Task Wizard starts; click Next.

4. The Scheduled Task Wizard displays a list of applications that it has found on your system. The application that you need is not listed. Click Browse.

5. The Select Program to Schedule window appears. From this window, you can navigate to the program, batch, or script file that you want to run. Navigate to the D: drive, and select the desired file. Click Open to continue.

6. The Scheduled Task Wizard prompts you to type in a name for the task. Type "DB Sort". Next, you will need to select how often to perform this task. There are selections for:

➤ Daily

➤ Weekly

➤ Monthly

➤ One Time Only

➤ When My Computer Starts

➤ When I Log On

7. Because the DB administrator wants to run this batch file every day, select the Daily radio button. Click Next.

8. You are given options to set the time for the task. Set the start time to 11:59 P.M. Click Next.

9. Enter the name of an account that has the proper authority to run the batch file and the appropriate password. Because the batch file you are running has to access Active Directory objects, it needs administrative access. Enter an account with Administrator rights in the format *domain\userid*. Type in the password twice, and then click Next.

10. You will receive a summary of the options that you selected to schedule this task. Review the options. If any options need to be changed click Back to return to the previous screens. Click Finish to complete the task.

Jeff completed this task, and then used Task Scheduler log to monitor it over the next few days.

13

Project 13.2
To add users to Active Directory via scripting, perform the following steps:

Jeff decided to use the **For** command to parse the space-delimited data input file with the following format to create the user accounts.

```
C:\>type filename
Asmith Ann Smith
Tjones Terri Jones
```

Using the /f switch with the **For** command will parse the data that it reads from the text file and pass it to the replaceable parameters, which you add to the **NET USER** command like this:

```
C:\>type addusers.cmd
For /f "tokens=1,%" %X in (filename) do net user %X  /add /
  fullname:"%%Y"
```

1. Create the addusers.cmd batch file using the previously mentioned commands and syntax.

2. Select Start | Programs | Accessories, and then select the Command Prompt.

3. Run the command file.

After Jeff added the new users to Active Directory, he requested that they all log on and change their password from blank to something that was acceptable on the network.

Project 13.3
To migrate printers to Active Directory, perform the following steps:

Because the old print server could not be upgraded to Windows 2000, Jeff had to perform some additional steps.

1. Install and configure Windows 2000 Server on the new print server machine.

2. Create a script to migrate the printers from the old print server to the new one. Fortunately, Microsoft has supplied a script to automate the addition of non-Windows 2000 printers. The pubprn.vbs script is provided in the \winnt\System32 folder.

   To use the script, the syntax is

   ```
   cscript pubprn.vbs <servername> dspath
   ```

   As an example, the following command publishes all the printers on the Topeka print server. The printers will be published in the Marketing organizational unit (OU) container in the Sasnak domain.

   ```
   cscript pubprn.vbs topeka "LDAP://ou=marketing,dc=sasnak,dc=com"
   ```

   The script can also be used to publish a single printer.

   ```
   cscript pubprn.vbs \\topeka\HP5
   "LDAP://ou=marketing,dc=sasnak,dc=com"
   ```

The pubprn.vbs script will publish only the following subset of the printer's attributes:

➤ Comment

➤ Location

➤ Model

➤ UNC Path

3. Select Start | Programs | Accessories, and then select the Command Prompt.

4. Call the pubprn.vbs script using the previously mentioned syntax.

Jeff made sure that all of the printers were migrated over properly; he then retired the old print server.

Project 13.4
To add a legacy logon script, perform the following steps:

1. Open Active Directory Users And Computers by selecting Start | Programs | Administrative Tools | Active Directory Users And Computers.

2. In the console tree, double-click the container of the user accounts that you want to add the logon script to.

3. Locate the user objects in the right pane of the console, then hold down the control key, and select the ones you want to add the logon script to.

4. Right-click your highlighted selections. A pop-up menu appears.

5. Select Properties. The User Properties window appears.

6. In the User Properties window, select the Profile tab.

7. In the Login Script field of the Profile window, enter the path and the name for the logon script (\winnt\sysvol\sasnak.com\scripts*commandfilename.cmd*).

8. Click OK to save.

9. Log on as one of the users that the script was assigned to, and check that the script functions correctly.

Jeff then closed his notepad for the day and went home to celebrate a job well done!

13

CHAPTER FOURTEEN

MANAGING WINDOWS 2000 SERVER

After completing this chapter, you will be able to:

✓ Work with the Microsoft Management Console (MMC)

✓ Manage Windows 2000 using Administrative Tools utilities

✓ Manage Windows 2000 using Control Panel utilities

M anaging a Windows 2000 Server requires intimate knowledge of the tools and utilities used to control every aspect of a network environment. These tools are found within the Control Panel and in the Administrative Tools section of the Start menu (there is also a link to Administrative Tools in the Control Panel). Thorough knowledge of these tools can aid you in performing any administrative task, including access control, performance monitoring, hardware installation, system management, service configuration, and more. This chapter examines each of the administration and management tools native to Windows 2000 Server.

MICROSOFT MANAGEMENT CONSOLE

Windows 2000 has adopted a new utility infrastructure that most of the system administration and management tools are built upon. This infrastructure is known as the *Microsoft Management Console (MMC)*. The MMC offers a standardized interface through which controls can be added to manipulate and interact with any object on the local system or network. The MMC simplifies Microsoft's native tools and allows third-party vendors to quickly and easily build interfaces for their proprietary devices and applications that can be directly integrated with other administrative tools. The MMC itself is little more than a display console and a programmatic shell; it offers no native control or administrative capabilities. Admin controls are added to the MMC through *snap-ins*. A snap-in is a tool designed to interact with a single type or group of objects. Multiple snap-ins can be combined to create a multitool utility where most or all common tasks can be performed through a single utility. An example of such a multiple snap-in configuration is the Computer Management tool found in the Administrative Tools section of the Start menu.

An MMC console is a "document" of the MMC that hosts one or more snap-ins. Each MMC can have one or more consoles loaded at any given time, in much the same manner as an Office application can load multiple documents. Many snap-ins can be expanded or enhanced through the use of specialty *extensions*. An extension simply offers additional functions or capabilities to an object-specific snap-in.

In many cases, an MMC snap-in can be used to manage objects locally or remotely. When working with remote systems, you must have administrative privileges or delegated access on the remote system.

MMC is not a completely new element. It was first introduced to the Windows NT platform via the Windows NT 4 Option Pack. The MMC was first used to host the snap-in for controlling Internet Information Server 4. Microsoft has plans to include the MMC in Windows Millennium (the third edition of Windows 98).

The MMC shell can be launched independently of any snap-ins, but, in such a state, it offers no administrative capabilities. Launching an empty MMC is performed through the Start|Run command or a command prompt using the execution string "mmc". This will open the MMC shell (see Figure 14.1).

The MMC shell has a menu bar offering Console, Window, and Help menus. The Console menu contains the following commands:

➤ *New*—Closes an existing MMC shell and opens a new MMC shell with an empty console.

➤ *Open*—Opens an existing console window stored in an MSC file.

➤ *Save*—Saves the current console to its MSC file.

➤ *Save As*—Saves the current console into a new MSC file.

➤ *Add/Remove Snap-In*—Adds or removes snap-ins from the current console.

➤ *Options*—Sets the mode for the console (as described later this chapter).

➤ *Exit*—Closes the MMC.

The Window menu contains the following commands:

➤ *New Window*—Creates a new console window.

➤ *Cascade*—Arranges open console windows in a cascading fashion.

➤ *Tile Horizontally*—Arranges open console windows in a tiling fashion.

➤ *Arrange Icons*—Arranges minimized console window icons.

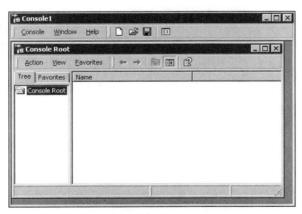

Figure 14.1   An empty MMC shell.

The Help menu contains common commands to access help, jump to Web resources, and display version information about MMC.

An empty console window is displayed by default within the MMC shell. The console window offers a menu bar with Action, View, and Favorites menus. The Action menu contains commands based on the context of the selected node or subelement. The View menu contains common commands that you can use to alter the icon display of the console. The Favorites menu is used to add shortcuts to console and snap-in elements.

A console has several important elements in addition to its menu bar. It also includes a button toolbar, console tree (also referred to as a scope pane), and details pane. The button toolbar varies based on the context of a selected snap-in or subelement within the console tree or details pane. The console tree displays the organization and relationship of snap-ins. The specific items present in this area are known as *nodes*. The details pane, located to the right of the console tree, displays the subelements of a selected console node.

From a blank console window, any native or third-party snap-in can be added into the display. After a snap-in is loaded into a console window, it can be immediately used to perform its programmed functions. In most cases, you'll want to organize and configure your snap-ins, then save them as MSC files for later use. Some of the snap-ins included with Windows 2000 are:

➤ Active Directory Schema

➤ ActiveX Control

➤ ADSI Edit

➤ Certificates

➤ Component Services

➤ Computer Management

➤ Device Manager

➤ Disk Defragmenter

➤ Disk Management

➤ Event Viewer

➤ Fax Service Management

➤ Folder

➤ Group Policy

➤ Indexing Service

➤ IP Security Policy Management

➤ Link to Web Address

➤ Local Users and Groups

➤ Performance Logs and Alerts

➤ Removable Storage Management

➤ Resource Kits

➤ Security Configuration and Analysis

➤ Security Templates

➤ Services

➤ Shared Folders

➤ SIDWalker Security Manager

➤ System Information

➤ WinMgmt Control

The preceding snap-ins are used in the various predefined tools and utilities found in the Control Panel or Administrative Tools. However, you can use the same snap-ins to create a customized control and management system that closely matches the methods you employ to manage systems. To do so, issue the Add/Remove Snap-In command from the Console menu, then click Add to access the Add Standalone Snap-In dialog box (see Figure 14.2).

14

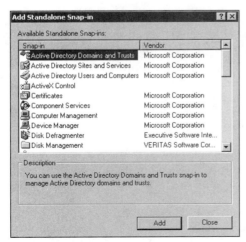

Figure 14.2   The Add Standalone Snap-In dialog box.

On the Console menu, the Options menu is used to define a name for the console and set the console mode. The mode determines how much change control a user has over a console. The four modes are:

➤ *Author Mode*—Users can add and remove snap-ins, create new console windows, view a console tree, and save altered versions of the console, if desired. This is the default mode for MMC consoles.

➤ *User Mode: Full Access*—Users can create new console windows and view a console tree, but users are prevented from adding or removing snap-ins and saving altered versions of the console.

➤ *User Mode: Delegated Access, Multiple Windows*—Users can create new console windows, but users are prevented from accessing portions of the console tree, adding or removing snap-ins, and saving altered versions of the console.

➤ *User Mode: Delegated Access, Single Window*—Users are prevented from creating new console windows, accessing portions of the console tree, adding or removing snap-ins, and saving altered versions of the console.

After you've selected a console mode, save the console under a new file name. Keep in mind that once you save a console under a User Mode setting, you cannot change the mode to Author Mode. Once a console is saved in a User Mode format, it can be safely distributed for nonadministrators to use.

ADMINISTRATIVE TOOLS

Most of Windows 2000's native administration and management utilities are MMC consoles. These utilities are found mainly in the Administrative Tools section of the Control Panel (see Figure 14.3) or Start menu. Windows 2000 Server's MMC console tools include:

➤ *Active Directory Domains And Trusts*—Manages domains and trusts. Functions performed through this utility include defining domain manager, setting the domain mode, and creating trusts. Details on this tool can be found in Chapters 9 and 12.

➤ *Active Directory Sites And Services*—Manages services, sites, and replication. Details on this tool can be found in Chapter 9.

➤ *Active Directory Users And Computers*—Manages users, groups, and computers. Details on this tool can be found in Chapter 12.

➤ *Component Services*—Manages COM+, scripted tasks, interprocess transactions, and scalable component applications. This was previously the Microsoft Transaction Server. Details on this tool can be found in the *Windows 2000 Server Resource Kit* and the IIS 5 Software Developers Kit.

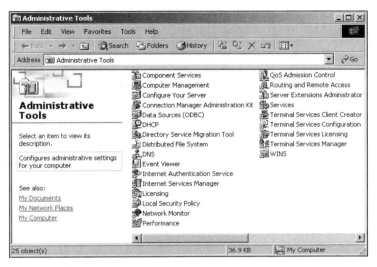

Figure 14.3 Administrative tools.

➤ *Computer Management*—Manages various aspects of the local computer system, including event details, drive configuration, services, and more. Details on this tool can be found later in this chapter.

➤ *Data Sources (ODBC)*—Manages DSNs (Data Source Names) used by services and applications to interact with databases. Details on this tool can be found in the *Windows 2000 Server Resource Kit.*

➤ *DHCP*—Manages the dynamic client configuration service for a domain. Details on this tool can be found in Chapter 8.

➤ *Distributed File System*—Manages the Distributed file system service for a domain. Details on this tool can be found in Chapter 4.

➤ *DNS*—Manages the name resolution service that associates domain names with Internet Protocol (IP) addresses. Details on this tool can be found in Chapter 8.

➤ *Domain Controller Security Policy*—Manages the security policy for domain controllers. Details on this tool can be found in Chapter 11.

➤ *Domain Security Policy*—Manages the group policy for a domain. Details on this tool can be found in Chapter 11.

➤ *Event Viewer*—Manages the event details recorded by Windows 2000. Details on this tool can be found later in this chapter.

➤ *Internet Services Manager*—Manages the Internet information services of Web and File Transfer Protocol (FTP). Details on this tool can be found in Chapter 10.

14

➤ *Licensing*—Manages the licensing of Windows 2000 and related applications. Details on this tool can be found later in this chapter.

➤ *Local Security Policy*—Manages the local group policy for a system. Details on this tool can be found in Chapter 11.

➤ *Network Monitor*—Gathers information on network packet data for network troubleshooting purposes.

➤ *Performance*—Manages the monitoring of system performance, records logs of activity, and issues performance alerts. Details on this tool can be found in Chapter 6.

➤ *Routing And Remote Access*—Manages routing and remote access for a server. Details on this tool can be found in Chapter 10.

➤ *Server Extensions Administrator*—Manages FrontPage server extensions. Details on this tool can be found in the *Windows 2000 Server Resource Kit*.

Note: *Configure Your Server is not an MMC console tool; instead, it is a multimenued wizard that you can use to configure a server. Details on this tool can be found in Chapters 3, 9, and 10.*

Services is not an MMC console; it is an applet (however, it appears as a snap-in within the Computer Management tool). See the Control Panel section later in this chapter.

Telnet Server is not an MMC console; it is a text-based menu system used to configure and manage the Telnet server service. Details on this tool can be found in Chapter 10.

Other tools might appear within Administrative Tools based on added Microsoft or third-party components. However, the preceding list is an exhaustive list of the default utilities that appear on a Windows 2000 Server domain controller.

Computer Management

Computer Management (see Figure 14.4) is a utility located in Administrative Tools. It is an MMC console with a variety of snap-ins that offer administration and management control over numerous components and objects within a computer system. The capabilities of Computer Management are separated into three sections—System Tools, Storage, and Services And Applications.

The section labeled *System Tools* contains six snap-in tools:

➤ *Event Viewer*—This utility is used to view and manage Windows 2000's log files. This utility is the same utility found in the Start menu under Programs | Administrative Tools | Event Viewer. Details on this tool can be found later in this chapter.

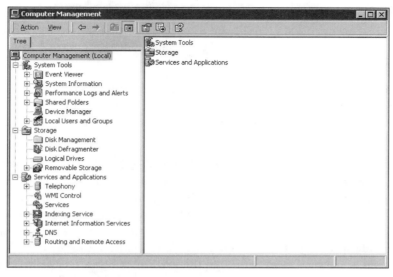

Figure 14.4   Computer Management.

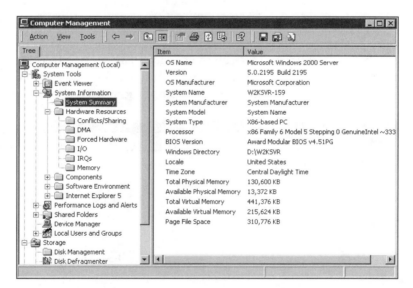

Figure 14.5   The System Information utility in Computer Management.

➤ *System Information*—This utility is used to examine and display information in the System Summary (see Figure 14.5), Hardware Resources, Components, Software Environment, and Internet Explorer 5 nodes. This utility is only able to display the current status, value, or setting of the various objects; it cannot be used to configure or alter any displayable settings. The most useful portion of this utility relates to hardware resources.

The currently used and available system resources of DMA, I/O address, IRQ, and memory addresses are listed along with any conflicts. This utility is the same utility found in the Start menu under Programs | Accessories | System Tools | System Information.

➤ *Performance Logs and Alerts*—This utility is used to record logs of performance activity and scan for performance alerts. This is the same tool found through the Performance tool of Administrative Tools. Details on this tool can be found in Chapter 6.

➤ *Shared Folders*—This utility is used to manage shares (see Figure 14.6). From here, new shares can be created, and existing shares can be managed. Share management includes changing a share's comment, changing its simultaneous user limit, specifying whether caching of its contents is allowed, changing permissions on the share, and changing permissions on the file-level object itself. Under the Shares node, both normal and hidden shares are displayed, and, through this section, you can access a share's Properties dialog box. Under the Sessions node, a list of all users currently accessing shares is displayed. Under the Open Files node, a list of all files currently being accessed is displayed.

➤ *Device Manager*—This utility is used to manage devices, drivers, and hardware configuration. Through the Device Manager (see Figure 14.7), drivers can be updated, conflicts resolved, and devices added or removed from hardware profiles. This is the same utility accessed by pressing the

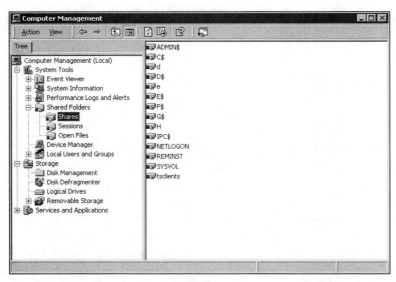

Figure 14.6 The Shared Folders utility in Computer Management.

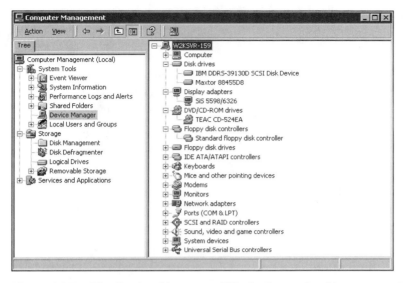

Figure 14.7 The Device Manager utility in Computer Management.

Device Manager button on the Hardware tab in the System applet. Details on this tool can be found later in this chapter.

➤ *Local Users and Groups*—This utility is used to manage local users and groups. It is disabled on Windows 2000 Server when Active Directory is installed.

The section labeled *Storage* contains four snap-in tools:

➤ *Disk Management*—This utility is used to manage hard drives. It can be used to create volumes and various types of volume sets, format volumes, assign drive letters and mount points, and more. Details on this tool can be found in Chapter 7.

➤ *Disk Defragmenter*—This utility is used to reduce the fragmentation of Windows 2000 volumes. Details on this tool can be found in Chapter 7.

➤ *Logical Drives*—This utility is used to access information about logical drives, specifically the same information as seen on the General and Security tabs of a volume's Properties dialog box. Details on this tool can be found in Chapter 7.

➤ *Removable Storage*—This utility is used to manage libraries of removable media, such as floppies, tapes, CDs, CDRs, and CDRWs. Details on this tool can be found in Chapter 7.

The section labeled *Services And Applications* contains a varying number of snap-in tools, based on the installed services and applications. Some of the tool you might see here include:

➤ *DHCP*—This utility is used to manage the dynamic client configuration service for a domain. This is the same tool as DHCP in the Administrative Tools. Details on this tool can be found in Chapter 8.

➤ *Telephony*—This utility is used to manage communication providers. This is the same tool as the Advanced tab in the Phone And Modem applet. Details on this tool can be found in Chapter 10.

➤ *Services*—This utility is used to manage services. This is the same tool as the Services tool in Administrative Tools. Details on this tool can be found later in this chapter.

➤ *Indexing Service*—This utility is used to manage the indexing service. Details on this tool can be found in Chapter 10.

➤ *Internet Information Services*—This utility is used to manage the Web, FTP, and Simple Mail Transfer Protocol (SMTP) services of IIS 5. This is the same tool as Internet Service Manager in Administrative Tools. Details on this tool can be found in Chapter 10.

➤ *DNS*—This utility is used to manage the name resolution service that associates domain names with IP addresses. This is the same tool as DNS in Administrative Tools. Details on this tool can be found in Chapter 8.

Event Viewer

Windows 2000 log files are managed and viewed through the Event Viewer. The Event Viewer is available as an element of Computer Management and as its own tool in Administrative Tools. The Event Viewer (see Figure 14.8) manages the three standard Windows NT/2000 log files—System, Application, and Security—as well as several application or service-specific logs, such as Directory Service, DNS Server, and File Replication Service. The Event Viewer can view logs from the local system or any remote system (assuming proper access permission on the remote system).

The log files record *event details*. An event detail is a document that records information about occurrences within the Windows 2000 environment. A wide range of occurrences can trigger the creation of an event detail. These include audit events, failed services, rebooting, starting of services, functions of an application, changes in group policy, and system errors. Each event detail includes relevant who, what, when, and where specifics, including:

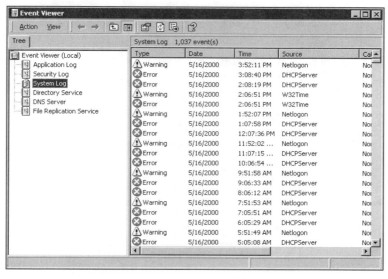

Figure 14.8 The Event Viewer.

➤ Date

➤ Time

➤ Type

➤ User

➤ Computer

➤ Source

➤ Category

➤ Event ID

➤ Description

➤ Data

Most logs contain three types of event details:

➤ *Information event detail*—Identified by a thought bubble containing a blue *i*.

➤ *Warning event detail*—Identified by a yellow triangle containing an exclamation point.

➤ *Error event detail*—Identified by a red circle containing a white *X*.

The Security log only contains success and failure event details based on enabled audit options. Every log file viewed through the Event Viewer can be

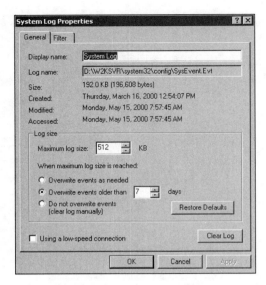

Figure 14.9 A log file's Properties dialog box, General tab.

customized. The Properties dialog box for a log has a General tab and a Filter tab. The General tab (see Figure 14.9) displays information and provides the following functions:

➤ Shows the display name of the log.

➤ Displays the path and file name of the log.

➤ Specifies the current size of the log.

➤ Specifies the date the log was started.

➤ Indicates the last date the log was modified.

➤ Indicates the last date the log was read or written to.

➤ Displays the maximum size the log can grow, set in kilobytes.

➤ Enables you to define, when the log file becomes full, whether to overwrite events as needed, only overwrite events older than a specific number of days, or stop recording into the log until manually emptied.

➤ Enables you to use low-speed connection management schemes for the logs being stored over a slow connection.

➤ Allows you to restore the default settings.

➤ Enables you to clear the log file.

Each log file has its own Properties dialog box and each can have different settings defined.

The Filter tab of a log's Properties is accessed both through the Properties command on the Action menu and the Filter command on the View menu. The Filter tab (see Figure 14.10) is used to reduce the types of event details displayed through the Event Viewer. Reducing the number of displayed items can help you locate specific information. Options to filter event details include:

➤ Event Types, including Information, Warning, Error, Success Audit, and Failure Audit options

➤ Event Source

➤ Category

➤ Event ID

➤ User

➤ Computer

➤ From *first event*, *time*, or *date*

➤ To *last event*, *time*, or *date*

Another useful element of the Event Viewer can be access by selecting the Find command on the View menu. The Find feature can be used to search for keywords or text strings contained within a selected log. The search parameters can include the same elements as for a filter in addition to a keyword or text string.

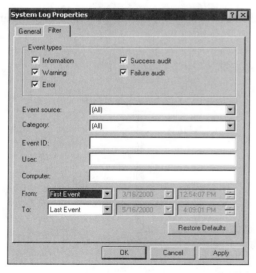

Figure 14.10 A log file's Properties dialog box, Filter tab.

Licensing

The ability for users to legally connect to a Windows 2000 Server and use network-enabled BackOffice or third-party applications is managed by the Licensing utility. Licensing manages the number of simultaneous users based on the total number of use or access licensing purchased and installed on a Windows 2000 Server. This tool can manage licensed usage for any application that registers with it. This includes many Microsoft BackOffice and other add-on products for Windows 2000 as well as many third-party products. The Licensing utility (see Figure 14.11) is launched from the Administrative Tools section of the Start menu or the Control Panel.

Two types of licensing can be used on Windows 2000—Per Server and Per Seat. Client access licenses are granted to the server with Per Server licensing. This means that a single client computer can connect to the server for each installed license. This also restricts the client access license to a single server, the one on which it is installed. Client access licenses are granted to the client with Per Seat licensing. This means that a client can connect to any server on the network for each installed license. Smaller networks or networks with few servers can use Per Server licensing. Larger networks or networks with many servers should use Per Seat licensing. Windows 2000 licensing can be converted from Per Server to Per Seat once if your needs change, but it cannot be reversed without reinstalling the operating system (OS).

The Licensing utility's tabs are:

➤ *Purchase History*—This tab displays the history of purchased and installed licenses expansions per product.

➤ *Products View*—This tab displays the total number of Per Seat and Per Server licenses for each product.

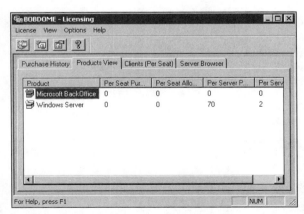

Figure 14.11   The Licensing dialog box, Products View tab.

➤ *Clients (Per Seat)*—This tab displays information about which client-based licenses are being used and for which products.

➤ *Server Browser*—This tab displays the settings of licensing on other servers on the network.

Through the Advanced submenu of the Options menu, *license groups* can be created and managed. A license group is used to grant or restrict access to client access licenses when the total number of users, computers, and licenses are not in synch. For example, consider a system with 300 users, 150 computers, and 100 client access licenses. Further, on this system, 20 users must always be able to access a product. To license this setup, you could use license groups to assign 20 licenses to a group whose members are the 20 special users, and use another license group for the remaining users and license.

Services

Services are the background applications or processes that offer some sort of resource or perform a necessary function for local or network activities. Services range from the print spooler to the security authentication system to the messenger service that is used to display pop-up messages. The Services utility is used to manage how services behave within the Windows 2000 environment. The Services utility (see Figure 14.12) can be accessed either through the Administrative Tools directly or as a subelement of Computer Management.

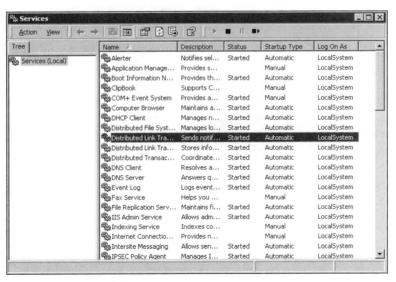

Figure 14.12 The Services utility.

Every installed service, whether active or not, is listed in the Services utility. As shown in Figure 14.12, a service's name is listed along with other items, including a description, activation status, startup type, and security context (Log On As).

The activation status of a service can be blank, Started, or Paused. A Started status indicates that the service is running and performing its tasks. A Paused status indicates the service was running and has been paused. A paused service remains in memory and its allocated system resources are retained. A blank status indicates that the service is not active and is not in memory. All services that are not launched during bootup are inactive until manually started. Services that are Started or Paused can be stopped.

A service's startup type defines how or when a service is started. The possible settings are automatic, manual, or disabled:

➤ *Automatic startup*—Indicates the system will attempt to start the service as soon as its requirements are present. A service's requirements might include other services (known as *dependencies*), system resources, specific processes, an application launch, or a specific logged-on user account.

➤ *Manual startup*—Indicates that the service is not started automatically by the system during bootup, but any process, application, user, or other service can start the service at any time.

➤ *Disabled startup*—Indicates that the service cannot be initiated by the system or by a user; this effectively prevents a service from being launched by accident. Simply returning a service's startup type to automatic or manual enables the service's ability to be executed.

A Log On As entry indicates the user account that will be used to initiate or launch the service as well as provide the service's security context. Most system-controlled and native Windows 2000 services are set to use the LocalSystem account. This means, the service will be launched with system-level access. Some nonessential services can be altered to a less endowed user account, such as an administrator or domain user account. Always test such changes before implementing them on production systems. Many non-native Windows 2000 services, including other products from Microsoft and third-parties, can often be set to use a less-than-system-level user account to establish a security context.

Any listed service can be managed through its own Properties dialog box. A service's Properties dialog box is opened by selecting the service then issuing the Properties command from the Action menu. The General tab (see Figure 14.13) of a service's Properties dialog box includes:

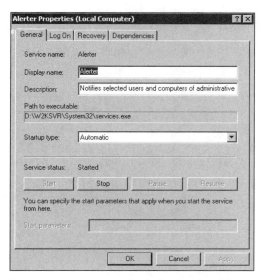

Figure 14.13   A service's Properties dialog box, General tab.

➤ Name of the service

➤ Definable displayed name for the service

➤ Definable description of the service

➤ Path to the service's executable

➤ Selectable startup type setting

➤ Buttons to start, stop, pause, and resume a service (these functions are not available for some services)

➤ A text box to provide command–line startup parameters

The Log On tab (see Figure 14.14) of a service's Properties dialog box includes:

➤ A radio button that enables you to select the logon credentials as the system or a user account

➤ A checkbox that enables you to allow the service to interact with the desktop

➤ Text fields that you can use to provide the username and password for a user account

➤ A list of hardware profiles and the enabled/disabled state of the service

➤ Buttons to enable and disable a service in a selected hardware profile

14

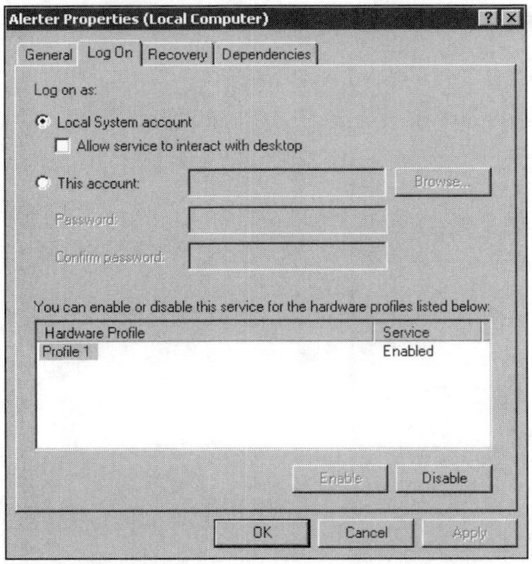

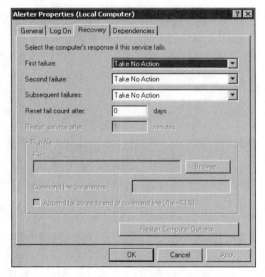

Figure 14.14 A service's Properties dialog box, Log On tab.

Figure 14.15 A service's Properties dialog box, Recovery tab.

The Recovery tab (see Figure 14.15) of a service's Properties dialog box includes:

➤ Pull-down lists to select the response for the first, second, and subsequent failures of a service. Response pull-down lists include options to Take No Action, Restart The Service, Run A File, and Reboot The Computer.

➤ A setting for how often to reset the failed count for a service.

➤ A setting for how long to wait before restarting a failed service.

➤ A field to provide the path and file name of a file to execute on a service failure, a field for command-line parameters, and a checkbox addressing whether to include the failed count as the last element of the command-line parameters.

The Dependencies tab (see Figure 14.16) of a service's Properties dialog box lists the services the service is dependent on (that is, required for execution) and the services that depend on this service. Keep in mind that if a service required by some other process fails, the process might fail or at least be unable to function normally.

CONTROL PANEL TOOLS

In previous incarnations of Windows, the Control Panel was the central repository of management tools. Windows 2000 retains a Control Panel with many familiar applets, a few new applets, and a few borrowed from Windows 98. Most of the local computer system configuration, installation, and troubleshooting tools appear in Control Panel. Specifically, most hardware-related control utilities are found in the Control Panel. The Control Panel (see Figure 14.17) is accessed via the Start menu (Settings | Control Panel), Windows Explorer, and My Computer. The Control Panel is really little more than a shortcut collection window where configuration tools are accessed easily. The Control Panel contains

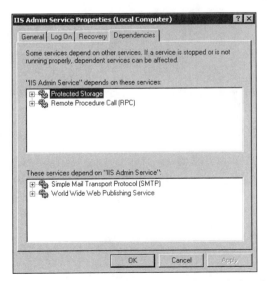

Figure 14.16   A service's Properties dialog box, Dependencies tab.

Figure 14.17 The Control Panel.

links to numerous default applets; however, the actual contents of the Control Panel varies based on the type of computer, the hardware present on the computer, installed services and applications, and the presence of some third-party products. The common applets found in Control Panel on most Windows 2000 Server systems are discussed in the following sections.

Accessibility Options

Windows 2000 offers alternate methods of communicating information through keyboards, sounds, display, mouse, and more through Accessibility Options. These features are designed to enable and improve system interaction for people who are visually, reading, or movement impaired. Some Accessibility Options include:

➤ *StickyKeys*—Enables use of Shift, Ctrl, and Alt with a single keystroke instead of holding the key down.

➤ *FilterKits*—Ignores quickly repeated keystrokes or keys held down for a long period of time.

➤ *SoundSentry*—Displays a visible signal whenever a sound is generated.

➤ *HighContrast*—Sets color schemes to high-contrast display.

➤ *MouseKeys*—Enables you to use the number keypad to control the mouse pointer.

For more information on Accessibility Options, refer to the Accessibility Options applet, online Help information, or the *Windows 2000 Server Resource Kit*.

A⧉⧉⧉ove Hardware

Work⧉⧉⧉ith hardware installation, removal, and troubleshooting is made simple through the Add/Remove Hardware applet/wizard. This tool can be used to add new devices, troubleshoot existing devices, uninstall devices, and temporarily remove or eject devices. The applet wizard walks you through each of these processes step by step. Most hardware is automatically detected and installed at bootup. When not automatically installed, the applet wizard can be used to install any type of device. When adding a device, the wizard searches your system for the new device and attempts to perform an installation automatically. If necessary, you'll be prompted to select the device from a list and provide drivers. Troubleshooting a device is simple, because devices that are not working properly are displayed with a yellow warning or red error icon. Uninstalling a device removes the drivers from the system. Removing or ejecting a device disables the drivers but retains them in the system for the future return of the device.

Add/Remove Programs

Adding and removing Windows 2000 components and third-party software is managed through the Add/Remove Programs applet. The Add/Remove Programs applet (see Figure 14.18) offers three buttons to gain access to its functions:

➤ *Change Or Remove Programs*—Allows you to access a display of installed programs. From this display, each installed program can be changed (if the setup tool for the program supports changes) or removed. This display also includes data such as the amount of disk space consumed by the program and the level-of-use frequency (which can be frequently, occasionally, or rarely).

➤ *Add New Programs*—Enables you to accesses a window to launch the installation of new programs from a floppy, CD, the Microsoft Update Web site, or a network software distribution point.

➤ *Add/Remove Windows Components*—Opens the Windows Components Wizard where native Windows 2000 components can be added or removed by marking the listed item's checkbox (and subcontents' checkboxes).

Administrative Tools

The management tools created through the use of MMC consoles and snap-ins are contained within the Administrative Tools element of the Control Panel. This link contains the same elements as the Start menu's Administrative Tools element. Details on the contents of this element are discussed earlier in this chapter.

14

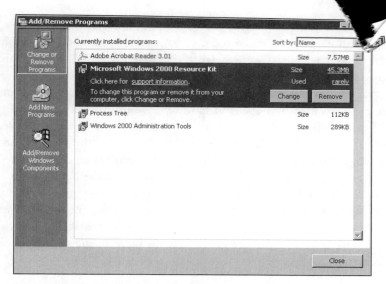

Figure 14.18 The Add/Remove Programs applet.

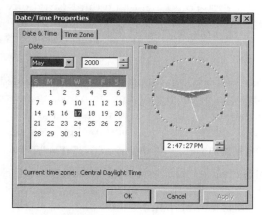

Figure 14.19 The Date/Time applet.

Date/Time

Altering a computer system's date and time is performed through the Date/Time applet (see Figure 14.19). This applet is used to change the calendar date (month, day, year), clock time (hour, minute, second, AM/PM), and time zone (on the Time Zone tab).

Display

Controlling video adapters, colors, screen savers, and more is handled through the Display applet. The controls on each of this applet's tabs are:

➤ *Background*—Sets images to be displayed as desktop wallpaper.

➤ *Screen Saver*—Sets the screen saver, inactivity time period before a screen saver is launched, and whether the screen saver is password protected. Further, this option grants quick access to the monitor's power saving features configuration dialog box.

➤ *Appearance*—Sets the color of windows, desktop, and dialog boxes to predefined or custom schemes.

➤ *Web*—Enables or disables Active Desktop, adds and removes elements to be displayed, and configures the properties for each element.

➤ *Effects*—Sets desktop icons and enables or disables various visual effects, such as menu transition effects, large icons, and show window contents while dragging.

➤ *Settings*—Sets the color depth and screen resolution of the display, used to manage multidisplay layouts (up to nine displays), and grants access to advanced controls for adapter and monitor drivers and configuration settings.

Two or more displays can be used with Windows 2000 to enhance the size of the desktop, show full-screen video, or zoom in on selected desktop areas. After multiple adapters are installed, the Settings tab of the Display applet shows a monitor icon for each adapter. These icons can be arranged into any rectangular configuration. Each individual adapter can have a unique color depth and screen resolution. However, multiple display usage has several requirements:

➤ Only AGP and PCI video adapters are supported.

➤ Motherboards with built-in video adapters can be used, but only as secondary adapters.

➤ Windows 2000 should be installed with a single video adapter. Additional adapters should be installed afterward.

Fax

Faxing can now be performed from Windows 2000 without any additional software. The Fax applet enables you to configure the following settings:

➤ *User Information*—Provides typical cover sheet data.

➤ *Cover Pages*—Enables you to create or add cover sheets for use.

➤ *Status Monitor*—Configures notification.

➤ *Advanced Options*—Launches the Fax Service Management Console, opens Fax Help, and adds a Fax Printer.

14

The Fax Service Management Console is used to configure sending and receiving options, such as number of rings and the level of logging of fax activities.

Faxing is enabled automatically when a fax-capable modem or device is installed. Faxing functions in the same manner as printing, except that a fax device cannot be shared. To fax a document, select the Fax printer. Answering faxes can only be performed manually by default. To enable automatic fax reception, use the Fax Service Manager Console. For details on faxing, see the online help.

Folder Options

Configuring how Windows Explorer and My Computer display file and folder information through their interfaces is controlled through the Folder Options applet. This configuration dialog box is also accessible through the Folder Options command of the Tools menu from either Windows Explorer or My Computer. The configuration options available on the tabs of the Folder Options applet are:

➤ *General*—Specifies whether to use Active Desktop or Windows classic desktop, enables Web content in folders or Windows classic folders, opens folders in the same window or new window, or opens with a single or double click.

➤ *View*—Sets which advanced settings (such as Hide Extensions, Show Hidden Files, and Display Full Path) are enabled for one or all folders.

➤ *File Types*—Associates file extensions with applications or viewers.

➤ *Offline Files*—Configures the caching of network files and folders for use when offline.

Fonts

Font management is performed through the Fonts applet. This interface lists all installed fonts and can be used to add new fonts or remove existing fonts.

Game Controllers

Joysticks, steering wheels, and speed pedals can be installed and configured through the Game Controllers applet. New devices are easily added by pulling the device drivers from the Windows 2000 CD or a vendor-provided disk. Existing devices can be configured through vendor-created dialog boxes. Existing devices can also be removed through the Game Controllers applet.

Internet Options

The various functions and features of Internet Explorer can be managed through the Internet Options applet. This interface is also accessible through the Internet Options command on the Tools menu in Internet Explorer or by opening the Properties dialog box of the Internet Explorer icon on the desktop. The Internet Options applet controls how Internet Explorer functions. The following tabs display in the applet and are used to configure Internet Explorer's settings:

➤ *General*—Sets the home page; defines temporary file storage location, size, and force purge; sets days to retain access history; and alters configuration of colors, fonts, languages, and accessibility options specific to Web access.

➤ *Security*—Defines the contents of the four Web zones to determine if software is accepted from Web sites, form data can be submitted, and cookies are used.

➤ *Content*—Configures the Content Advisor to block sites, manages certificates to prove your identity, configures AutoComplete, and defines your online identity.

➤ *Connections*—Sets which connections (modem and/or LAN) are used to gain Internet access; also allows for configuration of those connections.

➤ *Programs*—Associates Internet services with applications or viewers.

➤ *Advanced*—Configures IE-specific advanced features for accessibility, browsing, HTTP 1.1, Microsoft VM, multimedia, printing, searching, and security.

Keyboard and Mouse

Configuring how the keyboard and mouse I/O is handled by Windows 2000 is performed through the Keyboard and Mouse applets, respectively. Keyboard settings include repeat delay for held-down keys and how quickly the cursor blinks. Mouse settings include tracking acceleration and the double-clicking speed.

Licensing

The Licensing applet is the same tool found in Administrative Tools. Details on this tool are discussed earlier in this chapter.

Network and Dial-Up Connections

Local and dial-up network connections are managed through the Network And Dial-Up Connections applet. This tool can also be accessed through the Start menu (Settings | Network And Dial-Up Connections). Details on this tool can be found in Chapter 8.

14

Phone and Modem Options

Configuration of dialing properties and modems is managed through the Phone And Modem Options applet. This applet is used to define dialing locations, dialing rules, and modem configuration as well as configure RAS (Remote Access Service) and TAPI (Telephony API) drivers and services. Details on this tool can be found in Chapter 10.

Power Options

A computer's ability to save power, especially when using a battery, is managed through the Power Options applet. For desktop systems, Power Options can be used to define timeouts for powering down the monitor and hard drives. Doing so can prolong a machine's lifespan by being powered down when not in active use. For notebook or other portable systems that can operate from batteries, Power Options offer controls over hibernation and other device-specific power saving features. This applet offers several predefined power saving schemes and the ability to define custom schemes.

Printers

The Printers element of the Control Panel is the same as the Start menu Printers command in the Settings section. The Printers element opens the Printers folder, where printers and print queues are managed. Details on this tool can be found in Chapter 4.

Regional Options

Differences in conventions for numbers, currency, time, and dates are configured through Regional Options. This applet offers predefined configurations for various geographic locations, languages, and countries as well as the ability to create custom conventions. The Regional Options applet is also used to define the base language for a system as well as install any secondary or alternate languages to be used.

Scanners and Cameras

Digital cameras and scanners are managed through the Scanners And Cameras applet. This tool is used to install vendor-provided drivers for these devices if Windows 2000 does not automatically detect and install the device on bootup. After a device is installed, vendor-supplied configuration dialog boxes can be accessed.

Scheduled Tasks

The automation of batch files and launching of programs is managed via the Task Scheduler. The Scheduled Tasks applet displays a list of all defined tasks and access to the Add Scheduled Task Wizard. This applet offers the same interface as the Scheduled Task command in the Programs | Accessories | System Tools section of the Start menu. Tasks can be scheduled to launch automatically at a specific time, when a system event occurs, with a specific user's credentials, only when the system is idle, only when not running from batteries, and more. Details on this tool can be found in Chapter 13.

Sounds and Multimedia

The audio and multimedia capabilities of Windows 2000 are managed through the Sounds And Multimedia applet. This applet is used to associate sounds with system events, use or create sound schemes, set preferred playback and record devices, and access multimedia device properties (in the same manner as through the Device Manager).

System

Many important system management and control functions are contained within or accessed from the System applet. The System applet is probably the most important applet within the Control Panel. The available tabs and functions in the System applet include the following:

➤ *General*—Displays information about the system version, registration, and computer type.

➤ *Network Identification*—Displays the current system name and domain/ workgroup membership. The Network ID button is used to change the domain and workgroup membership. The Properties button is used to change the name of the computer or change the domain and workgroup membership. Both buttons are disabled on Windows 2000 Server domain controllers, because neither the computer name nor the domain can be changed on a domain controller.

➤ *Hardware*—Enables you to access the Add/Remove Hardware applet (via the Hardware Wizard button; details on this tool are presented earlier in this chapter), the Driver Signing Options dialog box (via the Driver Signing button), the Device Manager, and the Hardware Profiles dialog box.

➤ *User Profiles*—Enables you to manage roaming user profiles. Details on this tool appear in Chapter 12.

➤ *Advanced*—Enables you to access the Performance Options dialog box, the Environmental Variables dialog box, and the Startup and Recovery dialog box.

The following sections provide information about the preceding tools that are not covered elsewhere in this book.

14

Driver Signing Options Dialog Box

The Driver Signing Options dialog box is used to configure how a system handles hardware drivers. Microsoft initiated a new feature where hardware drivers are validated by their hardware labs. You can configure Windows 2000 to never install anything but signed drivers, warn you when an unsigned driver is about to be installed, or use any driver without warning. This tool is used to help maintain system integrity by preventing the installation of unapproved or untested device drivers.

Device Manager

Installed hardware can be configured and removed via the Device Manager. This tool displays a list of all installed hardware. In the Properties dialog box of each device, you can view device information, launch the troubleshooter, enable and disable a hardware profile, configure device-specific properties, remove or update drivers, and more. Devices that are not functioning properly or are in conflict with another device are highlighted with a yellow triangle or a red stop sign. In addition to listing devices by type, the Device Manager can also list devices by connection, resources by type, and resources by connection.

Hardware Profiles

Portable computers that have removable or undockable hardware can benefit from hardware profiles. A hardware profile defines which device drivers are enabled for each specific hardware configuration. One hardware profile can disable a NIC (network interface card) when not connected to the network, another can disable the modem when connected to the network, and yet another can enable peripheral support only when docked. All Windows 2000 systems have a default hardware profile. Additional hardware profiles are created by copying an existing profile, then booting into the profile and altering which devices and services are enabled for the profile. After two or more profiles are present on a system, each time the computer boots, Windows 2000 will attempt to match a hardware profile with the detected hardware. If a match is not found, you can be prompted to select from the existing profiles before the default profile is used.

Performance Options

The general system optimization for a computer system is set in the Performance Options dialog box. This system setting is set to background services for Windows 2000 Server systems and applications for Windows 2000 Professional systems.

The Performance Options dialog box also grants access to the Virtual Memory dialog box through the Change button. The Virtual Memory dialog box (see Figure 14.20) is where the size, number, and location of the paging file(s) is

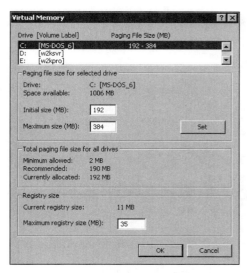

Figure 14.20 The Virtual Memory dialog box.

controlled. By default, Windows 2000 Server's paging file is 64MB larger than the amount of physical RAM present at the time of installation placed on the boot partition. You can move, delete, and add additional paging files by selecting a drive and altering the initial and maximum sizes, then pressing Set. Paging files are always placed in the root directory of a drive. The initial size is the amount of drive space preallocated for the paging file. The maximum size limits how large the system can expand the paging file as needed. Setting both sizes to 0 deletes the paging file from the selected drive.

Environment Variables

Various system- and user/application-specific environmental variables are managed through the Environment Variables dialog box (see Figure 14.21). The default values listed in this dialog box are typically correct and should not be changed. However, you might encounter some applications that require modification to a variable to function correctly.

Startup and Recovery

Defining the default operating system to boot and configuring how the system reacts to stop errors is performed on the Startup And Recovery dialog box (see Figure 14.22). Any operating systems defined in the Boot.ini file can be selected as the default OS via the Default Operating System pull-down list. The amount of time the boot menu is displayed can be set in seconds or disabled entirely. When a stop error occurs, the system automatically writes an event to the Application log. You can enable other actions, including:

Figure 14.21   The Environment Variables dialog box.

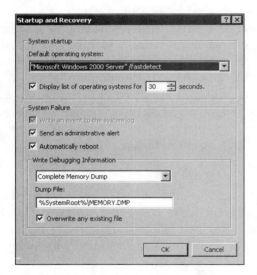

Figure 14.22   The Startup And Recovery dialog box.

➤ Sending an administrative alert

➤ Rebooting automatically

➤ Recording a dump file of debugging information

In most cases, recording a dump file is useless, because the data it contains is only useful to a trained system engineer. The write debugging options are none, small memory dump (64KB), kernel memory dump, and complete memory dump. The dump files are written in the main Windows 2000 system directory.

CHAPTER SUMMARY

Windows 2000 is managed through its tools. In addition to the Control Panel applet types of utilities common with previous versions of Windows, Windows 2000 includes Microsoft Management Console snap-in tools. MMC consoles can be customized to contain the utilities you use most often.

Numerous preexisting MMC console configurations exist in the Administrative Tools section of the Start menu and Control Panel. These include Active Directory Domains And Trusts, Active Directory Sites And Services, Active Directory Users And Computers, Component Services, Computer Management, Data Sources (ODBC), DHCP, Distributed File System, DNS, Domain Controller Security Policy, Domain Security Policy, Event Viewer, Internet Services Manager, Licensing, Local Security Policy, Performance, Routing And Remote Access, and Server Extensions Administrator.

The Control Panel tools included with Windows 2000 are Accessibility Options, Add/Remove Hardware, Add/Remove Programs, Administrative Tools, Date/Time, Display, Fax, Folder Options, Fonts, Game Controllers, Internet Options, Keyboard, Licensing, Mouse, Network And Dial-up Connections, Phone And Modem Options, Power Options, Printers, Regional Options, Scanners And Cameras, Scheduled Tasks, Sounds And Multimedia, and System.

REVIEW QUESTIONS

14

1. Which saved mode of an MMC console will allow users to open new console windows, but prevent them from accessing portions of the console tree, adding or removing snap-ins, and saving altered versions of the console?

   a. Author Mode

   b. User Mode: Full Access

   c. User Mode: Delegated Access, Multiple Windows

   d. User Mode: Delegated Access, Single Window

2. Which of the following management tools are MMC snap-in based? [Choose all that apply]

   a. Active Directory Users And Computers

   b. Services

   c. Event Viewer

   d. Internet Options

3. Which utility or applet collectively includes the abilities to view log files, display configuration information, manage shared folders, defragment a disk, configure services, and more?

   a. System

   b. Computer Management

   c. Configure Your Server

   d. Network And Dial-Up Connection

4. Which of the following are Event Viewer features and abilities? [Choose all that apply]

   a. Automatic intrusion detection

   b. Display filtering

   c. Searchable event details

   d. Looping log files management

5. Which type of licensing should a large network with numerous Windows 2000 Servers employ?

   a. Per Seat

   b. Per Server

6. A license group is used to grant or restrict access to client access licenses when the total number of users, computers, and licenses are not equivalent.

   a. True

   b. False

7. Which of the following are included as service configurations? [Choose all that apply]

   a. Launching within the context of a specific user account

   b. Preventing other services or applications from launching a specific service

   c. Launching command-line startup parameters

   d. Configuring automatic termination after a specified time period

8. Which of the following actions can a system perform if a service fails once, twice, or repeatedly? [Choose all that apply]

   a. Restart the service after a specified time period

   b. Launch a program or batch file

   c. Start a Counter Log

   d. Reboot the computer

9. If a service required by other applications or services to perform essential operations or functions fails, the dependant processes might not be able to continue operating normally.

   a. True

   b. False

10. Which of the following are offered by Windows 2000 as alternate methods of communicating information to enable and improve system interaction for people who are visual, reading, or movement impaired? [Choose all that apply]

    a. Ignoring quickly repeated keystrokes

    b. Allowing use of Shift, Ctrl, and Alt with a single keystroke

    c. Flash an element on the screen whenever a sound is played

    d. Use the numeric keypad to control the mouse pointer

11. Which Control Panel applets can be used to install devices? [Choose all that apply]

    a. Sounds And Multimedia

    b. Add/Remove Hardware

    c. Scanners And Cameras

    d. Game Controllers

12. Which utility or applet should be used to install drivers for most hardware, when not automatically detected and installed upon bootup?

    a. Computer Management

    b. Device Manager

    c. System

    d. Add/Remove Hardware

14

13. The Add/Remove Programs can be used to install applications from floppies, CDs, network distribution points, and the Microsoft Update Web site.

    a. True

    b. False

14. How many displays can or should be used on Windows 2000 during initial installation?

    a. 1

    b. 3

    c. 6

    d. 9

15. Without additional third-party products, which of the following fax capabilities does Windows 2000 offer? [Choose all that apply]

    a. Auto answer

    b. Transmit from any print-enabled application

    c. Network sharing of fax services

    d. Log fax activities

16. If you regularly use several languages in documents and for system configuration, which utility or applet should be used to install support for the languages?

    a. System

    b. Regional Settings

    c. Computer Management

    d. Configure Your Server

17. The Driver Signing Options dialog box is used to control which drivers can be used on a Windows 2000 system. This control offers the ability to restrict drivers only to those certified by Microsoft, define several trusted vendors from which to accept drivers, allow unsigned drivers after warning about their use, and allow any drivers without any warning.

    a. True

    b. False

18. What tools can be used to determine which system resources, such as IRQs, are in use or are free and available? [Choose all that apply]

    a. Device Manager

    b. Power Options

    c. System Information

    d. Add/Remove Hardware

19. Which of the following are true of hardware profiles? [Choose all that apply]

    a. Upon each bootup the system attempts to automatically match a hardware profile with detected hardware.

    b. Only portable systems have hardware profiles.

    c. Services can be enabled or disabled in a hardware profile.

    d. To alter the configuration of a hardware profile, you must boot a machine using the hardware profile you want to modify.

20. When a stop error occurs, which of the following can be triggered? [Choose all that apply]

    a. Automatic reboot

    b. Dump the state of the memory to a file

    c. Launch a program or batch file

    d. Disk defragmentation

REAL-WORLD PROJECTS

Josh was hired as a part-time systems administrator at a small firm. The president of the company raised concerns about a number of network management issues that she asked Josh to address. On the list of major concerns were the following:

➤ The need for a simplified management interface for the network services

➤ The ability to view system events in realtime

➤ Management of network resources

➤ Limiting the number of users to the number of licenses available

➤ Management of network services

➤ Installation of new applications and limiting downloads of unsigned software

➤ Managing hardware for portable systems

14

After perusing the network, Josh decided to first begin by building a custom Microsoft Management Console (MMC) interface for the network.

> **WARNING!** Make sure that the steps outlined in these projects are performed on a test machine or with test accounts to avoid causing any problems with active user accounts and resources.

Project 14.1
To customize MMC, perform the following steps:

1. Select Start | Run, type "mmc", and press OK. The MMC shell opens with a blank console.

2. Click the Console menu, then click the Add/Remove Snap-In command. The Add/Remove Snap-In dialog box displays.

3. Click Add.

4. Select a snap-in from the list.

5. Click Add. The Add Standalone Snap-In dialog box displays.

6. As necessary, respond to additional prompts for context or configuration information specific to the selected snap-in.

7. Repeat Steps 4 through 6 until all desired snap-ins are added.

8. Click Close

9. Click OK. This returns you to the console that is now displaying your added snap-ins.

10. Click the Console menu, then click the Save As command.

11. Select the location and provide a name for the MSC file.

12. Click Save.

After building the custom console, Josh showed the company president how to view system events so that if anything happened while he was away from the office, users can gather troubleshooting information.

Project 14.2
To view system information, perform the following steps:

1. Open Computer Management from the Administrative Tools.

2. Expand the System Tools section, if it's not already expanded.

3. Select System Information within the System Tools section.

4. Double-click the System Summary item in the right pane.

5. Information about your system displays in the right pane. Review the information.

6. Click the Hardware Resources item in the left pane.

7. Double-click the IRQs item in the right pane.

8. The system's IRQ assignments display in the right pane. Review the information.

9. Select the Conflicts/Sharing item in the left pane.

10. A list of any problems or shared resources displays in the right pane. Review the information.

11. Explore the other elements of System Information, and take note of the data you see in case you need it in the future.

12. Close the Computer Management window by clicking the close button (the X) in the title bar.

The next project Josh decided to tackle was that of management of network shares so that unauthorized users could not view sensitive network data.

Project 14.3
To manage local shares, perform the following steps:

1. Open Computer Management from the Administrative Tools.

2. Expand the System Tools section, if it's not already expanded.

3. Expand Shared Folders within the System Tools section.

4. Select the Shares item. A list of normal and hidden shares displays in the right pane.

5. Issue the New File Share command from the Action menu. The Create Shared Folder Wizard opens.

6. Click the Browse button.

7. Locate and select a folder to share.

8. Click OK.

9. Provide a share name and a description.

10. Click Next.

14

11. Set the permission level for this share: All Users Have Full Control, Administrators Have Full Control And Other Users Have Read-Only Access, Administrators Have Full Control And Other Users Have No Access, or Custom Permissions.

12. Click Finish. The share is created.

13. When prompted whether to create another share, click No. Notice the new share appears in the right pane.

14. Select the Sessions item. A list of all users and systems accessing shares on the system displays in the right pane.

WARNING! Make sure that you are not terminating a needed session before performing the next step. This step may cause a user to lose data if not managed correctly.

15. Select a user or computer from this list (if applicable). Issue the Close Session command from the Action menu to terminate the session.

16. Select the Option Files item. A list of all files being used over shares on this system displays in the right pane.

17. Close the Computer Management window by clicking the close button (the X) in the title bar.

Josh then wanted to make sure that a record was kept of system events so that he could view system information from days that he was not present in the office. Therefore, Josh decided to set up a system log to note any system events and their details.

Project 14.4
To use Event Viewer, perform the following steps:

1. Open the Event Viewer from the Administrative Tools.

2. Select the System log. A list of events from this log displays in the right pane.

3. Double-click an information event. Notice the details about this event contained within the event detail.

4. Click OK to close the event detail window.

5. Next, repeat Steps 3 and 4 for a warning and an error event, if they are present in the log. You might need to scroll down the list of event details to find examples of these event types.

6. Issue the Properties command from the Action menu. The System Log Properties dialog box displays.

7. Alter the maximum log size to 2048K.

8. Select the Overwrite Events As Needed radio button.

9. Click OK.

10. Issue the Filter command from the View window. The System Log Properties dialog box opens with the Filter tab selected.

11. Select only the Information event type checkbox.

12. In the Computer field, type in the name of the local system.

13. Click OK. The Event Viewer now only displays information events for the local computer.

14. Close the Event Viewer window by clicking the close button (the X) in the title bar.

To make sure that Windows 2000 Server licensing was properly established, Josh used the Licensing utility provided with Windows 2000.

Project 14.5
To use Licensing, perform the following steps:

Note: Only perform this project if you are installing real licenses that you have purchased. If you have not purchased licenses, contact your license reseller before continuing.

1. Open the Licensing utility from the Administrative Tools.

2. Select the Products View tab.

3. Notice the current number of licenses for Windows Server.

4. Select the Purchase History tab.

5. Issue the New License command from the License menu. The New Client Access License dialog box opens.

6. In the Product pull-down list, select Windows Server.

7. Set the quantity field to the number of additional licenses you've purchased.

8. Select Per Seat or Per Server. This selection will not be available on Per Seat mode systems.

9. Type a comment for the set of licenses.

10. Click OK.

11. Check the I Agree checkbox, then click OK. The added licenses are now listed on the Purchase History tab.

14

12. Select the Products View tab. The number of licenses available for Windows Server should be increased by the number of licenses just installed.

13. Issue the Exit command from the License menu.

Per the company president's request, Josh then turned his attention to management of network services.

Project 14.6
To manage services, perform the following steps:

1. Open Services from the Administrative Tools.

2. Locate and select the Print Spooler service.

3. Issue the Properties command from the Action menu. The Properties dialog box for this service opens.

4. Click the Stop button. The service stops.

5. Click the Start button. The service restarts.

6. Click the Pause button. The service halts.

7. Click the Resume button. The service restarts.

8. Select the Log On tab.

9. Select the This Account radio button.

10. Use the Browse button to locate and select the Administrator account.

11. Click OK.

12. Provide the password for the Administrator account.

13. Select the Recovery tab.

14. Change the First Failure pull-down list to Restart The Service.

15. Change the Second Failure pull-down list to Restart The Service.

16. Change the Subsequent Failure to Reboot The Computer.

17. Set the Reset fail count to 1 day.

18. Select the Dependencies tab. View the dependencies for the service.

19. Click OK to close the Properties dialog box and save changes.

20. Close the Services window by clicking the close button (the X) in the title bar.

Next on the list of things to do was to install a custom application for the accounting department. Josh used the built-in Windows 2000 Add/Remove Programs applet to make sure that the program was properly installed.

Project 14.7
To install a new application, perform the following steps:

1. Open the Add/Remove Programs applet from the Control Panel.

2. Click the Add New Programs button.

3. Insert the distribution CD or first floppy for the application into the appropriate drive on the computer.

4. Click the CD or Floppy button. The Install wizard opens.

5. Click Next.

6. The wizard scans the CD or floppy for a known installation startup file (such as setup.exe or install.exe). If one is found, its path and file name display. If one is not found, use the Browse button to locate the correct startup file.

7. Click Finish.

8. The installation routine for the application is started. Follow its prompts.

9. If asked to reboot your system when the installation is complete, do so.

10. Close the Add/Remove Programs applet by clicking the Close button.

11. Close the Control Panel by clicking File | Close.

To ensure that users didn't install unsigned software from the Internet, Josh set up the system so that only trusted software is installable on the network.

14

Project 14.8
To manage driver signing options, perform the following steps:

1. Open the System applet from the Control Panel.

2. Select the Hardware tab.

3. Click the Driver Signing button. The Driver Signing Options dialog box opens.

4. Select the Block—Prevent Installation Of Unsigned Files radio button.

5. Click OK to close the Driver Signing Options dialog box.

6. Click OK to close the System applet.

7. Close the Control Panel by clicking on the File menu and selecting Close.

Finally, Josh needed to manage hardware settings for portable company computers. He established these settings through the Hardware tab of the System applet.

Project 14.9
To manage hardware profiles, perform the following steps:

1. Open the System applet from the Control Panel.

2. Select the Hardware tab.

3. Click the Hardware Profiles button. The Hardware Profiles dialog box opens.

4. Select the profile that exists by default named Profile 1 (Current).

5. Click Copy.

6. Type in a name for the new hardware profile.

7. Click OK.

8. Reboot the system using the Shut Down command on the Start menu.

9. When prompted, select the newly created hardware profile using the arrow keys.

10. Press Enter to boot with the selected hardware profile.

11. Log in.

12. Open the System applet from the Control Panel.

13. Select the Hardware tab.

14. Click the Device Manager button. The Device Manager opens.

15. Locate and select a device to disable in the current hardware profile.

16. Issue the Properties command from the Action menu.

17. Change the Device Usage pull-down list from Use This Device (Enable) to Do Not Use This Device In The Current Hardware Profile (Disable).

Note: To reenable a device in a hardware profile, change the Device Usage setting from Do Not Use This Device In The Current Hardware Profile (Disable) to Use This Device (Enable).

18. Click OK.

19. Repeat Steps 15 through 18 for each device to be removed from (or added back into) the hardware profile.

20. When completed, close the Device Manager and close the System applet.

21. Shut down the system using the Shut Down command on the Start menu.

22. While the system is powered off, change the hardware configuration of the system to match the enabled (or disabled) components of the new hardware profile.

23. Power on the system. The new hardware profile should be automatically selected and used to boot.

24. Log in.

25. Repeat this entire project to create other hardware profiles.

14

CHAPTER FIFTEEN

SAMPLE TEST

Question 1

What is the best method to use for encrypting a compressed file?

- ○ a. Ensure you are a member of a group with administrative privileges, and use the Advanced Attributes button to set encryption settings
- ○ b. Decompress the file, and use the Advanced Attributes button to set encryption settings
- ○ c. Set up a recovery agent to encrypt the file
- ○ d. Move the file to a folder that is encrypted

Question 2

Assume you have assigned the following permissions to the AccData folder:

- ➤ *Authenticated Users group*—Allow standard Read permission
- ➤ *AccDept group*—Allow standard Read and Write permissions
- ➤ *TempStaff group*—Deny Full Control
- ➤ *Administrators group*—Allow Full Control

Tom, a temporary staff member, is in the TempStaff group. What access will he have to the files in the AccData folder?

- ○ a. He will only be able to view the names of files and the contents of the files.
- ○ b. He will have Full Control over all the files.
- ○ c. He will have no access.
- ○ d. He will only be able to view some files and make changes to those files.

Question 3

Which of the following operating systems can be upgraded to Windows 2000 Server? [Check all correct answers]

❑ a. Windows NT Server 3.51

❑ b. Windows 98

❑ c. Windows NT 4 Workstation

❑ d. Windows NT 4 Server

Question 4

Which of the following are scripting errors? [Check all correct answers]

❑ a. Syntax

❑ b. Logic

❑ c. Overflow

❑ d. Runtime

Question 5

Which of the following systems support Dfs root shares? [Check all correct answers]

❑ a. Windows 2000 Advanced Server domain controller

❑ b. Windows NT 4 domain controller

❑ c. Windows NT 4 standalone server

❑ d. Windows 2000 standalone server

Question 6

Where is the Partition Knowledge Table (PKT) stored on a domain-based Dfs?

○ a. Active Directory

○ b. Registry

○ c. MMC

○ d. NDS

Question 7

Susan has a Windows 2000 Server with one hard disk and one partition, formatted as FAT16. She wants to convert the hard drive from a basic disk to dynamic, but she is not able to. Why is this? [Check all correct answers]

- ❑ a. Dynamic disks only support striped sets.
- ❑ b. She needs to use NTFS as the file system.
- ❑ c. You cannot upgrade a volume that is the system or boot volume.
- ❑ d. The workstations are Windows 98, so the server knows that these systems cannot access a dynamic disk and does not permit the upgrade.

Question 8

How can you determine which users are currently connected to a share on a server?

- ○ a. MMC|Shares
- ○ b. Computer Management, Shared Folders|Sessions
- ○ c. Active Directory Users And Groups|Users
- ○ d. MMC|Open Files

Question 9

Which of the following advanced boot options allow network access over PC card NICs? [Check all correct answers]

- ❑ a. Safe Mode with Networking
- ❑ b. Safe Mode with Command Prompt
- ❑ c. Enable VGA Mode Boot
- ❑ d. Last Known Good Configuration

15

Question 10

Which of the following is the default service used by Windows 2000 for name resolution?

- ○ a. WINS
- ○ b. DHCP
- ○ c. DNS
- ○ d. IGMP

Question 11

How can you change a serial mouse on COM1 to a Plug and Play PS/2 mouse?

○ a. Plug the new mouse into the PS/2 port. Windows 2000 Server will automatically detect it, and you can start to use it.

○ b. In the Control Panel, double-click Mouse, and, on the Hardware tab, click Properties. On the Driver tab, click Update Driver, and follow the prompts.

○ c. In the Control Panel, double-click Mouse, and, on the Hardware tab, click Properties. Change the ports from COM1 to PS/2.

○ d. Windows 2000 Server does not support PS/2; purchase a USB mouse device.

Question 12

In which of the following domain modes are universal groups allowed to contain other universal groups?

○ a. Passive mode

○ b. Active mode

○ c. Native mode

○ d. Mixed mode

Question 13

Which of the following events cause the kernel to preempt a thread's execution? [Check all correct answers]

❑ a. The thread has run the duration of the quantum.

❑ b. The thread has returned to a waiting state.

❑ c. The thread is terminated by the Process Manager.

❑ d. A thread with a higher priority requires service.

Question 14

An important difference between Windows 2000 group policy and Windows NT 4 system policy is that:

○ a. If a GPO is removed, the configuration settings specified by the GPO are also removed from the computers' Registries. System policy changes to the Registry persist after the system policy has been removed from the domain.

○ b. Group policy can configure settings for users and computers. System policy can only configure settings for users.

○ c. Group policy processes the computer configuration before a user logs on. System policy processes the computer configuration after a user logs on.

○ d. Group policy cannot be applied to Windows NT 4 clients.

Question 15

Which of the following multiprocessing techniques is used by Windows 2000?

○ a. Asymmetric

○ b. Context-switching

○ c. Symmetric

○ d. Demand paging

Question 16

In Windows 2000 and NetWare (using GSNW) communication, which NetWare configurations are supported? [Check all correct answers]

❏ a. Active Directory

❏ b. Bindery

❏ c. Universal Directory Service

❏ d. NDS

15

Question 17

Which port does the Administration Web Site use?

○ a. 80

○ b. 81

○ c. 8080

○ d. A random port assigned during setup

Question 18

Which of the following are true of hardware profiles? [Check all correct answers]

- ❏ a. Upon each bootup, the system attempts to automatically match a hardware profile with detected hardware.
- ❏ b. Only portable systems have hardware profiles.
- ❏ c. Services can be enabled or disabled in a hardware profile.
- ❏ d. To alter the configuration of a hardware profile, you must boot a machine using the hardware profile you want to modify.

Question 19

What is the name of the feature for every object in Active Directory, which describes exactly where the object is located and what its name is?

- ○ a. Account object
- ○ b. Distinguished name
- ○ c. Object share
- ○ d. Account summary

Question 20

Where is scheduled task data created using the **AT** command stored?

- ○ a. .job file
- ○ b. Registry
- ○ c. .tsk file
- ○ d. %windir%

Question 21

What is the method of adding service packs to Windows 2000 installation files known as?

- ○ a. Hotfixing
- ○ b. Routing
- ○ c. Slipstreaming
- ○ d. Upgrading

Question 22

Which of the following translates private IP addresses to public IP addresses for communication over the Internet?

- ○ a. VPNs
- ○ b. NAT
- ○ c. Router
- ○ d. Bridge

Question 23

Which of the following still occur as background tasks after System Monitor is closed? [Check all correct answers]

- ❑ a. Realtime graphing of performance data
- ❑ b. Log files
- ❑ c. Alteration of a counter's scale
- ❑ d. Alerts

Question 24

Which of the following devices can be managed using SNMP (assuming that they are SNMP-compliant)? [Check all correct answers]

- ❑ a. Server
- ❑ b. Router
- ❑ c. Hub
- ❑ d. Stereo

15

Question 25

Which of the following are Event Viewer features and abilities? [Check all correct answers]

- ❑ a. Automatic intrusion detection
- ❑ b. Display filtering
- ❑ c. Searching on event details
- ❑ d. Manage looping log files

Question 26

Which of the following hidden shares provides the named pipes when administering a server remotely?

○ a. ADMIN$

○ b. IPC$

○ c. PRINT$

○ d. PIPES$

Question 27

What is the authentication protocol for Windows 2000 computers in a Windows 2000 domain?

○ a. Kerberos

○ b. NTLM

○ c. MSCHAP

○ d. Certificates

Question 28

Once Terminal Services is configured to operate in the Remote Administration mode, how can it be converted to the Application Server mode?

○ a. Run the Add/Remove Windows Components Wizard, and choose the Application Server Mode radio button

○ b. In the Terminal Services Configuration Application, click the Convert button

○ c. Uninstall Terminal Services, reboot the system, and reinstall Terminal Services

○ d. This cannot be done

Question 29

A user, Sally, moves an uncompressed file that is located in a folder on her Windows 2000 Professional hard drive to the Windows 2000 Server's compressed "work storage" folder. All volumes are NTFS. What happens to the file during the transfer?

○ a. The file changes its attributes to the new parent folder and is automatically compressed.

○ b. An error message appears on Sally's computer stating that the file is in an incompatible state and needs to be changed to a compatible one.

○ c. The file retains its attributes and remains uncompressed.

○ d. The server's folder changes its attributes and becomes decompressed.

Question 30

A Group Policy Object can be linked to which of the following? [Check all correct answers]

❑ a. Site

❑ b. Security group

❑ c. Domain

❑ d. Organizational unit

Question 31

Which of the following is supported when running Setup in a command prompt window on a Windows 95 system? [Check all correct answers]

❑ a. **/u**

❑ b. **/unattend**

❑ c. **/s:**

❑ d. **/r:**

Question 32

By default, which group must you be a member of to schedule tasks using the **AT** command?

○ a. Power Users

○ b. Administrators

○ c. Server Operators

○ d. Backup Operators

15

Question 33

The addresses assigned to the physical memory have no limitation except the 32-bit address length.

○ a. True

○ b. False

Question 34

You want to upgrade a Windows NT 4 Server to Windows 2000 Server. The server has a 4GB hard drive (one partition), 200MHz CPU, 64MB of RAM, and 24x speed CD-ROM drive. All the hardware is listed on the Windows 2000 Server HCL. What do you need to change?

○ a. Replace the hard drive with one that has at least 10GB of space

○ b. Replace the 233MHz CPU with one that is at least 500MHz

○ c. Add an additional 64MB of RAM

○ d. Nothing

Question 35

Which of the following is the binary representation of 137?

○ a. 01100111

○ b. 10001001

○ c. 10110001

○ d. 10010001

Question 36

Windows 2000 includes several administration tools, such as:

Computer Management

System applet

Active Directory Users And Computers

(continued)

Question 36 (continued)

Each of the preceding tools can be used to perform several tasks. Match each of the following tasks with the appropriate tool:

View event details

Record Counter Logs

Define path to user's roaming profile directory

Defragment disks

Alter service credentials

Change domain membership

Access the Device Manager

Manage shares

Create hardware profiles

Create new users

Alter Startup And Recovery

Question 37

A group policy is used to control aspects of security on a Windows 2000 system. Several subdivisions of a group policy include:

Password Policy

User Rights Assignment

Security Options

Identify the group policy subdivision each of the following controls can be found in:

Allow the ejection of NTFS media

Store passwords using reversible encryption for all users in the domain

Enable loading and unloading of device drivers

Rename administrator account

Disable the Ctrl+Alt+Del requirement for logon

Shut down system immediately if unable to log security audits

Allow adding workstations to domain

Enforce password history

Allow access to this computer from the network

15

Question 38

The following two default user accounts are on Windows 2000:

    Administrator

    Guest

Identify which of the following characteristics are true for each account:

    Blank password by default

    Can be locked out and disabled

    Can be renamed

    Cannot be delegated

    Cannot be deleted

    Cannot be locked out or disabled

    DES cannot be used and Kerberos is required

    Disabled by default on Server and Professional

    Password cannot be stored with reversible encryption

    Password never expires

    Requires non-blank password on domain controllers

    Smart card cannot be required

Question 39

Windows 2000 Server domain controllers can be deployed in two modes:

    Native mode

    Mixed mode

Identify which types of user groups are present on a Windows 2000 Server domain controller when configured for either of these modes:

    Domain local

    Global

    Universal

    Built in

    System

    Special Identities

Question 40

Windows 2000 uses security on files and shares to control access. These are generally known as:

NTFS security

Share security

Each of the preceding security control objects can be configured on a user or group basis for various access or permission levels. Match the following possible access levels with the preceding security control objects:

Change Permissions

Create Files/Write Data

Create Folders/Append Data

Delete

Delete Subfolders and Files

Full Control

List Folder/Read Data

List Folder Contents

Modify (or Change)

Read

Read & Execute

Read Attributes

Read Extended Attributes

Read Permissions

Take Ownership

Traverse Folder/Execute File

Write

Write Attributes

Write Extended Attributes

15

Note: *Case studies are a new testing technique Microsoft uses in some of its tests. Although you probably won't encounter case studies in the Core Four exams, a case study is included in this practice test because it is a valuable way to reinforce the material you've learned.*

Case Study

BigBolts, Inc. has a company network that hosts over 3,000 clients and 200 servers. BigBolts decided to migrate to a Windows 2000–based network from its current Windows NT–based network. The existing network used by BigBolts uses only Windows NT 4 Servers for servers, but it employs Windows NT 4 Workstation and Windows 98 as desktop clients.

Current LAN/Network Structure

All the Windows NT 4 Server systems are 200MHz Pentiums with 256MB of RAM and 20GB of drive space. The hardware in use on the desktop clients is quite broad, ranging from minimal requirements through high-end systems capable of 3-D rendering and multimedia editing.

All users on the BigBolts network have customizable roaming user profiles. This includes mapping user home directories to network shares. The system administrators have attempted to store all data on network servers. This ensures that everything is protected by the daily backups. Only the data on servers is included in these backups, so users are encouraged to keep important data on network servers.

Planned Upgrades

As BigBolts continues to expand, it needs to build in support for a 50 percent expansion. It has already considered dividing the network into multiple domains to accommodate a growing user base and to separate administration functions by physical location.

After BigBolts installed four Windows 2000 Servers as domain controllers and six Windows 2000 Servers as file servers, it decided to migrate the Windows NT and Windows 98 clients to Windows 2000 Professional.

BigBolts recruited several new managers who will regularly travel to each of BigBolts's remote manufacturing plants to perform inspections, obtain performance data, and create production reports. This information is to be communicated to the main office on a daily basis. These roving managers will also be working in the office one to two days each week. BigBolts elected to assign each manager a mobile computer with the ability to connect to the LAN locally and remotely as needed. However, the company's security policy strictly requires that no system connected to the LAN locally have the ability to bypass the imposed security with a modem connection.

After several months, BigBolts has a mixed network consisting of Windows 2000 and Windows NT 4 systems both as servers and workstation clients. The network is divided into three domains. New procedural and departmental guidelines now require some cross-domain administration to be performed.

Question 41.1

The first step BigBolts will take in its migration process is to bring 10 new Windows 2000 Servers into the network. Which of the following must be true in order for the network migration to eventually be successful? [Check all correct answers]

❑ a. A Windows 2000 Server domain controller needs to be installed to replace the existing Windows NT 4 PDC.

❑ b. All Windows 2000 Servers acting as domain controllers must be configured to operate in native mode.

❑ c. All Windows 2000 Servers added to the network must be domain controllers.

❑ d. The new computers used to host Windows 2000 Server must have at least 133MHz Pentium processors, 128MB or more RAM, and at least 1GB of free drive space.

Question 41.2

Which method of deployment will cause the least amount of administrative overhead and retain as much of the user environment and system configuration as possible?

○ a. Deploy via RIS using boot disks at each client.

○ b. Launch the setup from each system manually from a locally present CD-ROM.

○ c. Initiate a network upgrade install from a logon script that uses an unattend.txt file and a UDF to fully automate the installation process.

○ d. Use a disk imaging tool to force distribute new client drive images.

15

Question 41.3

After several months, BigBolts completed the migration of clients to Windows 2000 Professional, and more than half of the servers are now Windows 2000 Servers. However, due to some custom applications and a few third-party tools essential to business operation, the remaining systems must remain Windows NT 4 Servers. Which of the following are now true? [Check all correct answers]

❑ a. All Windows 2000 Server systems should be reconfigured to function in native mode.

❑ b. The vendors of the third-party tools should be contacted about work-arounds, upgrades, or new versions that function properly on Windows 2000.

❑ c. The in-house programmers should be assigned the task of porting the custom applications over to Windows 2000.

❑ d. All Windows NT 4 Servers should be taken offline immediately.

Question 41.4

BigBolts has begun to streamline its business practices, which includes maintaining tighter control over business data and requiring all clients to use the same applications to manipulate data. Which major feature of Windows 2000 would allow BigBolts to perform or enforce these new practices with software?

○ a. Routing And Remote Access Service

○ b. Networking And Dial-Up Connections

○ c. Hardware Profiles

○ d. IntelliMirror

Question 41.5

What feature or ability of Windows 2000 can be used to allow the mobile computers to function as needed both when connected and disconnected to the office LAN?

○ a. Routing And Remote Access Service

○ b. Networking And Dial-Up Connections

○ c. Hardware profiles

○ d. Roaming user profiles

Question 41.6

Which mechanism in Windows 2000 can allow an administrator from one domain to manage security in another domain?

○ a. IntelliMirror

○ b. Trusts

○ c. Routing

○ d. Active Directory

Question 41.7

Once BigBolts enabled trusts among all Windows 2000 domains, only the trusting domain can use resources from the trusted domain.

○ a. True

○ b. False

Question 41.8

BigBolts needs to automatically deploy new client systems. It wants to be able to plug in the new system to the network and allow an automated system to perform installation and configuration, so a user can sit down and log in. This capability is brought to Windows 2000 through:

    IntelliMirror

    Remote Installation Service

Match the following activities or capabilities with the preceding services:

    Boot with RIS disk

    Enforce group policy

    Select an installation image

    Install software on demand

    Redirect user folders

15

Question 41.9

The BigBolts's roving managers need to have custom hardware profiles defined. What is the correct order in which hardware profiles are created?

 A copy of the default hardware profile is created.

 Windows 2000 Professional is installed.

 Enable or disable drivers and services.

 Change the hardware configuration.

 Boot with the new hardware profile.

 Watch as the system automatically selects a hardware profile.

 Shut down the system.

Question 41.10

The Control Panel includes several types of applets, including:

 Applets to install and configure hardware

 Applets to just configure hardware

Match the following applets with one of the preceding types (note that all items might not be used):

 Add/Remove Hardware

 Display

 Fax

 Accessibility Options

 Game Controllers

 Keyboard

 Mouse

 Phone and Modem Options

 Power Options

 Printers

 Scanners and Cameras

 Sounds and Multimedia

CHAPTER SIXTEEN

ANSWER KEY

1. b	18. a, c, d	35. b
2. c	19. b	36. *
3. a, d	20. b	37. *
4. a, b, d	21. c	38. *
5. a, c, d	22. b	39. *
6. a	23. b, d	40. *
7. b, c	24. a, b, c, d	41.1. a, d
8. b	25. b, c, d	41.2. c
9. a, d	26. b	41.3. b, c
10. c	27. a	41.4. d
11. b	28. a	41.5. c
12. c	29. c	41.6. b
13. a, d	30. a, c, d	41.7. b
14. d	31. b, d	41.8. *
15. c	32. b	41.9. *
16. b, d	33. b	41.10. *
17. d	34. c	

Question 1

Answer b is correct. Compressed files cannot be encrypted. You must first decompress the file, then encrypt its contents through the file's Properties | Advanced Attributes area. Answers a, c, and d are incorrect, because compressed files cannot be encrypted; these settings are mutually exclusive.

Question 2

Answer c is correct. Tom will have no access; he has been denied Full Control. Answers a, b, and d are incorrect, because Tom is a member of the TempStaff group, which has been assigned the Deny Full Control permission. Therefore, he cannot view or control any of the contents in the AccData folder.

Question 3

Answers a and d are correct. Windows NT 4 Server and Windows NT Server 3.51 can be upgraded to Windows 2000 Server. Answers b and c are incorrect, because Windows 98 and Windows NT 4 Workstation cannot be upgraded to Windows 2000 Server.

Question 4

Answers a, b, and d are correct. Syntax, logic, and runtime are common script errors. Answer c is incorrect; overflow is a common error in Network and Dial-Up Connections regarding network overload.

Question 5

Answers a, c, and d are correct. Windows 2000 Advanced Server, Windows NT 4 standalone servers, and Windows 2000 standalone servers can support Dfs root shares. Answer b is incorrect. Although Windows NT 4 systems can participate in the Dfs structure, only standalone servers can host Dfs roots.

Question 6

Answer a is correct. The PKT for a domain-based Dfs is stored in the Active Directory. The PKT is not stored in the Registry or the MMC; therefore, answers b and c are incorrect. Answer d is incorrect; NDS is the directory structure for NetWare.

Question 7

Answers b and c are correct. The drive must be formatted with NTFS, and the volume must not be the system or boot volume to upgrade to a dynamic disk. Answers a and d are incorrect because having a disk that is a striped set and the type of client that accesses the disk is irrelevant.

Question 8

Answer b is correct. The Sessions node within the Shared Folders portion of the Computer Management console provides a list of users currently connected to the shares on the computer. The list of currently active user sessions cannot be found through MMC | Shares, Active Directory Users And Groups | Users, or MMC | Open Files. Therefore, answers a, c, and d are incorrect.

Question 9

Answers a and d are correct. You can enable PC card NIC access booting into Safe Mode with Networking and the Last Known Good Configuration. Neither Safe Mode with Command Prompt nor Enable VGA Mode Boot allows network access; thus, PC card NICs cannot be used with the boot options.

Question 10

Answer c is correct. By default, Windows 2000 uses DNS for name resolution. WINS, DHCP, and IGMP are not the default name resolution services; therefore, answers a, b, and d are incorrect.

Question 11

Answer b is correct. In the Control Panel, double-click Mouse, and, on the Hardware tab, click Properties. On the Driver tab, click Update Driver, and follow the prompts.

16

Question 12

Answer c is correct. Universal groups can only be created when the domain is functioning in native mode. Passive and active modes are fictitious; therefore, answers a and b are incorrect. Universal groups are not allowed in mixed mode; therefore, answer d is incorrect.

Question 13

Answers a and d are correct. The kernel will preempt a thread's operation when the amount of processing time specified by the quantum has expired or when a thread with higher priority is waiting for service. Answers b and c are incorrect, because, if the thread returns to a waiting state on its own or is terminated by the Process Manager, preemption is not required.

Question 14

Answer d is correct. Group policy and local security policy cannot be applied to Windows NT 4 computers. Answers a, b, and c are false statements and are therefore incorrect.

Question 15

Answer c is correct. Windows 2000 utilizes symmetric multiprocessing to provide the most efficient use of all available processors. Windows 2000 does not use asymmetric, context-switching, or demand paging multiprocessing; therefore, answers a, b, and d are incorrect.

Question 16

Answers b and d are correct. NetWare servers only support Bindery and NDS. NetWare does not support Active Directory; therefore, answer a is incorrect. Universal Directory Service is not supported; therefore, answer c is incorrect.

Question 17

Answer d is correct. The Administration Web Site uses a random port assigned during setup. Because the selected port is random, answers a, b, and c are incorrect.

Question 18

Answers a, c, and d are correct. Windows 2000 automatically attempts to find a hardware profile that matches system hardware at bootup. In addition, services can be enabled or disabled in hardware profiles. Finally, you must boot into a system using a hardware profile you want to modify. Answer b is incorrect, because hardware profiles are supported by systems other than portable systems.

Question 19

Answer b is correct. The name of the feature for every object in Active Directory, which describes exactly where the object is located and what its name is, is the distinguished name.

Question 20

Answer b is correct. The scheduled task data that is created using the **AT** command is stored in the Registry. Scheduled task data is not stored in .job files, .tsk files, or in %windir%; therefore, answers a, c, and d are incorrect.

Question 21

The correct answer is c, slipstreaming. A hotfix is a minor correction to an application; therefore, answer a is incorrect. Routing has to do with packet delivery; therefore, answer b is incorrect. Upgrading consists of a full-blown operating system update; therefore, answer d is incorrect.

Question 22

Answer b is correct. Network Address Translation (NAT) translates private IP addresses to public IP addresses for communication over the Internet. Answer a is incorrect; virtual private networking (VPN) is a method used to securely access a private network over the Internet. Answers c and d are incorrect; routers and bridges are hardware devices, not address resolution services.

Question 23

Answers b and d are correct. Only logs and alerts continue to function when System Monitor is closed. Realtime performance tracking and counter alteration depend on System Monitor; therefore, answers a and c are incorrect.

16

Question 24

Answers a, b, c, and d are correct. Assuming that they are compliant with the Simple Network Management Protocol (SNMP), all these devices can be managed.

Question 25

Answers b, c, and d are correct. Event Viewer can filter, search, and overwrite old elements in a log. Event Viewer does not offer automatic intrusion detection; therefore, answer a is incorrect.

Question 26

Answer b is correct. Named pipes are provided by the IPC$ hidden share. Named pipes are not provided by the ADMIN$, PRINT$, or PIPES$ shares; therefore, answers a, c, and d are incorrect.

Question 27

Answer a is correct. Kerberos would be used in a pure Windows 2000 domain environment. NTLM is provided for compatibility with older Microsoft operating systems. Therefore, answer b is incorrect. MSCHAP transmits authentication information in plain text and is not recommended. Therefore, answer c is incorrect. Certificates prove identity after authentication; therefore, answer d is incorrect.

Question 28

Answer a is correct. Run the Add/Remove Windows Components Wizard, and choose the Application Server Mode radio button. Terminal Services cannot be converted to Application Server mode through the Terminal Services Configuration Application or by uninstalling and reinstalling Terminal Services; therefore, answers b and c are incorrect. Because this operation can be performed, answer d is incorrect.

Question 29

Answer c is correct. When moving a file from one folder to another, the file retains its state regardless of the state the folder is in. The file will not inherit the attributes of the new parent folder; therefore, answer a is incorrect. No error message will appear; therefore, answer b is incorrect. The folder on the server will not change attributes; therefore, answer d is incorrect.

Question 30

Answers a, c, and d are correct. GPOs can only be linked to sites, domains, and organizational units. Groups can be used to filter the effect of a GPO; therefore, answer b is incorrect.

Question 31

Answers b and d are correct. Both **/unattend** and **/r:** are only available using winnt32.exe, which must be run in a command prompt window on a system running Windows 95/98/NT4. The **/s:** switch is available from both versions of the installation; therefore, answer c is incorrect. The **/u** switch is not available; therefore, answer a is incorrect.

Question 32

Answer b is correct. To schedule tasks using the **AT** command, you must be a member of the Administrators group. By default, the Power Users, Server Operators, and Backup Operators groups cannot schedule tasks with the **AT** command; therefore, answers a, c, and d are incorrect.

Question 33

Answer b is correct. The address assignments available for the physical memory are limited by the amount of memory installed. Therefore, answer a is incorrect.

Question 34

Answer c is correct. The minimum requirement for Windows 2000 Server is 128MB of RAM. Answers a and b are optional and not required, because they surpass the minimum requirements for the hard drive size and processor speed. Because answer c is correct, answer d is incorrect.

Question 35

Answer b is correct. 10001001 is the binary representation of 137. None of the other options is the binary equivalent of 137; therefore, answers a, c, and d are incorrect.

Question 36

The correct answer is:

Computer Management

    View event details

    Record Counter Logs

    Defragment disks

    Alter service credentials

    Access the Device Manager

    Manage shares

16

System Applet

>   Change domain membership

>   Access the Device Manager

>   Create hardware profiles

>   Alter Startup and Recovery

Active Directory Users And Computers

>   Define path to user's roaming profile directory

>   Create new users

Question 37

The correct answer is:

Password Policy

>   Enforce password history

>   Store passwords using reversible encryption for all users in the domain

User Rights Assignment

>   Allow access to this computer from the network

>   Allow adding workstations to domain

>   Enable loading and unloading of device drivers

Security Options

>   Allow the ejection of NTFS media

>   Disable Ctrl+Alt+Del requirement for logon

>   Shut down system immediately if unable to log security audits

>   Rename administrator account

Question 38

The correct answer is:

Administrator

>   Can be renamed

>   Requires non-blank password on domain controllers

Cannot be locked out or disabled

Cannot be deleted

Password never expires

Password cannot be stored with reversible encryption

Smart card cannot be required

Cannot be delegated

DES cannot be used and Kerberos is required

Guest

Can be renamed

Blank password by default

Can be locked out and disabled

Cannot be deleted

Disabled by default on Server and Professional

Question 39

The correct answer is:

Native mode

Domain local

Global

Universal

Built in

System

Special Identities

Mixed mode

Global

Built in

System

Special Identities

16

Question 40

The correct answer is:

NTFS Security

Traverse Folder/Execute File

List Folder/Read Data

Read Attributes

Read Extended Attributes

Create Files/Write Data

Create Folders/Append Data

Write Attributes

Write Extended Attributes

Delete Subfolders and Files

Delete

Read Permissions

Change Permissions

Take Ownership

Full Control

Modify

Read & Execute

List Folder Contents

Share Security

Full Control

Change

Read

Question 41.1

Answers a and d are correct. To complete or move forward with migration, the Windows NT 4 PDC needs to be replaced with a Windows 2000 Server domain controller. Any computer used to host Windows 2000 Server must have at least 133MHz Pentium processors, 128MB or more RAM, and at least 1GB of free drive space. In this situation, the Windows 2000 Server domain controllers should be in mixed mode, not native mode. Therefore, answer b is incorrect. Not all Windows 2000 Servers brought into the existing network must be domain controllers. Windows 2000 Servers can serve as file or application servers without hosting Active Directory. Therefore, answer c is incorrect.

Question 41.2

Answer c is correct. Only the listed option of initiating a network upgrade installation from a logon script that uses an unattend.txt file and a UDF to fully automate the installation process will cause the least amount of administrative overhead and will retain as much of the user environment and system configuration as possible. RIS will format the client drive in most cases, thereby eliminating the upgrade option. Therefore, answer a is incorrect. Launching the setup manually is administratively intensive, plus it does not indicate to start an upgrade installation. Therefore, answer b is incorrect. Using a disk imaging distribution system will lose all existing data and configuration. Therefore, answer d is incorrect.

Question 41.3

Answers b and c are correct. Looking for application upgrades and reauthoring custom applications for Windows 2000 are requirements to complete the migration to Windows 2000. Switching the Windows 2000 systems to native mode will prevent users from continuing to access resources on the Windows NT Server systems. Therefore, answer a is incorrect. Windows NT 4 and Windows 2000 Servers can function in the same network without problems; taking the Windows NT 4 Servers offline is unwarranted. Therefore, answer d is incorrect.

16

Question 41.4

Answer d is correct. IntelliMirror can be used to manage all user data so it remains on network servers, and it can distribute approved software to clients as needed. Routing And Remote Access Service, Networking And Dial-Up Connections, and Hardware Profiles do not offer these abilities. Therefore answers a, b, and c are incorrect.

Question 41.5

The correct answer is c. Hardware profiles can be used to configure the system so that the modem is not functional when connected to the office LAN. Routing And Remote Access Service, Networking And Dial-Up Connections, and Roaming user profiles do not offer features to allow a mobile computer with a modem to be connected to the LAN locally and not violate the security policy. Therefore, answers a, b, and d are incorrect.

Question 41.6

Answer b is correct. Trusts allow administrators from one domain to manage security in another. IntelliMirror, routing, and Active Directory do not offer this ability. Therefore, answers a, c, and d are incorrect.

Question 41.7

Answer b is correct. The statement is false. Trusts in Windows 2000 are two-way transitive trusts.

Question 41.8

The correct answer is:

IntelliMirror

      Install software on demand

      Enforce group policy

      Redirect user folders

Remote Installation Service

      Boot with RIS disk

      Select an installation image

Question 41.9

The correct answer is:

1. Windows 2000 Professional is installed.

2. A copy of the default hardware profile is created.

3. Boot with the new hardware profile.

4. Enable or disable drivers and services.

5. Shut down the system.

6. Change the hardware configuration.

7. Watch as the system automatically selects a hardware profile.

Question 41.10

The correct answer is:

Applets to install and configure hardware

    Display

    Game Controllers

    Phone and Modem Options

    Printers

    Scanners and Cameras

Applets to just configure hardware

    Accessibility Options

    Fax

    Keyboard

    Mouse

    Power Options

    Sounds and Multimedia

Note: *The Add/Remove Hardware applet is not used in this solution, because it can only be used to install hardware, not configure it.*

16

ANSWERS TO REVIEW QUESTIONS

CHAPTER 1 SOLUTIONS

1. **c.** Windows 2000 utilizes symmetric multiprocessing to provide the most efficient use of all available processors.

2. **b.** Windows 2000 and Active Directory rely on the Kerberos (v5) standard for authentication. Windows 2000 is the first Windows operating system to natively support the Kerberos authentication standard.

3. **a, b.** Neither Windows 2000 Professional nor Windows 2000 Standard Server support clustering. This feature is available only with the high-end implementations of Windows Advanced Server and Datacenter Server.

4. **a.** All resources in Windows 2000 are referred to as objects.

5. **b, d.** The Security subsystem and the Enterprise Services subsystem are Windows 2000 user mode components.

6. **c, b, a, d.** Because the VMM bases its decision on which page of memory to move to the pagefile on the age of the pages currently in physical memory, the page with the highest age is moved first.

7. **b. False.** The address assignments available for the physical memory are limited by the amount of memory installed.

8. **b.** Although the I/O Manager handles most I/O, it is the Win32 subsystem that is responsible for keyboard and pointer device I/O.

9. **c.** The HAL provides the hardware specific programs required for Windows 2000 to operate on different hardware platforms.

10. **a.** The design structure of the WDM calls for a driver/minidriver combination.

11. **c.** The Unicode standard provides a single, extensive character map and was used as the basis for all Window 2000 components to facilitate implementation in countries outside the United States.

12. **d.** Although it is part of the TCP/IP protocol suite, it is the Lightweight Directory Access Protocol (LDAP) that serves as the native transport for Active Directory.

13. **c.** Although all of the utilities provide some remote management capabilities, Terminal Services is the new Windows 2000 feature that provides the most extensive remote administration capabilities.

14. **a.** The demand paging with clustering function of Windows 2000 retrieves not only the page that caused the page fault, but pages surrounding the offender in an effort to anticipate future requests and prevent additional page faults.

15. **b, c.** The kernel will preempt a thread's operation when the amount of processing time specified by the quantum has expired or when a thread with higher priority is waiting for service. If the thread returns to a waiting state on its own or is terminated by the Process Manager, preemption is not required.

16. **d.** In order to ensure that the code is standard for all drivers and that driver development by manufacturers is limited, Microsoft writes the class driver (also known as the driver in the driver/minidriver pair) in the WDM environment.

17. **c.** The Cache Manager effectively increases disk drive performance by storing write requests in memory and directly managing disk interaction.

18. **c.** The Hardware Abstraction Layer (HAL) interacts with system hardware on behalf of applications.

19. **b.** IPSec is a newly supported protocol for Windows 2000 that provides encrypted TCP/IP communication between devices on the network. It can also be implemented without the knowledge or intervention of end-users on the network.

20. **c.** The Primary Domain Controller and Backup Domain Controller model are no longer used in the Active Directory environment.

CHAPTER 2 SOLUTIONS

1. **b.** The second phase of planning involves determining where the company is going and its future requirements. This may involve conversations with all levels of management to fully understand your company's needs.

2. **c.** DDNS (Dynamic Domain Name System) is part of the TCP/IP suite.

3. **a.** Universal groups can only be created when the domain is functioning in native mode.

4. **b.** /unattend is only available using winnt32.exe, which must be run in a command prompt window on a system running Windows 95/98/NT4. You might be tempted to choose c as well, but it is available from both versions of the installation.

5. **a.** During the testing phase of implementation, test and work through those situations that you expect will cause the most difficulty. This will afford you extra time if needed to work through the problem before implementation.

6. **c.** The Windows 2000 Compatible certification indicates that the hardware was tested on the operating system prior to the final release of the software. The Designed for Windows 2000 certification indicates testing on the final release.

7. **d.** The Readiness Analyzer runs differently and provides different information on Windows NT systems than on Windows 95/98 systems.

8. **b.** Windows 3.x and 4.x backup domain controllers that participate in Active Directory are referred to as downlevel systems.

9. **b, d, c, a.** Windows 2000 Professional provides the lowest level of hardware support, whereas Windows 2000 Datacenter Server provides the highest level: 32-way SMP and 64GB of RAM.

10. **b.** Dfs links across domain boundaries can only be made to Dfs roots at this time. Future implementations will include midlevel junctions, allowing connections to be made between midlevel folders.

11. **a, b, c.** Windows 2000 supports mirroring and duplexing (RAID 1) and stripe sets with parity (RAID 5).

12. **a.** The term host server refers to the server on which a Dfs root resides.

13. **a.** The Microsoft Quality Labs are responsible for testing hardware supplied by the manufacturers for certification on the Microsoft operating systems and inclusion on the HCL.

14. **d.** In Active Directory, transitive trusts are created between domains in a tree.

15. **d.** IDE provides sufficient performance for a testing environment, but may not be able to support a full-blown server configuration.

16. **b.** A site represents the physical boundaries of a network and is used to streamline communication between domain controllers.

17. **d.** A domain is a logical representation of the network's operation and is used to partition the functions of the network.

18. **b.** Tactical applications or services are still of use to the company, but may not be providing the most benefit available.

19. **c.** With Windows 2000, the requirement for NetBIOS has been eliminated. Answer a is not correct because even in a Windows NT 4 environment, WINS was not required, but recommended.

20. **b.** Although Windows NT 4 systems can participate in the Dfs structure, only stand-alone servers can host Dfs roots.

CHAPTER 3 SOLUTIONS

1. **c.** SMS is the only distribution method that can be used for automated upgrades.

2. **b, d.** Using Windows 2000 boot disks or using the network method of installing Windows 2000 are alternative methods to installing Windows 2000 when the CD-ROM drive is not bootable.

3. **b.** Microsoft's site hosts the HCL at **www.microsoft.com/hcl/**.

4. **a.** Slipstreaming is a new method of adding service packs to Windows 2000 installation files.

5. **c.** The /cmd switch will run a specified command before the last stage of Setup.

6. **c.** The Administrator's name and password are set during the GUI portion of Windows 2000 Setup.

7. **a, b, d.** To use Sysprep, the machines should have identical HALs and mass storage controllers. Sysprep also requires a third-party disk duplication tool, such as GHOST.

8. **b.** UDF stands for uniqueness database file.

9. **a, b, c.** The disk to be partitioned is in the text-only portion of Setup.

10. **a, b, c, d.** Setup Manager can be used to create answer files, UDFs, Sysprep files, and remote installation files.

11. **a.** True. SMS can only be used to perform upgrades.

12. **b, d.** Windows NT 4.0 Server and Windows NT Server 3.51 can be upgraded to Windows 2000 Server.

13. **b.** Under most circumstances, the Everyone group should have Read access to the Windows 2000 source files on a network share.

14. **a, b, d.** UDFs can be created in Notepad or Setup Manager, and they are used as supplements to answer files.

15. **d.** Unlike the creation of boot disks in Windows NT 4, makeboot.exe must be used to create Setup boot disks.

16. **b.** False. There is no default UDF file.

17. **a, d.** The target computer must have a network connection and a mapped drive to the source files when installing Windows 2000 Server over a network.

18. **c.** The "-quiet" switch makes Sysprep run in a hands-off mode.

19. **a.** When used with a Windows 2000 CD, the answer file must be called winnt.sif.

20. **a, b, d.** A WWW Server, FTP Server, and administration files are included in IIS.

21. **b.** False. Windows NT 4.0 Server can be upgraded to Windows 2000 Server, but Windows NT 4.0 Workstation cannot.

CHAPTER 4 SOLUTIONS

1. **b.** Named pipes are provided by the IPC$ hidden share.

2. **a, b.** Active Directory provides a secure publication of network resources and makes it easy for end-users to find those resources.

3. **c.** Windows 2000 currently supports over 3,000 printers.

4. **a.** A printer is the physical hardware that prints material.

5. **a.** Microsoft's Basic Authentication scheme sends a user's name and password across a network in clear-text.

6. **b.** The Sessions node of the Computer Management console provides a list of users currently connected to the shares on the computer.

7. **a, b, d.** Depending on the configuration, IPC$, ADMIN$, and FAX$ are shares that may be automatically created when you install Windows 2000 Server.

8. **b.** Scripts access should be given to Web folders that contain documents that have scripting, but cannot run any executables.

9. **a, b, c, d.** Using My Network Places, using the Computer Management console remotely, mapping a network drive, and using a Web browser are all methods of accessing shares.

10. **b.** The Balance option should be used to optimize the computer for a mix of file sharing and network applications.

11. **b.** A printer pool is a print service that is set up to send a print job to the first available printer.

12. **a.** True. A Dfs host server can be a domain controller.

13. **a, b, d.** To replicate Dfs content automatically, you must have FRS, and you must be using a domain-based Dfs. The content must also be on an NTFS partition.

14. **c.** The print queue object can be used to monitor the performance of either a local or a remote printer.

15. **a.** Prune printers that are not automatically republished is a group policy that defines how to handle the automatic removal of printers when a non-Windows 2000 printer is no longer available on the network.

16. **a, b, c.** By default, shares give all users Read, Write, and Full Control access.

17. **b.** The Print Services For Macintosh service must be installed to share printers with Macintosh clients.

18. **d.** Only Read, Write, and Script source access can be assigned to Web-based shares.

19. **b, c.** By default, Server Operators and Administrators have access to the C$ share.

20. **d.** The PKT for a domain-based Dfs is stored in the Active Directory.

21. **b, c.** Full Control access allows a user to change NTFS permissions and take control of files and folders.

22. **b, d.** Both the File And Print Sharing service and the Distributed file system must be installed for Dfs to function.

23. **d.** Print, Manage Documents, and Manage Printer are the only three access types that can be assigned to printers.

24. **b.** A replica is a Dfs folder that is automatically replicated to another folder.

CHAPTER 5 SOLUTIONS

1. **d.** The minimum requirement for Windows 2000 Server is 128MB of RAM. Answers b and c are optional and not required because they surpass the minimum requirements for the hard drive size and processor speed.

2. **c.** Windows 2000 Server supports ACPI and is the preferred BIOS. Windows 2000 Server does support the legacy Advanced Power Management (APM) and Plug and Play devices will function, but not to their full capabilities.

3. **b, c.** The minimum requirement is a 12x CD-ROM and a 133MHz CPU.

4. **b, d.** Windows 2000 Readiness Analyzer and the HCL can be used to determine if a system can support Windows 2000 Server.

5. **d.** Answer d is the correct way to launch the application from the command prompt.

6. **b.** If the board is not listed on the HCL, it probably will not work with Windows 2000 Server. The HCL should always be checked first.

7. **a.** The minimum requirement for Windows 2000 Server is 256MB of RAM. Increasing the amount of RAM on the machine will improve performance.

8. **b.** False. Windows NT 4.0 Server does not support Plug and Play.

9. **b.** Answer b is the correct answer. Answer a is the first part of the process to reveal phantom devices.

10. **c.** You need to obtain a BIOS update from the system manufacturer if you experience any of the following:

    ➤ You cannot install Windows 2000 Server because of an ACPI BIOS error.

    ➤ After you install Windows 2000 Server, power management and Plug and Play functionality is not present.

    ➤ After you install Windows 2000 Server, power management and Plug and Play functionality is present, but does not work properly.

11. **a, b.** You can add new hardware through the Add/Remove Hardware applet found in the Control Panel. You can also have Windows 2000 Server Setup program find the hardware during setup by stopping the installation and replacing the driver with one that is on the HCL.

12. **c.** Windows 2000 Server only supports IEEE 1394 devices that are OHCI compliant, and therefore the best decision is to purchase a product that is clearly labeled as such. Although a manufacturer of a noncompliant device might eventually be able to build a driver that will allow the noncompliant device to work with Windows 2000 Server, this is just inviting trouble for your server.

13. **a, b.** Cable connections make up a large percentage of network connectivity problems. Checking to make sure the that network adapter card is properly seated is also a valid answer. If the product is on the HCL and is Plug and Play, it is very unlikely that Windows 2000 Server would assign a conflicting resource setting on a new system; therefore, answer d is not correct.

14. **b.** False. Windows 2000 Server is designed to use the new ACPI based system, whereas Windows 95 and 98 use the older legacy APM. Windows 2000 Server is backward-compatible with Plug and Play features associated with Windows 98.

15. **c.** The best answer to this question is c as it is the quickest and most reliable method. Not only will Windows Update automatically download and install the driver on your Windows 2000 Server, but it will also check the version you have against the updated driver. All drivers at Windows Update are digitally signed and have passed the WHQL tests. Although you might receive the correct updated driver (answers a, b, and d), there is the possibility that the driver has not passed the WHQL tests, and it is also possible that you have a more current version of the driver than the one that has been supplied.

16. **b.** You can manipulate the settings to be as stringent or lenient as you or your company desires. Although sending a memo to each user might work for some conscientious employees, you will still run the risk of an unsigned driver being installed by accident.

17. **a.** You should always use the administrative tools to make system changes. Manually working with the Registry could result in total system failure and might require that you reinstall Windows 2000 Server.

18. **b.** This is the correct procedure. Windows 2000 Server does not support PS/2 mouse devices.

19. **a, b, d.** Dr. Watson and the System Log in Event Viewer will contain information on problems that occurred. Removing any newly installed hardware will help isolate and locate the problem.

20. **a, b, c.** All of these options should be used when diagnosing a specific error message.

21. **b.** Using the tools provided with SMS Server is the best way to analyze a large network.

CHAPTER 6 SOLUTIONS

1. **a, b, c, d.** CPU utilization and number of processes is viewed on the Performance tab, CPU consumption per process is viewed on the Processes tab, and Kernel Mode process consumption of CPU resources can be viewed through the View menu.

2. **b.** This is a false statement. All objects have their own unique set of counters.

3. **a, c.** Only logs and alerts continue to function when System Monitor is closed.

4. **b, c.** The same interval is used for all counters, and logs can be recorded in text format. Counter logs are based on counters, not objects, and counters can be pulled from any system within a single log.

5. **b.** Only the Logical Disk object from this list is not enabled by default.

6. **b.** Two more than the number of elements in an object for a queue indicates a problem.

7. **a.** When Logical Disk: Avg. Disk Bytes/Transfer has a consistent value of 4KB, then most of the drive activity is caused by paging.

8. **c.** The System Monitor can only display 100 data points.

9. **d.** A reading of 80% utilization or more for the CPU may indicate a problem.

10. **a, c, d.** A message, a counter log start, and an event detail can all be performed when an alert is triggered.

11. **a, d.** A priority of 24, which is Real Time, is restricted to Administrators. A priority of 3 is not a defined execution priority for users; the closest is 4 for Low. A priority of 10 is AboveNormal and 6 is BelowNormal.

12. **a.** Windows 2000 Professional's Performance Options are preset to applications. Background services is the default for Windows 2000 Server. PWS and workgroup authentication are fictional settings.

13. **a, b.** Neither of these selections will load the PC card services; thus PC Card NICs cannot be used.

14. **a.** Only A indicates the correct ARC name for this scenario.

15. **a, c, d.** Copy, Daily, and Differential backups do not reset the archive bit.

16. **a.** This is a true statement.

17. **a, b, c, d.** All of these are capabilities of IntelliMirror.

18. **a.** This is a true statement.

19. **a, b, d.** Folder Redirection, home directory definition, and offline files are all required to ensure access to data both online and off.

20. **b.** This is a false statement. RIS can only deploy Windows 2000 Professional.

CHAPTER 7 SOLUTIONS

1. **b.** All files must be removed from the volume or transferred to another owner before a user can be removed from disk quotas.

2. **d.** Until the Ntuser.dat file is changed to Ntuser.man and the user account path is changed to *server**share*\username.man, the user profiles will not become mandatory.

3. **b.** Files that are compressed cannot be encrypted.

4. **a.** Only Windows 2000 NTFS can be used for disk quotas.

5. **a.** True. To display alternate colors, select My Computer | Tools | Folder Options | View Tab, and then check the Display Compressed Files And Folders With Alternate Color checkbox.

6. **d.** In this case, the decompressed size of the file is greater than 3MB, which is why the error message is occurring.

7. **c.** When moving a file from one folder to another, the file retains its state regardless of the state the folder is in.

8. **a, d.** Encryption and decryption are transparent to the user, so a user might not realize that the processes run in the background. A user can check the attributes of the file or folder to be sure it is encrypted or have another user try to access them.

9. **b.** When copying a file from one folder to another, the file takes on the state of the folder it is being copied to. In this case, b is the best answer because copying the file to the server's compressed folder will automatically compress it. Answer d will work because the file is compressed prior to copying and because the target folder is compressed, the file will not be changed. However, this adds a lot of unneeded work and is not the best solution for the question.

10. **a, c.** A roaming user profile is stored locally at the workstation, as well as on the server. When a user logs in, the locally cached profile is compared to the server's and if the server has a newer profile, it will be copied to the workstation.

11. **d.** Only NTFS is supported by Windows 2000 for compression. Any transfers from NTFS to FAT will result in a file losing its compression state. Answer a might have been correct if both computers were using NTFS, but Windows 98 cannot be formatted in NTFS, making this answer incorrect.

12. **b.** Check the disk and defragment it once a month (or more if the disk is heavily used).

13. **a.** The network administrator (or designated recovery agent) will be able to use the recovery agent to restore the file. Answer d, although intriguing, is a fabrication (as far as we know anyway!).

14. **d.** Moving files and folders that are rarely used to a tape backup is the best method. If the backup tape is an easily accessible device, like an Iomega Zip drive, this is even better. Answer a is not recommended because there could be vital information in the files, even though they are not used often. Answer b will not work against his disk quota because it is the file's actual size, not its compressed size that is measured. Answer c is an alternative, but not the best answer in this case.

15. **b.** Compressing files and folders that are not used often is the best choice. By compressing these files, you keep disk performance and degradation to a minimum.

16. **b.** Data compression can provide more space on a drive, but if done on a heavily used server, access time to the files and folders will be reduced. Answer c is not correct because it does not matter if the target file is compressed or not; the process to transfer the file from the server to the workstation remains the same.

17. **d.** You should encrypt at the folder level, so temporary files that are created when editing will also be encrypted.

18. **a.** Disk Management is an MMC snap-in tool, which replaces Disk Administrator.

19. **b, c.** You need to use NTFS, and the volume must not be the system or boot volume to upgrade to a dynamic disk.

20. **a.** Event Viewer will log the date and time of the infraction, but does not keep statistics about the user after that.

21. **c.** Users can log on to several machines using roaming profiles. A problem occurs when they make changes to profiles while logging on and off because the changes may be lost. For example, a user logs on to machine 1, and then machine 2. While on machine 1, the user makes changes to his profile, and then logs off. The profile is then saved on the server. On machine 2, the user makes no changes to the profile and then logs off machine 2. The profile on machine 2 is then saved on the server. So the changes made to the profile from machine 1 have been overwritten, or in other words, lost.

CHAPTER 8 SOLUTIONS

1. **c.** NAT translates private IP addresses to public IP addresses for communication over the Internet.

2. **d.** 10001001 is the binary representation of 137.

3. **b, d.** NetBEUI and NetBIOS services are provided for legacy application support.

4. **c.** ARP associates IP addresses to physical addresses.

5. **d.** CIFS ensures file integrity.

6. **a, b.** 255.255.0.0 and /16 represent a Class B subnet mask.

7. **c.** The default route directs all host traffic not specified in the routing table.

8. **b.** MUP provides support for multiple redirectors on a single computer.

9. **a.** OSPF is the link state protocol for TCP/IP.

10. **a.** RRAS provides Windows 2000 VPN components.

11. **a.** Mailslots are used for broadcast messaging.

12. **d.** NWLink is Microsoft's implementation of Novell's primary protocol. You may be tempted to choose AppleTalk and NetBIOS also. However, the Windows 2000 implementations of these protocols are fully supported and licensed by the manufacturer. NWLink, on the other hand, requires manipulation before it can operate in the NDIS environment.

13. **d.** DHCPOffer uses the combination of source IP address/destination physical address.

14. **d.** DHCPRelease is used to terminate a lease.

15. **c.** Winsock is used to implement Quality of Service.

16. **a.** IAS uses the RADIUS standards.

17. **a.** TCP operates at the Transport layer of the OSI model.

18. **b.** When the lease is 50 percent complete, the client sends a DHCPRequest to the server from which the lease was obtained.

19. **b.** The Session layer creates a virtual circuit between sending and receiving processes.

20. **b.** Wake-on-LAN initializes the computer when a signal is received from another computer.

21. **a.** Networks on which the sending host dictates the route data takes across the network are called source routing networks.

22. **c.** ATM uses the NDIS LAN Emulation intermediate driver.

23. **a.** The TDI boundary layer is not represented by a software component and represents the interface between services and protocols.

24. **a.** RPC provides communication paths between processes running on the same computer.

25. **c.** DNS is the default service used by Windows 2000 for name resolution.

26. **a, d.** PPTP and L2TP are used by Windows 2000 to create private, tunneled connections.

27. **b.** A metric is included in a routing table entry to assist the router in determining the best path for the data.

28. **a.** UDP provides connectionless datagram transport.

CHAPTER 9 SOLUTIONS

1. **a, c.** NetWare servers only support Bindery and NDS.

2. **c.** A collection of AppleTalk Systems is known as a zone.

3. **d.** SNA is only available using Host Integration Server 2000.

4. **c.** Although it is the quickest way, it is not the most efficient way.

5. **c.** FSM and PSM rely on AppleTalk to function.

6. **b.** False. The protocol used with GSNW is NWLink.

7. **b.** Each system on an AppleTalk network is known as a node.

8. **b.** The Apple implementation of AppleTalk over Ethernet is known as EtherTalk.

9. **c.** Forksize is not a feature of the MacFile utility.

10. **a, b, c, d.** Assuming that they are SNMP-compliant, all can be managed using SNMP.

11. **c.** The protocol used with GSNW is NWLink.

12. **a, c.** NTFS is only required if GSNW is used as a gateway. GSNW will work over any physical media supported by both systems.

13. **c.** MIB is the acronym for management information base.

14. **d.** The Apple implementation of AppleTalk over Token Ring is known as TokenTalk.

15. **a.** Unix usually uses the NFS file system.

16. **b.** Windows 2000 usually uses the CIFS file system to share files.

17. **a.** True, although these are one and the same product, GSNW can be used only as a client.

18. **c.** The Apple implementation of AppleTalk over LocalTalk is known as LocalTalk.

19. **b.** False, GSNW allows Windows 2000 systems to connect to NetWare servers to access file and print resources.

CHAPTER 10 SOLUTIONS

1. **b.** SNMP is not an IIS service.

2. **d.** SiteA and SiteB use different port numbers and Host Headers.

3. **c.** Use the Permissions Wizard to configure Web site permissions.

4. **a.** True. The ISM (HTML) can be used to restart Web services.

5. **d.** A random port is assigned to the Administration Web Site during setup.

6. **b.** False. Because the applications are actually running on the server, and many clients can connect at once, the Application Server mode uses more processing power than the Remote Administration mode.

7. **b.** Two concurrent administrators can connect to Terminal Services running in Remote Administration mode.

8. **a, c, d.** A policy can be used to set remote policy properties that allow or deny access based on time/day and the protocol used. In addition, it can specify the phone number to be dialed by the user.

9. **c.** Gateway Server is not one of the configuration options for RRAS.

10. **b.** False. Terminal Services can be installed and uninstalled without reinstalling the operating system.

11. **b.** While a static IP address is ideal, it is not a requirement for IIS.

12. **b, c, d.** MS-DOS is not supported for connecting into Terminal Services. All Windows versions are.

13. **a.** To convert from Remote Administration mode to Application Server mode, run the Add/Remove Windows Components Wizard, and choose the Application Server Mode radio button.

14. **b.** False. Not all applications run in Application Server mode.

15. **c.** By default, a Web server uses port 80.

CHAPTER 11 SOLUTIONS

1. **a, b, c.** GPOs can only be applied to sites, domains, and organizational units. Groups can be used to filter the effect of a GPO.

2. **c.** To improve GPO performance, disable Computer Configuration in a GPO that only has User Configuration settings configured.

3. **d.** The GPO settings are removed from the computers. The computers will revert to settings configured manually on the computers if no other GPOs are being applied to it.

4. **b, d, i.** You can specify the Block Inheritance option of an organizational unit. You can specify the No Override option for a GPO. You can use Deny Apply Group Policy for a Security Group.

5. **a.** It prevents all GPOs from the parent containers applying to a particular organizational unit.

6. **b.** You can force a GPO propagation event to refresh the settings on a computer using the command **secedit /refreshpolicy machine_policy**. GPOs are refreshed every 90 ± 30 minutes on client computers and every 5 minutes on domain controllers.

7. **d.** The Local Security Policy first, then site policies, and then domain policies, with OU policies last.

8. **c.** The computer starts, the computer policy is applied, and startup scripts run. All computer settings are configured before the user logs on. The user logs on, the user policy is applied, and logon scripts run.

9. **d.** Secedit.exe can be used to configure or analyze security settings on a computer.

10. **b.** You cannot use a security template to define settings for computers formatted with the FAT file system; the computer to which a template applies must be formatted with NTFS.

11. **d.** Group Policy and Local Security Policy cannot be applied to Windows NT 4 computers.

12. **a, c.** General Permissions and Specialized Permissions can be configured on NTFS.

13. **b, d.** Auditing and a standard permission called Modify & Delete are provided by NTFS.

14. **c, d.** If you deny Full Control to the Everyone Group, no one will be able to access the folder. Denying Read permission takes precedence over Allow. If Terry has Full Control of the folder, she can change the permissions for files that she does not want other users to access.

15. **a.** A new file is created in the process, so the file will inherit the permissions set for the Archives folder.

16. **b.** A new file is not created in this move process because the move takes place on the same partition, so the file will retain the permissions it had in the Schedule folder.

17. **c.** Tom will have no access; he has been denied Full Control.

18. **c.** You will have no access; Everyone has been denied Full Control.

19. **c.** She needs to enable Audit Object Access in the Audit Policy of the Local Security Policy before she can configure auditing for the folder.

20. **a.** EFS, or Encrypting File System, enables encryption of sensitive data.

CHAPTER 12 SOLUTIONS

1. **c.** Kerberos would be used in a pure Windows 2000 domain environment.

2. **a, b, d.** NTLM is used in mixed environments and for authentication when logging on locally to a Windows 2000 member server or Professional computer.

3. **d.** Kerberos uses a symmetric secret key to encrypt authentication information when a user logs onto a Windows 2000 domain using a password.

4. **c.** Sessions tickets are issued to the client computer for each service that the user wishes to connect to.

5. **b.** To use Active Directory, promote at least one Windows 2000 server to a domain controller. Active Directory will automatically be installed. All the computers in the network do *not* have to be running Windows 2000.

6. **a, d.** Local user accounts do not need to be configured on computers. Users must still supply a password. The KDC can verify that a user has submitted the correct password, and Kerberos then provides the client computer with appropriate keys to encrypt subsequent authentication information.

7. **c, d.** Local user accounts can only access resources on the machine on which they were created and you can use one of the System Tools in Computer Management to create local user accounts.

8. **b.** The users container cannot contain OUs, nor can Group Policy be applied to it. Using OUs gives you greater flexibility and control. Passwords should be complicated. You use Active Directory Users And Computers to create domain user accounts.

9. **b, c.** Initials are optional. You can use the same word for many fields on the first wizard screen when creating a user. The logon and pre-Windows 2000 logon names do not have to be the same, but it will make your work easier.

10. **c.** The Log On To button is used to specify computers from which a user may log on, not the time. To assign group membership, use the Members Of tab. You cannot configure a date on which an account will automatically be enabled. You can only configure a date on which an account will be disabled.

11. **d.** You want users to receive the same profile, irrespective of the computer from which they log on.

12. **a, b.** Dial-in settings and all the settings on the tabs related to Terminal services.

13. **c.** You will always be prompted to enter a password when you copy an account. You normally disable a template account for security reasons, so answer a is incorrect.

14. **a.** Computer accounts are only needed for Windows 2000 and Windows NT computers; Windows 95/98 computers do not require them. Use Active Directory Users And Computers to create computer accounts.

15. **d.** Active Directory is the directory service used by Windows 2000 domains.

16. **b.** An Active Directory distinguished name refers to every object's name and location.

17. **d.** There is one Global Catalog per forest.

18. **c.** Domains are not related to the physical structure and can span WAN links.

19. **b.** The administrator cannot *lock out* an account; only Windows 2000 can do that. The account lockout duration is the amount of time that the account remains locked out. The account lockout threshold determines how many incorrect passwords a user can enter before being locked out. A value of zero means no lockout will occur.

20. **d.** The most efficient way to accommodate the 10-character password requirement and ensure that all passwords are changed monthly is to create one domain, create OUs for each department, and place the users in appropriate OUs. At the domain level, create and apply two Account Policies called All Users Account Policy and RD Account Policy, respectively. Make sure that the RD Account Policy is applied before the All Users Account Policy. Configure the RD Account Policy with the appropriate password settings and ensure No Override is enabled. Configure the Users Account Policy with the appropriate password settings and ensure that the No Override checkbox is cleared. For the R&D OU, ensure Block Inheritance is checked.

CHAPTER 13 SOLUTIONS

1. **b, c.** The **AT** command can be used to schedule tasks in both Windows NT 4 and all editions of Windows 2000.

2. **d.** The scheduled task data that is created using the **AT** command is stored in the Registry.

3. **a.** The scheduled task data that is created using the Windows 2000 Task Scheduler is stored in .job files.

4. **a.** True. Tasks that are created using the **AT** command can be viewed and modified using the Task Scheduler. However, once they have been modified using the Task Scheduler, they can no longer be viewed or modified using the **AT** command.

5. **d.** To schedule tasks using the **AT** command, you must be a member of the Administrators group.

6. **c.** To schedule tasks using the Task Scheduler tool, at the very least, you must be a member of a group that has sufficient permissions to complete the task.

7. **b, c.** Both the Task Scheduler log and the Notify Me Of Missed Tasks option can be used to help in the diagnosis of problems with the Task Scheduler.

8. **b, c.** The Task Scheduler logs show when the task was started and also the exit code from the task, which can be used to determine if the task completed successfully.

9. **b, c.** WSH includes both the VBScript and the JScript scripting engines.

10. **a, b.** The scripting engine to use with the script can be set on the command line, or by default, the script file name extension will be used to reference the correct scripting engine.

11. **a.** True. The common objects supplied with WSH can be used with any scripting language that plugs into WSH.

12. **a, c.** Active directory can be manipulated via ADSI or the LDAP using any programming language including WSH.

13. **b.** False. All attributes can be changed via scripting.

14. **a, b, d.** Syntax, logic, and runtime are the three common scripting errors.

15. **b.** False. The Microsoft Script Debugger was designed to debug the scripts that were used with Internet Explorer.

16. **b.** False. In Windows 2000, scripts are stored in the SYSVOL, so that they can be easily replicated between domain controllers.

17. **b.** False. In certain instances, the MS-DOS batch language has several advantages including being small and fast, and allowing for easy batch file creation.

18. **b.** False. The enhancements added to the batch language in Windows 2000 are minimal.

19. **b.** False. There is no such thing as the Microsoft Script Editor. Logon scripts and batch files can be created using any text editor.

20. **a, b.** Legacy Logon Scripts and Group Policy Logon and Logoff scripts are supported. There is no such thing as Scheduled Scripts or Logoff scripts.

21. **b.** False. As in previous versions of Windows, logon scripts are optional.

22. **b, c.** The **AT** command and the Task Scheduler are the two methods of scheduling tasks in Windows 2000.

23. **d.** The only advantage that the **AT** command has over the Task Scheduler tool is that the **AT** command can be scripted.

24. **c.** When using the **AT** command with anything other than an .exe file, the command must be prefaced with cmd /c. Also, the explicit path of the file must be given.

CHAPTER 14 SOLUTIONS

1. **c.** User Mode: Delegated Access, Multiple Windows allows users to open new console windows, but prevents users from accessing portions of the console tree, adding or removing snap-ins, and saving altered versions of the console.

2. **a, c.** Active Directory Users And Computers and Event Viewer are MMC snap-in based utilities.

3. **b.** Computer Management collectively includes the abilities to view log files, display configuration information, manage shared folders, defragment a disk, configure services, and more.

4. **b, c, d.** Event Viewer can filter, search, and overwrite old elements in a log. It does not offer automatic intrusion detection.

5. **a.** Per Seat licensing is better suited for larger networks with many servers.

6. **a.** True. A license group is used to grant or restrict access to client access licenses when the total number of users, computers, and licenses are not equivalent.

7. **a, b, c.** Service configuration includes Log On As, startup type, and command-line startup parameters. Services cannot be terminated by a time limit; only Scheduled Tasks can be terminated by a time limit.

8. **a, b, d.** A failed service can initiate a service restart after a specified period of time, launching of a file, or a reboot. Only alerts can trigger the start of a Counter Log.

9. **a.** True. If a service required by other applications or services to perform essential operations or functions fails, the dependent processes might not be able to continue operating normally.

10. **a, b, c, d.** Accessibility Options provide for all of the listed capabilities.

11. **b, c, d.** Add/Remove Hardware, Scanners And Cameras, and Game Controllers are applets that can be used to install hardware. Sounds And Multimedia cannot be used to install hardware.

12. **d.** The Add/Remove Hardware applet should be used to install drivers for most nondetected hardware.

13. **a.** True. The Add/Remove Programs can be used to install applications from floppies, CDs, network distribution points, and the Microsoft Update Web site.

14. **a.** Only a single display should be used during initial installation. After installation, up to nine displays can be used.

15. **a, b, d.** The only listed ability not supported by the native fax within Windows 2000 is network sharing of fax devices.

16. **b.** Regional Settings can be used to install additional language support.

17. **b.** False. The false element in the statement is the ability "to define several trusted vendors from which to accept drivers"; the rest of the statement is true.

18. **a, c.** Device Manager and System Information can both be used to determine the use status of system resources. The View selections of Resource By Type and Resources By Connection of the Device Manager are designed specifically for this purpose.

19. **a, c, d.** All systems have a hardware profile—the default hardware profile. In most cases, administrators will only define additional hardware profiles on portable systems.

20. **a, b.** When a stop error occurs, the system can automatically reboot, and a dump file is created in addition to the mandatory event detail in the Application log and the optional administrative alert.

OBJECTIVES FOR EXAM 70-215

Installing Windows 2000 Server	Chapter(s):
Perform an attended installation of Windows 2000 Server	3
Perform an unattended installation of Windows 2000 Server	3
• Create unattended answer files by using Setup Manager to automate the installation of Windows 2000 Server	3
• Create and configure automated methods for installation of Windows 2000	3
Upgrade a server from Microsoft Windows NT 4	3
Deploy service packs	3
Troubleshoot failed installations	3

Installing, Configuring, and Troubleshooting Access to Resources	Chapter(s):
Install and configure network services for interoperability	4
Monitor, configure, troubleshoot, and control access to printers	4
Monitor, configure, troubleshoot, and control access to files, folders, and shared folders	4
• Configure, manage, and troubleshoot a standalone Distributed file system (Dfs)	4
• Configure, manage, and troubleshoot a domain-based Distributed file system (Dfs)	4
• Monitor, configure, troubleshoot, and control local security on files and folders	4
• Monitor, configure, troubleshoot, and control access to files and folders in a shared folder	4
• Monitor, configure, troubleshoot, and control access to files and folders via Web services	4
Monitor, configure, troubleshoot, and control access to Web sites	4

Configuring and Troubleshooting Hardware Devices and Drivers	Chapter(s):
Configure hardware devices	5
Configure driver signing options	5
Update device drivers	5
Troubleshoot problems with hardware	5

Managing, Monitoring, and Optimizing System Performance, Reliability, and Availability	Chapter(s):
Monitor and optimize usage of system resources	6
Manage processes	6
Set priorities and start and stop processes	6
Optimize disk performance	6
Manage and optimize availability of System State data and user data	6
Recover System State data and user data	6
• Recover System State data by using Windows Backup	6
• Troubleshoot system restoration by starting in safe mode	6
• Recover System State data by using the Recovery Console	6

Managing, Configuring, and Troubleshooting Storage Use	Chapter(s):
Monitor, configure, and troubleshoot disks and volumes	7
Configure data compression	7
Monitor and configure disk quotas	7
Recover from disk failures	7

Configuring and Troubleshooting Windows 2000 Network Connections	Chapter(s):
Install, configure, and troubleshoot shared access	8, 9
Install, configure, and troubleshoot a virtual private network (VPN)	8
Install, configure, and troubleshoot network protocols	8, 9
Install and configure network services	8, 9, 10
Configure, monitor, and troubleshoot remote access	10
• Configure inbound connections	10
• Create a remote access policy	10
• Configure a remote access profile	10
Install, configure, monitor, and troubleshoot Terminal Services	10
• Remotely administer servers by using Terminal Services	10
• Configure Terminal Services for application sharing	10
• Configure applications for use with Terminal Services	10
Install, configure, and troubleshoot network adapters and drivers	8, 9

Implementing, Monitoring, and Troubleshooting Security	Chapter(s):
Encrypt data on a hard disk by using Encrypting File System (EFS)	**11**
Implement, configure, manage, and troubleshoot policies in a Windows 2000 environment	**11**
• Implement, configure, manage, and troubleshoot Local Policy in a Windows 2000 environment	**11**
• Implement, configure, manage, and troubleshoot System Policy in a Windows 2000 environment	**11**
Implement, configure, manage, and troubleshoot auditing	**11**
Implement, configure, manage, and troubleshoot local accounts	**12**
Implement, configure, manage, and troubleshoot Account Policy	**12**
Implement, configure, manage, and troubleshoot security by using the Security Configuration Tool Set	**11**

Appendix B

APPENDIX C

STUDY RESOURCES

This appendix provides information about additional resources you can use to further your study and understanding of Windows 2000.

BOOKS

The following are books specific to Windows 2000:

➤ Minasi, Mark, et al. *Mastering Windows 2000 Server*. Sybex, February 2000. $49.99. ISBN: 0-78212-774-6. This book is written by *NT Magazine* columnist Mark Minasi and is full of excellent information.

➤ *Microsoft Windows 2000 Server Resource Kit*. Microsoft Press, January 2000. $299.99. ISBN: 1-57231-805-8. This book and CD set includes invaluable additional detailed documentation on Windows 2000. In addition, the CD includes many useful utilities.

➤ Russell, Charlie, et al. *Microsoft Windows 2000 Server Administrator's Companion*. Microsoft Press, January 2000. ISBN: 1-57231-819-8. This book details many of the complex features and capabilities of Windows 2000 Server. It's a great handbook for any network administrator.

➤ Boswell, William. *Inside Windows 2000 Server*. New Riders, December 1999. ISBN: 1-56205-929-7. This is an excellent guide for installation and general administration.

➤ Tittel, Ed, et al. *Windows 2000 Server for Dummies*. IDG, April 2000. ISBN: 0-76450-341-3. This is an excellent beginner's resource for Windows 2000 Server.

WEB SITES

The following are Web sites with useful Windows 2000 information. Some of these sites are focused on Microsoft certification. Although not all of these include Windows 2000 Server–specific information currently, they should soon.

➤ **209.207.167.177**—Offers braindumps on various certification exams. A braindump is a person's recollection of what they saw on an exam. Keep in mind that this information is not always accurate and is not condoned by the certification vendors.

➤ **www.activewin.com**—A resource page for PC and Windows products and information.

➤ **www.hardcoremcse.com**—Offers MCSE study materials, including online sample questions.

➤ **www.internexis.com/mcp**—A peer discussion and chat site for certification students.

➤ **www.jsiinc.com/reghack.htm**—A collection of hundreds of tricks, tips, scripts, hacks, and utilities to get Windows 2000 (and Windows NT) to perform functions not built in by Microsoft.

➤ **www.mcpmag.com**—The official *Microsoft Certified Professional Magazine* Web site.

➤ **www.mcsetutor.com**—Offers lots of MCSE self-study materials, including book reviews, tests, tips, and FAQs.

➤ **www.microsoft.com/train_cert**—The official Microsoft certification Web site.

➤ **www.mous.net**—The home page for the Microsoft Office User Specialist (MOUS) program.

➤ **www.searchwin2000.com**—A "global" search tool that can help you locate specific information related to products for or problems with Windows 2000.

➤ **www.veriworld.com**—Offers online testing and a personalized progress evaluation.

➤ **www.win2kworld.com**—Collects Windows 2000 headlines from numerous sources and offers peer discussion groups and lots of links to other sites.

➤ **www.winntmag.com**—The official *Windows 2000 Magazine* Web site.

➤ **www.winsupersite.com**—A useful resource for general Microsoft OS information, such as news announcements, FAQs, reviews, and technology showcases.

APPENDIX D

WINDOWS SCRIPT HOST COMMANDS AND SYNTAX

As mentioned in Chapter 13, you can use the Windows Script Host (WSH) to automate administrative tasks in Windows 2000. This appendix uses the information found in the WSH 2.0 documentation. The Help file is available as a free download from **http://msdn.microsoft.com/scripting/windowshost/ wshdoc.exe**.

*Note: Microsoft reorganizes its Web site on occasion and this URL may not currently be valid. If it is not valid, go to the MSDN site at **http://msdn.microsoft.com/**, and click the scripting option.*

Four sections are listed in this appendix:

➤ WSH Elements

➤ WSH Methods

➤ WSH Objects

➤ WSH Properties

Each of these subjects is discussed in the following section. Each component is defined and its syntax listed.

WSH ELEMENTS

WSH elements define the different boundaries of the script. An object, for example, would be surrounded by the <object> element field.

<?job ?>

The *<?job ?>* parameter is used by XML to specify which attributes should be used for error handling. This component's syntax is as follows:

```
<?job error="flag" debug="flag" ?>
```

<?XML ?>

Use the *<?XML ?>* parameter to force the file to be parsed as XML. This component's syntax is as follows:

```
<?XML version="1.0" [standalone="DTDflag"] ?>
```

<job>

Use the *<job>* parameter if one or more jobs needs to be executed from within a single script file. This component's syntax is as follows:

```
<job [id=JobID]>
job code
</job>
```

<object>

The *<object>* component allows for the definition of objects to be referenced by the script. This component's syntax is as follows:

```
<object id="objID" [classid="clsid:GUID" | progid="progID"] />
```

Note: GUID and progID are optional commands.

<package>

The *<package>* element contains within it the code used to identify multiple jobs in a WSH (.wsf) control file. This component's syntax is as follows:

```
<package>
WSH code goes here
</package>
```

<reference>

The *<reference>* XML element points to an external type library. This component's syntax is as follows:

```
<reference [object="progID"|guid="typelibGUID"] [version="version"] />
```

Note: In the preceding code, version is an optional parameter.

<resource>

The *<resource>* element allows you to specify data that is independent of the script and should be kept as such. This component's syntax is as follows:

```
<resource id="resourceID">
value
</resource>
```

\<script>

The *\<script>* element allows you to create XML scripts to define how your script will execute. This component's syntax is as follows:

```
<script language="language" [src="strFile"]>
Script
</script>
```

WSH METHODS

WSH methods can be thought of as tasks. To perform a task on an object, you must call on its method. For example, to create a shortcut object, you would call on the CreateShortcut method.

AddPrinterConnection

The AddPrinterConnection method allows you to map a local resource to a remote printer. This component's syntax is as follows:

```
Object.AddPrinterConnection strLocalName, strRemoteName
[,bUpdateProfile] [,strUser] [,strPassword]
```

Note: *in the preceding code, [,bUpdateProfile], [,strUser], and [,strPassword] are optional parameters.*

AddWindowsPrinterConnection

The AddWindowsPrinterConnection method adds a printer connection to Windows 2000 and NT. This component's syntax is as follows:

```
Object.AddWindowsPrinterConnection(strPrinterPath)
```

AppActivate

By executing the AppActivate method, an application Window appears. This component's syntax is as follows:

```
Object.AppActivate title
```

Close

The Close method closes an open stream. This component's syntax is as follows:

```
Object.strStream.Close
```

ConnectObject

The ConnectObject method connects the object's event sources to specified functions. This component's syntax is as follows:

```
Object.ConnectObject strObject, strPrefix
```

CreateObject

The CreateObject method creates an object. This component's syntax is as follows:

```
Object.CreateObject(strProgID[,strPrefix])
```

Note: In the preceding code, [,strPrefix] is an optional parameter.

CreateShortcut

The CreateShortcut method creates a shortcut. This component's syntax is as follows:

```
Object.CreateShortcut(strPathname)
```

DisconnectObject

The DisconnectObject method disconnects any open (or connected) object. This component's syntax is as follows:

```
Object.DisconnectObject obj
```

Echo

The Echo method sends specified information to a dialog box. This component's syntax is as follows:

```
Object.Echo data
```

EnumNetworkDrives

The EnumNetworkDrives method returns the values of the currently mapped network drives. This component's syntax is as follows:

```
ObjNetDrives = object.EnumNetworkDrive
```

EnumPrinterConnections

The EnumPrinterConnections method returns the values of the currently connected network printers. This component's syntax is as follows:

```
ObjPrinters = object.EnumPrinterConnections
```

ExpandEnvironmentStrings

The ExpandEnvironmentStrings method returns the value of the requested environment variable. This component's syntax is as follows:

```
Object.ExpandEnvironmentStrings(strString)
```

GetObject

Use the GetObject method to return an automation object. This component's syntax is as follows:

```
Object.GetObject(strPathname)
```

GetResource

The GetResource method returns the value of a resource that is defined in the *<resource>* element. This component's syntax is as follows:

```
Object.GetResource(resourceID)
```

LogEvent

The LogEvent method can be used when information needs to be logged into the Windows 2000 event log or the wsh.log file. Six log types exist: 0 is used for success, 1 for error, 2 for warning, 4 for information, 8 for successful audit, and 16 for failed audit. This component's syntax is as follows:

```
Object.LogEvents(intType, strMessage)
```

MapNetworkDrive

Use the MapNetworkDrive method to map a network drive. This component's syntax is as follows:

```
Object.MapNetworkDrive strLocalName, strRemoteName
```

Popup

The Popup method displays a pop-up message. This component's syntax is as follows:

```
IntItem = object.Popup (strText)
```

Quit

The Quit method is used to exit the script with a specified error. This component's syntax is as follows:

```
Object.Quit
```

Read

Use the Read method to read a specific number of characters from the data stream and return the resulting string. This component's syntax is as follows:

```
Object.strStream.Read(characters)
```

ReadAll

The ReadAll method reads the entire data stream and returns the resulting string. This component's syntax is as follows:

```
Object.strStream.ReadAll
```

ReadLine

The ReadLine method reads the entire line in the data stream and returns the resulting string. This component's syntax is as follows:

```
Object.strStream.ReadLine
```

RegDelete

The RegDelete method deletes data from the Registry. This component's syntax is as follows:

```
Object.RegDelete strName
```

RegRead

The RegRead method reads data from the specified Registry entry and returns the Registry key or value named by *strName*. This component's syntax is as follows:

```
Object.RegRead (strName)
```

RegWrite

The RegWrite method writes data to the specified Registry entry. This component's syntax is as follows:

```
Object.RegWrite(strName, value)
```

Remove

The Remove method deletes the specified environmental variable. This component's syntax is as follows:

```
Object.Remove(strName)
```

RemoveNetworkDrive

The RemoveNetworkDrive method disconnects a mapped network drive. This component's syntax is as follows:

```
Object.RemoveNetworkDrive strName
```

RemovePrinterConnection

The RemovePrinterConnection method disconnects a connected network printer. This component's syntax is as follows:

```
Object.RemovePrinterConnection strName
```

Run

The Run method can be used to execute a new process. This component's syntax is as follows:

```
Object.Run (strCommand)
```

Save

The Save method saves a shortcut. This component's syntax is as follows:

```
Object.Save
```

SendKeys

The SendKeys method simulates key presses on the keyboard. This component's syntax is as follows:

```
Object.SendKeys str
```

SetDefaultPrinter

The SetDefaultPrinter method can be used to set the default printer for the system. This component's syntax is as follows:

```
Object.SetDefaultPrinter strPrinter
```

Skip

The Skip method can be used to skip over a specified number of characters. This component's syntax is as follows:

```
Object.strStream.Skip(characters)
```

SkipLine

The SkipLine method can be used to skip to the next line in the stream. This component's syntax is as follows:

```
Object.strStream.SkipLine
```

Sleep

The Sleep method pauses the script for a specified number of milliseconds. This component's syntax is as follows:

```
Object.Sleep (intTime)
```

Write

The Write method writes the specified string to the output stream. This component's syntax is as follows:

```
Object.strStream.Write (strString)
```

WriteBlankLines

The WriteBlankLines method writes a specified number of blank lines to the stream. This component's syntax is as follows:

```
Object.strStream.WriteBlankLines (intNumLines)
```

WriteLine

The WriteLine method writes a specified string and newline character to the output stream. This component's syntax is as follows:

```
Object.strStream.WriteLine
```

WSH OBJECTS

WSH uses an object model type of architecture. This means that in order to use WSH to make modifications to your system, you will need to access these objects. For example, the WshNetwork object makes it easier for a script to connect and disconnect from network resources.

WScript

The WScript object is used to create and read objects. It can also be used to find out information about the script host. These objects can include the execution mode and the path of the script host.

WshArguments

The WshArguments object returns the collection of command-line parameters available.

WshEnvironment

The WshEnvironment object returns the values stored as environmental variables in the operating system. These values can include the temp directories and the Windows directory.

WshNetwork

The WshNetwork object is used to connect to the network. It enables you to connect to and disconnect from network printers and shares.

WshShell

The WshShell allows you to create new objects, set up environmental variables, and create shortcuts.

WshShortcut

The WshShortcut object can be used to create shortcuts.

WshSpecialFolders

Using the WshSpecialFolders object, you can get the paths for some of the special folders stored in Windows including the Start menu, the My Documents folder, and the Favorites folder.

WshUrlShortcut

The WshUrlShortcut object is used to create shortcuts to URLs, rather than to local and network files.

WSH PROPERTIES

Each object has properties assigned to it. For example, the Description property returns the value of the description of the shortcut property. Each object has its own set of properties.

Application

The Application property returns the Idispatch interface. This component's syntax is as follows:

```
Object.Application
```

Appendix D

Arguments

The Arguments property returns a point to the WshArguments collection. This component's syntax is as follows:

```
Object.Arguments
```

AtEndOfLine

AtEndOfLine can be used to determine if the stream pointer is at the end of the line. This component's syntax is as follows:

```
Objec.strStream.AtEndOfLine
```

AtEndOfStream

AtEndOfStream can be used to determine if the stream pointer is at the end of an input stream. This component's syntax is as follows:

```
Object.strStream.AtEndOfStream
```

Column

The Column property may be used to return the column number of the current character position. This component's syntax is as follows:

```
Object.strStream.Column
```

ComputerName

The ComputerName returns the value of the name of the computer on which the script is being executed. This value returns a string. This component's syntax is as follows:

```
Object.ComputerName
```

Count

The Count property returns the total number of enumerated items. This component's syntax is as follows:

```
Object.Count
```

Description

Description allows for the description of a shortcut object to be assigned. This component's syntax is as follows:

```
Object.Description
```

Environment

The Environment object returns the WshEnvironment object. This component's syntax is as follows:

```
Object.Environment
```

FullName

The FullName property returns the full path for the shortcut object or .exe file. This component's syntax is as follows:

```
Object.FullName
```

Hotkey

Use the Hotkey property to assign a keyboard shortcut to the shortcut object. This component's syntax is as follows:

```
Object.HotKey = strHotKey
```

IconLocation

The IconLocation property can be used to return the location of the icon of a shortcut object. This component's syntax is as follows:

```
Object.IconLocation = strIconLocation
```

Item

Use the Item property to return the specified item from a collection. This component's syntax is as follows:

```
Object.Item(Collection)
```

Length

The Length property returns the string value of the number of enumerated items. This component's syntax is as follows:

```
Object.Length
```

Line

The Line property returns the current line number in an input stream. This component's syntax is as follows:

```
Object.strStream.Line
```

Name

The Name property returns the friendly name of the WScript object. This component's syntax is as follows:

```
Object.Name
```

Path

The Path property returns the folder where the CScript.exe or WScript.exe files reside. This value returns a string. This component's syntax is as follows:

```
Object.Path
```

ScriptFullName

The ScriptFullName property returns the full path of the script that is currently being executed. This component's syntax is as follows:

```
Object.ScriptFullName
```

ScriptName

The ScriptName property returns the name of the script that is currently being executed. This component's syntax is as follows:

```
Object.ScriptName
```

SpecialFolders

The SpecialFolders property provides the WshSpecialFolders Object, which provides access to built-in folders, such as the NetHood, Recent, and Programs folders. This component's syntax is as follows:

```
Object.SpecialFolders(objWshSpecialFolders)
```

StdErr

The StdErr property returns the error output of the current stream. This error output is write-only information. This property only works with CScript.exe. This component's syntax is as follows:

```
Object.StdErr
```

StdIn

The StdIn property returns the input of the current stream. This input is read-only information. This property only works with CScript.exe. This component's syntax is as follows:

```
Object.StdIn
```

StdOut

The StdOut property returns the output of the current stream. This output is read-only information. This property only works with CScript.exe. This component's syntax is as follows:

```
Object.StdOut
```

TargetPath

The TargetPath property allows you to set a path to the shortcut's object executable file. This component's syntax is as follows:

```
Object.TargetPath
```

UserDomain

The UserDomain property returns the value of the domain name that the system is currently logged into. This value is returned as a string. This component's syntax is as follows:

```
Object.UserDomain
```

UserName

The UserName property returns the value of the currently logged on username. This value is returned as a string. This component's syntax is as follows:

```
Object.UserName
```

Version

The Version property returns a value that is equal to the version of the WSH that is installed on the system. This component's syntax is as follows:

```
Object.Version
```

WindowStyle

When working with shortcut objects, the WindowStyle property returns the window style of the object. A value of 1 displays the window, a value of 3 maximizes the window, and a value of 7 minimizes the window. This component's syntax is as follows:

```
Object.WindowStyle = intWindowStyle
```

WorkingDirectory

When working with shortcut objects, the WorkingDirectory property returns the working directory value. This component's syntax is as follows:

```
Object.WorkingDirectory = strWorkingDirectory
```

WINDOWS 2000 SUPPORT TOOLS

This appendix introduces some of the utilities available for Windows 2000. It is important to realize that this list is just a subset of some of the utilities that are available for Windows 2000 administration and is not a complete list.

Before purchasing any of these utilities, download and test a trial version to ensure that the utility performs that tasks required for your unique situation.

BACKUP SOFTWARE

Obviously, one of the most important aspects of Windows 2000 administration is keeping a current backup of data available for use at all times. This section examines some of the available third-party backup tools for Windows 2000.

ArcServeIT from Computer Associates

ArcServeIT is one of the most popular and powerful backup solutions. It backs up Exchange and SQL with special add-on tools. Prices vary, but cost is generally around $1,500. For more information, visit **www.ca.com**.

BackUpExec from Veritas

BackUpExec was previously owned by Seagate Software. It is one of the top backup tools in the industry and offers specialized tools to back up open files, SQL databases, and Exchange Servers. BackUpExec costs $99. For more information, visit **www.veritas.com**.

Double-Take from NSI Software

Double-Take is a powerful, realtime replication server. It replicates data from multiple locations to a central location. Double-Take costs $1,995. For more information, visit **www.nsisoftware.com**.

Open File Manager from St. Bernard Software

Open File Manager is a great utility dedicated to backing up open files. It costs $750. For more information, visit **www.stbernard.com**.

PowerSync from LinkPro Technologies

PowerSync provides automatic file synchronization, replication, backup, and remote mirroring. It costs $1,795. For more information, visit **www.linkpro.com**.

UltraBac from BEI Corporation

UltraBac offers powerful enterprise-class backup software for $795. For more information, visit **www.ultrabac.com**.

DISK DUPLICATION UTILITIES

The following product enables disk duplication for complete mirrors of system data.

Ghost from Symantec

Ghost is an extremely powerful and fast system imaging application. For more information, visit **www.symantec.com**.

EXCHANGE TOOLS

The following utilities provide advanced features for Microsoft Exchange.

CAMEO from MicroData Group, Inc.

CAMEO monitors corporate email and ensures that policies are being followed. It costs $395. For more information, visit **www.microdata.com**.

MELIA from MicroData Group, Inc.

MELIA monitors the amount and type of messages being sent from your Exchange servers. It costs $495. For more information, visit **www.microdata.com**.

FAXING SOLUTIONS

The following tools offer increased fax capabilities for Windows 2000.

Faxination Enterprise Server from Fenestrae

Faxination allows for the sending and receiving of faxes directly from the desktop. Pricing information was unavailable. For more information, visit **www.fenestrae.com**.

FAXMaker from GFi

FAXMaker uses a native connector to connect faxing capabilities into Exchange. Faxes can be sent and received from every user. FAXMaker costs $349. For more information, visit **www.gfifax.com**.

RightFax from RightFax

RightFax Enterprise Suite v6.0 is a fully integrated server-based fax solution that lets users send and receive faxes directly from their network workstations. Pricing information was unavailable for this product. For more information, visit **www.rightfax.com**.

NETWORK MANAGEMENT UTILITIES

The following tools offer advanced management functions for Windows 2000.

DirectoryAnalyzer from NetPro

DirectoryAnalyzer ensures the health of your Active Directory. It allows the administrator to control what "tweaks" are done to maintain a healthy Active Directory. Prices start at $14 per license. For more information, visit **www.netpro.com**.

Event Log Monitor by TNT Software

Event Log Monitor is a tool that can be used to collect event log messages, monitor them, and notify you of problems. This tool can monitor multiple servers in your organization. Prices start at $245. For more information, visit **www.tntsoftware.com**.

Hyena by Adkins Resource

Hyena is a powerful utility that provides centralized administrative features for most Windows 2000 services, including all printing tasks, on your network. Prices start at $199. For more information, visit **www.adkins-resource.com**.

LAN Licenser by ABC Systems and Development

One of the biggest problems facing organizations is ensuring that they are using the correct number of software licenses they have purchased. LAN Licenser monitors and controls software licenses on a network and can control when specific applications can be executed. LAN Licenser is priced at $1,350. For more information, visit **www.abcsystems.com**.

LanExplorer by Intellimax Systems

LanExplorer is a Windows 95/98/NT/2000–based LAN and Internet protocol analyzer. It allows the administrator to capture packets sent on the network for troubleshooting purposes. LanExplorer starts at $599. For more information, visit **www.intellimax.com**.

Sniffer Portable Analysis Suite by Network Associates

Sniffer Portable Analysis Suite is another protocol analyzer. It is a powerful tool for analyzing network traffic patterns and bottlenecks. Pricing information was unavailable for this product. For more information, visit **www.sniffer.com**.

PERFORMANCE MANAGEMENT UTILITIES

The following products offer advanced performance management tasks for Windows 2000.

Diskeeper by Executive Software

Diskeeper is currently the most popular disk defragmentation tool. In fact, its basic version is included with Windows 2000. A more advanced version is available from Executive Software and is a must for all systems running Windows 2000. Prices start at $44.95 for Windows 2000 Professional. For more information, visit **www.diskeeper.com**.

Performance Gallery by Demand Technology Software

Performance Gallery is a utility that automatically monitors performance of your network systems and alerts you if any problems occur. Prices start at $1,999. For more information, visit **www.perfgal.com**.

Speed Disk by Symantec

Speed Disk is another defragmentation utility for Windows 2000. It works on FAT and NTFS partitions. Speed Disk pricing starts at $50. For more information, visit **www.symantec.com**.

SuperSpeed NT by SuperSpeed.com

SuperSpeed NT is a utility that improves disk performance by not only defragmenting drives, but by also caching commonly accessed data. SuperSpeed NT starts at $649. For more information, visit **www.superspeed.com**.

TrafficMax by Intellimax Systems

TrafficMax allows the administrator to set warnings for network traffic. When traffic reaches a specified maximum, the administrator is notified. Prices start at $995. For more information, visit **www.intellimax.com**.

PRINTING UTILITIES

One of the biggest jobs an administrator performs deals with printing. These Windows 2000 tools help to simplify that job.

Print Console by Software Shelf International

Print Console centralizes control of all printer activity on a network. It supports Windows, Unix, OS/2, and Macintosh operating systems. Print Console prices start at $395. For more information, visit **www.printconsole.com**.

Print Manager Plus by Software Shelf International

Print Manager Plus is another powerful print queue manager that allows an administrator to also set quotas on printing. Prices start at $495. For more information, visit **www.printmanagerplus.com**.

REMOTE CONTROL

With the number of systems most administrators have to support, these tools simplify the tasks involved by allowing for remote control of systems.

ControlIT by Computer Associates

ControlIT is a full-featured remote control application. It allows the administrator to remotely manage systems on the network. Prices start at $199. For more information, visit **www.ca.com**.

LapLink 2000 by Laplink.com

LapLink 2000 started out as a method of connecting laptops. It is now an excellent remote control utility that offers powerful file transfer options. LapLink 2000 is priced starting at $170. For more information, visit **www.laplink.com**.

NetOp by CrossTec

NetOp is designed with the help desk in mind. Powerful scripting facilities are included in the product. NetOp pricing starts at $160. For more information, visit **www.crossteccorp.com**.

PcAnywhere by Symantec

PcAnywhere is one of the most popular remote control tools on the market today. It offers both server and client versions. With PcAnywhere, a single gateway system can be set up for remote control of multiple systems. PcAnywhere prices start at $170. For more information, visit **www.symantec.com**.

Appendix E

ReachOut by Stac Software

ReachOut is a remote control utility that also allows for remote control access through a browser. Prices start at $170. For more information, visit **www.stac.com**.

Remote Administrator by Famatech

Although Remote Administrator does not have some of the features of its more expensive counterparts, it is extremely fast and inexpensive. Remote Administrator prices start at $25. For more information, visit **www.famatech.com**.

RemotelyAnywhere by 3AM Laboratories

RemotelyAnywhere offers no client software. Instead, all remote control and remote management utilities are executed through a Web server/browser. Prices start at $99. For more information, visit **www.remotelyanywhere.com**.

SECURITY TOOLS

Securing your server is one of the most important tasks you must perform. Although Windows 2000 offers some powerful safety features, these tools can add to that arsenal.

BlackICE Defender by Network ICE

BlackICE Defender is a very powerful, yet simple stealth firewall solution. It hides your systems from the Internet. BlackICE Defender prices start at $40. For more information, visit **www.networkice.com**.

CyberwallPLUS by Network-1 Security Solutions

CyberwallPLUS is a great firewall from one of the biggest makers of security-based software. It is one of the most advanced Windows 2000–based solutions available. Pricing information was unavailable for this product. For more information, visit **www.network-1.com**.

NTSec by Pedestal Software

Many administrators want simple but powerful utilities for administrating their systems. NTSec is such a utility. In fact, it is a great collection of command-line tools for setting and controlling security. NTSec prices start at $130. For more information, visit **www.pedestalsoftware.com**.

Secure Copy by Small Wonders Software

Secure Copy not only copies files and folders on NTFS partitions, it also maintains all security rights. Prices start at $299. For more information, visit **www.smallwonders.com**.

Security Explorer by Small Wonders Software

Security Explorer is a great tool for analyzing your security. It finds and fixes security holes. Security Explorer prices start at $379. For more information, visit **www.smallwonders.com**.

SFProtect 2.0 by Agilent Technologies

SFProtect 2.0 monitors your network regularly for security holes. Prices start at $995. For more information, visit **www.agilent.com**.

STAT by STAT

STAT is a great tool that detects and corrects over 800 Windows vulnerabilities. Prices start at $795. For more information, visit **www.statonline.com**.

STORAGE MANAGEMENT TOOLS

As an administrator, it is imperative that you be able to monitor and control your system's storage. These tools for Windows 2000 help to simplify those tasks.

DiskAdvisor by W. Quinn Associates

DiskAdvisor reports on storage usage and trends on your systems. Prices start at $395. For more information, visit **www.wquinn.com**.

File Rescue by Software Shelf International

File Rescue is a utility that restores deleted Windows 2000 files and folders. Prices start at $75. For more information, visit **www.file-rescue.com**.

FileScreen 2000 by W. Quinn Associates

FileScreen 2000 controls which files are allowed to be saved on your servers. It blocks unwanted file types, such as images, movies, and sounds. FileScreen 2000 prices start at $195. For more information, visit **www.wquinn.com**.

QuotaAdvisor by W. Quinn Associates

QuotaAdvisor is a powerful utility for monitoring, managing, and enforcing disk quotas on your systems. Prices start at $595. For more information, visit **www.wquinn.com**.

UnDelete by Executive Software

UnDelete recovers deleted files and folders from FAT and NTFS partitions. Pricing for this tool begins at $250. For more information, visit **www.executive.com**.

SYSTEM ADMINISTRATION TOOLS

As networks become more and more complex, the task of managing them becomes more and more difficult. These Windows 2000 tools make these tasks a little easier to perform.

Aelita Enterprise Suite by Aelita Software

Aelita Enterprise Suite is a full-featured suite of utilities for managing your entire network. Its tools include domain migration tools, emergency repair disk tools, and so on. Pricing was unavailable for this product. For more information, visit **www.aelita.net**.

AutoShutdown by Barefoot Productions

AutoShutdown allows you to configure your server to shut down automatically based on very specific criteria. AutoShutdown prices start at $25. For more information, visit **www.barefootinc.com**.

Enterprise Configuration Manager by ServerWare

Enterprise Configuration Manager (ECM) is a tool for monitoring and preventing network configuration problems. Enterprise Configuration Manager prices start at $500 per license. For more information, visit **www.serverware.com**.

Intact Account Manager by TNT Software

Intact Account Manager lets you give some of your power users more control than is normally allowed. It moves some of the basic administration tasks to a junior administrator. Pricing was unavailable for this tool. For more information, visit **www.tntsoftware.com**.

OpalisRobot by Opalis

OpalisRobot is an extremely powerful system management and automation application. It is used to automate very complex tasks and execute them according to a set schedule. Prices start at $999. For more information, visit **www.opalis.com**.

UltraAdmin by Dorian Software Creations

UltraAdmin is a single utility that centralizes all major administrative tasks. UltraAdmin prices start at $175. For more information, visit **www.ultraadmin.com**.

VIRUS PROTECTION APPLICATIONS

One of the biggest causes for lost system time is due to viruses. Viruses can render your entire network unusable. These Windows 2000 tools are a must to protect your network from such virus attacks.

InoculateIT by Computer Associates

InoculateIT is one of the most popular antivirus programs available today. Prices start at $30 per license. For more information, visit **www.ca.com**.

VirusScan by McAfee

VirusScan is another popular antivirus program available. VirusScan prices start at $30 per license. For more information, visit **www.mcafee.com**.

Norton Antivirus by Symantec

Norton Antivirus is also a popular antivirus program. Included in this program is an auto update feature that updates the virus signature files from either the Internet or a locally detected system. Prices start at $36. For more information, visit **www.symantec.com**.

GLOSSARY

Access Control List (ACL)
A list that defines user rights for resources.

Active Directory
A centralized resource and security management, administration, and control mechanism in Windows 2000, which is used to support and maintain a Windows 2000 domain. The Active Directory is hosted by domain controllers.

Active Directory Domains and Trusts
A Windows 2000 utility used to create and manage domains and trusts. It allows an administrator to perform operations, such as setting the domain name's operation manager, changing a domain's mode, creating trusts between domains, and defining a managing user account.

Active Directory Sites and Services
A Windows 2000 utility used to configure server settings, site settings, and replication.

Active Directory Users and Computers
A Windows 2000 utility used to create and manage users, groups, and computers within a domain.

Administrator
A built-in Windows 2000 account that can perform a full array of management functions.

answer file
A file that contains a complete set of instructions for installing Windows 2000 unattended. User interaction is not required.

AppleTalk
The Apple Macintosh network protocol stack.

Application log
Records various application specific details.

asymmetric multiprocessing
A process in which the operating system assigns a process to a specific processor, often based on the type of process.

AT (automated task)
A way of programming an operating system to perform management functions automatically.

audit policy
A Windows 2000 component that specifies which events are recorded in the Security log of the Event Viewer.

auditing
The recording of the occurrence of a defined event or action.

authentication
A Windows 2000 process that confirms a user's identity via a username and password before allowing the user to log onto the system.

baseline
A measurement of normal system operation.

basic disks
Standard hard disks.

boot.ini
The text file that tells a computer how to load an operating system and creates the Windows 2000 boot loader's menu.

Cache Manager
A Windows 2000 component that accepts read/write requests from the CPU, stores them in memory, and controls processes in the background.

class driver
A piece of software that supplies basic driver interfaces and functions that define broad parameters for specific types of devices.

cluster
A group of computers (individually called cluster nodes) that are configured to operate as if they were a single system. Clusters are used to provide load balancing and fault tolerance.

Component Services
The renamed Microsoft Transaction Server, it is used to deploy and control COM+, automate tasks using scripting or programming languages, manage transactions between processes, and create scalable component-based applications.

compression
The process of compacting data to save disk space.

Computer Management
A Windows 2000 utility that offers single interface access to several commonly used local computer management utilities, such as Event Viewer, Disk Management, and the Services applet.

context switching
An operating system's capability to allow a thread to execute until it is forced to wait for available resources or until the operating system interrupts its operation. At the point that the thread ceases

operation, the operating system saves its context and loads the context of another thread. Once the new thread's context is loaded, it continues execution. This process is repeated indefinitely until there are no more threads to process.

Control Panel
A collection of tools, called applets, within Windows 2000, where most system and hardware configuration take place.

Counter list
A Resource Kit utility that outputs a list of all the counters installed on a system to a file. This data can be very useful in ensuring that specified logs run on all systems in the network by comparing the counters installed on those systems.

CryptoAPI version 2
An application programming interface that enables applications to encrypt or digitally sign data.

CScript
A command-line based scripting engine that is included with Windows 2000.

Data Link Control (DLC)
A low-level network protocol designed for IBM connectivity, remote booting, and network printing.

Data Sources (ODBC)
A Windows 2000 utility used to define DSNs (Data Source Names) employed by applications and services to access database management systems in the domain.

defragmentation
The process of reorganizing files so they are stored contiguously on the hard drive.

delegation
A new feature in Windows 2000 that enables an administrator to specifically assign certain administrative tasks to another user or group.

demand paging
The process of the operating system requesting free pages of memory for an active application from RAM.

Device Manager
A Windows 2000 administrative tool used to install, configure, and manage hardware devices.

Disk Cleanup
A tool used to regain access to hard drive space by deleting temporary, orphaned, or downloaded files, emptying the Recycle Bin, compressing little-used files, and condensing index catalog files.

Disk Management
The MMC snap-in used for drive management.

distinguished name (DN)
A unique name that identifies an object and its location on a network.

Distributed file system (Dfs)
A Windows 2000 Server service that manages shared network resources in a single hierarchical system.

domain
The main structure of Active Directory. A domain is a grouping of objects that are administered as a single unit. By placing objects within one or more domains in an organization, the organization's physical structure can be duplicated.

domain controller (DC)
A computer that authenticates the domain logons and maintains a Windows 2000 domain's Active Directory, which stores all information and relationships about users, groups, policies, computers, and resources.

Domain Controller Security Policy
A Windows 2000 utility used to configure and define the security policy for all domain controllers.

Domain Name Service (DNS)
A naming system used to translate host names to IP addresses and to locate resources on a TCP/IP-based network.

Domain Security Policy
A Windows 2000 utility used to configure and define the security policy for a domain.

driver
A device-specific software component used by an operating system to communicate with a device.

Driver signing
All drivers from Microsoft and approved vendors are signed. A signed driver is one whose integrity is verified by Microsoft and digitally approved for installation. Windows 2000 can be configured to refuse to install any nonsigned drivers.

dynamic disks
A hard disk that can only house dynamic volumes created through the Disk Management administrative tool. Dynamic disks do not include partitions or logical drives, and they cannot be accessed by DOS.

Dynamic DNS (DDNS)
Automates the addition and removal of systems in DNS.

Dynamic Host Configuration Protocol (DHCP)
A protocol that automates dynamic assignment of IP addresses to clients.

Emergency Repair Disk (ERD)
A disk that can be used to repair a failed system; it is created through the Backup utility.

Encrypting File System (EFS)
A file system supported by Windows 2000 that provides encryption of data stored on NTFS volumes.

encryption
A method of scrambling data to protect it from anyone who doesn't have a decryption key.

Glossary

event
A system occurrence that warrants user notification or logging.

Event Viewer
Used to view and manage the logs of Windows 2000.

Executive Services
The collection of kernel mode components for operating system management.

Extensible Authentication Protocol (EAP)
A protocol that provides remote user authentication.

fault tolerance
An operating system's capability to guarantee data integrity after a hardware failure, power outage, or other system failure.

file allocation table (FAT)
The file system originally introduced with DOS; it does not provide file system security features.

File System Manager
Controls file systems and hard drive activities including writing, reading, disk repair, drive partitioning, drive configuration, and drive construction.

forest
A collection of one or more trees in Active Directory.

fragmentation
The division of data into two or more parts, where each part is stored in a different location on the hard drive. As the level of fragmentation on a drive increases, disk performance decreases.

FrontPage 2000 Server Extensions
Microsoft offers a Web site authoring application known as FrontPage 2000. This application is available as either a standalone application or as one of the applications in the Office 2000 Premium suite of applications. Some of the specialized features of FrontPage require a component to be executed on the server. These components can include search pages, counters, and other specialized components. These components will not run properly unless the Web server supports the FrontPage 2000 Server Extensions. When this option is installed, all Web sites hosted on the server can support FrontPage 2000–developed Web sites. However, these extensions can be disabled on a per Web site basis.

fully qualified domain name (FQDN)
A friendly name that consists of a host and a domain name, including top-level domain, such as www.microsoft.com, which is linked to an IP address, such as 207.46.130.45.

global catalog
A replica of every domain and object within the same forest of an Active Directory.

global group
A group that exists throughout a domain that can only be created on a Windows 2000 Server.

Graphical Device Interface (GDI)
The software component that interacts with the Windows 2000 printing system on behalf of applications.

Graphics Device Drivers
Passes graphical instructions created by the gdi32.dll to video and printer drivers that create the software interface to the actual video and printing hardware.

Group Policy
An MMC snap-in that manages a variety of user settings, including software settings, Windows settings, and security settings.

Hardware Abstraction Layer (HAL)

A loadable kernel-level .dll (called Hal.dll; stored in the *%systemroot%*\system32 folder on a Windows 2000 computer) that provides the low-level interface to the hardware of the computer on which Windows 2000 is installed.

Hardware Compatibility List (HCL)

A list of hardware devices that are supported by Windows. A version of the HCL is found on the Windows 2000 Server distribution CD, but a Web site version is updated regularly at **www.microsoft.com/hwtest/hcl/**.

hardware profile

A software component that specifies custom device settings used on computers. Upon startup, Windows 2000 automatically loads the hardware profile that is suitable for the hardware present on a system.

HKEY_CLASSES_ROOT

A Registry key that contains the value entries that define the relationships between file extensions (i.e., file formats) and applications. This key is actually just a redirector to the HKEY_LOCAL_ MACHINE\Software\Classes subkey.

HKEY_CURRENT_CONFIG

A Registry key that contains the value entries used to control the currently active hardware profile. This key is built each time the system boots by duplicating the contents of the HKEY_LOCAL_ MACHINE\System\CurrentControlSet\ HardwareProfiles\### subkey relative to the active hardware profile.

HKEY_CURRENT_USER

A Registry key that contains the value entries specific to the currently logged on user. This key is built each time a user logs on by duplicating the user-specific subkey from the HKEY_USERS key and the NTUSER.DAT/.MAN file from the user's profile.

HKEY_LOCAL_MACHINE

A Registry key that contains the value entries specific to the local computer hardware. The contents of this key are not dependent on a user account or any applications, services, or processes in use.

HKEY_USERS

A Registry key that contains the value entries for all users who have ever logged onto a system plus a default user profile for new users that do not already have a user profile.

hotfixes

Software releases that are used to fix any major bugs or security holes in an operating system.

I/O Manager

A Windows 2000 software component that manages all I/O channels including file systems and devices.

IntelliMirror

A network desktop-management system that allows administrators to retain control over systems not permanently connected to the network. Each time a computer logs back onto the network, the domain's group policies are reinforced, software is added or removed, and user data files are updated.

Internet connection sharing

Built into Windows 2000's routing support is a basic proxy server. This tool can be used to grant Internet access to a small network without requiring additional hardware or applications. Plus, the network clients are automatically configured to use the shared connection.

Internet Information Services (IIS) 5

The latest generation of Microsoft Internet Information Server version 5 included with Windows 2000. IIS offers a solid platform for building personal Web pages through true distributed, dynamic Web sites. IIS integrates with the Windows 2000 system,

Glossary

seamlessly granting Web administrators access to networked resources, security, and management controls.

Internet Protocol Security (IPSec)
A secure, industry-standard protocol that works with and provides security for TCP/IP.

Internet Services Manager
A Windows 2000 utility used to manage Internet information services, such as Web and FTP.

Internet Services Manager (HTML)
Allows the administrator to configure and control IIS over the Internet. This is the application used to configure the Internet Information Server in previous versions of IIS. The Windows 2000 version allows the administrator to perform nearly all the same tasks that he or she could perform using the IIS snap-in.

Internetwork Packet Exchange/ Sequenced Packet Exchange (IPX/SPX)
The protocol used on Novell NetWare networks.

IPC (Interprocess Communication)
A Windows 2000 software component that manages all transactions between server and client processes, both within the local computer and with remote computers.

Kerberos Version 5
An encryption authentication protocol employed by Windows 2000 to verify the identity of a server and a client before data is transferred.

kernel mode
The level of Windows 2000 where objects can only be manipulated by a thread directly from an application subsystem.

Key Distribution Center (KDC)
A Kerberos service that issues ticket-granting tickets and service tickets for domain authentication.

Layer 2 Tunneling Protocol (L2TP)
A protocol that creates a secure connection, relying on other encryption methods (such as IPSec) for communication.

lease
A measurement of time that an IP address assigned by DHCP is assigned to a client.

Licensing
A Windows 2000 utility used to configure and manage the license of Windows 2000 and installed applications.

Lightweight Directory Access Protocol (LDAP)
An access protocol for Active Directory protocol.

LMHOSTS
A text file that maps IP addresses to NetBIOS computer names.

load balancing
A mechanism that provides more efficient utilization of the network by balancing incoming TCP/IP traffic between servers, most often Web servers, by using windows clustering.

Local Security Policy
The Windows 2000 control mechanism that is used to configure and define the security policy for a local system including password restrictions, account lockout, audit, user rights, security options, public key, and IP security.

logical printer
The software component that provides print services in Windows 2000.

Master Boot Record (MBR)
The first sector on a disk that contains executable code and a partition table, which stores information about the disk's primary and extended partitions.

Media Access Control (MAC) address
A unique address assigned to a network interface card.

Microsoft Challenge Handshake Authentication Protocol Version 2 (MS-CHAP v2)
An authentication protocol developed by Microsoft for remote user authentication via remote access or dial-up connections.

Microsoft Management Console (MMC)
A new standardized Web–capable management interface. Most of the Windows 2000 administration tasks are accessible through an MMC snap-in.

mixed mode
A domain setting that enables communication between Windows 2000 domain controllers and Windows NT domain controllers.

mount point
A directory on an NTFS volume that is used as an access point to a volume that does not have an assigned drive letter.

MS-DOS subsystem
An environmental subsystem provided to support DOS applications.

multicast scopes
A range of IP addresses that can be assigned to multicast DHCP clients by DHCP.

multiprocessing
The ability of an operating system to use more than one microprocessor.

multithreading
A software design that allows applications to to run multiple threads concurrently.

native mode
A domain setting signifying that all domain controllers on a network are using Active Directory.

NetBIOS Extended User Interface (NetBEUI)
A native Microsoft networking protocol that is being phased out with Windows 2000 due to its inability to be routed, making it unusable for enterprise networks.

Network Address Translation (NAT)
An Internet standard that enables a LAN to use one set of IP addresses for internal traffic and a second set of addresses for external traffic.

Network Monitor
A Windows 2000 utility used to view and troubleshoot data packets.

Network News Transfer Protocol (NNTP)
A new feature in Windows 2000 that allows a Windows 2000 Server to become a Usenet or NNTP server. As with FTP, the server can then operate with any other server using the same protocol, regardless of the operating system.

New Technology File System (NTFS)
The preferred file system of Windows 2000 that supports file-level security, encryption, compression, auditing, and more.

nonpreemptive multitasking
A process in which individual applications maintain control over their threads using the CPU.

Novell Directory Services (NDS)
A distributed database on NetWare servers that maintains network resource information.

NWLink
The Microsoft implementation of IPX/SPX.

object
Every component of the Windows 2000 operating environment including printers, groups, and server processes is an object.

Object Manager
A Windows 2000 component that manages object naming and security functions. It also allocates system objects, monitors their use, and removes them when they are no longer needed.

Glossary

Offline Files
A Windows 2000 feature that allows mobile Windows 2000 users to access shared files and folders even when they are not connected to the network.

Open Shortest Path First (OSPF)
A routing protocol that propagates routing information.

organizational unit (OU)
A container used to organize objects into logical administration groups. Organizational units can contain objects, such as users, groups, printers, computers, applications, file shares, and other organizational units.

OS/2 subsystem
An environmental subsystem provided to support OS/2 character-mode applications.

paging file
A file, called pagefile.sys, used by the Virtual Memory Manager as a temporary storage container for inactive memory pages.

Password Authentication Protocol (PAP)
A connection negotiation protocol that passes authentication information in clear text, which is not very secure.

PDC emulator
A Windows 2000 domain controller that acts as though it is an NT Server domain controller to systems that do not support Active Directory.

Plug and Play
A technology that allows an operating system to recognize a device, install the correct driver, and enable the device automatically.

Plug and Play Manager
A Windows 2000 component that manages all Plug and Play–compliant devices and their associated drivers.

Point-to-Point Tunneling Protocol (PPTP)
A protocol used in virtual private networking that allows remote users to access a network over the Internet securely.

policy
A component that automatically configures user settings.

POSIX.1 (Portable Operating System based on Unix) subsystem
An environmental subsystem provided to support POSIX.1 text-only applications.

Power Manager
This component manages the power conservation capabilities of Windows 2000 (mostly used by laptop computers).

preemptive multitasking
An operating system's ability to interrupt a thread during its execution.

print monitor
The printing component that manages printers and print jobs on the server as well as print job scheduling and priority.

process
An executable set of commands designed to perform a specific set of steps, allowing access to system resources, such as files and hardware devices.

Process Manager
This component manages the creation, disassembly, and maintenance of processes.

program
An executable collection of one or more threads, their code, and other information.

Public Key Infrastructure (PKI)
The settings involved in the management of digital certificates and public and private cryptography keys.

quantum
The predetermined amount of time that a thread runs.

quotas
An assignment in Windows 2000 that limits the amount of disk space available to individual users.

Recovery Console
A command-line control system used in system recovery in the event of a failure of a core system component or driver. Through the Recovery Console, simple commands can be used to restore the operating system to a functional state.

redirector
A Windows 2000 component that distinguishes between local and network resource requests and directs network traffic accordingly.

Redundant Array of Independent Disks (RAID)
A drive configuration of multiple drives in which data is written to all drives to distribute the workload. For fault tolerance in striped volumes, parity information is added to the written data to allow for drive failure recovery.

REGEDIT
The 16-bit Registry editing program.

REGEDT32
The 32-bit Registry editing program.

Registry
The hierarchical database that stores all Windows 2000 system information.

Remote Access Service (RAS)
Part of the Routing And Remote Access Service (RRAS) suite of protocols for Windows 2000. This suite of protocols allows an administrator to connect clients to the network through a direct dial-up connection (RAS) or a secure Internet connection (virtual private networking).

Remote Installation Preparation (RIPrep.exe) wizard
An application used for remote OS installation, where an administrator can take an entire image of one Windows 2000 Professional machine and install that image onto other workstations.

Remote Installation Service (RIS)
A service that allows clients to be easily installed across the network by booting from a Pre-Boot Execution Environment (PXE) ROM NIC or a boot floppy. The installation routine can be fully automated once the destination computer is turned on, or a full or partial user interaction required installation can be customized.

reverse lookup
A query process in which the IP address of a computer is translated to its DNS name.

ScanDisk
A native tool used to discover and correct problems on hard drives. Both physical and logical errors can be detected by ScanDisk.

schema
The objects and classes as well as their attributes in Active Directory.

scopes
The range of IP addresses that can be leased to clients by DHCP.

Security Accounts Manager (SAM)
A Windows 2000 service that maintains user and group account information.

security identifier (SID)
The unique identification number assigned to computer accounts on a Windows 2000 network.

Security log
Records details about security occurrences and audit events.

Security Reference Monitor
This component manages the security services including authentication, resource access, and group memberships.

Glossary

service packs (SPs)
A collection of hotfixes and add-ons to fix bugs or improve features in an operating system.

Simple Mail Transfer Protocol (SMTP)
A protocol that is used when one server is sending a message to another. This protocol is not used by client systems to pick up delivered messages; that task is assigned to either the Post Office Protocol version 3 (POP3) or Internet Message Access Protocol version 4 (IMAP4).

site
An Active Directory component that enables administrators to manage and organize the Active Directory.

slipstreaming
A new way of applying service packs. Slipstreaming ensures that updated files will be used so that service packs need only be applied once.

snap-ins
The consoles that can be added to the Microsoft Management Console to manage Windows 2000 features.

Spooler Service
The service that is responsible for passing a print job to the print monitor.

superscopes
A feature that allows DHCP to use multiple scopes of IP addresses for client assignments on the same physical subnet.

symmetric multiprocessing
The capability of an operating system to allow any process to be run on any processor, ensuring that the operating system uses all available processor resources.

Sysdiff
The Windows 2000 utility used to take a snapshot of a basic installation and, after changes have been made, record the changes, and then apply them to another installation.

Sysprep
A tool used to duplicate an entire hard drive. This tool is useful when installing Windows 2000 onto multiple identical systems that require identical configurations.

System log
Records details about hardware and software issues related to Windows 2000 itself and installed drivers.

Task Scheduler
A Windows 2000 component that automates the execution or launch of programs and batch files based on time and system conditions.

Terminal Services
Windows 2000 includes native Terminal Services (previously available to Windows NT only as an add-on), which allows thin clients to be employed as network clients. Terminal Services grants remote access to applications and offers limitation controls over application access.

thread
A set of commands within a program and is the entity to which the operating system grants processor time.

time-to-live
The amount of time that a packet is held before being discarded.

Trace Dump
A Resource Kit utility that gathers information in a trace log file (or a real-time trace) and outputs it into a .csv file. A .csv file then allows the data to be imported into an Excel spreadsheet and manipulated.

Trace Log
A Resource Kit utility that allows an administrator to start, stop, or enable trace logs from the command prompt. This allows for trace logs to be included in startup or login scripts.

Transmission Control Protocol/ Internet Protocol (TCP/IP)
The most popular protocol suite in use today, originally based on the network protocols developed by the Department of Defense. TCP/IP is the protocol used on the Internet.

trees
A collection or group of one or more Windows 2000 domains.

unattended installation
A Windows 2000 installation that uses a previously made script to install the OS without user interaction.

uniqueness database file (UDF)
A text file that contains a partial set of instructions for installing Windows 2000, which specifies settings for individual users. Used to supplement an answer file when only minor changes that don't require a new answer file are needed.

user mode
Components that operate in user mode are responsible for interaction between the user and the operating system. User mode components are granted limited access to the computer's resources and must make all resource requests through components operating in kernel mode.

virtual memory
A Windows 2000 service that stores memory pages not currently in use by the system in paging files on the hard drive, which frees up memory for other uses. Virtual memory also hides the swapping of memory from applications and higher-level services.

Virtual Memory Manager (VMM)
A Windows 2000 software component that manages virtual memory, including physical RAM and paging files.

virtual private network (VPN)
An extension of a network that can be accessed securely through a public network, such as the Internet.

Web-Based Enterprise Management (WBEM)
The Distributed Management Task Force (DMTF) initiative included in Windows 2000 via Windows Management Instrumentation (WMI), which grants the administrator the ability to remotely manage, configure, and control nearly every aspect of systems and networks from software to hardware.

Win16 subsystem
An environmental subsystem is designed to support Windows 3.x, Windows for Workgroups 3.11, and Win16 Windows 95 applications in a simulated Windows 3.x environment.

Win32 subsystem
An environmental subsystem required by Windows 2000. Win32 supports many essential functions including maintaining the user's desktop environment and providing a standard interface for graphical and user device I/O.

Window Manager
This component manages the input (mouse and keyboard) and display of windowing and dialog boxes.

Windows 2000 Advanced Server
The enhanced version of Windows 2000 Server that provides improved support for application and Web services through expanded hardware support, network load balancing, and application fault tolerance through two-node *clustering*.

Windows 2000 Backup
The built-in backup program in Windows 2000.

Glossary

Windows 2000 Datacenter Server
The Windows 2000 Server version that expands on the Advanced Server features. Datacenter Server is designed for the largest enterprise networks; it provides 32-node network load balancing and 4-node clustering.

Windows 2000 Executive
The collection of high-level system services in Windows 2000.

Windows 2000 Professional
A high-performance, secure operating system for network client computers.

Windows 2000 Server
The latest version of the server operating system from Microsoft, which is designed to provide file, print, and application sharing in a networked environment.

Windows Driver Model (WDM)
A portion of the Windows architecture that allows device manufacturers to create drivers that conform to a consistent standard, which is supported by Windows 98 and 2000. The WDM is supported by Windows 98 and Windows 2000.

Windows file protection
An automated protection measure that prevents in-use system files, such as SYS, DDL, OCX, TTF, and EXE, from being overwritten by other programs or installation routines.

Windows Installer Service (WIS)
A Windows 2000 component that manages application installation and removal by applying defined setup rules.

Windows Internet Naming Service (WINS)
A service that dynamically maps IP addresses to NetBIOS computer names used by Microsoft operating systems other than Windows 2000.

Windows Script Host (WSH)
Native scripting capabilities of Windows 2000 that grant administrators a wider set of automation options. Most tasks can be accomplished through command-line utilities. Using WSH, an administrator can automate many redundant tasks.

winnt.exe
The 16-bit Windows 2000 installation program that can be run on 16-bit operating systems.

winnt32.exe
The 32-bit Windows 2000 installation program that can be run on 32-bit operating systems.

WScript
The 32-bit, Windows-based scripting engine included with Windows 2000.

zone
A subtree of a DNS database.

INDEX

M

R

V

X

Z

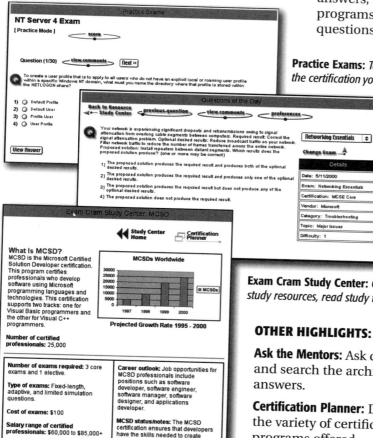

WHAT'S ON THE CD-ROM

The *MCSE Windows 2000 Server Exam Prep*'s companion CD-ROM contains the testing system for *MCSE Windows 2000 Server Exam Prep*, which includes 50 questions. Additional questions are available for free download from **ExamCram.com**; simply click on the Update button in the testing engine. You can choose from numerous testing formats, including Fixed-Length, Random, Test All, and Review.

System Requirements

Software

➤ Your operating system must be Windows 95, 98, NT4 or higher.

➤ To view the practice exam, you need Internet Explorer 5.x.

Hardware

➤ An Intel Pentium, AMD, or comparable 100MHz processor or higher is recommended for best results.

➤ 32MB of RAM is the minimum requirement.

➤ Available disk storage space of at least 10MB is recommended.